PORTFOLIO & RESOURCE INTRODUCTION TO DESIGN AND TECHNOLOGY

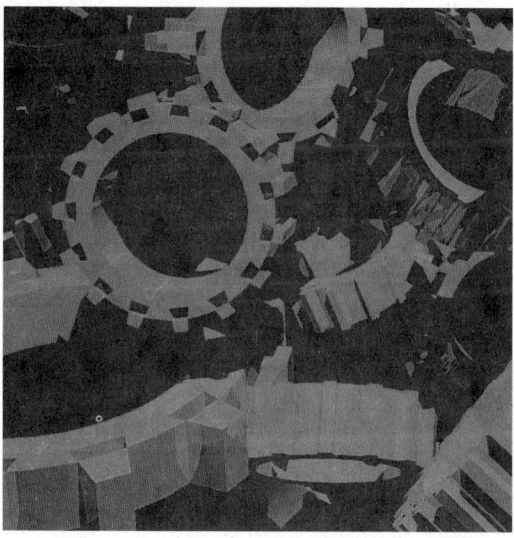

TODD, TODD, McCRORY

Ronald D. Todd, Ph.D.
School of Engineering ■ Department of Technological Studies ■ Trenton State College ■ Trenton, New Jersey

Karen Rohne Todd, Ph.D.
Department of Home Economics ■ Montclair State University ■ Montclair, New Jersey

David L. McCrory, Ph.D.
Technology Education ■ West Virginia University ■ Morgantown, West Virginia

JOIN US ON THE INTERNET
WWW: http://www.thomson.com
EMAIL: findit@kiosk.thomson.com

A service of I(T)P®

Thomson Learning®
TOOLS

I(T)P® An International Thomson Publishing Company

Cincinnati • Albany • Bonn • Boston • Detroit • London • Madrid • Melbourne • Mexico City • New York
Philadelphia • Pacific Grove • Paris • San Francisco • Singapore • Tokyo • Toronto • Washington

Copyright © 1996
by Thomson Learning® TOOLS
an International Thomson Publishing Co.

I(T)P

The ITP logo is a trademark under license.

For more information, contact:

Thomson Learning® TOOLS
5101 Madison Road
Cincinnati, OH 45227

International Thomson Publishing
Berkshire House
168-173 High Holborn
London, WC1V7AA
England

Thomas Nelson Australia
102 Dodds Street
South Melbourne 3205
Victoria, Australia

Nelson Canada
1120 Birchmont Road
Scarborough, Ontario
M1K 5G4, Canada

International Thomson Publishing GmbH
Konigswinterer Str. 418
53227 Bonn
Germany

International Thomson Publishing Asia
221 Henderson Bldg. #05-10
Singapore 0315

International Thomson Publishing Japan
Kyowa Building, 3F
2-2-1 Hirakawa-cho
Chiyoda-ku, Tokyo 102
Japan

The text of this publication, or any part thereof, may be reproduced for use in classes for which *Introduction to Design and Technology* is the adopted textbook. It may not be reproduced in any manner whatsoever for any other purpose without permission in writing from the publisher.

ISBN: 0-538-64468-0

1 2 3 4 5 6 7 8 9 MZ 00 99 98 97 96

Printed in the United States of America

Publisher: Brian J. Taylor
Project Manager/Acquisitions Editor: Suzanne F. Knapic
Production Coordinator: Jean Findley
Editor: Carol Spencer

Acknowledgments

This book, like most good design and technology activities, draws heavily on the work and ideas of others. We would like to thank the following individuals for their gracious assistance during the preparation of the book and the Portfolio and Activities Resource. They made significant contributions to the content, process, and activities of the book, thus enriching the learning experiences for the readers.

CONTRIBUTING AUTHORS

John Wells, Assistant Professor, Department of Technology Education, West Virginia University, Morgantown, West Virginia

Alan Paul, Senior Lecturer, Design and Technology, The Nottingham Trent University, Nottingham, England

Contributors

Peter Bartcherer, Director, Design and Imaging Studio, Drexel University Philadelphia, PA

Tim Brotherhood, QLS-STEP Staffordshire Technology Education Programme, Stafford, England

Paul Devine, Chair, Department of Technology Education, Glasgow High School, Glasgow, DE

Leonard Finegold, Professor of Physics, Drexel University Philadelphia, PA

John Hindhaugh, Teacher Advisor, QLS-STEP Staffordshire Technology Education Programme, Stafford, England

Catherine Houghton, Teacher, Department of Biology Glasgow High School, Glasgow, DE

Pat Hutchinson, Editor-in-Chief, TIES Magazine, Trenton State College, Trenton, NJ

Richard Kimbell, Professor of Design and Technology, Goldsmiths College, University of London

Geoffrey Oliver, Senior Lecturer, In-Service Department Unit, Charlotte Mason College, Lancaster University Cumbria, England

Edward Rockel, Professor of Biology Trenton State College, Trenton, NJ

Peter Sellwood, Consultant in Design and Technology, Bath, England

Phillip Forrest-Smith, Design Consultant, Nottingham, England

Richard Tufnell, Design and Technology, Middlesex University, London, England

The authors would like to thank the following individuals for their help and interest:

Norm Asper, Andrew Birkin, Frank Capelle, John Cave, Catherine Farrup, Keith Finkral, Ted Gill, Hazel Hannant, Harry Hess, John Hutchinson, John Karsnitz, Larry Kelly, Ken Maskell, Jamie Mulligan, Gordon Pritchett, Ray Shackelford, Ben Sprouse, Melvin Sprouse, Barbara Stala, Roni Todd, Victor Vinci, Jeff Wagoner, and Cindy Yayac.

Additionally, we would like to thank the editors and researchers who played such an essential role in bringing this effort to a successful conclusion.

Sue Knapic, Carol Spencer, Joni Noe, and Suzanne Murphy

Finally, we would like to thank those companies that have provided information and resources to support select of the learning activities:

Cambridge University Press

Economatics (Education) Ltd.

K'NEX Inc.

Modern School Supplies

Plastruct Inc.

Science Instruments Co.

Unilab, Inc, a Division of Philip Harris plc.

Contents

UNIT ONE — DESIGN AND TECHNOLOGY

Chapter 1   *Introduction to Designing and Problem Solving*   **1**
    Using the Design Loop and the IDEATE Model   12

Chapter 2   *Designing, Documenting, and Drawing*   **21**
    Design Considerations   21
    Documenting Techniques   22
    Drawing Techniques   26
    Pictorial Drawings   29
    Plan Drawings   37
    Presentation Techniques   44
    Presentation Portfolios   56
    Review and Enrichment   57

Chapter 3   *Models and Model-Building*   **59**
    Types of Models   59
    Model-Making   60

UNIT TWO — THE RESOURCES OF TECHNOLOGY

Chapter 4   *Tools, Mechanisms, and Machines*   **79**
    Tools and Mechanisms   79
    Linkages   83
    Fluid Mechanisms   93
    Electromechanical Mechanisms   97
    Machines   100
    Skill Assessment and Inventory   102

Chapter 5 Materials and Materials Processing **105**
Characteristics of Materials 105
The Structure of Materials 110
Function of Materials 113
Conversion of Materials 118

Chapter 6 Energy and Energy Processing **133**
Sources of Energy 133
Forms of Energy 140
Conversion of Energy 148
Fluid Mechanisms 169
Electromechanical Mechanisms 171

Chapter 7 Information and Information Processing **179**
Signals—Information for Machines 179
Symbols—Information for Humans 200
Using Symbols in Design and Technology 204

Chapter 8 Humans as Designers and Consumers **213**
Designing for Humans 213
Design and Technology Activities 214
Humans and Materials, Energy and Information 223
Designing for Humans 229
Humans as Decision Makers 236

Chapter 9 Time, Space, Capital, and Management **237**
Time, Place, and Space 237
Capital—Human and Monetary 252
Management of Resources 259

UNIT THREE THE SYSTEMS OF TECHNOLOGY

Chapter 10 Physical Systems — 279
- Construction Systems — 279
- Transporting Systems — 301
- Production Systems — 311
- Producing and Manufacturing — 314
- Design Activities—Research and Development Projects — 316

Chapter 11 Biotechnology Systems — 323
- Stages of Development — 323
- Cells and Genetics Engineering — 331
- Bioprocessing — 337
- Biotechnology in Agriculture — 345
- Bioethics — 350

Chapter 12 Communication Systems — 351
- Senders and Receivers — 351
- Transmitting Through Media — 351
- Feedback — 363
- Forms of Communicating — 365

Chapter 13 Control Technology Systems — 389
- Control Systems — 389
- Integrated Circuits — 399
- System Outputs — 405
- Integrated Systems — 426

UNIT FOUR   THE IMPACT OF TECHNOLOGY

Chapter 14   *Investigating, Developing, and Improving*   **431**
    Investigating Through Exploring   431
    Investigating Through Forecasting   434
    Expanding Knowledge for Improving Future Investigations   442
    Developing—Putting Knowledge to Work
    Improving—Making Things Better   443

Chapter 15   *Consequences and Decisions*   **447**
    Looking Toward the Future   447
    Decisions—Making Tough Choices   455

Appendix A   *Isometric Grid*   **463**

Appendix B   *Suggested Model-Making Materials*   **464**

Appendix C   *Properties of Materials*   **465**

Appendix D   *Common Adhesives*   **466**

Appendix E   *Adhesives Application Chart*   **468**

Appendix F   *Common Plastics and Polymers*   **469**

Appendix G   *Units of Measure*   **470**

Appendix H   *Trigonometric Functions*   **471**

Appendix I   *Designing a Computer-Controlled System*   **472**

Appendix J   *Selected Reference Books and Resource Materials*   **484**

Appendix K   *Selected Publishers and Vendors of Technology Education Resource Materials*   **490**

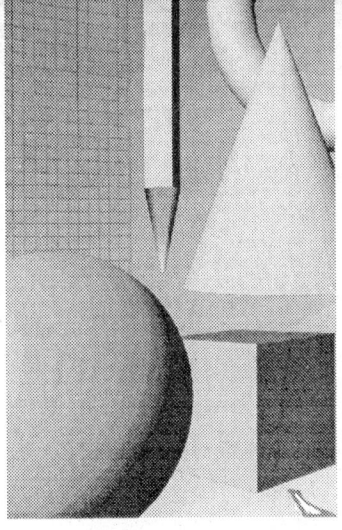

Introduction to Designing and Technology

OVERVIEW FOR STUDENTS

In your work in this course of study, you may find that the designing and technology (D&T) approach is different from the approach used in classes you have previously taken in high school. The following chart shows some of these differences of what you would experience as a student through standard and design and technology approaches.

The Differences for Students between Standard and Design and Technology Approaches to Learning

Standard Approach	D&T Approach
• students assume passive role in learning	• students assume active role in learning
• students often engage in memorization of unrelated facts and figures	• students usually learn facts and concepts as they relate to real problems
• students often work alone	• students often work in teams
• students seldom share what they are learning	• students often share what they are learning
• students seldom work on real problems	• students often work on real problems
• students seldom become the classroom expert in a topic of study	• students often become the classroom expert in a topic of study
• students usually work on restricted topics and problems	• students often work on open ended topics and problems
• students seldom set their own pace of learning	• students often set their own pace of learning
• students seldom direct their own process of learning	• students often direct their own process of learning

D&T results in a different kind of program. It provides activities that are different from standard schooling, and it helps to develop a different set of skills that you will find helpful as you live and work, both now and in the future.

Design and Technology Programs

D&T places value on	D&T engages students in	D&T helps students gain competence with
application	instruction	resources
progression	investigation	interpersonal skills
collaboration	invention	information
empowerment	interpretation	systems
		technology

THE CURRICULAR DESIGN OF D&T

The curricular design of D&T underscores the importance of four related ideas—*application, progression, collaboration,* and *empowerment*. Each of these will be considered in turn, below.

Application The D&T course is shaped significantly by the concept of application. What you learn you are expected to apply. Knowledge and skills that you gain are intended to be put to work. This means you will spend less time memorizing facts and figures in the D&T course, and more time finding and using information and data that you need to complete a problem or project.

Through the activities of the D&T course, you will also find that being able to recall various bits of knowledge is quite different than being able to synthesize and use that knowledge. For example, you may know such concepts in mathematics as "pi", "rate, time, and distance", or "slope". You may be able to use them to solve math problems. Your level of understanding of these concepts will increase significantly as you use them in real problems, however. Designing and developing "playground and fairground rides" or an "energy efficient personal transport system" requires a deeper understanding of such concepts.

As much as possible, the D&T activities are designed to help you apply what you are learning, and to help you realize how useful and powerful applied knowledge can be. The D&T approach is perfectly suited to the emerging national movement in education that gives more attention and importance to what students can do, rather than focusing primarily on what they know.

Progression In this book, important concepts in design and technology will be introduced, and revisited. For example, you will encounter the idea of "materials" and how they can be changed. As you move through the D&T experiences, you will progressively gain more insight into the nature of materials and become more skilled in their use.

The experiences provided in this course are intended to help you move from lower to higher levels of understanding and skills. Additionally, the experiences are intended to provide a structure of technology and an approach to problem solving that will help you to continue learning after you have completed your schooling.

Collaboration Many D&T activities will require that you and your classmates work together to solve a problem, complete a project, or accomplish an objective. In these instances, a great deal of the success of your work and the grade you will receive will depend on how well all of you work together.

As the D&T course progresses, the class will move from simple collaborative tasks to more complex and demanding tasks. Concurrently, you will be introduced to approaches that will help you gain skills in cooperative team work.

Empowerment "Empowering" you as a student means you gain the essential skills and resources that allow you to solve increasingly difficult problems. Through a planned program of experiences, you will be helped progressively to take charge of your own study. As you gain these skills, you will be less dependent on your teacher and others for specific directions on how to proceed. Rather, as you become more experienced in the D&T approach and more skilled in asking questions, you will progressively use other people as outside consultants and collaborators rather than guides.

Reaching an adequate level of empowerment means you have developed important skills in identifying problems and asking questions. In many cases, you will find that asking the right questions will be a major part of solving a problem. People who have not learned to solve problems, are more likely to depend on others for answers and solutions. Empowerment can be equated with independence and competence in thought and action, an important goal of the D&T course.

THE D&T ACTIVITIES

The D&T program is intended to help you gain important knowledge and skills by engaging you in four general types of activities—*instruction, investigation, invention,* and *interpretation*.

Instruction Some of your D&T activities will focus primarily on helping you gain knowledge needed to pursue a problem or project. Such activities are intended to help you learn established facts, ideas and concepts that are important to D&T activities. In these instances, the activities are designed to help you gain this new knowledge as effectively and efficiently as possible.

Some of the instructional activities will be quite familiar to you because of their similarity to the learning activities you have experienced in standard classes and courses. Other activities are designed to help you gain new insights into different aspects of D&T. For example, through different activities, we want you to learn that all machines are similar. As you come to understand these similarities, you will never encounter a machine that is totally strange to you, even those that have not yet been invented. This insight about machines will provide a valuable analytic tool as you work with or improve a machine.

Investigation In many of the D&T activities you pursue, you will find that the related knowledge is neither complete or organized. In these circumstances, investigative rather that instructive learning strategies will be more appropriate. In some instances, you may engage in scientific inquiry. In these instances, you will be trying to gain some insight into a topic or subject of interest or searching for answers to specific problems.

Through your work in inquiry, you will learn more about how the natural world operates. In some instances, you may find this new knowledge to be useful in your D&T work. In other instances, you may find the new knowledge to be exciting and fulfilling, but you may not be able to put that knowledge to immediate use. Both results are quite acceptable.

In your D&T related work, you may engage in research and investigation related to a problem you are trying to solve. In some of these instances, you may be engaged in "inquiry" to learn more about the scientific facts, concepts and principles that relate to your project or problems that you have encountered in your efforts. For example, if you design and develop a bioreactor to make ginger ale, you may become very interested in the biotechnology processes that take place in producing the ginger ale. You may decide to go beyond what you need to know about the related processes and learn more about other biological processes.

In other instances, your D&T work calls for more practically driven research and development. Perhaps you want to know which of several new adhesives work best to hold parts of a machine or a toy together. You can design a test to collect data on how well the different adhesives perform. Both of these instances deal with investigation and inquiry—one is to add to your general knowledge, the other to add to your practical knowledge.

Invention In a D&T course there are many opportunities to apply what you have learned to creative endeavors. Inventive activities are what they suggest, the opportunity for creating unique ways of implementing a process, solving a problem, or completing a project. Inventive endeavors can include design activities, design briefs, R&D projects, and the like. These endeavors can range from small efforts to large-scale projects. In some instances, the inventive solutions are complex and sophisticated; in others, simple and elegant.

Inventive solutions are often the result of trying things that fail. Failure in D&T is to be expected. If your solutions are always successful, you may be staying too much with predictable answers. Inventive solutions often push beyond the boundaries of accepted answers and explore untried and more risky possibilities. Although failure is more common in this "pushing of the boundaries," there is also a greater possibility of success in finding truly inventive solutions to your D&T problems. Part of your responsibilities in this D&T program is to push the boundaries of accepted ideas and solutions. You may find it a little incongruous that in a D&T course "to succeed, you must also fail."

As suggested above, in an inventive pursuit there is no single right answer. Instead, there are a variety of answers or solutions that may be appropriate. A good solution fulfills a few of the identified criteria or specifications. The "best" solution, however, scores fairly well on achieving all the criteria and specifications. Best solutions often represent a "trade-off" across the different criteria. This is referred to as "optimizing" the criteria and includes the search for the most inventive solutions that can fulfill the criteria and specifications that you have established.

Interpretation In this D&T course only learning and remembering what you have been taught is not sufficient. You must also rethink and reconstruct what you have learned so that it makes sense to you and so that it matches the real world and new problems.

In your D&T work, you will be expected to gain more insights into what you are doing, as a means of moving your own learning to a higher level of understanding. You will also be expected to share the results, progress and problems of your efforts with others. To do either of these activities will require that you gain skills in analyzing and interpreting what is taking place.

Most demanding is the rethinking of your previous knowledge based on new insights you have gained. In these instances, you will be interpreting your experiences for yourself. These insights will be invaluable as you reconstruct your ideas on a subject. This is an important part of your own learning, during and beyond this course. Research on learning makes it clear that we are unable to transmit much knowledge, especially higher level insights to other people. Each of us must go through the process of rethinking what we have learned and how it may support, enhance, or perhaps replace earlier, incomplete, or sometimes faulty ideas.

RECONSTRUCTING WHAT WE KNOW

Reconstructing What We Know.

People often have ideas of how things operate. These ideas appear to be correct because they work. This is not always the case, and the following example is a personal account of the wrong ideas I had about how a heating system operated.

When I was young, I had a mental picture (concept) that the thermostat that controlled the hearing system was a type of "heat faucet or valve" to be turned on and off. If it was cold, I reasoned, I could turn on the thermostat and allow a certain amount of heat to run into the room. When it got warm enough, I could then turn off the faucet and stop the heat.

The interesting thing was, this "conceptual model" worked, at least to a certain extent. Turn the thermostat up = heat flows. Turn the thermostat off = no heat flows. The model provided me with an explanation of what was taking place. The inadequacies and inaccuracies of the model became evident, however, when I wanted to design and develop a "temperature control" system for a small greenhouse. For example, I found out that a thermostat does not sense heat but operates on sensing temperature.

A thermostat operates by sensing the temperature in the room. If the temperature drops below a desired level, the thermostat switches on the furnace. The furnace will operate until enough heat has been introduced into the room to raise the temperature reading in the thermostat. When the desired temperature is reached, the thermostat turns off the furnace. And so it continues, turning on or off, as needed, depending upon the temperature of the room.

When I realized that my model of a working heating system was inadequate, I had to rethink my model and make changes in it. In this case, part of the model (the control aspect) was incorrect, and I had to replace the idea of a faucet of the model with a different device. After considerable thought and experimentation with the ideas, I used the analogy of a little mechanical man in the thermostat that would lean one way when he became warm would turn off an electrical switch to stop the furnace from running. Similarly, if he became cold he would lean the other way to turn on the switch, thus turning on the furnace. I had improved my understanding of operating systems. My "conceptual model" was improved, and later was improved again when I replaced the little mechanical man with a switch that would move as it got warmer or cooler. Other changes in this model were necessary as I began to develop control systems, and particularly when I began to teach others how to design and develop them.

You may find it interesting to explore what "conceptual models" you use to explain events such as the operation of a heating system. You are certain to encounter instances where you explain how something operates, but your concept may be inaccurate or incomplete. In those instances where you find you are using an inadequate model, you can begin to question, analyze and improve it. As indicated earlier, this is called "interpretive" thinking.

RECONSTRUCTING WHAT WE KNOW CONTINUED

For example, as you design and build things you will discover that some of these concepts don't work. We encourage you in your interpretive learning activities, described earlier, to make notes in your portfolios and take the time to rethink these ideas. All of us do this and different times. It is called "reconstructing"[1] our knowledge. D&T activities and thinking will help you "reconstruct your knowledge" to build new models that are more adequate and powerful in helping you explain how the natural and designed world actually operates. (R.T.)

[1] Constructivism refers to a theory of how people learn. The name was developed by cognitive scientists to describe the process of how people change, modify and rebuild meaning from what they learn. Reconstruction relates to the rebuilding of "mental structures" that adapt to or accommodate what we know and what we are learning.

STUDENT CAPABILITIES

A major goal of the D&T program is to help you develop your capabilities in areas seen as essential for working and living in the world of the future. As the workplace continues to change, new competencies will be required of individuals who are to enjoy a productive, full, and satisfying life. A number of these competencies were identified in a major study completed by a "blue ribbon panel of experts from business and industry."[2] The study identified five general competencies related to using resources, interpersonal skills, information, systems, and technology. Additionally, the panel identified three foundation competencies related to basic skills, thinking skills, and personal qualities. These competencies are described below.

The know-how identified by SCANS is made up of five competencies and a three-part foundation of skills and personal qualities that are needed for solid job performance. These include:

COMPETENCIES — effective workers can productively use:

- **Resources** — allocating time, money, materials, space and staff;
- **Interpersonal Skills** — working on teams, teaching others, serving customers, leading, negotiating, and working well with people from culturally diverse backgrounds;
- **Information** — acquiring and evaluating data, organizing and maintaining files, interpreting and communicating, and using computers to process information;
- **Systems** — understanding social, organizational, and technological systems, monitoring and correcting performance, and designing or improving systems;

[2] The study supported by the United States Department of Labor is called the SCANS report (the Secretary's Commission on Achieving Necessary Skills). This 1994 report described the changes seen in the workplace and the skills that would be necessary for those who were to succeed in that changing workplace.

- **Technology** — selecting equipment and tools, applying technology to specific tasks, and maintaining and troubleshooting technologies.

THE FOUNDATION — competence requires:

- Basic Skills — reading, writing, arithmetic and mathematics, speaking, and listening;

- Thinking Skills — thinking creatively, making decisions, solving problems, seeing things in the mind's eye, knowing how to learn, and reasoning;

- Personal Qualities — individual responsibility, self-esteem, sociability, self-management and integrity.

INTRODUCTION TO THE D&T ACTIVITIES

Within this book, you will engage in a variety of activities, shown graphically in the conceptual map that follows. You will see several different shapes and titles are used. Let us consider each of them in turn.

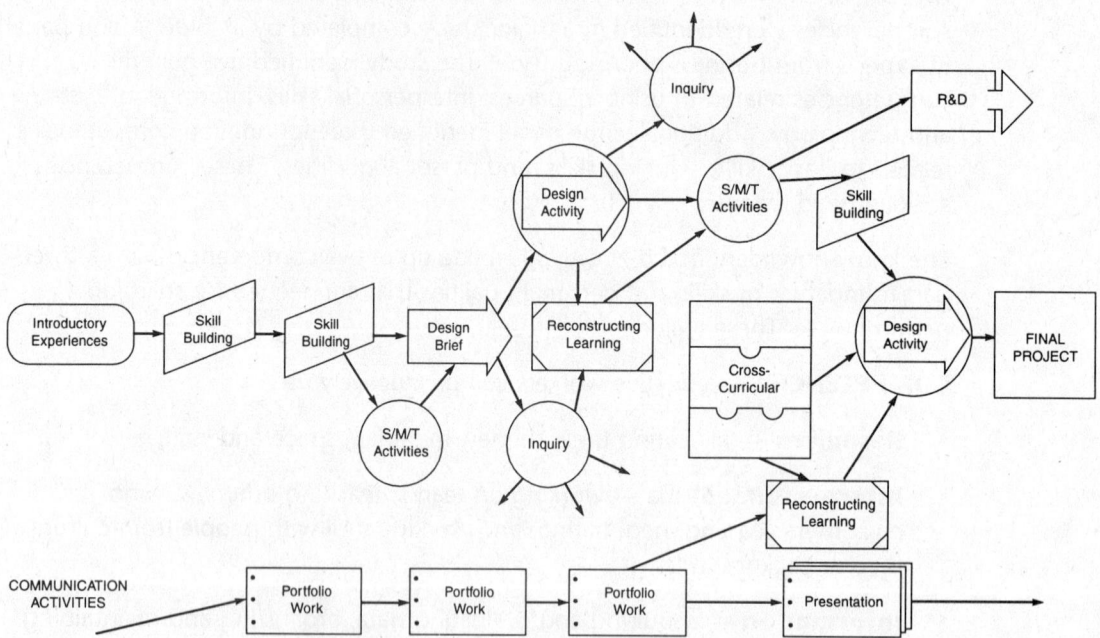

Conceptual Map

Design and Development

These activities represent the major focus of this course. Most of the activities are designed to help you gain, use and improve your skills and knowledge about design and development. Through the planned sequences of activities you will become more comfortable and better able to tackle progressively more complex and demanding problems.

The activities start with *Introductory Experiences*. These activities are designed to help you understand what D&T is about and how D&T problems are pursued. These activities will help provide the foundation for going on with more interesting and demanding activities.

Skill Building activities are introduced next. These include the work you will do in developing skills in such areas as sketching, drawing, and modeling.

Two related activities are then considered—*Design Activities and Design Briefs*. *Design Activities* are somewhat general in nature and set the context and general directions within which you will pursue a creative effort of developing solutions to problems. *Design Briefs* are more specific. Design Briefs spell out in more detail of what you are to do in pursuing a recognized problem.

Integrated Learning Integrated activities are designed to help you make connections that are often undeveloped between different areas of study. The major attention here is given to integrating science, mathematics and technology and to making connecting other subjects across the curriculum.

S/M/T Activities refers to those projects you will pursue that require understanding and application of concepts and skills of science, mathematics and technology to complete a project or implement a solution to a problem. These activities are very powerful because you will have the opportunity to see what you know in science and math be put to work and through that application will learn more.

S/M/T activities can be set in a variety of contexts. Some are set in historical contexts, such as the development of Morse's telegraph, the emergence of the steam engine or the evolution of automation, where the intent is to help you better understand how an invention or development came about. In many cases, the new inventions created a need for more scientific understanding. For example, the area of scientific study called "thermodynamics" that deals with heat and heat flow, was almost nonexistent and of only modest importance until the steam engine was developed. However, when steam boilers began blowing up, causing losses of property and life, the government intervened to provide support for research and investigation into thermodynamics as a body of important knowledge. This was not the first time, nor would it be the last, that governmental actions would shape policy on scientific and technological practice.

In other instances of S/M/T, the intent will be to show how the three areas of knowledge work together in real world instances. Consider for example what is required in the design and development of a playground slide, an elevator, or a bioreactor for making ginger ale. In these instances, the technology provides the means of translating ideas into physical form, the science provides insights into how the object, system or environment works, and the mathematics provides a means of describing (quantifying) the devices—their size, their operation and their results.

Cross Curricular activities refer to those initiatives that link with many of the school subjects you study. One example might be a joint theater and/or video production. A second example, might be a community improvement project such as helping to establish a recycling system. Another might be a collaborative study that would support the development of historical exhibit of the region where you live. Other examples might be the design and development of a product for needy children, the homeless or the elderly. There are almost countless examples that your school might consider instituting to enhance cross-curricular links between subjects.

Research and Investigation The longer-term goal of the D&T course is to help you become more skilled in pursuing investigative study. You should view these skills as essential competencies for living and working in the coming century. Two specific types of investigative study are identified and described—inquiry, and research and development.

Inquiry refers to investigative study related to science. Through inquiry activities you will learn more from your own study and investigation of a topic or a phenomenon than from being taught such content by someone else. Inquiry skills are important because in many cases you may pursue the study of an area or topic that has been previously studied. Inquiry skills will also serve you well in later life as you face circumstances and problems that have no predetermined answers and solutions.

Research and Development (R&D) refers to investigative activities that tend to be rather practical. R&D activities focus on fairly specific problems, such as the adhesive testing problem mentioned earlier. R&D problems are similar to D&T problems, but tend to be more technical in nature and may give less attention given to the design aspect of the work. In many instances, these two type of activities will look very much alike and will require many of the same skills and talents.

Communication Activities The final activities and competencies described here relate to your ability to represent, discuss and convey ideas to others. The success of your D&T work will depend on your ability to share information with others. Through your D&T activities you will gain skills and experience in (1) sketching, drawing, modeling and other visual means of communicating, (2) discussing, sharing and explaining, ideas within small groups, and (3) presenting, demonstrating and defending ideas to large groups of people.

In your *Portfolio Work*, you will use and develop many of your graphic communication skills. You will learn how to use sketching and drawing and other graphic skills to help you develop your own ideas and plans. You will also use these skills in the documentation and development of the designs you undertake. You will use your portfolio as a means of showing what you have learned in science, math and other subjects as they relate to the problems and projects you have completed. Finally, you will use your portfolio work to help reflect on the problems you have encountered, and to use this to rethink and reconstruct your knowledge about technology and other related subjects.

Finally, the D&T course will engage in Presentation work. Making presentations can initially be very intimidating. You will find, however, that in the topics you undertake in your D&T work you will know more about it that anyone else. Consequently, it will become easier, and rather exciting to share with others what you have learned in your work. Progressively, you will move from informal sharing of your ideas and work with a classmate or your teacher, to more formal sharing through large-group or video presentations.

Hopefully, you will enjoy the D&T course and its activities and that you will gain new knowledge and skills related to technology and design. We wish you good luck in your studies and in the applying what you will be learning to creative solutions to a wide range of problems and projects.

UNIT One

Design and Technology

CHAPTER 1
Introduction to Designing and Problem Solving

Technology is an activity that uses what we know to produce what we want and need. This book is intended to help you learn about technology by examining technology from the standpoint of:

- its *processes*—the **design** approach to problem solving,

- its *knowledge*—the understandings gained by people about the **design, resources, systems,** and **impacts** of technological activities,

- its *results*—the major technological **products, systems,** and **environments,** and

- its *impacts*—some previously identified **consequences** and **projections** for future developments.

Designing and problem solving are the processes by which ideas and knowledge are translated into something tangible. It provides a plan about how to make and improve on the product. Within this course, the design loop is represented by the word IDEATE.

When you use the design loop, you will move back and forth through the steps several times, depending on the complexity of the problem.

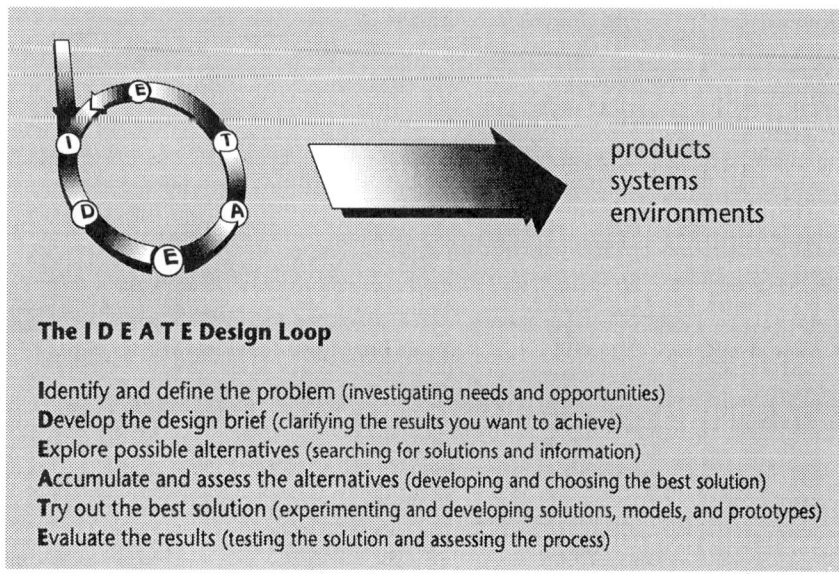

The I D E A T E Design Loop

Identify and define the problem (investigating needs and opportunities)
Develop the design brief (clarifying the results you want to achieve)
Explore possible alternatives (searching for solutions and information)
Accumulate and assess the alternatives (developing and choosing the best solution)
Try out the best solution (experimenting and developing solutions, models, and prototypes)
Evaluate the results (testing the solution and assessing the process)

As indicated in the text, going through the same process several times is called **reiteration**, with each cycle through the process called an **iteration**. This process will be made easier by asking yourself a set of questions as you pursue your work. An example Guide for Design Questions is provided below.

GUIDE FOR DESIGN QUESTIONS

Identify and Define the Problem—*Investigating Needs and Opportunities*
- Did you identify a problem that represents a real need or potential opportunity?
- Did you set the problem within a larger context or situation?

Describe the Design Brief—*Clarifying Results You Want to Achieve*
- Did you develop specifications and criteria such as time, cost, materials, size/shape, special function, user(s), and place of use?

Explore Possible Alternatives—*Searching for Solutions and Information*
- Did you conduct an adequate investigation?
- Did your research help clarify the needs, wants, and opportunities of the design?
- Did you generate a number of possible and diverse solutions?

Assess the Alternatives—*Choosing the Best Solution*
- Did you use a systematic approach to assessing the possible alternatives?
- Did you compare and rank the alternatives before choosing the best solution?

Try Out the Best Solution—*Experimenting and Developing Solutions, Models, and Prototypes*
- Did you conduct experiments and tests on your design and its operation?
- Did you engage in modeling and prototyping your proposed answer?

Evaluate the Results—*Testing the Solution and Assessing the Process*
- Did you conduct appropriate testing of your finished product?
- Did you collect, analyze, and report the essential data on the product?
- Did you assess its operation and your efforts in developing the product?

The Guide for Design Questions is provided to help you ask and answer better questions in your design work. For the activities that follow, you may wish to deal with another problem that Aunt Sarah has in her home. Although she gets around fairly well, she tends to forget where she leaves things. She is specifically concerned that she misplaces her portable phone and can only find it when someone calls and the phone rings. Can you help her deal with this problem? Use the worksheets that follow to guide your work on this problem or one you and your teacher choose.

Identify and Define the Problem

Investigating Needs and Opportunities. As you engaged in your design and technology work, did you identify a problem that represents a real need or potential opportunity? Did you set the problem within a larger context or situation?

What needs does the problem represent?

What opportunities does the problem represent?

What is your problem statement?

Problem Statement:

Describe the Design Brief

Clarifying results you want to achieve. In describing the design brief, did you develop specifications and criteria such as time, cost, materials, size/shape, special function, user(s), and place of use?

Design Brief:

Specifications:

Explore Possible Alternatives

Searching for Solutions and Information. As you pursued your design, did you conduct an adequate investigation? Did your research help clarify the needs, wants, and opportunities of the design? Did you generate a number of possible and diverse solutions?

Possible Alternatives

Unit 1 Design and Technology

Assess the Alternatives

Choosing the Best Solution. As you worked on your design, did you use a systematic approach to assessing the possible alternatives? Did you compare and rank the alternatives before choosing the best solution?

ASSESSMENT OF SPECIFICATIONS WORKSHEET

Specifications for the Design: (from page 7)	Alternatives*				
	I	II	III	IV	V
a) _____	___	___	___	___	___
b) _____	___	___	___	___	___
c) _____	___	___	___	___	___
d) _____	___	___	___	___	___
e) _____	___	___	___	___	___
f) _____	___	___	___	___	___
Average**	___	___	___	___	___

*   Rank alternatives on a scale of 1–5.
    (1= poor, 2 = fair, 3 = acceptable, 4 = good, 5 = excellent)

** Mark apparent best solution.

Try Out the Best Solution

Experiment and Develop Solutions, Models, and Prototypes. In this phase of your design work, did you conduct experiments and tests on your design and its operation? Did you engage in modeling and prototyping your potential answer?

Solutions, Models, and Prototypes:
    Fabrication (actual devices, photos, drawings, or videos)

Evaluate the Results

Test the Solution and Assess the Process. Did you conduct appropriate testing of your finished product? Did you collect, analyze and report the essential data on the product, its operation, and your efforts in developing the product?

Test Solutions, Models, and Prototypes:

Assess the Process:

Evaluating and assessing your results will help you develop your final report on how well your product performs. Some of the specific questions you will ask as you evaluate your project and as you prepare your report will include the following:

CHECKLIST FOR EVALUATION OF DESIGN

- How well does the design perform?
- How good does the design look, aesthetically?
- How safe is the product to use?
- How adequate was our plan of work?
- How easy or difficult was the construction?
- Was the most appropriate method of construction used?
- Were the most suitable materials used?
- Was the cost more or less than expected?
- How can I/we improve my/our design?
- How can I/we improve my/our overall effort?

ENRICHMENT DESIGN AND TECHNOLOGY ACTIVITIES

There are several design and technology activities you can try out at this time. Suppose you and one of your classmates were April and Enrique's friends and you joined their team. Given the design brief and the specifications that April and Enrique developed, consider the following:

- Identify at least three alternative solutions you would suggest.
- What source could you use to get good information on each of these alternative solutions?
- Use the checklist from the previous page and assess each of your proposed solutions.
- Which solution to the problem seems to be best and worth exploring further?
- Make a sketch of your proposed solution and what it would look like.
- How would you go about testing your proposed solutions?
- What are some of the strengths and weaknesses of your solution?
- Write a short statement describing those strengths and weaknesses in comparison to April and Enrique's solution using magnetic labels.

REVIEW AND ASSESSMENT ACTIVITIES

- List and describe the general steps in the design loop.
- Identify a problem that addresses how tools are displayed in your school facility.
- Develop a design brief to solve that problem for a specific tool.
- Develop specifications for the tool display device.
- Generate several alternative solutions to your problem.
- Assess which of the alternative solutions is potentially the best.
- Develop plans for how you would build the device or a model of it
- Describe how you would evaluate the product of your work.

The formats that are provided on the following pages should help you go through a design problem. The formats are provided as reminders of the type of questions that need to be posed and answered. The sequence of events in problem solving is far more involved and complex than going through a set of steps in a mechanical fashion. You will find it necessary to move back and forth through the steps as you continue the design process. That "give and take" and "uncertainty" better represents the design process. The formats are to help you reconstruct and record some of the major phases of development in a design problem.

USING THE DESIGN LOOP AND THE IDEATE MODEL

Identify and Define the Problem—Investigating Needs and Opportunities

- *Did you identify a problem that represents a real need or potential opportunity?*
- *Did you set the problem within a larger context or situation?*

Problem Statement:

Describe the Design Brief—Clarifying Results You Want to Achieve

- *Did you develop specifications and criteria such as: time, cost, materials, size/shape, special function, user(s), place of use?*

Design Brief:

Specifications:

Explore Possible Alternatives—Searching for Solutions and Information

- *Did you conduct an adequate investigation?*
- *Did your research help clarify the needs, wants and opportunities of the design?*
- *Did you generate a number of possible and diverse solutions?*

Research and Investigation:

Generate Possible Solutions:

Assess the Alternatives—Choosing the Best Solution

- *Did you use a systematic approach to assessing the possible alternatives?*
- *Did you compare and rank the alternatives before choosing the best solution?*

ASSESSMENT OF SPECIFICATIONS WORKSHEET

Specifications for the Design:

Alternatives*

	I.	II.	III.	IV.	V.
a)	—	—	—	—	—
b)	—	—	—	—	—
c)	—	—	—	—	—
d)	—	—	—	—	—
e)	—	—	—	—	—
f)	—	—	—	—	—
	—	—	—	—	—
Average**	—	—	—	—	—

* Rank alternatives on a scale of 1-5.
(1= poor, 2 = fair, 3 = acceptable, 4 = good, 5 = excellent)

** Mark the apparent best solution.

Try Out the Best Solution—Experimenting and Developing Solutions, Models, and Prototypes

- *Did you conduct experiments and tests on your design and its operation?*
- *Did you engage in modeling and prototyping your proposed answer?*

Develop Test, Model, or Prototype:

Evaluate the Results—Testing the Solution and Assessing the Process

- *Did you conduct appropriate testing of your finished product?*
- *Did you collect, analyze, and report the essential data on the product?*
- *Did you assess its operation and your efforts in developing the product?*

CHECKLIST FOR EVALUATION OF DESIGN

(Selected specific questions to ask as you evaluate your project and work.)

- How well does the design perform?

- How good does the design look, aesthetically?

- How safe is the product to use?

- How adequate was your plan of work?

- How easy or difficult was the construction?

- Was the most appropriate method of construction used?

- Were the most suitable materials used?

- Was the cost more or less than expected?

- How can I/we improve my/our design?

- How can I/we improve my/our overall effort?

- Others?

CHAPTER 2: Designing, Documenting, and Drawing

In designing, you translate your ideas into things and your thoughts into action. This is the process part of technology, and it is done in order to satisfy human wants or needs.

As you develop your ideas, it is helpful to get them out of your head and into a more tangible form by sketching, writing, or composing. Communicating ideas to others can be expanded and enhanced by adding visual or auditory representations.

In design and technology activities, it is important that you keep records of your ideas and work by "thinking on paper." Documenting can help prevent you from losing good ideas. Keeping track of when you did the design work includes notations on the date you made the notes and drawings. This is important when "ownership" is proven through copyrighting or patenting.

Freehand sketching can be used to record ideas and share them with others. Initial sketches include only partial thoughts and ideas. Attention to line, shape, and form can be used to achieve different effects. Lines can be used to show ideas such as restfulness, texture, movement, growing, chaos, and distance.

Many objects can be drawn by using their basic geometric shapes. Patterns and tessellations are included in many designs. A square can be rendered as a cube, a triangle as a cone or a pyramid, and so on. This approach becomes very important as you represent objects in three-dimensional forms in sketches and drawings.

DESIGN CONSIDERATIONS

A successful design should function properly. It should also be attractive to the users. Attractiveness is more than looking good. The users of a design may experience it through a range of senses to include sight, hearing, touch, taste, and smell. Designs that are attractive are said to have aesthetic appeal. If the design conveys the message or has the effect it is supposed to, it is considered to have aesthetic effectiveness.

Aesthetic design is accomplished partly through the use of visual design elements. These elements (point, line, shape, form, texture, and color) are used to translate ideas into objects of effective appearance. Aesthetic designs are also enhanced through the use of visual design principles (proportion, balance, harmony, contrast, and pattern).

Effective designs are also achieved through appropriate applications of ergonomics principles that help insure the designs are usable by the intended users. As you design things for people, four main factors must be considered and investigated. These are size (the relation of the object and the part of the body that will be involved with the thing being designed), movements (the moves that a human must make while using the designs, energy requirements (strength, stamina, and endurance), and sensory responses (the reactions of the people to the design).

DOCUMENTING TECHNIQUES

In design and technology activities, it is important that you keep records of your ideas and work by "thinking on paper." Documenting can help prevent you from losing good ideas. Keeping track of when you did the design work includes notations on the date you made the notes and drawings. This is important when "ownership" is proven through copyrighting or patenting.

You can document your work using logs, journals, reports and portfolios. Journals provide a general record of events and are technical diaries with entries made on a daily or periodic basis. Journals include personal observations, notes, drawings, and other entries that record the work of your progress. Logs are somewhat more formal and serve as a daily record of what happens each day in the conduct of your project. Reports and portfolios provide information on the progress or results of a project. You can use a variety of page layouts for a portfolio.

Drawings are essential for recording ideas that can not be described in words alone. Drawings allow you to express ideas of what something will look like before it is actually made. Drawings will help you think through how a product or device will work. Your drawings can help to isolate problems that might be encountered in an object's operation or in the construction of that object. As you will see later in this chapter and elsewhere throughout this book, drawing requires skill. Drawings are an indispensable part of design and technology work.

Notes are helpful to add to sketches and drawings as you are capturing ideas and communicating with others. You can use notes to help remember what you had in mind, to show how different parts might go together, how a material might be shaped or formed, how moving parts might interfere with each other, or where something might not be altogether safe. Sketches and drawings with explanatory notes are valuable as memory tools and for communicating your ideas to others.

DESIGN ACTIVITIES—RECORDING IDEAS THROUGH DRAWINGS

The drawings below represent some of the ideas of a designer. The designer has been asked to help solve a specific problem often encountered in an elementary classroom—the need for table space at selected times, but the need to have open, clear floor space at other times. How might you approach this problem, and what will your ideas look like in sketches and drawings?

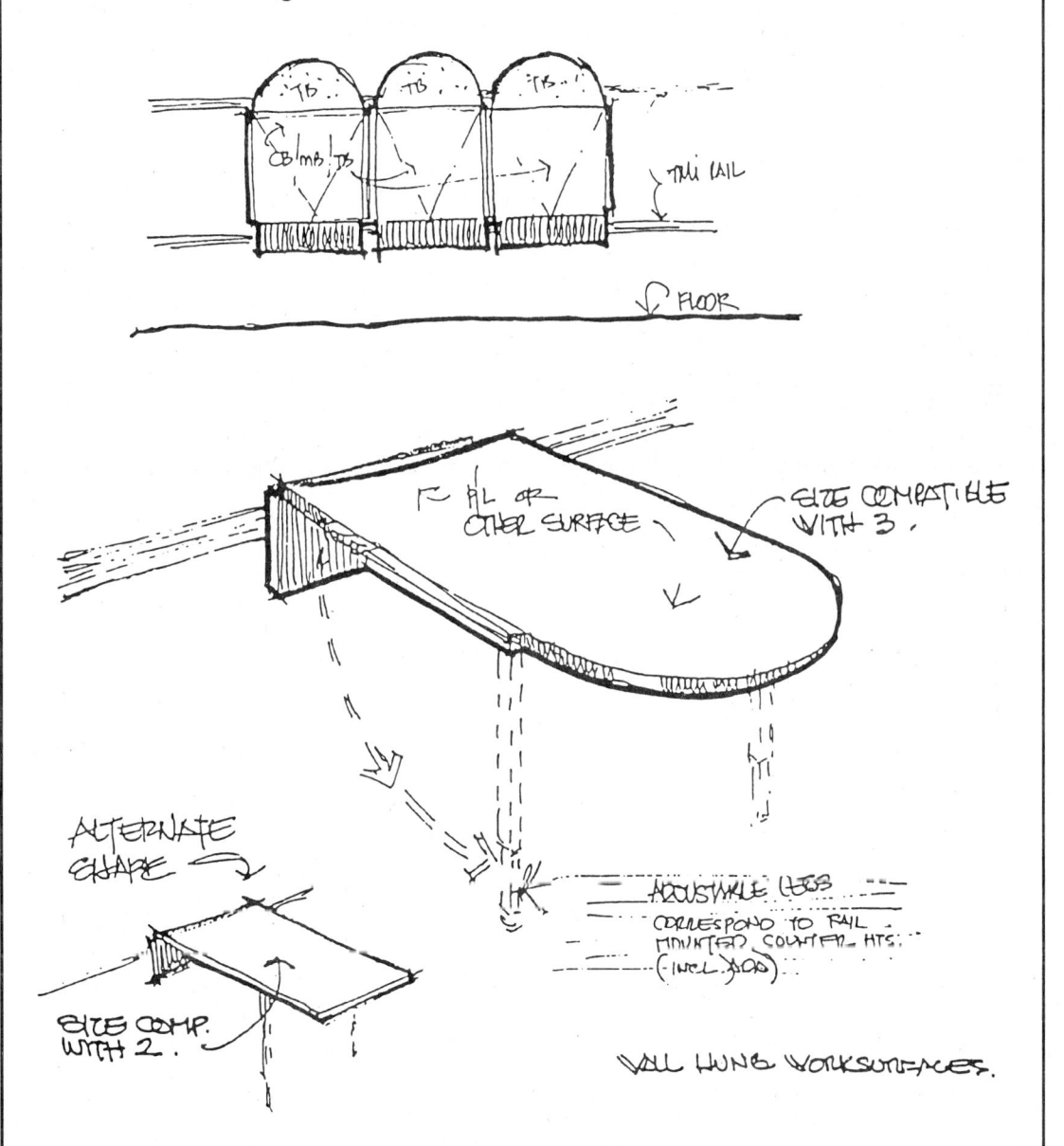

Notice how some of the notes included by the designer are a form of "shorthand". The note "TB" refers to "tackboard". What do you think CB MB refers to in the top drawing? The note "P/L" refers to plastic laminate. What might the other notations represent? What do the numbers "2" and "3" refer to? Hint: Remember the client/user.

DESIGN ACTIVITIES—IDEAS FOR NOTES AND NOTATIONS

Illustrated below are examples from your text of notes and notations.

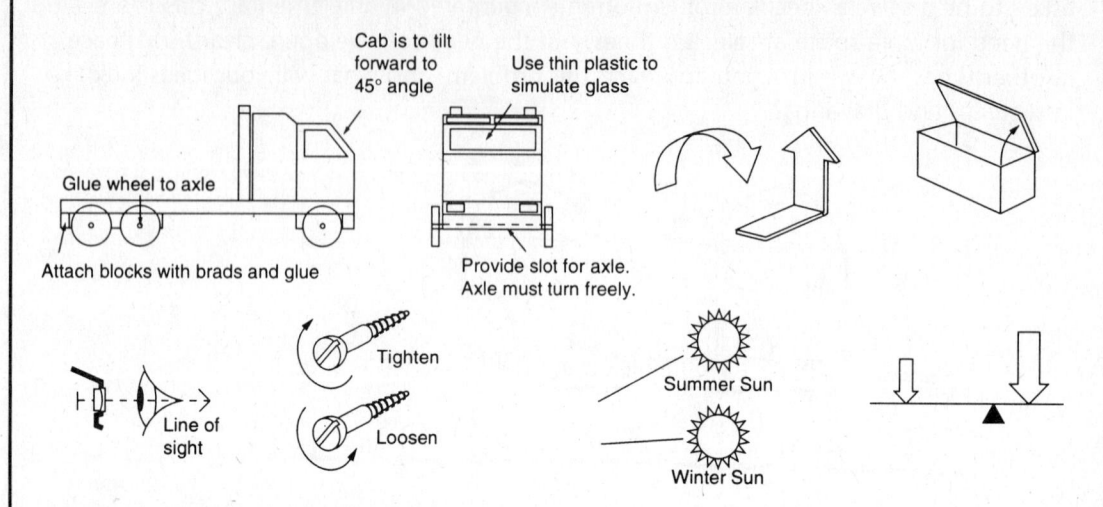

Develop a collection of other examples that others have used in making notes and notations on their drawings. Add ideas of your own that will help explain how a device operates. What notes and notations would be helpful in describing how a device or project might be constructed?

Developing Plans and Timelines

Plans play an important part in helping you understand and keep track of what lies ahead. Often problems can be averted or solved through good planning. Many different types of plans are available. The Gantt timeline identifies the necessary activities in the sequence in which they need to be done.

PROJECT TIMELINE

Month	Jan.	Feb.	Mar.	April	May	June	July	Aug.	Sept.	Oct.	Nov.	Dec.
Activity												
1.												
2.												
3.												
4.												
5.												
6.												
7.												
8.												
9.												
10.												
11.												
12.												
13.												

DRAWING TECHNIQUES

Freehand sketching can be used to record ideas and share them with others. Initial sketches include only partial thoughts and ideas. Attention to line, shape, and form can be used to achieve different effects. Lines can be used to show ideas such as restfulness, texture, movement, growing, chaos, and distance. In the space provided, try your hand at using lines to represent the following ideas: direction, movement, noise, strength, depth, or feelings of anger or fear. When you draw straight lines by freehand, you will keep your wrist locked and move your whole arm across the paper with each stroke you make.

Practice drawing vertical, horizontal, and diagonal lines. Experiment with drawing them close together and spaced farther apart. Experiment with drawing lines that range from light to heavy.

Horizontal

Vertical

Diagonal

If you hold your pencil at a shallow angle, you can draw broad lines. Experiment to see what effects you can achieve with different lines from broad to very fine.

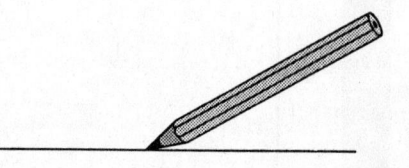

You will find that if you draw two points on a piece of paper, your mind tends to link them with an imaginary line. You can use this approach to help you in your drawing. Dots have been used in the illustration below to help in drawing a chair and table. By using dots, you can get a quick image of an object before you draw it. This approach is particularly helpful because you can change the object easily by simply moving or changing the dots.

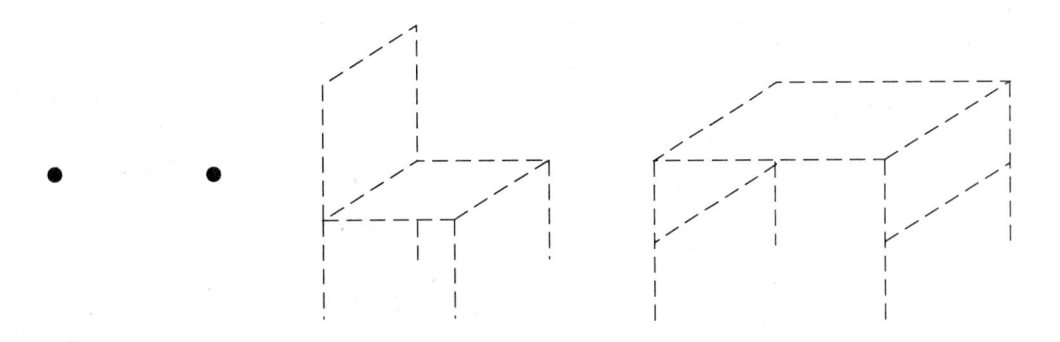

Using Curved Lines

When you draw long, curved lines, you should lock your wrist as you did for straight lines. You will use your elbow as a pivot as you swing your arm across the page.

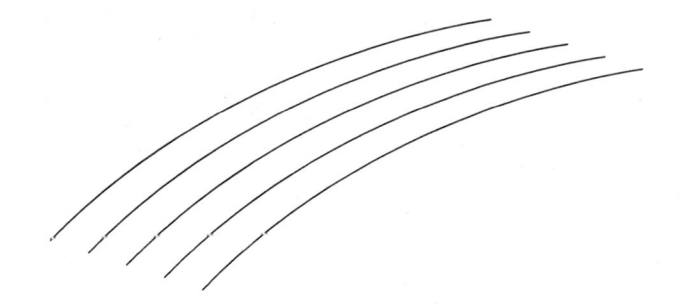

When you draw tighter curves, you can use your wrist as the pivot and draw the curve by moving your hand in an arc or curve. In the space provided, practice drawing a variety of curved lines. Try to create a range of lines from fine to broad.

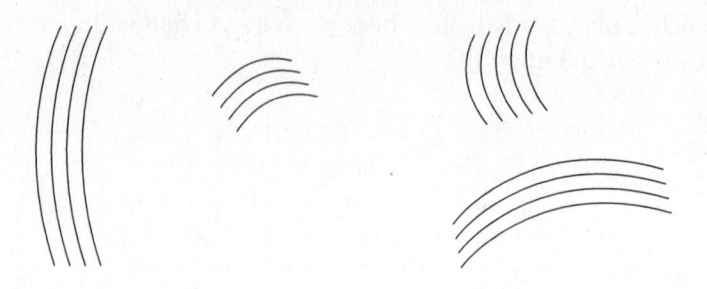

Curved lines are also used to create contour lines that link points of equal height. The most common use of contour lines is on maps, but contour lines can also be used to show that something has form or three dimensions. Examples of both uses are shown below. Experiment with both approaches to show the contour of different objects.

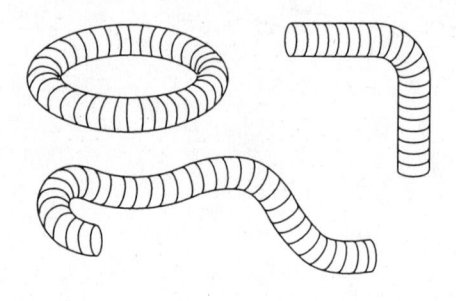

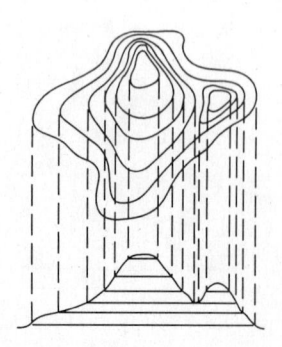

PICTORIAL DRAWINGS

Pictorial drawings include one-point perspective, two-point perspective, isometric drawings, and oblique drawings. Oblique drawings allow you to develop pictorial drawings by using slanted (oblique) lines. These lines can be drawn mechanically which, with practice, will help you generate a drawing fairly quickly. Isometric drawings are pictorials that are usually drawn mechanically by using three equal angles. The use of these angles makes isometric drawings similar to two-point perspective drawings. Developing pictorial drawings by freehand can be considerably easier by using a transparent box, or crating, technique to visualize the object more easily and keep the drawing in proportion. Developing pictorial drawings by freehand can also be made easier by using grid paper.

Pictorial drawings can help you represent objects as you see them, but the realism achieved by using angled lines makes it difficult to get true measurements from pictorial drawings. Non-pictorial drawings serve as a plan or working drawings for something you wish to build. They provide the dimensions, materials, and information for fabrication and assembly that are necessary to actually build the object represented in your design.

One-Point Perspective

An important part of drawing in perspective is placing the objects correctly on the paper. Usually, you will draw things that are quite small. They should be placed below eye level because you normally look down on them. When you draw buildings, they should be placed at or just above eye level. The drawing below shows a box drawn in one-point perspective. Refer to Figure 2.25 in your text and complete a similar drawing of an object you or your teacher choose.

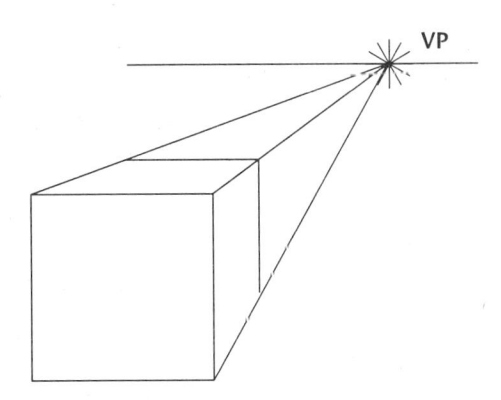

Two-Point Perspective

Two-point perspectives are used regularly in representing objects pictorially. With practice, you can become quite good at showing objects in realistic form. The drawing below shows a box in two-point perspective that is placed at, above, and below eye level. Complete a two-point perspective drawing of the television set with the screen facing to the left. Feel free to replace the TV with an object you want to include in your portfolio.

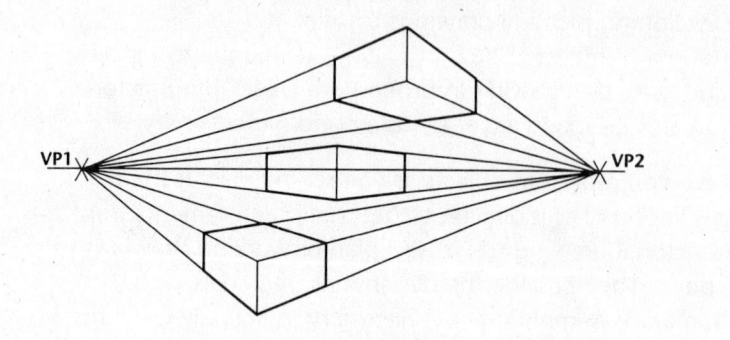

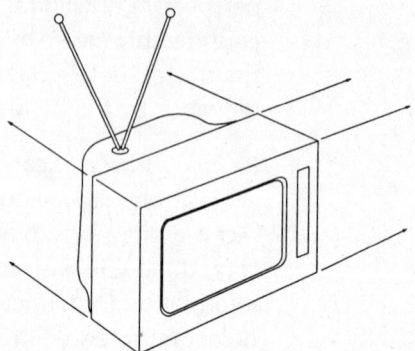

Your drawing in perspective will improve as you gain skill in looking closely at the objects you will draw. Most objects seem to be made of simple geometric shapes and solids such as squares, cubes, rectangles, circles, cylinders, and spheres.

NOTE: When you draw a large object or something closer, you may need to place the vanishing points off the page.

Oblique Drawings

Oblique drawings are useful as pictorial drawings because they give a sense of perspective, but they allow you to draw the front view in its true size. This drawing shows a step block in oblique form. Refer to Figure 2.27 in your text and complete an oblique drawing of a house, a desk, a tool, or other object of your choice.

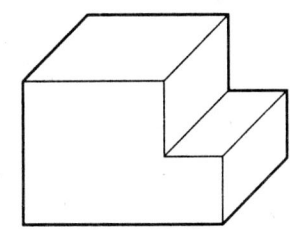

Isometric Drawings

Isometric drawings are easy to draw and to understand. The drawing below shows a block in isometric. Remember, isometric drawings do introduce a certain amount of distortion, but the overall effect is still quite acceptable. Refer to Figure 2.28 in your text and complete an isometric drawing of a toy, tool, package, or other object of your choice.

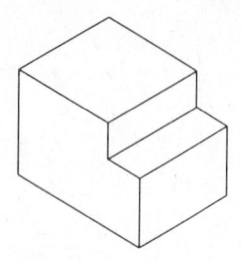

NOTE: (a) All vertical lines on an object are also vertical on the drawing. (b) The lines that are horizontal on the object are drawn at 30°. (c) Draw all lines in scale with their actual, or true, length. (All lines might be one-half their true length.)

Crating Techniques

You will find that representing objects in pictorial drawings will be much simpler if the objects are reduced to their basic shapes. Once you have determined the shape, the object can be drawn within the crate. Crating can be used with any of the 3-D drawing techniques that have been introduced—oblique, isometric, or perspective.

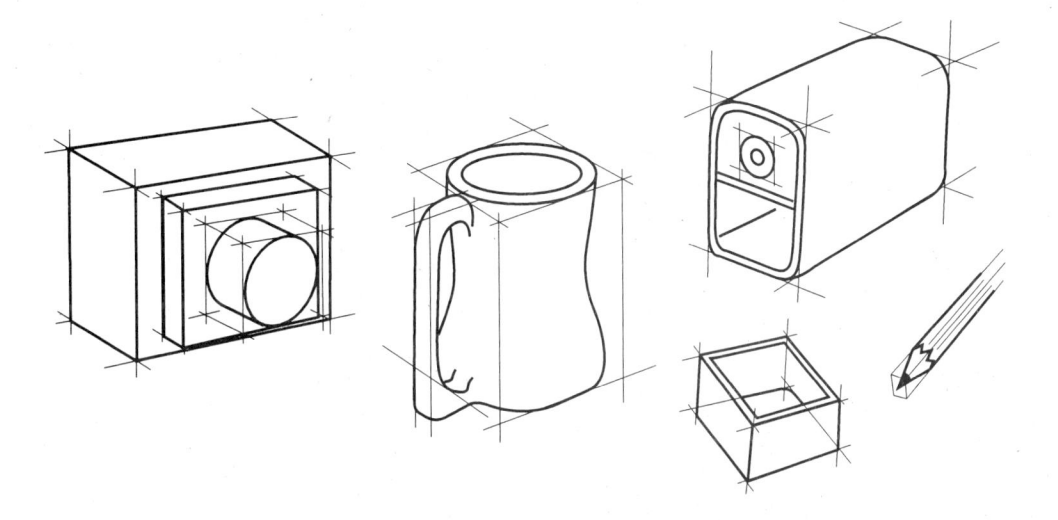

Refer to Figure 2.29 in your text and then draw each of the above objects, or others of your own choice, in freehand oblique, isometric, or perspective form.

You should draw the crating with light lines using the pictorial technique you believe is best. You can then finish drawing the object and add the appropriate details.

Drawing Circles in Pictorial Views

You can draw circles in perspective with templates or by freehand. Each circle is actually drawn at an angle and forms an oval or ellipse. They can be drawn mechanically with templates as shown below.

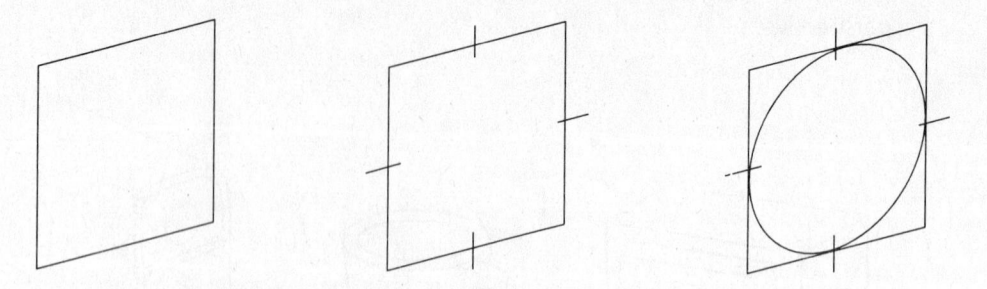

You can also draw circles in perspective by using the following technique.

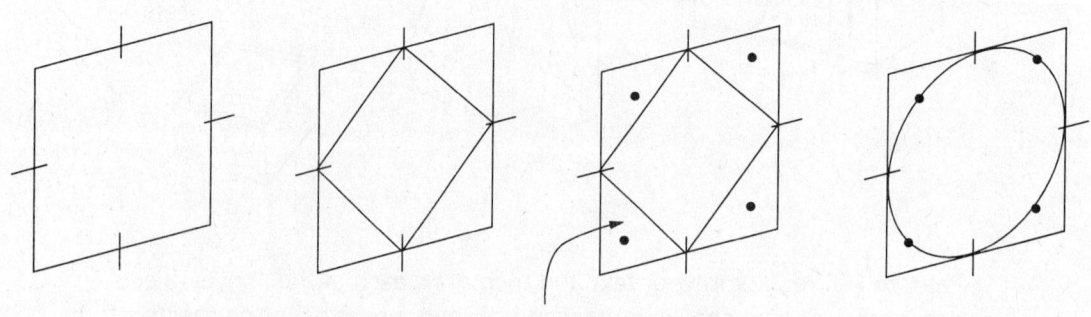

NOTE: Place the dots in the center of these triangles.

You may find it helpful to practice drawing ellipses on the faces of the cube provided below.

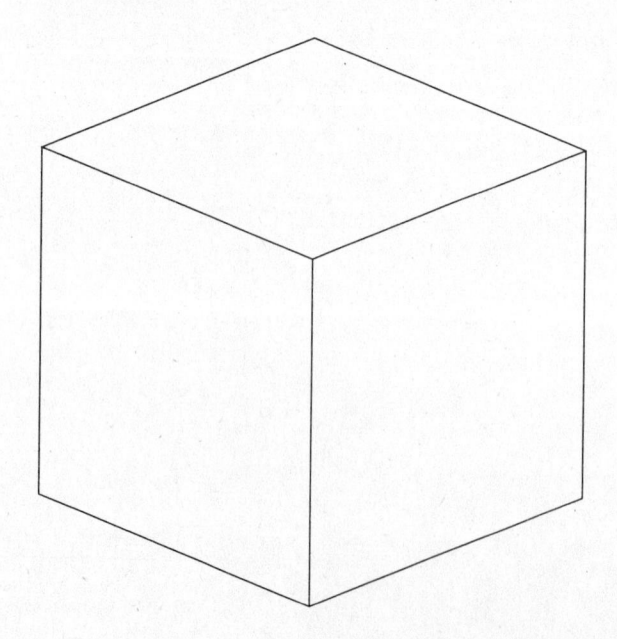

Using Grids for Pictorial Drawings

With a little practice, isometric drawings are fairly easy to understand. As indicated before, they are simplified pictorials. The grid paper included at the end of the chapter provides lines for you to follow as you complete your drawing. To create an isometric drawing, complete the following steps:

1. Draw the edge of the object closest to you. The length of the line is the same as the length of the edge.

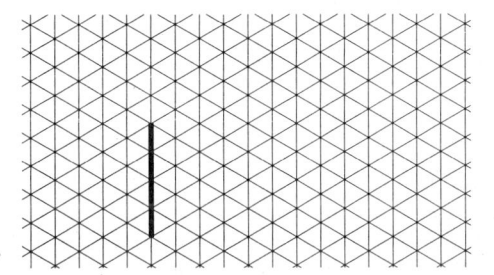

2. Now draw the right side (as you look at the object). Draw a line for the top edge and the bottom edge. These are at 30° and are the actual length of the side.

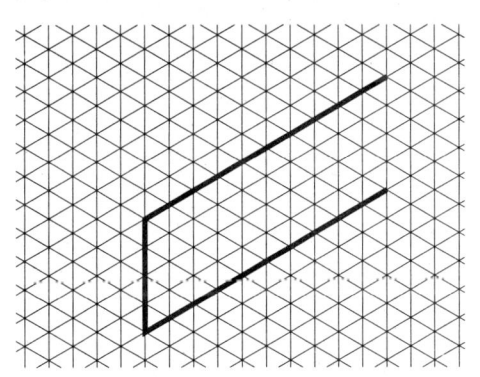

3. Draw the left side of the object. The two lines are also at 30° and are the actual length of the left side.

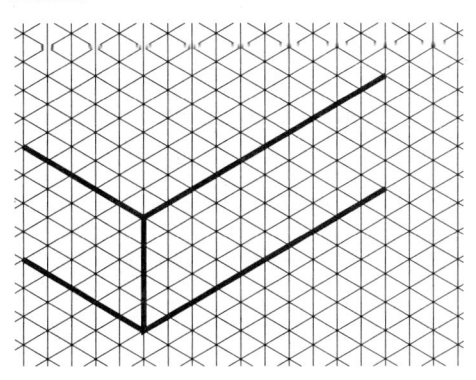

4. Draw the vertical lines at the right and left of the object.

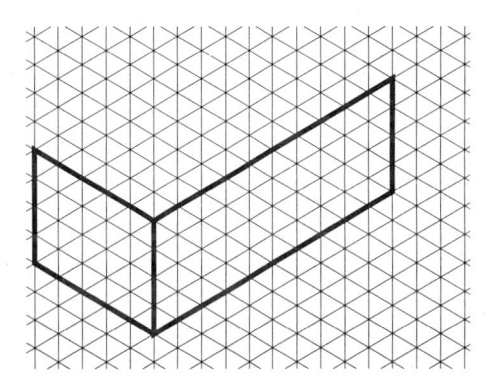

5. Add the final lines to complete the drawing. These lines are also drawn at 30° and are true length.

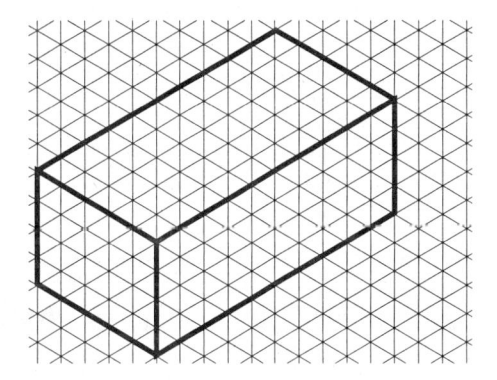

You can improve your drawings if you place a plain sheet of paper on top of the grid paper. Grids used in this manner are called backing sheets. Place a sheet under your drawing paper and use the grid lines to guide your sketching. When the backing sheet is removed, your drawing will appear as though you sketched it freehand on plain paper. Experiment with different grids to match the style of drawing you want. Also use a sheet with horizontal lines as a guide for your handwriting or lettering.

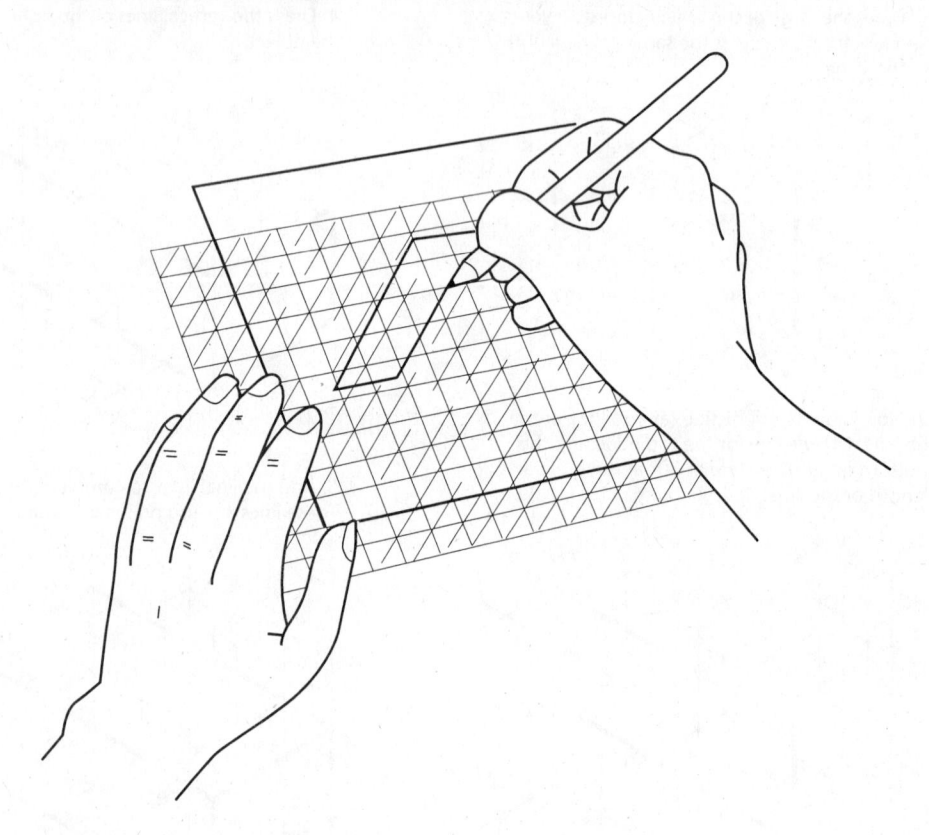

Using Grids for Reducing and Enlarging Drawings

In some cases, you will need to enlarge or reduce the scale of an object. You may not have easy access to a copier that will do the job, and you can accomplish satisfactory results by using grids, as shown in the examples below. The size of the grid in Drawing 1 will depend primarily on how large you wish to make the finished drawing. The size of the grid in Drawing 2 will depend on how small you want to make the finished drawing. You can draw both grids directly on the paper, or you can draw the grids on tracing paper if you do not want the grids to show.

(1)

(2)

Enlargement

Reduction

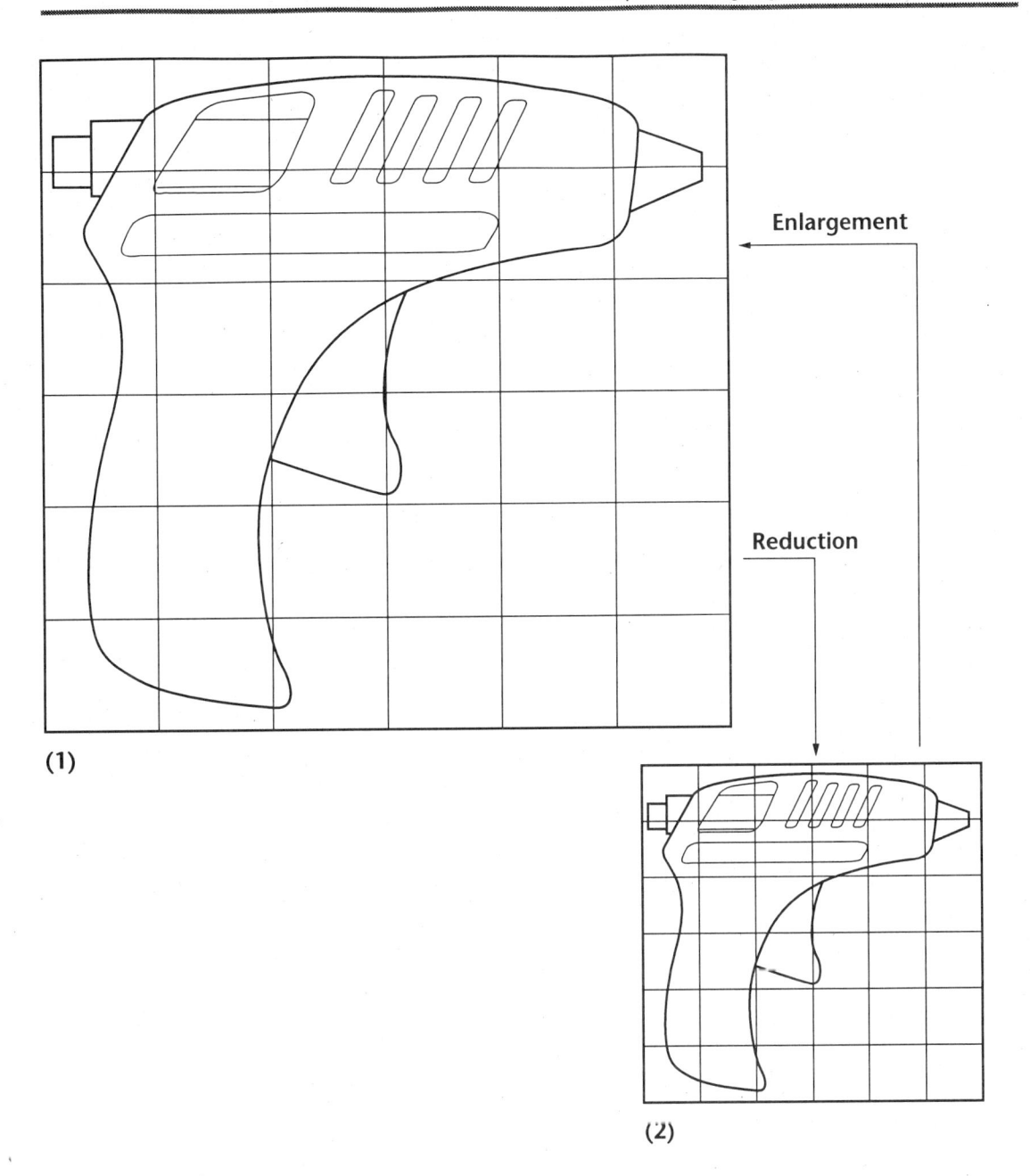

PLAN DRAWINGS

The most common plan drawings used in design and technology are orthographic projections. These projection techniques help you create a flat drawing of the top (often called the plan view), the side view or elevation, and the end view or elevation. Dimensions are added to provide important information to make the object.

Several other drawing techniques are useful for different purposes in your planning of design and technology projects. These include sectional, exploded view, or cutaway drawings.

Orthographic Projection Techniques

Go through the following steps to create an orthographic drawing of a toy truck (see Figure 2.31 in your text). Draw all horizontal lines with a T-square or parallel rule and draw the vertical and diagonal lines with a triangle. You may use a drafting machine if one is available.

If the object can not be drawn full-size, convert the dimensions to scale. It is good practice to make a quick sketch, or a thumbnail sketch, of the views of the drawing and how they will fit on the paper before you start.

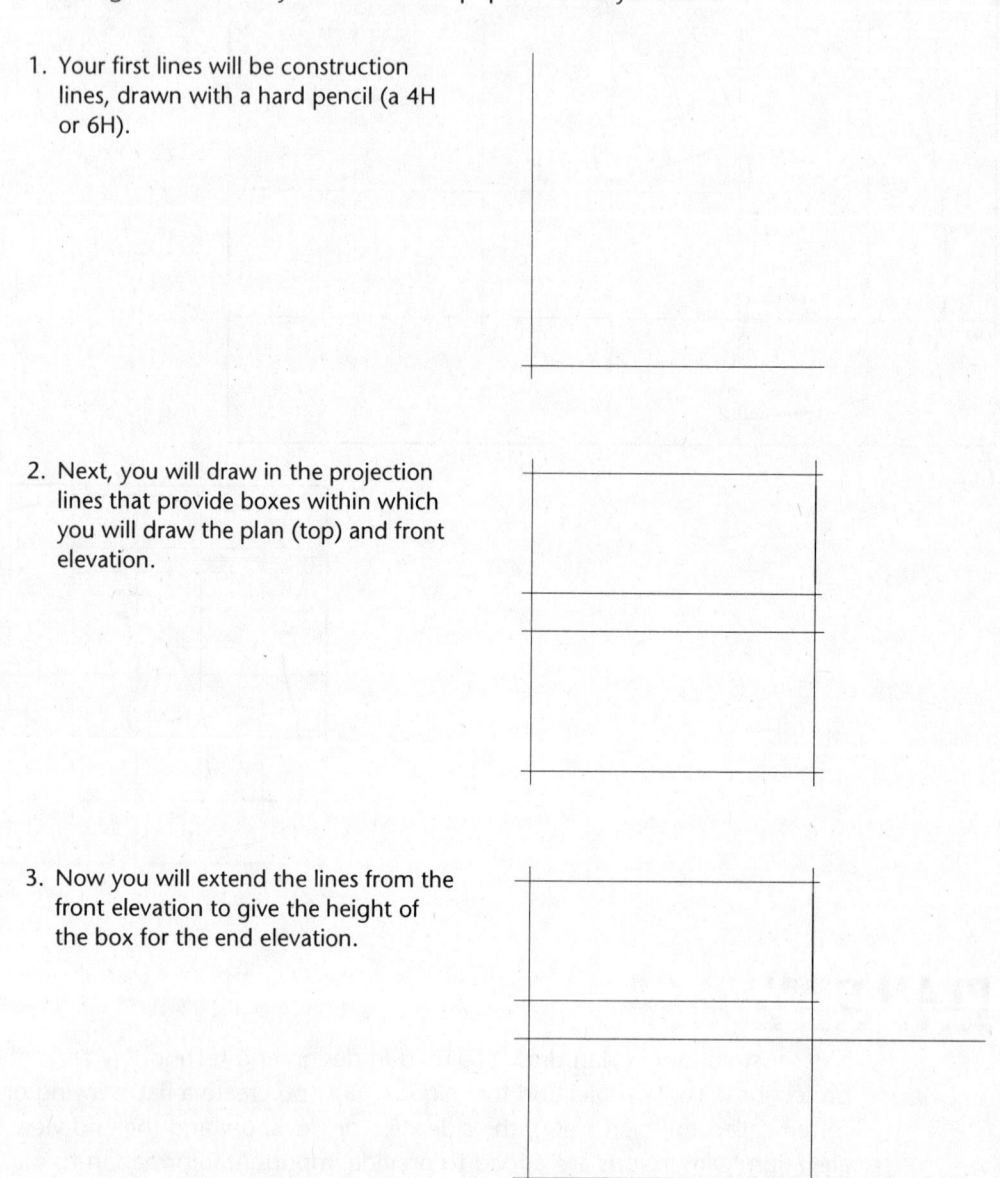

1. Your first lines will be construction lines, drawn with a hard pencil (a 4H or 6H).

2. Next, you will draw in the projection lines that provide boxes within which you will draw the plan (top) and front elevation.

3. Now you will extend the lines from the front elevation to give the height of the box for the end elevation.

Chapter 2 Designing, Documenting, and Drawing **39**

4. Next, draw a line at 45° from the front elevation. You will use this line to project the width of the object from the plan view. Projecting these lines forms the box for the end elevation. The three views are now set.

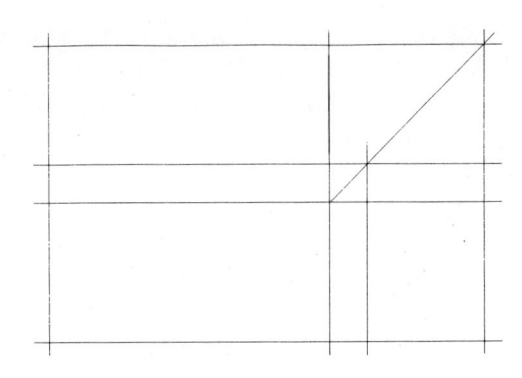

5. Show the center of all circles and symmetrical objects with a center line. A center line is a thin line with dashes at the center of the circle. Use the cross of the centers to draw in all the full circles. Use a compass with HB lead.

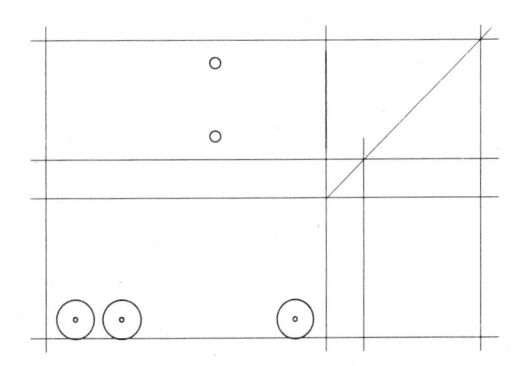

6. Now add the rest of the detail. Your drawings will be more accurate if you develop the habit of using your instruments to transfer dimensions from one view to another. This practice is more accurate than making extra measurements.

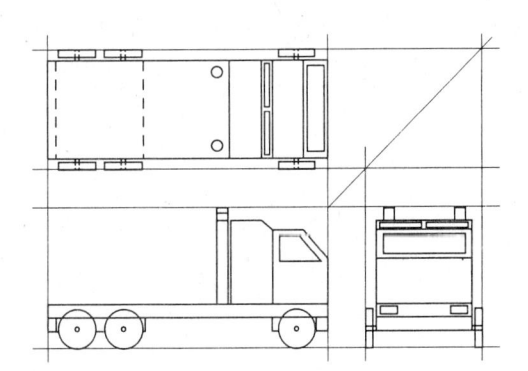

7. Draw in outline with a 2H pencil. You should make sure that corners meet exactly and do not cross. Do not press too hard on the pencil.

Sometimes, details cannot be seen because they are hidden inside or behind another part. In this drawing, you cannot see the holes that hold the exhaust stacks or the holes in the wheels for the axles. These are hidden lines and are drawn with a 4H pencil as short dashed lines. Remember that plan drawings allow you to see edges and shapes in their actual length and size. Plan drawings allow you to draw objects as though you were looking straight at each surface of the object. By drawing with right angles and perpendicular lines, each view is seen in its true shape.

DRAWING ACTIVITIES—ADDING DIMENSIONS

If you or someone else are to make the object you have drawn, you will need to add dimensions. There are some accepted rules to dimensioning a drawing. Dimensions have been included in the drawing of the toy truck according to these rules. You will want the dimensions to be clear and easy to read, but not dominate the drawing.

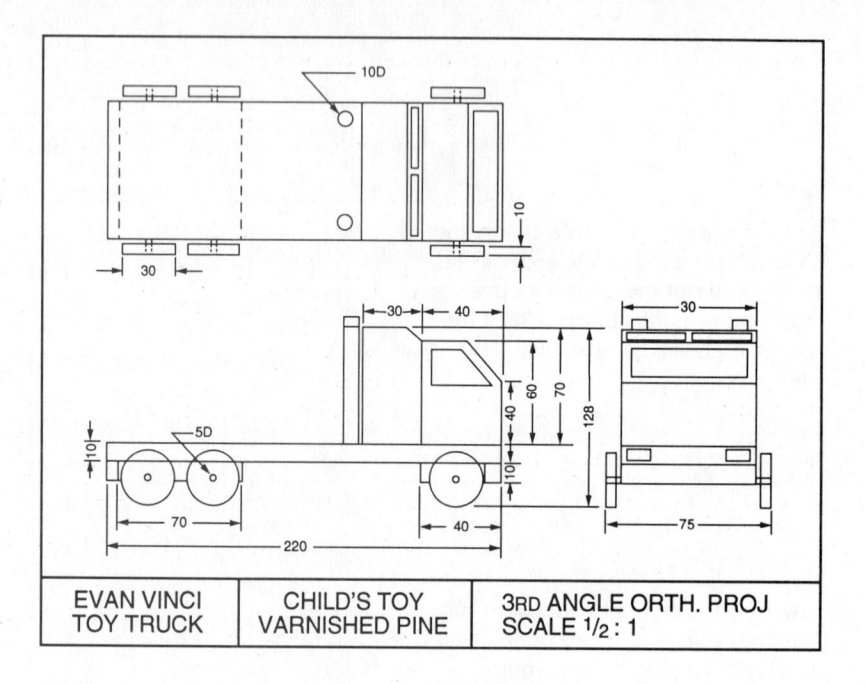

| EVAN VINCI TOY TRUCK | CHILD'S TOY VARNISHED PINE | 3RD ANGLE ORTH. PROJ SCALE 1/2 : 1 |

Key Points

- You should use a harder pencil to draw the dimension lines lighter than the outline of the objects.

- You should include all dimensions necessary to define the object.

- You should not include a dimension more than once.

- You should draw the projection and dimension lines, as shown in these examples.

- You should make the arrowheads clear, slender, solid, and no more than 3 mm or 1/8" long.

- You should learn to dimension in millimeters.

- You should add dimensions to be read from the bottom and the right-hand side. (Look at the example drawings.)

- You should dimension circles as shown in these examples.

DRAWING ACTIVITIES—ADDING DIMENSIONS CONTINUED

Information

Your drawing of the toy truck can be completed by adding a title block. The block contains important information about the drawing, including the title of the object, type of projection used, scale, materials to be used to make the object, name of the person making the drawing, date, and the drawing or reference number, if there is one. You can improve the appearance of your drawing further by adding a border. (See the finished drawing of the toy truck on the previous page.) The drawing is done in a scale of $1/2:1$ (sometimes called half-scale). Can you determine how long the truck would be on the actual finished drawing?

Exploded View Drawings

Exploded view drawings are used to help show all the parts of an object, particularly if the parts are difficult to see. For example, exploded views can be used with isometric drawings. Parts are projected out along the 30° or 90° axes.

The parts can be fully separated or overlapped if space is limited, but they should be aligned properly to show how they go together.

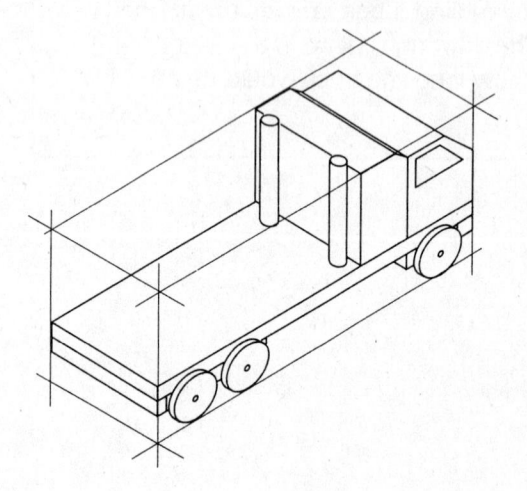

The drawing at the left shows the toy truck within the basic isometric box (with the projected lines shown).

The drawing below shows the start of an exploded drawing of the truck. Complete the drawing with all the parts aligned along the projection lines.

Include the necessary explanatory notes to help someone use the drawing to assemble the parts to make a completed truck.

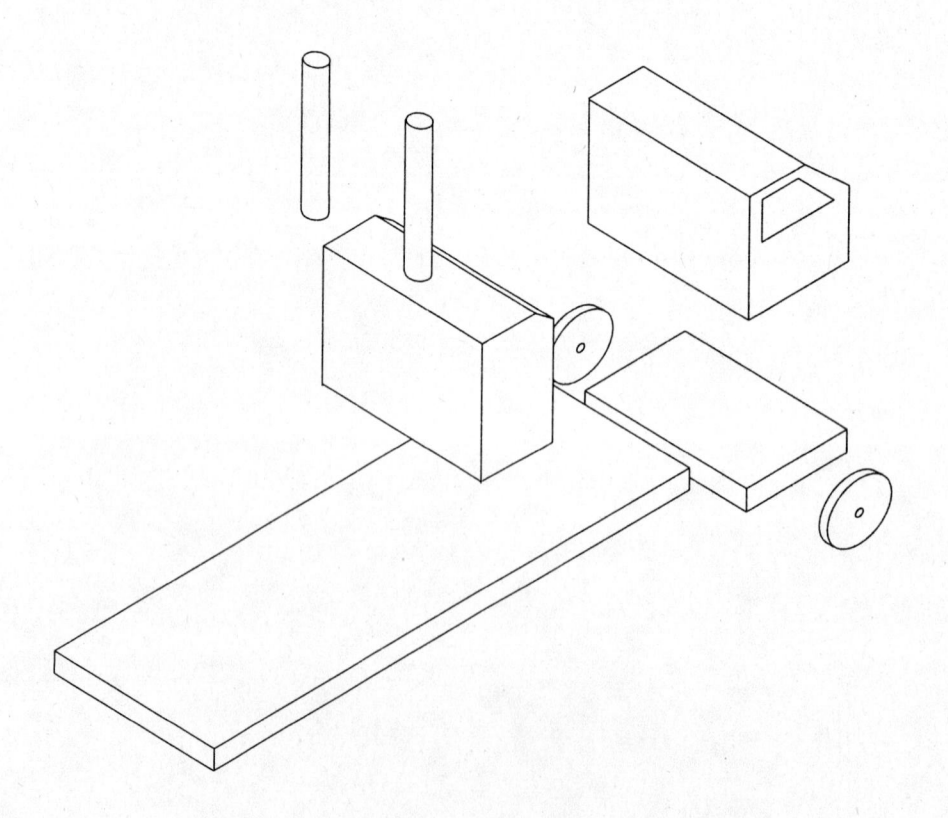

Sectional Drawing

In some instances, we need a drawing that shows the details that are hidden inside an object. Sectional drawings are made as though the object was being cut apart, or sectioned. See Figure 2.32A in your text for an example of a sectional drawing. Using the pictorial drawing below, develop a sectional drawing in the space provided. Remember to use "hatch lines" that are usually slanted at 45° to represent where the cut or section has been made. If necessary, hatch lines can be drawn at 30°.

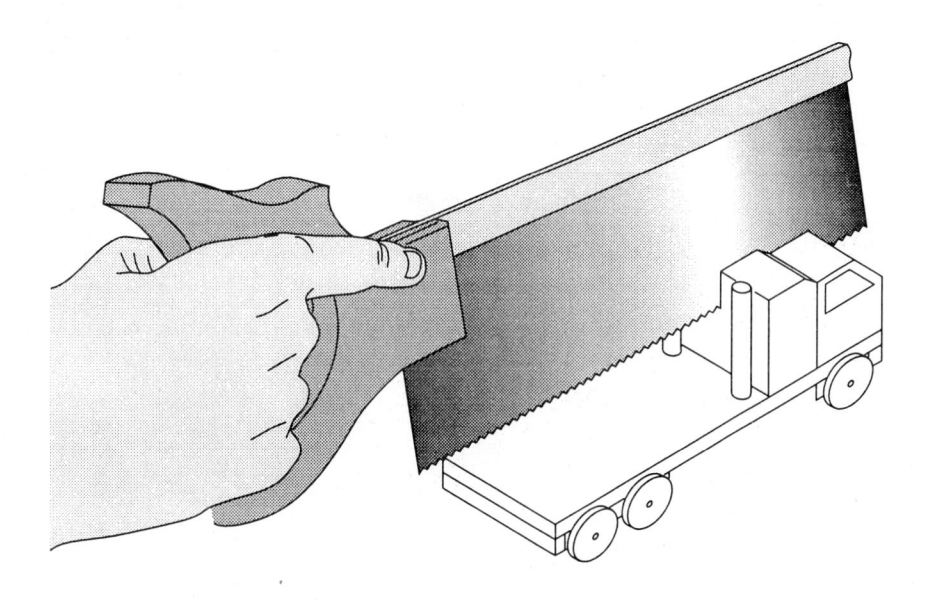

PRESENTATION TECHNIQUES

Different presentation techniques can be used to add realism to your drawings or draw attention to specific parts of the drawing that are particularly important. The careful use of shading with a pencil will allow you to produce realistic effects by creating different tones. Varying the degree of pressure on the pencil produces light, dark, and a range of mid-tones.

In order to add shading to pictorial drawings, you need to understand how light is reflected from the object and where lighter and darker shades appear. Pencil shading can represent these differences. Standard forms used to create drawings of complex objects include the cube, cylinder, cone, pyramid, and sphere. These forms can be combined to help you develop more complex forms in your drawings.

Concepts learned about primary, secondary, and tertiary colors, complementary and contrasting colors, and color wheels can be applied to add realism and impact to your drawings and illustrations.

Graphics refers to the general approach of presenting information in a visual form. Specifically, graphics include the presentation of data in charts, graphs, statistics, schematics, maps, sequence drawings, and the like.

Shading by Steps

Practice shading by steps in the spaces provided.

Dark   Light

Continuous Shading

Practice continuous shading in the spaces provided.

Dark Light

Rendering a Cube by Shading

A cube has six faces, but only three of the faces show in a pictorial drawing. If the light comes from the upper-left, the top of the cube gets the most light and the right side, the least. Light falling on the right side will be mid-tone. (See Figure 2.34 in your text.) Determine a different direction of light than in Figure 2.34 and render the cube provided below.

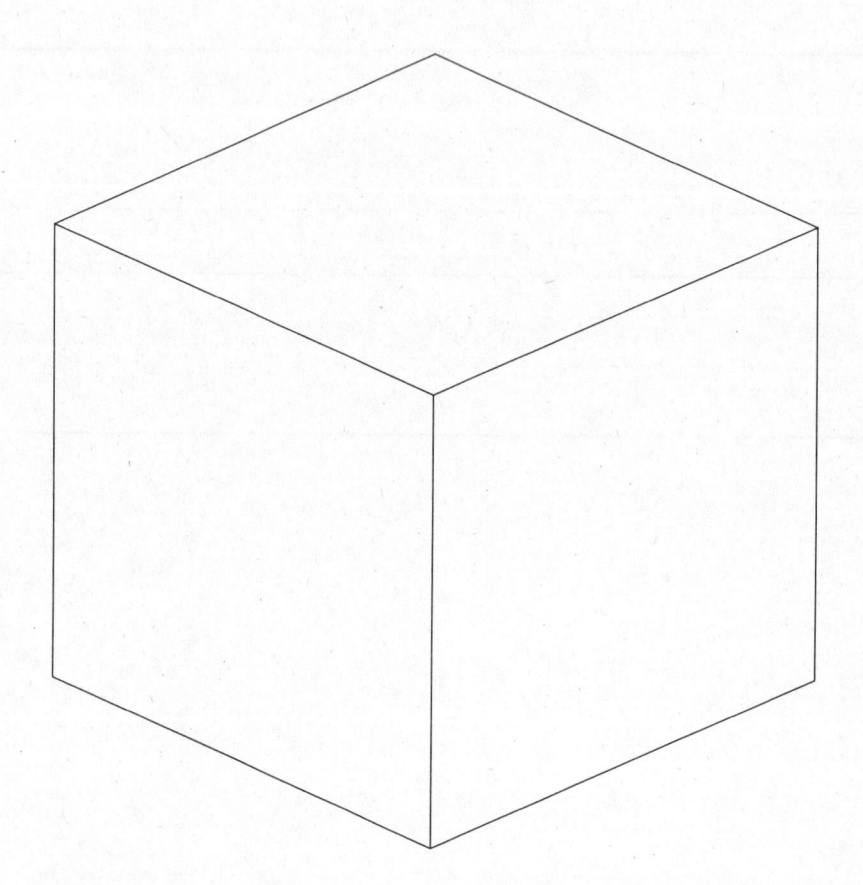

Rendering a Pyramid by Shading

Prisms and pyramids are somewhat similar to cubes in that they are regular solids. Prisms have the same shape in their cross-section and all along their length. Pyramids are similar to prisms but they come to a point, sometimes called an apex. Shading a prism or pyramid uses the same techniques as in shading a cube. Refer to Figure 2.34 in your text. Determine a different direction of light and render the pyramid provided below.

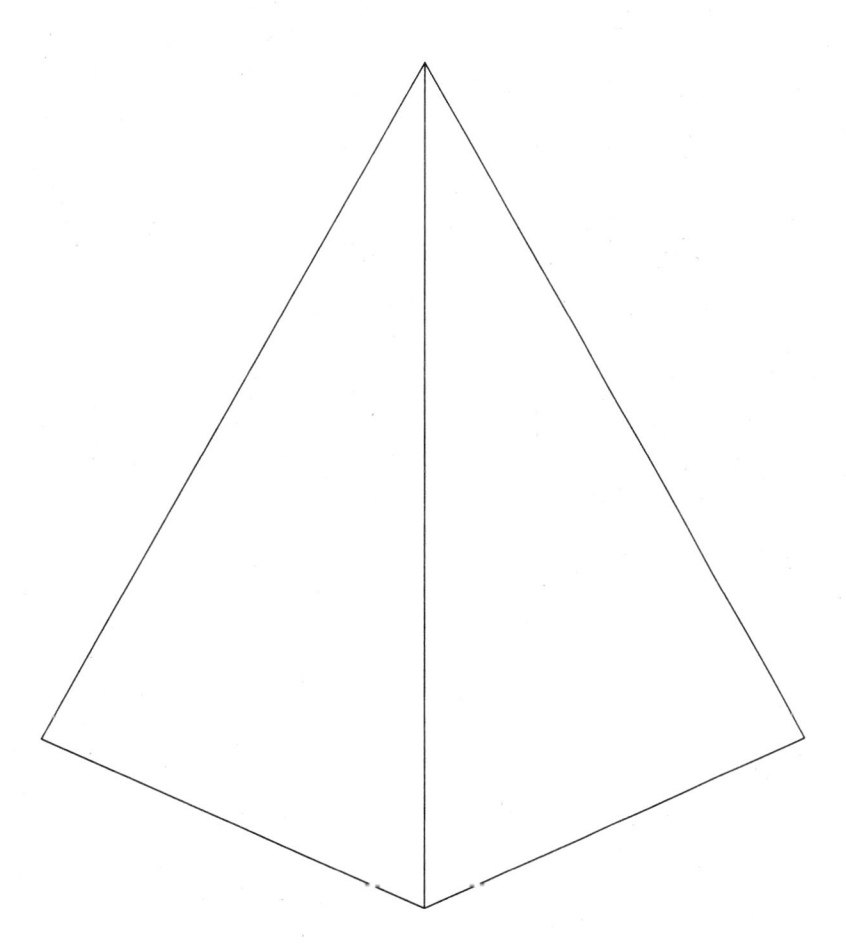

Rendering a Cylinder by Shading

Cylinders are shaded by using some new ideas as well as some of the shading techniques described previously. You should add almost no shading to that part of the drawing facing the light source. (See Figure 2.35 in your text.). You should add shading to the cylinder progressively to make it darker as the surface moves farther away from the light source. The use of continuous shading becomes very important in rendering cylinders and other curved surfaces. Select a direction for the light to shine on the cylinder and render the drawing provided here.

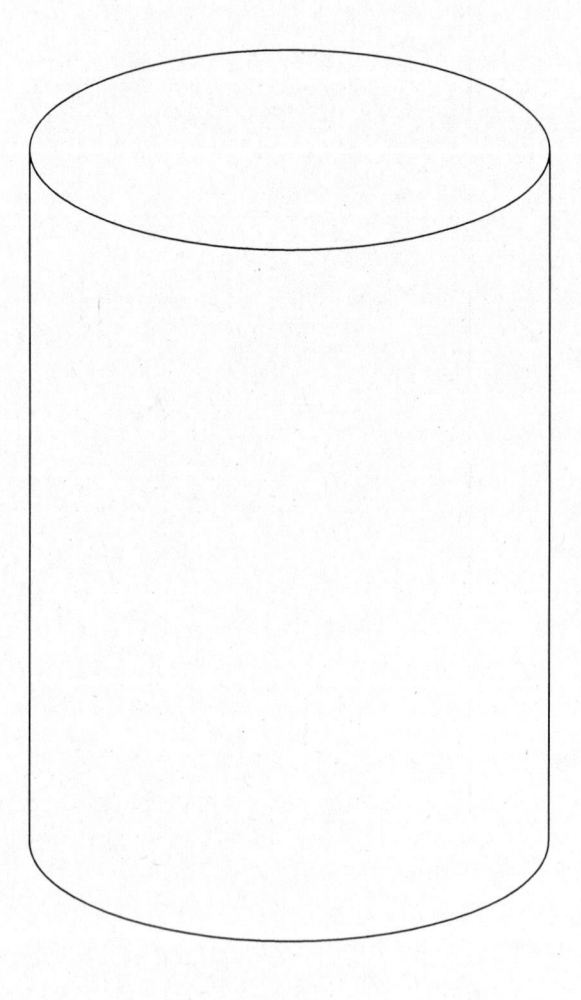

Rendering a Cone by Shading

You can shade a cone in a manner very similar to a cylinder. The biggest difference is the shape of the lightest part of the shaded surface. The lightest part must have a triangular shape that reaches from the apex to the base. (See Figure 2.35 in your text.) You must maintain this shape by shading the rest of the surface at a slight angle. The basic triangular shape of the cone is matched to add realism to the drawing. Use continuous shading to render the cone provided here.

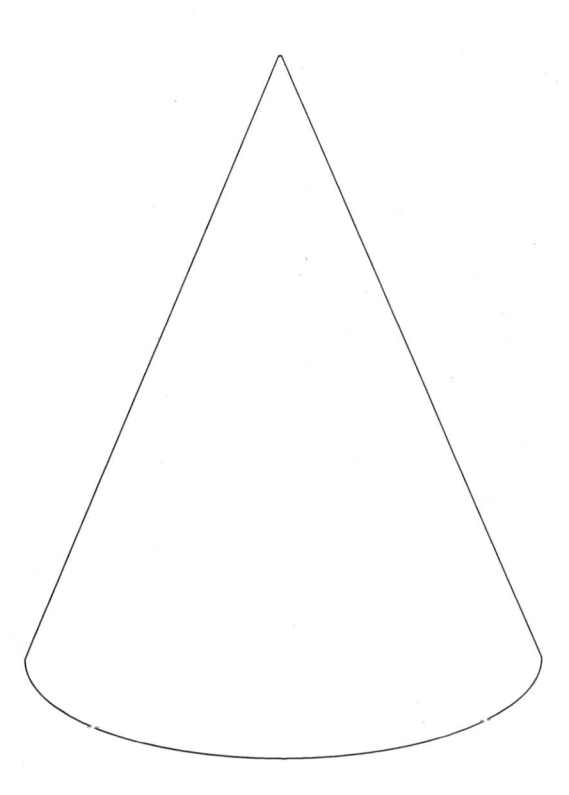

Rendering a Sphere by Shading

As you shade a sphere, you will leave a light shape or spot that is circular. (See Figure 2.36 in your text.) You do this because the sphere is based on a circular shape. You will shade your sphere in a circular manner, becoming darker as the surface of the sphere curves away from the source of light. Choose a direction for the light hitting the sphere and render the drawing below.

Using Highlights

You will use highlights to show different shades and light reflections. You will find highlights helpful in portraying form. Reflections are a natural part of nearly everything we see and they add realism to the forms we are drawing. (See Figure 2.37 in your text.) As with previous drawings you have completed, reflections are influenced by the shape of the object. This is especially noticeable in the cone, cylinder, and sphere. You will actually exaggerate highlights to represent a line or point of bright, reflected light.

The drawing of a humane mouse trap, shown at left, has been rendered to represent plastic. Note the use of highlights on the edge. Add highlights to the rendering of the personal communicator below to represent a bright light coming over your right shoulder as you are viewing it. Use a white pencil to create the highlight. You might also wish to experiment with using a small brush and white correction fluid to create brighter highlights.

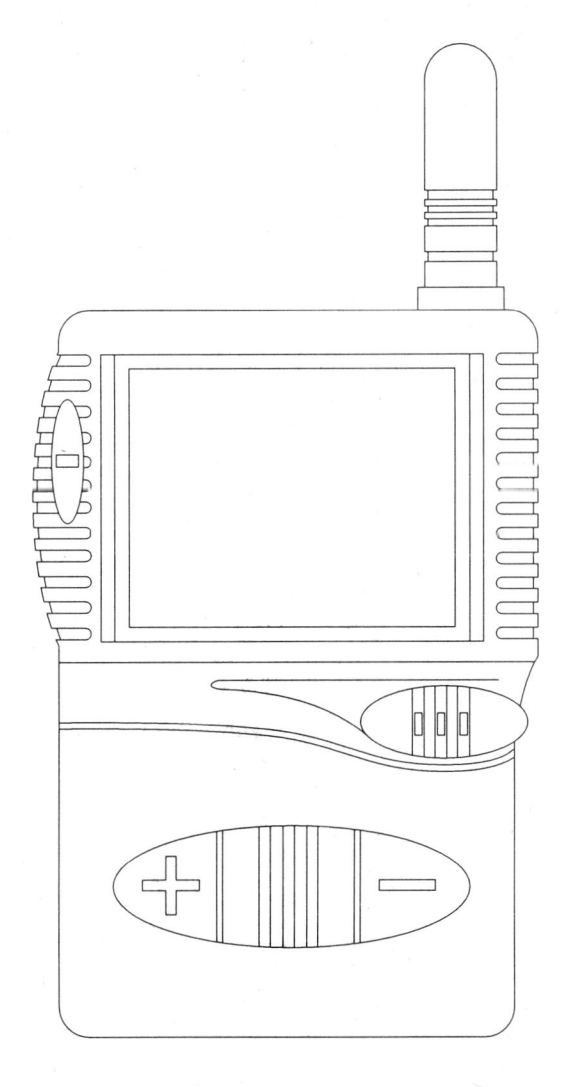

Using Outlining

Outlining emphasizes objects and makes them stand out. A technique that adds emphasis is to use thick lines for only the outside edges of the object. The use of color also makes the product stand out and attract more attention. Use outlining in black and in color to make an object of your choice be more prominent.

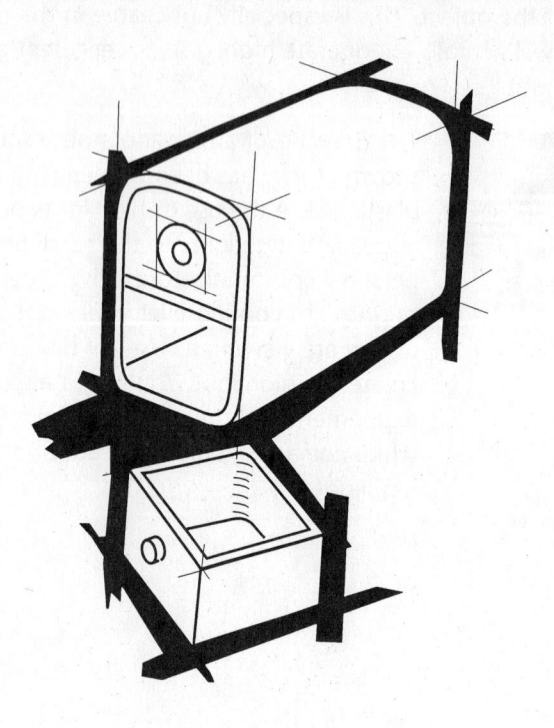

Shading with Color Pencils

Color pencils utilize the same skills you developed in shading with regular pencils.

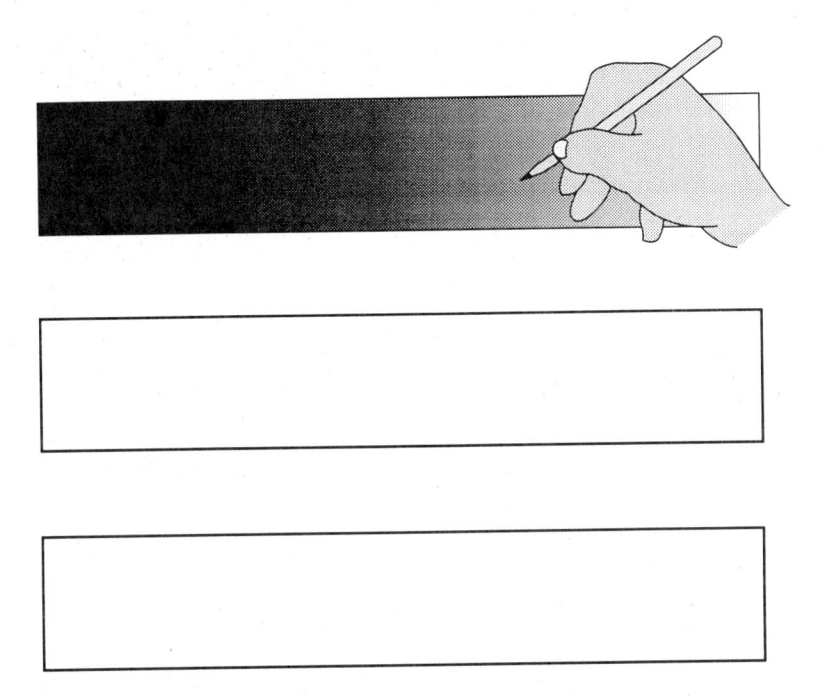

Create a range of colors and a full range of secondary and tertiary colors by using only three pencils, one for each of the primary colors.

Use three primary colored pencils (red, yellow, blue) to create the primary and secondary colors in the overlapping circles at the right. What color is created where all three circles and colors overlap? You may want to compare your results with comments made related to Figure 2.7 in your text.

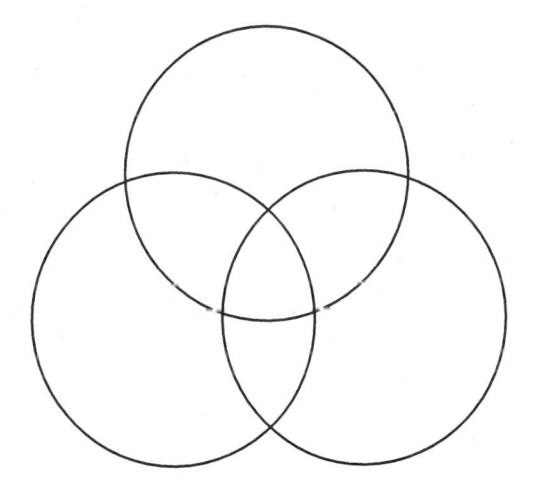

Using Color Markers

Refer to Figures 2.40 and 2.41 in your text to see some of the uses of color to help improve the communication potential of your drawings. Practice using the different applications of color markers on some of the drawings you have already completed. Determine if the color and technique help to produce the power and effect that you want.

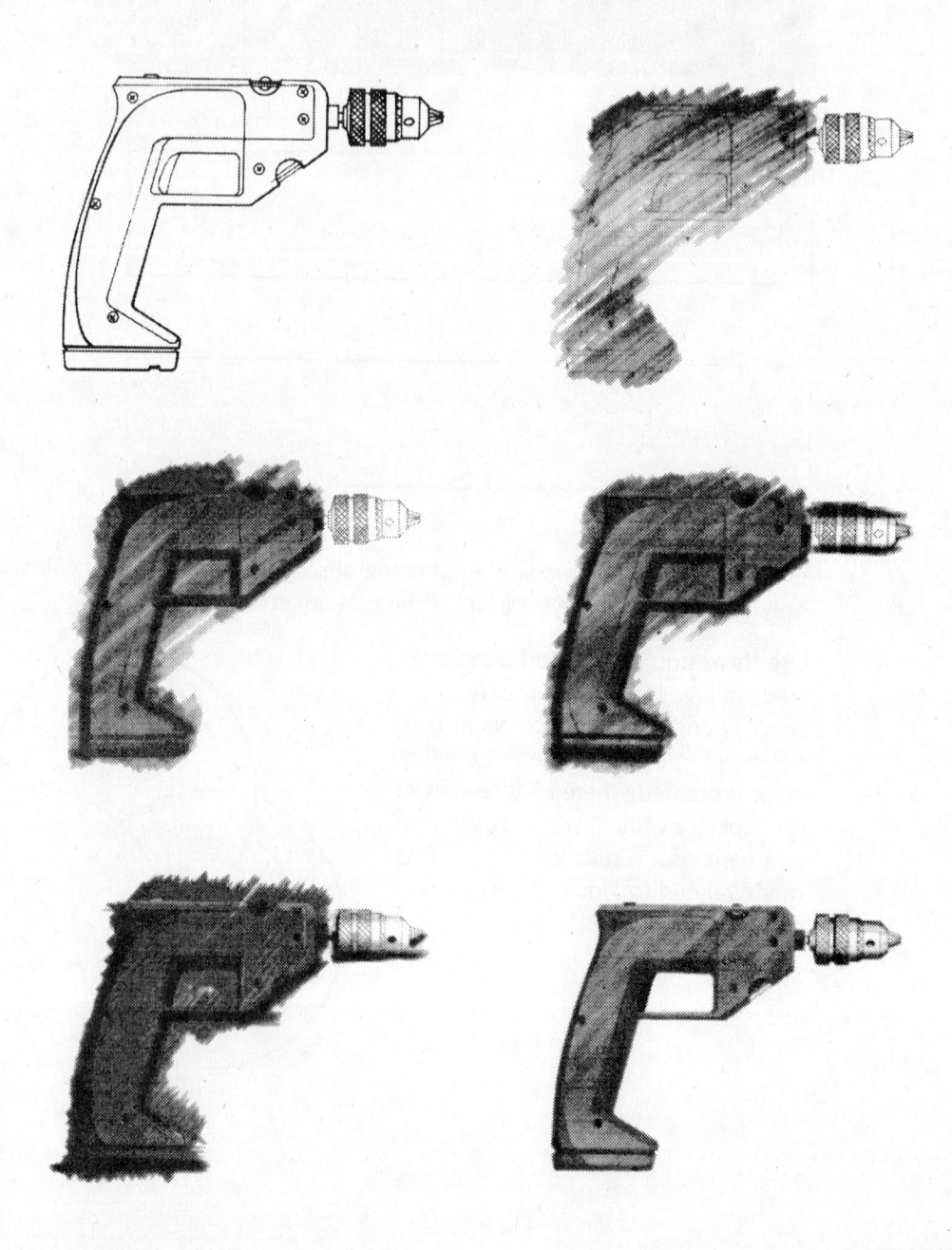

Chapter 2 Designing, Documenting, and Drawing **55**

Using Graphics to Present Information

Graphics refers to the means you can use to present information in visual forms. Graphic methods can include presentation of data in charts, graphs, statistics, schematics, maps, sequence drawings, and the like. Select one of the methods shown below that is appropriate for presenting information related to one of your projects. Develop your own version to present the data in an effective and interesting manner. You may also want to refer to the graphic tools introduced in Chapter 9 of this book. Those tools for Total Quality Management make extensive use of presenting information in visual form.

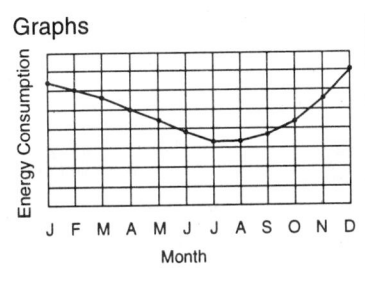

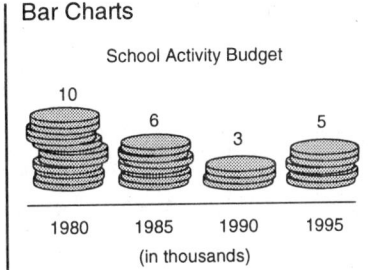

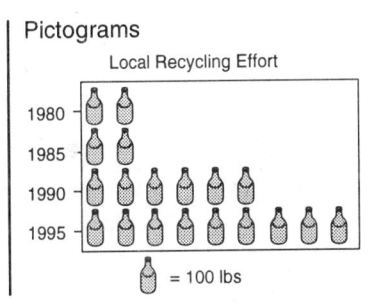

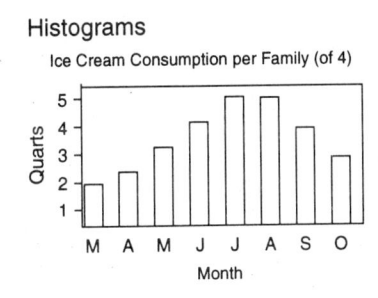

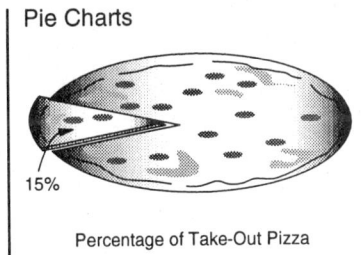

Graphs
Energy Consumption by Month (J F M A M J J A S O N D)

Bar Charts
School Activity Budget
1980: 10, 1985: 6, 1990: 3, 1995: 5
(in thousands)

Pictograms
Local Recycling Effort
1980, 1985, 1990, 1995
= 100 lbs

Histograms
Ice Cream Consumption per Family (of 4)
Quarts by Month (M A M J J A S O)

Pie Charts
Percentage of Take-Out Pizza — 15%

Presenting Information Graphically

PRESENTATION PORTFOLIOS

Developing a portfolio to present a summary of your work will be easier if you follow a general outline from the very beginning. The portfolio is a compilation of the records that you keep in various forms throughout your design and problem-solving process. By organizing these sketches, drawings, and other records and placing them in a sensible order on your page formats, your portfolio will take on a more professional format and will help present your work as a meaningful whole.

You were introduced to how a portfolio could be organized using the IDEATE model. The plan for organizing a portfolio is presented below. You may wish to refer to the sample portfolio shown later in this book.

ORGANIZATION OF A PORTFOLIO— USING THE IDEATE MODEL

Title Page

Introduction
Provide the background for your problems.
(Describe the situation and context of the problem.)

Describe the Problem
Identify and define the problem.
(Describe how you investigated the needs and opportunities.)

Design Brief and Specifications
Develop the design brief and specifications.
(Describe how you clarified the results you wanted to achieve.)

Research and Investigation
Explore possible alternatives.
(Portray how you conducted your search for information, resources, and solutions.)

Selected Solution
Accumulate and assess the alternatives.
(Describe how the best solution was chosen and developed. Why is this the best?)

Implementation and Development Work
Try out the best solution.
(Describe your experiments as you develop solutions, models, and prototypes.)

Final Testing and Overall Evaluation
Evaluate the results.
(Present how you tested your solution. How did you assess the process used in solving the problem? What is your overall satisfaction with the results and the process?)

The following are the suggested pages of the sections of a portfolio:

(a) Title Page
(b) Introduction—Situation
(c) Problem and Context
(d) Design Brief and Specifications
(e) Research and Investigation
(f) Alternative Solutions
(g) Selected Solution
(h) Implementation and Development Work
(i) Models/Prototypes
(j) Final Testing
(k) Overall Evaluation

As you work on your portfolio, you will want to use drawings, notes, models, color, digitized images, regular photos, and other graphic techniques wherever they will help communicate to others. Effective use of graphics can help explain what your design is to do, how you went about solving your problem to realize your design, and how you assessed the effectiveness of your product and your own effort. You may also wish to refer to pages 377–382 in Chapter 12 of this book to see sample pages from a student portfolio. You may also find it helpful to refer to Figure 2.43 in your text for a graphic overview of a portfolio and to the sample page formats on the following page.

REVIEW AND ENRICHMENT

As you complete your work in this chapter, you should refer to the Interaction of Hand and Mind model shown in Figure 2.44 in your text. The sketches, drawing, and other graphic techniques are important means for clarifying and sharing your thoughts and ideas. Finally, there are a range of Enrichment Activities, a Design Brief, and Review and Assessment Activities provided on pages 52 and 53 in your text that can help you further develop your graphic skills.

Portfolio Formats

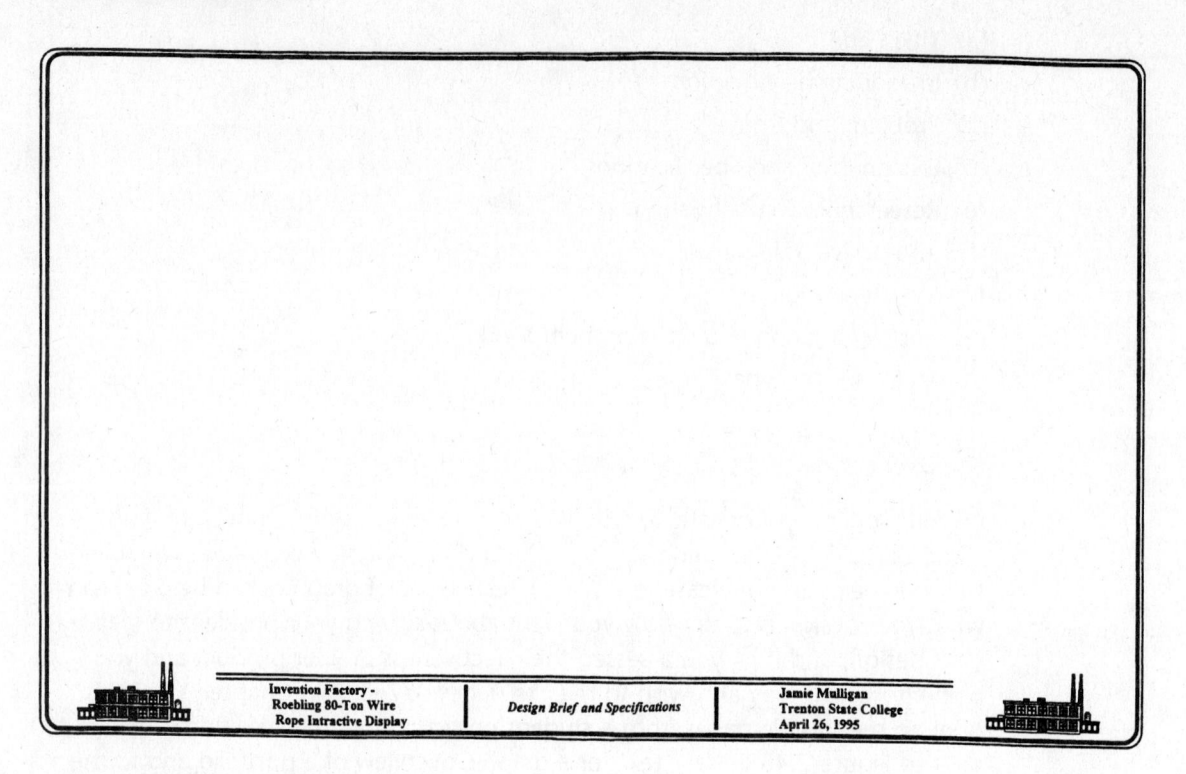

Invention Factory -
Roebling 80-Ton Wire
Rope Intractive Display

Design Brief and Specifications

Jamie Mulligan
Trenton State College
April 26, 1995

Portfolio Formats

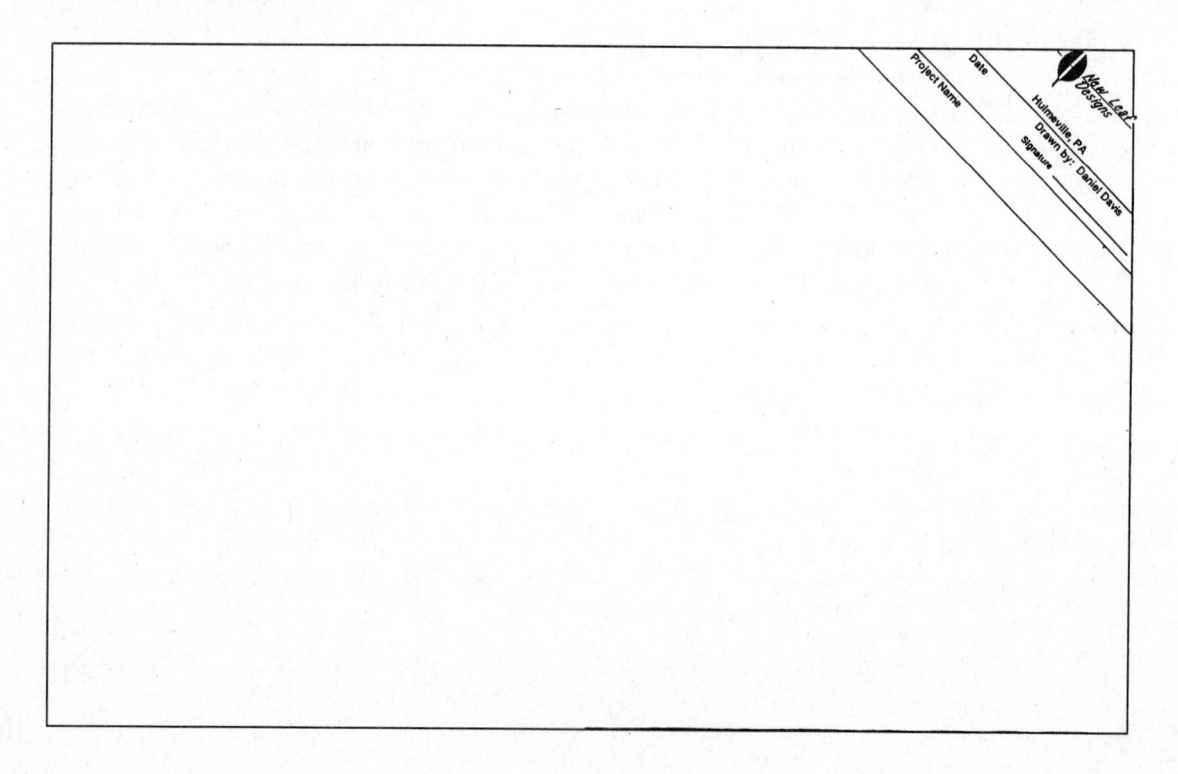

Date
Project Name
New Leaf Designs
Hulmeville, PA
Drawn by: Daniel Davis
Signature

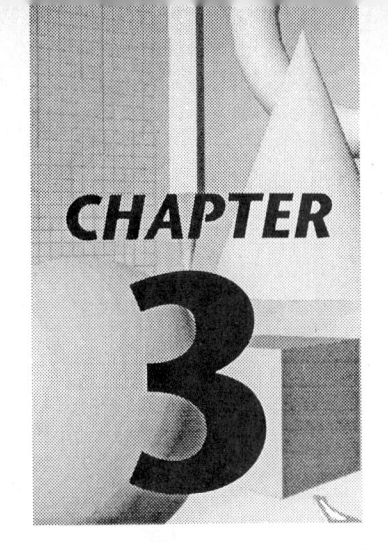

CHAPTER 3
Models and Model-Building

Transforming your ideas into a model is an important way for communicating with others, turning your ideas into real objects, and seeing ways to improve your ideas and plans. All models are simplified representations of something from the real world. Three types of models include physical models, conceptual models, and theoretical models.

TYPES OF MODELS

Conceptual models are used to make sense out of the real world. We build models to help us categorize ideas and things that help us understand the world in which we live. We also use conceptual models to help us transfer what we already know to explain and explore something new and unfamiliar.

In your design and technology work, you will use conceptual maps as models that show the connection and positions of objects and ideas in relationship to each other. You will use two specific types of conceptual maps—the question web and the planning web.

In your design and technology work, you will also use theoretical models. Theoretical models spell out in some detail how the parts of the model work together as a way of describing how the theory works. If a theoretical model can be expressed as a formula, it can be used on a computer to model the process or event.

Physical models are three-dimensional representations that tend to be either functional, appearance, or production models. Types of functional models include structural, mechanical, electronic, and systems models. Structural models show how the parts of a structure fit together. Many are static and do not involve movement. Structural models can provide the frameworks that support mechanical and electrical components for creating dynamic models. A wide range of materials and a variety of kits can be used for designing and construction.

Mechanical models show how mechanical parts fit and work together. Linkages, gears, pulleys, cams, pneumatic cylinders, and other devices may be required to produce the desired movements. Electronic models show how electrical and electronic parts will be assembled and tested. Real components can be placed on a solderless breadboard, often called an electronic prototyping board. You can use these boards to test whether an electronic circuit actually operates, before you spend the time and money to build it.

Systems models illustrate how subsystems are to be assembled and demonstrate or suggest how the system will actually operate. Smaller parts of a large system can be built to see if that subsystem actually operates and how all parts of a system work together. Electronic models and systems models are more complex than many other models.

For example, appearance models are used to show what an object will look like when it is produced. Well-built architectural models, teamed up with the creative use of photography and videos, can provide simulated trips, indicate what changes the new building will take on over time, and show larger environments in which the building will be located.

Before you produce a product in quantity, you will want to see if all the produced parts are as similar as possible. A production model can serve as a master in developing the tooling necessary for manufacturing the product in quantity. The production model is used to ensure that any new tooling is the same as the original tooling, when parts wear out and must be replaced.

Prototype models are developed to represent the finished product, system, or environment as accurately as possible. Prototypes, as final models, allow the designer to test out a product before it is actually fabricated or put into production.

MODEL-MAKING

The materials used in developing models are not complex, nor do they need to be expensive. Many models are made from two-dimensional materials. The word *development* is often used in design and technology to describe how a three-dimensional form is made from two-dimensional (flat) materials.

Fabrication involves making models from materials that need to be processed to create the desired model. The materials must be cut, shaped, formed, assembled, and then finished in some appropriate manner. Cutting and shaping materials can be done through a variety of processes, using appropriate tools. Forming refers to the processes that are used to change the form of materials without necessarily removing any of the material.

Computer models provide a dynamic function that allows the object to be manipulated and modified as needed. Physical modeling is possible through computer-controlled processes, such as stereo lithography and rapid deposition modeling (RDM).

Conceptual models, such as the conceptual map, show the connection and positions of objects in relationship to each other. Theoretical models are similar to conceptual models but are more specific. The theoretical models that will be most useful to you are those that can be expressed by using numbers in a formula.

Chapter 3 Models and Model-Building **61**

DESIGN ACTIVITIES—STRUCTURAL MODELS

Each of the systems that can be used to develop structural models has different characteristics and capabilities. For example, some allow you to build structures very quickly by using snap connections. Some are assembled using threaded fasteners and are, therefore, slower to use but result in stronger structures.

Analyze the following systems provided by your teacher and identify what you believe are the most positive and least positive characteristics of each. Attempt to answer such questions as: What makes the system good or easy to use? What makes it difficult to use? What would I tell someone else about this system to help them use it or decide whether buy it?

Structural System	Most Positive Characteristics	Least Positive Characteristics
Lego-Dacta		
Lasy		
Fisher Technik		
Polymek		
K'nex		
Inventa		

DESIGN ACTIVITIES—STRUCTURAL MODELS CONTINUED

Using each of the systems that are available in your school, design and develop the tallest structure possible, the strongest, the lightest, the most flexible, and the most rigid. Analyze how each system performs in each of the five applications shown in the chart below. Rank each system on a 5-point scale where 1 = poor performance and 5 = excellent performance. Record your findings in the spaces provided below. You will want to record your observations in your log or journal, using drawings, notes, and appropriate notations. You will use this information as you select the most appropriate system for your future model-building activities.

Structural System	Best Application for:				
	Tallest	Strongest	Lightest	Most Flexible	Most Rigid
Lego-Dacta					
Lasy					
Fisher Technik					
Polymek					
K'nex					
Inventa					

DESIGN ACTIVITIES—
DEVELOPING MECHANICAL MODELS

Identify a toy that operates mechanically. Without taking it apart, try to figure out how it works. Make several sketches of how the parts might move and work together. With the materials provided by your teacher, construct a model to represent how the toy operates.

The systems you have available for developing mechanical models will also have different characteristics and capabilities. Some of the systems use snap connections that will allow you to build mechanisms very quickly; others will be slower to use but provide more rugged mechanisms. In a manner similar to your activities with structural systems on page 62, analyze the mechanical systems and identify what you believe are the best and worst characteristics of each. Using each of the systems, design and develop gearing that will lift the heaviest weight possible, lift a light weight as fast as possible, and move an object as slow as possible.

Identify what other mechanical movements are possible with the construction systems. As before, record your findings using drawings, notes, and notations to help you select the most appropriate system for building mechanical models in future activities.

Mechanical System	Most Positive Characteristics	Least Positive Characteristics
Lego-Dacta		
Lasy		
Fisher Technik		
Polymek		
K'nex		
Inventa		

DESIGN ACTIVITIES—DEVELOPING APPEARANCE MODELS USING POLYSTYRENE BLOCKS

To develop your skills in building appearance models, refer in your text to Figure 3.16 of the Personal Communicator System. Using the materials provided by your teacher, and the procedures shown below, develop an appearance model for that product or for a product you have designed.

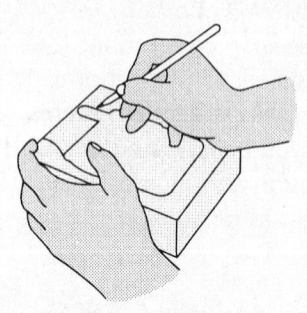

(1) Attach top and side views of the Personal Communicator (P.C.) to polystryene block.

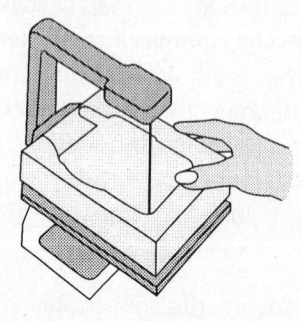

(2) Cut out shape of the P.C. from polystyrene block.

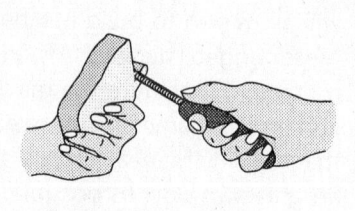

(3) Shape and smooth the polystyrene block.

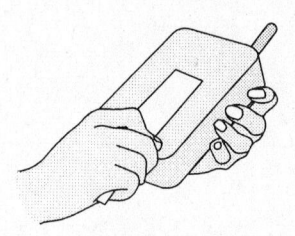

(4) Use modeling putty to get smooth shape of P.C.

(5) Coat the polystyrene with Lite Spackle™.

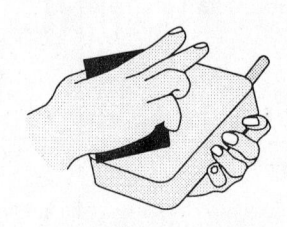

(6) Sand spackle to smooth finish. (Do not sand through to polystyrene.)

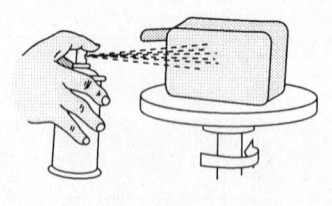

(7) Spray paint surface of P.C. to final color.

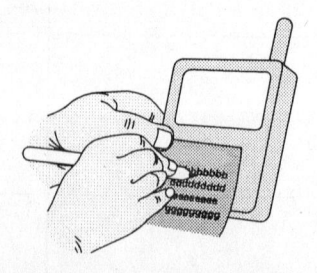

(8) Add letters, numbers, and other details to P.C.

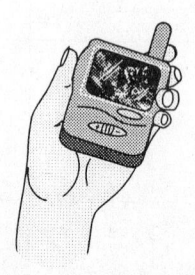

(9) Add colored picture and clear plastic to represent TV image.

DESIGN ACTIVITIES—FABRICATING APPEARANCE MODELS USING POLYSTYRENE SHEETS

You can use different techniques to fabricate appearance models of your design projects. Some of the processes shown below are in sequence, while many are not. You should plan a sequence of processes that are most appropriate for your project work.

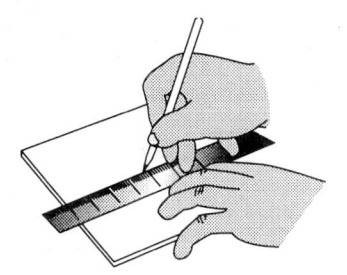

(1) Lay out the shape and size of the model parts on a polystyrene sheet.

(2) Cut out shapes using the appropriate saw or cutter.

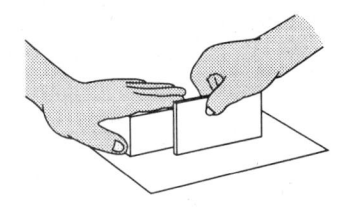

(3) Snap the piece of polystyrene along the score marks.

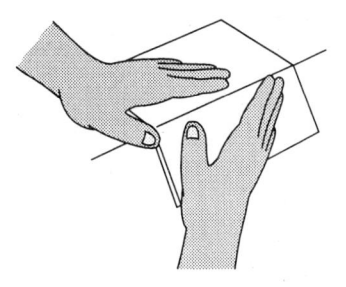

(4) Sand the edges of the parts. Smooth as shown above.

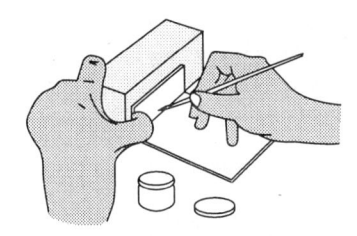

(5) Join the polystyrene pieces with adhesive or solvent. (Be sure to use adequate ventilation.)

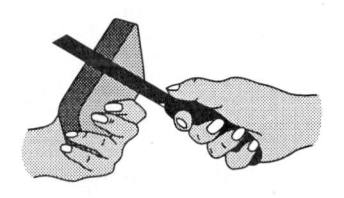

(6) Shape and smooth polystyrene with files and other tools.

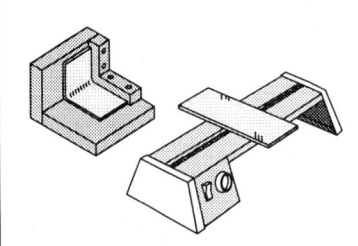

(7) Use a strip heater to get a straight bend.

(8) Form polystyrene sheet by using a mold to get desired shape.

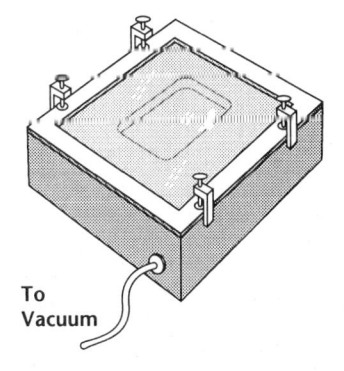

(9) Form sheet materials using vacuum forming processes.

DESIGN ACTIVITIES—
DEVELOPING APPEARANCE MODELS

Many products that are currently being sold could be improved in appearance and performance. The outer appearance of a product is important because it is the first contact the user has with the product. The image of the product, its effect on the user, the placement of the controls, the ease of reading them are a few aspects of appearance that can often be improved. Collect one or more products that are no longer operating, or secure a product from those provided by your teacher. Analyze the product and determine what changes you would make in its appearance. Develop an outline drawing of the product and reproduce several copies of the drawing on a copier. Develop several alternatives designs for the product. (These should include the use of elements and principles of visual design discussed in the preceding chapter.)

Consider the following ideas to add realism to your models:

- Use self-adhering labels to create buttons and details.

- Use remnants of adhesive labels to add details.

- Use relief lettering to give 3-D effects on your model.

- Use rub-on (dry transfer) low-relief lettering and details.

- Use strip lettering (Dyno-tape) to create labels.

- Use self-adhering vinyl materials to simulate wood, Formica™, etc.

- Use small objects (from charm bracelets/toys) for added detail.

- Use real components and devices to add details.

After choosing the best design, construct an appearance model that incorporates your proposed changes. Add the sketches and drawings as visual documentation of your work to your portfolio. You may also want to take a photo, or grab a frame of a video of your model and print it out to add it to your portfolio. Copy one of these and attach it in the space provided below.

DESIGN ACTIVITIES—
DEVELOPING APPEARANCE MODELS

With your teacher, identify a building that is being planned in the community. Contact the mayor's office, or appropriate agency, and propose that a model of the building or project be built, if none is available. Secure drawings and plot plans of the grounds on which the building will be constructed. Construct an architectural model of the proposed building.

You will find that using scale model parts can be particularly helpful in adding details to your building model. In specialty catalogs, such as those available from Plastruct, Inc., you will find a wide range of parts that are used in architectural models. You can add such details to a building model as trees, shrubs, vehicles, and humans. You can also use scale models of furniture and equipment to add to the realism of your models (see Listing of Resources in the Appendices at the end of this book.

DESIGN ACTIVITIES—DESIGNING A MODELING AREA

Your school may not yet have a modeling area or it may not be as good as you would like. Working in groups as assigned by your teacher, develop a three-dimensional model of a proposed modeling area for your school facility. The illustration below, from Figure 3.11 in your text, can be used for ideas. If possible, the dimensions and location of the actual space for the proposed facility should be considered. Attention should also be given to creating an aesthetically appealing area. You should use appropriate ideas and techniques that you learned through previous activities in the course.

DESIGN ACTIVITIES—DEVELOPMENTS: BUILDING MODELS FROM TWO-DIMENSIONAL MATERIALS

Figure 3.14 in your text showed how a development was generated for the 3-D model of the Trenton State College electric car. Developments are useful for creating 3-D models quickly and inexpensively out of sheet materials.

Design and construct a development using sheet materials to create a model of the car. Next develop an object of your choice or one that is assigned by your teacher.

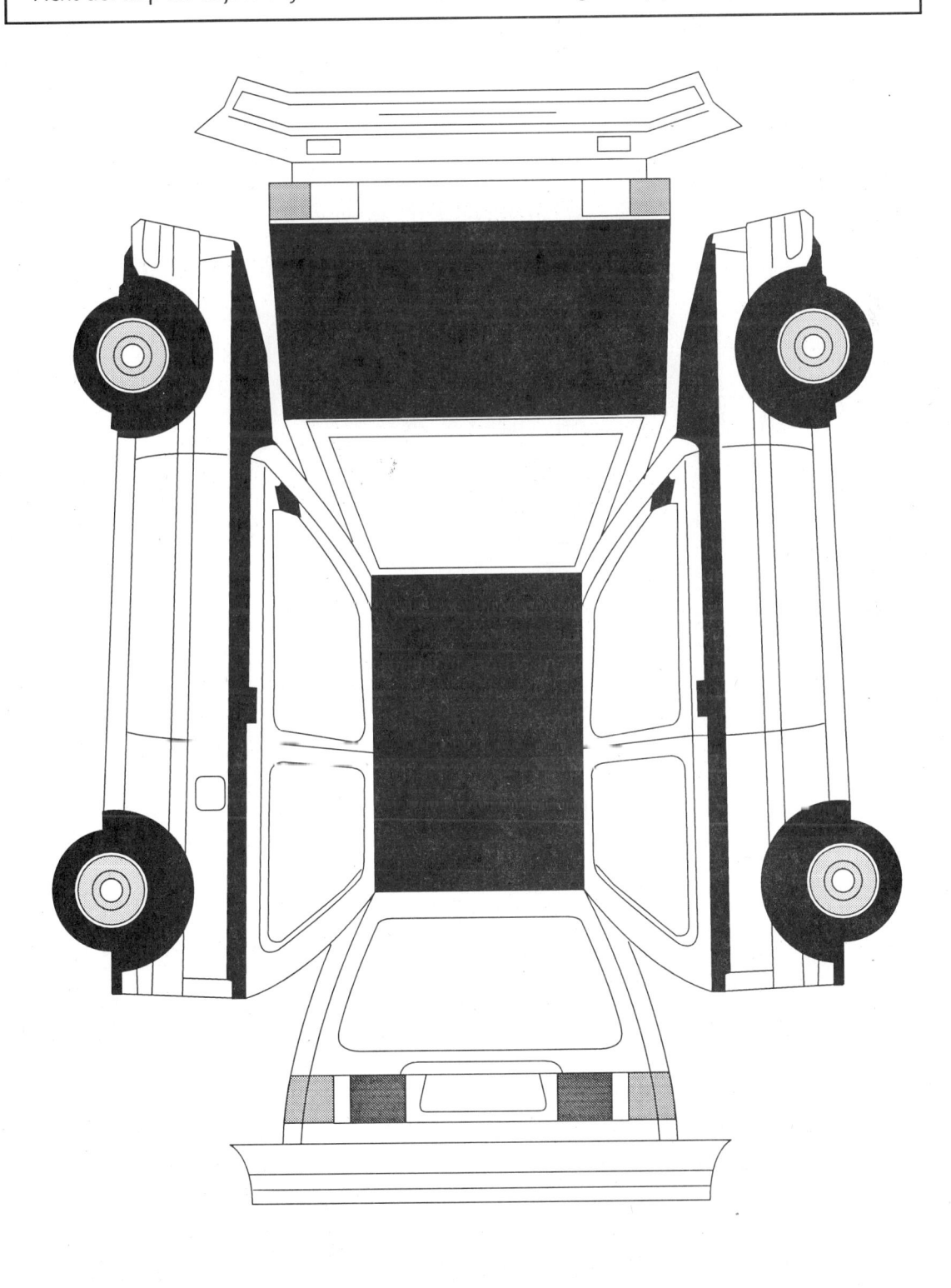

DESIGN ACTIVITIES—CONSTRUCTING A PACKAGE FROM TWO-DIMENSIONAL MATERIALS

The use of developments is also very helpful in creating models of packages. In many instances, packages are special boxes designed so that they can be cut out of a single piece of card material. Design and develop a package, formed from a single piece of card stock the size of a sheet of notebook paper, that will hold the largest object possible.

Collect several different packages. Carefully take each package apart so that it will lie flat on the table. Analyze how each package was constructed and determine which of the approaches you plan to apply. You can form the package by folding the material and gluing the box together at the appropriate places—usually with tabs.

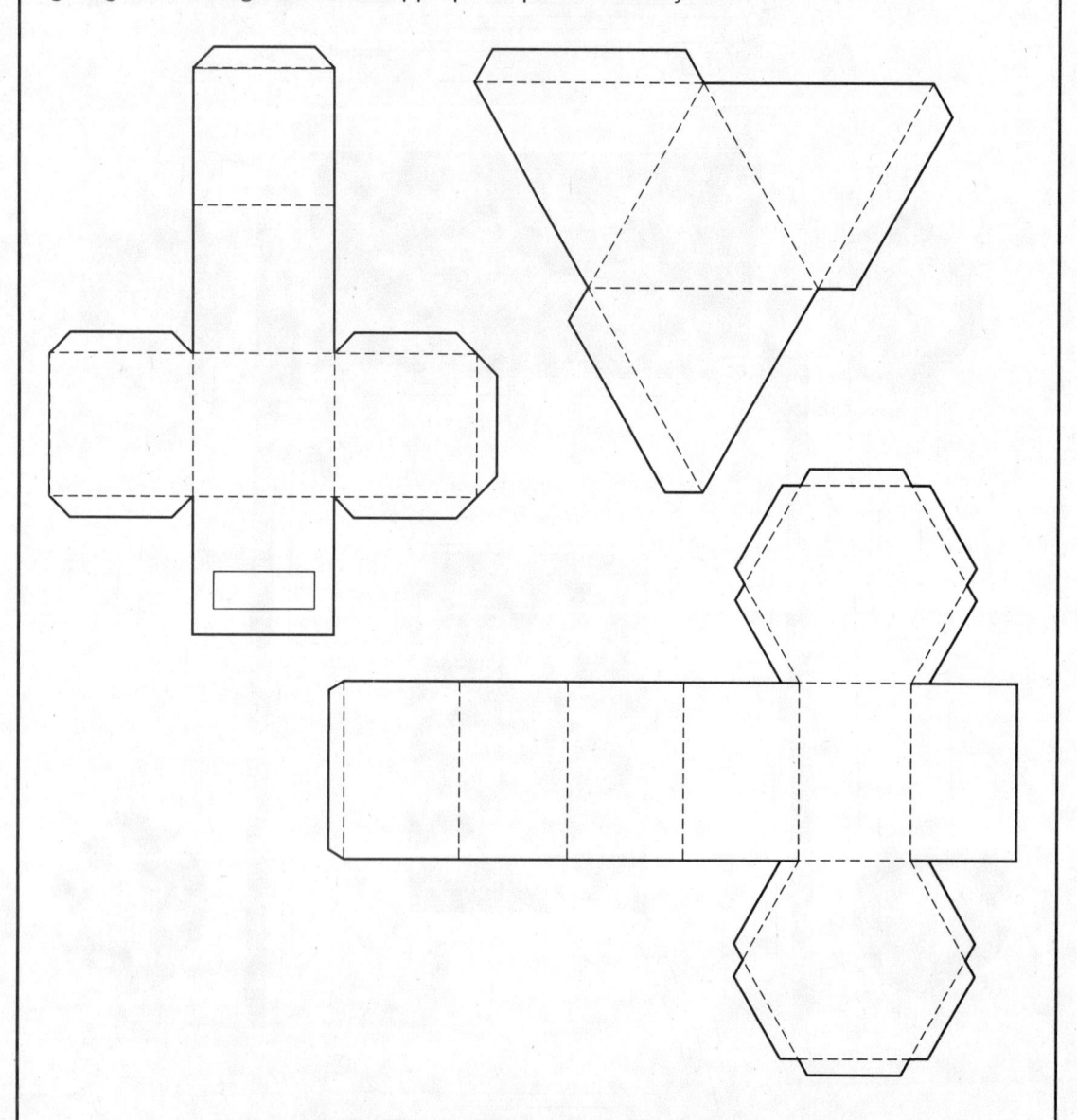

Enlarge one of the above drawings and fabricate a package to hold an object the size of a baseball. You may want to refer to Figure 3.13A and 3.13B in your text for guidance.

DESIGN ACTIVITIES—BUILDING MODELS FROM CONSTRUCTION KITS

Using one of the available construction kits, develop a functional model of a device that includes movement. This might include a model of an amusement park ride, an elevator or escalator, a conveyor system for moving feed to livestock or storage, or a system for handling and cleaning dirty dishes in the school cafeteria. Make a sketch, take a photo, or grab a frame of a video of your model. Attach this visual documentation of your work in the space provided below.

DESIGN ACTIVITIES—DEVELOPING MODELS USING A COMPUTER

Computer models provide a dynamic function that allows the object to be manipulated and modified as needed. The object below was developed as a computer generated model from a Swedish company. The "Toy Factory®" is a program that has been available for use in schools for several years. It has the capability of providing two dimensional development that can be used to create three-dimensional forms. Computers are also able to create three-dimensional forms directly. An example of such 3-D models is shown in Figure 3.17 in your text.

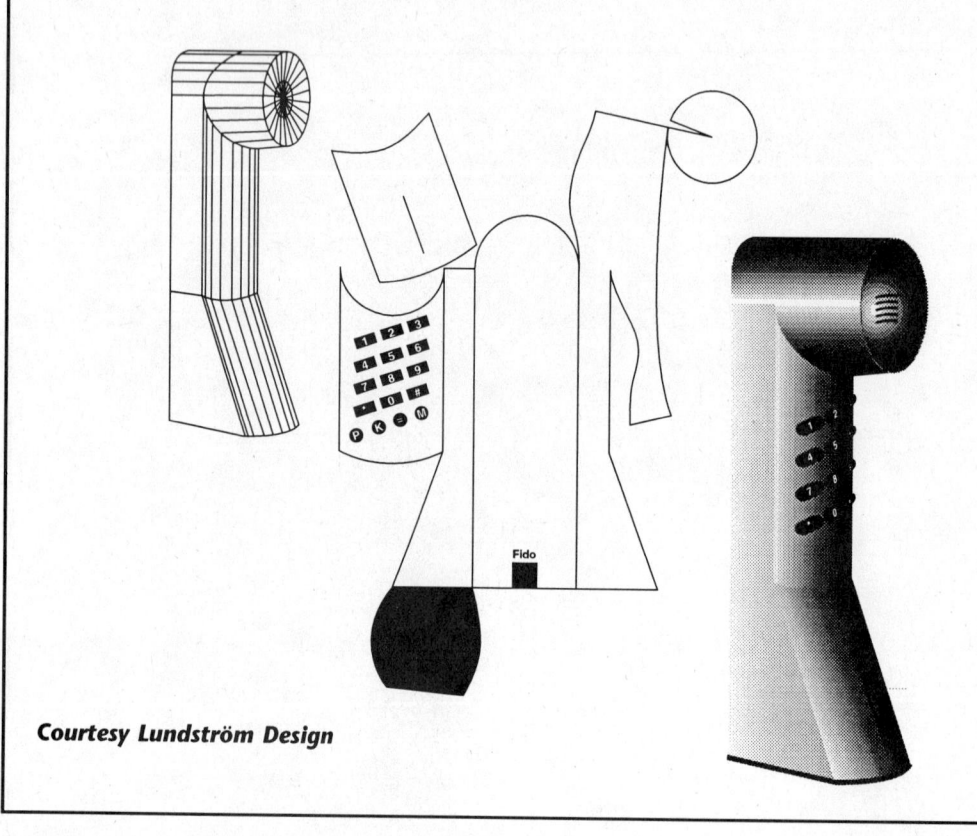

Courtesy Lundström Design

DESIGN ACTIVITIES—DEVELOPING CONCEPTUAL MAPS

Conceptual models and maps provide you a means of getting ideas recorded so you can think about them more clearly or so that you can discuss the ideas with others. Figures 3.3A and 3.3B in your textbook, presented two conceptual maps developed by a group of teachers and students. You and your classmates have been asked to take on a community service project. Some of the potential projects might include setting up an urban garden area, improving a walking or biking trail, the production and presentation of a play at a retirement center, or the design and production of a toy to be used at a day-care center, to mention only a few. Select one of these projects or use one of your own choosing.

On a large sheet of paper provided by your teacher, develop one map to help the group identify what activities might be included in the project. Develop a second map, or web, to help generate questions to guide you and your group as you investigate and develop possible solutions. Make a reduction of your work and paste it in the space below.

A question web

A planning web

DESIGN ACTIVITIES—COLLECTING MATERIALS FOR MODEL BUILDING

The checklist below identifies a range of special and common materials that can be very useful in your work. As you learn to use these materials, you will be able to save time and effort and also reduce the cost of your model-building activities. Space is provided to inventory the materials to determine if you need (N) more, have an adequate (A) or a surplus (S) supply.

Working in groups, as assigned by your teacher, use the Checklist of Materials for Making Models provided at the end of this chapter. Identify the materials from the list that are already available to the class. Develop a display that labels and shows samples of each material. Identify those materials that are currently not available. Conduct a survey in the community for possible sources of scrap or surplus materials. As a class, develop a collection of other possible materials that might be added to the checklist. Develop a storage system for the model-building materials that is linked to the display and the labeled materials.

Checklist of Materials for Making Models

Sheets of:
- (N)(A)(S) foamcore
- (N)(A)(S) corraflute
- (N)(A)(S) polystyrene
- (N)(A)(S) polyvinyl chloride
- (N)(A)(S) Plexiglas™
- (N)(A)(S) Lucite™
- (N)(A)(S) Perspex™
- (N)(A)(S) cardboard
- (N)(A)(S) card *(different weights and colors)*
- (N)(A)(S) paper *(different weights and colors)*
- (N)(A)(S) cloth *(different weights and colors)*
- (N)(A)(S) textiles *(plaids, stripes, and solids)*
- (N)(A)(S) imitation leather *(different weights and colors)*
- (N)(A)(S) wood veneer
- (N)(A)(S) aluminum foil
- (N)(A)(S) copper foil
- (N)(A)(S) fabric swatches
- (N)(A)(S) wallpaper catalog
- (N)(A)(S) sandpaper
- (N)(A)(S) cork
- (N)(A)(S) floor tile
- (N)(A)(S) transparent film-clear
- (N)(A)(S) transparent film-colors
- (N)(A)(S) shrink-wrap plastic
- (N)(A)(S) others

Block materials:
- (N)(A)(S) rigid foam plastic
- (N)(A)(S) flexible foam plastic
- (N)(A)(S) high-density Styrofoam™
- (N)(A)(S) balsa wood
- (N)(A)(S) basswood
- (N)(A)(S) other woods
- (N)(A)(S) others

Rod and tube materials:
- (N)(A)(S) toothpicks
- (N)(A)(S) shish kebab sticks
- (N)(A)(S) cocktail sticks
- (N)(A)(S) drinking straws
- (N)(A)(S) dowel rods
- (N)(A)(S) pipe cleaners
- (N)(A)(S) cardboard tubes
- (N)(A)(S) pieces of plastic pipe
- (N)(A)(S) spools
- (N)(A)(S) Popsicle™ sticks
- (N)(A)(S) tongue depressors
- (N)(A)(S) round and square dowel
- (N)(A)(S) others

Balls and spherical materials:
- (N)(A)(S) plastic cups, spools, and knobs
- (N)(A)(S) marbles

Chapter 3 Models and Model-Building **75**

DESIGN ACTIVITIES—COLLECTING MATERIALS FOR MODEL BUILDING CONTINUED

- Ⓝ Ⓐ Ⓢ Ping-Pong™ balls
- Ⓝ Ⓐ Ⓢ wooden beads
- Ⓝ Ⓐ Ⓢ plastic balls
- Ⓝ Ⓐ Ⓢ ball bearings
- Ⓝ Ⓐ Ⓢ others

Adhesives:
- Ⓝ Ⓐ Ⓢ rubber cement
- Ⓝ Ⓐ Ⓢ contact cement
- Ⓝ Ⓐ Ⓢ PVA (polyvinyl acetate)
- Ⓝ Ⓐ Ⓢ polystyrene cement
- Ⓝ Ⓐ Ⓢ acrylic cement
- Ⓝ Ⓐ Ⓢ hot glue
- Ⓝ Ⓐ Ⓢ caulking materials
- Ⓝ Ⓐ Ⓢ others

Mechanical fasteners:
- Ⓝ Ⓐ Ⓢ brads
- Ⓝ Ⓐ Ⓢ pins
- Ⓝ Ⓐ Ⓢ staples
- Ⓝ Ⓐ Ⓢ rivets
- Ⓝ Ⓐ Ⓢ binding posts
- Ⓝ Ⓐ Ⓢ eyelets and studs
- Ⓝ Ⓐ Ⓢ thread and needle
- Ⓝ Ⓐ Ⓢ cord
- Ⓝ Ⓐ Ⓢ others

Molding materials:
- Ⓝ Ⓐ Ⓢ plasticine
- Ⓝ Ⓐ Ⓢ clay
- Ⓝ Ⓐ Ⓢ papier maché
- Ⓝ Ⓐ Ⓢ flour polymer *(bread and glue)*
- Ⓝ Ⓐ Ⓢ ready-mixed fillers
- Ⓝ Ⓐ Ⓢ powdered fillers
- Ⓝ Ⓐ Ⓢ plastic wood
- Ⓝ Ⓐ Ⓢ modeling materials
- Ⓝ Ⓐ Ⓢ others

Lettering:
- Ⓝ Ⓐ Ⓢ dry transfer lettering
- Ⓝ Ⓐ Ⓢ vinyl cutout lettering
- Ⓝ Ⓐ Ⓢ molded plastic letters
- Ⓝ Ⓐ Ⓢ embossed lettering
- Ⓝ Ⓐ Ⓢ others

Tapes:
- Ⓝ Ⓐ Ⓢ drawing tapes *(different weights and colors)*
- Ⓝ Ⓐ Ⓢ car stripping tapes
- Ⓝ Ⓐ Ⓢ others

Finishes:
- Ⓝ Ⓐ Ⓢ varnish
- Ⓝ Ⓐ Ⓢ spray paints
- Ⓝ Ⓐ Ⓢ car touch-up paints
- Ⓝ Ⓐ Ⓢ nail polish
- Ⓝ Ⓐ Ⓢ latex paints
- Ⓝ Ⓐ Ⓢ acrylic paints
- Ⓝ Ⓐ Ⓢ others

Mechanical and electrical components:
- Ⓝ Ⓐ Ⓢ balloons
- Ⓝ Ⓐ Ⓢ syringes
- Ⓝ Ⓐ Ⓢ wire
- Ⓝ Ⓐ Ⓢ batteries
- Ⓝ Ⓐ Ⓢ small motors
- Ⓝ Ⓐ Ⓢ switches
- Ⓝ Ⓐ Ⓢ others

Mechanical construction kits:
- Ⓝ Ⓐ Ⓢ K'nex
- Ⓝ Ⓐ Ⓢ Lego
- Ⓝ Ⓐ Ⓢ Lasy
- Ⓝ Ⓐ Ⓢ Fischer Technik
- Ⓝ Ⓐ Ⓢ Mecanno
- Ⓝ Ⓐ Ⓢ Polymek
- Ⓝ Ⓐ Ⓢ others

Real objects:
- Ⓝ Ⓐ Ⓢ small knobs
- Ⓝ Ⓐ Ⓢ electric cords
- Ⓝ Ⓐ Ⓢ liquid crystal displays
- Ⓝ Ⓐ Ⓢ calculator keypads
- Ⓝ Ⓐ Ⓢ others

UNIT TWO

The Resources of Technology

CHAPTER 4

Tools, Mechanisms, and Machines

All technological activities involve the use of tools, mechanisms or machines. The term "tools" refers not only to hand tools, but all types of mechanisms, devices (mechanical, fluidic, optical, and electrical), and machines. Tools are used to extend human capabilities in order to convert materials, energy, and information into other desired and useful forms.

Tools provide the processes for using a variety of inputs to accomplish a set of outputs. The first step in using a tool is to identify the output you want and whether the tool/device/machine can accomplish this. Second, identify the process involved and what needs to occur in order to change the materials, energy, or information. Third, identify the input (the resources) required to complete the process.

TOOLS AND MECHANISMS

Tools, mechanisms, and related devices can take many different forms. One of the most common ideas used in mechanical tools is the "principle" of the lever. The "concepts" of the lever also apply to the wheel, the wedge, and the other simple machines.

The principle of the lever is a key element to understanding tools, mechanisms, and machines. Levers are simple devices that involve four related ideas:

(a) The load is the force to be moved by the lever.

(b) The fulcrum is the pivot, or the point around which the lever turns.

(c) The force is the effort that is applied to the lever.

(d) The moment is the length of the leverage arm (from the fulcrum to the force or from the fulcrum to the load).

Where you place the fulcrum (pivot), load, and force (effort) will determine what class of lever will result—1st, 2nd, or 3rd class.

Linkages are used to transmit forces and motion of appropriate and manageable size from a force applied as an input. Simple linkages take two forms—those producing motion in the same direction as the input force and those producing motion in the opposite direction of the input force. The bell crank lever is a common form of linkage used to change a backward or forward motion to a motion that moves to the right or left.

Wheels represent a continuous lever that pivots around the axle (fulcrum). Wheels and axles transmit circular motion and can take the form of belts and pulleys, sprockets and chains, and gears. The crank or windlass is an application of the wheel and axle, seen in steering wheels and lifting devices.

Belts and pulleys are slight variations of the wheel and axle and can link two or more pulleys that are some distance apart. Flat belts and toothed belts are used with pulley systems and work in the same way as sprockets and chains.

Gears and gear trains are used to transmit the motion of one shaft to another, in order to change direction or speed. Spur, idler, bevel, miter, worm, and rack and pinion gears are often used in machinery. Gear trains are formed by combining pairs of gears so that they mesh with each other to change the speed (torque). Cams are able to change their motion into another type of motion. The raised portion on a cam is called a lobe which acts like a wedge that causes the cam follower to move.

DESIGN ACTIVITIES—LEVERAGE, INCLINATION, AND ROTATION

Many of the tools that are used in design and technology are variations of the lever and its different forms—sometimes called the simple machines. All mechanical tools apply one or more of the simple machines and operate on the concepts of leverage, inclination, and/or rotation.

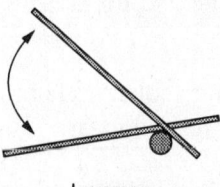

Leverage    Inclination 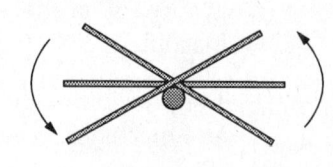   Rotation

- On the sheets provided on the following pages, identify and draw examples of tools that apply the concepts of leverage, inclination, and rotation.

- For each example, indicate the outputs that can be achieved by using that tool or device.

- For each example, indicate the inputs that are required for the tool or device to operate.

- Share your ideas with classmates; develop as many examples as possible and add the ideas and examples of your classmates to your collection.

DESIGN ACTIVITIES—TOOLS AND DEVICES THAT USE THE CONCEPT OF LEVERAGE (THE LEVER)

Identify the input and output of each of the levers shown below.

Input	Process	Output
long radial movement	Hammer	short radial movement, large mechanical advantage
	Scissors	
long radial movement with low force	Wheelbarrow	short radial movement with high force
	Microswitch	
	Shovel	
short linear movement with medium force	Tweezers	short linear movement with low force
	(Others)	

INTEGRATED S/M/T ACTIVITIES—IDENTIFYING AND ANALYZING CLASSES OF LEVERS

In the space provided, add examples of other devices that apply the lever in their operation. Organize the devices using the three classes of levers. Try to show two very different examples within each of the three classes of levers.

Arrange the components of load, fulcrum, and effort in the different orders that are found in 1st, 2nd, and 3rd class levers. Identify different examples of each of the different classes of levers. Share these ideas with your classmates. Trade your ideas so all of you have as big a collection of examples as possible.

	Example #1	Example #2
1st Class Lever	Effort Fulcrum Load	Effort Fulcrum Load
2nd Class Lever	Effort Load Fulcrum	Effort Load Fulcrum
3rd Class Lever	Fulcrum Effort Load	Fulcrum Effort Load

LINKAGES

The purpose of a **linkage** is to transmit forces and linear motion of appropriate and manageable size from a force applied as an input. Simple linkages take two forms—those producing linear motion in the same direction as the input force and those producing linear motion in the opposite direction of the input force.

In some of your design work with mechanical devices, you may have to change the direction of the linkages. The **bell crank lever** allows you to create force and motion that operates at a right angle. For example, you can use the bell crank lever to change a motion directly away from you to a motion that moves to the right or left.

Refer to the devices and components shown in Figure 4.6 in your text and revisited on the following page.

DESIGN BRIEFS—LINKAGES AND LEVERAGES

Using the devices and components referenced above as a starting point, design and assemble linkages that will provide:

- an output force that is greater than the input force,
- an output motion that is greater than the input motion,
- an output force that is equal to and in the same direction as the input force,
- a rotary output motion from a linear input motion, and
- a back and forth motion to a left and right motion.

INTEGRATED S/M/T ACTIVITIES

Using the devices that you designed in the above activity, show how you would modify them to achieve:

- an output force that is twice as great as the input force,
- an output motion that is three times greater than the input motion,
- an output force that moves in the same direction as but that is one-quarter of the input distance, and
- a large sidewise (left and right) motion from a small back and forth motion.

DESIGN ACTIVITIES—TOOLS AND DEVICES THAT USE THE CONCEPT OF LEVERAGE (LINKAGES)

Identify the input and output of each of the linkages shown below.

Input	Process	Output
rotary movement	Reverse motion linkage	short linear movement
small or large movements	Pantograph linkage	magnified or reduced movement
_____	Push-pull linkage	_____
_____	Treadle linkage (crank & slider)	_____
_____	Toggle linkage	_____
_____	(Others)	_____
_____	(Others)	_____

DESIGN ACTIVITIES—TOOLS AND DEVICES THAT USE THE CONCEPT OF INCLINATION (THE WEDGE)

Identify the input and output of each of the wedges shown below.

Input	Process	Output
high impact, short movement	Chisel	Short movement, cutting action
linear movement	File	linear cutting action
	Saw	
	Plane	
	Wire cutters	
	(Others)	
	(Others)	

DESIGN ACTIVITIES—TOOLS AND DEVICES THAT USE THE CONCEPT OF INCLINATION (THE INCLINED PLANE)

Identify the input and output of each of the inclined planes shown below.

Input	Process	Output
vertical & horizontal force	Ramp	vertical lift and horizontal movement
linear (horizontal) reciprocating movement	Linear cam	linear (vertical) reciprocating movement
	Inclined conveyor	
	Ratchet	
	Staircase	
	(Others)	
	(Others)	

DESIGN ACTIVITIES—TOOLS AND DEVICES THAT USE THE CONCEPT OF INCLINATION (THE SCREW)

Identify the input and output of each of the screws shown below.

Input	Process	Output
	Clamp	linear, high pressure (force)
short rotary motion of screw wheel	Compass	radial placement (movement) of compass legs
	Scissors jack	
	Micrometer	
	Screws	
	(Others)	
	(Others)	

Applications of the Lever

Other applications of the lever can take many different forms, including the wheel and axle, crank or windlass, belts and pulleys, and toothed belt and pulley, and sprockets and chains are similar to belts and pulleys, and cams and gears. Complete the analysis activities that follow on pages 89–92 and then complete the following activities.

ENRICHMENT DESIGN AND TECHNOLOGY ACTIVITIES

Using pulleys, chains and sprockets, and/or gears, design and model devices that:

- increase the output rotary speed of a fan relative to the input by a factor of 2,
- increase the output rotary speed of a fan by a factor of 10,
- increase the MA of an elevator by a factor of 10, and
- increase the MA of an elevator by a factor of 200.

INTEGRATED S/M/T ACTIVITIES

If you are able to lift 100 pounds using one pulley, you can lift 200 pounds with two pulleys, 400 pounds with four pulleys, and so on. This does require more time, however, because more pulleys require more loops of rope. Determine how much more rope you will need to pull through the pulleys to move the same distance with two and four pulleys. Will this allow you to increase the MA? Why? Will this allow you to increase the amount of work done? Why?

Chapter 4 Tools, Mechanisms, and Machines **89**

DESIGN ACTIVITIES—TOOLS AND DEVICES THAT USE THE CONCEPT OF ROTATION (THE WHEEL)

Identify the input and output of each of the wheels shown below.

Input	Process	Output
rotary movement	Valve	short linear movement
rotary movement	Doorknob	linear movement of lock mechanism
	Pizza cutter	
	Steering wheel	
	Carts	
	(Others)	
	(Others)	

DESIGN ACTIVITIES—TOOLS AND DEVICES THAT USE THE CONCEPT OF ROTATION (PULLEYS)

Identify the input and output of each of the pulleys shown below.

Input	Process	Output
rotary motion with large motion and low force	Pulley	rotary motion with small motion and high force
rotary, high torque motion	Belt sander	linear, inline motion (sanding operation)
	Conveyor	
	Drill press (stepped pulley)	
	Clothesline	
	(Others)	
	(Others)	

DESIGN ACTIVITIES—TOOLS AND DEVICES THAT USE THE CONCEPT OF ROTATION (GEARS, SPROCKETS, AND CHAINS)

Identify the input and output of the gears or sprockets shown below.

Input | **Process** | **Output**

_____ | Spur gears | short radial, high-power movement

rotary motion | Bevel gears | rotary motion at angle to input motion

_____ | Worm gear | _____

_____ | Rack and pinion | _____

_____ | Sprocket and chain (Chain is incomplete) | _____

_____ | (Others) | _____

_____ | (Others) | _____

DESIGN ACTIVITIES—TOOLS AND DEVICES THAT USE THE CONCEPT OF ROTATION (CAMS)

Identify the input and output of each of the cams shown below.

Input	Process	Output
rotary motion	Pear-shaped cam	short radial, high-power movement
rotary motion	Cam with large dwell	rotary motion at angle to input motion
_____	Snail shell cam	_____
_____	Heart-shaped cam	_____
_____	Eccentric cam	_____
_____	(Others) _____	_____
_____	(Others) _____	_____

FLUID MECHANISMS

A source of power that is used in machines comes from force applied to fluids—compressed gases and liquids. Pneumatics deal with producing movement through the use of compressed air. When high forces are required, liquids such as oil are used rather than air. Using liquids under pressure is called hydraulics. Pneumatics and hydraulics are widely used in industry in the machines that are used to manufacture products. Also, many of the products use fluidics to do work. The major mechanisms and machines used in fluid power include compressors, air motors, cylinders, valves, flow regulators, and reservoirs or accumulators. Refer to Figure 4.13 in your text for illustrations and descriptions of key pneumatic devices.

Compressors and pumps are required to operate pneumatic devices and systems. Air motors produce rotary motion from the force of compressed air. Cylinders are the most used pneumatic components for producing linear movement and force. Pneumatic cylinders are either single action or double action.

Valves are devices used to control the operation of air motors and cylinders. Flow regulators control the amount of air entering a cylinder or other air-operated mechanism. Reservoirs (accumulators) are used for storing air and creating a time delay in the operation of a pneumatic system.

DESIGN ACTIVITIES—FLUID POWER MECHANISMS (POWER SOURCES AND DEVICES)

Identify the input and output of each of the fluid power devices shown below.

Input	Process	Output
air at low pressure	Compressor	air at high pressure
fluid under pressure (on) pressure (off)	Single-action cylinder	linear, high force, motion, low force return
	Double-action cylinder	
	Accumulator	
	Shock absorber	
	(Others)	
	(Others)	

DESIGN ACTIVITIES—FLUID POWER MECHANISMS (CONTROL DEVICES)

Identify the input and output of each of the control devices shown below.

Input	Process	Output
linear force, fluid under pressure	Push-button 3-port valve	fluid supplied to one port and controlled device
electrical signal, fluid under pressure	Solenoid-operated 3-port valve	fluid supplied to two ports and controlled device
_____	Flow restrictor	_____
_____	Shutoff valve	_____
_____	Amplifying valve	_____
_____	(Others)	_____
_____	(Others)	_____

DESIGN BRIEFS

You have been asked to help design a display that will include an animated figure that will move slowly back and forth in a slow and controlled fashion. Identify the devices from Figure 4.13 in your text that you would use.

Design and sketch a pneumatic circuit using the above devices to create the back and forth motion needed for the display. Can you modify the circuit to introduce a time delay before the figure returns to its starting point?

INTEGRATED S/M/T ACTIVITIES

Two pneumatic cylinders are shown below. Determine the following:

- Which one can apply the most force?
- Which one can apply the longest motion?
- Which one will return to the start position when air pressure is removed?
- Does the double-acting cylinder create more force when it is extending than when it is retracting? If so, why?

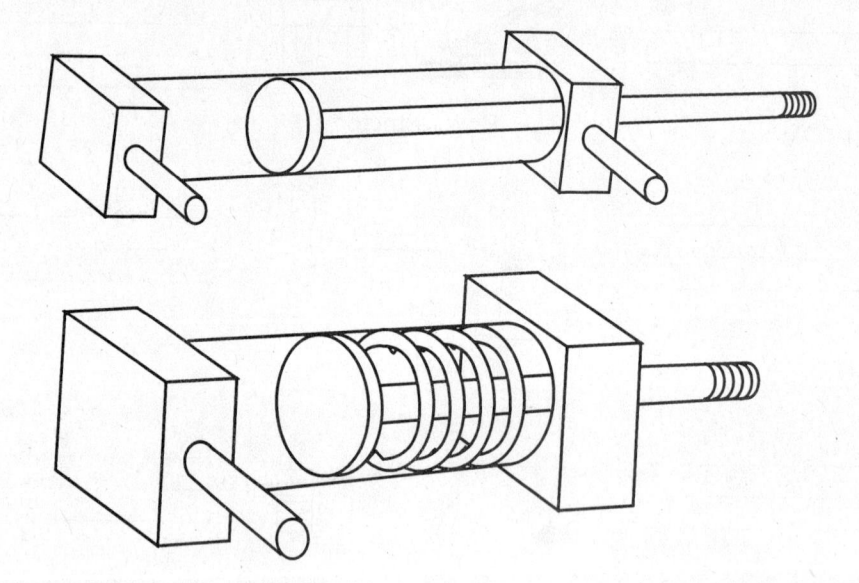

ELECTROMECHANICAL MECHANISMS

Electromechanical devices use electricity to create motion, and in some instances use motion to create electricity. Creating motion from electricity is accomplished by harnessing the magnetic fields that are produced around a wire that is carrying electric current. The attraction of unlike **magnetic poles** and the repulsion of similar poles provides a push and pull that will cause an electric motor to rotate. Electromechanical mechanisms are basically of two types: power devices and control devices.

Electromechanical devices use electricity to create motion, or they use motion to create electricity by moving a coil of wire through a magnetic field. Electric motors are most commonly used to create rotary motion. Motors come in two standard types: direct current (DC) and alternating current (AC). Stepper motors will move a small step each time a signal is sent to the motor. Stepper motors are useful in robotic and computer-driven applications. The linear motor moves in a straight line along a track that is laid out like a long series of magnetic coils.

Solenoids operate when an electric current is passed through a coil of wire, causing a strong magnetic field. Solenoids are used to create a short linear movement electrically. Electric generators operate when a moveable coil is turned within a magnetic field, causing an electric current to flow.

DESIGN ACTIVITIES—ELECTROMECHANICAL DEVICES (POWER DEVICES)

Identify the input and output of each of the electromechanical devices shwon below.

Input	Process	Output
electrical power, amperage and voltage	Motor	rotary, high-speed motion
electrical energy, low voltge and amperage	Light-emitting diode (LED)	visible light, voltage drop
_____	Generator	_____
_____	Light bulb	_____
_____	Solenoid	_____
_____	(Others)	_____
_____	(Others)	_____

DESIGN ACTIVITIES—ELECTROMECHANICAL DEVICES (CONTROL DEVICES)

Identify the input and output of each of the control devices shown below.

Input	Process	Output
physical movement (off condition)	Switch	closing or opening control circuit (on condition)
physical movement	Variable resistor	increasing/decreasing of resistance
_____	Light-dependent resistor	_____
_____	Thermistor	_____
_____	Transistor	_____
_____	(Others) _____	_____
_____	(Others) _____	_____

MACHINES

Machines are developed by combining different subsystems into an interrelated system. All machines are similar in that they all have these subsystems: 1) the structure and cover system to provide protection for the user and the parts of the machine, 2) the energy transmission system to transmit energy from one place to another, and 3) the control system to provide guidance and control to direct the operation and movement of the machine. The function of machines is to convert materials, energy, or information into new forms.

Machines change materials from an existing form to a new form. Specifically, you can use machines to change the characteristics of a material so that the material better fulfills the purpose you have in mind. You may choose a machine and its related process that will make the material tougher, softer, more flexible, or more brittle, depending on what you are trying to accomplish.

Machines are also used to change energy from one form to a more usable form. In converting energy, it is necessary that you think of the final form of energy you want to provide and the form of energy you have to start with. If you need energy in the form of heat, and you have electrical energy available, you can then identify the devices that you might use to convert the electrical energy into heat energy.

Finally, machines are used to change information to new forms. Machines allow you to change information by converting materials into new symbols. You can also use information in the form of signals to control the operation of a machine.

DESIGN ACTIVITIES—MACHINE ANALYSIS AND CLASSIFICATION

All machines have three basic subsystems—energy transmission, structure and cover, and control. Most simple machines use humans to provide part of one or more of the three subsystems. The more sophisticated the machines, the less human involvement is required to operate the machines.

You will work in teams of three, with each of you responsible for one of the machine subsystems. As a team, you will need to assign a subsystem to each of you. Consider the following and complete the Machine Analysis Form on the next page.

Work first as individuals to:

- identify each of the three subsystems for your machine
- determine which parts of the machine belong to your subsystem
- identify which parts you think are shared by the subsystems

Work now as a group to reach agreement on:

- what the three subsystems for your machine are
- which parts of the machine belong to which subsystem
- which parts are shared by the subsystems

Work again as a group to determine:

- the changes that can be made in materials, energy, and/or information by your machine
- the primary function that your machine can accomplish
- the alternative functions that your machine could accomplish

MACHINE ANALYSIS FORM

Name of machine _____

Your name _____ Members of your team _____

Subsystem you are responsible for _____

Class _____ Date _____

Name of Machine Part	Energy Transmission	Structure and Cover	Control

Primary Machine Function

Alternative Machine Functions

SKILL ASSESSMENT AND INVENTORY

To help in the management of the course and as a means for you to keep track of your progress, a form for an Inventory of Tools/Devices/Machines Uses and Skills, is provided for the tools and machines you will use in your design and technology work. In some instances, you may discover a tool that would help you complete a job, but one you do not know how to use. In these instances, it is essential that you receive instructions from your teacher on how to use the tool. When indicated by your teacher, you can add the name of this and other new tools to your inventory.

A space is provided for you to write the name and make a sketch of the tool. A second space is provided for you to add the use and output of the T/D/M (tool, device, or machine). Finally, a space is provided for you to identify the level of skill you have acquired in using the T/D/M. You are to shade in the bar to represent the level of skill you believe you have gained. Your teacher will then mark and initial your form, indicating agreement or disagreement with your self-assessment.

INVENTORY OF TOOLS/DEVICES/MACHINES USES AND SKILLS

Name and sketch of tool	Use and output of T/D/M	Your skill level (shade bar) none　low　med.　high Comments:
Name and sketch of tool	Use and output of T/D/M	Your skill level (shade bar) none　low　med.　high Comments:
Name and sketch of tool	Use and output of T/D/M	Your skill level (shade bar) none　low　med.　high Comments:
Name and sketch of tool	Use and output of T/D/M	Your skill level (shade bar) none　low　med.　high Comments:
Name and sketch of tool	Use and output of T/D/M	Your skill level (shade bar) none　low　med.　high Comments:

(Reproduce as required.)

DESIGN ACTIVITIES—ANALYZING DEVICES THAT USE THE CONCEPT OF

*_____

Input	Process	Output
_____		_____
_____		_____
_____	_____	_____
_____		_____
_____		_____
_____		_____
_____	_____	_____
_____		_____
_____		_____
_____	_____	_____
_____		_____
_____		_____
_____	_____	_____
_____		_____
_____		_____
_____	_____	_____
_____		_____
_____	_____	_____

* Insert concept of: Leverage, Inclination, Rotation, Power or Control.

CHAPTER 5: Materials and Materials Processing

This chapter explores (1) the **characteristics** of materials, (2) their **structure,** (3) their **function,** and (4) the **conversion** of materials to change those characteristics, structures and functions.

CHARACTERISTICS OF MATERIALS

All materials have characteristics or properties, such as being strong, tough, soft, rough, heavy, or brittle. Designing potential solutions to a technological problem involves selecting materials with appropriate characteristics. Some materials, which we classify as chemical elements, are made of only one type of atom. Most materials are combinations of elements. These are called compounds and are made up of many molecules. Each molecule, however, is made of atoms of specific elements and all molecules in that compound are alike. Atoms and molecules (material units) combine in sensible ways. Some material units have almost no attraction for each other. Some have tremendous forces of attraction. Other material units fall somewhere between these extremes.

Materials can have many characteristics. An important characteristic in your design and technology work is the strength of the materials. Strength of materials relates to how well a material holds up under tension, compression, shear, and torsion. (These are called tensile, compressive, shear, and torsion strength of materials, respectively.) You will remember that the idea of torque was introduced in Chapter 4 as the force that is needed to create a circular motion. Shear is the force needed to create a cutting action.

These drawings show the concept of testing a material for tensile and compressive strength.

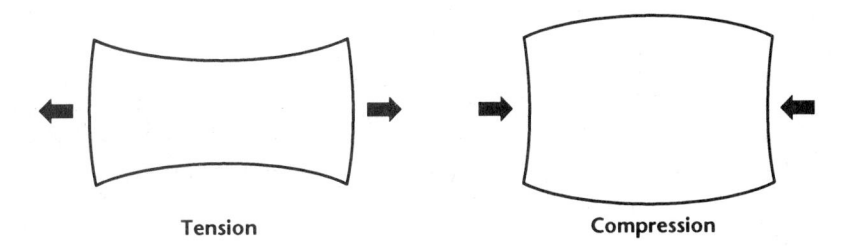

Tension   Compression

DESIGN BRIEFS— MATERIAL TESTING OF TENSILE AND COMPRESSIVE STRENGTH

Using the specific material sample assigned by your teacher, determine if it should be tested for tensile or compressive strength or both. Design a device that can be used to determine its strength.

- If appropriate, determine the tensile strength of the material.
- If appropriate, determine the compressive strength of the material.
- Determine how the other types of strength of the material could be tested.
- List some ways in which each material might be put to other uses.

Design and build a structure, using only three sheets of thin card stock, 36" of tape, and a pair of scissors, that will support a common house brick as high off the ground as possible. After you have built your structure, test it and then:

- Determine which parts fail first and why. Do the parts tear or crumple?
- Determine which parts of the structure require compressive strength.
- Determine which parts of the structure require tensile strength.
- Determine how the structure can be improved.
- Examine one of the chairs you use in school and determine where the most compressive strength is needed. Where is the most tensile strength needed? Identify where the chair is subjected to twisting actions and needs the most torsion strength. Will the person always be sitting still and be a static load? When might the chair be subjected to a moving or dynamic load? Use the information gained through your analysis to propose design changes to make the chair stronger.

INTEGRATED S/M/T ACTIVITIES

Tensile Testing of Materials

- Determine the load required to pull a material sample apart.
- Measure and calculate the cross-section size of the material sample.
- Determine the load required to break (dislocate) the sample. Express this in pounds per square inch.
- Determine the load required to dislocate the sample in Newtons per square centimeter.

Compression Testing of Materials

- Determine the load required to break a material by squeezing (compressing) it.
- Measure and calculate the cross-section size of the material sample.
- Determine the load required to break the sample in pounds per square inch.
- Determine the load required to dislocate the sample in Newtons per square centimeter.

Characteristics/Properties of Materials

- What is the difference between the characteristics of strength and stiffness?
- What new characteristics can you add to the list started at the beginning of the activities in this chapter?

On the worksheets provided on the following pages, several different characteristics of materials are identified and illustrated. As you work with new materials within the activities in this chapter, identify the major characteristics for each material. Add the name of each new material in the space provided. For each new material space, a general five point scale, ranging from high to low, is provided. Analyze and estimate the general level for each new material. Record your estimate by placing an arrow along the scale to designate whether the material is "high" in the specific characteristic or "low."

	Name of material	High (characteristic) Low
		5 4 3 2 1
Strength	wood-balsa	_____^__
Stiffness	wood-balsa	_____^_____

Over the length of this course, you should accumulate a range of new materials that you can use in your design and technology work. Materials are chosen because they have specific characteristics and they can do specific jobs. The experiments and design activities in this section, and the observations you make and the notes you keep, will help you do a better job of choosing the best materials for your designs.

DESIGN ACTIVITIES—MATERIAL CHARACTERISTICS/ PROPERTIES AND TESTING

	Name of Material	High (characteristic) Low
Strength		5 4 3 2 1
Stiffness		5 4 3 2 1
Hardness		5 4 3 2 1
Toughness		5 4 3 2 1
Malleability		5 4 3 2 1
Elasticity		5 4 3 2 1
Flexibility		5 4 3 2 1
Brittleness		5 4 3 2 1

DESIGN ACTIVITIES—MATERIAL CHARACTERISTICS/PROPERTIES AND TESTING CONTINUED

	Name of Material	High (characteristic) Low
Workability		5 4 3 2 1
Conductivity		5 4 3 2 1
Porosity		5 4 3 2 1
Reflectivity		5 4 3 2 1
Absorption		5 4 3 2 1
Transmission		5 4 3 2 1
Flammability		5 4 3 2 1
Density		5 4 3 2 1

(Develop more sheets as needed.)

THE STRUCTURE OF MATERIALS

The basic building units of materials can be combined in different ways. Some materials are made of units connected in long chains, called polymers. These chains are held together by the molecular forces of attraction. Wood is made largely of long cellulose molecules; and plastics are synthetic polymers, very similar to wood.

INTEGRATED S/M/T ACTIVITIES

Measure your height. Use a piece of butcher paper that is at least as long as you are tall. Lay out a graph using inches or centimeters. Plot your size over the period of approximately 30 minutes you would be in the incredible shrinking machine. Plot the size you would be after each minute. Consider each minute as a step in your shrinking process.

How many steps can you actually plot on the chart? When did the steps get so close together that you could not discern a difference in the plots? How could you improve the chart to help you and others understand how small you would become?

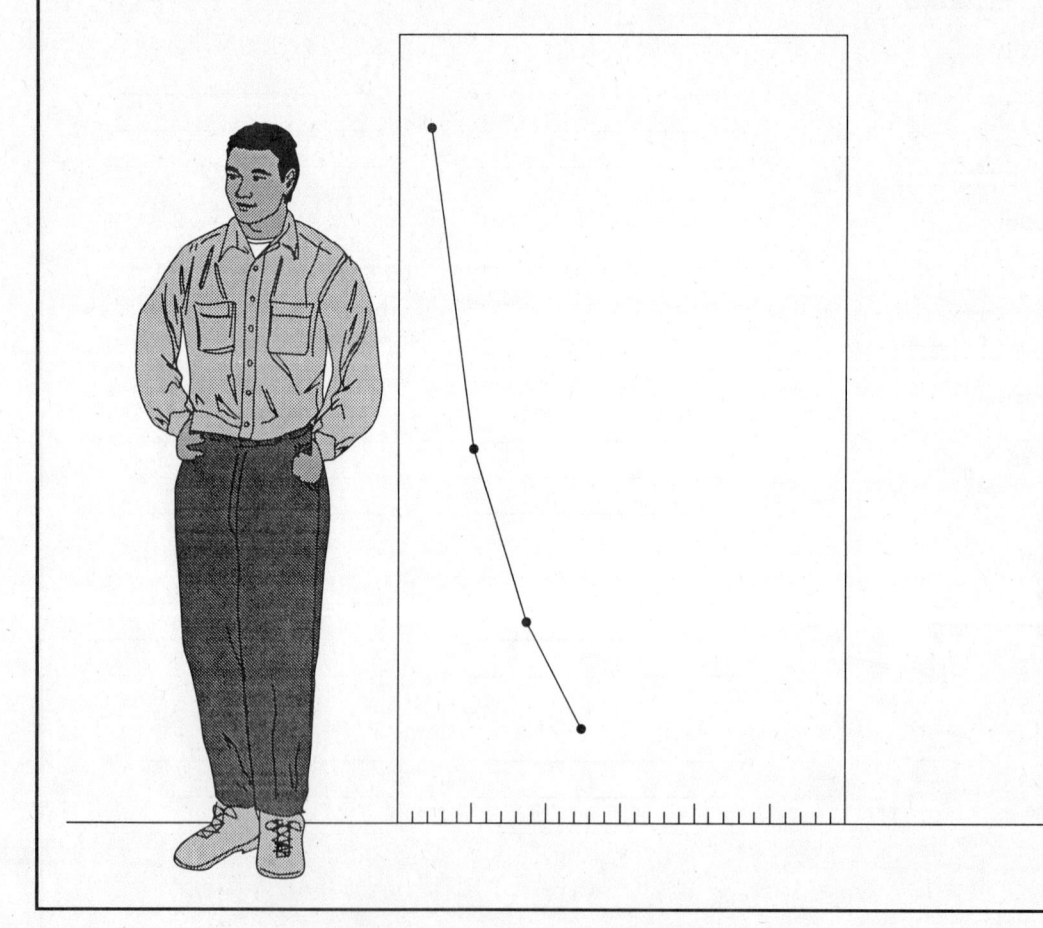

Not all materials form chains or have a grain direction when they bond together. Some molecules bond into tiny platelets that slip and slide easily over each other. Materials that are comprised of platelets usually have good properties of pliability, a property that is usually lost when the materials are heated.

Some materials have crystals that form a grain that can be rearranged by processing while cooling. This property of metals makes them very useful for forming and shaping. In metals, atoms pack together to form molecules in a simple manner. You can build a model of a metal molecule by using spheres as the atoms. Some metals have atoms that are stacked together in the shape of cubes. Other materials pack together in a six-sided, hexagonal shape.

Materials often look very different from each other, yet in some ways all materials are quite similar. We need to understand what it is that makes materials similar. Use your imagination as you read the vignette about the incredible shrinking machine on page 108 of your textbook.

DESIGN BRIEFS—MODELS OF MATERIALS

Using the techniques shown in your text (see Figure 5.3A, 5.4 and 5.6), develop a model of a molecule of one of the common materials provided by your teacher. With your teacher and your class, select one of the compounds and develop a model of it using the materials provided. Compare the models of different compounds developed by your class. Use the periodic table in your text to identify the atoms in your compound. Label the compound with the appropriate symbols.

DESIGN BRIEFS—CHAINS OF MOLECULES

With your teacher, determine which of the polymer plastics you will develop as a model. Using the modeling materials provided, build a model of your polymer. (Initially, develop a model of one mer [monomer] or molecule of your polymer.)

Discuss with your classmates the models that were built.

- Show how the structure of the material and the presence of long molecules help determine the characteristics of that material.

- Test actual sample pieces of real polymers.

- Which of the materials have good tensile strength?

- Which of the materials tend to be flexible?

- Which of the materials tends to be more rigid?

- Check the Appendix on Materials and Properties and refer to the section on plastics and polymers. What help does this information provide as you choose materials for your designs?

DESIGN BRIEFS—CLOSE PACKING OF MATERIALS

One of the most useful kinds of materials with **crystals** is metals. The crystals form a grain that can be arranged in the desired form by processing while cooling.

In metals, atoms pack together to form molecules in a simple manner. You can build a model of a metal molecule by using spheres as the atoms. Some metals seem to have atoms that are stacked together in the shape of **cubes**. Other materials pack together in a six-sided, **hexagonal** shape.

Refer to the illustrations in Figure 5.8 in your text (shown in part below). Using the materials provided by your teacher, develop a model that shows close packing of materials. Develop models of body-centered cubes, face-centered cubes, and close-packed hexagons.

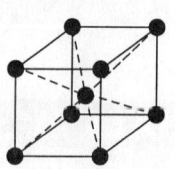

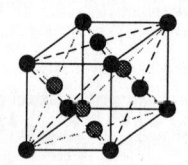

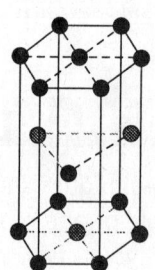

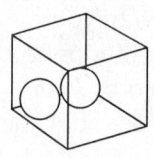

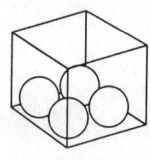

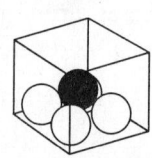

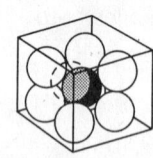

Body-centered cube   **Face-centered cube**   **Close-packed hexagon**

Develop a model that illustrates what happens with close-packed and loose-packed materials. What difference do you think there would be in processing close-packed and loose-packed materials?

FUNCTION OF MATERIALS

Materials can be grouped into four categories. They can be considered as monolithic, amorphous, material systems, and dynamic materials. Monolithic materials are made of only one ingredient, element, or compound. They do not change during use. There are two kinds of monolithic materials: natural and basic.

Amorphous materials lack any specific structure or organization. Their structure and form are not organized as in crystalline or string-like molecules. These materials are rather nondescript and disorganized in their form.

Material systems are two or more materials that differ in form, that become a new, more desirable material when they are combined. All material systems fall within two categories: material mixtures and material layers.

Dynamic materials change during use. There are three types of dynamic materials: metamorphic, expandable, and functional. Metamorphic materials change slowly from their original characteristics to something different as they are used. Expandable materials are of two types, those that flex and those that foam. Flexible materials can expand and contract. Most foaming materials expand only once. Functional materials change back and forth from one state to another as an outside force is applied and then removed.

Many materials are really parts of families of materials. For example, the term "plastics" is a name for a family of related materials. This family includes many types of plastics such as vinyl, styrene, and acrylic. We use such terms as metal, food, ceramic, textile, and wood to indicate families of materials. One important material family is the ferrous metals. These are irons and steels.

We mix various ingredients in various amounts to make different types of cakes, as well as to make different types of materials such as ceramics and steels. Each type of new material is made from the same basic components, in varying amounts. The amount of the basic ingredient and specific additional materials will change the properties of the outcome (the new material). Recipes or formulas have been developed to ensure consistent production of the materials, each designed to do different jobs and make different products.

On the next two pages are design activities related to identifying **material systems.** The first asks you to identify different examples of **mixtures**. The second asks you to identify examples of **layers**.

DESIGN ACTIVITIES—MATERIAL SYSTEMS SHOWING MIXTURES

Examples

Composite

Diffused

Dispersed

Fiber reinforced

Alloys

Powder compacted

(Others)

(Develop more sheets as needed)

Chapter 5 Materials and Materials Processing **115**

DESIGN ACTIVITIES—MATERIAL SYSTEMS SHOWING LAYERS

Examples

Sandwiched

Cladded

Bonded

Coated

Laminated

(Others)

(Develop more sheets as needed)

The design activity that follows is intended to help you understand how **dynamic materials** change during use. As indicated earlier, there are three types of dynamic materials: **metamorphic, expandable,** and **functional. Metamorphic** materials change slowly from their original characteristics to something different. **Expandable** materials either flex or foam. Flexible materials expand and contract while most foaming materials expand only once. **Functional** materials change back and forth from one state to another as an outside force is applied and then removed. These changes take place with no moving parts.

DESIGN ACTIVITIES—IDENTIFYING DYNAMIC MATERIALS SHOWING METAMORPHIC, EXPANDABLE, AND FUNCTIONAL EXAMPLES

Examples

Metamorphic

Expandable

Functional

(Others)

(Develop more sheets as needed)

DESIGN BRIEFS

Understanding the different functions of materials is important if you and your classmates are to use materials effectively in the design and development of products and structures. In order to share what you learn about materials and their functions, collect samples of different materials. Design and develop a display of materials that presents and describes each of the following:

- natural and basic materials—monolithic and amorphous
- material systems—mixtures and layers
- dynamic materials—metamorphic, expandable, and functional

Analyze the products provided by your teacher and determine the different materials that are used in the manufacture of their parts. Next:

- categorize each of the parts according to the materials used,
- identify which parts might perform better if changed to a different material, and
- write a short defense of why the new material would be better for the part.

INTEGRATED S/M/T ACTIVITIES

Function of Materials

- Devise and conduct simple tests to determine the structure of the samples of materials you collected (crystals, platelets, polymers, or amorphous).

- Using a microscope, see if you can determine whether the material samples you have collected are comprised of crystals (grains), platelets, or polymers, or if the material is amorphous in form.

- Develop drawings to represent the structure of your material samples.

CONVERSION OF MATERIALS

Your design and development work will involve changing the characteristics, structures, and functions of materials. In the design part, you will need to plan and choose the processes by which you will change the materials. In the development or making part, you will actually use the processes to fabricate the model or prototype of your solution.

The term "process" refers to a sequence of actions that lead to some result. Materials can also be converted not only to form new materials, but also to generate energy, and to create information. All three types of processes (conversion of materials, energy, and information) are similar and involve **sequence, action, changes,** and **results.** These are the four essential parts of any **process.**

The **sequence of actions** involves placing the right materials together in the proper places and treating them in a certain way over a given time. The **change** in materials may be one of four kinds, indicated in the next paragraph. The **result** is the desired outcome—a conversion of materials, information, or energy to new forms as products, environments or systems.

The activities provided on the following pages will focus on four categories of processes that can be used to change materials. These include (1) **adding** materials to each other, (2) **separating** materials, (3) making **contour changes,** or (4) making **internal changes.**

Addition Processes

Adding materials together can form a new material or product that combines the characteristics of the ingredients. The addition of materials falls into the four categories of (1) **mixing**, (2) **joining** or **fastening**, (3) **coating**, and (4) **weaving** or **interlacing.**

Materials Separation Processes

Separation processes involve removing materials, most often using a **wedge**-shaped tool driven by a mechanical **force** that generates some waste in the form of a **chip**. Some processes use a wedge that does not create a chip. Other processes operate without relying on force.

DESIGN BRIEFS—MATERIALS CONVERSION ADDITION AND SEPARATION OF MATERIALS

Addition—In the design and development work you will be doing, it is important that you know which materials conversion processes are appropriate to use in the making of the models, prototypes, and products. To provide you with a better background for this work, design and develop reference pages for your portfolio. Through drawings, narratives, and examples taken from old magazines, develop a short presentation for each of the following addition of materials processes—(1) **mixing**, (2) **joining** or **fastening**, (3) **coating**, and (4) **weaving** or **interlacing.** For each example included, illustrate it and write an explanation of how the materials are added to each other and why that process was selected.

Separation—Design and develop a reference page for the following separation of materials processes—(1) **with and without a wedge,** (2) **with and without a chip,** and (3) **with and without force.**

Using the examples provided by your teacher, determine which of the above processes are used for the addition of materials. Determine which are used for the separation of materials. Develop an alternative approach for one of the products you analyzed in the activities on page 120.

DESIGN ACTIVITIES—ADDITION OF MATERIALS

Mixing

Joining/fastening (adhesion)

Joining/fastening (cohesion)

Coating

Weaving/knitting/ interlacing

Examples

(Develop more sheets as needed)

DESIGN ACTIVITIES—SEPARATION OF MATERIALS WITH AND WITHOUT A WEDGE, CHIP, AND FORCE

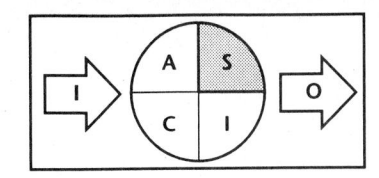

Tool/Process	Wedge with	Wedge without	Chip with	Chip without	Force with	Force without
Chiseling						
Sawing						
Planing						
Hot wire cutting						
Shearing						
Drilling						
Piercing						
Sanding						
Filing						
Broaching						
Milling						
Scraping						
Bleaching						
Washing						
Etching						
Developing						
Screening						
Winnowing						

DESIGN ACTIVITIES—SEPARATION OF MATERIALS WITH AND WITHOUT A WEDGE, CHIP, AND FORCE

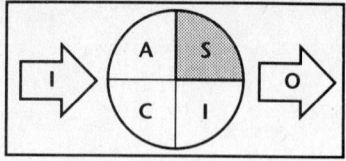

Tool/Process	Wedge with	Wedge without	Chip with	Chip without	Force with	Force without

(Develop more sheets as needed.)

INTEGRATED S/M/T ACTIVITIES

- Use sample materials and sample adhesives provided by your teacher. Adhere two pieces of the materials with each adhesive. Use the test device provided by your teacher, and determine how much force is required to break the adhesive bond.

- Develop a chart to show the relative strength of the different adhesives when applied to different materials.

- Compare your results of these tests with those of your classmates and discuss how and why the results are similar and different.

- If you were to repeat this testing, what factors (variables) would you want to control to ensure that this is a fair test of the strength of the adhesive bond only.

- Using a cutting tool and sample pieces of wood, plastic, and fabric provided by your teacher, determine the force needed to cut (shear) the samples.

- Develop a chart to show the relative strength of the different materials (with the grain, across the grain, and diagonally across the grain — on the bias).

- Identify if there are any factors that interfere with you making accurate measurements on these tests. How would you take these into account?

Contour Change Processes

Contour change processes alter the outside or surface of materials without removing or adding any materials. There are five general types of contour change processes: **casting, extruding, forming, pressing,** and **molding.**

Internal Change Processes

Some processes are used only to make changes inside materials. These processes are often used to create specific characteristics in the materials. They include thermal, mechanical, magnetic, chemical, acoustical, optical, and electrical processes.

DESIGN ACTIVITIES—CONTOUR CHANGE OF MATERIALS

Examples

Casting

Extruding

Forming

Pressing

Molding

(Develop more sheets as needed)

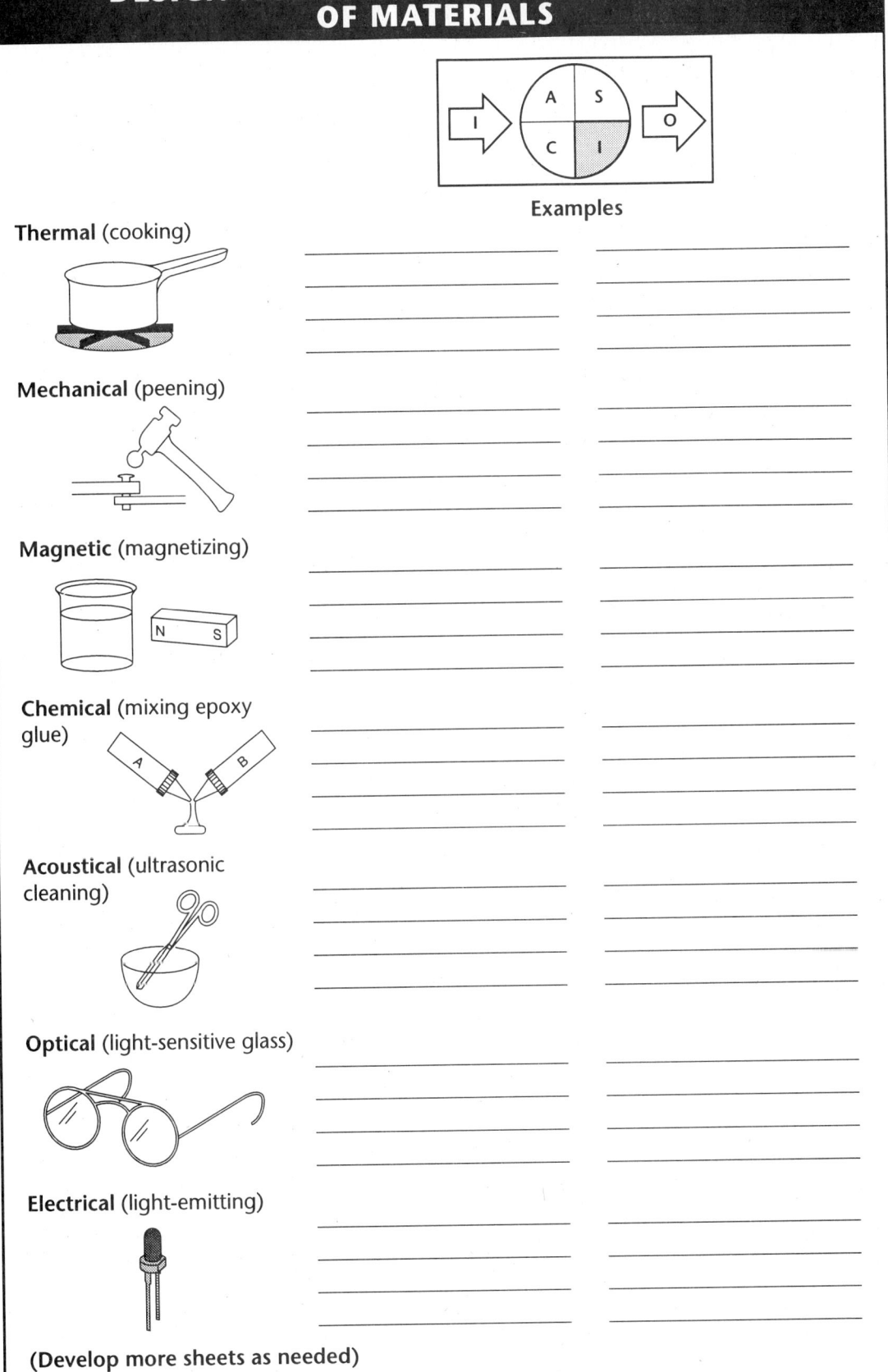

DESIGN ACTIVITIES—INTERNAL CHANGE OF MATERIALS

Examples

Thermal (cooking)

Mechanical (peening)

Magnetic (magnetizing)

Chemical (mixing epoxy glue)

Acoustical (ultrasonic cleaning)

Optical (light-sensitive glass)

Electrical (light-emitting)

(Develop more sheets as needed)

DESIGN BRIEFS—MATERIALS CONVERSION—CONTOUR AND INTERNAL CHANGE OF MATERIALS

Contour Change—It is important that you know which materials conversion processes are appropriate when you wish to modify the shape (contour change) and structure (internal change) of materials. Design and develop reference pages for your portfolio that include drawings, narratives, and examples to illustrate each of the contour changes—**casting, extruding, forming, pressing,** and **molding.** Use the drawings and examples you have identified on page 124 as a starting point.

Internal Change—Design and develop a reference page for each of the following internal change processes—**thermal, mechanical, magnetic, chemical, acoustical, optical,** and **electrical.** Use the drawings and your work on page 125 as a starting point for this activity.

DESIGN ACTIVITIES—DEVELOPING MATERIALS TESTING AND APPLICATIONS SHEETS

In your design and technology work, you will make many decisions about materials to use in your designs. You will choose a material based on its characteristics and the function it is to perform. The following activities are designed to help you and your classmates learn more about materials and how to select them. Working in teams, you will use the IDEATE model to design and develop information sheets on different characteristics (properties) of materials. The first two steps of the design process are described below. You will need to complete the remainder of the process.

The I D E A T E Design Loop

Identify and define the problem (investigating needs and opportunities)

Develop the design brief (clarifying the results you want to achieve)

Explore possible alternatives (searching for solutions and information)

Accumulate and assess the alternatives (developing and choosing the best solution)

Try out the best solution (experimenting and developing solutions, models, and prototypes)

Evaluate the results (testing the solution and assessing the process)

Focusing on the property designated by your teacher, or on a property selected by your group, complete the design process started below. Remember, at the end of these activities your group will display your work and share your ideas with your class. They will also share their work with you. As a class you will have developed a set of Materials Testing and Applications Sheets that all of you can use in your design work.

Developing Materials Testing and Applications Sheets

Problem Statement:

Choosing materials to use in a design problem requires some knowledge about the characteristics and properties of materials. Because time in this course is limited, it is difficult working alone to learn everything required to make good decisions in selecting materials.

Learning about materials and sharing what has been learned with classmates could help save time and might help show the similarities of materials and their properties.

Design Brief:

Design and develop a display that describes one material property of materials and that illustrates the tests that can be used to determine if a material has that property.

DESIGN ACTIVITIES—DEVELOPING MATERIALS TESTING AND APPLICATIONS SHEETS CONTINUED

Specifications:

a) The displays should focus on key questions regarding the property of materials. Sample questions would include the following:

- What is the property?
- What makes a material have that property?
- How can that property be controlled?
- What problems are caused by the property?
- What uses can be made of the property?
- What can be done to the design to increase that property?

b) The displays should make extensive and effective use of drawings, symbols, and other graphics.

c) The displays should be limited to one panel of 17" x 22".

d) The information on the displays should fit on a 11" x 17" sheet that can fit into your notebook or portfolio.

e) Safety suggestions for each of the proposed tests should be developed and highlighted.

f) Each display and sheet should be usable by other groups in the class that have not been involved in their development.

Listed below are some of the characteristics or properties of materials to be researched and then designed and developed for display.

strength	stiffness	hardness	toughness
malleability	elasticity	flexibility	brittleness
workability	conductivity	porosity	reflectivity
absorption	transmission	flammability	density

Refer to the following pages to see some suggested simple tests of these properties.

DESIGN ACTIVITIES—DEVELOPING MATERIALS TESTING AND APPLICATIONS SHEETS CONTINUED

Materials Testing and Applications from British Petroleum Notebook

Similarities in Materials Conversion Processes

All the materials conversion processes change the way the materials are bonded together. These processes involve sequences, actions, changes, and results, the four essential parts of any process and are used to create new bonds, break bonds, or modify existing bonds in some way. Key points in the conversion processes are the actions you use to change the materials.

Materials are converted into useful objects through the processes that the tools and machines perform on those materials. As indicated before, tools and materials interact through one or more different **processes**. Processes are the sequence of actions that lead to some result. Processes can be used to reach a desired goal or output, such as new energy, information, or materials. The next section examines the characteristics and structure of materials, followed by a section on the function of materials. This background should help you select and use specific materials processes to create the characteristics required in your designs.

ENRICHMENT DESIGN AND TECHNOLOGY ACTIVITIES

Building upon the activities you have completed related to materials and material processing, develop an exhibit of one of the material characteristics identified below:

- strength—compression, tension, shear, and torsion
- stiffness, hardness, brittleness, ductility, toughness, and density
- thermal properties of conductivity and expansion
- electrical properties of resistance and conductivity
- magnetic properties of natural and induced magnetism
- optical properties of transparency, translucency, and opacity
- properties of reflection, radiation, and absorption of heat and light

Obtain from your teacher samples that represent the different characteristics and functions of materials. Identify which of the samples fit best in the categories of properties in your exhibit.

DESIGN BRIEFS

Using the information and findings recorded in the exhibit you and your classmates have developed, choose and complete one of the following design briefs:

- Design and develop a model of a piece of clothing that will conserve body heat by reducing wind penetration.
- Disassemble and analyze a simple product, such as a toy. Determine the materials used in its manufacture and the appropriateness of each. Choose one of the products and illustrate how you would improve its design through the materials and processes used for its production.
- Revisit the design project on the seesaw from the preceding chapter. If the seesaw was to be made of wood, what properties would be most appropriate? What specific woods are most suitable? Remember to take into account the availability and cost of the different woods.
- You have been asked to determine which material would be best for the seesaw— wood, metal, or plastics—based on the criteria of strength, weight, cost, comfort of the user, and durability. How would you determine which material is most appropriate? What specific material would you choose?
- Using your new knowledge of materials, look at a range of products—toys, furniture, clothing—and predict what part of the products will fail first.
- What design changes would you propose in the products to improve their performance?

INTEGRATED S/M/T ACTIVITIES

Obtain from your teacher samples that represent the different characteristics and functions of materials.

- Test each of the samples and rank order them in terms of their strength — compression, tension, shear, and torsion.
- Rank order the samples in terms of their properties of stiffness, hardness, brittleness, ductility, toughness, and density.
- Test and rank order the samples in terms of the thermal properties of conductivity and expansion; electrical properties of resistance and conductivity; magnetic properties of magnetism; and optical properties of transparency, translucency, and opacity.
- Finally identify which samples exhibit the best properties of reflection, radiation, and absorption of heat and light.

CHAPTER 6
Energy and Energy Processing

Energy is available to us from several sources and can be converted from one form to another for storage and use. This chapter focuses on (1) sources of energy, (2) forms of energy, and (3) conversion of energy into more useful forms. Energy is an essential resource for all technological activities.

Energy is given off when bonds are broken between atoms or molecules of materials and the bonds are reformed to make new materials. The bonds may be broken rapidly, such as in burning or rapid oxidation, or through a slower chemical process called slow oxidation.

SOURCES OF ENERGY

Energy can be found in many different forms, but the basic source of all energy is the bond between material units. Large usable reservoirs of energy are called primary sources from which other secondary sources derive their energy. The sun is a major primary source; solar collectors that capture the heat from the sun or plants that use its light and heat to grow are examples of secondary sources.

Solar energy is radiated from the sun. Solar energy includes visible light, infrared waves, microwaves, ultraviolet, and several other energy wave forms, as well as atomic particles. Solar energy provides all our energy, except what comes from nuclear and geothermal sources. Wind power, most water power, fossil fuels, and fuel from plants or animals are sources of energy derived from solar energy.

Geothermal energy is a vast reservoir of heat that comes from molten rock called magma. We use only a very small amount of the heat from this geothermal energy source because there are few places where the molten rock has been pushed up close to the Earth's surface.

Wind is one of our primary energy sources. The movement of the Earth itself and of the air, as it heats and cools, creates high and low energy differentials. These, in turn, cause the movement of air or wind. The larger the energy difference between the high and low pressure zones, the greater is the speed or flow of the winds.

Energy from moving water can be traced to two influences of the sun on the Earth—gravitation and evaporation. The forces of gravity between the sun and

Earth create moving water in the form of tides or tidal energy. Energy, as heat from the sun, causes water to evaporate. This water eventually falls back to Earth as rain that can be stored in natural and artificial reservoirs.

Although tidal energy is linked with the sun, it is one of the few forms of energy that does not depend on radiated solar energy. The tides draw their energy from the gravitational forces of the sun and moon. The gravity of the sun and the moon serve to make oceans pulse in long, steady counts.

Nuclear energy results from tearing the nucleus of the atom apart (fission) or from combining the nucleus of one atom with the nucleus of another (fusion). The forces that hold the nucleus of an atom together are extremely powerful.

Fossil fuel takes the form of peat, coal, oil, shale, petroleum, or natural gas. Energy is released when material bonds of the fuel are broken during burning.

Biological energy is based on solar energy and chemical energy. There is great variation in the efficiency of plants and animals that use and provide biological energy. The energy is stored in the plants and is referred to as biomass. Biomass processes provide an alternative to some of the uses of fossil fuels.

DESIGN ACTIVITIES—MASS, FORCE, WORK DONE, AND POWER

In some design and technology problems, determining mass, force, work accomplished, and power required will be important to completing your design. The illustrations below help to clarify what is meant by mass and force.

| 1,000 cc Water at 4° C | Mass = 1 kilogram* |

| 1 kg ↓ 10 N | Force exerted due to gravity = 9.81 newtons = 10 newtons |

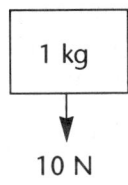

* 1 kg = 2.2 lb.   ** 1 N = .22 lb.

By using force and distance, it is possible to indicate the amount of work that has been done. The illustration below shows this relationship.

1m ↕ 1N   Work Done   A force of 1 N applied over a distance of 1 meter (m) = 1 newton meter (N-m)
1 N-m = 1 joule (J) of work
(E.g., force of 4 N applied across 2 m = 8 joules of work.)

Power refers to the rate of work done and is illustrated below:

1 N applied across 1 m, in 1 second = 1 watt

E.g., 10 N applied across 2 m in 2 seconds = $\frac{10 \times 2}{2}$ = 10 watts

10 N applied across 4 m in 1 second = $\frac{10 \times 4}{1}$ = 40 watts

DESIGN ACTIVITIES—SOURCES OF ENERGY

You and your team members are to design and develop a device or system to use the energy from one of the sources identified. These sources will include solar energy, energy from movement of the wind, energy from moving water, energy from heat sources (simulated magma and nuclear energy), energy from fossil fuels, energy from biomass, and energy from food.

In the illustrations that follow are different means for measuring the amount of energy that your device or system can produce. For this problem, the output of your design must indicate how much weight it can lift, how much electricity it can generate, or how much heat it can generate.

Each of your designs should be developed as a working model with a display of the operation and principles underlying the device or system. Include illustrations and descriptions of historical developments that preceded your proposed designs.

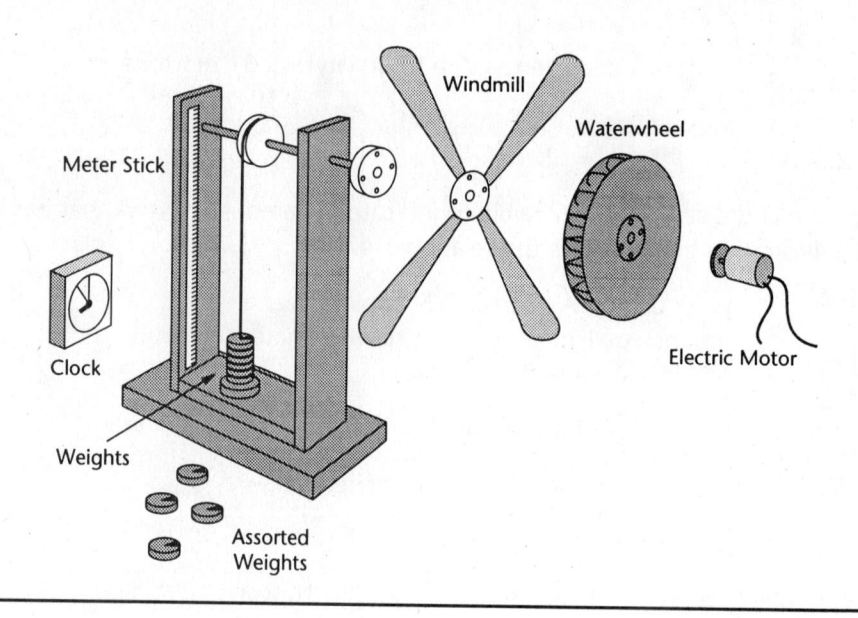

DESIGN ACTIVITIES—MOVEMENT-PRODUCING TEST DEVICES

For designs that deal with movement, you will need to identify how much weight the device can lift. Express this weight (force) in terms of newtons (N). (Here on Earth, the weight of one kilogram exerts a force of 10 N.) Determine how high your device can lift this weight. Calculate the work done when:

work done = force x distance moved (in the direction of the force)

$\quad$ W = f x d (Work is expressed in units called joules [J])

If your device can lift 300 grams a distance of 75 centimeters, you would then calculate:

work done	= 300 grams x 75 cm	300 grams = 0.3 kilogram
		(because 1 kg weighs 10 N, 0.3 kg = 3 N)
	= 3 N x 0.75 m	100 g = 0.1 kg = 1 N
	= 2.25 J	

If you want to express this in terms of power, you must consider the time it takes to do the work. If your device took 5 seconds to move 300 grams 75 cm, its power would be:

power = rate of doing work = $\dfrac{\text{work done}}{\text{time required (seconds)}}$ (expressed in joules per second)

$\qquad\qquad\qquad\qquad\quad = \dfrac{2.25 \text{ J}}{5 \text{ s}} \quad = .45 \text{ J/s}$

Using Your Devices:

Refer to the description and examples of mass, force, work done, and power provided above.

Determine how much weight your device can lift. _____ N

Determine how high your device can lift this weight. _____ cm

Calculate the work done by your device. _____ J

Calculate the power capability of your device. _____ J/s

DESIGN ACTIVITIES—ELECTRICITY-PRODUCING TEST DEVICES

For your designs that generate electricity, you will need to express your findings in terms of electrical power (watts). Remember that the unit of one joule per second (J/s) is also expressed as a watt, named after James Watt, designer of early steam engines. Knowing that 1 watt = 1 J/s will allow you to compare the power produced as electrical energy with the power produced as mechanical energy. Power related to electricity is expressed as:

power = voltage x current,   or   P = V x I

where   power is measured in watts (W)
        voltage is measured in volts (V)
        current is measured in amps (A or I)

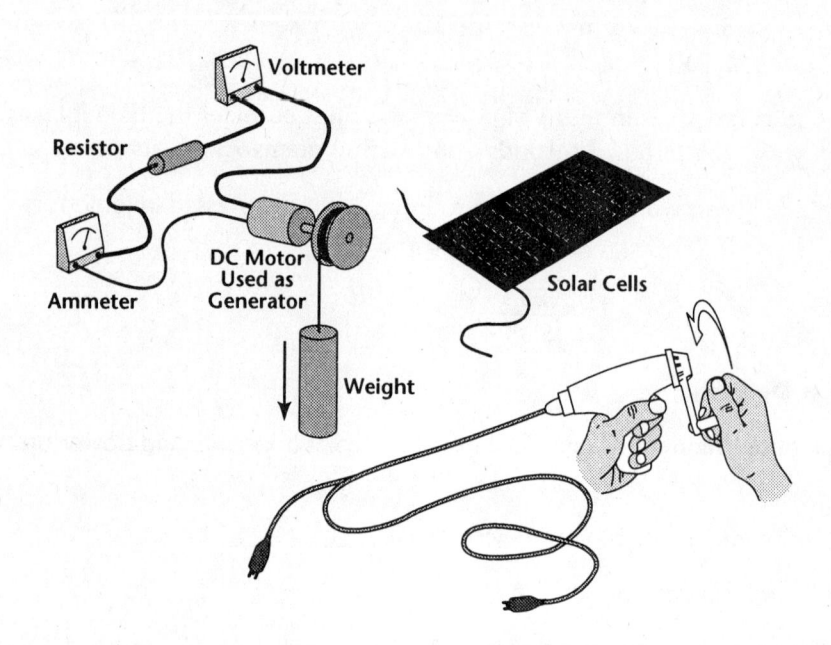

For Your Devices:

Determine how much current your device can generate. _____ A

Determine how much voltage your device can generate. _____ V

Calculate the power output of your device. _____ W

DESIGN ACTIVITIES—HEAT-PRODUCING TEST DEVICES

For designs that produce heat, you will need to express your findings in terms of calories (cal). A calorie (cal) was originally designated as the heat required to raise a gram (1 g) of water one degree Celsius (1°C). The specific measure of a calorie is now accepted internationally to be equivalent to 4.187 J. Use a test device similar to the one illustrated here to stir the water in the insulated container to see how much heat the different devices can generate in calories (cal).

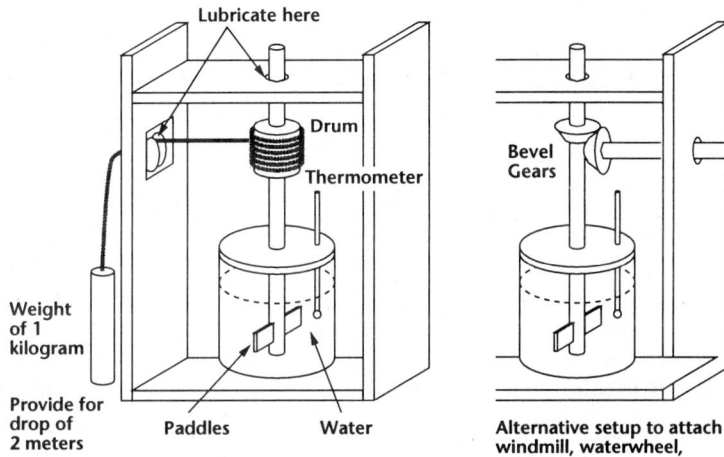

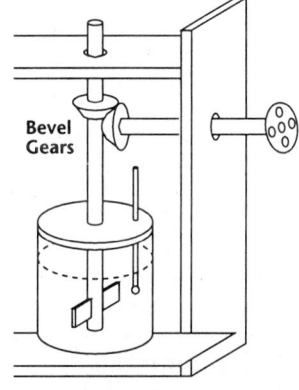

NOTE: Be sure to insulate the container.

- Using these data, calculate the calories of heat generated by the movement caused by the device being tested. (It is helpful to express calories in terms of joules, the unit used for all types of energy. One (1) calorie = 4.18 joules.)

For Your Devices:

Determine the increase in temperature caused by your device. _____ °C

Determine the mass of water used in the test device. _____ g

Determine how many calories your device can generate. _____ cal

Determine how many joules of energy your device generated. _____ J

Determine the power produced by your device. _____ J/s

FORMS OF ENERGY

The energy spectrum introduced in your textbook (see Figure 6.8) provides a way of looking at the major categories of energy forms. The energy spectrum has six major bands, ranging from matter in one direction to energy in the other direction. The bands are atomic, chemical, mechanical, electromagnetic, radiant, and cosmic. Most applications of energy are from the middle of the energy spectrum—mechanical and electromagnetic—with some use of chemical, radiant, and thermal energy. Atomic energy comes from the immensely hard nucleus that is held together with immensely high energy bonds.

Chemical energy is released through processes such as burning, photosynthesis, and digestion. Through chemical processes, energy stored in high-energy bonds within molecules is released and new molecules are formed that contain lower-level energy bonds. The excess energy that is released can often be detected as heat.

Thermal energy is found in all the energy bands. Thermal energy relates to the level of kinetic energy of the molecules of a material. Heat energy is produced by almost all energy conversion processes, either as a by-product or as the desired form. Heat is transferred by three means: conduction, convection, and radiation.

Two concepts related to thermal energy come into play when materials are converted back and forth from solids, liquids, or gases. The first, the latent heat of evaporation, requires additional energy to overcome the attraction between the bonds. In the second, the latent heat of fusion, the additional heat must be removed to allow the material to condense or solidify.

There are several key ideas related to mechanical energy. Kinetic energy is needed to cause the movement of matter. Potential energy refers to storing energy that can be converted to kinetic form to create motion.

The use of compression and tension can cause movement in materials. This process will change the internal structure and produces rhythmic vibrations. The number of vibrations in one second is called frequency and is measured in cycles per second, now known as Hertz (Hz). There is a physical limit to mechanical vibration, and higher frequencies overlap into the electromagnetic band of the spectrum. In this overlap, we find alternating electric current.

Rotating the coils of a generator in a magnetic field is a common means of generating frequencies up to 7,000 Hz. Frequencies above 7,000 Hz normally must be produced by other devices such as ultrasonic transducers used to generate sound frequencies greater than 20,000 Hz.

The frequency of energy waves increases through the spectrum of radio waves, television waves, and microwaves. Devices that generate higher frequencies are needed to produce infrared energy and visible light.

High energy forms can be very dangerous to humans. Light from lasers, ultraviolet from the sun and some lamps, and X rays can cause injury or disease. Protective materials, shields, and glasses are needed to block the radiation and prevent damage.

We have a few tools that use or generate energy in the radiant band. We know very little about using cosmic energy, and there is concern for potential side effects for humans and other life forms.

INTEGRATED S/M/T ACTIVITIES

Energy in the nuclear bonds in the nucleus can be released by splitting the nucleus (fission), or by combining nuclei (fusion). In either process, the resulting final total nuclei actually weigh a little bit less than the total nuclei did at the start of the process. The energy released by this change of mass (m) is very large and is determined by Einstein's law, E=mc², where c is the speed of light, or 3×10^8 meters per second*. Let us consider what happens when the very small mass of a period at the end of a sentence is converted entirely into energy. The mass was estimated as one millionth of a gram. If the energy were electricity, it could operate a 100-watt lightbulb for about ten days. The following calculations determine the potential energy output of that mass.

NOTE: one millionth of a gram = 1×10^{-6} grams

$E = mc^2$

$E = 1 \times (10^{-6}$ grams$) (3 \times 10^8$ meters/sec$)^2$ Note: convert the grams to kilograms

$\dfrac{10^{-6}}{10^{+3}} = 10^{-9}$ kilograms

$= 1 \times (10^{-9}$ kg$) (3 \times 10^8$ meters/sec$)^2$

$= 1 \times (10^{-9}$ kg$) (9 \times 10^{16}$ meters/sec$)$

$= 9 \times 10^7$ joules/second

$= 90,000,000$ joules/second (or 90,000,000 watts or 9×10^7 watts, or 90 Megawatts)

It will be helpful to remember that the unit of one joule per second (J/s) is also expressed as a watt (W). You may want to refer to page 151 in your text.

*NOTE:

Very large or very small numbers are awkward to work with when written out. For example, the speed of light can be written as 300,000,000 meters per second. This can be written in "Scientific Notation" as 3×10^8. [This is a shorthand way of saying 3 x (10 x 10 x 10 x 10 x 10 x 10 x 10 x 10), which when multiplied out will be 300,000,000.]

As an example of a very small number, the mass of the period at the end or a sentence, as described above, is estimated as being one millionth of a gram (or .000,001 gram). This can be written in scientific notation as 1×10^{-6}. [This is a shorthand way of saying $1 \times (\dfrac{1}{10} \times \dfrac{1}{10} \times \dfrac{1}{10} \times \dfrac{1}{10} \times \dfrac{1}{10} \times \dfrac{1}{10})$ or $1 \times \dfrac{1}{1,000,000}$. When this is written out it is .000,001. It is obviously easier to write and calculate as 1×10^{-6}.

INTEGRATED S/M/T ACTIVITIES

Suppose in the preceding example, you use all 90,000,000 joules in one second. Since 1 watt = 1 J/s, you can express the above time rate of using energy (i.e., power) as 9×10^7 watts. It is more convenient to use kilowatts, the standard measure for electrical power.

$$9 \times \frac{10^7}{10^3} = 9 \times 10^4 \text{ kw}$$

or = 90,000 kw

This can be converted to kilowatt hours by dividing by 3,600 (the number of seconds in an hour).

$$= \frac{90,000}{3,600} \text{ kw} = 25 \text{ kwh}$$

The energy could be converted to mechanical form and used to lift a person. If the individual weighed 50 kg, the energy in the mass of a period would lift the person about 180 km in the air, or about the altitude of a low-orbit satellite. Does this sound believable?

Use the formula for work done, force, and distance below to calculate the height a 50-kg weight could be lifted.

W = F x D   where   W = work done (mc^2)

$D = \frac{W}{F}$ F = 50 kg = 500 N*
                   D = distance (height)   (with scientific notation)

$D = \frac{90,000,000 \text{ J}}{500 \text{ N}}$ or $D = \frac{9 \times 10^7 \text{ J}}{5 \times 10^2 \text{ N}}$

D = 180,000 m $D = \frac{1.8 \times 10^5 \text{ m}}{1 \times 10^3}$

D = 180 km

                                                        $D = 1.8 \times 10^2$ or 180 km

Based on these calculations, determine how much energy there is in a single sheet of paper. Also determine how much energy is in a double cheeseburger, a large order of French fries, and a milkshake.

If you have access to a sensitive electronic scale, you could determine the mass of a period. Use a computer to generate a page of periods or dots. Weigh the paper before and after the printing. Determine the increase in mass and then calculate the mass of a single dot. Use Einstein's law to calculate the total energy in the mass of your dot.

* NOTE: A force will be required that can lift the 50 kg. Remember that force is expressed in newtons (N), so a 500 N force will be required to lift a 50 kg weight.

INTEGRATED S/M/T ACTIVITIES CONTINUED

Note: as indicated in the preceding **INTEGRATED S/M/T ACTIVITIES**, a number can be written in regular or scientific form.

For example:

$$90,000,000 \text{ watts} = 90,000 \text{ kw} = 9 \times 10^4 \text{ kw}$$

This conversion to kilowatts can be done as:

$$\frac{90,000,000 \text{ watts}}{1,000} = 90,000 \text{ kw}$$

or as:

$$\frac{9 \times 10^7 \text{ watts}}{1 \times 10^3} = 9 \times 10^{7-3} = 9 \times 10^4 \text{ kw.}$$

In this example, *dividing* the large numbers is accomplished by *subtracting* the exponents (7-3 = 4).

In the problem concerning Einstein's law $E = mc^2$ presented on page 151, multiplying large numbers is accomplished by adding the exponents. For example, when the speed of light (3×10^8 meters/second) is calculated as $(3 \times 10^8)(3 \times 10^8)$ the result is (9×10^8 meters/sec.).

In the next step of the problem, you determine E by calculating $(1 \times 10^{-9} \text{ kg})(9 \times 10^{16}$ meters/sec.). This is accomplished by adding the exponents

$$E = 1 \times 9 \times 10^{(-9+16)} \text{ joules/second}$$
$$= 9 \times 10^7 \text{ joules/second}$$
$$= 9 \times 10^7 \text{ watts}$$

INTEGRATED S/M/T ACTIVITIES

Research and Investigation on Chemical Energy

Devices that use chemical energy take many different forms. Consider one of the following topics or devices for individual or small group research and investigation. The topics include batteries, fuel cells, food, fossil fuels, and cold light. You may be interested in investigating some of the materials conversion processes identified in the materials chapter. Several chemical processes were identified including bleaching, washing, etching, and developing. What other chemical processes can you identify that are used in the design and technology course? For example, when you use soldering as a thermal process for creating a mechanical fastener, no mention appears to be made of chemical processes. The terms "resin" and "flux" are used, however. These are chemicals that are used in soldering. "Resin core solder" indicates that the chemical is inside the solder. Flux is a chemical that is added to the metal parts just before the parts are soldered together. In both instances, the chemicals are used to keep the metal clean and shield it from oxygen which interferes with the soldering process. What other examples can you find?

Caution—Remember, most chemical processes are safe, but some can be quite dangerous and can hurt you.

DO ALL EXPERIMENTS ONLY UNDER THE SUPERVISION OF YOUR TEACHER!

INTEGRATED S/M/T ACTIVITIES

Research and Investigation on Thermal Energy

After water has reached a boiling point, the temperature stays the same (even though heat is still being added) until all of the water has turned to gas (water vapor). The temperature remains constant, while the energy that is added will equal the latent heat of evaporation. The same phenomenon occurs as you take the heat away from the water vapor to convert it back to water. The process is similar as water is cooled sufficiently to freeze and turn to ice. The energy that is extracted from the fluid must equal the latent heat of fusion.

The concepts of latent heat of evaporation and fusion are put to use in liquids called coolants. These coolants readily absorb heat and, in doing so, turn to gases. What is required for good coolants? What is meant by the term "heat transfer"? What practical examples have you seen as applications of that concept? How do these ideas relate to devices such as heaters and coolers? What are some of the examples of heaters and coolers you see or come into contact with during the course of a regular day?

INTEGRATED S/M/T ACTIVITIES

Movement, Inertia, and Potential and Kinetic Energy

The following concepts, developed by Sir Isaac Newton, are very useful in explaining movement. Set up and conduct the experiment shown in the illustrations below.

A—In the absence of force, an object at rest will stay at rest. In Figure (A), place the driving weight at rest as shown. In this case, the vehicle will remain at rest. Wind the string around the pulley on the drive wheels until the weight is at rest at the top. This arrangement has high potential energy. What is the amount of energy that is stored in the raised weight? (Be sure that the end of the string is not attached to the axle permanently so that the vehicle can continue to coast.) How far do you estimate that the vehicle will move while the weight is falling? How far do you estimate the vehicle will travel while it is coasting?

B—Objects in motion tend to stay in motion. Figure (B) shows the weight in motion and the vehicle in motion. The weight will continue to drop (stay in motion) until it hits the vehicle base. The energy from the falling weight will cause the vehicle to move. The vehicle will tend to stay in motion until the forces of gravity and friction slow it down and eventually cause it to stop. If the weight is moving, the potential energy is being converted into kinetic energy. Measure how far the vehicle travels while the weight is falling. Measure how far the vehicle travels while coasting.

C—For every action, there is an opposite and equal reaction. Figure (C) illustrates some of the actions and reactions. The action of the falling weight (down) pulls the drive rope (up). The up action of the role causes the pulley to turn down (rotate). The rotary action of the pulley causes the attached wheel to turn against the floor. The pushing action of the wheel tread against the pushing reaction of the floor causes the vehicle to move. Identify where energy is lost in this process through friction, wind drag, slippage, and other factors. Identify ways in which you could improve the operation of the vehicle. Set up an experiment for making some of your proposed changes, one at a time, to see if they work. Record the information from your experiments so you can compare how your changes compare with the operation of the original vehicle. Will you need to construct two or more vehicles for your experiments?

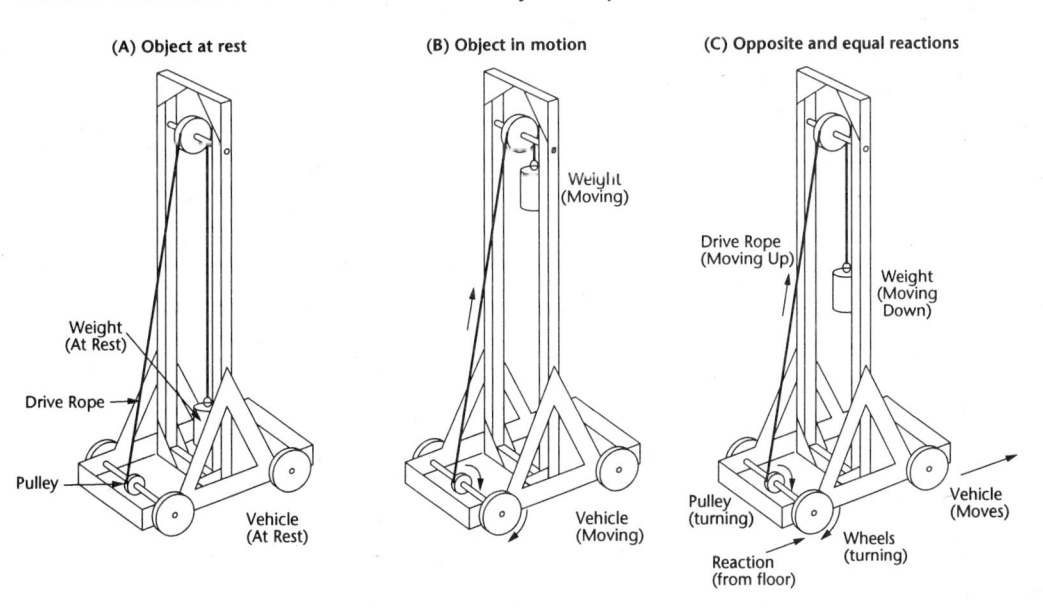

(A) Object at rest
(B) Object in motion
(C) Opposite and equal reactions

You may consider conducting experiments using other forms of mechanical energy—rubber band, mousetrap, windup spring, gravity as raised weight of stored water, compressed air, etc.

INTEGRATED S/M/T ACTIVITIES

Humans and the Energy Spectrum

There are many different forms of energy included in the energy spectrum. The spectrum was described as a clothesline on which to hang the major categories of energy. Of those forms of energy, six are the most common and available for people to use. These include chemical, thermal, mechanical, sound, electrical, and light. All of the energy forms can have undesired effects on humans if the amount of exposure exceeds the levels of human tolerance.

- Record each of the examples from the activities you complete on the Energy Sources form provided at the end of this chapter.

- Use the descriptions and illustrations to develop your own applied version of the energy spectrum.

- Refer to the illustration of the Environmental Tolerance Zones (ETZ) provided on the following page.

- Match the factors of the ETZ that relate to specific categories on the energy spectrum.

- Identify and record the different devices that use or emit energy that falls within each of the 16 zones.

- Select one of the 16 categories to investigate. Identify which devices/machines fall within the tolerance zones (shaded area) shown on the diagram. Plot a point or a line that shows the potential range of the impact.

- Work as a group or class to design and develop a display that illustrates the range from "comfort to tolerance limit" for the ETZ factors.

- Design and develop a display that illustrates the range from "comfort to tolerance limit" for one of the ETZ factors.

NOTE: You will want to return to this work later as you study about humans and how they relate to, and are affected by, the resources and systems of technology.

Environmental Tolerance Zones

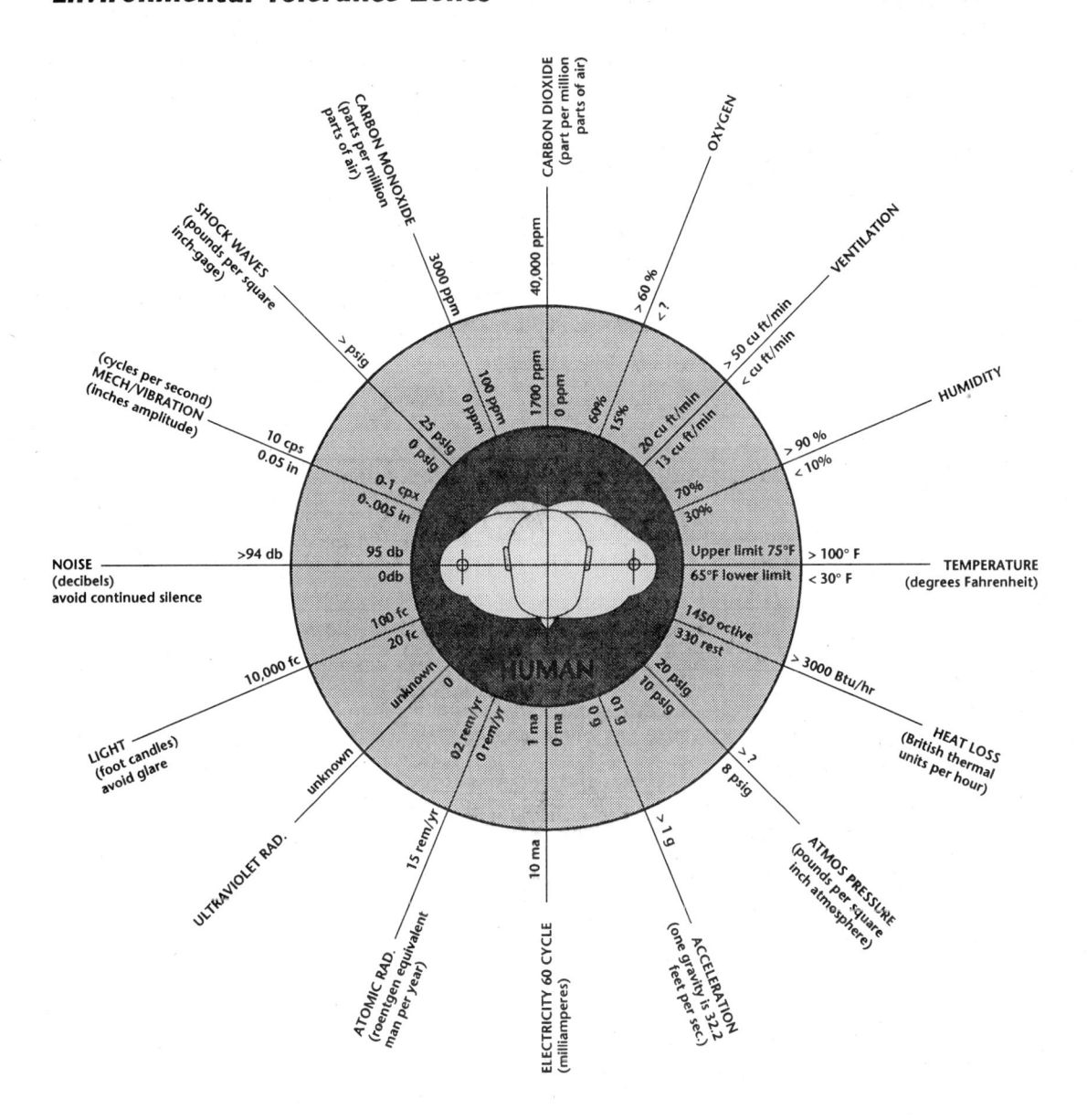

CARBON MONOXIDE (parts per million parts of air): 3000 ppm / 100 ppm / 0 ppm

CARBON DIOXIDE (part per million parts of air): 40,000 ppm / 1700 ppm / 0 ppm

OXYGEN: > 60% / < ? / 15%

VENTILATION: > 50 cu ft/min / < ? cu ft/min / 20 cu ft/min / 13 cu ft/min

HUMIDITY: > 90% / < 10% / 70% / 30%

TEMPERATURE (degrees Fahrenheit): > 100° F / < 30° F / Upper limit 75°F / 65°F lower limit

HEAT LOSS (British thermal units per hour): > 3000 Btu/hr / 1450 active / 330 rest

ATMOS PRESSURE (pounds per square inch atmosphere): 20 psig / 8 psig / > ?

ACCELERATION (one gravity is 32.2 feet per sec.): 10 g / .01 g / > 1 g

ELECTRICITY 60 CYCLE (milliamperes): 10 ma / 1 ma / 0 ma

ATOMIC RAD. (roentgen equivalent man per year): 15 rem/yr / 0.2 rem/yr / 0 rem/yr

ULTRAVIOLET RAD.: unknown / unknown / 0

LIGHT (foot candles) avoid glare: 10,000 fc / 100 fc / 20 fc

NOISE (decibels) avoid continued silence: >94 db / 95 db / 0 db

MECH/VIBRATION (cycles per second) (inches amplitude): 10 cps / 0.05 in / 0.1 cps / 0.005 in

SHOCK WAVES (pounds per square inch-gage): > psig / 25 psig / 0 psig

HUMAN

CONVERSION OF ENERGY

As you design and plan the objects you wish to build, you need to determine the energy requirements. You are most likely to use mechanical, fluid, and electrical systems in your design and development work. Conversion of energy means that energy is being changed from potential or stored energy to kinetic energy, or from kinetic energy back to potential energy.

To be able to use energy, it must be stored and made readily available. The storage of some forms of energy is difficult and therefore it must be converted to other forms for storage. Examples of chemical energy storage include batteries and hydrogen gas; mechanical energy storage is found in water storage, compressed air, and the flywheel; and thermal energy storage is found in heat and cold storage devices.

Batteries use chemical processes to convert materials into the flow of electrons. Similarly, the flow of electrical current can cause materials in some rechargeable batteries to convert back to their original state. Hydrogen gas is produced by electrolysis—the chemical process that uses the flow of electricity to separate the hydrogen and oxygen as gases. The hydrogen can then be stored for conversion back into electricity later when burned as a fuel. Hydrogen can also be used in fuel cells to produce electrical energy through chemical processes.

Water storage has been used for many years when dams were built on rivers to create reservoirs. The potential energy in the mass of the water from the reservoir provides mechanical energy that can be used to turn electrical generators. The electricity that is generated can also be used to pump water back into the storage reservoirs during periods of low demand for electrical power for later use.

The kinetic energy in the spinning mass of a heavy flywheel can be used as mechanical energy to drive a generator that will then produce electrical energy. Flywheels can also be used as a source of mechanical energy to propel a vehicle.

Air under pressure provides potential energy for doing work. With appropriate devices, the energy in the compressed air can be put to practical use for doing work through the movement of cylinders, air motors, and other devices.

Heat storage is accomplished in standard and solar buildings, where selected materials in the buildings are used to absorb heat during the heat of the day. This heat is then released into the interior of the building as the outside temperature drops. Cold storage is a common use for storing food and other perishable materials. Cold storage can be seen as the reverse of heat storage. For example, cold storage can be used to extract heat from the interior of the building as the outside temperature climbs.

DESIGN ACTIVITIES—CONVERTING ENERGY FOR STORAGE

Storage devices can take many different forms. These may be as common as the stretching of a rubber band, the winding of a spring, the compressing of air into a tank, accumulator, or cylinder, the raising of a weight vertically, or the charging of a battery or capacitor. In your design and technology projects, you will be involved in designing devices and systems that convert energy into storable forms and then convert that energy again into other usable forms using the Energy Conversion Chart below.

INPUT

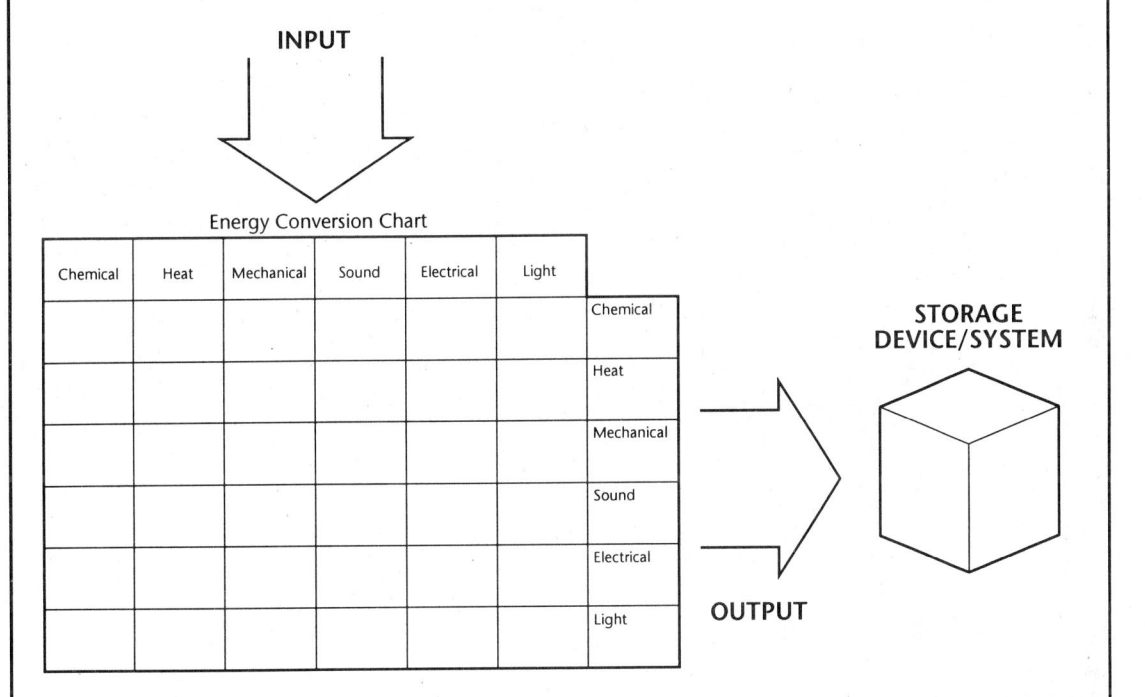

Energy Conversion Chart

Chemical	Heat	Mechanical	Sound	Electrical	Light
					Chemical
					Heat
					Mechanical
					Sound
					Electrical
					Light

OUTPUT → **STORAGE DEVICE/SYSTEM**

DESIGN ACTIVITIES—CONVERTING ENERGY FOR STORAGE CONTINUED

INPUT	PROCESS	OUTPUT	STORAGE DEVICE/SYSTEM
Mechanical Movement Magnetism	Generator	Electrical Power	Battery (chemical)
Mechanical Air	Compressor	Air under Pressure	Air Tank (Mechanical)
Solar Energy	Thermal wall	Heat	Brick, Stone, Water (Thermal Mass)
Solar Energy Water Carbon Dioxide	Plants	food	Vegetables, fruits (Chemical, Bio-mass)

Converting Energy for Use

When energy is used, it is generally converted from one form to another through **converters** or **transducers**. We will consider transducers in the following chapter on Information, but most of our attention in the remainder of this chapter will be on **converters**. **Converters** use one energy form to produce a new form or to change the nature of the original energy form. The number and types of energy converters is very large and includes all living plants and animals, as well as all tools, mechanisms, and machines.

The illustration below indicates how the output of an energy conversion process can provide the input to another process. For example, coal as a fuel can be converted through a chemical process to produce heat as an output. This heat can serve as an input for a process that involves cooking, drying, or heating, or it may cause a change in materials for a subsequent process.

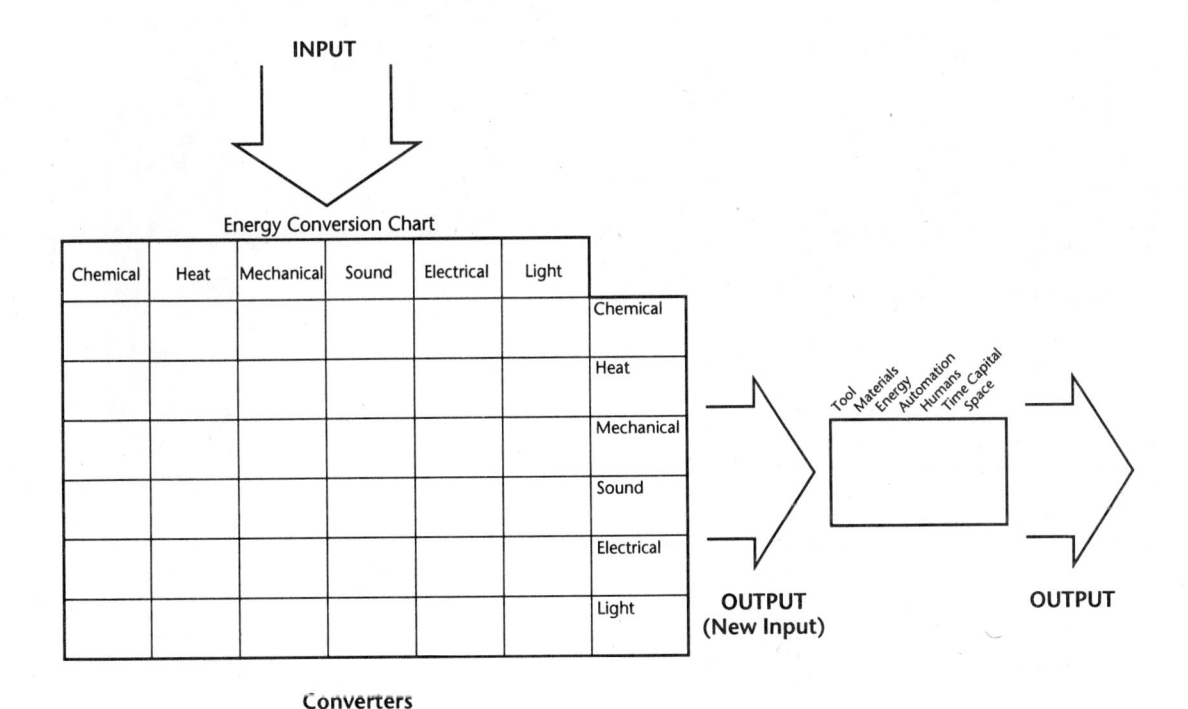

Energy Conversion Chart

Chemical	Heat	Mechanical	Sound	Electrical	Light	
						Chemical
						Heat
						Mechanical
						Sound
						Electrical
						Light

Converters

INPUT → OUTPUT (New Input) → [Tool, Materials, Energy, Automation, Humans, Time, Capital, Space] → OUTPUT

Each time the energy is changed from one form to another, some loss of energy (entropy) occurs. Energy that is lost can go to several forms, but most often it produces heat. Many of the activities designed to maintain a system or machine are attempts to slow down or repair the effects of unwanted heat in the form of friction.

Much of the heat from an engine is not put to practical use and is considered lost. If a device converts one energy form to another with a small energy loss, the process is considered efficient. Energy conversion often will go through several steps, losing usable energy at each step.

DESIGN ACTIVITIES—CHART ON ENERGY CONVERSION

In this chart, a variety of devices are included that can be used to change energy from one form to another. The chart is intended to be read from the top (INPUT) and then to the right (OUTPUT). The examples are only representative and are not exhaustive. Based on your study and design work in this course, add other examples to your own Energy Conversion Chart.

Input

	Chemical	Heat	Mechanical	Sound	Electrical	Light	Output
	plants, food	fermentation, cooking	implosion	hearing	electrolysis, batteries	photosynthesis	Chemical
	fuels, furnace	heat exchanger, heat pump	friction brake	sound absorber	toaster, heat lamp, spark plug	incandescent light, sunlamp, solar collector	Heat
	gunpowder, rocket, gas engine, animal muscle	diesel, gas, and steam engines	flywheel, pendulum, waterwheel	ultrasonic cleaner	solenoid, relay, electric motor	electroscope	Mechanical
	hearing, explosion, smoke detector	explosion, flame tube	voice, musical instrument	megaphone	loudspeaker, thunder, electric horn	movie sound track, video disk	Sound
	batteries, electrolysis, electroplating	thermistor, thermopile, thermocouple	generator, alternator, power plants	microphone, telephone, hearing	diode, rectifier, transformer	solar cell, photoelectric cell	Electrical
	candle, oil lamp, phosphorescence	fire, arc lamp, lightbulb	flint and steel, sparks from friction	sound absorber	fluorescent light, incandescent light, television, light-emitting diode	laser, light wave repeater	Light

Mechanical energy is used when muscles do some work. Many tools and machines are designed to provide mechanical advantage (MA) to decrease the amount of energy provided by the person or animal supplying the muscle power. As an object is moved by a lever, it passes through part of a circular arc. Movement in a circular direction is caused by turning forces, sometimes called torque.

The crank and windlass are common devices that move in a circle around a pivot. Cranks and windlasses are used to provide a mechanical advantage for moving something in a rotary motion. The MA of a crank depends on the length of the arm of the crank. A long arm (a large moment) provides a larger MA; a short arm (a small moment) provides a smaller MA.

A pulley can be considered as a lever in the form of a wheel with the arms of the pulley the same length (equal to the radius of the pulley). In this sense, pulleys are a form of Class 1 levers. A single pulley does not provide a mechanical advantage but, when used as a lifting device, serves to change the direction of the effort and the load. If the force on the effort and the force on the load are the same, the pulley system is said to be in equilibrium and the pulley will remain at rest. If additional effort is applied, the load will start to rise.

INTEGRATED S/M/T ACTIVITIES—FORCES IN EQUILIBRIUM

You have already studied some of the major ideas and skills related to mechnical systems, and it is appropriate now to revisit some of these ideas and apply them to the conversion of energy. The principle of the lever involves four related ideas: load, fulcrum, force, and movement.

(a) The **load** is the force to be moved by the lever.
(b) The **fulcrum** is the pivot, or the point around which the lever turns.
(c) The **effort** is the force that is applied to the lever.
(d) The **moment** is the turning effort acting around the fulcrum.

Conduct the experiments below to show that the loads at rest in A, B, and C will stay in place so long as the downward force (gravity) is the same as the upward force (support). How would you describe that the forces are balanced and the object is in equilibrium and will remain at rest? How would you describe that the system shown in (D) is in equilibrium? How much additional force is required to overcome that equilibrium and create the desired movement? What changes would you make in the experiments to help you compare which of the instances will require the greatest increase in force to overcome inertia and change and equilibrium of the device?

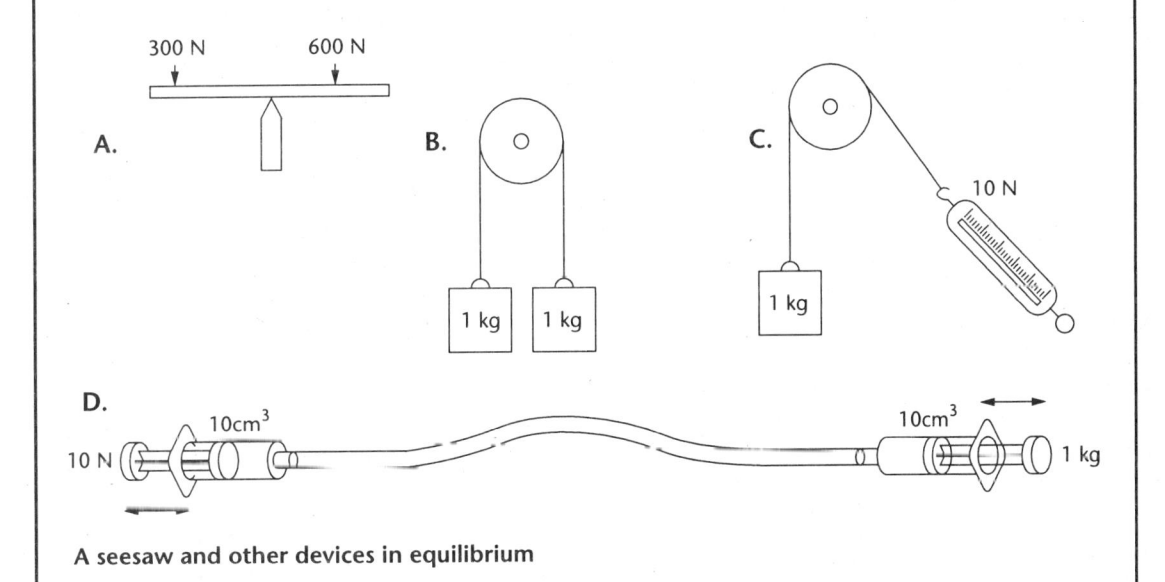

A seesaw and other devices in equilibrium

DESIGN ACTIVITIES—CONVERTING ENERGY FOR USE

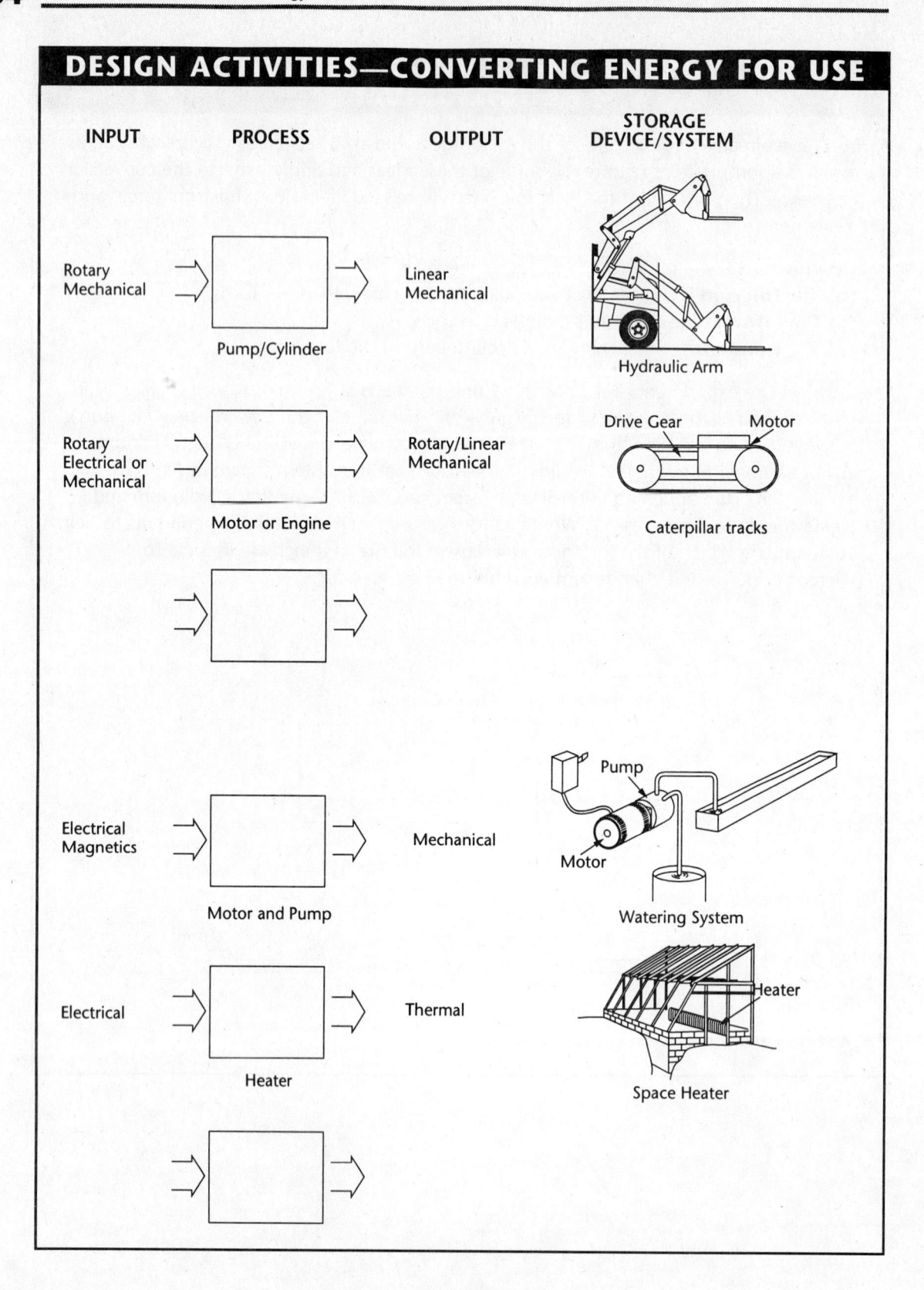

INPUT	PROCESS	OUTPUT	STORAGE DEVICE/SYSTEM
Rotary Mechanical	Pump/Cylinder	Linear Mechanical	Hydraulic Arm
Rotary Electrical or Mechanical	Motor or Engine	Rotary/Linear Mechanical	Caterpillar tracks (Drive Gear, Motor)
Electrical Magnetics	Motor and Pump	Mechanical	Watering System (Pump, Motor)
Electrical	Heater	Thermal	Space Heater

INTEGRATED S/M/T ACTIVITIES—TURNING FORCES AND MOMENTS

Each person on a seesaw creates a turning effect (see Figure 6.15 in your textbook). The turning force around a point is described in the following equation:

turning force = force x distance from the pivot

The units of the quantities in all of the equations will be expressed in terms of a:

turning force (or moment)	newton meters (N-m)
force	newtons (N)
distance	meters (m)

Solve the following problems involving the use of turning forces, distances, and points of rotation (pivots).

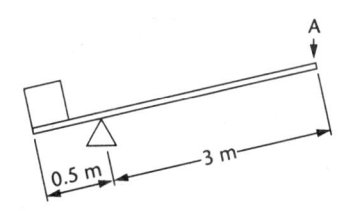

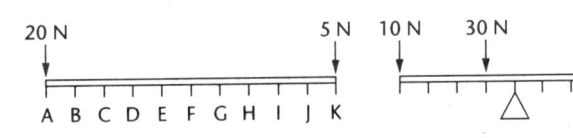

(1) What turning force must be applied to the lever at point A to bring it into balance (equilibrium)?

(2) Where would you place the pivot (fulcrum) on the beam to make it balance?

(3) What turning force must be applied to point B to balance the lever?

NOTE: A special term (moment) is sometimes used to describe turning forces. As you will see in the following activities, the moment will equal the force when multiplied by the distance.

moment = force x distance

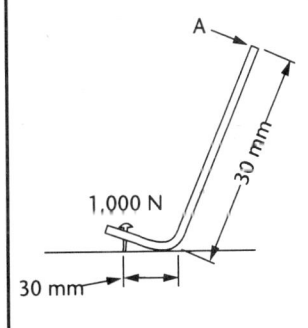

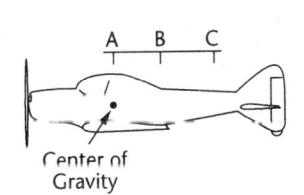

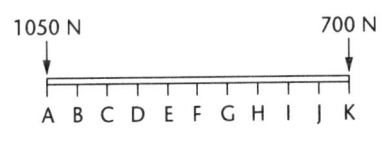

(4) What force must be applied at point A on the handle of the pry before the nail will move?

(5) Where would you place a heavy load in the airplane to create a moment that will make the airplane balanced while in flight?

(6) Where should the pivot be on the seesaw to balance the bar moments created by the riders?

DESIGN ACTIVITIES—DETERMINING THE PROPERTIES AND EFFICIENCY OF A LEVER

To determine the output efficiency of a lever, it is necessary to measure the effort required to move the load. In the illustration below, the effort of 11 N acting through a distance of 1 m is required to move a load of 20 N a distance of .5 m.

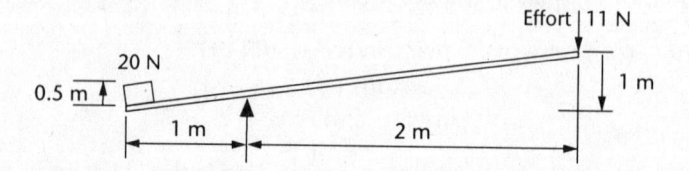

NOTE: The calculations of velocity ratio, mechanical advantage, and efficiency for the lever are shown below.

$$\text{Velocity Ratio} = \frac{\text{Distance Moved by Effort}}{\text{Distance Moved by Load}} = \frac{1 \text{ m}}{0.5 \text{ m}} = 2$$

$$\text{Mechanical Advantage} = \frac{\text{Load}}{\text{Effort}} = \frac{20 \text{ N}}{11 \text{ N}} = 1.8$$

$$\text{Efficiency} = \frac{\text{Work Out}}{\text{Work In}} \times 100\%$$

$$= \frac{20 \text{ N} \times 0.5 \text{ m}}{11 \text{ N} \times 1 \text{ m}} \times 100\%$$

$$= \frac{10 \text{ N-m}}{11 \text{ N-m}} \times 100\%$$

$$= 90\%$$

OR

$$\text{Efficiency} = \frac{\text{MA}}{\text{VR}} \times 100\%$$

$$= \frac{1.8}{2} \times 100\%$$

$$= 90\%$$

DESIGN ACTIVITIES—CONVERTING ENERGY/ VELOCITY RATIO

As indicated in your text, velocity ratio applies to many different applications (see pages 87 to 90) These include wheels and axles, pulley systems, gears systems, chains and sprockets, and inclined planes. Example applications of each are presented below.

Pulley drive systems. The equation for pulley drive systems is expressed as:

$$\text{velocity ratio} = \frac{\text{circumference of driven pulley}}{\text{circumference of driver pulley}}$$

Or, if more convenient, as:

$$\text{velocity ratio} = \frac{\text{diameter of driven pulley}}{\text{diameter of driver pulley}}$$

1. If the circumference of the driven pulley is 38 cm, and the circumference of the driver pulley is 13 cm, what is the VR? _____ If the diameter of the driven pulley is 7 cm and the diameter and the diameter of the driver pulley is 19 cm, what is the VR? _____

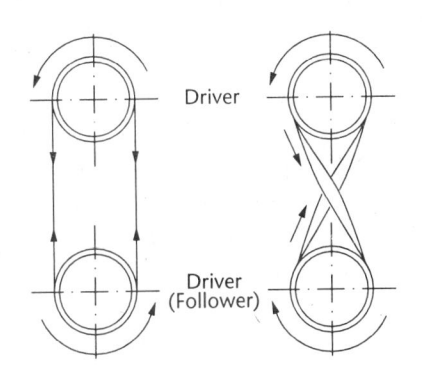

NOTE: The arrangement in the diagram on the right above provides a larger angle of wrap and helps to reduce the slippage of the belt and results in less loss of power. This arrangement also reverses the direction of the drive pulley.

2. The use of step pulleys is common in drill presses to provide different rotary speeds. The drawing at the right shows a common arrangement that provides three different speeds.

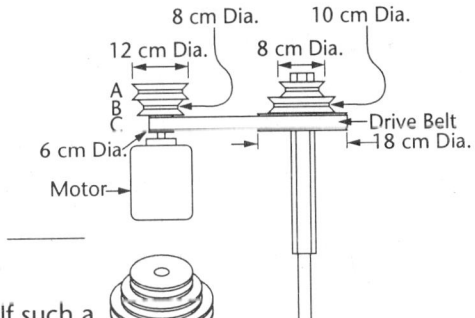

    a. Which position provides the fastest speed? _____
       Which provides the slowest speed? _____

    b. Many drive motors operate at 1,740 rpm. If such a motor is used, what will be the highest speed possible? _____

       What will be the lowest possible speed? _____

Sprocket drive systems. The equation for sprocket drive systems is expressed as:

$$\text{velocity ratio} = \frac{\text{number of teeth on the driven sprocket}}{\text{number of teeth on the driver sprocket}}$$

DESIGN ACTIVITIES—CONVERTING ENERGY/ VELOCITY RATIO CONTINUED

1. If the driver sprocket A has 12 teeth and the driven sprocket B has 36, what is the VR? _____ If the driver has 36 and the driven has 12, what is the VR? _____

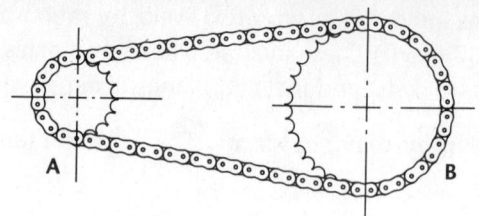

(Remember, ratios are expressed as 4:1; 1:8, and the like.)

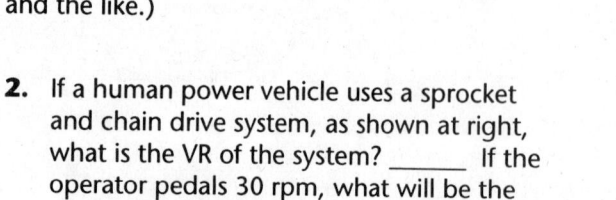

2. If a human power vehicle uses a sprocket and chain drive system, as shown at right, what is the VR of the system? _____ If the operator pedals 30 rpm, what will be the speed the vehicle will move across the ground? _____ At 45 rpm, what will be the speed? _____

Circumference of Wheel = 290 cm

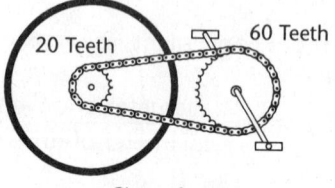

Gear drive systems. The equation for gear drive systems is expressed as:

$$\text{velocity ratio} = \frac{\text{number of teeth on the driven gear}}{\text{number of teeth on the driver gear}}$$

3. If the driver gear has 30 teeth and the driven gear had 15, what is the VR? _____
If the driver has 12 and the driven has 48, what is the VR? _____
If the driver is a worm gear and the gear wheel has 72 teeth, what is the VR? _____

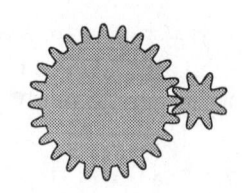

NOTE: A velocity ratio is often expressed as a gear ratio.

To determine the velocity or gear ratio of a gear train, it is necessary to consider how the gears work together as pairs. In the gear train below, gears B and C are attached to each other. In such cases, gears A and B provide one ratio and gears C and D provide a further gear reduction.

$$\text{Gear ratio} = \frac{\text{number of teeth on gear B}}{\text{number of teeth on gear A}} \times \frac{\text{number of teeth on gear D}}{\text{number of teeth on gear C}}$$

4. Calculate the ratio of the gear train shown at the right. _____

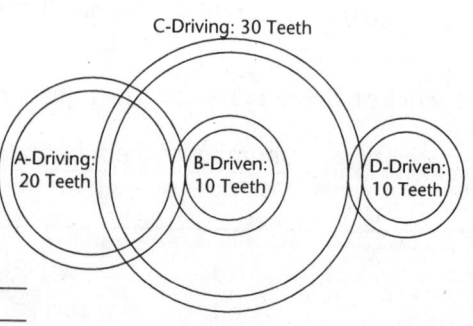

A-Driving: 20 Teeth
B-Driven: 10 Teeth
C-Driving: 30 Teeth
D-Driven: 10 Teeth

5. For the following gear sizes, calculate the gear ratios:

Gear sizes	A	B	C	D	
Gear train	20	10	30	10	
1	12	48	12	48	= _____
1	36	12	36	12	= _____
1	19	72	11	36	= _____

DESIGN ACTIVITIES—CONVERTING ENERGY/ VELOCITY RATIO CONTINUED

Inclined plane systems. The equations for inclined plane systems are expressed as:

$$\text{mechanical advantage} = \frac{\text{load}}{\text{effort}} = \frac{\text{weight pressing down vertically}}{\text{force required to push the load up the slope}}$$

and

$$\text{velocity ratio} = \frac{\text{distance moved effort}}{\text{distance moved by load}} = \frac{s}{h}$$

1. If the weight of the load is 50 kg, and the pushing force is 400 newtons, what is the MA provided? _____ If rollers are added to reduce friction, and the pushing force now required is 250 newtons, what is the MA now? _____ How can the MA for an inclined plane be increased? _____

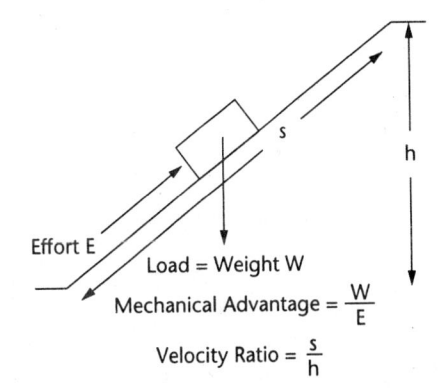

2. For the above circumstances, if the distance moved is two meters, and the 0.5 meter, what will be the VR? _____ How can the VR be increased? _____

Effort E
Load = Weight W
Mechanical Advantage = $\frac{W}{E}$
Velocity Ratio = $\frac{s}{h}$

DESIGN BRIEF—PUTTING YOUR IDEAS TO WORK

You have been asked to work in a design group that has the responsibility of providing a means for moving physically challenged and elderly people from one floor to another in a six-story building. Your team has been asked to develop a working model of an elevator as a possible solution. You have been asked to create the movement of the elevator so it moves from one floor to another in the same scale of time as the finished, full-sized elevator would.

NOTE: If a full-sized elevator takes 10 seconds to move from floor to floor, your model elevator should take 10 seconds to move from one floor to another.

- Using the modeling kits provided, develop the working model so that it travels at the required speed.

- Also using the modeling kits, develop a working model that shows how the elevator doors would open at an appropriate rate of speed.

- Identify some of the problems you can anticipate if the modeled solutions were to be translated into a full-sized prototype.

- Document the calculations you do to determine the gear reduction required of the gear train for your elevator.

- Most elevators use a counterbalance to make the elevator. You might apply that concept to your design.

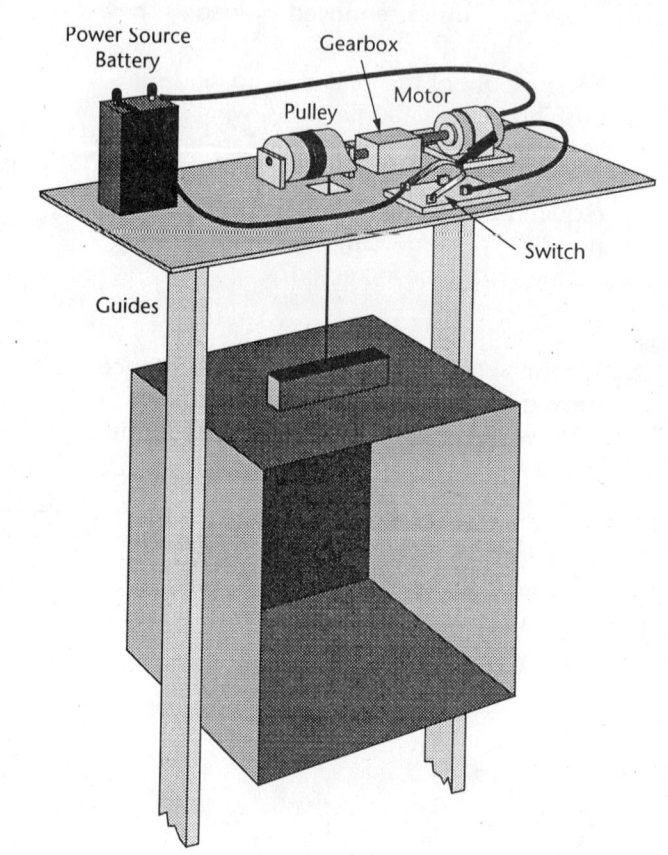

A conceptual illustration of an elevator

NOTE: You may find it helpful to refer back to the section of this chapter on pulleys in equilibrium as a simplified version of a counterbalance for an elevator.

INTEGRATED S/M/T ACTIVITIES

For the model elevator and doors you are developing, determine the following:

- What will be the speed that your model elevator will move from floor to floor?
- If you use a small Lego motor for your model, what type and size gears will you use in the gear train?
- What will be the VR between the output of the motor (or the turning worm gear) and the final output shaft turning the drum on the lift?
- What will be the MA gained through the gear train?
- If the motor is not big enough, what size will you need to substitute for it?
- How would you incorporate a counterbalance to improve your design?
- Suppose you decide to use a rack and pinion to operate the elevator door. What gear ratio will you need to achieve an appropriate speed for the door?

As an enrichment activity, conduct the following investigation on the power required to operate a system similar to yours.

- Determine the electrical power used to drive the motor with the rate of mechanical work done by the lift.
- Determine the efficiency of the system.

NOTE: See the following page for an example problem using a gear train and drum lifting system.

INTEGRATED S/M/T ACTIVITIES—LIFTING WITH A GEARED WINCH

The lifting system (the gear train and drum) shown in the elevator problem is often called a winch. The example below illustrates a geared winch being used to lift a load of 40 newtons. (The winch has two gears—one with 25 T and the other with 50 T.) To lift the 40 N load a distance of 1 m, an effort of 25 N acting over a distance of 2 m is required.

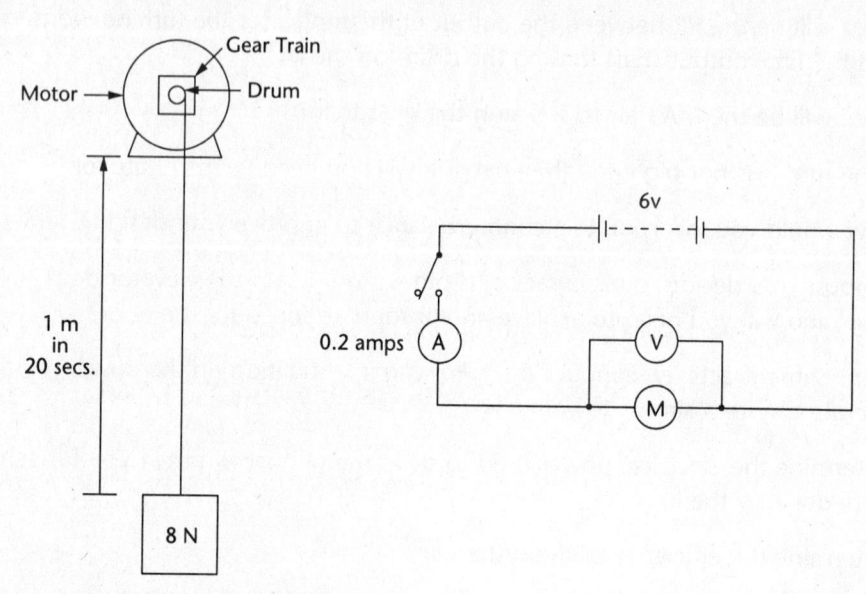

The following show the calculations for determining the velocity ratio, the mechanical advantage, and the efficiency of the winch.

<u>Work Done</u> = Force × Distance Moved

= 8 N × 1m

= 8 N-m or 8 Joules

NOTE: 1 Joule/second = 1 watt

<u>Rate</u> of Working = <u>Power</u>

= 8 Joules in 20 secs.

= $\frac{8 \text{ Joules}}{20 \text{ Secs}}$ = 0.4 watts

Comparing Power In and Power Out

= 6V × 0.2A = 1.2 watts   0.4 watts

Efficiency = $\frac{\text{Power Out}}{\text{Power In}} \times 100\%$

= $\frac{0.4}{1.2} \times 100\%$ = 33.3%

Determine the work done, power, and efficiency of the winch you designed for your elevator.

Work done = _____   Power = _____   efficiency = _____%

What changes in work done, power, and efficiency did you observe after introducing a counterbalance into your design?

RELATED S/M/T ACTIVITIES—PULLEYS AND GEAR TRAIN CALCULATIONS

In order to complete the elevator design problem, you will need to develop a gear train that will move the elevator car from floor to floor at a speed comparable to a real elevator. For this example, the distance from one floor to another is 5 meters and the time of travel should be 8 seconds. The motor you will use provides a shaft output of 2,000 rpm. In the examples below three transmission arrangements are illustrated. The first two use pulley arrangements; the third uses a worm gear.

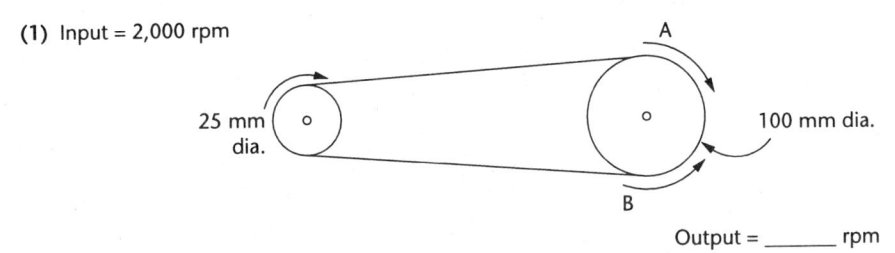

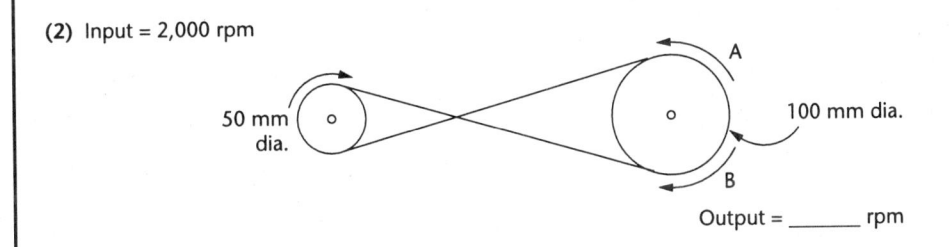

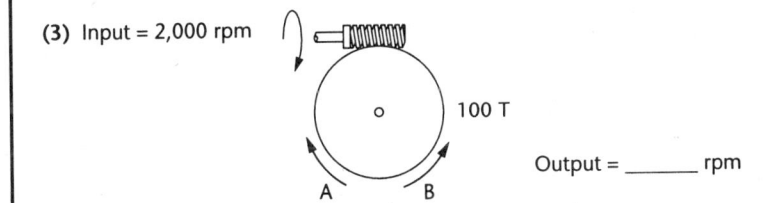

(1) Input = 2,000 rpm

25 mm dia.   100 mm dia.

Output = _____ rpm

(2) Input = 2,000 rpm

50 mm dia.   100 mm dia.

Output = _____ rpm

(3) Input = 2,000 rpm

100 T

Output = _____ rpm

What direction (A or B) does the output pulley or gear turn in each of the above instances?

(1) _____   (2) _____   (3) _____

Of the three arrangements, which is the most promising for the elevator design problem?
(1) _____ (2) _____ or (3) _____ ?

Why?

RELATED S/M/T ACTIVITIES—GEAR TRAIN CALCULATIONS CONTINUED

After you add the drum to your system, you find the rate of movement of the elevator car still a little too fast. To slow the rate of movement down, you decide to use a gear train. Three gear trains are shown below.

(1) 10T → 25T → 50T, 2,000 rpm
Output = _____ rpm
Direction of rotation _____

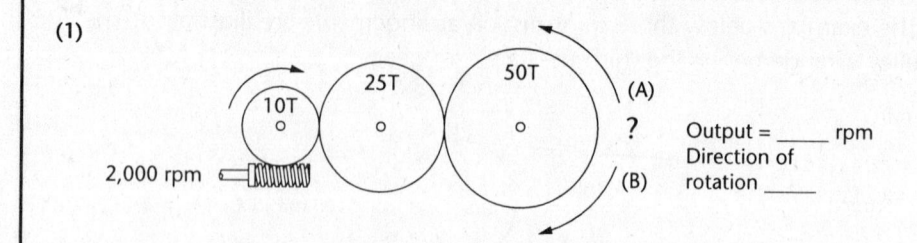

(2) 25T → 10T → 25T, 2,000 rpm
Output = _____ rpm
Direction of rotation _____

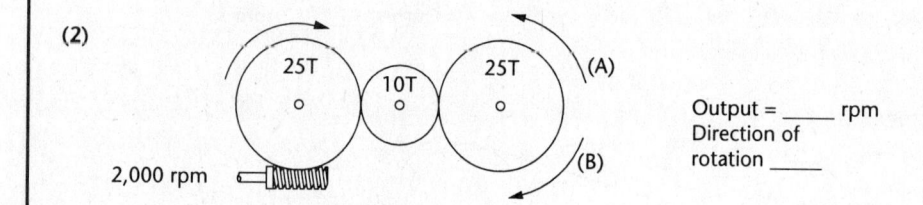

(3) 10T → 30T/10T (locked) → 50T, 2,000 rpm
Output = _____ rpm
Direction of rotation _____

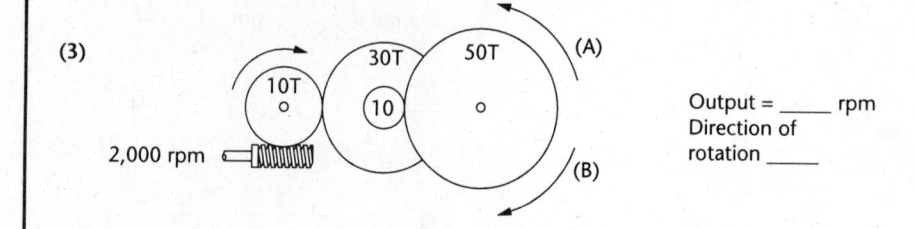

NOTE: In example 3, the middle gears (30 T and 10 T) are locked together and rotate as one.

Determine the direction of rotation for each of the gear trains. Determine the output speed (in rpm) for each of the gear trains.

DESIGN ACTIVITIES—CONVERTING ENERGY BY RACK AND PINION

Rack and pinion gears provide the capability of converting rotary motion to linear motion or linear to rotary motion. The basic function of a rack and pinion, as shown in Figure A, is to convert a back and forth motion to a circular motion, or as shown in Figure B, to change a circular motion to a back and forth, linear motion.

The movement of the rack is determined as:

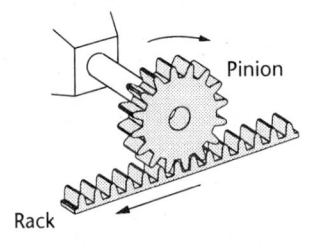

$$\text{movement of rack} = \frac{\text{number of teeth on pinion} \times \text{number of times pinion turns}}{\text{number of teeth per meter on rack}}$$

(A) The rotating motion of a pinion causing a linear motion of the rack

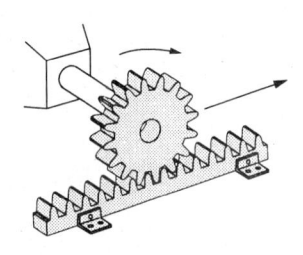

(B) A linear motion of a rack causing a rotation of the pinion

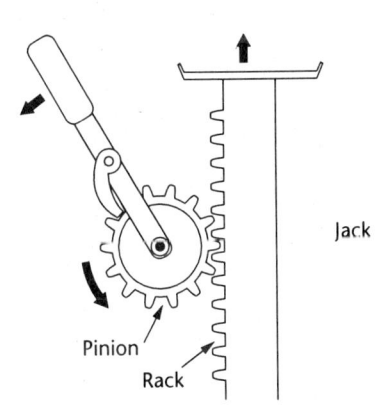

(C) The rotating pinion on the jack causing a linear lifting motion

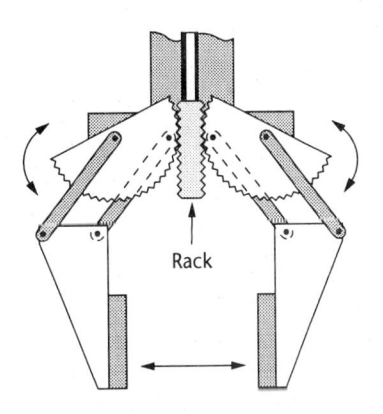

(D) A linear motion of a double-toothed rack causing a rotation of the pinions and the movement of the gripper

1. The jack in Figure C has a handle that is 60 cm in length and turns the pinion gear with 14 teeth. The pinion meshes with the rack gear. The radius of the pinion is 8 cm. The distance between the teeth on the rack is 0.5 cm. What is the MA of the jack? _____ How far does the jack move in a vertical direction for each complete turn of the pinion? _____ If 25% of the work that is done in lifting the load by the jack is used to overcome the force of friction, what force is required to lift a load of 1,000 kg? _____

DESIGN ACTIVITIES—CONVERTING ENERGY BY RACK AND PINION CONTINUED

2. Use the illustration shown in Figure D as a suggestion for the design of an end effector, or hand of a robot. Build a model of the device using cardboard and some of the real gears provided by your teacher. Determine how far the rack must move to open and close the jaws completely. If you decide that a force of 10 N is required for your design, what force must be applied to the rack? _____

3. What changes in the design do you think would improve the operation of the end effector? _____

INTEGRATED S/M/T ACTIVITIES—USING PULLEYS

Something interesting happens when a single pulley is connected so that it is moveable. With the resources provided by your teacher, set up such an arrangement so that the pulley is supported by the rope as shown in the illustrations below.

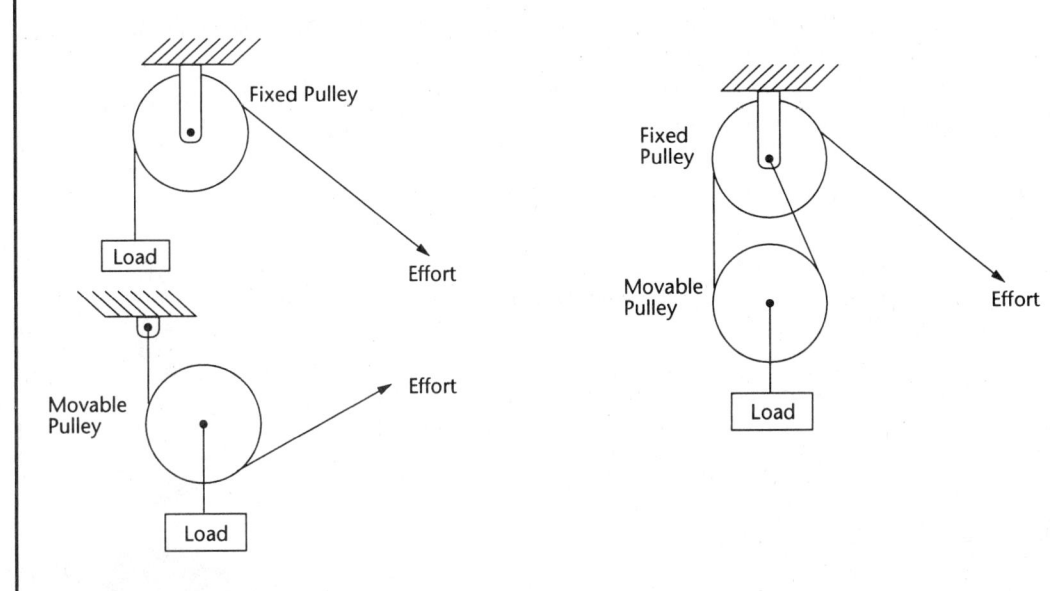

- Measure the weight of the load to be lifted.

- Place the load on the pulley and lift it, measuring the force that is necessary to move the load.

- Lift the load and measure the distance it moved.

- Measure how much rope you had to pull through the pulley to move the load through that distance.

- From this data, determine the MA and VR provided by a single movable pulley.

- From what you have learned, how would the MA of a pulley system relate to the number of pulley wheels that were used? How would MA relate to the number of times the rope loops back and forth between the pulleys?

DESIGN ACTIVITIES—PULLEYS AND MA

Apply the concepts you have learned about using pulleys to improve the operation of the elevator model developed earlier. Can you reduce the size and complexity of the gear train? What advantages and disadvantages will using a pulley system present?

To achieve a higher mechanical advantages, you may want to use multiple pulleys. The illustration in illustration A below shows a hand-operated set of pulleys, often called blocks and tackle, with the pulleys making up the block and the rope serving as the tackle. Illustration B shows a concept of how the elevator drive motor might be connected to the pulley system.

1. If all the pulleys are the same size, what will be the velocity ratio of a block and tackle that has six pulley wheels? _____ What will be the VR of a system that uses four pulley wheels? _____

The velocity ratio can be determined by comparing how far the cable is moved with how far the load is moved, as represented by the following formula:

$$\text{velocity ratio} = \frac{\text{input distance}}{\text{output distance}}$$

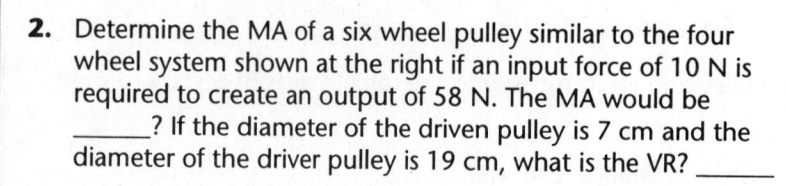

2. Determine the MA of a six wheel pulley similar to the four wheel system shown at the right if an input force of 10 N is required to create an output of 58 N. The MA would be _____? If the diameter of the driven pulley is 7 cm and the diameter of the driver pulley is 19 cm, what is the VR? _____

The MA for pulleys can be determined by comparing the input force and the output force, as represented by the following formula:

$$\text{mechanical advantage} = \frac{\text{output force}}{\text{input force}}$$

3. What is the MA of the four pulley block and tackle shown at the right, if an input force of 16 N is required to move a load of 50 kg? _____

4. If the Velocity Ratio of a block and tackle system is 12:1 and it requires an effort force of 600 N to lift a 650 Kg load, what is the efficiency of the system?

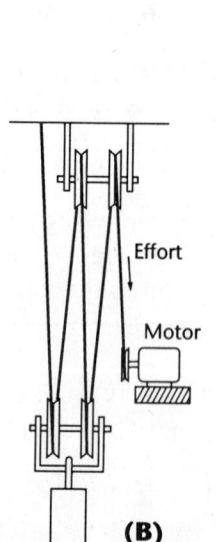

NOTE: The arrangement of pulleys and ropes known as blocks and tackle were used extensively on large sailing boats for raising and lowering the huge sails. The first mass-production system was developed to produce blocks by the thousands for the British navy.

FLUID MECHANISMS

INTEGRATED S/M/T ACTIVITIES—GENERATING FORCE WITH A COMPRESSOR AND PISTON

Compressors are used to provide air at increased pressure. Cylinders are the most common means of using air pressure to create and apply movement and force. Air pressure is measured in newtons per square meter. When using a pneumatic or hydraulic cylinder to apply force, the amount of force must be compatible with the capability of the piston. These calculations will be done in metric measurement, involving meters and newtons.

As you prepare to calculate the force generated by a piston, you will need to know the pressure of the air supply and the piston area. This will allow you to determine the following:

$$\text{pressure} = \frac{\text{force}}{\text{area}} \quad \text{or} \quad P = \frac{F}{A}$$

where pressure is measured in N/mm^2
force is measured in newtons (N)
area is measured in square millimeters (mm^2)

Based on the above, it follows that

$F = P \times A$

The area (A) of a round piston = $pi \times r^2$ or $= \frac{pi \times d^2}{4}$

where r = radius of piston in millimeters
d = diameter of piston in millimeters
pi = 3.142

If you study the above formula, it shows that the greater the pressure, the higher the force on the piston. Similarly, if the area of the piston is increased, the force on the piston will be increased.

In your work, the cylinders and their pistons are going to be very small. It will be easier, therefore, to measure the pistons in square millimeters rather than square meters. One square meter is equal to 1,000,000 square millimeters, or:

$1,000,000 \ N/m^2 = 1 \ N/mm^2$

Caution—High pressures of air or liquid can be dangerous.
BE CAREFUL WHEN USING FLUID POWER!
DO NOT POINT AIR HOSES OR CYLINDERS AT ANYONE!

DESIGN BRIEF—DEVELOPING A PNEUMATIC DEVICE FOR MOVING MATERIALS

You have been asked to help develop a pneumatic device that will move packages from a conveyor line to a loading operation where the products will be placed on a pallet for transportation to users by truck.

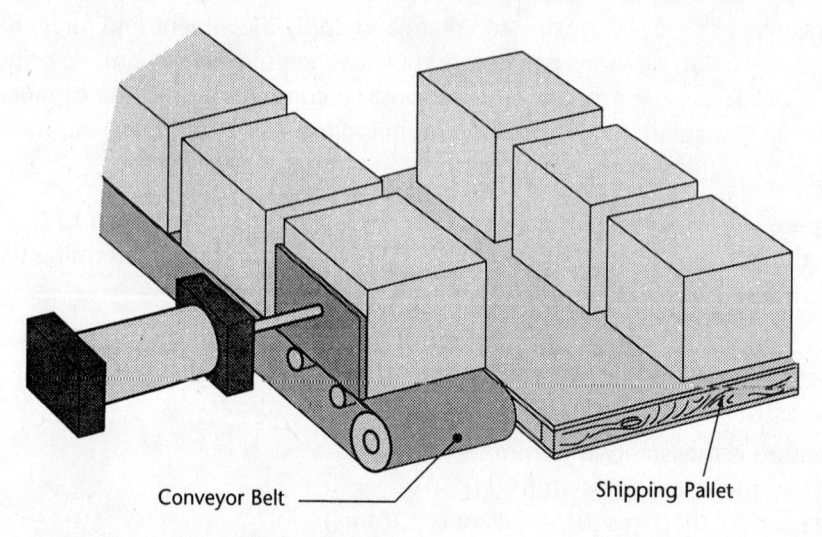

A general drawing of the packaging line

Conveyor Belt — Shipping Pallet

The packages weigh 25 kilograms each. You have been asked to determine the diameter of the pneumatic cylinder that will be needed to move the packages. You have also been asked to build a working model of the system.

1. A source of air pressure of 50,000 N/m² is available to service the pneumatic device. The air cylinder will need a stroke of 60 cm to move the packages the required distance. What is the minimum diameter of the cylinder to move the packages, one at a time, onto the loading station?

The air pressure of 50,000 N/m² can be converted to N/cm² by dividing by 10,000, or it can be converted to N/mm² by dividing by 1,000,000.

An air pressure of 50,000 N/m² = _____ Nmm²?

If the packages weigh 25 kg, a force of 250 N will be needed to move them one at a time. Use the equation below to determine the area of the cylinder needed.

Force = pressure × area

Area = _____ ?

DESIGN BRIEF—DEVELOPING A PNEUMATIC DEVICE FOR MOVING MATERIALS CONTINUED

This can be converted to the diameter of the cylinder needed by using the following equation:

area = πD, or

$D = \dfrac{\text{area}}{\pi}$

D = _____ mm?   D = _____ inches?

2. What size cylinder would be needed if the packages weighed 56 kg, the air pressure supplied was 100,000 N/m^2, and the air cylinder needed a stroke of 80 cm to move the packages the required distance? Determine the minimum diameter needed for the cylinder to move the packages, one at a time, onto the loading station?

ELECTROMECHANICAL MECHANISMS

The forces of magnetism can be converted to electrical energy, which in turn can be converted to mechanical energy for movement. This movement can be expressed as heat, light, or sound, as well as the physical movement of a load.

Electrical power refers to the rate at which electrical energy is converted into another form of energy. Electrical potential energy is measured in joules and electrical power is measured in watts. One watt of electrical power is equivalent to one joule per second.

Resistors, by design, are able to withstand the heat they generate when electricity flows through them. All resistors have a power rating within which they will operate. If that rating is exceeded, the component will burn out or fail. Resistors come in many different values of resistance (electrical sizes). This means that some are manufactured to have a few ohms of resistance while others have many, many ohms of resistance.

INTEGRATED S/M/T ACTIVITIES—USE AMMETER AND VOLTMETER IN CIRCUITS

In your design and development work, you will make direct measurements of two properties of electricity—the current (amperes) and the force (voltage). The design activities that follow will help you gain some important skills in using ammeters and voltmeters.

With the materials provided by your teacher, complete the exercises below which show how to use ammeters and voltmeters. After you have completed the activity, refer to your textbook to see if you have placed an ammeter or voltmeter into a circuit to get appropriate and usable readings.

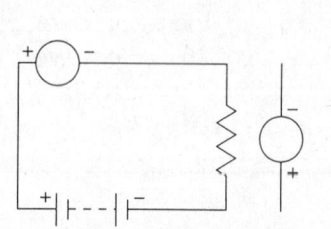

Ammeter Readings

Ammeter	Reading (A)
A_1	2.5 A
A_2	___ A
A_3	___ A
A_4	___ A

(A) Draw an ammeter and a voltmeter correctly into this circuit.

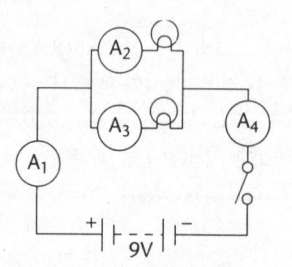

(B) Ammeter in series with legs of parallel circuit.

(C) Ammeter readings in legs of the circuit.

Which meter does the electrical current actually flow through? In Figure B, which of the ammeters will be registering the same readings—A_1 and A_2, A_1 and A_3, or A_1 and A_4? Which have equal readings—A_2 and A_1, A_2 and A_3, or A_2 and A_4? In Figure C, complete the current readings for the example provided. How do the readings of A_1 and A_4 compare? How do the readings of A_2 and A_3 compare to A_1?

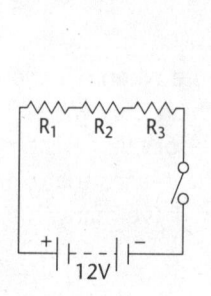

Voltmeter Readings

Voltmeter	Reading (V)
V_1	12 V
V_2	___ V
V_3	___ V
V_4	___ V

(A) Draw in a voltmeter to check the voltage of the battery. Add a voltmeter to check pd across R_2.

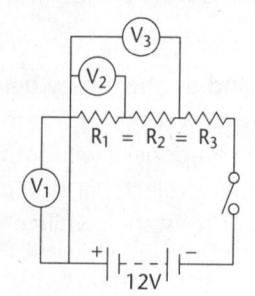

(B) If the resistance of R_1, R_2, and R_3 are the same, what will be the pd across each?

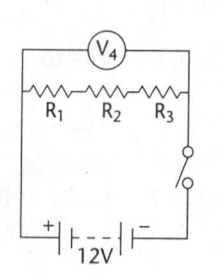

(C) What will be the voltmeter reading across all three components?

(D) What are the voltmeter readings (V_1, V_2, V_3, and V_4) across each of the components?

What is the voltage drop (pd) across each of the different components? How do these amounts compare to the total voltage drop of the circuit? How can you determine the pd across each component or series of components?

INTEGRATED S/M/T ACTIVITIES—USING OHM'S LAW

Resistance can be determined by measuring the voltage across a component and the current flowing through it. By using Ohm's Law, you can determine the relationship of voltage, current, and resistance. Resistance was originally indicated by the letter Omega (Ω), but since computers have come into common use, the letter R is used. Ohm's Law indicates that:

voltage = current × resistance or $V = I \times R$

You can rearrange this formula so that:

resistance = $\dfrac{\text{voltage}}{\text{current}}$ or $R = \dfrac{V}{I}$

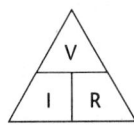

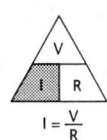

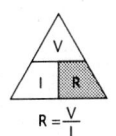

There are many instances when it is important to reduce current flow through the use of a resistor. The example below shows a resistor used to reduce the voltage to a light emitting diode (LED). LEDs are small devices that normally operate at about 2 volts and require 20 mA to function. (One mA is equal to 1/1,000 of an ampere.) To ensure that the voltage is correct for the LED, it is placed in series with a resistor. The circuit below is powered by a 9-volt battery and 7 volts must be dropped over the resistor so that 2 volts are available to operate the LED. Use Ohm's Law to calculate the size resistor that is required.

When two or more components are placed in a circuit as shown at right, they form a potential divider. They divide the voltage from the battery between them. If the LED requires 2 v, then the resistor must create a drop of 7 v. As indicated above, the LED requires about 20 mA to operate.

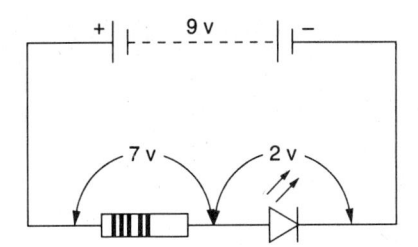

The value of the resistor can be calculated as:

$R = \dfrac{V}{I} = \dfrac{7}{.020} = 350$ ohms

Resistors come in standard values and you can select a 350-ohm resistor. You can refer to Figure 6.28 in your text to see what the color code will be for this resistor.

INTEGRATED S/M/T ACTIVITIES—COMBINING RESISTORS

Resistors can be combined in series, as shown in the illustration below. The total resistance in this circuit is determined by adding the resistance of all the parts. Using the components and materials provided by your teacher, set up the circuit below and determine its total resistance.

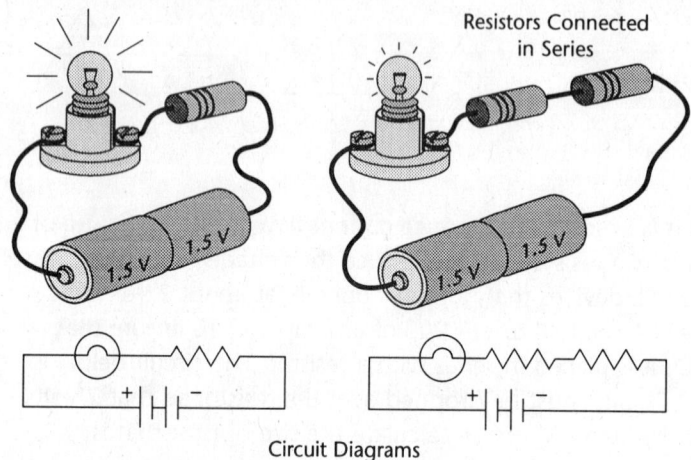

Resistors Connected in Series

Circuit Diagrams

What is the formula for the total resistance in a series circuit?

RT =

Resistors can also be combined in parallel as shown below.

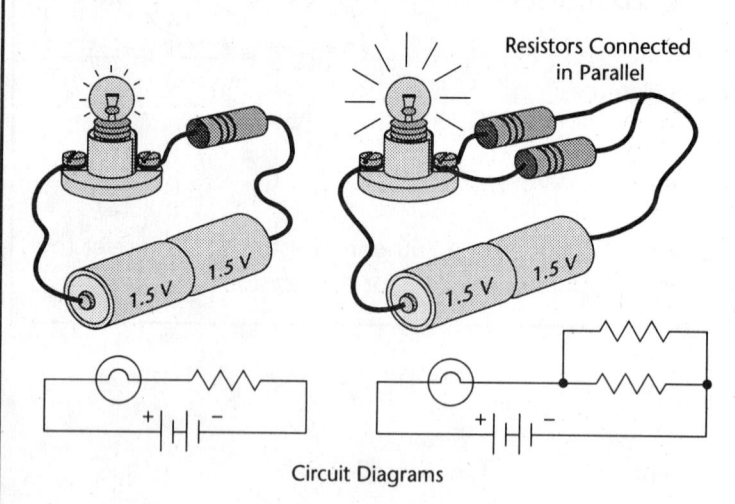

Resistors Connected in Parallel

Circuit Diagrams

What is the formula for the total resistance in a parallel circuit?

$\frac{1}{RT}$ =

NOTE: The chart and directions provided in your text show the codes and process for determining the resistance of a resistor.

DESIGN BRIEF—DEVELOPING YOUR ENERGY CONVERSION CHART

The Energy Conversion Chart, introduced earlier in this chapter, will be most useful in your design and technology work if you add instances and examples that mean something to you. Use the blank format of the Energy Conversion Chart provided on the following page. Make sketches and name the devices that you have used, as well as the processes and devices that you have learned about in the class. Enter other devices and processes as you proceed in your individual and class activities.

Develop a second Energy Conversion Chart to help you record the sensors and transducers you use. The chart will provide a means of identifying and describing what devices can be used when you continue your more in-depth study of how information (signals) are actually samples of energy forms.

ENERGY CONVERSION CHART

	Chemical	Heat	Mechanical	Sound	Electrical	Light
Light						
Electrical						
Sound						
Mechanical						
Heat						
Chemical						

ENRICHMENT DESIGN AND TECHNOLOGY ACTIVITIES

Design Briefs

- Identify five different tools you use at home or in school that operate on electricity. Determine how much energy can be provided by each tool and which does the most work for the electrical energy used. Place the tools in rank order of most efficient to least efficient. Determine what changes you might make in the tool with the poorest efficiency to improve its performance.

- Identify what you would eat in the morning as your favorite breakfast. Determine where each of the products for that breakfast was grown, processed, and packaged. Discuss what forms of energy were used to grow, prepare, and deliver the food to your table. Design and develop a display that shares this information with others. What changes would you propose to improve the efficiency of this system?

- Design a safety card that identifies the key safety features of a tool or machine. The card should help people understand the precautions that should be taken or the protection that should be used to shield the user from the energy used by the machine. Consider the protection required for electrical energy, thermal energy (extreme heat or cold), microwave energy, or mechanical energy in the form of moving gears, belts, pulleys, motors, and cutting tools.

- Using electricity and gas bills, determine how much energy is being used in your home each day and each month. Can you determine the difference of the energy use between the seasons, particularly winter and summer?

- Although the Earth receives more energy from the sun each month than the energy stored in the known fossil fuel reserves, solar energy remains underutilized in this country. Design and construct models of different devices and systems that will put energy from the sun to practical use.

- Identify and record the kinds and amount of foods you consume in a 24-hour period. Determine the calorie content of the different foods you have eaten. Identify the activities you do during the same day, and determine the calories used for that day.

REVIEW AND ASSESSMENT ACTIVITIES

- For each of the following prime sources, identify at least one example of application: solar energy, geothermal energy, movement of air, movement of water, atomic energy, fossil fuels, and energy from living things.

- Describe the differences between slow and rapid oxidation and provide an example of each.

- Compare potential energy and kinetic energy as stored energy and energy in motion.

- Provide practical examples of devices or systems that fall within the categories of the energy spectrum — atomic, chemical, mechanical, electromagnetic, radiant, and cosmic.

- Describe how the latent heat of evaporation and the latent heat of fusion can represent energy that is wasted or energy that is stored.

- Different forms of energy can be detected by humans with their unaided senses. Identify these forms and describe how humans detect and use these energy forms.

- Identify the additional examples you would add to the Energy Conversion Chart.

- There are many important terms related to energy and its use. Describe the following and provide an example that shows the application of entropy, friction, efficiency, and equilibrium.

- Describe and illustrate how mechanical advantage (in the use of levers) involves loads, moments, and moment arms.

- Describe and illustrate how mechanical advantage and velocity ratio are related.

- Compare the differences and similarities of using wheels and axles, belts and pulleys, and chains and sprockets.

- Describe and illustrate how mechanical advantage operates in pneumatics systems.

- Describe and illustrate the relationship between force and pressure.

- Describe how the resistance in series circuits differs from resistance in parallel circuits.

- There are a number of important concepts related to electromagnetism such as amps, ohms (resistance), potential difference, voltage, and EMF. How do these different concepts relate to each other?

- Consider energy that is stored as potential energy. Identify specific examples and devices that can be used to store energy in a mechanical, electrical, and fluid (pneumatic, hydraulic) form.

- What is meant by the idea of converting energy into information? What do transducers have to do with this process?

CHAPTER 7
Information and Information Processing

Since the first messages were sent, information has been processed and used. The accumulation of knowledge itself is a product of information processing and use. As humans perceive, store, and retrieve information, they do so with symbols. Signals and symbols are the basic building blocks of information as we communicate ideas and control actions.

Through symbols we share our experiences and their meaning with other humans. Symbols represent something more than the symbol itself—they infer meaning. Symbols are the signs used by humans and machines to communicate with humans.

SIGNALS—INFORMATION FOR MACHINES

Signals are intended to cause action. Signals are the signs or impulses to communicate or control machines by humans or by other machines. All technological events require information as a resource.

In the previous chapter on Energy, sensors and transducers, as special energy converters, take a small sample of energy and change that energy into information (signals) for communicating with or controlling a machine. These signals (the input) are modified and changed (by the process) to create some form of action (the output). The sensor or transducer is the major link between energy and information. Signals are generated by these devices that sample a form of energy—such as heat, light, sound, or movement—and convert that energy into a usable signal.

Signals are put together into codes that machines can be programmed to understand. Codes used with machines must be prearranged and cannot vary from their original form and meaning. Codes allow people to make sense out of signals.

One of the most common means of sensing and switching mechanical energy is the cam. The cam has a specific shape that contains certain information that will determine how long something is turned on or off. Another common device for switching mechanical energy on and off is a clutch. The clutch can be released at any time to turn off the machine.

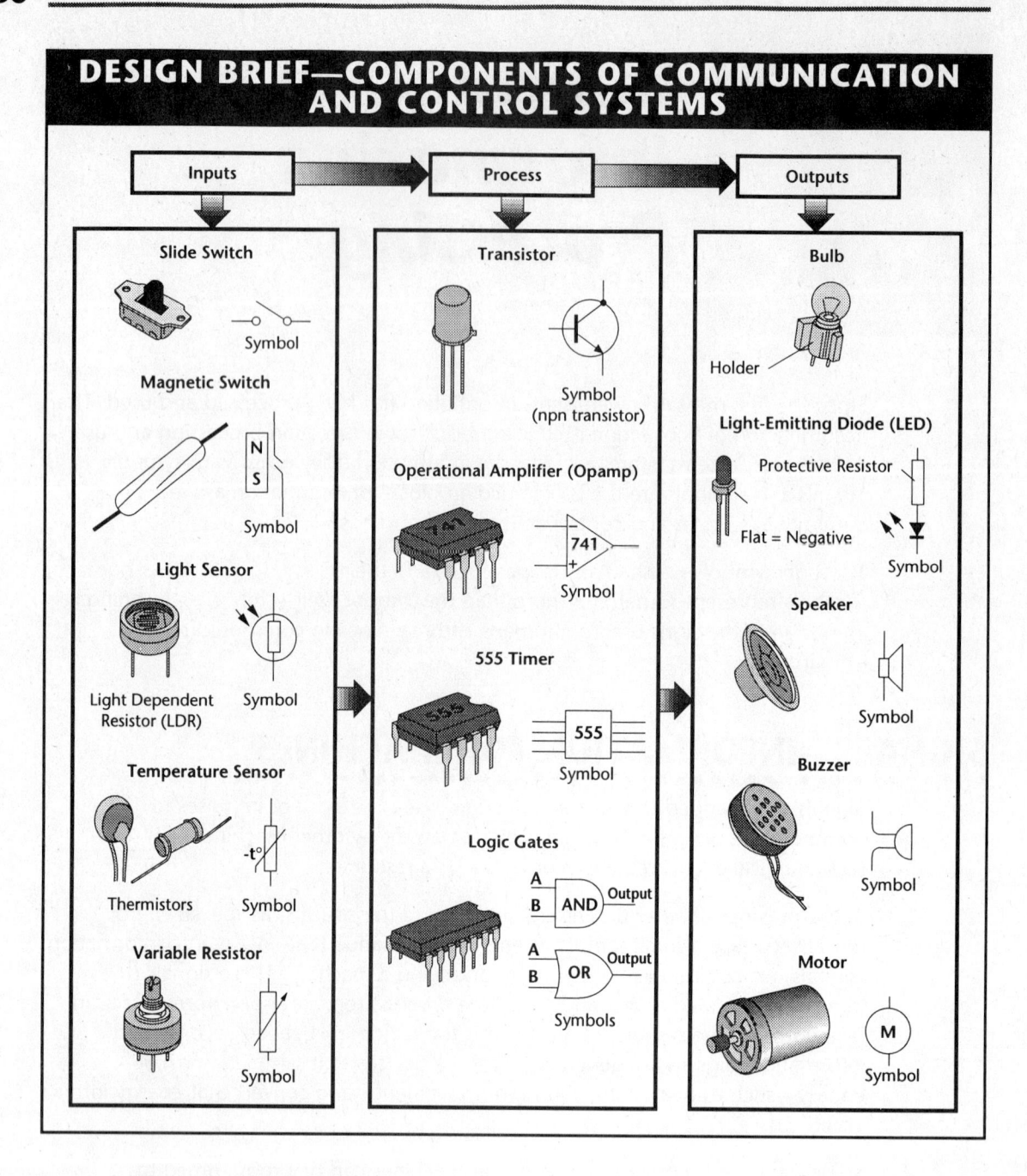

DESIGN BRIEF—COMPONENTS OF COMMUNICATION AND CONTROL SYSTEMS

Inputs → **Process** → **Outputs**

Inputs

Slide Switch
Symbol

Magnetic Switch
N S
Symbol

Light Sensor
Light Dependent Resistor (LDR)
Symbol

Temperature Sensor
Thermistors
-t°
Symbol

Variable Resistor
Symbol

Process

Transistor
Symbol (npn transistor)

Operational Amplifier (Opamp)
741
Symbol

555 Timer
555
Symbol

Logic Gates
A, B → AND → Output
A, B → OR → Output
Symbols

Outputs

Bulb
Holder

Light-Emitting Diode (LED)
Protective Resistor
Flat = Negative
Symbol

Speaker
Symbol

Buzzer
Symbol

Motor
M
Symbol

DESIGN ACTIVITIES—SENSORS AND SWITCHES—HOW THEY WORK

As you continue your design and technology work, identify any new sensors and switches you discover. Use drawings, notations, and descriptions to record how each device operates. Remember, you will use these in some of your designs, so you will need to keep good records of your collection of devices.

Sketch or drawing (with name of device)	Description of how the device works (input energy needed to operate the device and output provided by the device)	Notes and observations
Micro Switch	The micro switch is operated when force is applied to the arm of the device. It is operated with a small (micro) movement or force. The micro switch provides a digital, on/off output. Typically has a 5 A rating. Requires about 100-200 grams of force to operate.	
Reed Switch	The reed switch is a magnetically operated control device. It operates when a magnetic field is strong enough to cause the reeds in the switch to make contact with each other. Maximum current is 0.5 A. The reed switch provides a digital on or off output.	
Thermistor	Thermistors operate on temperature change. As the temperature increases, the resistance of the thermistor decreases. The thermistor provides an analog output that varies as the temperature being sensed varies.	
Optoswitch-slotted	The slotted optoswitch operates when a beam of light is interrupted, sending a signal to the transistor component of the switch. The built-in diode operates on 1.7 volts at 20 milliamps. The transistor is rated at 5 volts and 10 milliamps.	
Microphone (resistance)	This microphone operates as the sound level increases and the carbon in the mike is compressed, and its resistance is lowered allowing a flow of current. It provides an analog output from the changes as level of sound and resistance varies. Its rating is about 0.001 v at 1 kHz.	

DESIGN ACTIVITIES—SENSORS AND SWITCHES—HOW THEY WORK CONTINUED

Sketch or drawing (with name of device)	Description of how the device works (input energy needed to operate the device and output provided by the device)	Notes and observations
Photocell	The photocell contains materials that are sensitive to light energy. This device operates on changes in light. As the light level increases and decreases, the materials in the photocell produce a small flow of current. The photocell provides an analog output that varies as the level of light and current flow varies.	
Light-Dependent Resistor (LDR) Symbol	The LDR contains materials that are sensitive to light energy. As the light level increases and decreases, the resistance of the semi-conducting materials similarly increases and decreases. The LDR provides an analog output that varies as light level and resistance varies.	

Note: A blank form titled **Sensor and Transducer Chart** is provided at the end of this chapter. As you continue your investigations and experiments with sensors and transducers, you will find it helpful to record each device under the category of energy form it is able to detect. You will see that for some energy forms there are only a few devices, while others have many.

The output section of the chart focuses on devices with electrical output, since electricity is the primary energy form used in communication and control. Historically, the most used form was mechanical in nature. In the future, it is anticipated that light or optical energy will be used much more commonly.

DESIGN ACTIVITIES—SENSORS AND SWITCHES— HOW THEY WORK CONTINUED

Sketch or drawing (with name of device)	Description of how the device works (input energy needed to operate the device and output provided by the device)	Notes and observations
Sketch Name _____		
Sketch Name _____		
Sketch Name _____		
Sketch Name _____		
Sketch Name _____		
Sketch Name _____		

(Develop more sheets as needed)

DESIGN ACTIVITIES—SYSTEMS INPUTS AND OUTPUTS

You have become part of a small team that will be responsible for the developing systems that can be used for the remote control of machines. As a part of that work, you are expected to know the different types of **inputs** and **outputs**, how they can be used, and how they operate.

From the components provided by your teacher, identify which are the input components. (You may want to refer to the section on signals, starting on page 192 in your textbook and to your notes from earlier activities in this chapter.) Work as a team to determine what changes in resistance (or other electrical property) take place in each input and output device as you use them. Record any changes you can detect in the spaces on the worksheet provided on page 186)

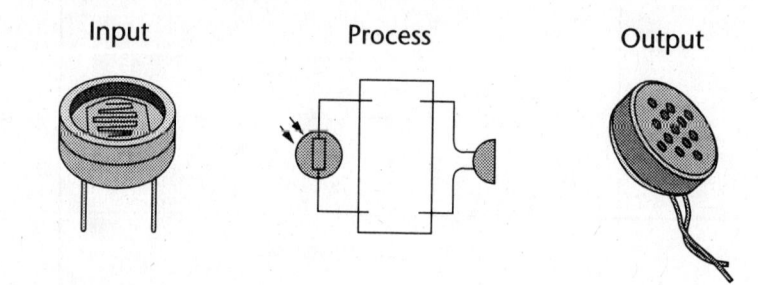

Input   Process   Output

Name <u>Light-Dependent resistor (LDR)</u>

Energy present <u>lighted state</u>   ohms

Energy absent <u>darkened state</u>   ohms

Energy variable _____

Identify change made in input device when used to sample energy form.

Name <u>Electric Buzzer</u>

Device on (min.) low level ____v

Device on (max.) high level ____v

Device on (var.) _____v

Identify energy required to operate output device.

From the same set of components, identify which ones are output components. Using the low-voltage power source provided by your teacher, test to see if you can make each device operate. Record the data on the minimum (low level) required for operation of the device, the maximum (high level).

NOTE: Some input and output devices operate with digital response (on, off) and some with analog (variable) response. For analog devices (input or output), record the variable energy required to make them operate. Record this data in the appropriate spaces.

INTEGRATED S/M/T ACTIVITIES

Devices, like the light-dependent resistor illustrated on the previous page, operate because the material used in their design and manufacture can change. The cadmium sulphide used in the LDR is affected by light energy. For the other input and output devices, determine the following:

- What is the energy form that caused the device to change?
- What is the minimum energy level needed to make the device change?
- What is the nature of the change that happens in each device?
- What other devices operate in a similar manner and might be added to the list?

DESIGN ACTIVITIES—REFERENCE DATA ON OPERATION OF INPUT PROCESSES AND OUTPUT DEVICES

(Drawing and name of input device)   (Drawing and name of output device)

INPUT	PROCESS	OUTPUT

Name _____
Energy present _____
Energy absent _____
Energy variable _____
Identify change made in input device when used to sample energy form.

Requires processor that operates on:
High resistance _____
Low resistance _____
Variable resistance _____

Name _____
Device "on" (min.) _____
Device "on" (max.) _____
Device "on" (var.) _____
Identify energy required to operate output device.

INPUT	PROCESS	OUTPUT

Name _____
Energy present _____
Energy absent _____
Energy variable _____
Identify change made in input device when used to sample energy form.

Requires processor that operates on:
High resistance _____
Low resistance _____
Variable resistance _____

Name _____
Device "on" (min.) _____
Device "on" (max.) _____
Device "on" (var.) _____
Identify energy required to operate output device.

INPUT	PROCESS	OUTPUT

Name _____
Energy present _____
Energy absent _____
Energy variable _____
Identify change made in input device when used to sample energy form.

Requires processor that operates on:
High resistance _____
Low resistance _____
Variable resistance _____

Name _____
Device "on" (min.) _____
Device "on" (max.) _____
Device "on" (var.) _____
Identify energy required to operate output device.

(Develop more sheets as needed.)

Chapter 7 Information and Information Processing **187**

DESIGN ACTIVITIES—DEVELOPING PROCESSOR UNITS

Processors use the input of switches and sensors and convert that input into signals that cause output devices to function. As indicated in your text and below, two circuits are used regularly as processors. One circuit operates as the resistance of a sensor increases; the other operates as resistance decreases.

Use the electronic modeling systems provided by your teacher and construct the processor unit shown in Figure A.

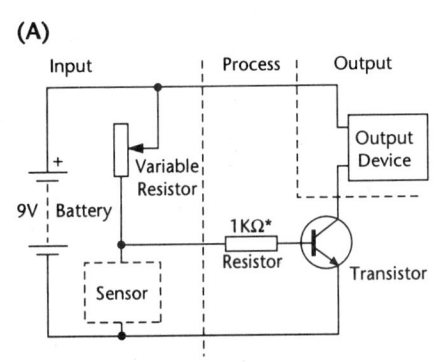

(A)

Operates on increase of sensor resistance
*1KΩ = 1000 ohms

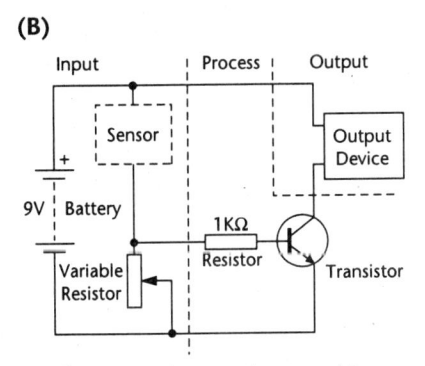

(B)

Operates on decrease of sensor resistance

Refer to the data sheets you developed earlier on input and output devices. Select an output device that will operate on 9 volts or less and connect it as shown in Figure A. Select a sensor that will provide an increase in resistance and connect it as shown. Adjust the variable resistor and see if you can make the output device operate.

Reverse the sensor and variable resistor to conform to the diagram shown in Figure B. Can you make the circuit work with the sensor in this position?

Test the different input devices with each output device you have available. Determine which can work because of an increase in resistance of the sensor and which can operate because of a decrease in resistance. Record your notes and observations about the processor units in your journal. Which of the circuits could be used with the LDR and buzzer shown on page 184?

See if you can make both of the circuits work with the LDR and buzzer. How might this setup be useful? What applications would be possible with these circuits?

In the following activity, you will see how the operation of these devices relates to the input, process, and output signals they generate.

DESIGN ACTIVITIES—DETERMINING SIGNAL STRENGTH

As indicated several times, signals are an essential requirement for controlling machines or for allowing machines to communicate with each other. Each input, process, and output device requires a specific kind of signal to operate. Designing a control system will be much easier for you if you know what kind of signal a device or circuit produces or requires. To facilitate your work, a set of shorthand symbols will be used to represent how an electrical signal is changing.

1. Electrical signals that change in strength from a low level to a high level are represented as:

2. Electrical signals that change in strength from a high level to a low level are represented as:

3. Electrical signals that alternate continually between a high level and a low level are represented as:

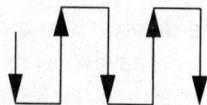

On the following pages, you will be introduced to several activities related to the processor units developed in the preceding activity. The processor units will be used with a variety of input and output devices. Working first with a processor unit that operates on an *increase* of resistance, you will determine and record the change in signal strength for each variety of input and output device. You will then repeat the procedure with a processor unit that operates on a *decrease* of resistance. These activities will lay the foundation for activities and applications in later chapters, particularly the chapter on control.

DESIGN ACTIVITIES—DETERMINING INPUT SIGNAL STRENGTH

Set up the circuit shown below and connect the voltmeter (V) as shown in the drawing. For the devices listed below, determine the voltage (high/low and actual reading) and the signal strength of each.

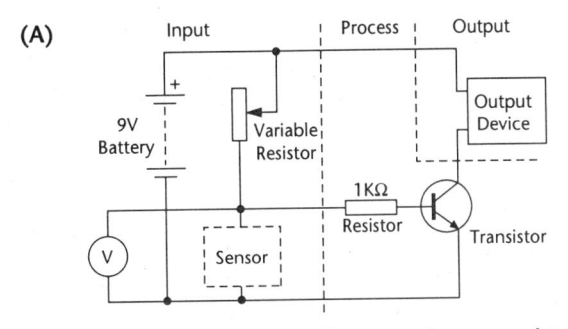

(A)

Processor unit that operates on increase of sensor resistance

Device	State (on/off)	Voltage (high/low)	Voltage (reading)	Signal (strength)	Notes and Observations
Slide switch	on				
	off				
Magnetic switch	on				
	off				
LDR	light				
	dark				
Thermistor	hot				
	cold				
Variable resistor	min.				
	max.				
Optoswitch	light				
	dark				
Microphone	loud				
	quiet				
Others _____					
_____					
_____					

DESIGN ACTIVITIES—DETERMINING INPUT SIGNAL STRENGTH CONTINUED

As in the preceding activity, set up the circuit shown below and connect the voltmeter (V) as shown. Determine the voltage (high/low and actual reading) and the signal strength of each device.

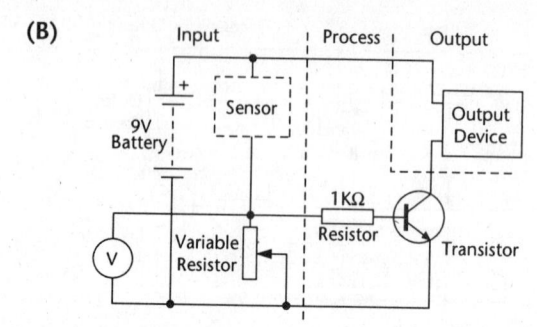

(B)

Processor unit that operates on decrease of sensor resistance

Device	State (on/off)	Voltage (high/low)	Voltage (reading)	Signal (strength)	Notes and Observations
Slide switch	on				
	off				
Magnetic switch	on				
	off				
LDR	light				
	dark				
Thermistor	hot				
	cold				
Variable resistor	min.				
	max.				
Optoswitch	light				
	dark				
Microphone	loud				
	quiet				
Others _____					
_____					

DESIGN ACTIVITIES—DETERMINING OUTPUT SIGNAL STRENGTH

Set up the circuit provided below and connect the voltmeter (V) as shown. Determine the voltage (high/low and actual reading) and the signal strength of each output device.

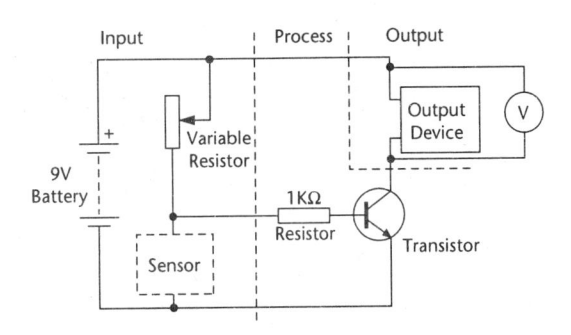

Processor unit that operates on increase of sensor resistance

Device	State (on/off)	Voltage (high/low)	Voltage (reading)	Signal (strength)	Notes and Observations
Light	on				
	off				
LED	on				
	off				
Speaker	loud				
	quiet				
Buzzer	loud				
	quiet				
Motor	run				
	stop				
Solenoid	on				
	off				
Others _____					
_____					
_____					

DESIGN ACTIVITIES—DETERMINING OUTPUT SIGNAL STRENGTH CONTINUED

Set up the circuit provided below and connect the voltmeter (V) as shown. Determine the voltage (high/low and actual reading) and the signal strength of each output device.

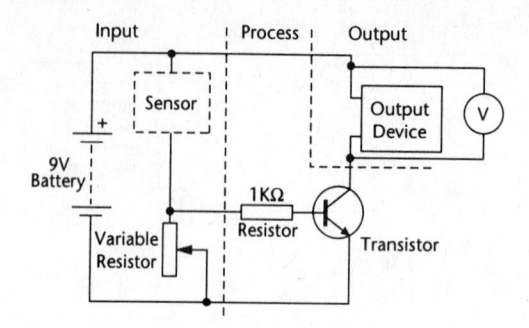

Processor unit that operates on decrease of sensor resistance

Device	State (on/off)	Voltage (high/low)	Voltage (reading)	Signal (strength)	Notes and Observations
Light	on				
	off				
LED	on				
	off				
Speaker	loud				
	quiet				
Buzzer	loud				
	quiet				
Motor	run				
	stop				
Solenoid	on				
	off				
Others _____					
_____					
_____					

DESIGN ACTIVITIES—DETERMINING PROCESSOR SIGNAL STRENGTHS

Set up the circuit provided below and connect the voltmeter (V) as shown. Determine the voltage (high/low and actual reading) and the signal strength across the sensor and across the process device (in this case, the transistor).

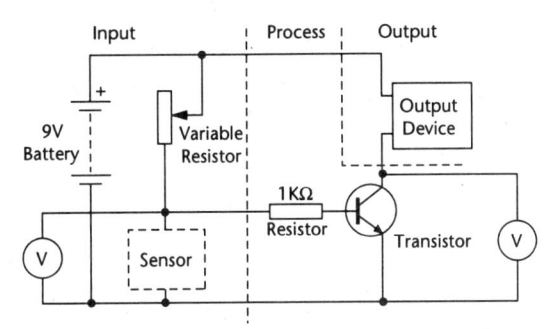

Processor unit that operates on increase of sensor resistance

Device	State (on/off)	Voltage (high/low)	Voltage (reading)	Signal (strength)	Notes and Observations
Sensor	on				
	off				
Transistor	on				
	off				

DESIGN ACTIVITIES—DETERMINING PROCESSOR SIGNAL STRENGTHS CONTINUED

Set up the circuit provided below and connect the voltmeter (V) as shown. Determine the voltage (high/low and actual reading) and the signal strength across the sensor and across the process device (in this case, the transistor).

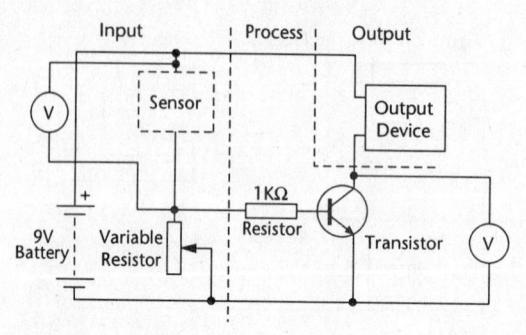

Processor unit that operates on decrease of sensor resistance

Device	State (on/off)	Voltage (high/low)	Voltage (reading)	Signal (strength)	Notes and Observations
Sensor	on				
	off				
Transistor	on				
	off				

DESIGN ACTIVITIES—USING LOGIC CIRCUITS AS PROCESSOR UNITS

Signals provided by single-purpose processor circuits like the above have interesting but limited applications. Combining signals from several sensors and processors provides for more sophisticated circuits. This is done using logic gates to give machines decision-making capabilities.

For the logic circuit shown below, determine whether the voltage outputs are high or low. Record that information in the spaces provided below.

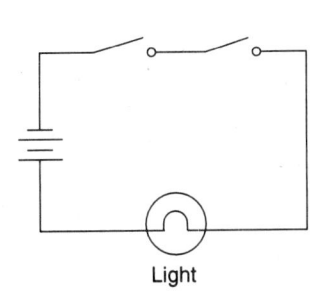

(A) Simple AND circuit

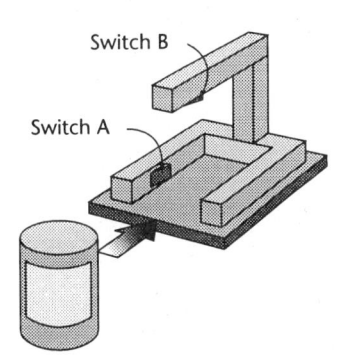

(B) An AND circuit for Aunt Sarah

(C) A truth table for an AND circuit

Switch A	Switch B	Bulb	Voltage	A	B	Output	Voltage Output
off	off	off	low	0	0	0	_____?
off	on	off	low	0	1	0	_____?
on	off	off	low	1	0	0	_____?
on	on	on	high	1	1	1	_____?

NOTE: The truth table for this AND circuit includes more information than necessary. (Refer to Figures 7.13 and 7.14 in your textbook.)

DESIGN ACTIVITIES—USING LOGIC CIRCUITS AS PROCESSOR UNITS CONTINUED

For the logic circuit shown below, determine whether the voltage outputs are high or low. Record that information in the spaces provided below.

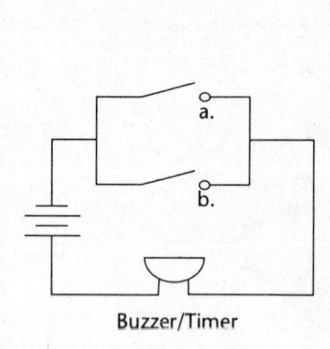

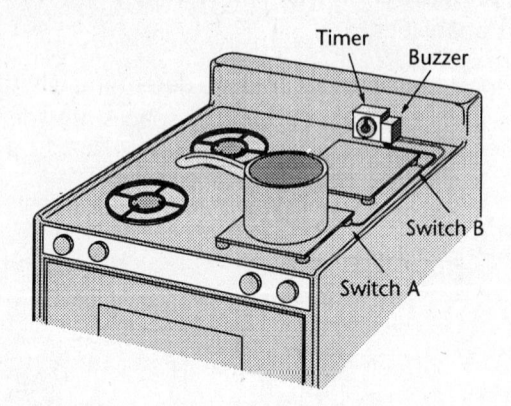

(A) An OR circuit

(B) An application of an OR circuit

(C) A truth table for an OR circuit

A	B	Output	Voltage Output
0	0	0	_____ ?
0	1	0	_____ ?
1	0	0	_____ ?
1	1	1	_____ ?

DESIGN ACTIVITIES—APPLYING LOGIC GATES AND SYSTEMS

Based on your new knowledge of logic gates and logic systems, you have been asked by April and Enrique to help improve their design for identifying cans in Aunt Sarah's kitchen. They believe that a relatively simple device could be designed and developed that would help Aunt Sarah check the contents of a can by its size.

After some experimentation, the three of you come up with an idea to add two additional switches to the overhead arm so the device could be used to measure cans of three different heights, as shown in the sketches below. The design of the logic system should signal Aunt Sarah by buzzer for the shortest cans, by bell for the medium-sized cans and by both buzzer and bell for the tallest cans.

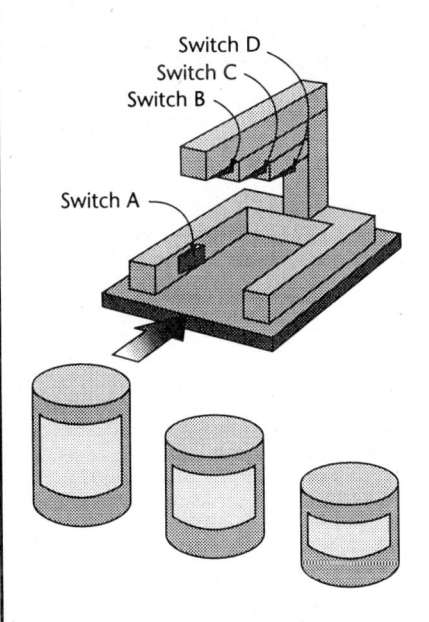

(A) Device to measure width and heights of three can sizes

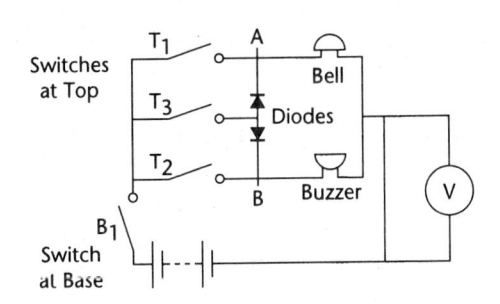

(B) Schematic of switches on the bottom (B_1) and switches on the top arm (T_1, T_2, T_3)

Determine the voltage readings at Point A and B in the drawing. Determine if the bell, buzzer, or both sound for each switch.

NOTE: The use of diodes was introduced in electrical circuit B. Why? What happens without them?

Switch	State of Switch	A	B	Outputs		Notes and Observations
				Bell	Buzzer	
T1						
T2						
T3						

DESIGN ACTIVITIES—APPLYING LOGIC GATES AND SYSTEMS CONTINUED

Identified below are example problems within which you can apply the content introduced in this chapter. You may choose to pursue one or more of these problems now, or you may undertake a similar problem that emerges from your own work later in the course. You will find that the *Microelectronics For All (MFA)* logic systems, if available, will be helpful in solving the following problems. If the MFA system is not available, you should use simple logic gates for the problems.

- Design and develop a safety system that will not allow you to start the engine of a lawn tractor, or a motor bike unless someone is in the seat and the clutch is depressed.

- Design and develop a safety system that will not allow the engine to run if someone lifts the hood on the tractor or removes any safety guard from either machine.

- Design and develop a safety system to sound a beeper when the tractor is moved in reverse.

- Design and develop a system that can be used with a mechanized display that will not allow the display to operate until the viewers have deposited two coins in the coin slot.

- Design and develop a system that will not allow the first action on the stage to begin unless the theater curtain has been opened.

- Design and develop a system that will not allow the mechanized production to start until the viewer has deposited a quarter and a nickel in the coin slot.

- Design and develop a system to monitor the levels of liquid nutrients supplied automatically by pump to plants in a greenhouse.

- Design and develop a system for monitoring when the roots of the plants in the greenhouse have become too dry.

- Design and develop a system that can monitor the temperature of the greenhouse.

- Design and develop a system to monitor pH levels of water and nutrients used in the greenhouse.

INTEGRATED S/M/T ACTIVITIES—HISTORY OF SCIENCE AND TECHNOLOGY

Communicating over long distances was very difficult until Samuel Morse invented the telegraph. This was an important development during the westward movement in the United States and the settling of the western states and territories.

The early telegraphs required that an operator be on duty to send and receive messages in Morse code. This code was a language system used to send and receive messages through a wire, but someone had to be at the receiving end, waiting, or the message would be missed. Morse developed a simple recording machine that helped solve the problem and allowed the receiving operator to decode the message from the recorded message.

NOTE: There is an error in this drawing, if it represents what Morse actually built as his first operating model. Can you identify what is wrong?

The recording machine made a mark on the paper tape as it was pulled past a marking pen. Every time a signal was sent, an electromagnet drew the arm forward. The pen made a mark each time a signal was transmitted. The record of the message was a long tape of these marks.

Morse's telegraph and recorder

- Recorder
- (1) Transmitter
- Battery
- (2) Electromagnet
- (3) Pendulum with Pencil
- (4) Marks Recorded on Paper Strip

Your teacher may wish to have the class work on a History of Technology Exhibit that can be used in the school. Working in small groups as assigned, develop a working model of Morse's telegraph and recorder. Design and develop the necessary illustrations and signs to help others understand how the devices worked and some of the impacts that resulted from the development and use of the telegraph.

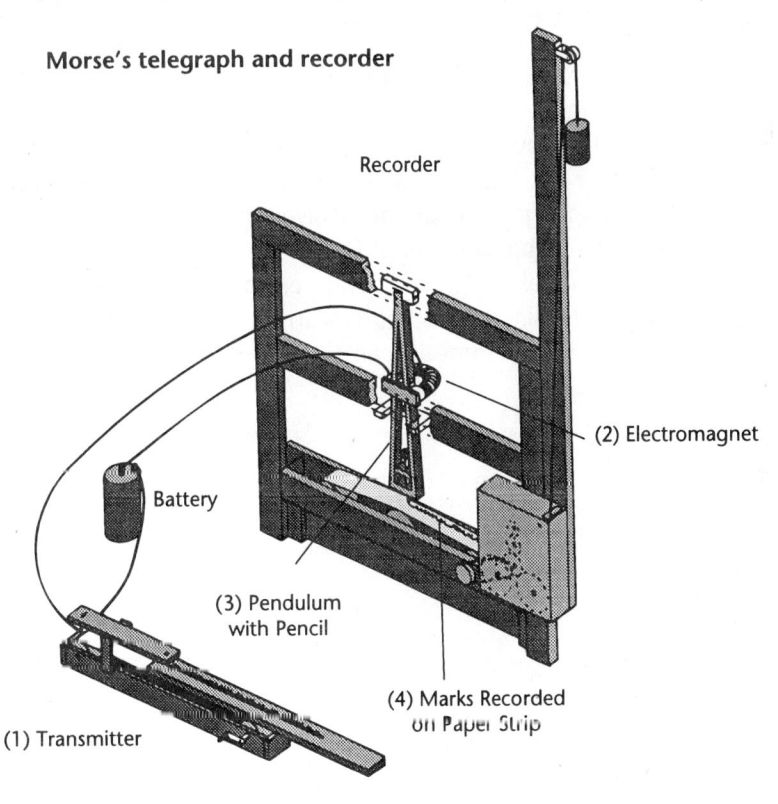

SYMBOLS—INFORMATION FOR HUMANS

Symbols have inferred meaning; they stand for something. Symbols only have meaning and communicate information if the person who receives the symbols can interpret them. Centuries ago, people attempted to talk with others in their group and developed oral language systems. Words came to stand for the actual object. Expressions, gestures, and other movements and sounds came to symbolize emotions and actions. Communication of information depends on shared agreement on meanings. Later, the development of the alphabet, pictographs, numbers, and other symbolic systems meant that information could be saved, transported, and exchanged.

Communication can take place among humans, between humans and machines, and between machines. When a machine is to be controlled by information, the human must try to think like a machine. Each step of the process must be considered objectively and logically. Information must be broken down from the symbols a person might understand into tiny bits of data.

If you are to communicate through symbols, it is not enough to only understand each symbol you use; you must know the code for symbol sequences as well. You need to know how to use the code and symbols to create the messages you want to share with others. Each symbol has a limited meaning, but collectively a symbol system can provide an impressive amount of information. One of the most familiar systems is the alphabet of letters we use in our writing and reading. The simplicity of the alphabet belies its long period of development. Our number system went through a similar evolution. Many symbol systems have been developed to help those involved in design and development activities communicate ideas easily and effectively.

DESIGN ACTIVITIES—LOGOS AND PICTOGRAMS

Some symbols are relatively easy to understand and use because they have a limited meaning. Logos and pictograms usually have a single meaning. Logos are developed as a graphic representation of an organization. Several pictograms are shown in Figure 7.20 of your text. Logos, with or without pictograms, are used to give an organization a readily recognizable visual image. Each image is intended to convey a desired message concerning the organization.

- Identify at least five products or companies that use a recognizable logo or pictogram. Draw or attach a copy of the images in the spaces provided below.
- Analyze the messages you think the logos shown below are trying to convey.
- Determine what ideas the logo designers were trying to get across to people who see the logos.
- Determine which logos or pictograms appear to be most successful in representing visually what the company or product is about.
- Design and develop a logo or pictogram for something you think is a marketable

Logo/Pictogram	Message	Idea to be Conveyed	Degree of Success

DESIGN ACTIVITIES—UNDERSTANDING SYMBOL SYSTEMS

The illustration below, introduced in your textbook, includes several different symbol systems. Identify each of the systems and what the specific images represent and record your answers below.

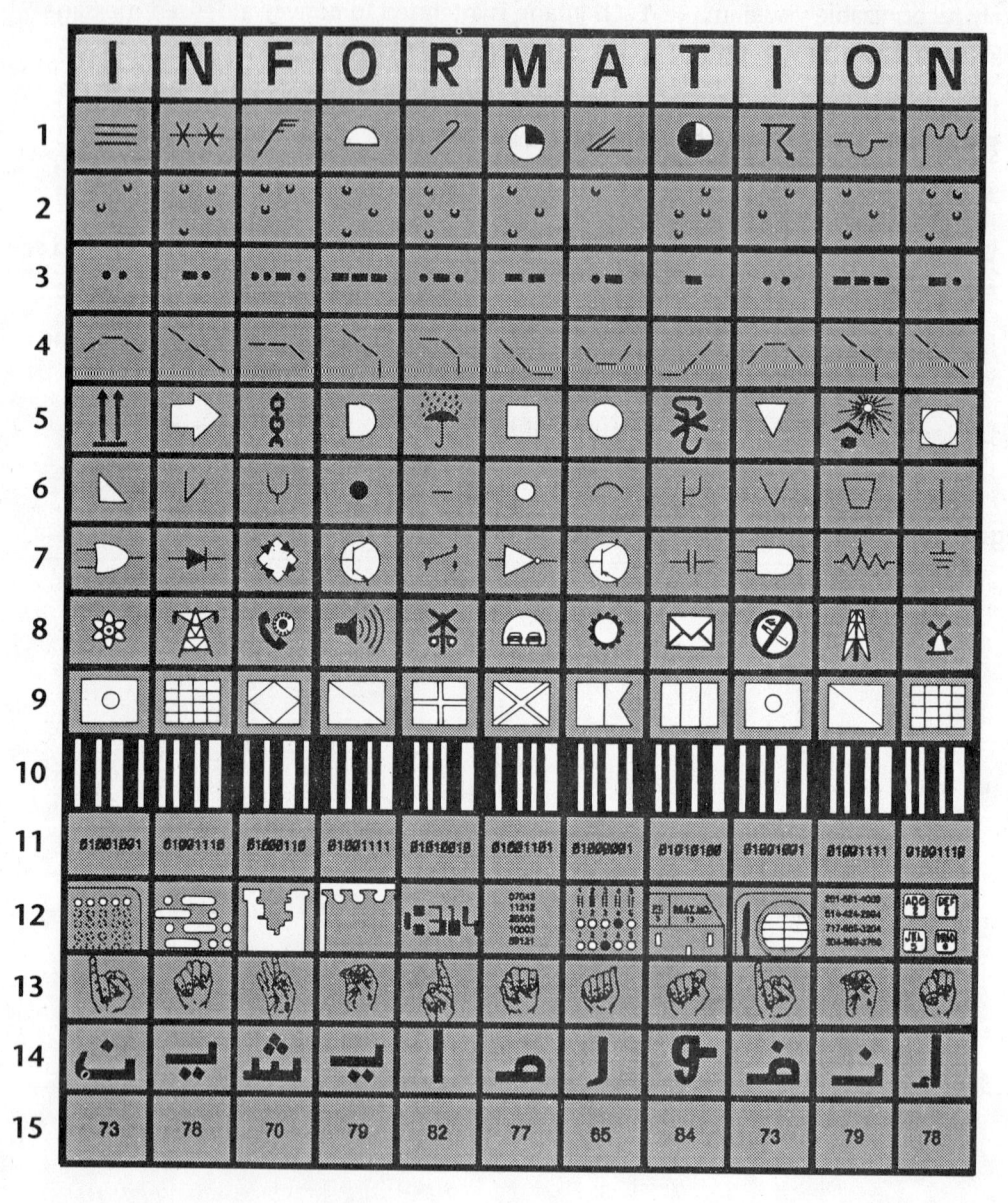

1. _____   2. _____   3. _____
4. _____   5. _____   6. _____
7. _____   8. _____   9. _____
10. _____   11. _____   12. _____

You can check your responses with the answers provided in your text. (See Figure 7.30.)

DESIGN ACTIVITIES—DESIGNING SYMBOL SYSTEMS

- Design and develop a symbol system that would be useful in design and technology.

- Identify and use a current symbol system for communicating ideas about your design and technology work. What suggestions would you make to improve the symbol system?

- Develop a drawing and symbolic representation of an electronic system you developed.

- Design a symbol that will help draw attention to the safe use of a tool or machine.

- Design a symbol that will help people understand a basic concept of a tool or

- Design a symbol system for a major sporting event.

- Design a symbol system to help store and retrieve resources provided in your technology facility.

INTEGRATED S/M/T ACTIVITIES—SYMBOL SYSTEMS AND THEIR USES

- Design and conduct a survey of how people react to and use tools, and machines.

- Conduct research on the psychology of how people use symbols.

- Conduct research on how people learn.

USING SYMBOLS IN DESIGN AND TECHNOLOGY

In some design work, we will need to measure things and group them by name. You may want to know how many people voted "yes" and how many voted "no." You might want to know how many females and how many males responded to a survey. Because this level of measurement only uses names, it is called nominal.

The next level of measurement is when you place things in order from most to least. This is called the ordinal level of measurement. For example, by conducting a survey to determine what people like to eat, you may be able to describe people's preferences, from most to least liked.

The third level of measurement is called interval and requires measurements that use equal units. In this case, you may report the number of people who actually bought each selection from your menu.

A fourth level of measurement is called the ratio level. This level requires an actual zero. It is important to note that some interval levels of measurement allow scores to be less than zero. For example, you can go in debt—have less than zero money. Interval and ratio levels of measurement allow us to add, subtract, calculate averages, and determine proportions. The ratio level also allows us to make much more precise comparisons.

During your designing process, you will need to select a unit of measurement that yields an appropriate amount of precision. If the design is to address the needs or wants of only one person for only one time, or if the required resources are not very expensive, little precision may be necessary. When designs address the needs of many people, or are to be replicated in several places on many occasions, several issues should be considered.

At several points in your design and problem-solving activities, you will need good information to help you in making decisions. You will need to organize that information in order to make sense of it and to share it with others. At this point, it could be said that you are using information in order to diagnose the problem and its dimensions.

As your work progresses, you will gather information to predict the effectiveness of different strategies for solving the problem. In these instances, you know a given solution may not work all the time, but just how well does it perform usually? How much error is acceptable?

In the testing phase, when evaluating your design solution, you will want to test it several times. Gathering the performance data on your solution is essential if you are to decide how to improve the design.

INTEGRATED S/M/T ACTIVITIES—LEVELS OF MEASUREMENT PUT TO USE

You will recall that April and Enrique had to decide on just how precise they needed to be in their design project for Aunt Sarah. They wanted to ensure that Aunt Sarah could find and identify a can of food from her cabinet and be accurate in her choice of cans as she prepares a meal, even though she cannot read any of the labels.

They considered one way to deal with the problem might be to designate different cabinet spaces for different foods. When someone delivers her groceries, they would simply put soups in one spot, vegetables in another, fruits in another, and meats in still another part of the kitchen cabinet. (see Figure 7.24 in your text). When Aunt Sarah goes to the cabinet closest to the door, she will know that cans of meat are there. This represents a nominal level of measurement.

April and Enrique were concerned that Aunt Sarah could tell the difference between cans of peas and cans of tomatoes. A higher level of precision will be needed because both will be in the vegetable area. They suggested that peas be bought in small cans and tomatoes in middle-sized cans. Vegetable juices were to be bought in large cans. Aunt Sarah could tell the vegetables by determining the size of the cans. This represents an ordinal level of measurement. (see Figure 7.25 in your text).

Rather than be dependent on other people to help her with shopping, Aunt Sarah wants to keep track of how many cans she uses of each food. When someone calls to see if there is something they can bring from the grocery store, she would like to know. Enrique and April designed a labeling system of raised, 3-D labels to place on each can, as shown in the figure below.

A storage system that provides integral and rated levels of measurements

Now, as Aunt Sarah uses a can of food, she can save the labels for reuse at a later time. Counting the labels from what she has used gives her a means of keeping track of her inventory of canned food. This data is at an interval level of measurement. This also satisfies the requirement for ratio level of measurement. She can say whether she used twice as many cans of pineapple as she did tuna. Her responses about what she needs to replenish her stock of foods can be much more precise.

INTEGRATED S/M/T ACTIVITIES—LEVELS OF MEASUREMENT PUT TO USE CONTINUED

To test and improve your designs, you will need to determine how accurate the data you collect must be. In some instances, it will be adequate if the data only provides you with general categories. In these instances, the nominal level of measurement will suffice. In other cases, higher levels of measurement may be needed. Examples of measurement levels are provided in the instances below.

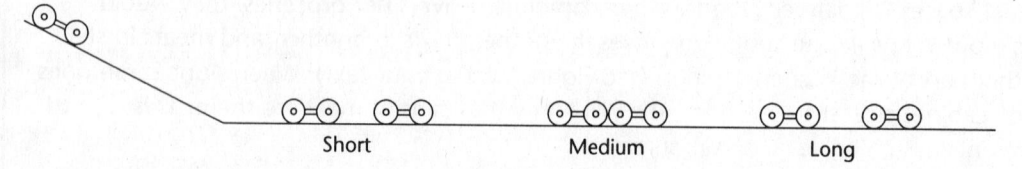

(1) Vehicle testing using nominal categories (short, medium, long). You might use this level early in your testing program to help see how your vehicle is performing. Nominal data is sufficient for this.

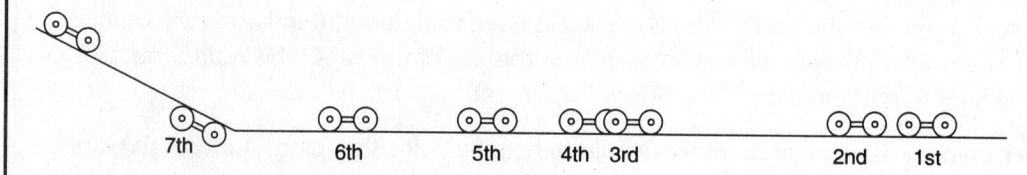

(2) Collecting test data at the ordinal level, noting how the vehicles placed (1st, 2nd, 3rd, ... etc.). As you work on improving your design, you will need more precise data to see if a specific change or innovation helps improve your vehicle performance as compared to earlier runs or to other vehicles.

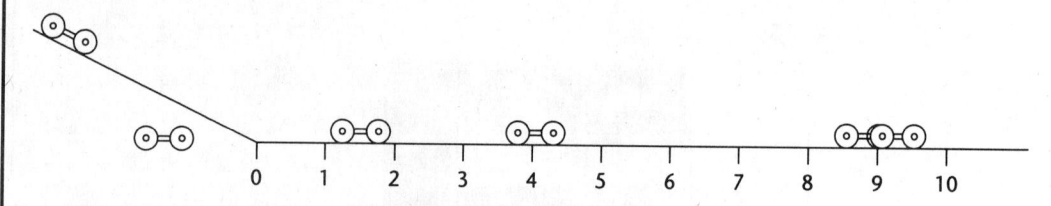

(3) Establishing an interval level of measurement. This example uses a linear measure that starts at the foot of the test ramp. (NOTE: If a car is unable to move or runs off the side of the ramp, it will have traveled a negative distance from the established zero point.

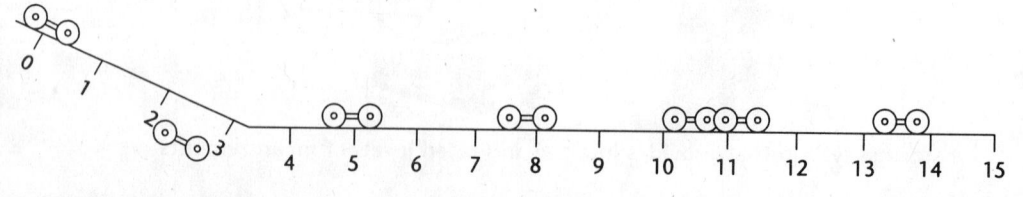

(4) Establishing a ratio level of measurement. This approach establishes the zero point at the top of the ramp. No vehicle that starts the test can travel less than zero distance.

INTEGRATED S/M/T ACTIVITIES—APPLYING LEVELS OF MEASUREMENT

Use the above examples in determining the data you might collect to:

- conduct tests on a boat hull,
- determine preferences people have for five different flavors of pancakes,
- determine if a new toy designed for children lives up to safety requirements, and
- determine how well a new tool does the job for which it has been designed.

Design and develop a hardware storage system for use in your design and technology facility that keeps track of materials through nominal, ordinal, interval, and ratio levels of measurement.

Design and develop a means of collecting data that will allow you to use at least the interval level of measurement in reporting on how well the production of food in a garden or a hydroponics greenhouse is progressing. Identify how you will gather data on how well the plants are growing, how different plants are producing, the potential income from the different crops, and the response of people to the food products you plan to grow.

GUIDE FOR DESIGN QUESTIONS

As you collect data on a Design and Technology project, you will need to collect appropriate data so that you can assess how sell your solution(s) fit your proposed design and intended purpose(s) and user(s). The following questions should be helpful to see what data will be needed at different steps in the design process.

Identify and Define the Problem—Investigating Needs and Opportunities

- What data can help you identify if a problem represents a real need or potential opportunity?

Describe the Design Brief—Clarifying Results You Want to Achieve

- What data will help you develop specifications and criteria such as time, cost, materials, size/shape, special function, user(s), and place of use?

Explore Possible Alternatives—Searching for Solutions and Information

- How will you know if you conducted an adequate investigation?
- What data will help you clarify the needs, wants, and opportunities of the design?

Assess the Alternatives—Choosing the Best Solution

- What data will help you use a systematic approach to assessing the possible alternatives?
- What data will help you compare and rank the alternatives before choosing the best solution?

Try Out the Best Solution—Experimenting and Developing Solutions, Models, and Prototypes

- What data from your experiments and tests of your design will be most useful in developing solutions?
- What data will help you develop a model or prototype of your proposed solution?

Evaluate the Results—Testing the Solution and Assessing the Process

- What data are essential to help you report on the testing of your finished product?
- What data will help you assess the operation of your solution and your efforts in developing that solution?

INTEGRATED S/M/T ACTIVITIES—UNITS OF MEASUREMENT

A great deal of work has gone into developing a common system of measurement to help us share information more readily. For example, most countries have adopted the metric system of measurement. The United States is one of the few countries in the world that uses an older, less flexible system of measurement. A few selected units of measurement, including distance, time, force, weight, mass, energy, and power, are listed below.

Quantity	Name of Unit	Symbol
Distance	meters	m
Time	seconds	s
Force	newtons	N
Weight	newtons	N
Mass	kilograms	kg
Energy	joules	J
Power	watts	W

What are the nonmetric equivalents of these units of measurement that are used in the U.S.?

Quantity	Name of Unit	Symbol
Distance	_____	_____
Time	_____	_____
Force	_____	_____
Weight	_____	_____
Mass	_____	_____
Energy	_____	_____
Power	_____	_____

DESIGN BRIEF—PRESENTING INFORMATION GRAPHICALLY

Charts, graphs, and maps are three useful means of organizing and sharing information. Data from the activities of this course can be collected, organized, and presented through these techniques. Listed below are several examples where information presented graphically could help communicate findings and relationships and comparisons that would be very difficult to share otherwise. Design and develop a chart, graph or map for one of this following instances, or one that related to your own work.

Using charts that can be used to show relationships

- the rate of growth related to selected vegetables and amount of fertilizers used
- plant productivity and amount of sunlight
- the area of reach of a high lift or a back-hoe shovel on a tractor
- the strength of an adhesive bond and the area of contact between the pieces of materials being attached
- the weight that can be supported by a structure and the area cross section of the support members of the structure

Using graphs to compare size (length, area, and volume)

- the amount of biomass materials that can be grown with different plants
- the amount of different vegetables produced based on size of the greenhouse
- the productivity and profits of strawberries and other selected plants
- the costs and profits of growing hydroponic vegetables compared to standard farming techniques
- the amount of food for a family and the size greenhouse required to raise crops for their own use

Using maps to present information

- the patterns of interest in different foods nationally
- the sources of raw materials nationally
- the areas of the world and the levels of deforestation
- the amount of cropland currently not used for farming in the United States
- the areas and levels of poverty and hunger in the United States

ENRICHMENT DESIGN AND TECHNOLOGY ACTIVITIES

Design Briefs

- From your experience in design and technology, design a portfolio format that represents symbolically one activity you wish to pursue or one product you wish to develop.

- Analyze the problems you have had in keeping your log and journal up to date. Design new page formats and methods to improve your record keeping.

- Mass transit systems, particularly bus and subway routes, tend to be difficult for new users to use. Design and develop a map and supportive brochure that would help a visitor from another country use the system easily and safely.

- Design and develop a survey questionnaire to collect information about a product you plan to develop. In the design of the survey and questionnaire, consider the following:

    What is the purpose of the survey?

    What information do you need?

    What people will you include in your survey?

    What specific questions do you plan to ask?

    How can you make the survey easy to analyze?

    How will the survey be conducted?

- Develop a plan that includes all the key steps required to implement the survey described above or to implement a project you plan to pursue.

- Design a graph or chart that conveys information gained from the survey questionnaire described above.

- Design and develop an electronic map to be used in a shopping mall that will help people find the destination of interest based on the products they want to purchase. All stores that sell a product should be identified when the user requests the information.

- Design and develop a map that will help people travel in your area on unmarked back roads, on streets within the largest city in the area, or on highways that have many entrance and exit points over a relatively short distance.

INTEGRATED S/M/T ACTIVITIES

- Identify common articles that can be used to help you and other students become familiar with the metric system of measurement. Develop a display of the objects and the related measures they represent.

- Identify the units of measure that are used for the sensors that have been introduced in this chapter.

- Develop a display of the standards of measurement that have been adopted internationally.

- Identify the levels of measurement—nominal, ordinal, and interval—as they apply to your classmates, the products you buy, or the project you are currently planning or implementing.

- The most common temperature scales we use are centigrade (C) and Fahrenheit (F). The zero point on these two scales is different and temperatures can fall below zero. The Kelvin (K) scale is based on absolute zero. Theoretically, temperatures below zero on this scale are impossible. Identify which levels of measurement (nominal, ordinal, interval, or ratio) are possible for each temperature scale, and describe why.

SENSOR AND TRANSDUCER CHART

Energy Forms — (Inputs)						
Chemical	Heat	Mechanical	Sound	Electrical	Light	Outputs
						Electrical
						(others)

CHAPTER 8: Humans as Designers and Consumers

DESIGNING FOR HUMANS

When designing a technological product, environment, or system for a human, it is useful to compare the body with a machine and its parts. The human structure and cover system includes our skeleton and skin. The skeleton forms a framework of bones which supports your body. Some parts of the skeleton, such as the skull and ribs, play both a support and cover function. The bones in your arms and legs act as levers that are moved by pulling muscles. Your skeleton provides a frame capable of being loaded with well over a ton of weight. The major part of the human's cover system is the skin, which provides a protective covering to keep out harmful germs and dirt, keeps itself moist and stretches as you move, repairs itself, keeps the temperature of your body within safe limits, and is waterproof.

The human energy transmission system includes our muscles, tendons, and cartilage. Since the human is self-propelled, the digestive system provides an inboard power plant to change food to energy and replacement materials. The muscles are attached to the bones by tendons and are controlled by nerves. Some muscles are much more powerful than others. The joints move only back and forth as a regular hinge and others move as a ball and socket hinge. They provide their own lubrication.

The human guidance and control subsystem includes the nervous system and all of the senses—sight, sound, smell, taste, and touch. Some parts of the body work automatically; other parts of our body require conscious guidance and control.

It is important to gather and use information about the user and the setting in which the product will be used. This includes the size, movement, reach, and strength. The human body has a tolerance limit. Beyond this limit, great discomfort, physical harm, and even death takes place.

Patterns of growth and development also influence a person's vulnerability and strength. Products and designs for people at different stages of growth need to consider the expected changes that will occur. Ergonomic calculations are needed for several stages if the product is to be used by people of all ages.

DESIGN AND TECHNOLOGY ACTIVITIES

Through the following activities, you will explore some of the essential aspects of humans as related to the process of design and development. Initial activities will help you understand the major ergonomic dimension of humans and some applications to the design of products, systems, and environments for human use. Additional activities will focus on human growth and development, humans as material, energy, and information users, humans as learners, and humans as decision makers.

DESIGN ACTIVITIES—COLLECTING ERGONOMIC DATA

With a partner, and using the tools and devices provided by your team, measure and record the ergonomic dimensions on the appropriate form that follows. After you have completed the measurements, compile this data in chart form and add your numbers to those of your entire class. Check with your teacher to see if information has been collected on other classes or from other schools. If so, compile and analyze this larger data set to determine the average (50th percentile) of the different measurements. Determine the measurements of the 95th percentile and the 5th percentile of student size.

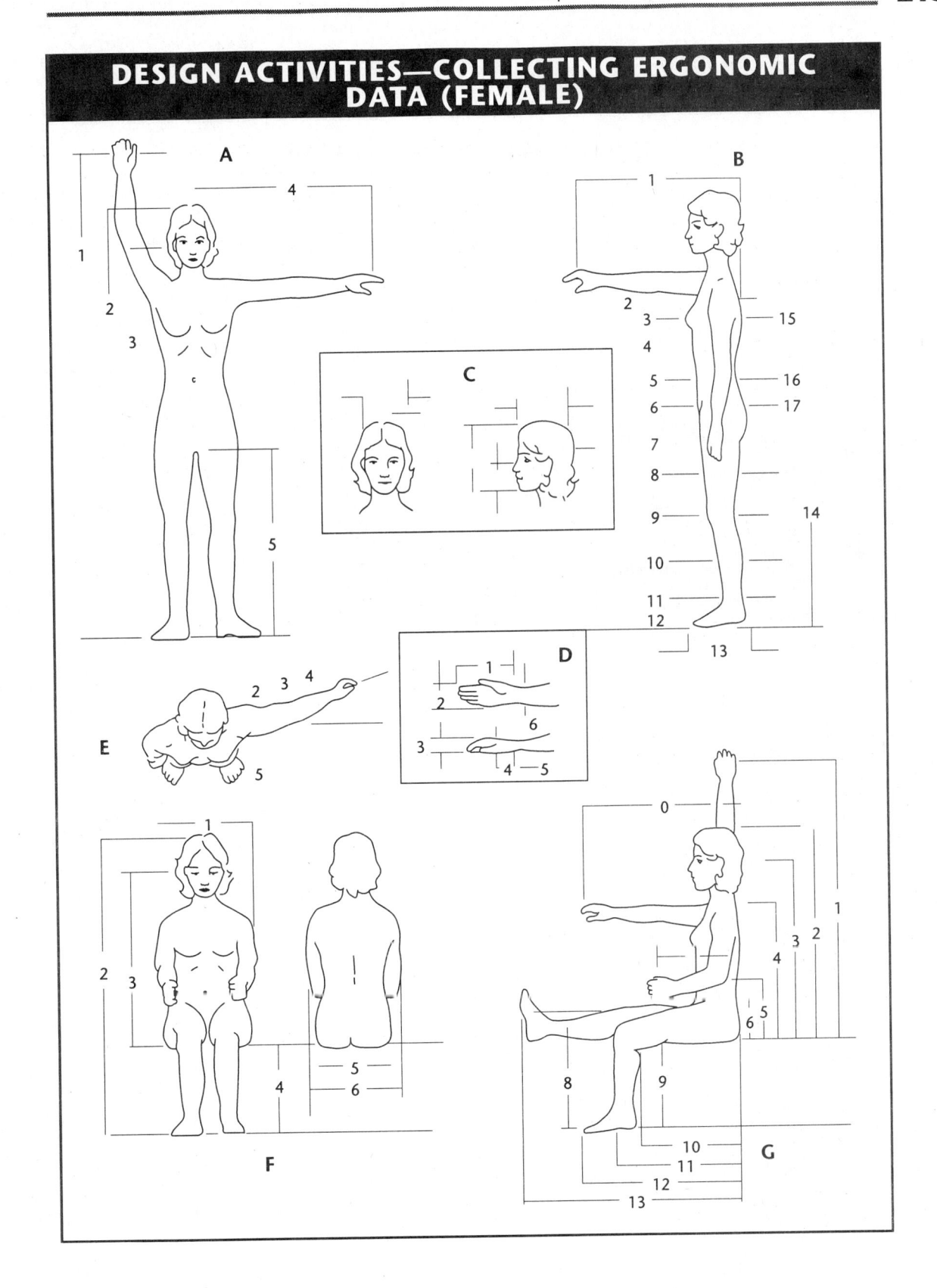

Chapter 8 Humans as Designers and Consumers **215**

DESIGN ACTIVITIES—COLLECTING ERGONOMIC DATA (FEMALE)

DESIGN ACTIVITIES—COLLECTING ERGONOMIC DATA (FEMALE) CONTINUED

FEMALE HUMAN BODY DIMENSIONS FORM

	Dimensional Element	Dimension (in inches except where noted)			
		5th Percentile	95th Percentile	Yours	Class Average
	Weight	102 lb.	150 lb.		
A	1 Vertical reach 2 Stature 3 Eye to floor 4 Side arm reach from CL to body 5 Crotch to floor	69.0 60.0 56.0 27.0 24.0	81.0 69.0 64.0 28.0 30.0		
B	1 Forward arm reach 2 Shoulder circumference 3 Chest circumference (bust) 4 Lower chest circumference 5 Waist circumference 6 Hip circumference 7 Upper thigh circumference 8 Thigh circumference 9 Knee circumference 10 Calf circumference 11 Ankle minimum circumference 12 Ankle circumference 13 Foot length 14 Elbow floor	24.0 * 30.0 * 23.6 33.0 * 19.0 * 11.7 * 7.8 8.7 34.0	35.0 * 37.0 * 28.7 40.0 * 24.0 * 15.0 * 9.3 10.2 46.0		
C	1 Head width 2 Interpupillary distance 3 Head length 4 Head height 5 Chin to eye 6 Head circumference 7 Neck circumference	5.4 1.91 6.4 * * 20.04 *	6.1 2.94 7.3 9.0 4.25 22.7 *		
D	1 Head length 2 Hand width 3 Hand thickness 4 Hand circumference 5 Fist circumference 6 Wrist circumference	6.2 3.2 0.84 * 9.1 5.5	7.3 4.0 1.14 * 10.7 6.9		
E	1 Arm swing, aft 2 Upper Arm circumference 3 Elbow circumference 4 Forearm circumference 5 Foot width	40 degrees * * * 3.2	40 degrees * * * 3.9		
F	1 Shoulder width 2 Sitting height to floor (std chair) 3 Eye to floor (std chair) 4 Standard chair 5 Hip breadth 6 Width between elbows	13.0 45.0 41.0 18.0 12.5 11.0	19.0 55.0 51.0 18.0 15.4 23.0		
G	0 Arm reach (finger grasp) 1 Vertical reach 2 Head to seat 3 Eye to seat 4 Shoulder to seat 5 Elbow rest 6 Thigh clearance 7 Forearm length 8 Knee clearance to floor 9 Lower leg height 10 Seat length 11 Buttock-knee length 12 Buttock-toe clearance 13 Buttock-foot length	22.0 39.0 27.0 25.0 18.0 4.0 3.5 14.0 17.0 13.5 13.0 18.0 27.0 34.0	33.0 50.0 38.0 32.0 25.0 12.0 6.0 18.0 22.0 18.8 23.0 27.0 37.0 49.0		

Note: Except on critical dimensions round measurements off to nearest inch.

* STANDARDIZED DATA NOT AVAILABLE

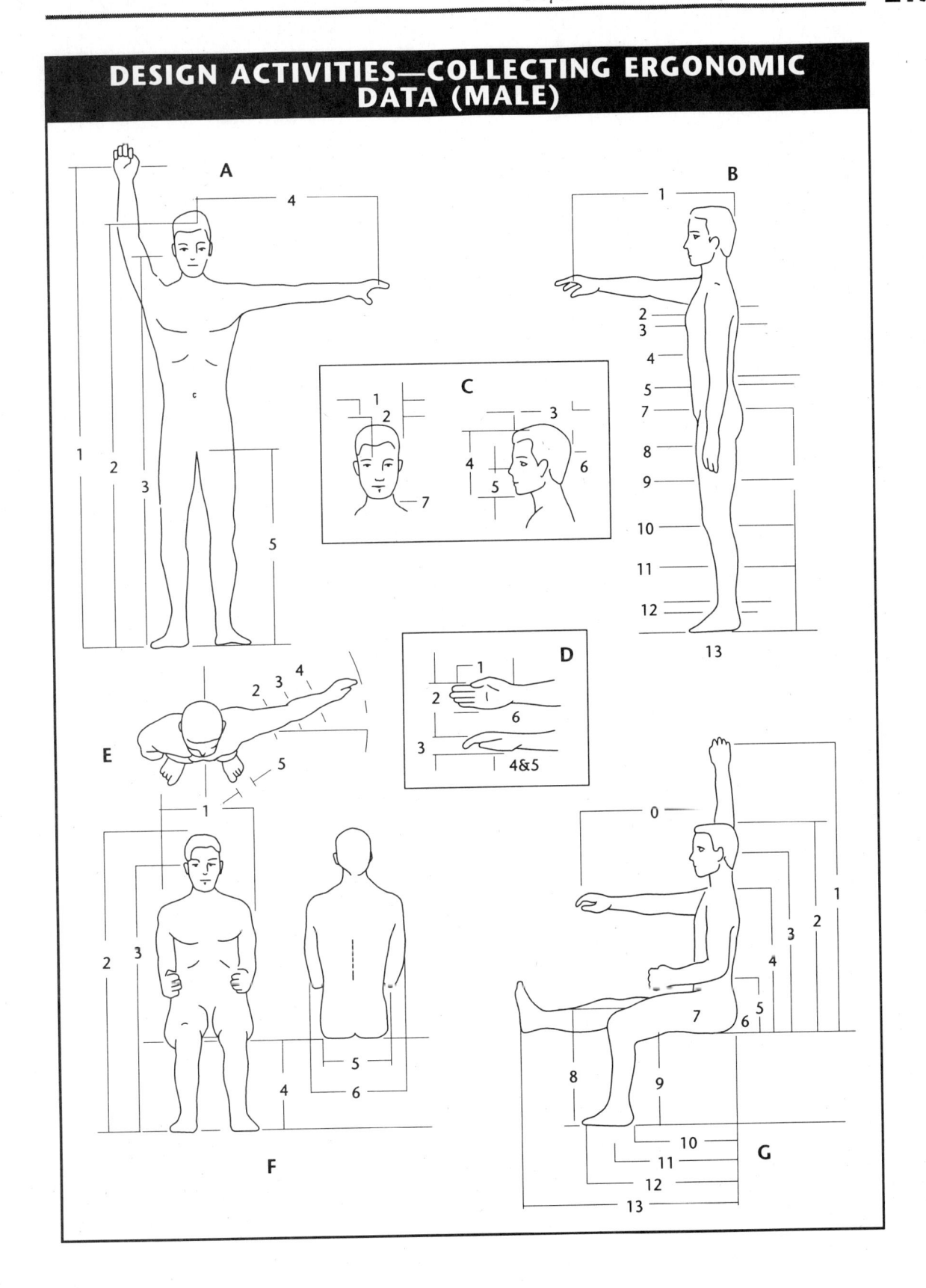

Chapter 8 Humans as Designers and Consumers **217**

DESIGN ACTIVITIES—COLLECTING ERGONOMIC DATA (MALE)

DESIGN ACTIVITIES—COLLECTING ERGONOMIC DATA (MALE) CONTINUED

MALE HUMAN BODY DIMENSIONS FORM

	Dimensional Element	Dimension (in inches except where noted)			
		5th Percentile	95th Percentile	Yours	Class Average
	Weight	132 lb.	201 lb.		
A	1 Vertical reach 2 Stature 3 Eye to floor 4 Side arm reach from CL to body 5 Crotch to floor	77.0 65.0 61.0 20.0 30.0	89.0 73.0 69.0 34.0 36.0		
B	1 Forward arm reach 2 Shoulder circumference 3 Chest circumference 4 Lower chest circumference 5 Waist circumference 6 Hip circumference 7 Upper thigh circumference 8 Thigh circumference 9 Knee circumference 10 Calf circumference 11 Ankle minimum circumference 12 Ankle circumference 13 Foot length 14 Elbow floor	28.0 * 35.0 * 28.0 34.0 * 20.0 * 13.0 * 8.0 9.8 41.0	37.0 * 43.0 * 38.0 42.0 * 25.0 * 16.0 * 10.0 11.3 46.0		
C	1 Head width 2 Interpupillary distance 3 Head length 4 Head height 5 Chin to eye 6 Head circumference 7 Neck circumference	5.7 2.27 7.3 * * 21.5 *	6.4 2.74 8.2 10.2 5.0 23.5 *		
D	1 Head length 2 Hand width 3 Hand thickness 4 Hand circumference 5 Fist circumference 6 Wrist circumference	6.9 3.7 1.05 * 10.7 6.3	8.0 4.4 1.28 * 12.4 7.5		
E	1 Arm swing, aft 2 Upper Arm circumference 3 Elbow circumference 4 Forearm circumference 5 Foot width	40 degrees * * * 3.52	40 degrees * * * 4.0		
F	1 Shoulder width 2 Sitting height to floor (std chair) 3 Eye to floor (std chair) 4 Standard chair 5 Hip breadth 6 Width between elbows	17.0 52.0 47.4 18.0 13.0 15.0	19.0 56.0 51.5 18.0 15.0 20.0		
G	0 Arm reach (finger grasp) 1 Vertical reach 2 Head to seat 3 Eye to seat 4 Shoulder to seat 5 Elbow rest 6 Thigh clearance 7 Forearm length 8 Knee clearance to floor 9 Lower leg height 10 Seat length 11 Buttock-knee length 12 Buttock-toe clearance 13 Buttock-foot length	30.0 45.0 33.8 29.4 21.0 7.0 4.8 14.6 20.0 15.7 14.8 21.9 32.0 39.0	35.0 53.0 38.0 33.5 25.0 11.0 6.5 16.2 23.0 18.2 21.5 36.7 37.0 46.0		

Note: Except on critical dimensions round measurements off to nearest inch.

* STANDARDIZED DATA NOT AVAILABLE

DESIGN ACTIVITIES—DEVELOPING ERGONOMIC MODELS

Some design projects—such as the design of playground equipment, the design of tools or toys, or the design of furniture—will involve the determination of appropriate size of the devices for the intended users. If your class decides to work on such a project for a kindergarten class or a sixth-grade class, you will need to acquire or access appropriate ergonomic data for children of these ages. You could repeat the process and make new ergonomic figures from these data, or you could turn to reference data on human dimensions, such as the *Measure of Man*, to create the new figures.

Your teacher will have the class work in three groups. One group will make models for their class, the second group will make models for the sixth-grade class, and the third will make models for the kindergarten class. Each group will form into three teams—one for the 95th percentile model, another for the 50th percentile, and a third for the 5th percentile. Use the appropriate data and draw to scale the parts of the ergonomic model, shown on the following page. With the materials provided by your teacher, develop and assemble the models.

DESIGN ACTIVITIES—CONSTRUCTING ERGONOMIC MODELS

On completion of this activity, you will have constructed a full-size and scale-size manikin of yourself and be able to (1) use the data from your charts of Body Dimensions to make a full-size and scale-size drawing of your body parts, (2) assemble the parts in working order, and (3) use the manikin-size sketches and full-size arrangements to help make simple design decisions.

1. Determine your height when sitting, dimension G-2 in the previous activity.

2. Get a square piece of cardboard 6" larger than this dimension. Be sure there are no creases in the piece of cardboard.

3. Mark a grid of 1" squares on the cardboard.

4. From the data recorded in the previous activity, make a tentative sketch of your body trunk, stopping at your chin.

5. Ask your teacher to check your sketch.

6. With permission from your teacher, have your teammate(s) sketch your silhouette as shown at right.

7. Transfer your silhouette to the cardboard by tracing on carbon paper, by making an indentation in the cardboard with a semi-sharp pencil, or by piercing the paper with a 4-penny nail.

8. Determine the length of your upper leg (dimension G-11 from your data charts), your lower leg (dimension G-8), upper arm (G-5 minus G-5), lower arm (G-7), foot length (B-13), and hand length (D-1).

9. Make a sketch of outline of your other manikin parts as shown on the next page. (Be sure to make 2 hands, legs, etc.)

10. Mark the holes and control grooves for the body parts included on the next page.

11. Carefully cut out all the parts.

12. Punch the holes for the joint pins.

13. Cut out the control grooves.

14. Assemble the manikin and test it for proper size and movement of parts.

15. Using the materials provided by the teacher, repeat steps 1-14 above to make two scale-model mannequins. One will be made to a scale of 1" = 4" and the other will be 1" = 8".

16. Using the support device provided by our teacher, place your full-size manikin in the operator's position at one of the machines.

17. Using one of your scale mannequins, sketch the machine in appropriate size on a sheet of drawing paper.

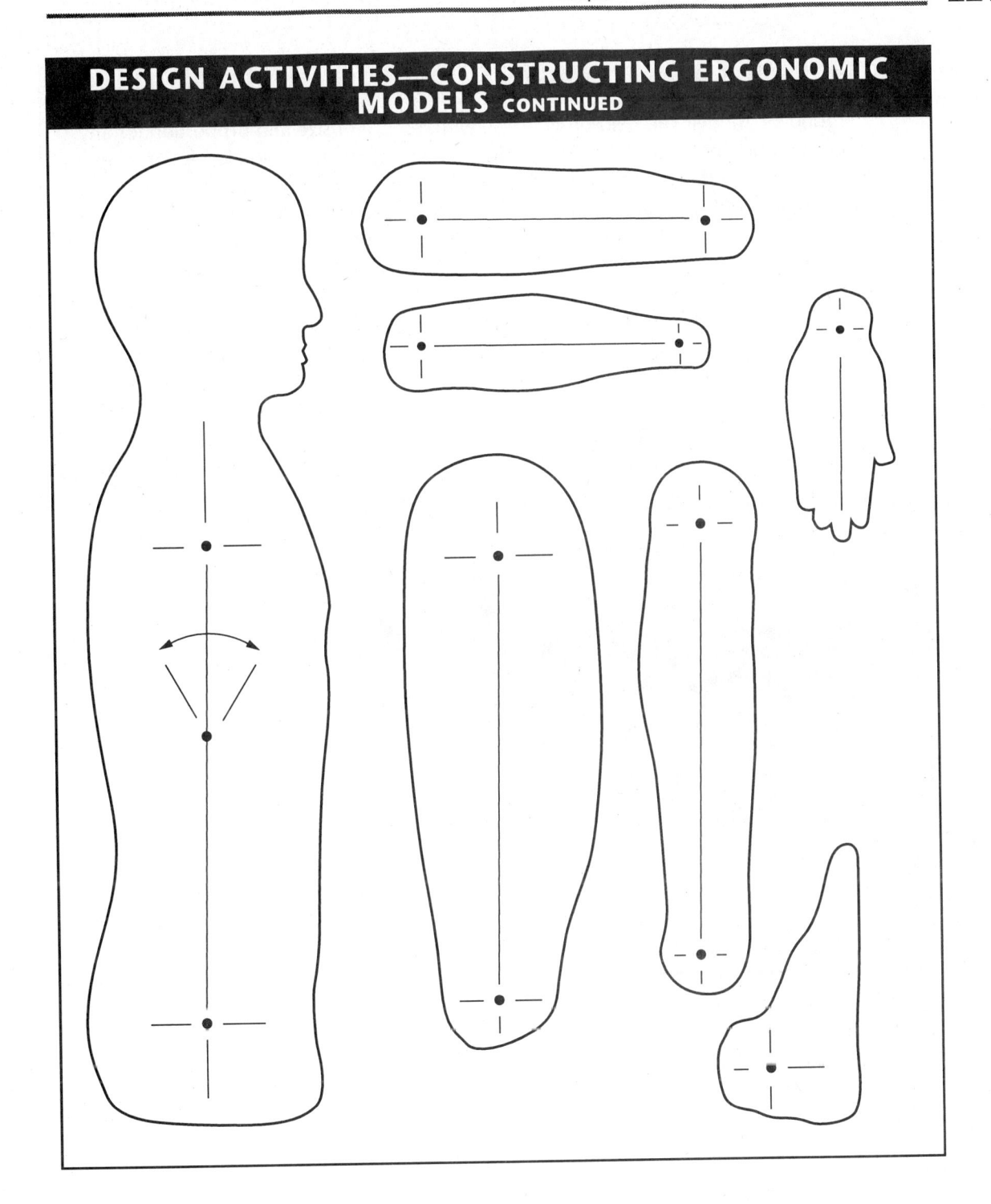

DESIGN ACTIVITIES—CONSTRUCTING ERGONOMIC MODELS CONTINUED

DESIGN ACTIVITIES—USING ERGONOMIC MODELS

The ergonomic models can help provide you with a sense of size and proportion for any object or product that you might develop for students of the three age levels. Develop a two-dimensional profile of a product or device, such as a bicycle or chair, that is to be used by students in kindergarten, sixth grade, or your own grade level. Attach the 2-D shape of the object to the gridded wall, as shown in the drawings below, and position your ergonomic models to determine if the products are of appropriate size and proportion for the intended users. Determine what changes will be necessary to improve the match of the products with the size of the students who will use those products.

HUMANS AND MATERIALS, ENERGY AND INFORMATION

Humans convert materials to products and resources such as other materials, tools, energy, and information. There is a continual exchange of materials between our bodies and the environment around us. Some organisms that come to live on and in us compete with our own cells for the nutrients we need. Understanding the needs and life cycles of these microscopic beings has led to new and better medicines to kill them or to resist their moving in. The human body's natural immune system protects us from some disease-causing organisms. Currently, the most effective protection from most diseases is the practice of everyday health habits.

Perhaps the most important material for human use is water, which is used for our own survival as well as for washing, cooking food, and many other uses. Ensuring the safety of water is a current, and very old concern.

Food is a form of material that we consume, burn, and store. Unused food is excreted as waste, along with the by-products of the food that is used. Currently, safety in food-handling is an important issue. Humans can satisfy their requirements for nutrients in many ways. Choice of the foods used to provide these nutrients and traditional ways of preparing, serving, and eating food varies greatly between cultures. The basic material requirements for food are the same, however.

A major activity of many people in developing nations is the production, storage, and preparation of food. This creates shifts in employment, and often the workers are growing food for export, rather than for their own use. The development of hybrid seeds and improved agricultural processes have increased the possibility of combating hunger in the world.

Materials are also used in clothing and other means of protecting the body. Clothing expresses many other aspects of the person and the social group and can be considered a synthetic skin. Many kinds of materials are used in shelters that protect us from outside forces, as well as to keep us warm or cool. We also use materials for adornment and self-expression, as well as destruction and waste.

Early technological activities were designed to replace human muscle power with other sources of energy. The early human was an essential part of the human/machine system and supplied the guidance and control, as well as energy. Energy is used to produce sound, to communicate thoughts and feelings, and to gain feedback from others and the environment.

The infinite complexity of the human's ability to receive, process, store, and retrieve information is unmatched by any other animal in the world. Many technological activities have been designed to correct for human tendencies in processing information.

Our senses gather information and our brain interprets it. In order to detect something, enough stimulation must be received. When too much stimulation occurs, the body acts to protect itself. The human brain seems to be programmed to process information in given ways. The brain seems to have cognitive templates that are used to screen and organize information. The information that is coming into the brain has to match our templates. If it does not, we will pay attention just long enough to make some adjustments. We delete and distort information—to fit what the brain expects to receive. If the experience will not fit the old pattern, then we have to change to learn. When there is not enough difference between the information coming in and what the brain expects, we generalize that there is nothing new. Learning, however, is a personal thing. And we approach a new situation with a preconceived notion of what we will find.

Information processing machines can be developed to correct for some of the prejudgments and expectations we bring. Technological devices and events have been developed to fill in these blanks and correct some of the distortions.

When we experience an event, the first level for processing information comes from the templates we have as human beings, as a species. The second level of filtering and organizing information is learned from our social groups and culture. The third is determined by our individual traits and experiences. After deleting, distorting, and generalizing at each level, we make sense out of the experience we have just had. The first screening comes through human sensory templates, the senses. The second filtering and organization is shaped by cultural expectations, especially those learned and remembered through language and labels. The next filtering comes through individual templates, including your own individual traits, past experiences, and interpretations. Even two humans from the same family, only a few years different in age, will disagree on what is "real."

DESIGN ACTIVITIES—IMPROVING THE QUALITY OF FOOD AND WATER

- Design a menu for an airline. Choose an airline and a route it flies on a regular basis. This menu should reflect the cultural preferences of the countries and regions to which the plane will fly. Be sure that the food is nutritionally sound, and aesthetically appealing in taste, temperature, texture, smell, color, and presentation to passengers. Consider factors of food availablity, food preparation, safety in handling, and cost. Consider also the changes that are to be expected in eating preferences of customers as well as the issues of serving a large number of people when working in such a confined space.

- Implement a plan for improving the safety of food that is served by the cafeteria/a local food truck/fast food restaurant/your own kitchen. Read food labels and identify the function of each ingredient. Research the function of additives and potential health risks for given people. Identify the most common illnesses caused by inadequate food-handling precautions. Obtain and analyze samples of foods under the microscope. Find out the FDA requirements and how food inspectors monitor food safety. Use the IDEATE model to develop and implement a plan that reflects your new understandings.

- UNICEF has chosen the availability of safe water as one of three focal points where they spend their resources dedicated to improving the lives of children throughout the world. Assess the safety of your own water supply. Compare this with the concerns in different parts of the world. Identify some of the technological proposals and current projects designed to increase the safety and availability of water in a given region.

DESIGN ACTIVITIES—CONDUCTING A SAFETY SURVEY

As a class, become a school safety consulting firm. Form groups to survey and assess safety aspects of areas of your school such as buildings, grounds, equipment, furniture, and the cafeteria. Identify potential hazards and unsafe practices. Design and make signs that use signals and symbols to communicate the potential hazards to the groups most likely to be affected. Take action to reduce the dangers, wherever possible. Talk with teachers, administrators, suppliers, and others who may need to change their products, delivery schedules, etc. Document your work and share it with other classes, the administrators, and other appropriate groups.

SAFETY ASSESSMENT FORM

As a class, become a school safety consulting firm. Form groups and choose one of the following to survey and assess.

Focus of Survey:

building _____ (which)   school grounds _____ (where)

equipment _____ (what)   furniture _____ (what)

traffic patterns _____ (where)   tools _____ (what)

traffic times _____ (when)   other _____ (identify)

NOTE: Describe any potential hazards and unsafe practices. Use descriptive terms and be very specific. Indicate the conditions under which you made the observations/assessments. Check your observations by making assessments more than once.

Source of Danger:

tools _____ materials _____

energy (its source) _____ (its use) _____

humans _____ use of space _____

Who Is Most Likely to be Affected:

students _____ children who might visit _____

elders who may use the facility _____ other people _____

the environment _____ other (identify) _____

DESIGN ACTIVITIES—DEVELOPING A SPECIAL NEEDS MENU

Create menus for two days for the following groups of people:

- nursery school (30 children-two groups of ten, ages 2-3, one group of ten, age 4-5, eight adults)

- elder day center (24 adults-three with diabetes, five with heart problems, 21 more than 70 years of age, three ages 35-55)

- sports team (18 high school football players in training camp, four coaches)

- weight reduction retreat (20 clients, ages 15-55, all with medical approval to enter the program, six workers for the retreat program)

First, develop daily plans for providing the basic nutrient needs for your group (use the food pyramid as your guide). Then identify the special needs of your group and modify the plan. Determine serving sizes. Calculate the nutritional components for each diet, using either a table showing the nutritional values of each food or a computer program designed for this analysis.

Calculate the costs for your menu. Survey two supermarkets for costs—one that is known to be expensive and one that is thought to be moderate in prices. Compare your work with that of other groups. Use feedback to modify your menu.

DESIGN ACTIVITIES—COMMUNICATING THROUGH CLOTHING

One way that people let others know about their values and attitudes is through the choice of nonverbal symbols, such as clothing, accessories, and other aspects of style and presentation of self.

In groups, choose one of the following messages a person might want to convey to others:

1. I am a down-to-earth, natural person who cares about the environment.
2. I want to impress others with my success, money, and fame.
3. I am interested in ideas and the life of the mind and do not care that much about how things look.
4. I am an active, energetic person who likes to move.
5. I want to belong and look like the in-crowd.
6. I don't want people to notice me; let me fit into the background.
7. I am just what you need as an employee. Hire me.

What are the values behind the message? What behaviors and objects reflect or symbolize these values?

- Design a complete outfit with accessories, hairstyle, cosmetics, etc.

Clothing Items

colors	line	textures/textiles
care and maintenance	source	cost

Accessory Items

colors	line	textures/textiles
care and maintenance	source	cost

Hairstyle   **Cosmetics**   **Other Symbols/Enhancements**

- Plan the total presentation.

- Draw the person in the outfit, find pictures in magazines to illustrate, or actually gather the items and have a fashion show or create an exhibit.

- In your design work, if you make a robot, ergonomic figure, etc., choose the message you want the character to represent. Decorate or dress the figure accordingly.

DESIGNING FOR HUMANS

Emotions are very important to our survival and learning. They supply motivation and the mental energy behind the decision to act or not to act. This is the "engine" that drives technological development. These emotions are only influenced, not determined, by what happens or the resources that a person has. Our beliefs, attitudes, and expectations filter perception of an event, and the labels and other symbols we use to categorize the experience are the major sources of the emotions we feel.

The choice of labels, colors, forms, shapes, and lines can be used to influence emotions and behaviors of others. Understanding more about a person increase the likelihood that the message you sent that will produce the result you want. Understanding yourself will help you resist the attempts of others to influence you in undesirable ways.

A strong emotion is an indication that what you perceive is not what you expected and the difference is very important to you. Taking the time to think about the ways you are processing information can help you respond to events in ways that are good for you in the long run.

Certain human needs are dominant at different ages. A person's experience in relationships with other people influences that person's chances for later development. The satisfaction of basic physical needs during the pregnancy, birth, and the first year of life influences a person's ability to trust others throughout life, as well as his/her chances for physical health and survival. People of all ages try to protect themselves when their survival is threatened.

Toddlers who have a sense of trust begin to explore their autonomy and test things out for themselves. Caretakers now must see to it that they are safe from dangers, poisons, and exposure to harmful materials and events. Even the most trusting and venturesome adults can be threatened, and safety becomes of primary concern.

The next level of development for trusting, confident preschoolers is to learn initiative by creating things and expressing ideas. The opinion of others is an important influence on the child who tries to gain approval for efforts.

Once a sense of physical well-being, safety, comfort, love, and belonging has been accomplished, people become more interested in achievement and using their unique abilities.

An emotionally healthy adult is motivated by higher-order concerns about more than themselves and the current time. People begin to strive for beauty, order, a sense of justice, and meaning. They have developed a strong sense of their own values and strive to share those values with other people. Achieving intimacy with others does not require that other people agree with them.

Once people are secure in having someone to share life with, they often become concerned about the well-being of all people and for the environment, both in the present and in the future. "Giving back" to future generations seems to be just and gives meaning to the person's own life. If people have reached middle and late adulthood with the previous needs satisfied to an adequate degree, they will be able to face their own mortality with a sense of pride in what they have done with their life. Their life has an integrity and seems to fit in the order of the cycle of life and death.

DESIGN ACTIVITIES—A NEW PRODUCT: COUSINS OF THE PET ROCK

- As a class, develop an idea for a product that is of little or no use to anyone.

- Form small groups to develop a marketing plan. Your teacher will assign your group one of the following stages of psychosocial development for your target customer:

    1. Learning to Trust—Basic Physical Needs
    2. Autonomy—Basic Need for Safety and Predictability
    3. Initiative—Social Need for Belonging
    4. Industry and Identity—Achievement
    5. Intimacy—Truth, Justice
    6. Generativity—Order and Beauty
    7. Integrity—Order and Beauty

- Research the characteristics of your target group of customers. Discuss and decide on the following:

    The expected age range _____ Customer's basic goals _____
    _____

    Customer is likely to work to get _____
    _____

    Customer is likely to work to avoid _____
    _____

- The product. (Remember that young children will have to convince their caretakers, who will probably be at a different developmental level.)
    _____
    _____

- Create the packaging of the product and the advertising campaign. Test out your plans with people from approximately the same target age groups.

- Compare your advertising campaigns with some of the ads you view every day on radio, TV, and other media.

INTEGRATED S/M/T ACTIVITIES

Select a different part of the world. In groups, do research about the lives of people your age in that region. Find out what technological products and activities are available to them. What types of tools, materials, energy sources, and information do they have access to? Write to a class or a pen pal, or communicate through e-mail. Find out as much as you can about what they like most and least to do, what their plans and hopes are, what their greatest concerns are and what they do for fun. Compare these findings with the answers your own classmates give to these questions.

DESIGN ACTIVITIES—EXTENDING HUMAN SENSES

For each of the following categories, identify three tools/devices/machines that have been produced to extend human senses:

Visual, to see:

tiny things

things far away

energy patterns

    heat

    sound

    movement

patterns

    slower

    faster

inside the body

around barriers

to correct for decreased function

to protect from too much stimulation and potential harm

other _____

other _____

Kinesthetic (haptic), to move:

in spite of physical barriers

with less potential harm

in hostile environments

inside the body

to correct for decreased function

to protect from too much stimulation and potential harm

other _____

    other _____

DESIGN ACTIVITIES—EXTENDING HUMAN SENSES CONTINUED

Auditory, to hear:
quiet sounds
low sounds
sounds from far away
things far away
inside the body
in spite of barriers
to correct for decreased function
to protect from too much stimulation and potential harm
other _____
other _____

Touch, to feel:
to correct for decreased function
to protect from too much stimulation and potential harm
to increase pleasure
to detect temperature
other _____
other _____

Olfactory, to smell:
to detect faint odors
to cover up unpleasant odors
to increase the amount
to decrease the amount
to protect from too much stimulation and potential harm
to form a more pleasant blend
other _____
other _____

Taste:
to form a more pleasant blend
to cover up unpleasant tastes
to detect small amounts
other _____
other _____

DESIGN ACTIVITIES—CONVERTING MATERIALS/INFORMATION/ENERGY FOR HUMAN USE

For each of the following categories, identify products that are designed to convert materials, information, and energy to enhance human survival, provide human needs, or satisfy wants:

Human survival and physical needs:

food

water

air

sleep

movement

elimination of wastes

temperature control

protection from disease

protection from injury

treat illnesses and injury

other _____

other _____

other _____

Satisfy wants:

increase stamina/strength

comfort

decrease amount of work

play

grasp

mobility

enhance memory

protection and security of resources

privacy

beauty

entertainment

justice and order

belonging

defy age

prolong life

enhance appearance

gain knowledge and explore

other _____

other _____

DESIGN ACTIVITIES—TECHNOLOGICAL PRODUCTS TO MEET HUMAN NEEDS AND WANTS

For each of the following products, identify a person who is likely to really want the product, and someone who is not likely to be interested. For the person who will be attracted to the product, identify whether the product is likely to be used to meet a need or a want. If you indicate a NEED, identify which developmental stage the person is likely to be trying to meet.

PRODUCT	WILL BE ATTRACTED	WON'T BE ATTRACTED	NEED/WANT
rollerblades			
electric fence			
gun			
teddy bear			
life insurance policy			
steak dinner			
running shoes			
encyclopedia			
bottle of milk			
designer outfit			
luxury car			
cosmetic surgery			
computer			
business suit			
collection of children's paintings			
diploma			
deed			
cardboard shelter			
plane ticket			
wrinkle cream			
wheelchair			
tennis racket			
skis			
latest stock market report			
alarm system			
other _____			
other _____			

INTEGRATED S/M/T ACTIVITIES—COGNITIVE TEMPLATES

What you are is what you perceive yourself to be.

A creature who is not familiar with humans as individuals, is making a visit to your home town. In groups, develop the messages you wish to convey that will help him/her understand you better. Discuss each of the following aspects:

- What is unique about being a human being? How does this influence how you perceive the universe and the ecology in which you, as a sample of humans, live?

- What is unique about your social climate and the culture in which you live? Identify the different types of groups that you, as a sample from your hometown, have experienced. What rules about human beings have you learned? Make as complete a list as you can of what people from your social group are expected to do and how you can predict they will behave. Contrast the subcultural groups that are represented in your town/city.

- As individuals, list the unique talents, interests, and capabilities that you each have. What do you want and work hardest to obtain? What do you want to avoid? Contrast this with younger people in your school, with the teachers, and with your grandparents or neighbors. List three major events that had an impact on who you are today.

- Develop an exhibit or display that illustrates a composite person from your class. Write out a script of what that person will communicate to the creature.

HUMANS AS DECISION MAKERS

With advances in communication and transportation, we have the ability to know what is happening in other parts of the world and even other parts of our universe. The importance of deciding on values, goals, and definitions of fairness are evident as we think of long-term consequences to our planet and all its people.

DESIGN ACTIVITIES—INVENTORY OF MATERIALS AND ENERGY USE

Keep a diary of all the materials and energy that you use in hour time segments at school, and at home before school, at home after school on a relatively typical day. Describe the activity. Then indicate whether the activity satisfed a need (N) or a want (W). List the materials used and then note whether they are natural (Na) or processed (P), from renewable (R) or nonrenewable sources (Nr). Identify the type of energy used, its source, and whether it is from renewable (R) or nonrenewable (Nr) sources.

ACTIVITY	N/W	MATERIALS	Na/P	R/Nr	ENERGY	R/Nr

CHAPTER 9
Time, Space, Capital, and Management

You can see the results of centuries of human design and problem-solving all around you. With any design and technology activity, people must decide (a) what they want/need; (b) the information, materials, tools, energy, and processes to use; (c) the time, space, and capital available; (d) the work to be done; and (e) how to tell if the results are satisfactory. In addition, management processes are needed for putting resources together in a way that achieves the desired outcomes.

TIME, PLACE, AND SPACE

Planning the use of time as a resource means deciding how to "spend" it to achieve our goals as efficiently as possible. Time is a resource that can be used and traded. When applied to time, the term entropy is used to discuss changes that occur over time. Systems tend to become disorganized, materials disintegrate, mistakes occur in reproducing the cells of living materials, and living organisms go through their expected life cycle. Humans try to slow down or stop some of this tendency toward disorganization and entropy. Management plans attempt to keep machines, systems, spaces, and groups of people functioning as originally intended. A good design accounts for maintenance and expected changes over the life span of the product. Plans to reclaim materials and recycle resources when products are no longer useful should be included in the original design.

In any technological event all processes require the resource of time. Often the process that takes the least amount of time, yet still achieves the desired outcome, is chosen. How people use their time depends on their own values and expectations. Some uses for time are already divided into fairly fixed, scheduled segments; others vary in the amount of time required. Some goals take many years of dedicated effort to achieve and are in sequential "layers" of accomplishments.

A sense of direction is based on our orientation to gravity and/or the center of the mass of whichever planet or spinning sphere we are on. People need a sense of living on a plane and an expected orientation in space. In addition, each of us wants some privacy, familiar space, and territory. Comfort is dependent on cultural and individual templates. A sense of crowding is also a matter of perception. The use of space can be planned to recognize these human needs and to achieve desired effects. Technological activities related to the use of space to provide shelter, security, belonging, and express personal preferences are numerous and often quite elaborate.

Societies differ greatly in their ideas about ownership and private vs. public property. In some social groups, complex documents for describing ownership have been developed.

In any technological event, there must be some space in which to conduct the activity. Once the sequence of steps is determined, the amount of space, the placement of tools and materials, and the amount of time needed for each step should be organized.

DESIGN ACTIVITIES—IMPROVING THE MANAGEMENT OF RESOURCES

There are two major components of a Total Quality Management (TQM) approach—philosophy and problem-solving/graphical techniques.

There are several common points in the operating philosophies of companies that are successful in using the TQM approach. They include the following:

- Improving quality by removing the cause of problems in the system inevitably leads to improved productivity.

- The person doing the job is most knowledgeable about the job.

- People want to be involved and do their jobs well.

- Every person wants to feel like a valued contributor.

- More can be accomplished by working together to improve the system than by having individual contributors working around the system.

- A structured problem-solving process using graphical techniques produces better solutions than an unstructured approach.

- Graphical problem-solving techniques let you know where you are, where the variations lie, the relative importance of problems to be solved, and whether the changes made have the desired impact.

- The adversarial relationship between labor and management is counterproductive and outmoded.

- Every organization has undiscovered "gems" waiting to be developed.

Problem-solving/graphical techniques fall into two major categories, as illustrated in the Venn diagram below. The techniques focus upon Problem Identification and Problem Analysis.

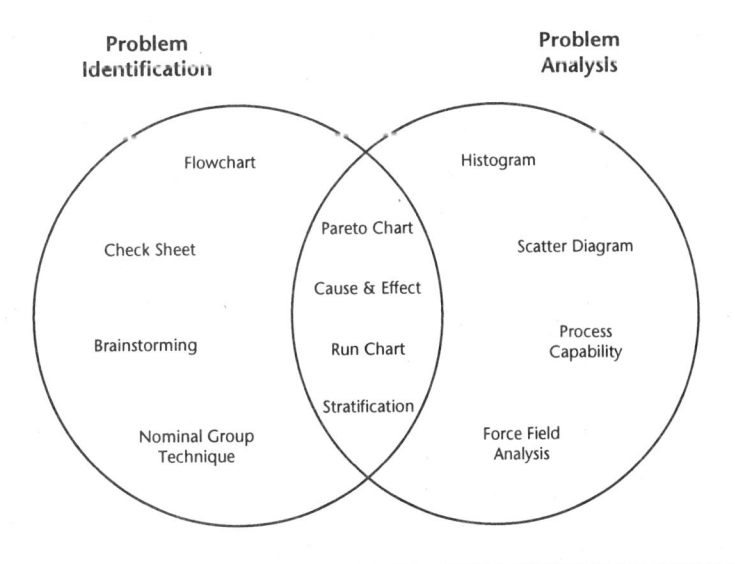

Problem Identification
- Flowchart
- Check Sheet
- Brainstorming
- Nominal Group Technique

Both (intersection)
- Pareto Chart
- Cause & Effect
- Run Chart
- Stratification

Problem Analysis
- Histogram
- Scatter Diagram
- Process Capability
- Force Field Analysis

DESIGN ACTIVITIES—IMPROVING THE MANAGEMENT OF RESOURCES CONTINUED

Below are examples of some of the problem-solving/graphical techniques that you will be able to use as you manage your own resources, or the resources of a group involved in a design project. Several of the techniques have already been introduced; others are introduced later in your textbook and activities.

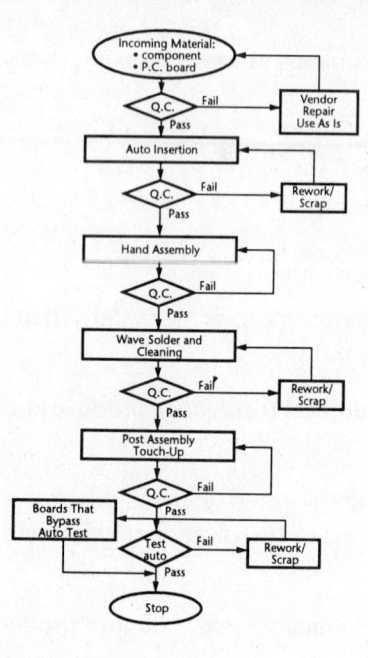

Flow Chart
A flow chart is a pictorial representation all the steps of a process. Flowcharting uses easily recognizable symbols to represent the type of processing being performed.

Check Sheet
Check sheets are used to help determine how often certain events are happening. The check sheet should make clear the event to be observed, the data to be collected, the time period over which the data will be collected, and the means used to insure the data will be collected in a consistent and honest manner.

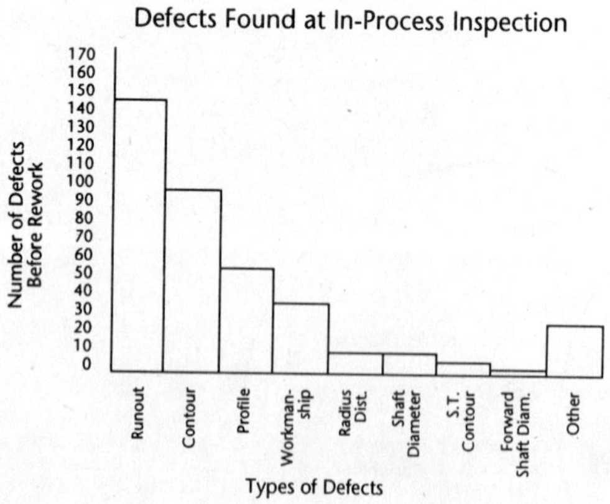

Pareto Chart
A Pareto chart is a special form of vertical bar graph that can help you determine which problems to solve and in what order they should be solved. The tallest bar is usually the most important problem to tackle.

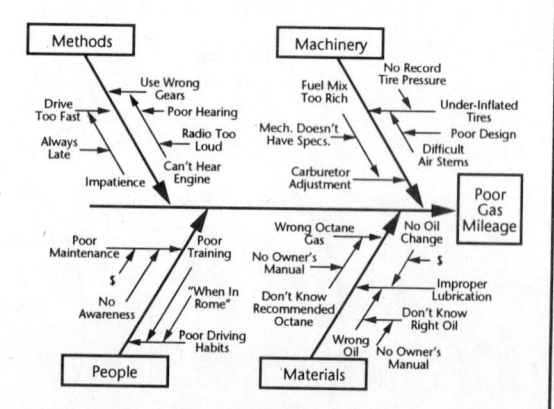

Cause & Effect Diagram—Daily Example
The Cause and Effect Diagram helps represent the relationship between some "effect" and all the possible "causes" influencing it. The effect or the problem is stated on the right side of the chart and the "causes" are listed on the left.

DESIGN ACTIVITIES—IMPROVING THE MANAGEMENT OF RESOURCES CONTINUED

Run Chart — Daily Example Family Expenditure/Month

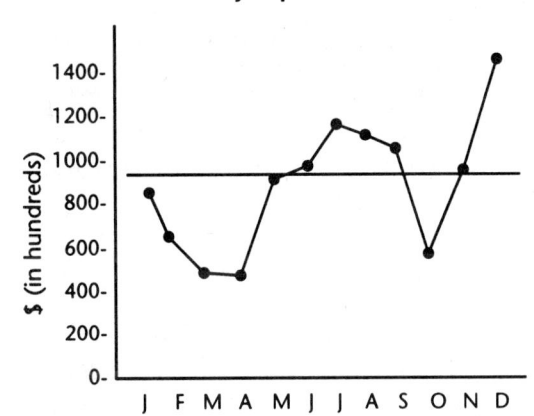

Histogram—Admin./Service Example Average Response Time To Patient Rings (1st Shift)

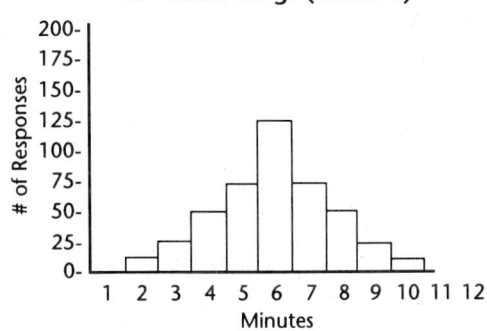

Run Chart
Run Charts are used to visually represent data. They are used to see whether or not the long range average is changing. Run charts are valuable to identify meaningful trends or shifts in the average—not based on chance.

Histogram
A Histogram is a vertical bar graph (like the Pareto chart) that takes measurement data (e.g., temperature, dimensions) and displays its distribution. Any repeated events will show results that vary over time. A Histogram helps reveal the amount of variation that a process has within it.

Height/Weight (100 Women)

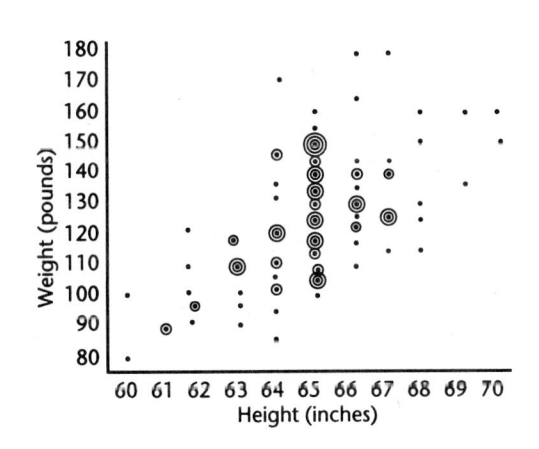

Operating Room Delays/Day

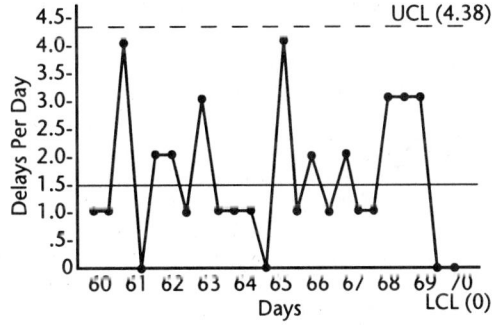

Scatter Diagram
A Scatter Diagram is used to study the possible relationship between one variable and another. The Diagram is to help test for possible "cause" and "effect" relationships. Remember, the Scatter Diagram does not prove if one variable causes another, but it can help to show if there is a relationship and how strong that relationship is.

Control Chart
A Control Chart is simply a run chart with statistically determined upper (Upper Control Limit) and possibly lower (Lower Control Limit) lines drawn on either side of the process average. It is important to note that, an "in control" process can produce "bad" as well as "good" products and services.

DESIGN ACTIVITIES—IMPROVING THE MANAGEMENT OF RESOURCES CONTINUED

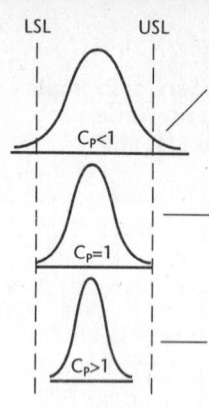

The process variation exceeds specification → defectives are being made.

The process is just meeting specifications. A minimum of .3% defective will be made, more if the process is not centered.

The process variation is less than specification; however, defectives might be made if the process is not centered on the target value.

Process Capability
Process capability helps achieve true improvement of a process by balancing the repeatability and consistency of the process with the capability of meeting the customer's requirements. By using Process Capability helps you control the variability of your process and place it within the specification limits.

NOTE: C_P is a simple process capability index that relates the allowable spread of the specification limits and the actual variation of the process.
USL = Upper Specification limit.
LSL = Lower Specification limit.

Brainstorming
Brainstorming can help you expand your thinking to consider all (or at least more) of the dimensions of a problem or solution. Brainstorming can be structured (with every person in a group giving an idea when it is their turn), or unstructured (with group members giving ideas as they come to mind).

The generally accepted guidelines for brainstorming are seen as the following:

- Never criticize ideas.
- Write each idea on a flip chart or blackboard.
- Write down the question or issue, so that everyone can agree on what the question or issue is.
- Record on the flip chart or board the words of the speaker; don't interrupt.
- Do it quickly; 5-15 minutes works well.

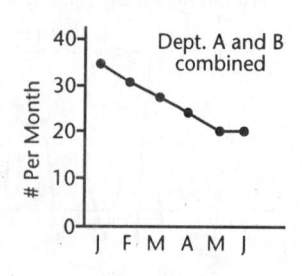

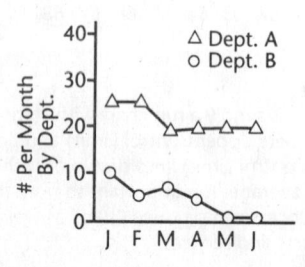

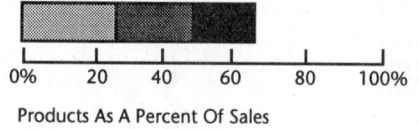

Stratification
Stratification is often very useful in analyzing data to find improvement opportunities. Stratification helps analyze cases in which data masks real facts, as in the above top example, which combines the number of minor injuries in two departments in a company. The second chart above bottom shows Dept. A to have more injuries than Dept. B.

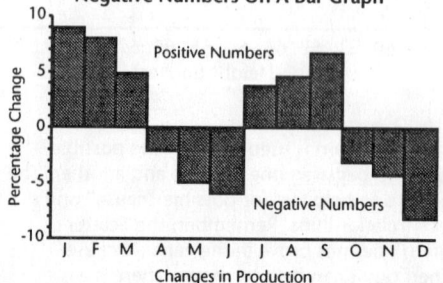

Charts/Graphs
Charts and graphs are used to improve the communication of problems, solutions and events to others. The choice of the specific approach to use often requires serious consideration of the data to be shared and the audience who needs to understand the data.

DESIGN ACTIVITIES—MANAGING CONFLICT

Every group of two or more people can expect to have conflict. Some ways of communicating tend to hurt the group's morale and ability to work together; other ways help them come to a solution that will increase the group's ability to get along and work together. The following is a list of rules for fair fighting and conflict resolution drawn from the work of the psychologist George Bach.

1. Be specific when you introduce a complaint. Accept that your own ideas and emotions are valid for you, but often are not the same as other's.
2. Don't just ventilate your feelings and gripes. Ask for a specific, feasible change that might produce an improvement.
3. Ask others for their viewpoint about your request.
4. Confine yourself to one issue at a time.
5. Do not be glib or intolerant. All viewpoints are valid for the person who owns and reports them.
6. Always consider a compromise.
7. Do not consider counterdemands until each point is resolved or until you mutually decide to table a point for later discussion, so that you can go on to another point.
8. Do not assume or try to read another's mind. Ask. Accept the other person's report of their feelings and ideas as valid for them.
9. Avoid labeling and sarcasm.
10. Confine the discussion to now and the future. Only bring up the past if you all agree that you can learn from it.
11. If there is a list of grievances, make a schedule of appointments to go over each one, one at a time.
12. Take time to think. It is better to table an issue and avoid snap judgments, than to have to redo faulty decisions.
13. Keep your eyes on the common goals of the whole group.

In groups, choose a setting in which conflicts often arise: workplace, school, neighborhood, home, classroom, with your friends. Choose two common issues that people in that setting argue about. From this list and from your research on mediation of conflict, create a script of helpful and hurtful things to say when dealing with those conflicts. Create an illustrated display of your fights and negotiations, role-play, and/or use video examples.

DESIGN ACTIVITIES—MANAGING YOUR OWN TIME

Choose a day of the week and keep track of how you spend your time.

WEEKDAY _____

TIME	Activity (describe)	CATEGORY*	MEETS GOALS?	WAYS TO IMPROVE
A.M.				
12:00	_____	_____	_____	_____
12:30	_____	_____	_____	_____
1:00	_____	_____	_____	_____
1:30	_____	_____	_____	_____
2:00	_____	_____	_____	_____
2:30	_____	_____	_____	_____
3:00	_____	_____	_____	_____
3:30	_____	_____	_____	_____
4:00	_____	_____	_____	_____
4:30	_____	_____	_____	_____
5:00	_____	_____	_____	_____
5:30	_____	_____	_____	_____
6:00	_____	_____	_____	_____
6:30	_____	_____	_____	_____
7:00	_____	_____	_____	_____
7:30	_____	_____	_____	_____
8:00	_____	_____	_____	_____
8:30	_____	_____	_____	_____
9:00	_____	_____	_____	_____
9:30	_____	_____	_____	_____
10:00	_____	_____	_____	_____
10:30	_____	_____	_____	_____
11:00	_____	_____	_____	_____
11:30	_____	_____	_____	_____

DESIGN ACTIVITIES—MANAGING YOUR OWN TIME CONTINUED

TIME	Activity (describe)	CATEGORY*	MEETS GOALS?	WAYS TO IMPROVE
P.M.				
12:00	_____	_____	_____	_____
12:30	_____	_____	_____	_____
1:00	_____	_____	_____	_____
1:30	_____	_____	_____	_____
2:00	_____	_____	_____	_____
2:30	_____	_____	_____	_____
3:00	_____	_____	_____	_____
3:30	_____	_____	_____	_____
4:00	_____	_____	_____	_____
4:30	_____	_____	_____	_____
5:00	_____	_____	_____	_____
5:30	_____	_____	_____	_____
6:00	_____	_____	_____	_____
6:30	_____	_____	_____	_____
7:00	_____	_____	_____	_____
7:30	_____	_____	_____	_____
8:00	_____	_____	_____	_____
8:30	_____	_____	_____	_____
9:00	_____	_____	_____	_____
9:30	_____	_____	_____	_____
10:00	_____	_____	_____	_____
10:30	_____	_____	_____	_____
11:00	_____	_____	_____	_____
11:30	_____	_____	_____	_____

*CATEGORIES (put the letter in the column that indicates how time was used)
B—caring for basic needs   I—self-improvement   H—helping others
R—recreation and leisure   P—paid work   F—family work   O—other (explain)

** Place an "X" beside activities you see as using your time wisely, to reach your goals.

*** Check those that you would like to change.

DESIGN ACTIVITIES—MANAGING YOUR OWN TIME CONTINUED

Choose a weekend day and keep track of how your spend your time.

WEEKEND DAY _____

TIME	Activity (describe)	CATEGORY*	MEETS GOALS?	WAYS TO IMPROVE
A.M.				
12:00	_____	_____	_____	_____
12:30	_____	_____	_____	_____
1:00	_____	_____	_____	_____
1:30	_____	_____	_____	_____
2:00	_____	_____	_____	_____
2:30	_____	_____	_____	_____
3:00	_____	_____	_____	_____
3:30	_____	_____	_____	_____
4:00	_____	_____	_____	_____
4:30	_____	_____	_____	_____
5:00	_____	_____	_____	_____
5:30	_____	_____	_____	_____
6:00	_____	_____	_____	_____
6:30	_____	_____	_____	_____
7:00	_____	_____	_____	_____
7:30	_____	_____	_____	_____
8:00	_____	_____	_____	_____
8:30	_____	_____	_____	_____
9:00	_____	_____	_____	_____
9:30	_____	_____	_____	_____
10:00	_____	_____	_____	_____
10:30	_____	_____	_____	_____
11:00	_____	_____	_____	_____
11:30	_____	_____	_____	_____

DESIGN ACTIVITIES—MANAGING YOUR OWN TIME CONTINUED

TIME	Activity (describe)	CATEGORY*	MEETS GOALS?	WAYS TO IMPROVE
P.M.				
12:00				
12:30				
1:00				
1:30				
2:00				
2:30				
3:00				
3:30				
4:00				
4:30				
5:00				
5:30				
6:00				
6:30				
7:00				
7:30				
8:00				
8:30				
9:00				
9:30				
10:00				
10:30				
11:00				
11:30				

*CATEGORIES (put the letter in the column that indicates how time was used)
B—caring for basic needs I—self-improvement H—helping others
R—recreation and leisure P—paid work F—family work O—other (explain)

** Place an "X" beside activities you see as using your time wisely, to reach your goals.

*** Check those that you would like to change.

DESIGN ACTIVITIES—MANAGING YOUR OWN TIME CONTINUED

- Calculate the percentage of time that you spent in each of the categories of activity.
- Make a pie chart of your time management and use.
- Compile class data and make a pie chart of usage for the class.
- Compare the average for the class with your own use of time.
- Create a plan for making your use of time more closely match your goals.

Several examples of time management plans are provided on the following pages. These include a Gantt chart, a Program Evaluation and Review Technique (PERT) chart and a Critical Path Methods (CPM) chart. Use these as examples and apply the techniques to managing the time required to complete your work in the next design project/problem you undertake. (You will want to refer to the reference books at the end of this document to identify sources of additional information and help on these time management techniques and their use.)

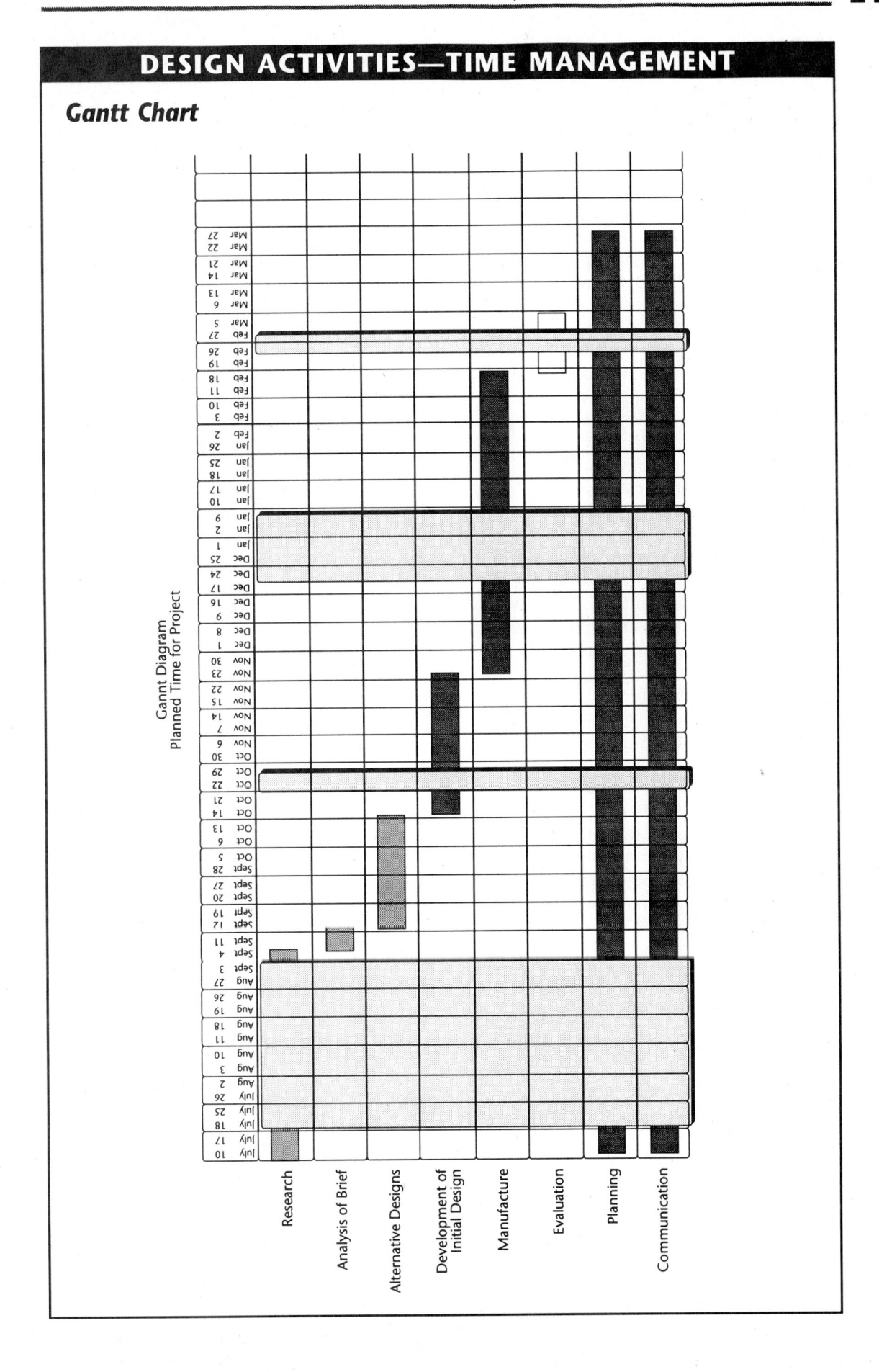

DESIGN ACTIVITIES—TIME MANAGEMENT

Gantt Chart

Gantt Diagram
Planned Time for Project

Activities:
- Research
- Analysis of Brief
- Alternative Designs
- Development of Initial Design
- Manufacture
- Evaluation
- Planning
- Communication

Time scale (weeks): July 10, July 17, July 18, July 25, July 26, Aug 2, Aug 3, Aug 10, Aug 11, Aug 18, Aug 19, Aug 26, Aug 27, Sept 3, Sept 4, Sept 11, Sept 17, Sept 19, Sept 20, Sept 27, Sept 28, Oct 5, Oct 6, Oct 13, Oct 14, Oct 21, Oct 22, Oct 29, Oct 30, Nov 6, Nov 7, Nov 14, Nov 15, Nov 22, Nov 23, Nov 30, Dec 1, Dec 8, Dec 9, Dec 16, Dec 17, Dec 24, Dec 25, Jan 1, Jan 2, Jan 9, Jan 10, Jan 17, Jan 18, Jan 25, Jan 26, Feb 2, Feb 3, Feb 10, Feb 11, Feb 18, Feb 19, Feb 26, Feb 27, Mar 5, Mar 6, Mar 13, Mar 14, Mar 21, Mar 22, Mar 27

DESIGN ACTIVITIES—TIME MANAGEMENT CONTINUED

PERT Chart (Program Evaluation and Review Technique)
1.0 Technology Education Program Development

1.1 Establish Program Objectives
    1.11 Establish selection criteria
    1.12 Identify objectives
        1.121 Analyze research data
        1.122 Determine need in field
        1.123 Analyze trends
    1.13 Organize objective
        1.131 Survey Advisory Group
    1.14 Justify objectives
        1.141 Apply criteria

1.2 Establish Data Bank
    1.21 Identify other similar technology programs
    1.22 Secure technology program objectives
    1.23 Secure technology program materials

1.3 Secure Consultants
    1.31 Identify interested people
    1.32 Screen individuals
    1.33 Select participants

1.4 Identify Supporting Materials and Media
    1.41 Identify grouping of objectives
    1.42 Identify potential materials

1.5 Match Available Materials and Specified Objectives
    1.51 Obtain available materials
    1.52 Analyze materials
    1.53 Identify objectives of materials
    1.54 Identify match of objectives
    1.55 Determine degree of match
    1.56 Modify materials to improve match
    1.57 Reject unsuitable materials

1.6 Identify Additional Needed Materials, Resources, and Equipment
    1.61 Identify unimplemented objectives
    1.62 Identify required curriculum units
    1.63 Specify required curriculum units
    1.64 Identify needed materials, resources and equipment

1.7 Revise Program, Resources, and Equipment
    1.71 Analyze feedback data
    1.72 Determine need for revision
        1.721 Revise appropriate courses
        1.722 Revise appropriate experiences
        1.723 Replace appropriate equipment

1.8 Formative Evaluation of Program and Procedures
    1.81 Implement assessment
    1.82 Introduce new feedback data to revision step

1.9 Summative Evaluation of Program and Procedures
    1.91 Establish evaluation procedures
    1.92 Conduct evaluation
    1.93 Collect evaluation data for final report

1.10 Install Program

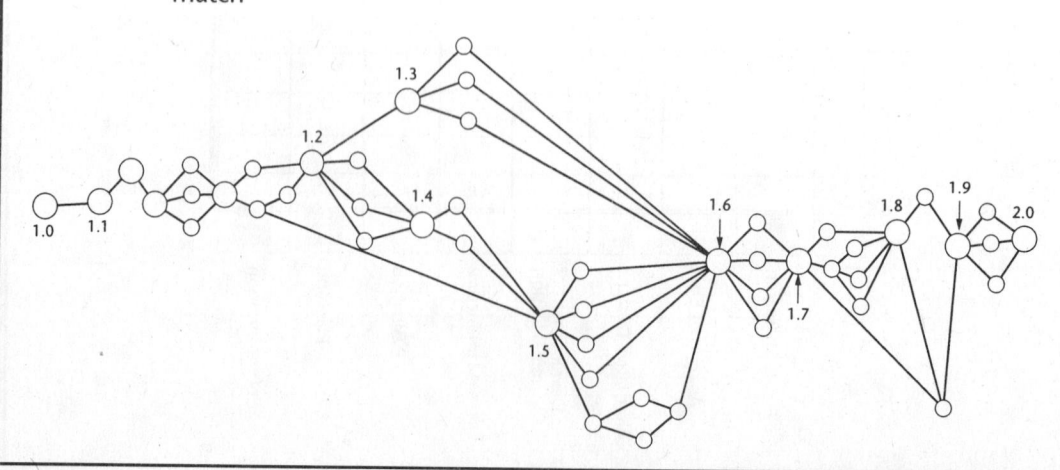

DESIGN ACTIVITIES—TIME MANAGEMENT CONTINUED

Critical Path Management (CPM)

To determine the "critical path", estimates of the time required for each activity must be made. Two estimates are usually made to determine the shortest and longest times. These can be used to determine the most likely time needed to complete a given activity or task. These times are recorded for each leg of the PERT chart and the longest set of branches is then identified. This is the "critical path" because any delay or extension of this path means the whole project will be delayed. Other paths will have more flexibility in terms of time to complete the activities. The critical path of the PERT chart is identified as a double (=======) line.

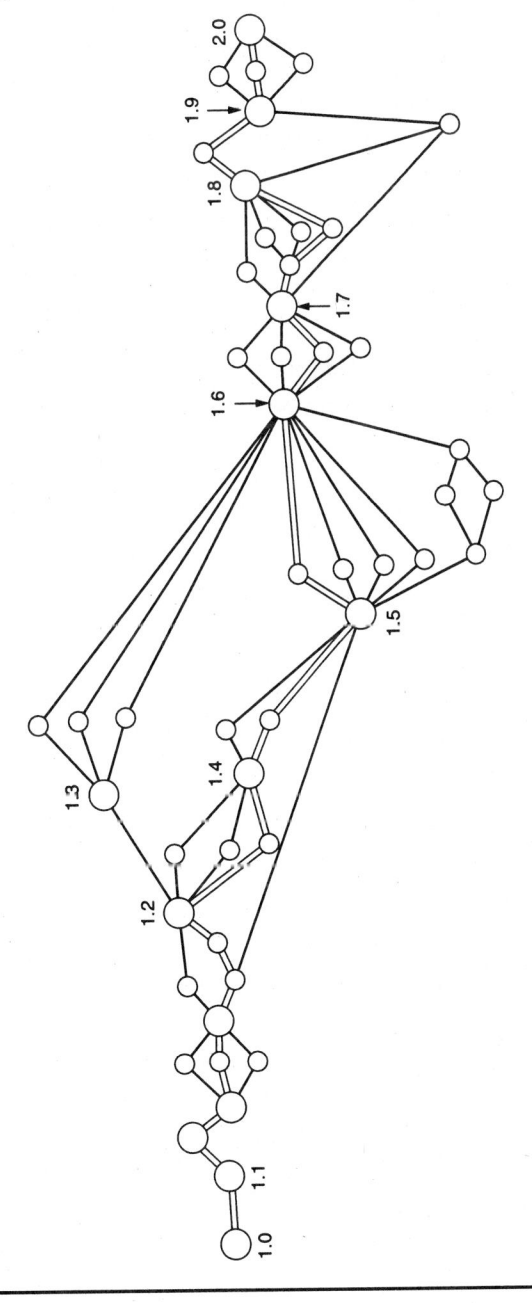

CAPITAL – HUMAN AND MONETARY

Resources that are scarce, transferable, measurable, and usable for production purposes have been called economic resources, also called capital. Resources consumed for purposes other than the production of goods and services are called noneconomic resources. The way in which decisions about capital are used varies from one culture to another. However, when an economic resource is in limited supply, the principle of "supply and demand" tends to govern the exchange. If the price gets high enough, people are willing to invest their resources to make the synthetic material or products.

The medium of exchange has changed over time, but the need to trade remains constant. People tend to specialize and develop skills, products, and resources in a few areas. This makes us dependent on each other for some of our wants and needs. Trade and exchange is necessary.

Most of the exchange of goods and services involves some kind of monetary resource. This is a symbol indicating that in the future, the money will be re-paid in some way. Even the most established monetary systems falls apart when the group no longer believes that the money is valuable. Even as economic capital is stored or used, it can grow or shrink as changes occur to supply, demand, and trust.

Today, credit cards, loans, and mortgages allow people to buy and use goods and services, even when they do not have the economic resources. Traditionally, wealth and capital consist of tangible items, such as gold, minerals and gems, land, raw materials, and an inventory of salable products. They are potential sources of income. Currently, a major form of wealth is in the form of information—records on a computer.

Another form of capital is human capital. People use their time, labor, and talents in exchange for monetary capital and goods. One form of human capital that does not usually result in monetary exchange is that used for family work. In the past, most of what a family needed was produced in the home. Now, many of the needed goods and services are purchased and a great deal of family work involves resource management and consumer decision making. Because family work does not involve a wage or monetary price, this resource is often overlooked when human capital is discussed. Yet more that one-half of the labor that is done in a society is personal and family work.

An investment in human capital often means that people spend time and other resources to improve their ability to work for pay, or to improve the quality of their performance. If there are many people who can do the same job, the amount they can charge for their labor will be low. The opposite is also true.

Most technological endeavors are accomplished by a group of people who contribute different types and amounts of capital. When there is a profit, there is often tension about what the contributions are worth and how the profit should be divided. These are all resource management decisions.

When there are many people to provide labor, few resources are spent on machines and the jobs are labor intensive. When very few people want to or are available to do physical labor, technological endeavors are likely to use machines and energy sources other than human muscle. These enterprises are called capital intensive. In both of the circumstances, there are some jobs in which there is no substitute for the human worker and other jobs that no one wants to do. As more and more work is done by machines, people must invest more in their human capital, learning new skills and adapting to changes.

People who provide the capital and those who have developed their intellectual and social skills tend to receive more monetary reward than do people who provide physical labor. On the same note, those who provide personal service often get paid less than people who do not actually see the client, but manage the workers and the organization.

DESIGN ACTIVITIES—CLASS "CLONE"

A biotechnologist has been commissioned to make a clone that represents the best traits and skills of you and your classmates. She wants to put information in her database.

- Talk to your school counselor about interest inventories, aptitude tests, and other instruments that are available for measuring traits, skills, and interests. List some of them and the types of scores they produce.

- Talk to a personnel director of a local company to find out how they assess applicants for jobs and for promotion in their company.

- Decide on the list of attributes that reflects the characteristics of the class. (Actually compile the data from various tests on class members, if you like.)

- Using your ergonomic figures from previous design briefs, decorate and/or dress the figure to reflect some of these traits.

- Write a marketing statement that will encourage an employer to hire your clone.

DESIGN ACTIVITIES—FAMILY WORK: TASKS FOR MANAGING A HOME

On the chart below, identify who does each of these tasks in your home. (See your text for the job description.) If your family hires the services of others to do the task, list the person who manages the job (finds help, pays for it, and monitors how well the job is done). Then find out how much each of the services would cost if you hired someone to do it at the going price in your community.

TASK	WHO DOES IT	WHO MANAGES IT	COST OF HELP
Buyer			
Health-Care Provider			
Tutor			
Manager			
Tailor			
Laundry Worker			
Driver			
Gardener			
Counselor			
Maintenance Worker			
Cleaner			
Cook/Caterer			
Waiter			
Errand Runner			
Accountant			
Interior Decorator			
Social Worker			
Dietitian			
Social Secretary			
Caregiver			

INTEGRATED S/M/T ACTIVITIES

- Calculate the income of each person who does family work, based on the approximate number of hours per week they use for family work, and the prevailing wage for such services in your community.

- In some countries of the world, each person is given a stipend (wage) based on their productivity or contribution to the economy. Household labor is not included, although it represents more that 40 percent of the labor in most societies. What would be the wage of a mother of young children in such a society?

- You have been asked to give expert testimony on behalf of a man who is suing the company whose negligence led to the permanent disability of his wife, the mother of two young children, ages 5 and 7. The company is willing to pay for lost salary. However, your job is to estimate the dollar amount of compensation for the loss of her contribution to family work each year. Use the information from your class analysis of family work as your starting point.

DESIGN ACTIVITIES—TIPS FOR MANAGEMENT OF COMPLEX JOBS

Use the following list of tips to manage the resources you need as you decorate for the prom/prepare a meal/produce a product from a design brief.

Management Tips	Proposed Actions
• Place equipment and materials so that they are easy to reach as you do the job. Sketch out the placement of all materials.	
• Plan the arrangement so that energy is used efficiently. Identify how the worker's body will be expected to move as the task is done.	
• Vary the parts of the worker's body that are stressed by the way you sequence the jobs. (Follow a job that requires lifting and moving with one that can be done while seated.)	
• Tasks that require little attention can be dovetailed with those that are more engaging, but that will tolerate interruptions. (Doing the laundry and your homework at the same time, for example.)	
• Jobs that can be expected to be distasteful or boring can be placed before a job that you do like. (Also, try to identify why you dislike the job and see if there is something that can be done about that.)	
• Schedule jobs that require skill and concentration and those in which mistakes will be costly at the time when you are most alert and full of energy.	
• Choose the day of the week that is likely to be matched to the requirements of the task. (Some jobs are best scheduled on Tuesday, rather than just after a weekend. Friday afternoon may not be a good time to start something new or to start an intricate project.)	
• Plan breaks and changes from a task that requires concentration to one that is less demanding.	

DESIGN ACTIVITIES—THE COST OF MONEY

Divide your class into groups to gather data from the following:

Three different banks

	1	2	3
types of accounts and restrictions			
savings interest			
cost of checks			
monthly fees			
interest on unsecured loans			
mortgage interest			
secured loans (what security is needed)			
safety-deposit box fee			
other fees and charges			
services provided			

Three different credit cards

	1	2	3
monthly or yearly charges			
interest rate per month			
actual interest rate per year			
penalty charges			
other fees and charges			
payment schedule			
closing date			
any special benefits			

ATM cards

	1	2	3
charges for cash			
charges for use with purchases			
advantages/disadvantages over credit cards			

MANAGEMENT OF RESOURCES

Managing money can help to ensure that your money "works" for you. The first step in the management of any resource is trying to figure out what is important, both for now and in the future. Some goals can only be accomplished over time, with the cooperation of others. The design and problem solving model learned in Chapter 1 can be used to improve the use of time, money, space, and human capital.

Some techniques of management can help people as they organize their work. Each separate job that must be done can be examined to determine the required amount of attention to safety, the importance of a high-quality outcome, the amount of skill required, the cost of mistakes, and other aspects of the process. The next step is to organize the jobs so that time, energy, and other resources are used most efficiently.

People have always had to work together in order to accomplish most of their goals. Therefore, how to gain the interest, motivation, and cooperation from groups of people are issues of management. Focusing on common goals, obtaining the best efforts from each individual, and issues of leadership and relationships between coworkers are major management decisions. Insights you have learned in living and working with others can help you understand organizations, even those as large as a major corporation or government.

Power, in terms of humans and group relationships, is the ability to influence the behavior of others. There are five basic types of power that can be used in managing group relationships: reward, punishment, referent, legitimate, and expert. Even in a group as small as two people, you can expect to have disagreement and conflict. How the issues are resolved determines the long-term health of the group process.

People who have the ability to give out rewards and punishments are able to influence others to act in the way they want. The kinds of rewards people work for differ according to their stages of life and whether their needs have been adequately satisfied previously.

Referent power comes not from who you are or what you can do, but from who you know. Expert power refers to the ability to influence someone based on the expert's knowledge and skills. Legitimate power is given to someone because of their role or the title of their position. This form of power works best when that person also has the expertise and skills that are expected to come with the role.

When people work together, a leader is usually needed, whether an informal or a formal one. In order to lead a group or organization, three types of skills are required: technical, human, and conceptual. Technical skills are those needed to do the actual task or make the product. Human skills involve communicating and motivating people to work together. Conceptual skills involve recognizing the bigger picture of the task, the people involved, and the organization. This includes the organization in relationship to others in society and trends and changes that can be expected to influence the functioning of the organization over time.

Technical skills are most evident in the leadership of the people who actually produce the outcome. Conceptual skills are demanded of those who are at the top of the organizational structure. No matter where in the leadership structure a person works, however, the need for good human skills remains. The actual people and jobs may be different, but the need for interaction and communication skills remains constant.

Some organizations are developed on a hierarchy, with each level more and more specialized. An organization chart is needed to show who is in charge of each specialized subgroup and where each person is on the hierarchy. Another approach to management views information from all levels of the organization as important in achieving products of high quality. Teams are formed to contain workers from all stages of production and distribution of the final product. Although each worker's job is specialized, they can see the results of their labor in the final product and contribute their understandings to the decisions that are made for the company as a whole. These management groups are sometimes called quality circles.

Underlying the management structure is a theory about the nature of human beings and their motivation to work. Some groups reflect the idea that people are basically trustworthy and want to have meaningful work. Another, contradictory idea about human beings and why they work is that people are basically lazy and will work as little as possible.

The functioning of an organization or group can be assessed by checking in four areas. First, to what degree does the group recognize that people are individuals and have a desire for personal recognition and growth? Secondly, every group needs rules that provide the structure and security of knowing what is expected. Are rules enforced fairly and consistently to all workers in the group?

The third aspect of a well-functioning group has to do with communications. The rules discussed above are clearly stated, are available to all, and are directly applied. In order to utilize individual contributions and ideas, people are encouraged to communicate emotions, ideas, and suggestions freely. In large organizations, workers are often expected to follow a chain of command, reflected in the organizational chart. The last aspect of a well-functioning group is the ability to gather resources from outside the group, as appropriate. No organization functions well as a closed system.

Time, space, labor, and capital are interrelated resources involved in technological events. Trade-offs and decisions are required in order to use resources effectively. Criteria for desired outcomes for both now and the future must be considered.

The management of resources has gone through many changes. Although introduced more than 50 years ago, the acceptance in this country of the Total Quality Management (TQM) approach has taken place only recently—the last decade or so of the twentieth century. The development and growth of TQM worldwide was largely due to the work of W. Edwards Deming, a statistician by training, who fervently believed that all workers want to be contributing and productive members of a corporation. Many leaders and workers in companies around the world have improved their work lives and their companies' products and services by adopting the TQM philosophy, tools, and techniques.

DESIGN ACTIVITIES—PLANNING FOR PRODUCTION

Select a product that you or one of your classmates have developed in previous design work. Divide your class into groups and each select one of the following resources.

- Develop a plan for what you will need in order to create a plan for putting the item into production. Identify the component parts of the product, the steps in its assembly, and the presentation of the final product.

    Time

    Space

    Tools

    Materials

    Energy

    Information

    Labor

    Money

- Create a marketing plan and identify how much to charge for the product in order to make a profit.

DESIGN ACTIVITIES—PLANNING FOR PRODUCTION
CONTINUED

For the product identified on the previous page, develop the production plan further by completing the following:

- Make a Gantt chart or a PERT chart to show the necessary tasks, their sequencing, and the approximate times for starting and finishing each.

- Make a note of the critical times; i.e., the times by which certain tasks must be done without hurting the outcome of the entire job. Develop a CPM chart for the process.

- Make the list of costs of materials, tools, labor, and space, making the costs as accurate as possible, based on actual market research.

- Use the list of tips for doing a complex task to set up a production and assembly plan. Make a sketch of the use of space and time from the beginning to the final product.

- Repeat the process as you draw up plans for marketing the product.

- Interview a manager of a production operation. Ask that your plan be criticized and then improve it.

- Incorporate as a company. Create your logo. Choose the management team and set up the production.

- Create job descriptions and decide on salaries and work conditions for each employee. Advertise, interview, and hire all needed personnel.

- Once you have put your product into production, form two different teams. One team will contain members from all stages of production and marketing; the other will be a team of supervisors/managers only, with the president of your company as the chair.

- Prepare portfolio entries for each of the steps above.

DESIGN ACTIVITIES—ASSESSING YOUR HUMAN CAPITAL

Often it takes more than just brains, good looks, and talent to get a good job or succeed in a career. The following characteristics have been shown to be factors in whether a worker succeeds in getting and keeping a job, as well as in getting pay raises and promotions. Answer the questions to indicate the degree to which the statement is true for you.

	Always	Sometimes	Seldom	Never
1. I show up on time.				
2. Once I agree to a job, I do it.				
3. I can find something of interest in a new job.				
4. I dress neatly and appropriately for work.				
5. I am a good listener.				
6. I can tell how someone feels before they tell me.				
7. I can get my ideas across to others.				
8. I stick with something until I finish.				
9. I do the job that is expected of me, even when I would rather quit.				
10. People can count on me to live up to my word.				
11. I go beyond what is required to create a better outcome.				
12. I can lose myself in my work and forget other things.				
13. When I start something, I give it my all.				
14. I can understand directions easily.				
15. When something goes wrong, I think through how I could improve my performance next time.				
16. I am honest and do not waste other people's time and other resources.				
17. I think most people are trustworthy.				
18. I look on the bright side of events and issues.				
19. I like to work.				
20. I like people.				
21. Other				
22. Other				

DESIGN ACTIVITIES—DETERMINING YOUR NEED FOR MANAGEMENT SKILLS

Interview a manager of an agency, business, or other group. Obtain answers to the following questions, as well as your own list of questions:

1. Describe your career path that led you to your current position.

2. When you started out, what were some of the reasons you obtained your job?

3. What special skills were required for you to succeed then?

4. When you were promoted, why were you selected over other people who were eligible? (Ask about each promotion, if appropriate.)

5. What new skills did you have to learn to do the job at that level? Where did you learn them? Were there any special people who guided and supported you as you learned?

6. What are your future plans?

7. What will you need to learn to do a good job at that level? How will you go about getting the skills and understandings you need?

8. Describe an ideal manager.

9. I have read that human skills are important at all levels of management. Do you agree? Give me some examples of times when a manager failed because of the lack of human skills. Also tell me about some times when skills in working with people made a difference in the success of the group.

10. I have read that it becomes less important to have the actual skills to produce a product as you go up the management ladder. Do you agree? Describe some experiences you have had that led to this opinion.

11. In my class, I learned that people at the top levels of management need more conceptual skills—the ability to see the big picture of how the whole organization fits together and fits in with the rest of the society and economy. Do you know any poor bosses who do not have enough of this skill? Any good managers that do? Describe what you have experienced.

DESIGN ACTIVITIES—"SAVING LABOR"

Identify examples of labor-saving devices or tools for use in the home or in production in industry or business. In groups, select one area for study about the machine and its impact on labor.

agriculture

housekeeping

cleaning and maintenance

food preparation

printing

other

- Read about or talk with people who remember what it was like to do the job before the device was made.

  What changes occurred in the lives of the workers?

  What are the required abilities of the person who operates the device/machine? What, if any, changes have occurred in the requirements for the following:

  time

  space

  standards for work

  money

  human capital of the worker/operator

- Identify the costs in money and time:
  - to purchase
  - to store
  - to maintain
  - to repair

- What are the advantages and disadvantages of switching from the old way to the new way of doing the job?

- As a class, come up with a new and improved version of one of the labor-saving devices.

DESIGN ACTIVITIES—PREPARING TO FIND A JOB

- Look in the Help Wanted ads of your local paper. Identify job titles that seem interesting. Call the listing and ask for a job description. (Indicate that you are from a class and not actually applying for the job.)

- Talk with your guidance counselor at school about the career path and requisite training and experience that will be required.

- Also ask your guidance counselor about tests and other ways to assess your own skills and interests.

- Write out a list of your own abilities and interests, to include the following:

  Would you like to work—with people in groups
  with people, but one at a time
  with people, but through media contact
  with machines
  with your hands and muscles
  outdoors
  by traveling and with different cultures
  with ideas and words
  and be able to move around a lot
  sitting in an office
  where the structure is informal
  where everyone knows what is expected
  in a formal organization with a clear structure
  with old people
     young people
     children
     adults
  making things
  selling things
  making changes in people, materials, ideas,
  producing tangible results
  where you make a lot of money
  where your job has a great
     deal of meaning to people's lives?

Write a statement of your skills, goals, experience, and special reasons why you should be considered for the job.

DESIGN ACTIVITIES—DESIGN YOUR PRIVATE SPACE

Everyone wants to have a home and a sense of space that is their own. You probably have such a place, a private space that is just yours or that you share with others. This activity is designed to help you identify how you use that space and ways in which you might improve your use of that space.

1. Describe the place where you feel most at home, where you can be yourself.
2. List all the activities that occur there (sleeping, reading, relaxing alone or with friends, etc.).
3. Identify all the functions this space should perform.
4. Make an inventory of the tools and materials you currently use or store here.
5. How often do you share that space with others?
6. Where do you keep your most personal and private things?
7. Sketch out your current arrangement of furniture and other things in your space.
8. What image of what your values or what statement about what you do you want others to know? Describe how your space and the decorations show this (or not).
9. Develop a model of your space in either 3-D form or on the computer.
10. Assess the degree to which your current arrangement and use of space meets your wants and needs.
11. Develop a plan for improving your use of space.
12. Develop a plan to decorate it to make it more comfortable, pleasing, and expressive of your style and interests. Use what you have learned about the principles of visual design and arrangement to make your room more aesthetically pleasing and functional.
13. Calculate the costs of the improvements you have indicated on your design for improving your personal space.

DESIGN ACTIVITIES—WHY DO PEOPLE WORK?

The assumptions that people have about why people work are important in determining the style of management an organization or group uses. Place a check mark in the column for each statement below to indicate what is true for you.

NOTE: You may want to refer back to the initial activity of this chapter on TQM.

STATEMENT	I HAVE BEEN TOLD THIS	PEOPLE I KNOW BELIEVE THIS	I BELIEVE THIS
1. People are born lazy. They work only if someone makes them do it.			
2. For people, working is as natural as playing and resting.			
3. People need to be told what to do.			
4. People will only do what the company wants them to do when they are afraid of getting caught and punished.			
5. It is not necessary to force people to work. When motivated, they are self-regulating and happy to work toward goals they agree with.			
6. The average person prefers to be told what to do, rather than figure it out for themselves.			
7. The average person wants to avoid responsibility.			
8. People have little ambition and work only for the money.			
9. People are motivated to work when they can see the results of what they do. Results are a form of personal achievement.			
10. The average person not only likes, but seeks responsibility.			
11. People can be highly imaginative and creative when they have the chance.			

DESIGN ACTIVITIES—SPACE AND ENVIRONMENTAL DESIGN

- Choose a public space or environment, such as a park, store, cafeteria, hospital, office, or school. Identify the functions that space must serve. Analyze current arrangements and evaluate the traffic flow, task sequences, barriers, and the elements of effective arrangement. Make a floor plan of the current arrangement. Make a floor plan for an improved arrangement.

- Analyze the use of color and lighting to create the effects that support the function of the personal and public spaces and environments in your designs.

- Identify the relative costs for renting and buying an office, factory, or other space in your geographical area. If relevant, compare costs in the urban, suburban, or mall site.

- Visit a site of a restoration effort in your own community. If you live in an area with buildings that are listed on a historic register, find out the history of the buildings.

- Identify a place in your community or area that is in the process of deterioration, or that is polluted. What forces have led to the pollution or deterioration? Form a community service group to clean up and fix up. Also identify and communicate with those in power to keep this from happening again.

DESIGN ACTIVITIES—CAPITAL AND BUDGETS

- It is estimated that approximately 1 trillion dollars a day crosses international borders—80 percent of which is speculation. Interview a banker or stockbroker and find out about plans for managing international trade.

- Create a display to indicate monetary systems from several countries and parts of the world. On the display, indicate the relative worth of the money systems.

- Design a form (such as a spreadsheet) to use in identifying the costs of materials and time that are needed for you to carry out your design and technology activities.

TYPES AND SOURCES OF POWER

- As a class, collect some ads from newspapers, magazines, and clips of advertisements from TV. Be sure to include ads from a variety of sources intended for diverse consumers. Also include ads for a variety of products and services.

- Group the ads according to the type of influence on the consumer's behavior (power) that is used:

    Reward: What benefit is being promised?

    Punishment: If the consumer does not buy or use the product or service, what punishment or deprivation might follow?

    Referent: Is the consumer promised that listening to the person who is doing the persuading will result in benefits from other(s) who are of higher status and authority?

    Legitimate: Is the consumer expected to buy or use the product or service because the person has a title or is in a position of authority?

    Expert: Is the person in the ad who is persuading the consumer a person who has the skills and understandings to actually assess the product and endorse its value?

- Change an advertisement you have collected to appeal to another type of influence over the consumer's purchasing behavior.

- The vast majority of western-produced television and radio (except for public broadcasting programs) is designed to deliver a consumer to the advertiser. Discuss how this influences the behavior and expectations of the audience for these commercially-driven shows.

DESIGN ACTIVITIES—ASSESSING THE HEALTH OF A GROUP

Group behavior can be studied to determine how well a group works together as a team. These factors will influence the morale of the group and its ability to accomplish its tasks. These aspects apply to many groups, whether they be a class, a family, a work team, or a friendship group.

Use the following checklist to assess the health of your class as a group, your family, your school, or a group you form to carry out a design project. Use a check mark to indicate how often the statement is true for you. Compare your answers with others in the group. Identify ways that you might improve group functioning.

FACTORS	Always	Sometimes	Seldom	Never
Individuality				
1. I can disagree with the group easily.				
2. We are all expected to give up our own opinions and obey the boss.				
3. I have to pretend to be someone I am not if I want to be accepted.				
4. It is easy to be myself in this group.				
5. The group values my unique insights and abilities.				
6. Everyone is treated like a number or a position, not a person.				
Communication				
1. If I want to be listened to, I must be careful about my language and voice quality.				
2. I can speak freely, without undue concern about language or tone of voice, in order to communicate my emotions and ideas to the group.				
3. There are things that are just not to be mentioned in this group.				
4. We talk about anything that is related to the group or to individual issues related to the group.				
5. When there is a conflict, all sides are listened to with respect.				

DESIGN ACTIVITIES—ASSESSING THE HEALTH OF A GROUP CONTINUED

FACTORS	Always	Sometimes	Seldom	Never
6. When there are disagreements, we talk to each other, but the people with the conflict do not talk directly to each other about the problem.				

Rules

	Always	Sometimes	Seldom	Never
1. We all know what is expected of us and of the group.				
2. People often do other people's jobs and are confused about their role.				
3. When there is a problem, the rules can be "bent," or suspended, in order to give the person some time to deal with it.				
4. Rules and policies are permanent, and things are to be done "according to the book" at all times.				
5. People who have the most talents and experience relevant to the task of the group provide the most leadership in developing and enforcing the rules.				
6. The rules are often different, depending on favoritism and special privileges based on such factors as gender, race, how much money they have, age, who the boss likes best, religion, etc.				

Use of Outside Resources

	Always	Sometimes	Seldom	Never
1. When a problem comes up that the group cannot solve, people are expected to hang together and try to look good, while we "tough it out."				
2. When a problem comes up that the group cannot handle, experts from outside of the group are called in.				

DESIGN ACTIVITIES—ASSESSING THE HEALTH OF A GROUP CONTINUED

FACTORS	Always	Sometimes	Seldom	Never
3. Group members are encouraged to communicate with other people from other groups and learn from them.				
4. A great deal of energy goes into trying to keep outsiders from knowing that we do not get along or do not know how to accomplish our task.				
5. Information about new ideas and resources and how other people are working is easy to get and people are expected to use as much information as possible.				
6. People in the group are expected to do things the way they have always been done, according to the instructions of the boss.				

INDIVIDUALITY AND INDEPENDENCE

The chart below was presented earlier relative to who does each of these tasks in your home. As you grow and mature, you will take more responsibility and become more independent in taking care of yourself. For each of the items, identify the level of individuality and independence you believe you have acquired. For each of the items that falls below a level you are willing to accept, identify what action you could take to gain appropriate skills and experiences.

TASK	SKILL AND EXPERIENCE LEVEL			Proposed Action
	Low	Moderate	High	
Buyer				
Health-Care Provider				
Tutor				
Manager				
Tailor				
Laundry Worker				
Driver				
Gardener				
Counselor				
Maintenance Worker				
Cleaner				
Cook/Caterer				
Waiter				
Errand runner				
Accountant				
Interior Decorator				
Social Worker				
Dietitian				
Social Secretary				
Caregiver				
Other				
Other				

ENRICHMENT DESIGN AND TECHNOLOGY ACTIVITIES

Design Briefs

- Select a product that you or one of your classmates have developed in previous design work. Create a plan for putting it into production. Estimate how much time, space, and capital you would need to start a business in which you make and sell the product.

- Gather data on the stock market for the same day, for the last five years. What social and economic events were happening at the time?

- Brainstorm the qualities of a valuable employee. Interview a manager of a small and a large corporation or business. Compare your list with that of the manager. Ask the managers what skills they find most important for their success as managers. Ask for examples in which they have had to use technical, human, and conceptual skills.

- Look in the Help Wanted ads of your local paper. Write a statement of your skills, goals, experience, and special reasons why you should be considered for the job.

REVIEW AND ASSESSMENT ACTIVITIES

- Identify the resources that must be managed in any design and problem-solving activity.

- Describe three ways products you use are designed to save time.

- In your own neighborhood, school, and home, identify at least five examples of places in which the space is reserved for a specific function.

- Define "capital," "capital intensive," and "labor intensive." Give examples.

- What is the relationship between psychological aspects, such as trust, and economic value of different forms of capital?

- Give examples in which you use money, time, and space for economic reasons and for non economic reasons.

- What are the types and sources of power?

- Describe the skills needed by a manager/leader at different levels of management.

- What are the assumptions behind hierarchical organization vs. flat organization of workers?

UNIT Three

The Systems of Technology

CHAPTER 10

Physical Systems

Three types of technological systems are the physical systems that help provide the goods and services people want and need. These systems are the interrelated activities of constructing, transporting, and producing.

Building various structures is called constructing. Structures can be classified into five basic types: supporting, sheltering, containing, directing, and transporting. Many structures combine more than one type. Supporting structures hold themselves and other things up. Sheltering structures hold themselves up and something else out. Containing structures hold themselves up and something else in. Directing structures control the flow of materials and humans going from one place to another. Transporting structures provide support and move themselves and something else.

CONSTRUCTION SYSTEMS

Construction must consider compression and tension forces, static and dynamic loads, design, and materials characteristics, regardless of the type of structure. Any structure must hold up its own weight and the weight of the materials it holds in, holds out, or carries away (usable load, or payload). Some of these loads act on the structure with a force called compression. This force causes the molecules of the material to squeeze together. Other parts of the load act with a force called tension. These stresses pull apart the molecules of the materials in the structure.

Most of the time, the structure must handle both types of force at once. A structure often is designed to balance these forces to achieve equilibrium. The triangular shape, called a truss, can be used as a brace and take advantage of this stable geometric form.

The materials and design of the structure must work with both static and dynamic weight. Static load is weight that does not move and includes the weight of the structure itself and of the objects or materials the structure must support. Dynamic load is weight that moves around. While moving, dynamic load may exert double or triple the load that it would if it were static.

One building technique uses the mass of materials, themselves, to provide necessary strength. Mass structures, such as dams, rely on their own weight to provide the strength needed to hold back the force created by the water they restrain. One kind of mass structure, the post and lintel structure, uses support columns (posts) and a stretcher across the top (the lintel).

A second building approach, the cantilever, is similar to an extended post and lintel where a side extends out beyond the support. A diving board is a simple instance of a cantilever structure. Another approach uses the arch to take advantage of the compressive strength of certain materials, such as stone and brick. Arches support loads far greater than could be supported by the same materials in a post and lintel structure.

The arch also served as the forerunner to the flying buttress, an external support to a building that works much like an extended arch. The flying buttress provides a mass to anchor, or support, the walls, arches, and roof.

Stones in an arch pack together under a load. They have high compression strength. On the other hand, rope tends to fold over itself when pushed together. Ropes have low compression strength, but they are very strong under tension. Early shipbuilders took advantage of this knowledge as they chose materials.

Sometimes materials are changed or developed to achieve the design purpose. New synthetic materials are light, but very strong. Even some of the conventional construction materials have been improved. There are many examples of materials systems used for construction. These materials systems take advantage of the characteristics of each material to improve the balance of tension and compression forces.

Supporting structures are usually anchored in one place. They are often built to provide a flat, usable surface, such as a floor. Examples are highways and building foundations. Additional support devices include footings, piles, and piers.

Poured footings, usually of concrete with metal reinforcing, are used when the earth can support the weight of the structure fairly easily. If a structure must be erected on ground that cannot support it, such as clay or sand, piles are driven through the soil until they reach bedrock. Bedrock is a layer of rock under the topsoil that does not shift as soil does.

Some supporting structures are designed to hold other tall structures. Towers are often truss structures that are built for height. Towers may be stabilized by the use of guy wires or cables. These wires provide stability and add little to the weight of the structure.

Sheltering structures often need little more strength than that needed to hold themselves up. Most sheltering structures have roofs. Some add walls, floors, and foundations. In geographic areas where there is a great deal of snowfall, the roofs and structures are constructed to withstand the extra weight. Likewise, roofs on shelters where severe storms and strong winds occur must be built to withstand those forces.

Inflatable structures are similar to large, durable balloons held up by air pressure. The inflatable building is a type of flexible shell that is relatively inexpensive and requires almost no support.

The Quonset hut, a common example of shell structures, is similar to a large barrel cut in half lengthwise and erected on a concrete or wood floor. Space frames, such as the geodesic dome, are similar to a combination of trusses and shell structures and can cover larger areas while using little material.

Containing structures serve not only to store materials, but also to restrain and direct materials. Our homes and buildings are often containing structures that help control the environment in which we live and work.

Storage structures take many different forms—water towers to store water, oil and gas tanks to store fuels, and grain elevators and silos to store feed for animals. Examples of containing structures used to direct materials are corrals and loading chutes, and levees used to control flood waters. Directing structures provide pathways that are important in the technological activity of transporting. Directing structures are used to contain materials and control their movement. Pipelines have been built in many parts of the world to carry gases, liquids, and some solids that have been mixed with liquids to form a slurry.

DESIGN ACTIVITIES—STRUCTURES ANALYSIS (TENSION AND COMPRESSION)

As you engage in designing a structure, it will be important to know the types of force that act on each of the component members of your structure. All structures change shape as they are subjected to external forces and loads. These external forces cause the components to stretch, compress, and bend, which creates internal forces within the members. These forces react against the external forces in specific, identifiable ways.

To analyze a structure, such as the simple wall crane shown below, you will need to identify which of the component members are under tension and which are under compression. You can identify the tension components by determining if the forces "along" a part are stretching or pulling it apart. If the forces "along" a part squash or push the part together, then it will be a compression component. The drawing below shows a simple structure supporting a load. Identify which way the forces are acting and which components are tension members and which are compression members.

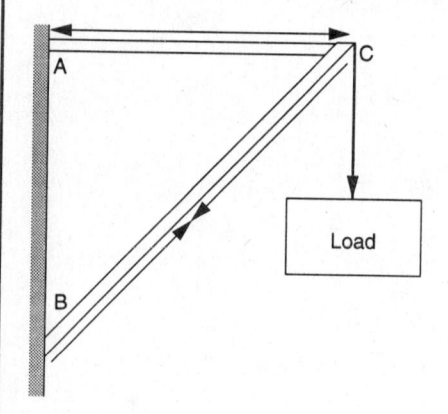

Component Member	Type of Component* (Tension, Compression)
AC	Tension ___ Compression ___
BC	Tension ___ Compression ___

Compression components are often called struts; tension components are called ties.

NOTE: You can determine which of the components of your structure are tension or compressive members by simply asking "If a part were cut in half, would the ends be pulled apart, or would they be pushed over each other?"

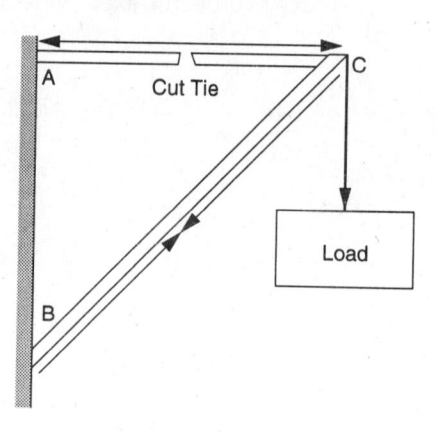

What happens when the tie is cut?

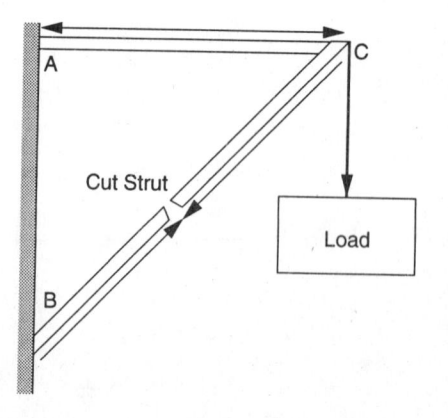

What happens when the strut is cut?

DESIGN ACTIVITIES—STRUCTURES ANALYSIS (BENDING)

The previous examples of the forces applied to the component were oriented "along" the length of the members. In many instances, the force on components will be "across" the members. In illustration (A) below, the force is acting upon the member at right angles to its length. In such circumstances, the member is called a beam, and the action is called a bending force.

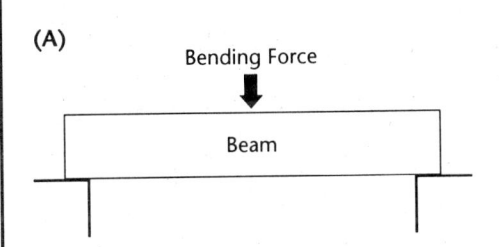

(A) Bending Force — Beam

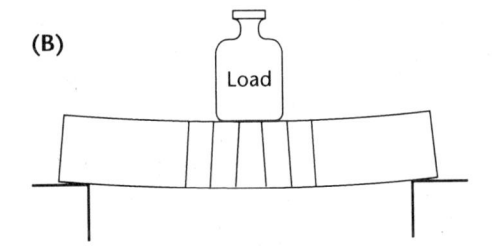

(B) Load

(C) Load

Use the foam materials provided by your teacher and draw the lines on the pieces as shown. Place a small weight on the foam beam (B) to create stress that will cause it to bend. Identify the part of the beam that is placed under tension (is being pulled apart), and which part of the beam is under compression (is being pushed together).

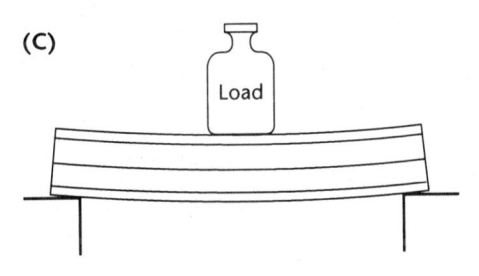

On beam (C), draw the lines along the length of the beam. These lines represent planes that run along and across the beam. Place the same weight used on beam (A) on beam (B). Can you determine which of the lines on the side of the beam gets shorter, which gets longer, and which remains about the same length? The line that remains the same length represents a neutral surface that remains unstressed. If a beam is loaded to the point that it will break, where will the break most likely be?

When a force is applied to a beam as shown in (D), the beam experiences a stress to some degree, at all points between point A and B. The greatest stress occurs at A, however—the point where the beam is most likely to break under the load. The bending moment is the product of the force and the distance between the force and the point of bending. What is the bending moment of point A? What is the bending moment of point C?

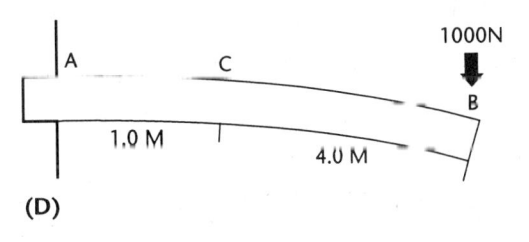

(D) 1000N at B, 1.0 M from A to C, 4.0 M from C to B.

NOTE: You may want to refer to Chapter 4 in your text to review the concept of moment.

DESIGN ACTIVITIES—STRUCTURES ANALYSIS (COMPRESSION, TENSION, AND BENDING)

Apply what you have learned in the previous activities and analyze the structures shown below to determine which of the components are under tension, compression, and bending forces. Add arrows to designate the direction of force acting upon each structural component.

(1)

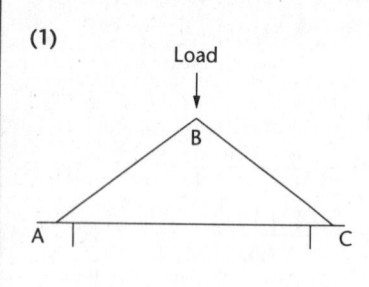

AB _____
BC _____
AC _____

(2)

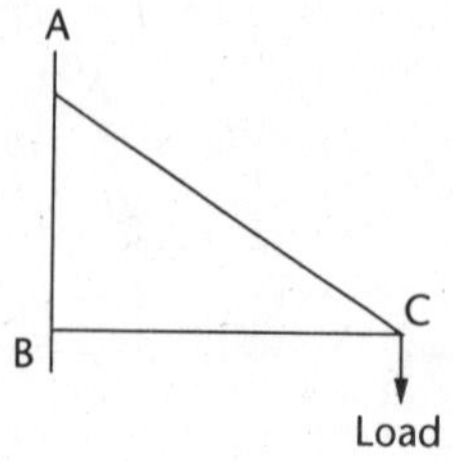

AB _____
BC _____
AC _____

(3)

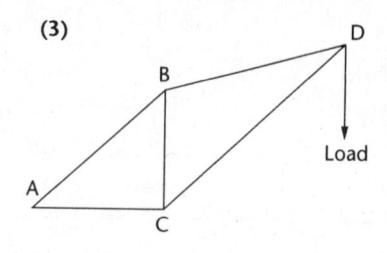

AB _____
BC _____
AC _____
BD _____
DC _____

(4)

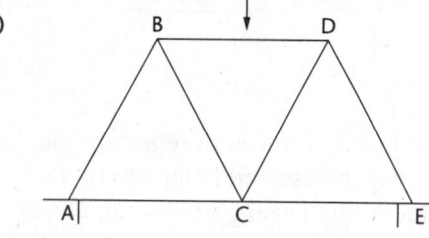

AB _____   CD _____
AC _____   CE _____
BC _____   DE _____
BD _____

(5)

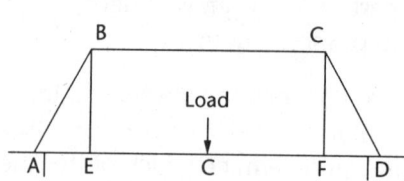

AB _____   BE _____
BC _____   CF _____
CD _____   EF _____
AD _____

(6)

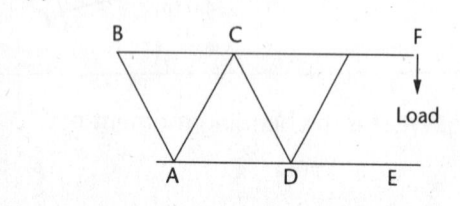

AB _____   CD _____
BC _____   CF _____
AC _____   DE _____
AD _____

(7)

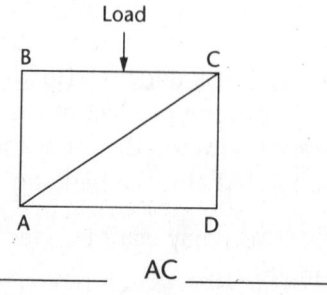

AB _____   AC _____
BC _____   CD _____
AD _____

DESIGN ACTIVITIES—USING TRIANGLES IN STRUCTURES (TRIANGULATION)

Use the Polymek components or other materials provided by your teacher to build the structures from the preceding illustration with the changes shown below. Use these structures to check how accurate you were in determining the tension, compression, and bending forces. Wherever possible, replace tension members with lengths of string, cord or other flexible materials. Can all of the tension members be replaced with these materials? Which of the structures on the preceding page have compression members? _____ Which of them have tension members? _____ Which have bending members? _____

If they are available, install forcemeters in each of the members of the structures. Determine the level of force that is acting upon each member. Do the force readings of the meters match the directions of force you identified in the preceding activities. Increase the load for each structure and chart the forces that act upon each of the members.

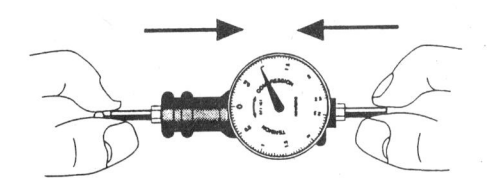

Force in "Compression"

Force in "Tension"

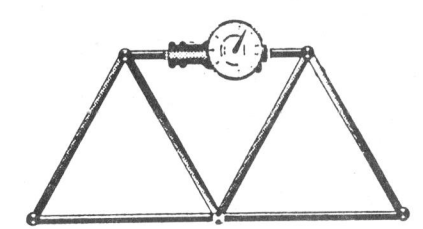

Structure with a forcemeter installed in one of its members.

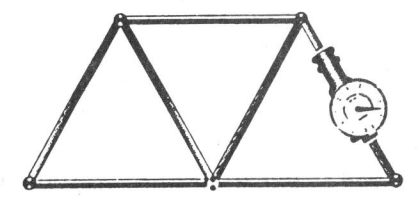

Forcemeter moved to a different structural member.

Courtesy of UNILAB™, Inc.

DESIGN ACTIVITIES—EQUILIBRIUM IN STRUCTURES (RESULTANT AND EQUILIBRANT FORCES)

In the Energy chapter, forces in equilibrium were introduced. (See Figure 6.14 in your Introduction to Design and Technology text and the Integrated S/M/T Activities on page 153 of the Portfolio and Activities Resource.) Objects and structures will remain at rest if the resultant and equilibrant forces are equal and act in the opposite directions.

In many cases, the forces acting on an object or structure may be the result of several forces. In some instances, the forces are added together; sometimes they are subtracted. For example, if you are riding a bike, you move forward because of the force you exert on the pedals (50 N), the force of the wind on your back (20 N), and the force of gravity due to a slight uphill grade (15 N). The resultant force drawn in scale is shown in the vector diagram below.

Vectors

| 50 N → | 20 N → | ← 15 N | or | Resultant (55 N) --------→ |

Scale: 1 cm equals 10 N

In the example shown below, the forces required to move the package onto a loading pallet are identified. See Figure 6.22 in your text. What is the resultant force that is necessary to overcome the individual forces and actually move the package? Construct a scale drawing that shows the individual forces and the combined resultant force.

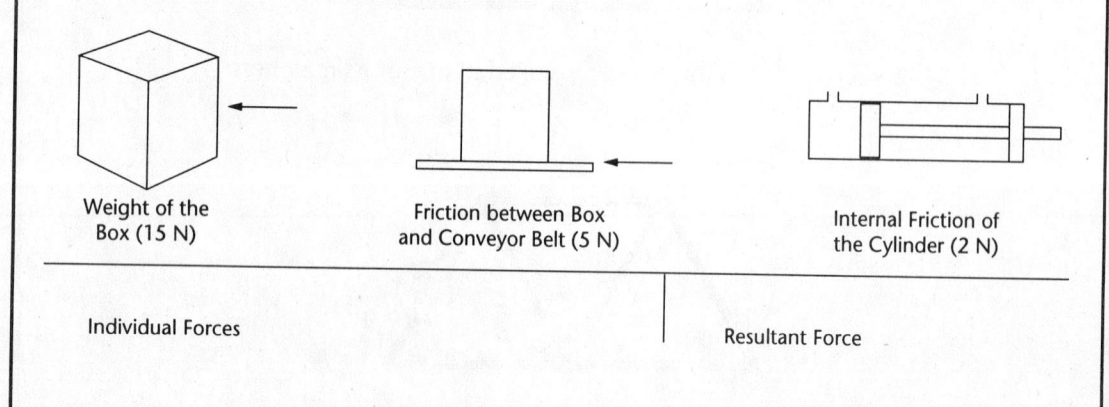

Weight of the Box (15 N)

Friction between Box and Conveyor Belt (5 N)

Internal Friction of the Cylinder (2 N)

Individual Forces | Resultant Force

INTEGRATED S/M/T ACTIVITIES—EQUILIBRIUM IN STRUCTURES (RESULTANT OF TWO ANGULAR FORCES)

A drawing of a sled being pulled by two people is shown below. In this case, the two friends are pulling unevenly, with one pulling more to the side and harder than the other. The diagram of two lines in (B) represents the two forces and the angle at which they are acting on the sled. The diagram in (C) shows the force lines drawn in scale. (In this instance, you have chosen a scale of 1 cm = 100 N.) The next step (D) shows the completed parallelogram. Finally, in (E) the diagonal between the two forces is drawn and measured. Using the same scale, you can convert the length of the line into newtons of force. (In a following activity on page 290, you will see how these diagrams can be labeled by using a standard approach called Bows notations.)

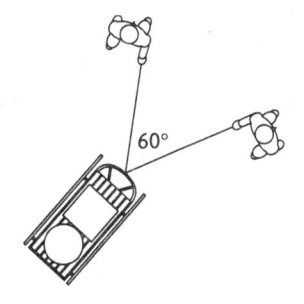

(A) Two people pulling a sled.

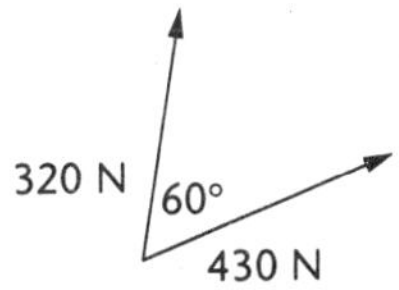

(B) Diagram representing the forces on the sled.

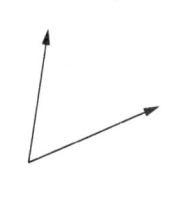

(C) Drawing the force lines to scale.

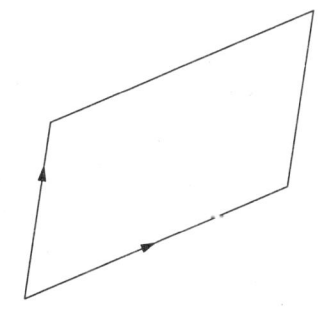

(D) The completed parallelogram.

(E) The parallelogram of forces showing the diagonal between the two forces as the resultant.

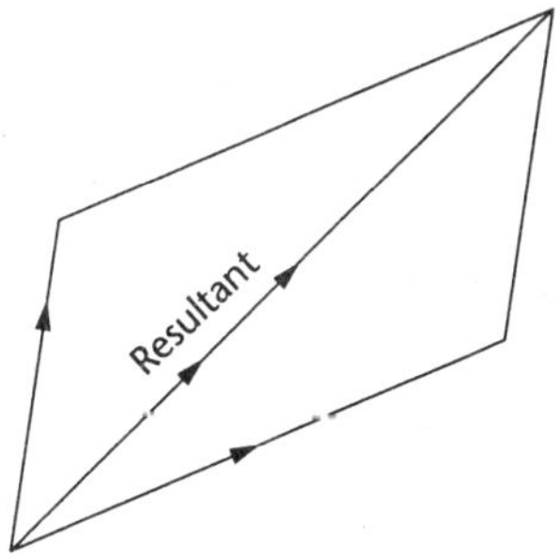

resultant length = 65 cm
force = 65 × 100 N
= 650 N

The illustration below shows an eyebolt embedded in a wall to hold guy ropes. As shown in the diagram, one rope exerts a force of 240 N and the other 380 N. What is the resultant force on the eyebolt? Can you determine at what angle the resultant force acts upon the eyebolt?

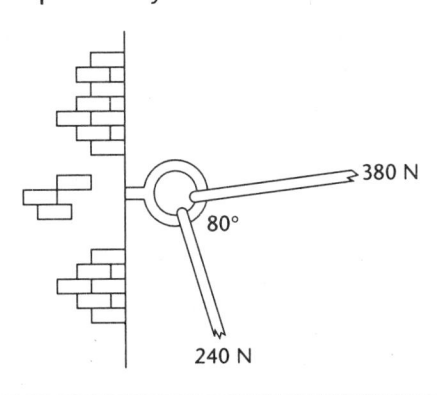

INTEGRATED S/M/T ACTIVITIES—CALCULATING FORCES

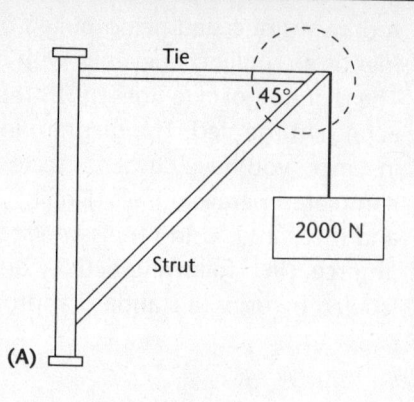

The illustration at the right (A) shows a post-mounted crane, drawn as a space diagram introduced in the previous activity on page 287. The device is to be used to lift heavy containers of water nutrients in your hydroponics greenhouse that weigh up to 500 pounds or 2000 N.

Your problem is to determine what force will be exerted on the tie and on the strut by a 2000 N load. The illustrations in (B), (C), and (D) below show how the solution to the problem is drawn.

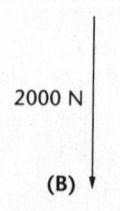

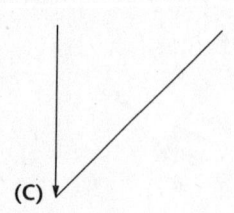

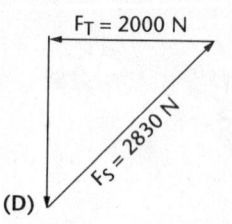

Follow the process yourself by drawing the space diagram shown in the circle above. First you must choose a scale (perhaps 1 cm = 10 N). You then draw, in scale, the known force generated by the load (2000 N). Next, draw a line parallel to the tie and a second line parallel to the strut. Your drawing should look like illustration (D) above. Now measure the length of the line for the tie and convert it to newtons. Record it as the tie force, or $F_T = 2000$. Next, measure the line for the strut and record it as $F_S = 2830$ N. Your finished drawing should include arrows that complete a path around the triangle. Now, with the materials provided by your teacher, build the crane structure and devise a test (in scale) to see if the forces are accurate.

Use the same process to draw the triangle of forces for a post-mounted crane in the design shown at right that will lift a load of 1500 N. Build a model of the crane to test your findings.

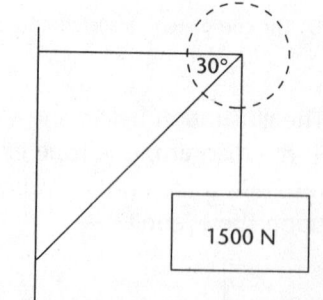

INTEGRATED S/M/T ACTIVITIES—CALCULATING FORCES CONTINUED

The components of the post-mounted crane form a right angle; consequently, the forces can be determined by using some simple trigonometry. The drawing below is the same as the one shown in illustration (D) on the preceding page. The relationship of the triangle can be expressed as:

$$\tan 45 = \frac{2000}{F_T} \quad \text{and} \quad \sin \text{ (or sin) } 45 = \frac{2000}{F_S}$$

The force generated in the tie can be expressed as $F_T = \dfrac{2000}{\tan 45}$

The force generated in the strut can be expressed as $F_S = \dfrac{2000}{\sin 45}$

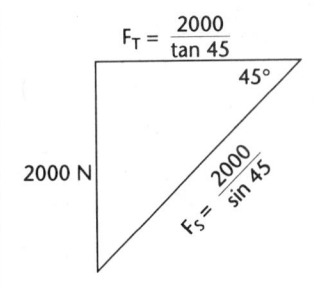

By looking up the values of tan 45 and sin 45 in the Appendix on trigonometric functions, you can substitute those values as:

$$F_T = \frac{2000}{\tan 45} = \frac{2000}{1.000} = 2000 \text{ N}$$

$$F_S = \frac{2000}{\sin 45} = \frac{2000}{0.707} = 2829 \text{ N}$$

Use the same process to complete the calculations for a crane that will lift a load of 1500 N, of the size shown in the problem illustrated on the preceding page.

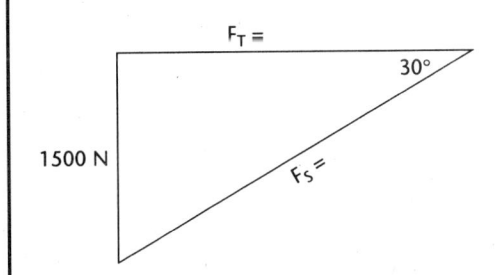

DESIGN ACTIVITIES—ANALYZING STRUCTURES USING BOW'S NOTATIONS

A good bit of your work in structures will be involved in designing framed structures. These frameworks are made up of struts, ties, bars, and rods that are pinned or joined together to make a rigid structure. Several frameworks are shown on page 293 in this text. You can see that the triangle is used in most structures. Such structures are often called triangulated frames.

To solve problems that involve triangulation—the process of using triangles for developing structures—it is essential that each structural member can be clearly named. An approach called Bow's notations provides a useful method for communication and problem-solving.

In the space diagram below, note that in (A) the space between each force is marked with a capital letter. Each force is identified by two letters. The 50 N force is designated as *AB* (the *A* is on one side of the line, and the *B* is on the other). The 45 N force becomes *BC* and the 30 N force becomes *CA*.

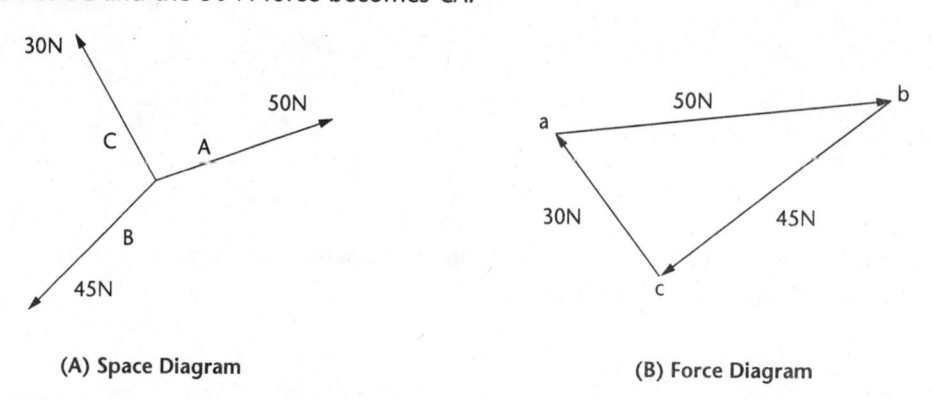

(A) Space Diagram

(B) Force Diagram

In the force diagram shown in (B), the forces are marked with lowercase letters. In this instance, the 50 N force is designated as *ab*, the 45 N force is designated *bc*, and the 30 N force is designated as *ca*. The force diagram is developed by drawing each of the force lines, as shown below. Starting with AB, draw a line in the direction of the arrow to generate line *ab*. Add an arrowhead, and from that point draw a line parallel to BC to generate line *bc*. Again add an arrowhead, and from that point draw a line parallel to BC to generate line *ca*. The three lines should be connected so that the arrows all point in a clockwise direction.

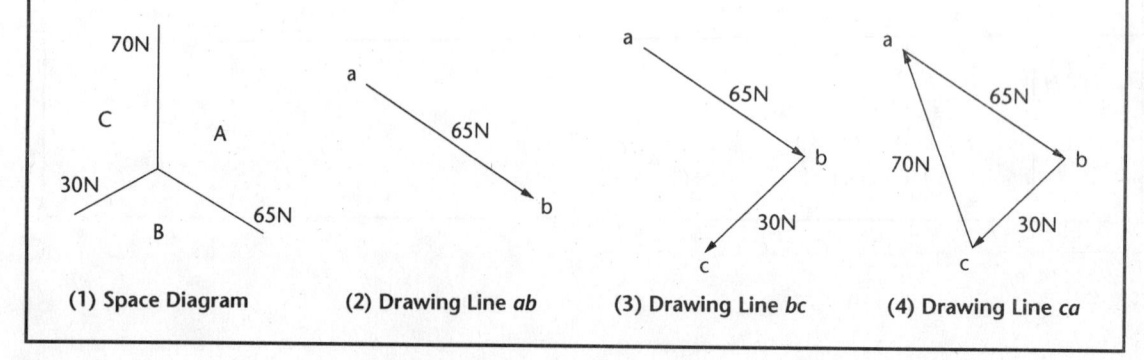

(1) Space Diagram (2) Drawing Line *ab* (3) Drawing Line *bc* (4) Drawing Line *ca*

DESIGN ACTIVITIES—ANALYZING STRUCTURES USING BOW'S NOTATIONS CONTINUED

The example below uses a roof truss from a greenhouse design to illustrate how the forces in a frame can be determined. Each truss is designed to support a load of 1000 N. To make your calculations simpler, the connectors are considered as pin joints forming corners, or nodes. All loads will be considered as acting at these corners (nodes).

Drawing of greenhouse truss (90°, 20°, 70°, Post)

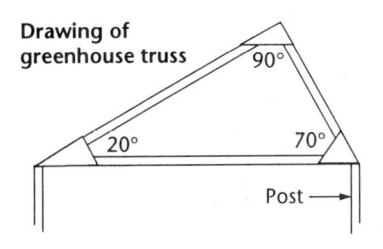

(1) Make a sketch of the space diagram

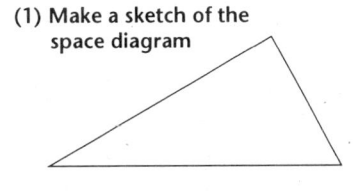

(2) Letter the diagram
1000 N Force (action) 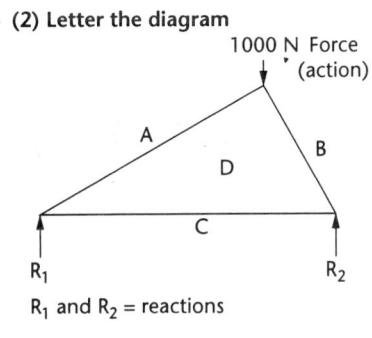
A, B, C, D
R_1 and R_2 = reactions

(3) Choose a scale for the drawing you will make.

10 N = 1 inch

(4) Select first node (a)

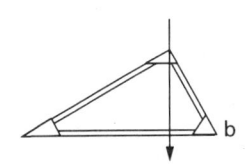

Note: Node "a" is selected because the weight of force (1000 N) applied as a downward load provides key information you need to start you drawing.

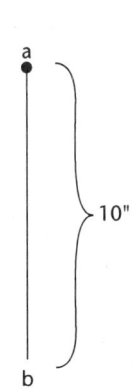

(5) Move to second node (b) and draw parallel line (b-d) as shown.

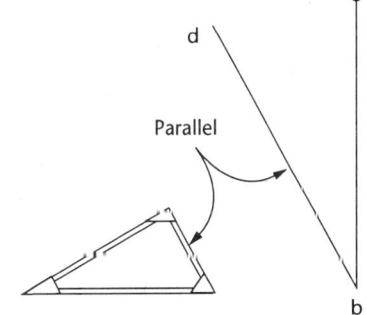

Parallel

Design Brief

Determine the forces in the truss shown at the right. Develop a space frame, a force diagram, and an information diagram for the truss.

Note: If you wish, you can check your calculations for the two preceding problems. Use the forcemeters introduced on page 287 of this text. Maintain the correct weight (in scale: 1000 N = 1 N and 5000 N = 5 N) and see what force and directions are measured in the different components.

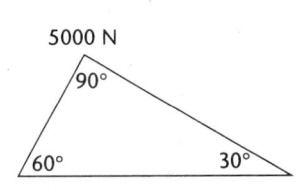

5000 N, 90°, 60°, 30°

DESIGN ACTIVITIES—ANALYZING STRUCTURES USING BOW'S NOTATIONS CONTINUED

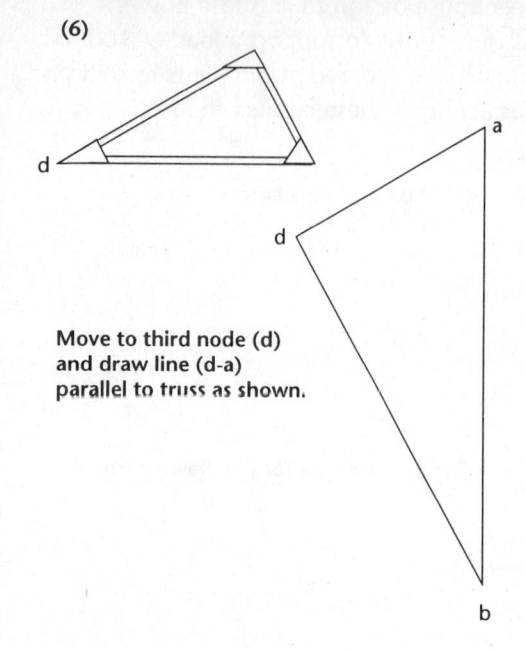

(6)

Move to third node (d) and draw line (d-a) parallel to truss as shown.

(7)

Remain at Node (d) and draw line (d-c) parallel to truss as shown.

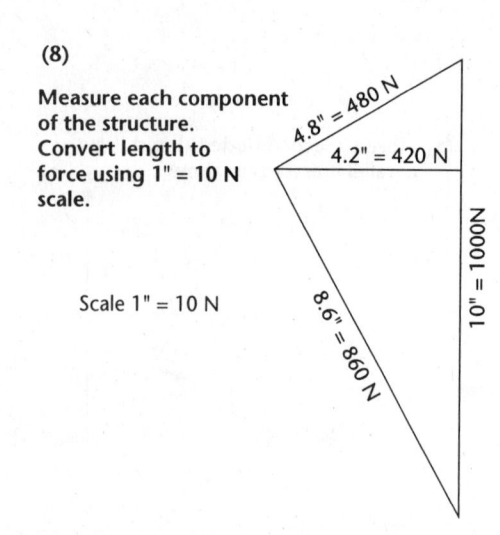

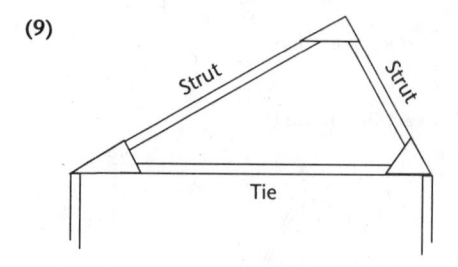

(8) Measure each component of the structure. Convert length to force using 1" = 10 N scale.

Scale 1" = 10 N

- 4.8" = 480 N
- 4.2" = 420 N
- 10" = 1000 N
- 8.6" = 860 N

(9) Determine if each component is a strut (compression) or a tie (tension).

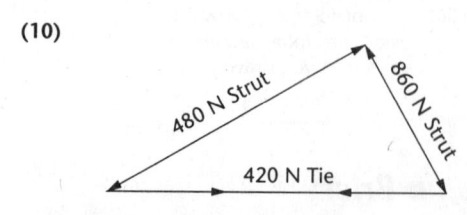

Strut, Strut, Tie

(10)

- 480 N Strut
- 860 N Strut
- 420 N Tie

Complete the information drawing.

Note: The numbers on the information diagram (480, 860, 420) represent the force acting on each member. These numbers are **NOT** the length of the member.

Chapter 10 Physical Systems **293**

DESIGN ACTIVITIES—ADDING STABILITY TO STRUCTURES

Below are several means of making structures more stable. Identify the advantages and disadvantages of each. Identify other examples of each approach to improving stability.

Illustrations		Examples	Examples
Solid Brace	Advantages		
	Disadvantages		
Internal Flexible Braces	Advantages		
	Disadvantages		
External Braces	Advantages		
	Disadvantages		
Rigid Frame	Advantages		
	Disadvantages		
Adding Sheathing (cover)	Advantages		
	Disadvantages		
The Triangle (truss)	Advantages		
	Disadvantages		

DESIGN ACTIVITIES—APPLICATIONS IN ADDING STABILITY TO STRUCTURES

Select and use the most appropriate method of bracing to strengthen your greenhouse structure. What contribution does the addition of the bracing make toward improving the structure? What are some of the problems that the method creates?

Select and apply the most appropriate method of bracing to strengthen your tower crane structure. What contribution does the addition of the bracing make toward improving the crane? What new problems does this method of bracing introduce into the crane structure? Why is the system you have chosen the best for the function your structure must perform?

INTEGRATED S/M/T ACTIVITIES

There are many questions that should be asked as you engage in designing and developing a structure. A few sample questions might include the following:

- What are some of the different shapes of braces that could be used to strengthen bridges?

- What are some of the types and shapes of braces that could be used to strengthen your tower bridge?

- Which of the above means do you think would be the best to use on your bridge problem?

- What contributes to making these braces stable?

- What contributes to making these braces strong?

- In testing a structure, you plan to use a can of sand to represent, or model, your weight. How much will the can of sand model weigh in pounds and newtons if it is one-tenth of your weight?

- Is there a difference when the object that represents your weight is placed gently on the bridge model as compared to dropping the object on the model?

- What are the advantages and disadvantages of constructing a greenhouse using a geodesic dome structure?

- What are the advantages and disadvantages of constructing a greenhouse using a truss roof structure?

- What are the advantages and disadvantages of constructing a greenhouse using an inflatable structure?

- Develop models of each and carry out appropriate tests to determine if the conclusions you have made above appear to be defensible.

DESIGN ACTIVITIES—TYPES OF CONSTRUCTION

Study the illustrations of post and lintel, cantilever, arch, and flying buttress structures. See if you can find several examples of each. What do you see as the advantages of each technique? What disadvantages do you see for each? Identify applications of each construction type.

Technique		Applications
Post and Lintel	Advantages	
	Disadvantages	
Cantilever	Advantages	
	Disadvantages	
Arch	Advantages	
	Disadvantages	
Flying Buttress	Advantages	
	Disadvantages	

DESIGN ACTIVITIES—USING ALTERNATIVE APPROACHES TO STRUCTURES

In addition to the more conventional structures, there are new approaches and variations on old approaches that can be used. In the illustrations below are four different approaches to structure design. As a class, work in four groups, with each group using one of the approaches to provide a large greenhouse for plants of your own choice. Design and develop a model of your greenhouse structure. Determine some of its advantages and disadvantages. Determine if there are parts of the country where your structure would perform best. Determine the general cost of the structure in terms of the ground space provided, the materials used, and the labor and construction costs.

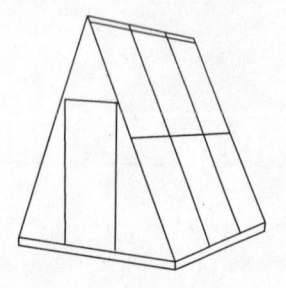

(1) "A" Frame

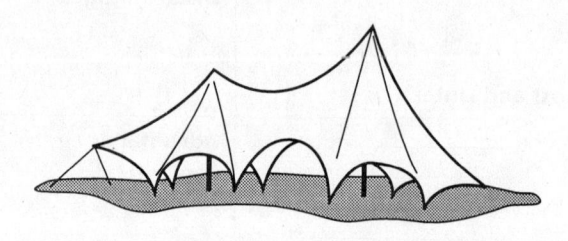

(2) Tented Structure

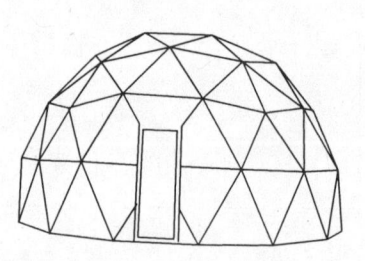

(3) Geodesic Dome

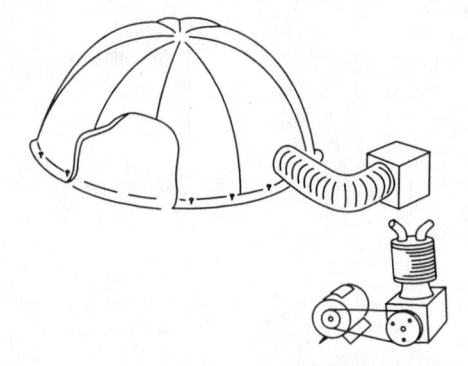

(4) Inflatable Structure

DESIGN ACTIVITIES—CONSTRUCTING A CRANE TO CARRY THE LOAD

A lumber import company has a lumber yard adjacent to a dock along a river. They require a crane that can off load the large bundles of lumber from the boats lying alongside the dock. The crane must be able to take the bundles from the hull of a boat and place them in an orderly fashion anywhere on the ground within the yard. In this instance, the lumber yard is 200 feet long parallel to the dock and 100 feet wide from the edge of the dock. The bundles of lumber weigh less than 2 tons and should represent little problem in terms of the weight to be lifted.

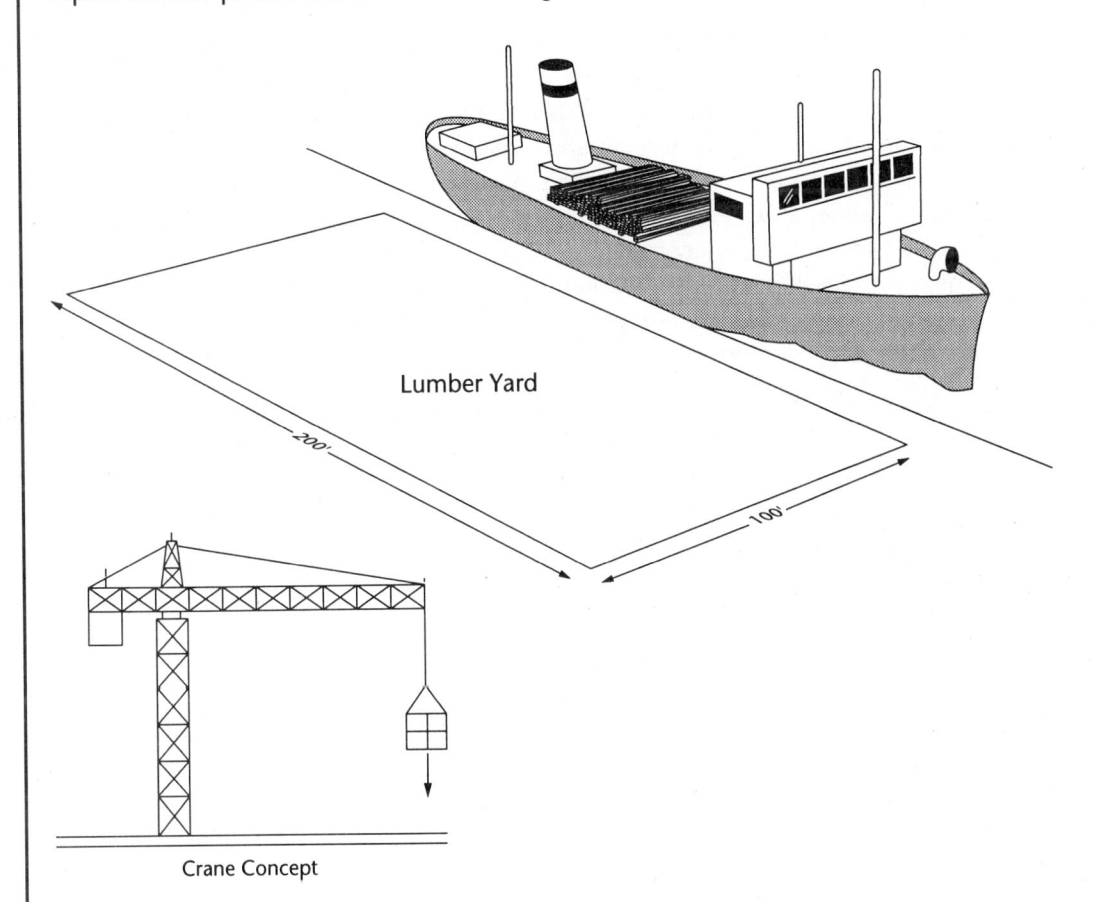

Lumber Yard

Crane Concept

Design a crane that can lift the loads and place them anywhere within the area described. The crane must be able to lift loads so that the bottom of bundle can clear a fifty foot obstacle, to ensure that the loads will clear the superstructure of the vessel.

NOTE: The illustrations above show a fixed tower crane with a long overhead boom or arm. Discuss whether this is an effective approach to the problem. What if the lumber yard was 200 yards long parallel to the dock and 20 yards wide from the edge of the dock, as described in your text? Would it be better to design a different approach, such as using a gantry crane that can move back and forth over the yard. What will be some of the drawbacks of a gantry crane? What do you propose as your best approach for this problem?

DESIGN ACTIVITIES—CHOOSING MATERIALS FOR STRUCTURES

To choose materials for different structures, you will find it helpful to know the characteristics of various materials you might use for a given structure. As indicated in the chapter on Materials in your textbook, there are many different characteristics of materials—strength, rigidity, flexibility, and others. The design of your structure will determine which characteristics are the most important. In many cases, the strength of a material is of prime concern.

You can determine the strength of many material by using a reference text or handbook on materials. You may also want to conduct tests on selected of the materials you plan to use. For example, the materials testing system illustrated below, available from the Unilab Inc., will allow you to test "controlled samples" to determine how strong a material is. The system, consisting of a straining unit and a readout device is designed to conduct a variety of tests (tensile, compression, bending, hardness). The straining device places a test "specimen" under strain and sends indications from the load cell to the readout device—either a meter unit or a computer screen. Supportive software is also available that can help you develop a graphic readout of the test results. Through using the materials testing device and software, you will become familiar with key concepts related to material strength, and more skilled in applying this knowledge to the structures you design.

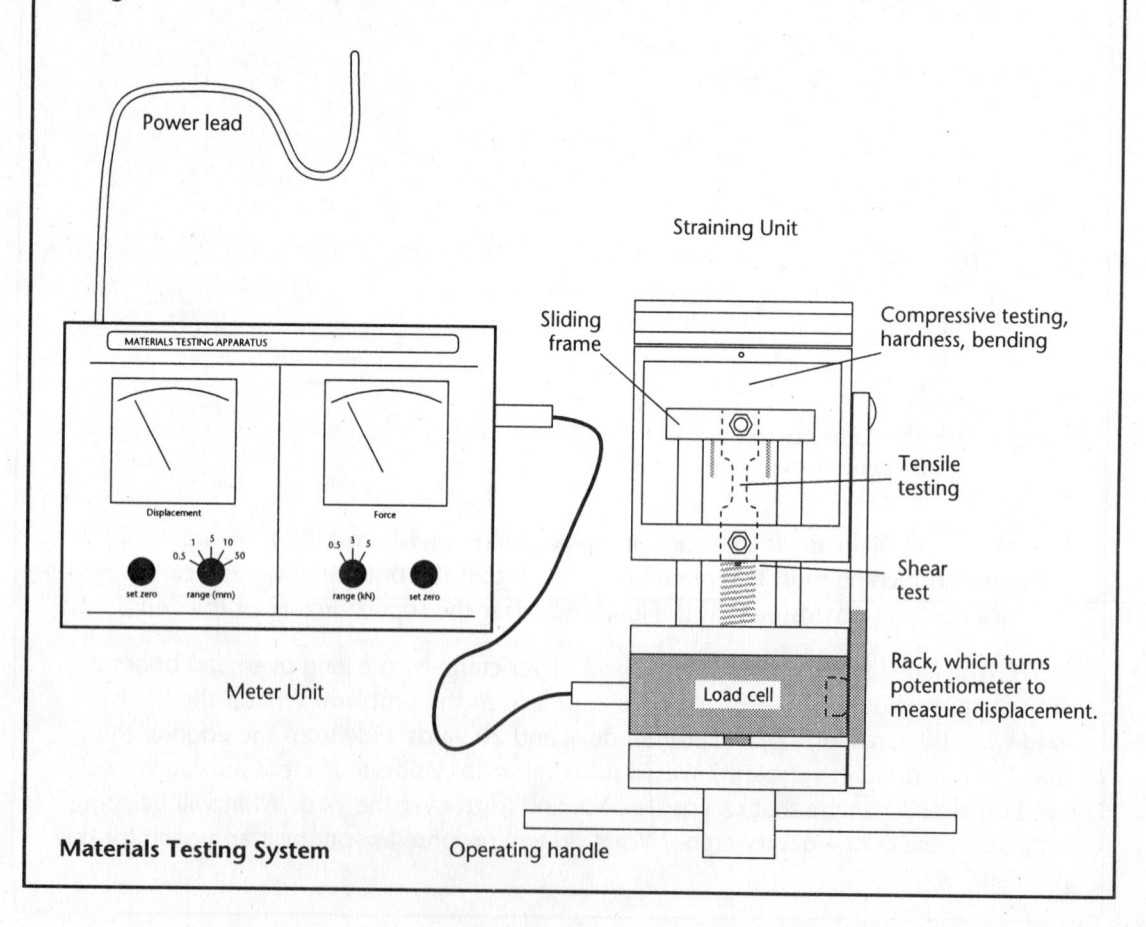

Materials Testing System

DESIGN ACTIVITIES—CHOOSING MATERIALS FOR STRUCTURES CONTINUED

The Straining Unit

Labels: Accessory mounting hole; Tapped holes for tensile specimens; Sliding frame; Rack retaining screw; Rack; Potentiometer and gear, driven by rack; Four locating pegs; Punch ejector pins; Fixed frame; Load cell; Shear punch; Electrical output to meter unit (5 pin DIN socket); Operating handle.

The Straining Unit (used for tensile testing)

Labels: Specimen clamped with two M6 bolts and washers; Rack attached to fixed frame; Rack drives gear to register displacement of the sliding frame.

The Specimen

14 mm; 2 mm radii; 10 mm Gauge length

NOTE: Specimen thickness is approximately 1 mm.

Fabric Testing Accessory

Accessories are fitted over the locating pegs and are secured by the countersunk M6 screw.

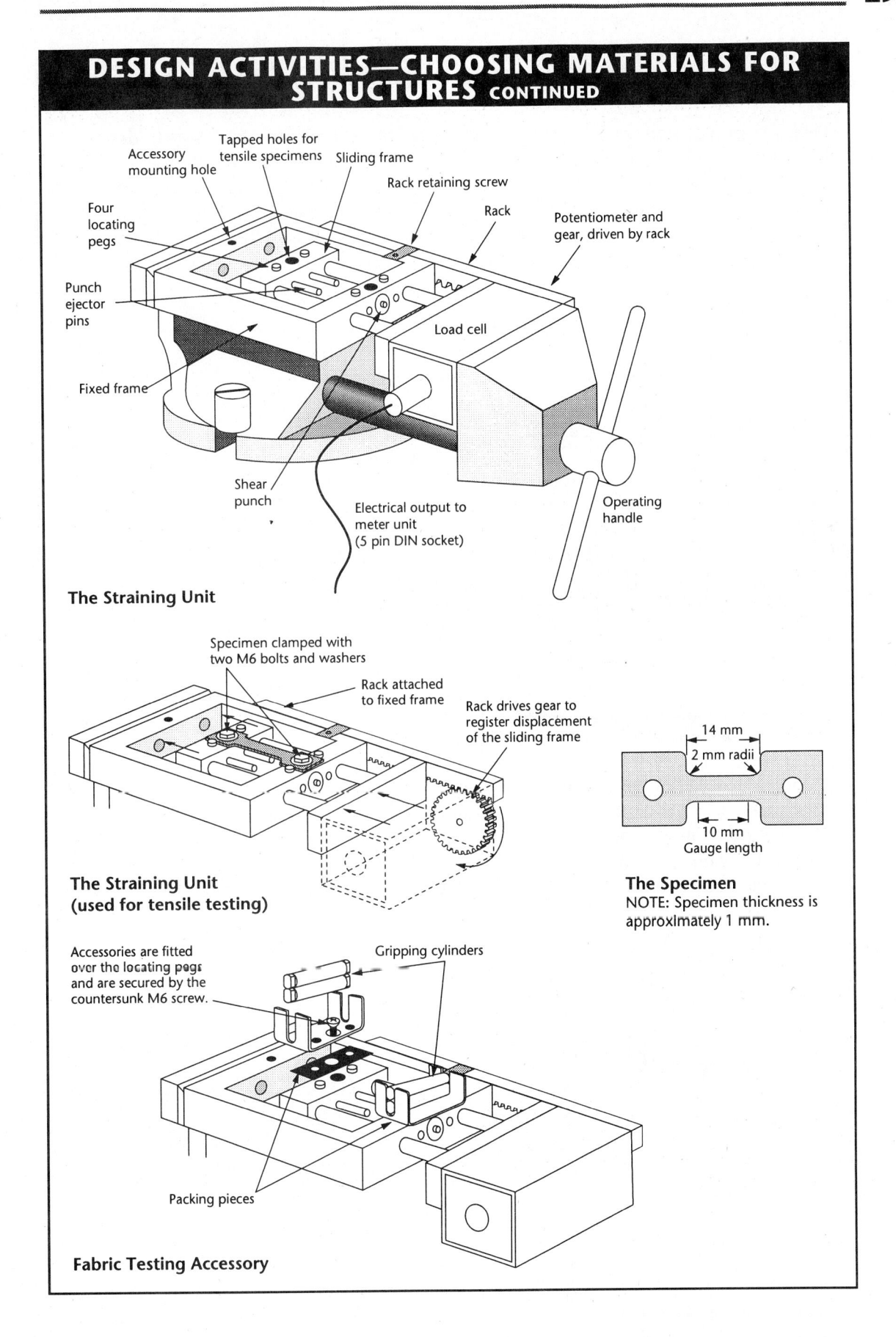

Labels: Gripping cylinders; Packing pieces.

DESIGN ACTIVITIES—DESIGNING BUILDINGS FOR EARTHQUAKE PRONE AREAS

Many populated parts of the world are vulnerable to earthquakes. The research, design and development of buildings with earthquake isolation foundations holds promise to make these structures safer. Investigate what is meant by isolation and what potential this idea might have to provide safer buildings. Refer to the illustration here and in Figure 10.9 in your text that shows a structure built from a conventional design and the same structure built to a design that will withstand forces caused by earthquakes. Use this approach as the basis for your own design and develop a working model illustrating your ideas for isolation devices.

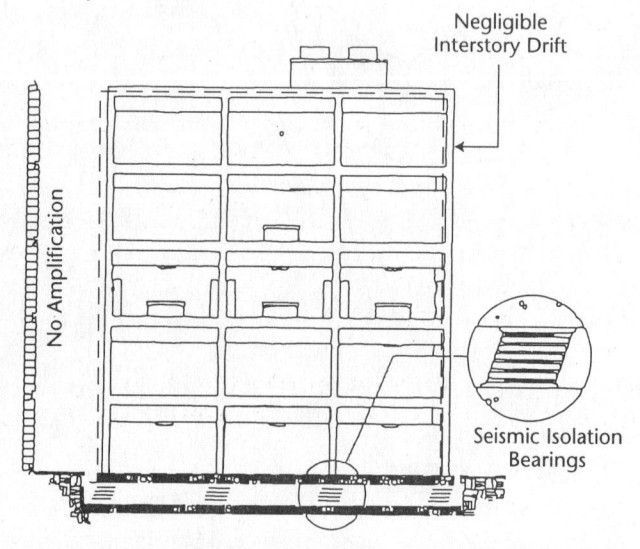

Concept of isolation

No Amplification

Negligible Interstory Drift

Seismic Isolation Bearings

Ideas for isolation devices

Another advances in the design of buildings for earthquake areas applies the concept of "dampening." As you pursue your investigation, it may be helpful to know an example of dampening is found in automobile shock absorbers to reduce the excessive movement of the car body on rough roads. You may want to experiment with this and other aspects of dampening of movement as a means of reducing the shifting of a building during and earthquake.

Concept of dampening

Large Mass

Energy-absorbing springs or hydraulics

Ideas for dampening devices

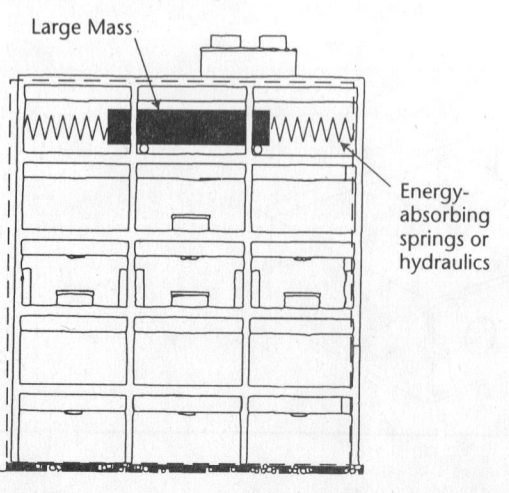

TRANSPORTING SYSTEMS

Transporting structures are portable containing structures. There are three basic types of transporting structures: floating, rolling, and flying. All structures are influenced directly by the materials, processes, and technological systems available to the builders at the time.

A rolling structure is made significantly different from a floating structure. Rather than the large surface areas over which the weight is distributed in floating structures, the load of rolling structures is focused on very small points of contact between the wheels and the surface supporting the vehicle.

Flying structures are a very different type of structure. Airships are somewhat similar to boats in that they follow the principles of specific gravity. The weight of the structure and its load must be less than the weight of an equal volume of the fluid (in this case, air) that supports it.

Airplanes, however, demanded new knowledge about how heavier-than-air structures could fly. It was necessary that the early developers understand that heavier-than-air vehicles could be lifted by the flow of air over their wings because of the partial vacuum it created. The wings of an airplane must be light in weight but also very strong to support the weight of the plane during flight.

Moving vehicles must be designed as impact structures. A car, plane, rocket, or boat must be designed as a high-impact structure that will collapse in a controlled fashion. The materials and design of the vehicle will help dissipate the mechanical energy that results from colliding with another vehicle or a nonmoving object.

Humans tend to be on the go, taking with them their materials and devices. Transporting is the technological activity in which people, machines, energy, materials, or other substances are moved from one place to another.

The key ideas in transporting are pathways, vehicles, loads, and purposes. The simplest transporting system may have the most controlled pathways. The vehicle travels in only one direction. Some transporting paths are more restricted than others.

Ways are the pathways from one place to another. Examples of ways include roadways, highways, seaways, and airways. Pathways differ in the number of directions they permit a vehicle to move. One-way transporting allows movement in only one direction. Examples include ski tows, escalators, slides, pipelines, aqueducts, and some conveyors. Two-way transporting allows travel in two directions. Examples include railroad tracks, office elevators, subways, and ferry boats that move along a fixed rope or chain as their guide track.

Three-way transporting allows movement in three directions. Examples include riverboats, skiers, motorcycles, and sailboats that uses square sails. Four-way transporting is the most widely used of any of the forms. Travel by foot, all-terrain vehicles, canoes, and rowboats allow four directions of movement.

Five-way transporting can be found in the air and the oceans. Fixed-wing aircraft can move in five directions, every way but in reverse. Some submarines, such as those that tow divers under water, travel in five directions. Six-way transporting is possible by helicopters, some submarines, and spacecraft. True sixth direction of movement removes the restriction of gravity. Consequently, the spatial reference that gravity provides is also removed.

Transportation requires separate vehicles and structures that can be used for containing and moving goods, materials, and/or people. These containers are often called the transportation unit. Examples are railroad cars and modular containers loaded on the bed of a truck. Some transportation units have their own power, or propulsion, while others must be attached to a power vehicle.

Vehicles such as the automobile, which combines a propulsion unit, with a container unit are relatively common. The automobile unites the engine and the passenger compartment (cargo space) into one combined unit.

Vehicles have limits to the cargo they can transport. In some instances, such as transporting potato chips, a vehicle can be filled in terms of space but carry only a fraction of its weight potential. In other instances, such as hauling bricks, plenty of space may be left in the vehicle after the maximum weight has been reached. The operational load is the total weight of the truck, driver, and anything other than the payload. The useful load would be potato chips or bricks hauled. Using lighter materials in the vehicle can help reduce the operational load and increase the useful load.

The goal in transporting is to use as few resources as possible to achieve the purposes. Time and speed of transporting may be of primary importance. Transporting people to work places an emphasis on speed to provide the most time possible for working, playing, or relaxing. Transporting strawberries for sale requires a different interpretation of time and whether the strawberries reach the market on schedule —at the point of ripeness and when the demand for strawberries is high.

The high cost of fast transporting, determined by a cost/benefit analysis, may outweigh the advantages of speed. The choice of transporting systems will be determined by which best meets the desired outcomes at the least cost, with the fewest undesired consequences, for now and for the future.

DESIGN ACTIVITIES—RESEARCH AND DEVELOPMENT PROJECTS

Developing Floating Transporting Structures

Conduct research and investigation into floating vehicles and how they operate in water. Conduct similar research on vehicles that float in air. With the insights gained through your research and investigation, pursue one or more of the following activities:

- Design a floating vehicle, to operate in water, that will carry the largest load at the least cost of energy to move it over great distances.

- Design a floating vehicle that will move heavy cargo (load) over long distances as quickly and economically as possible.

- Design a floating vehicle that will move people through the narrow waterways of a city, such as Amsterdam or Venice, as quickly and safely as possible.

- Design a floating vehicle that will operate on water and that will fulfill a set of purposes that you want to accomplish.

- Design a floating vehicle that will operate in air to lift a new steeple for a religious building. The steeple weighs 3,000 pounds and must be positioned on a base that is 30 meters above the ground.

- Design a floating vehicle that will operate in air and that will fulfill a set of purposes that you want to accomplish.

DESIGN ACTIVITIES—DESIGN BRIEF (DEVELOPING HIGH-SPEED, HUMAN-POWERED VEHICLES)

The chart below provides information on the draw and speed characteristics of human powered vehicles. Use this information as you design and develop models of proposed approaches to the most effective design for a track racing bike. (Your models should be built to a standard scale, such as 1" = 1' or 3 cm = 1 m.)

Conduct wind tunnel tests on your proposed design(s) to see which are most promising. Identify which of your designs should be developed further. What changes are appropriate in your design at this time? What will be your plan for pursuing your efforts further?

Drag & Speed Characteristics of Streamlined Human Powered Vehicles

Machine	Frontal Area m² (Area in ft²)	Drag Coefficient C_d	Percent Drag Reduction at 32 KPH	Required Power at 32Kph-Watts	Speed With No Power Increase-KPH (Increase-MPH)	Maximum Competition Speed-KPH* (Increase-MPH*)
Bare Bicycle	.50 (5.4)	.78	0	203	—	—
Bicycle Plus Front Fairing I	.55 (5.4)	.60	13%	177	33.5 (20.8)	54.72 (33.9)
Bicycle Plus Front Fairing II	.55 (5.9)	.52	22%	159	34.73 (21.5)	—
Palombo Supine Tricycle - Bare	.35 (3.8)	.77	26%	151	34.5 (21.4)	58.21 (33.9)
Van Valkenburg (Aeroshell Covers Upper Body)	.65 (7.0)	.32	34%	125	36.8 (22.8)	54.22 (33.6)
Aero plus Bottom Skirt	.68 (7.3)	.21	48%	97	39.8 (24.7)	74.85 (46.4)
Palombo Tricycle with Fairing	.46 (4.9)	.28	55%	92	40.9 (25.3)	71.42 (44.3)
Kyle Full Fairing	.71 (7.6)	.10	67%	68	46 (28.5)	74.77 (46.4)
Van Valkenburgh Prone Quadracycle with Fairing	.46 (4.9)	.14	68%	64	46.9 (29.1)	79.47 (49.3)

* Measured at the International Human Powered Speed Championships. From "Predicting Human Powered Vehicle Performance Using Eronometry and Aerodynamic Drag Measurements" Proceedings, International Conference on Human Powered Transportation, San Diego, 1979. Cheestar R. Kyle.

Courtesy *TIES Magazine*

DESIGN ACTIVITIES—DEVELOPING HUMAN-POWERED VEHICLES (SUBMARINE)

Use the idea for a water test tank below and design and develop a system for testing model submarines and boats.

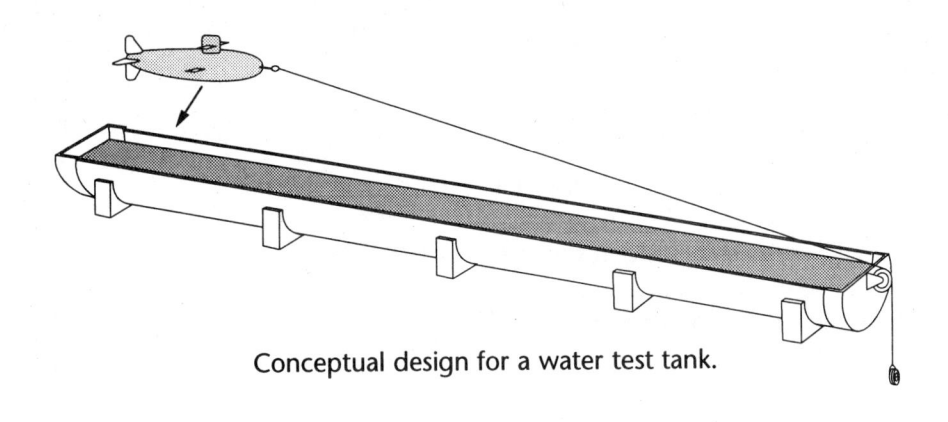

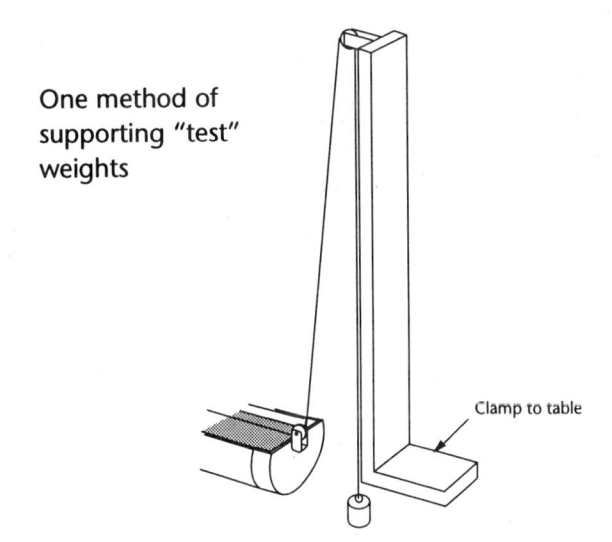

Conceptual design for a water test tank.

One method of supporting "test" weights

Clamp to table

Design and develop models of a human-powered submarine to determine the most effective shape for moving through water. Use your system to conduct water tank tests on your proposed design(s) to see which are most promising. Identify which of your designs should be developed further. What changes are appropriate in your design at this time? What will be your plan for pursuing your efforts further?

You may want to refer to the article on marine technology in the Jan/Feb 1996 issue of TIES magazine. If interested, you can get information on human-powered submarines by contacting the World Submarine Invitational '96, set your web browser to: **http://siolib-155.ucsd.edu/wsi/** or contact: Kevin Hardy, Co-Director, World Submarine Invitational '96, ph: (619) 534-6937. Internet: **khardy@ucsd.edu**

DESIGN ACTIVITIES—DESIGNING IMPACT STRUCTURES

Use the drawing provided by your teacher or develop one of your own from the example shown in Figure 3.14 of your textbook. After completing the drawing, cut out and assemble the car model. Design and develop a structure that will absorb the greatest amount of energy when tested on a stationary car-crash testing device similar to the one shown in the figure at the right.

Determine what materials will be most appropriate for dissipating the energy of the impact. Conduct experiments on the materials provided by your teacher to determine which materials are stiff and difficult to deform and which are more elastic and easier to deform. Which property will be most appropriate for your impact structure?

Test the car and its structure to see how well it works and how the design might be improved.

A pendulum-type car-crash test device

When you are ready, check with your teacher to test your car and structure in a moving car-crash device similar to the one in the figure below.

- Identify the science and technology concepts related to the impact structure problem.

- Identify which of the concepts you have applied properly and which you have applied improperly.

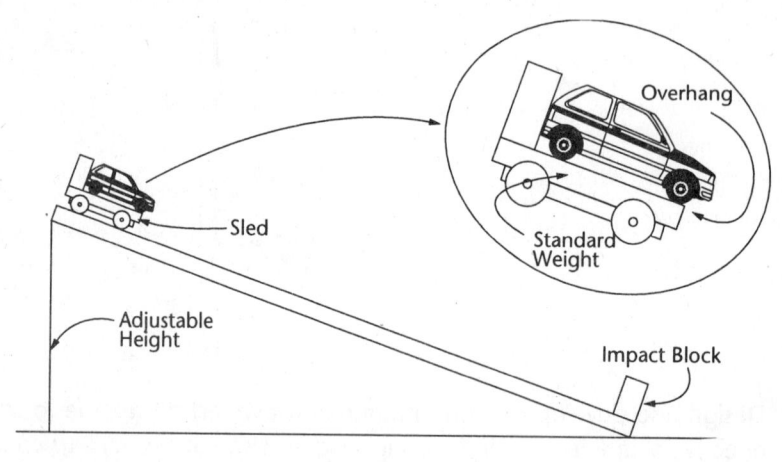

A moving sled-type car-crash test device

- Describe which of the concepts are most important in making your solution(s) to the above problem more effective.

- Describe how you can translate these concepts and apply them to improve your solution(s).

- Determine, through materials testing, what materials are most appropriate to use in your car model to provide the best cushioning during the impact from the crash tests.

DESIGN ACTIVITIES—MORE FREEDOM, LESS CONTROL

The mag-lev vehicle discussed in the chapter on Physical Systems in your text is an advanced form of two-directional transporting. Subways and trains are other more conventional means of transportation. The uniqueness of these systems is that part of the controls are built into the path. The flow of vehicles or materials is controlled by the pathway itself. Obviously, many more controls must be built into the tracks of a train or into a high-speed tube craft than into a slower pipeline or canal. Whether we are transporting eggs, bullets, or people, freedom of movement has both advantages and disadvantages. In transportation technology, more freedom means less control. Safety of the payload (including passengers) is a significant factor to consider. One solution is to turn the navigation and guidance of a vehicle over to an automatic system. Automatic guidance and control becomes more difficult and costly as the number of potential directions increases.

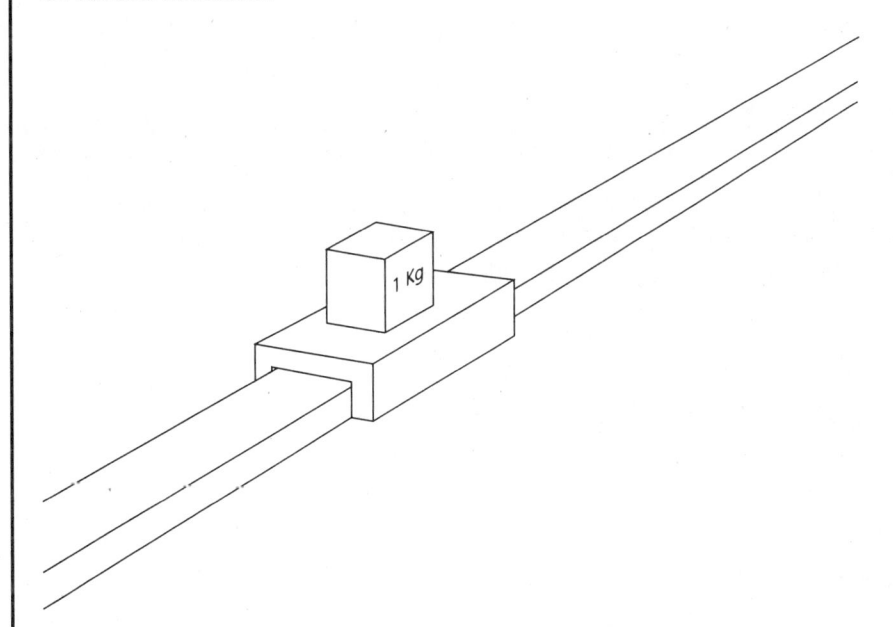

Design and develop a working model of a mag-lev system that is capable of transporting a load of one kilogram. Determine the most appropriate means for designing control of the vehicle into the pathways that will be used by the mag-lev vehicle. If you have time, design a method to stop the vehicle at designated places for receiving and discharging passengers.

DESIGN ACTIVITIES—TRANSPORTING STRUCTURES

You are challenged to build a glider to meet one of the two following briefs:

- Design a glider capable of flying along a straight path over a distance of at least 10 meters. The glider is to be made from thick paper or card and constructed by cutting, folding, and joining not more than two pieces of material.

- Design a glider capable of flying along a straight path over a distance of at least 30 meters. The glider may be made from a framework which supports a membrane covering.

In both the above activities, record your design on paper and include notes with your drawings which explain your design decisions. Evaluate the performance of your glider in terms of ease of construction, robustness of the glider, how well it meets the required performance, and the reliability of the flight path over a series of launches.

INTEGRATED S/M/T ACTIVITIES

An airplane's dynamic load and stress increase greatly as the plane moves through turns, dives, and pullouts. These movements must be made against the pull of gravity. These maneuvers increase the g-load of the plane. The g-load is the weight that must be pulled or lifted against Earth's gravity. A g-load of one (1 g) is equal to the plane's weight at rest or flying on the level. A plane pulling out of a dive has a g-load much greater than one. You may have felt these g-load forces if you were in an airplane as it took off and turned.

You may have also felt the opposite sensation when you jumped off a diving board, came down in an elevator really fast or sped down on a roller coaster. These are examples of negative g-loads, where the forces acting on you are less than the weight of gravity. How does this relate back to dynamic load? What does increasing the g-load do to an airplane in flight? Can you relate this to what happens to you when you ride a roller coaster? How would positive and negative g-loads affect the design of an airplane? How might you test the models you build for g-loading?

DESIGN ACTIVITIES—VEHICLES, LOADS, AND PURPOSE

Vehicles can be designed to perform a range of purposes and move many different loads. The vehicle shown in Figure 9.12 in your text was designed to move loads of toxic materials in a vast underground storage system. Operating by remote control will make it possible to handle the materials without subjecting human operators to exposure to the toxic materials.

The illustration below shows the model of a similar vehicle constructed of Fischer Technik™ components that is provided as part of the Jumpstart® materials developed by Economatics™ Ltd. that are available through Modern School Supply.™

Using the Economatic's buggy as a starting point, work in a small team to design a vehicle that will move and store barrels of toxic materials in an underground storage system. If time permits, you and your team can create a maze within which the vehicle must operate.

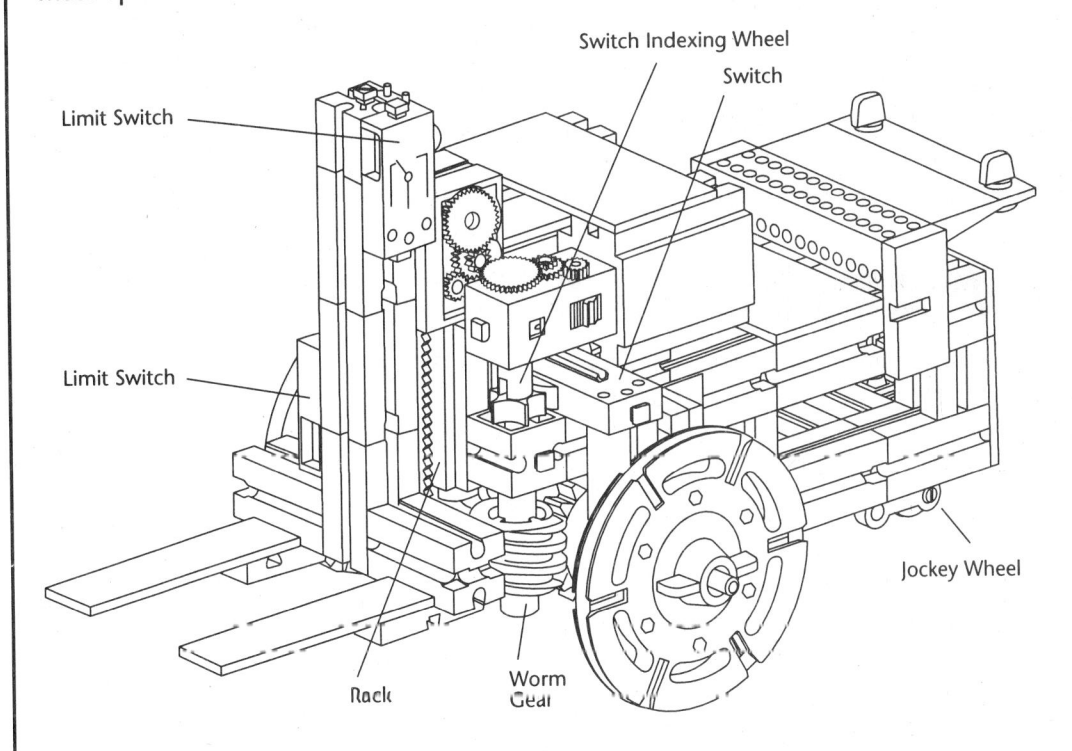

NOTE: This activity will be revisited in the Control chapter as part of the computer control systems.

INTEGRATED S/M/T ACTIVITIES

The freedom of movement of the space vehicle is possible until another planet catches the spacecraft in its gravitational field. Then a new reference plane is established. "Up" and "down" are in relation to the surface of that planet. The freedom of movement possible in outer space can pose some problems for space travelers. Without reference points, it is difficult to keep track of where you are going. It is also difficult to keep a sense of time. The sun does not rise and set in the 24 hour cycle of Earth. Artificial means must be designed to prevent disorientation.

All spacecraft have limitations on the amount of energy they can carry. Because the planets themselves move, nearby planets are the easiest targets and will be explored first. If we are to go into deep space, the exploratory craft cannot count on only the fuel it can transport. Energy from mechanical and electrical sources will be exhausted long before reaching the target. Breakthroughs in the utilization of energy from different portions of the energy spectrum expand the possibility of deep space travel. Devices for converting energy from solar power already look promising.

People will not be confined to the Earth for long. Time, speed, and available energy are critical in deciding where and for how long we might travel. As we leave our planet, the challenge of maintaining control along with freedom of movement will require new "ways."

DESIGN BRIEFS

People who will travel long distance in space or who will live and work in space for long periods of time will be more comfortable if they are in an environment that has a gravitational effect similar to that on Earth. A common approach to creating an artificial gravity field is to rotate the craft in a circle around a point so that the floor of the space craft moves along the outside of the circle. The centrifugal force can be matched to 1 g the normal force of gravity on Earth.

Design and develop a working model that illustrates how gravity of 1 g can be maintained in a space vehicle or colony. What rotation speed will be necessary for the model to operate properly? What will be the speed of rotation of the vehicle or space colony if it were full size? Would this approach be feasible, or would it take too much energy to keep the space structure rotating?

PRODUCTION SYSTEMS

Production includes any activity that yields or creates a product. These activities include extracting, harvesting, refining, producing, manufacturing, conservation, and recycling. Extracting minerals includes mining materials such as coal, salt, and diamonds. It also includes drilling and pumping such materials as gas, oil, water, and sulfur.

Extracting, Harvesting, and Refining

One method of mining is long wall mining. In this way, coal can be removed mechanically in large cuts, allowing the earth to settle and fill the open space, while requiring little or no support structures as protection from cave-ins. Another method is open pit, or strip, mining that is used to obtain gravel, coal, copper, diamonds, and other materials. A great deal of topsoil must be moved and huge ugly holes are often made. Open pit mining requires no air shafts and virtually no supports for cave-ins.

Reaching buried oil and pumping it to the surface is often a difficult and costly effort. Three general approaches are most used—regular pumping of oil, pumping heated liquids or solvents into the wells to liquefy oils too thick to pump regularly, and pumping water into wells to float the oil within reach of the pump intakes. Another new approach uses algae grown in ponds or in a factory. When placed in wells, these microscopic plants produce a slime around their cells that helps remove more oil from the underground rock particles.

Growing and harvesting is required to produce many of the materials used for food, shelter, clothing, and fuel. Over time, people have learned about the requirements for the growth of plants and animals, as well as other living organisms that affect their crops. Attempts to shield domestic plants and animals from their enemies led to techniques for weeding, trapping, and otherwise removing and resisting unwanted plants and pests.

A recent development involves growing and harvesting plants and animals that are too small to be seen without a microscope. Micro-algae are grown for such products as fish food, high protein/low cholesterol human dietary supplements, food colorings, thickeners, and vitamins.

Hydroponics is a method for growing plants inside a structure without soil. The nutrient-balance needed by the plants is provided in a solution that circulates over the plant roots. Light, temperature, and humidity are controlled, along with a careful watch for any signs of unwanted insects or disease-causing microbes. Foods can be grown year-round and in many locations—even space stations and caves.

Harvesting includes standard farming of land crops, as well as fish farming. Artificial structures are placed underwater to provide surfaces on which algae can grow. The algae, in turn, attract certain fish populations that can be harvested in highly efficient ways.

Many materials must be processed through refining before they can be used for human needs and wants. Refining of metals, fuels, and foodstuffs to make them more useful is common practice. Most metals are mined as ores and must be refined before use in manufacturing and construction. Most refining involves driving off excess oxygen through a process called reduction. A blast furnace is used to drive off oxygen from iron ore. This converts the ore to iron. Ceramic materials, such as Portland cement and limestone, are also reduced and refined.

Bauxite, the ore of aluminum, must be refined by passing electricity through the melted ore. This causes the melted aluminum to settle on the bottom of the furnace where it can be drawn off.

The refining of petroleum produces a range of usable fuels, as well as materials for manufacturing. Crude oils, such as hydrocarbons, fall into three main groups—the paraffins, the naphthenes, and the aromatics. Oil refining uses two types of processes—fractional distillation (the physical separation of the oil into several useful forms) and reforming through cracking and polymerization.

Coal can be refined to produce synthetic natural gas with many of the same properties as natural gas. Animal and plant wastes, as well as refuse from the products we use and consume, can be reclaimed and refined as a fuel, methane gas.

Foods are refined to remove impurities, to improve their characteristics for processing, and to improve their shelf life, nutritional value, and appearance. Flours, rolled oats, cornmeal, and sugar are examples of foods that are refined before use by humans.

INTEGRATED S/M/T ACTIVITIES—PRODUCTION AND EARLY DEVELOPMENTS IN MINING

The mining of raw materials such as flint, salt, and copper dates back many centuries. Before the sixteenth century, the major source of fuel was wood. In England, however, wood became scarce because it was used faster than it could be replenished. Wood became scarce once trees were cut down for fuel. You may recognize a similarity between the sixteenth century dilemmas and that are currently faced in some parts of the world. Now forests are being cut down in order to supply the energy and material needs of the population. As the population becomes larger, forests are cut down faster than trees can grow back. The amount of forestland is depleted and the ecological balance is threatened.

In the sixteenth century, before wood became scarce, mining was considered an affront to nature. When the need for an alternative fuel source became strong enough, mining coal became an acceptable method of extracting fuel.

Early mines were relatively small, shallow, and dangerous. Mines became deeper as better support structures were developed. Lifting devices, such as the one illustrated here, were needed as the mines got deeper. But deep mines had problems with ventilation, water, and transportation. The problem of removing water and getting sufficient air to the workers had to be addressed. Lifting the materials to the surface of the ground also required the development of new machines and structures. This new economic need contributed significantly to the development of the steam engine—a machine of major historical importance.

A—Reservoir. B—Race. C, D—Levers. E, F—Troughs under the water gates. G, H—Double rows of buckets. I—Axle. K—Larger drum. L—Drawing-chain. M—Bag. N—Hanging cage. O—Man who directs the machine. P, Q—Men emptying bags.

Design Brief

Conduct an investigation into the history of deep shaft and open pit mining in this country. Identify drawings and pictures of the different means of getting minerals out of the ground.

Develop working models of early human- and water-powered devices that were used for lifting materials and water out of early mines.

Develop working models of steam-operated devices for pumping water and lifting materials out of deep mines.

PRODUCING AND MANUFACTURING

Some energy devices are used to convert prime energy into secondary, more readily usable sources. These devices include solar energy units, geothermal devices, windmills, tidal-powered generators, hydroelectric power plants, nuclear reactors, fossil-fueled power plants, steam turbine generators, magneto hydrodynamic generators, and fuel cells. Solar energy can be used to generate heat or electricity. Solar cells, also called photovoltaic cells, are devices that convert the light of the sun directly into electrical energy.

Another prime source of energy with considerable potential for direct conversion is geothermal energy. In a limited number of locations on the Earth, wells can be dug to harness this heat, and steam escaping from cracks in the Earth can be captured directly.

The wind also has great potential as an energy source. Windmills must have some way of turning into the wind to maximize their power and control their speed.

Energy from water power is available in two major forms: mechanical and thermal. Mechanical energy exists in the movement of the waves, tides, and currents of the oceans. Thermal energy in water exists as a difference between the warm temperature of the surface water and the cold temperatures of water deep in the oceans. Few production systems have been developed to convert these sources.

Hydroelectric power plants use the driving force of moving water to produce energy. The water turbine is a logical development from early water-raising machines, such as the waterwheel.

The two major ways to produce nuclear energy are fission and fusion. Nuclear fission splits unstable atoms. Nuclear generating plants, called reactors, use fissionable materials to generate huge amounts of heat that is converted into steam to drive conventional electrical generators. Nuclear fusion uses reactors to bring materials together to produce vast quantities of clean energy. The major problems facing the large-scale development of nuclear fusion are initiating and controlling the extremely high temperatures of the process.

Fossil-fueled power plants are primarily large furnaces that burn coal, oil, or natural gas to generate heat to convert water to steam. The steam is used to drive a steam turbine that drives an electrical generator.

The magneto hydrodynamic (MHD) generator uses the electrical properties of a super-heated gas called a plasma. The plasma is passed through the magnetic field of a super magnet. The magnetic field captures the free ions from the plasma, causing electrons to flow, producing electrical energy.

The fuel cell converts hydrogen from the methane in natural gas into electrical energy. Currently, there is limited use of fuel cells as energy converters because of the cost of their manufacture and operation.

There are three types of manufacturing: custom producing of items, intermittent producing of batches of products, and the continuous production of products in mass. Custom manufacturing can operate on a small, medium, or large scale.

Intermittent manufacturing usually operates on a medium or large scale. Continuous or mass production can operate only on a large scale when a great quantity of a given item is produced.

Conservation and Reuse

Conservation may be less a problem of running out of resources, and more a problem of learning how to reclaim, recycle, and reuse the resources that are available. Many people, other than ecologists, are becoming aware of the need to conserve, reuse, and monitor the use of resources because they care about the future of the environment. Ecological concerns are beginning to change old throwaway habits.

Recycling and reuse systems have been developed so that many of the materials used for production can be recycled, reused, and reclaimed for future use. A key issue in the recycling process is the use of the reclaimed materials in making new products. If the system is to work effectively, all parts of the system must contribute. Consumers need to be convinced that the effort they make when they sort and recycle is worth it. Effective processes for reuse and reclaiming must be developed. Manufacturers need to be convinced that the use of reclaimed materials makes good business sense. Packaging can be designed to contribute as little waste as possible. Products can be designed so that when their useful life is ended, they can be taken apart and the materials can be reclaimed. The concept behind recycling is to "close" the system. The scrap, waste, or refuse from the system can be reintroduced and used again and again.

Waste and refuse can be considered as potential resources. Recycling can be established as a self-sustaining technological system.

DESIGN ACTIVITIES—RESEARCH AND DEVELOPMENT PROJECTS

There are many different projects you can pursue as a part of your study of the physical technologies. Several are suggested here, but they should be treated only as suggestions. If you are interested in planning and implementing your own research and development topic, you should talk with your teacher to see if the time, materials, and other resources will be available to complete the project. You may also want to talk with your teacher to explore other research and development topics that would be helpful in improving the design and technology program and facilities. For example, we have found that student research and development work with new materials and processes has helped to introduce these resources into the school program, thus benefitting all the people involved. There are many other instances similar to this example.

DESIGN ACTIVITIES—GROWING AND HARVESTING BY HYDROPONICS

Conduct the necessary research to determine what is required to raise vegetables using hydroponics (growing plants without soil). Determine which plants do well in a hydroponics system, and which do not. Conduct a test to see what differences there appear to be in vegetables grown hydroponically, as well as through standard methods.

DESIGN BRIEF—CONVERTING AND USING SOLAR ENERGY

Initiate the research and investigation on the different methods that are available to capture and use solar energy. Choose a method that is appropriate for your part of the country and that can be used to dry food, wood, or other materials. Determine which approach would be best to heat your home by solar energy and which could be best for cooling your home. Build a working model of one of these systems.

DESIGN BRIEF—CONVERTING USING WIND ENERGY

Determine some of the means by which wind can be converted to usable energy. Determine which of these means is most appropriate for use in your region. Design and develop a working model for capturing, converting, and using the wind energy. Determine how much energy you are able to convert in an hour at the different wind speeds prevalent in your area.

DESIGN ACTIVITIES—CONVERTING USING WATER POWER

Determine some of the means by which moving water can be converted to usable energy. Determine which of these means is most appropriate for use in your region. Design and develop a working model for capturing, converting, and using the water energy. Determine how much energy you are able to convert in an hour at the different speeds of flowing water that are available for use in your area.

DESIGN ACTIVITIES—PRODUCING AND USING ENERGY FROM A FUEL CELL

Initiate research and investigation into the operation of different fuel cells. Identify which of the fuel cells would be most appropriate in your home area. Determine some of the advantages and disadvantages of using this particular fuel cell. Determine what uses are most appropriate for the fuel cell. Determine the efficiency of the fuel cell and compare it to the cost of electrical energy and its cost in your school or your home. Build a physical model of one of the fuel cells. Determine if there is a fuel cell available in the technology facilities for you to use in your project.

DESIGN ACTIVITIES—DEVELOPING NEW PRODUCTS

A new company recently moved into your area and is very interested in developing new products for children. Wanting to take advantage of the creativity of young adults, the company approached the technology education department of your school with a proposal. Specifically, they are interested in producing kits, similar to the one illustrated in your textbook or ones of your own design, for young children (ages 5-11). The kits are intended to help young children understand and apply some of the key concepts of design and technology at a level appropriate to the age and development of the user. Three kits will be developed and produced, one for ages 5-7, one for ages 7-9, and one for ages 9-11.

When your design work is completed, make a sketch, take a photo, or grab a frame of a video of your model. Attach this visual documentation of your work in the space provided below.

DESIGN BRIEF

Select one of the age ranges above and, using the Design Loop as a guide, clarify what you plan to accomplish and how you will implement that plan. Some activities for each phase of the Design Loop are identified below:

Identify and define the problem.
- Clarify and investigate the needs and opportunities presented by the problem.
- Conduct interviews with one or more interested teachers and with children of that age.

Develop the design brief.
- Clarify the results you want to achieve.
- Describe and plan the types of activities that you think the children can do.
- Write the design brief that will guide your work.

Explore possible alternatives.
- Conduct a search for solutions and information.
- Consider several alternative experiences that children might use to learn about design and technology. Write out, illustrate, and print instructions for the activities.

Accumulate and assess the alternatives.
- Identify a range of alternatives.
- Consider each alternative and choose the best solution.

Try out the best solution.
- Experiment with the solution and translate it to a model and prototype.
- Determine items to be included in the kit—which will be bought and which will be made?
- List the sources and cost of each of the items you would buy.
- For those items you would manufacture, divide up the list among the class. Individually or in groups of two or three, do the following:
- Develop a plan for producing each of the items on your list, using the technology facility in your school.
- Compile the information from the plans of the class groups. Determine the required tools, materials, energy, information, people, space, time, and capital required for producing 100 kits.
- Design a production system that your class can actually carry out.
- Develop a package that will contain all the items and your instructions. Make the package safe, attractive, and efficient for use and storage.
- Conduct a pilot run and produce the 100 kits.

Evaluate the results.
- Test the solution and assess the process that was followed.
- Evaluate the overall effort. Include the assessment of (a) the finished items and kits, (b) the methods used to produce the product, (c) the work of the production team, and (d) your own participation and work as a team member.
- Test the kit by having children of the appropriate age, individually or in groups, use the product. Observe their behavior and interview them to get their reactions and suggestions. Be particularly alert to any safety hazards.
- Develop a report/presentation on improving the product and production system.

INTEGRATED S/M/T ACTIVITIES

- Identify the developmental characteristics of children who are potential users for your design and technology kit.

- Determine methods for testing materials and tools that will be included. How much strength of grip do children this age usually have? What tolerance limits will you build in? How strong should materials be? Devise tests for strength and durability.

- How much do kits such as this usually cost? Make a spreadsheet to show the costs of each item in the kit and the total amount for each kit. Calculate the differences in cost for a custom-made kit vs. those produced in batches of 20. Do the same for costs of batches of 100.

- Develop time lines and PERT charts for the production of the items, as well as for the assembly and production of the kits.

- Compare ergonomic statistics for the children ages 5-7 vs. ages 7-9 vs. ages 9-11, and determine how a specific product might differ for these age groups.

- Identify differences in safety concerns for each of the age groups of users. Design symbols that will warn the children of potential hazards. Identify what items will be excluded because of potential safety factors.

- Create instructions that can be understood by children who cannot read and by those who can read at a third-grade level. Count the number of syllables in the words you have used and the number of words per sentence. Simplify the instructions to create a clear, accurate message that is most likely to be understood by children with limited reading skills.

DESIGN ACTIVITIES

Design and develop a map showing the sources of the materials, parts, and components you used in the product selected in the previous activity, or from your own design and technology project. Show the most appropriate means for transporting these materials. For each of the different methods of transporting, calculate how long it would take for the materials to reach the site to fit into a Just-in-Time manufacturing plan. Determine which materials require quick delivery and which are less time-sensitive in their transportation. (Retain your maps for use in activities in Chapters 14 and 15.)

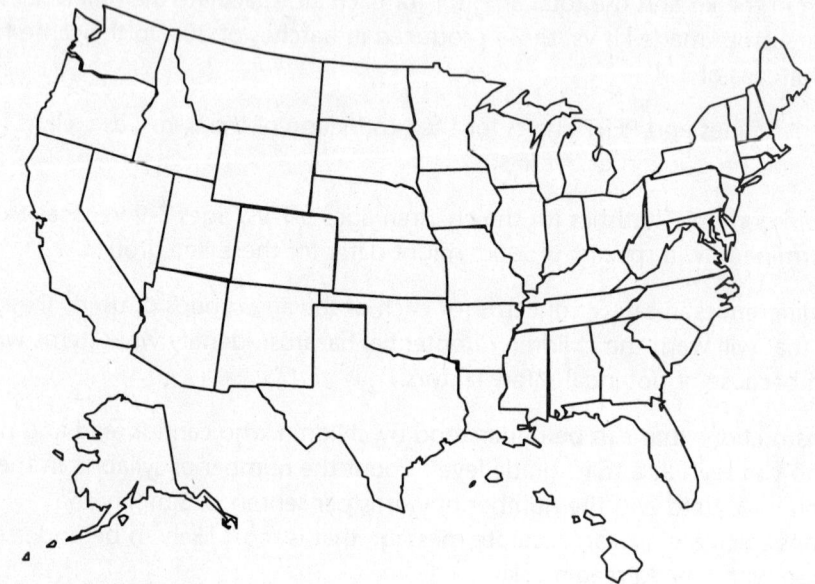

Map of the United States

Map of the World

ENRICHMENT DESIGN AND TECHNOLOGY ACTIVITIES

Design Briefs

- Design a shelter to take with you to the beach. The shelter should be light in weight so you can carry it easily. It should help you transport items from your home to the place on the beach where you will locate. Once you have opened it up, it should be big enough to contain you and the tools (radio, etc.) and materials (food, towels, etc.) you bring to the beach. It should shelter you from excess ultraviolet rays, heat, wind, and sand. The structure(s) should help your family and friends identify which shelter is yours. Develop a means of letting them know, from a distance, whether you would welcome their company or not. Remember, as you design the shelter, to consider the tools, materials, energy, information, time, money, and space requirements. Identify the human needs and wants the shelter should meet.

- Design a model of an electric, motor-powered vehicle that can operate on a sand table that simulates the surface of the Moon. The vehicle must be able to cross the sand table with a gross weight (vehicle, load, and driver) equal to 50 times the weight of the motor that is used to drive the vehicle. (The small electric motors available to you in school are usually small and lack significant torque. However, they do rotate at a high speed which can be used to your advantage in your design, through speed reduction arrangements that use a belt and pulley or a gear train for the drive system.)

- Design a meal that can be mass-produced and stored without refrigeration for use on an extended biking trip. List any instructions, including any required tools and materials, for making the meal more palatable before eating.

INTEGRATED S/M/T ACTIVITIES

- Calculate the weight that your vehicle would have on the Moon.

- Survey various batteries and motors to determine the power (wattage) each can generate. How much does each cost/cost to run? Determine the expected durability of each in terms of how long they could power the vehicle. If you were to add a solar cell booster, what change will be added to the vehicle's weight? Calculate whether the added weight will be offset by the added energy boost.

- Determine the energy needed for bike riders traveling 50 miles a day. What foods provide high energy and are efficiently digested? Which foods supply quick energy and which supply the body with energy slowly, for a longer duration?

CHAPTER 11

Biotechnology Systems

A technological revolution that is becoming more and more important is biotechnology. For centuries people have tried to learn more about living organisms in order to use this knowledge to enhance their lives. The quality of materials was improved, and destructive, sometimes life-threatening, outcomes could be avoided. With each advance in tools and materials, the ability to intervene and alter some life processes was possible.

The term biotechnology is defined as "any technique that uses living organisms, or parts of organisms, to make or modify products, to improve plants or animals, or to develop micro-organisms for specific uses." Biotechnology is currently being applied to such developments as:

(a) increasing the quality and output of food, both from plants and animals

(b) providing diagnostic tools for health care

(c) producing alternative energy sources

(d) tackling some environmental cleanup tasks

STAGES OF DEVELOPMENT

Biotechnology applications are reflections of the limits of the tools and materials that are available at a given time. With the development of microscopes came the ability to identify and study plants and animals (microorganisms) too small to be seen by the unaided eye. Recently, improvements in tools have allowed us to see into the structure of the cell itself and make it possible to change the rate and type of cellular growth.

Traditional biotechnology makes use of organisms, plant or animal, just the way they are found in nature, without altering them. However, procedures that made use of the understanding of growth processes were applied in order to increase the yield and quality of food, fiber, or other material derived from plants and animals. Attempts to control spoilage and illness were based on the knowledge of the time.

In the middle of the nineteenth century, Pasteur's investigation of the growth of these microbes, bacteria, and yeast led to the much more precise control of fermentation processes and better control of some diseases. Food preservation techniques, such as drying, salting, pickling, canning, refrigeration, and freezing, controlled the conditions needed for the growth of organisms that cause food to spoil.

People have always tried to explain and treat illness. Lister showed that germs (microorganisms) could be spread through contact with an infected person. Procedures for sanitation and sterilization decreased the spread of communicable diseases.

At approximately the same time, Mendel wrote about his systematic experiments on reproduction and the hereditary transmission of the characteristics of the parents to their offspring. Mendel also found mutations, the surprises that often occur in reproduction.

Records show that as far back as 6000 B.C., fermentation processes were used to make such products as bread, cheese, beer, and wine. Although people were not able to isolate the specific ingredients that produced the results they wanted, they observed and tried different approaches in order to improve the quality of the products.

At the next stage of biotechnological development, within the last century, more and more microorganisms have been identified. Production of specific enzymes and microbes was now done in the factory, so that greater quantities could be made in more controlled circumstances. During World War II, medicine was critically needed to treat the wounded and stop bacterial diseases. The mold that produced penicillin, an antibiotic that kills bacterial growth, was found. Through use of ultraviolet light and chemicals that caused mutation, the offspring of the original molds produce much greater quantities of penicillin than the parent molds could make.

In 1953, the structure of DNA was identified. This discovery was essential to the beginning of modern biotechnology because now technologists could develop the tools and processes that would alter the internal structure and functions of the organism itself. They could engineer the changes that were desired.

DESIGN ACTIVITIES—BIOTECHNOLOGY SURVEY

Complete the following survey—introduced in your textbook—to determine the daily contact you have with biotechnology. From the following list of activities, decide if there might be a biotechnology connection. Answer "yes" if you think biotechnology might be used in the activity, or "no" if it might not be used.

1. ____ Wash the dishes?

2. ____ Drink from a water fountain?

3. ____ Glue a plastic model together?

4. ____ Eat a steak?

5. ____ Throw away trash?

6. ____ Eat a cheeseburger?

7. ____ Drink a soft drink?

The answer to all the above questions is "yes"! From your textbook, determine how each of the activities are linked with biotechnology.

DESIGN ACTIVITIES—SELECTIVE BREEDING IN ANIMALS/PETS

For centuries, one of the major aspects of biotechnology has been the work done in the improvement of animals. The following are introductory biotechnology activities related to animal breeding that you might like to pursue:

- Either individually or in a small group, select an animal that has been grown either as a pet or for food or other products. Trace the changes in breeds or varieties over the last century.

- Identify ways in which selective breeding has been used in order to improve the desired characteristics of the breed. Find out about practices such as artificial insemination, surrogate mothering, etc. to ensure that the offspring have the desired characteristics.

- List some of the processes that have been developed to keep the animal population in check and to keep pets as healthy as possible.

- Visit a veterinarian or grower to find out about methods of disease control that have been improved over time.

- Contrast the agricultural practices found in countries with a high degree of technological development vs. those with very little.

- Compare an agribusiness approach vs. a family farm or ranch approach in terms of labor vs. capital-intensive processes, the amount of capital risk, and the potential yield of each.

- Read *Diet for a Small Planet*. Create a display that contrasts the process of growing animals in different countries of the world. Include different cultural attitudes toward eating meat. Also indicate differences in the degree to which the agricultural resources of the country will support the growth of different types of animals and plants.

DESIGN ACTIVITIES—GROWING CONDITIONS FOR YEAST

Many biotechnology processes depend upon yeast as an essential ingredient. The most common of these is the making of bread. Although some breads do not use yeast (or other leavening agents), most breads involve the use of yeast to produce gas to cause the bread to rise. The following activities are intended to show the role yeast plays in the making of bread:

- Use a standard recipe to make a yeast bread.

- Vary the recipe for the bread in the following ways:
    - add more sugar
    - include less sugar
    - add more fat
    - use different types of flour
    - add more yeast
    - include less yeast
    - knead longer than the recipe indicates
    - only stir until ingredients are mixed
    - increase the temperature for rising
    - decrease the temperature for rising
    - cover the dough during rising
    - leave the dough uncovered during rising
    - bake without waiting for the dough to rise

- With a microscope, observe and record the changes in the dough during the stages of fermentation and rising.

- Measure the differences in the characteristics of the bread produced under the different conditions for growth.

- Develop a plan for ensuring the quality of the next bread that you bake.

DESIGN ACTIVITIES—GINGER ALE MANUFACTURE

Ginger ale has been made for many years, both on a small, homemade scale and commercially. There are many standard recipes in recipe books that you can use in these activities for making ginger ale. The making of ginger ale provides another useful context for your design and technology work in the sense that you will design and make a bioreactor and then find out how to control it. You may also have the opportunity to compare batch production with semi-continuous flow systems. This is achieved by immobilizing the yeast in a harmless seaweed gel, called sodium alginate. This process, unlike some immobilization techniques, is easy to use, cheap, and avoids the use of toxic or dangerous chemicals. Once the yeast cells are fixed in this way, the sugar solution, containing the other ingredients, can be passed over the yeast beads. As this happens and the sugars diffuse into the beads, the yeast uses them in its respiration to produce alcohol and carbon dioxide, which passes out of the beads. The advantage of this technique is that the ginger ale is not contaminated with yeast, so there is not a costly downstream processing stage in which the yeast has to be separated from the ginger ale.

Many research and development projects can be devised around the process of immobilization. Some examples include the following: what effect does bead size have on efficiency; can the pore size be reduced by a partial drying of the beads to prevent cell leakage; can the beads withstand compression which would happen if the whole process was scaled up to commercial standards; and what is the optimum ratio of yeast to alginate in the bead?

You should only sample the ginger ale that is produced, and only if the equipment used was food grade and had not been used for other nonfood projects. The vessels should be sterilized before use with sodium hypochlorite tablets that are used for home brewing. These tablets should also be used to sterilize the vessel again after the ginger ale has been prepared.

If the immobilization technique is used then, as long as the calcium chloride is washed off the beads prior to use, there should be no hazard in the chemicals themselves. It is not recommended that students drink the ale in any quantity, but that they only taste small samples of the product.

The fermentation of ginger ale is only one context that could be used for this design activity. Another context is the production of fuel alcohol, such as that used in Brazil. Brazil now runs all its cars and trucks on alcohol made from the sugar cane it grows. In this case, using glucose as the food source will cause the yeast to produce alcohol even in the presence of air.

Large soda or pop bottles make good vessels. Even better are the large plastic containers used to provide bottled water for offices. Some of these hold five gallons of liquid, which provides a workable volume for a small bioreactor. The illustration on the next page shows a bioreactor developed for making ginger ale. Notice the motor driven paddle stirrer and the electrical heater that uses a ceramic resistor as the heat producing device.

DESIGN ACTIVITIES—GINGER ALE MANUFACTURE
CONTINUED

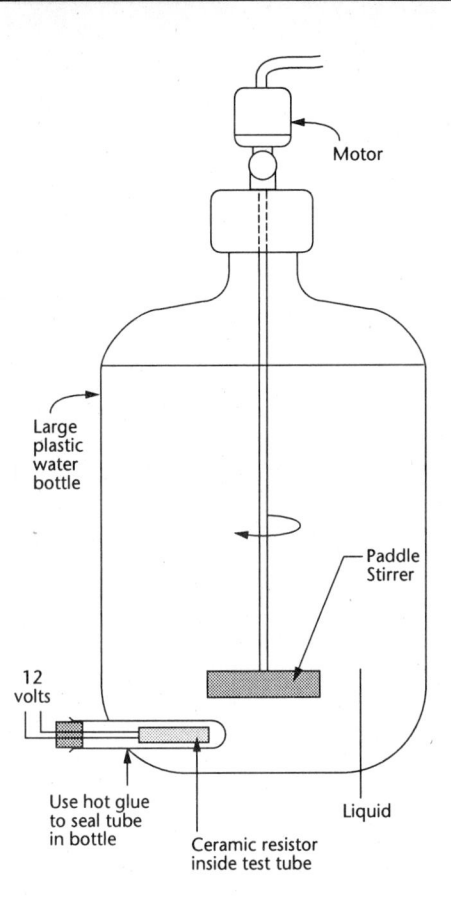

As noted earlier, heaters for bioreactors can be made using ceramic resistors. A more detailed treatment is included in the illustration at the right. This heating device can be used with temperature sensors and electronic systems to control the temperature inside the vessel. You can return to this activity when you move on to the chapter on control.

CAUTION: The test tube must be completely immersed in liquid before the power is turned on, or the heat may cause the test tube to shatter.

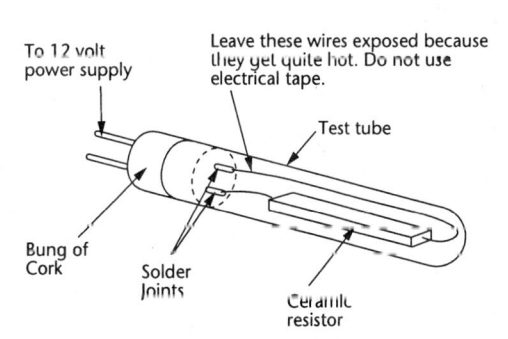

Ceramic resistor used as small heater.

Glass tubes packed with beads can provide the basis of a continuous flow bioreactor. The tubes can be fed with liquid in a number of ways. Peristaltic pumps are good, but tend to be expensive. Windshield washer pumps would work, but may not perform as well the cell numbers increase. A gravity feed would work well. The liquid could be returned to the vessel by a small water pump such as used for a windshield washer pump. The liquid could also be returned by an air-lift pump driven by a simple aquarium aeration pump.

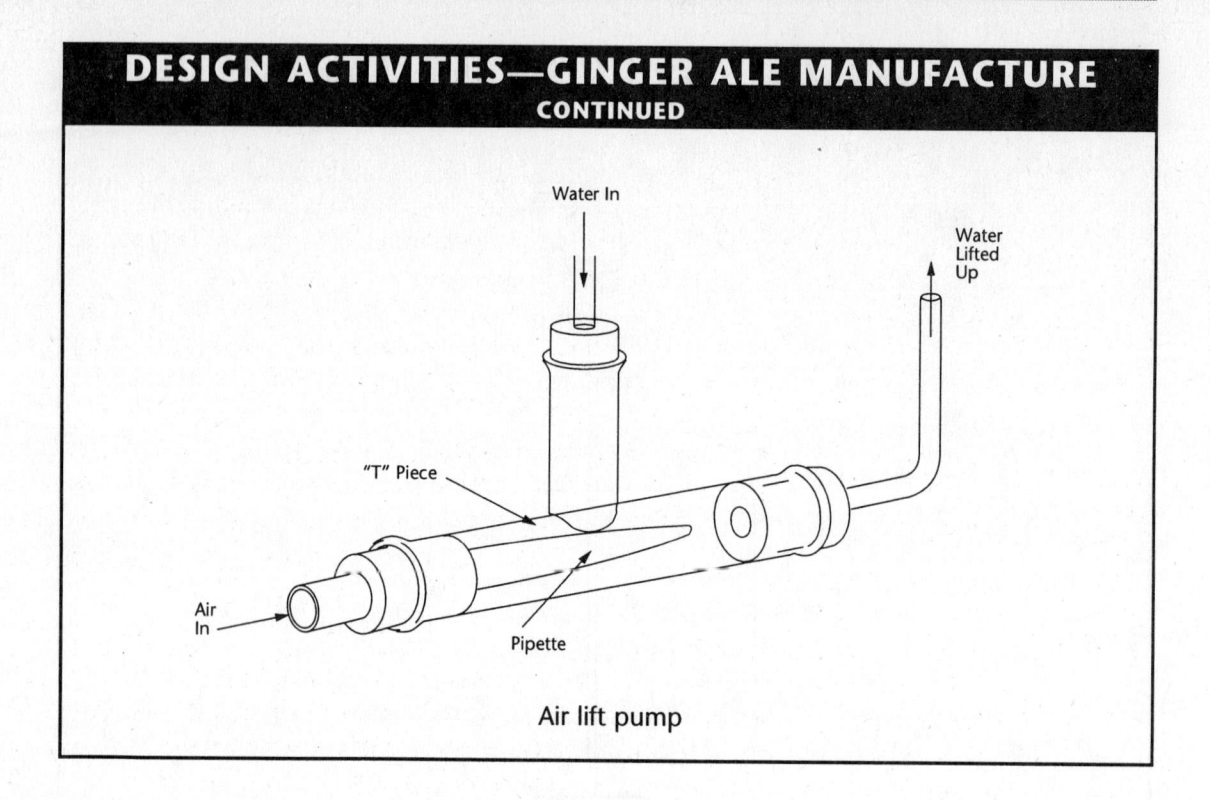

DESIGN ACTIVITIES—GINGER ALE MANUFACTURE
CONTINUED

Air lift pump

CELLS AND GENETICS ENGINEERING

All living things are made up of one or more cells as their basic building blocks. The average human body has more than one hundred billion individual cells, all living and working together as one unit. However in single-cell organisms, called microbes, each cell is able to perform all the functions necessary for its life and reproduction. When a cell divides, the strings of deoxyribonucleic acid (DNA) bunch together into chromosomes, which then make identical copies of themselves. The chromosomes pass on vital information to the new generation of organisms. The DNA strings contain many short segments known as genes, that carry the information cells need to make an enzyme or protein. With one-celled organisms, genes are contained on a single genome, or circular strand of DNA. The DNA is duplicated and, before the cell divides, a complete, identical strand is passed on to the new daughter cell.

Genetically engineering an organism involves moving the genes from one organism into the cell of another organism. A recombinant DNA (rDNA) contains the new genetic information that is passed on to its next generations. Bacteria resulting from further growth are called clones because each cell has identical DNA in its genome. Bioreactors are huge tanks where growing conditions such as temperature, nutrients, pH level, etc., are carefully maintained so that quantities of the genetically engineered product can be produced.

Currently, only relatively simple organisms can be altered through the rDNA process. Cells with a short life span tend to reproduce rapidly, producing many generations in a short period of time without the contamination of other genetic material.

Splicing genes first requires the isolation of the chromosomal DNA that has the desired gene, loosening the bond between the strands of DNA by using restriction enzymes, and then moving the DNA to another organism. The receiving organism has been prepared to accept the new strand. A second enzyme is then used to glue, or bond, the new combination into place. The foreign gene becomes part of the organism's genetic makeup, and the altered organism exhibits the characteristics of the new gene.

The Human Genome project hopes to identify the function of each segment of human DNA and produce a map that will decode all of the information contained in the DNA. Such a map will increase the potential to repair or make inactive genes associated with handicapping conditions, potential disease, and factors associated with gender, race, and sexual orientation.

DESIGN ACTIVITIES—GENETICALLY ENGINEERED FOODS

Recently, there have been many developments in the use of genetics to improve and expand the different kinds of food available for our use. The engineered tomato is an interesting example of how a plant and its fruit were designed or engineered. Consider one or more of the following activities:

- Read about the development of the engineered tomato that was planted in open fields in 1993. Interview a grocer or food broker in your area and see whether they stock the new tomatoes.

- Identify the reasons for the development and the controls that were placed on the growth of the tomatoes.

- Obtain the GRAS list—generally accepted as safe list for food ingredients and processes from the U. S. Food and Drug Administration (FDA). Find out the standards that are used by the FDA in deciding the list of additives and ingredients that must go on the label if products are to be consumed by people.

- Contrast this list with similar lists from governments in other countries. Identify the regulations that have been included in treaties such as NAFTA and other international trade agreements.

- Interview people from the two sides of the controversy and analyze the debate. Take a position and prepare a paper: Tomato soup companies should/should not be able to use engineered tomatoes in their soups without any additional warnings on their labels.

INTEGRATED S/M/T ACTIVITIES—EDIBLE FUNGI

For centuries people have eaten different kinds of fungi. One of the most common, yet uncommon, foods is the mushroom. You might like to pursue a study of mushrooms. If so, consider the following:

- Contact an English teacher to identify a novel or story in which poisonous mushrooms were used to kill or harm the victim.

- Identify the ways to distinguish between toadstools and mushrooms. Take a mushroom walk and pick as many varieties as possible.

- Visit or write to a mushroom production company to identify the kinds of microbes (and their sources) that are currently used in production.

- Identify the conditions needed to ensure that contaminants from the air, utensils, ingredients, etc., are controlled.

- Contrast the yield and the safety of mushroom farms vs. gathering mushrooms in the wild. Contrast the variety and availability given each condition.

DESIGN ACTIVITIES—BIOREACTOR: HOW TO CAUSE A STIR!

Bioreactors are essential devices in the study and use of biotechnology. They are used regularly in producing a wide range of products by bioprocessing techniques. Through the following activities, you will find out about:

- how large bioreactors are used in biotechnology to make all sorts of useful products;

- how bioreactors are designed to obtain the best possible yield of the product; and

- how to design for yourselves an impeller to stir a bioreactor, and how to decide whether or not it is a good design.

What Is a Bioreactor?

Bioreactors used to be called fermentors since they were most often used to ferment wine or ale. Today there are many different processes used in these containers, many of which need air. Therefore, these are not fermentation processes. Bioreactors are simply vessels in which a biological agent, perhaps cells or enzymes, are used to make something useful. A vessel in which you make yogurt, cheese, or wine is a bioreactor. However, in recent years, the bioreactor has come to mean a very high-tech vessel in which microbes grow under carefully controlled conditions to produce things like antibiotics, flavor enhancers, insulin, medicines, etc. Biotechnology industry has come to rely on bioreactors as the mini factories of the future in which microbes, often genetically engineered in some way, do all the hard work.

Vinegar is made in a traditional bioreactor. Formerly, the vessel was a large wooden cylinder filled with wood shavings. A vinegar cylinder or vat may be 30 feet high and 20 feet in diameter. In such a bioreactor, the bacterium *Acetobacter aceti* lives on the wood shavings and feeds on the alcoholic malt liquor, which is poured over the shavings. The alcohol is turned to acetic acid, or vinegar, which then has the typical malty flavor. In this bioreactor, the liquid is sprayed onto the wood at the top of the vessel, it trickles down to the base, and is then recirculated again. This happens many times until the batch of vinegar is ready. It is then filtered and cleaned through a process called downstream processing. Before the method of cleaning the vinegar was improved, tiny nematode worms could be seen swimming around in the vinegar. It is important that the bacteria have enough air to respire with, therefore, the vessel is not filled to the top with liquid.

There is now a more modern way of making vinegar, which involves a closed, stainless steel bioreactor. There are no wood shavings; the microbes just live in the liquid. The air has to be pumped into the vessel and the whole thing has to be stirred around to make the oxygen dissolve in the liquid. With this arrangement, it is crucial to have good mixing or the all-important bacteria would die.

Why do you think wine goes sour if it is kept for a few days after having been opened to the air?

INTEGRATED S/M/T ACTIVITIES

Find out about what things are made in modern bioreactors. You could use the library or newspapers to help you. Write a short account of how bioreactors are used in industry today.

DESIGN ACTIVITIES—USING MODERN BIOREACTOR

The vessels used in modern bioreactors are quite unlike the old-style vinegar vats. Everything that goes on in these modern vessels has to be carefully monitored and controlled so that the conditions are kept favorable for the growth and production of the product. A small laboratory scale bioreactor costs many tens of thousands of dollars. The scientists and engineers working on a new process have to be sure that they copy the results from the laboratory bench when it is scaled up to an industrial size. This is not easy to do, and often involves an intermediate, or pilot, scale model.

The conditions inside are monitored with sensors or probes measuring factors such as temperature, pH, and oxygen levels. The vessel has to be kept at the ideal temperature. This may involve warming it up, but more often requires a cooling jacket to take away the heat produced by the process. Additionally, ingredients will need to be added to and taken out of the bioreactor, all without letting the air in or out.

- Why is it vital that no microbes from outside get into the bioreactor? Why also is it important that nothing escapes from inside the bioreactor?

The ingredients and materials that are sometimes added include acid, alkali or more food (substrate). Samples are taken out from time to time to check the number or condition of the cells or the amount of the product that has been made.

Finally, sterile air has to be blown into the bioreactor. To help the oxygen dissolve fully, the air bubbles are smashed up with an inside propeller called an impeller. This works only if the cells are quite strong, such as with bacterial cells. More delicate plant cells need a more gentle way of stirring the contents of the vessel.

- Can you find out about other ways of mixing the contents of a bioreactor for plant or animal cells?

DESIGN ACTIVITIES—DESIGNING AN IMPELLER

The design of the impeller is crucial to the success of the whole process. Good mixing means good growth and more profits. Engineers often try out prototypes under non-sterile conditions to see how they will perform. For this design activity, you will need a plastic vessel (a soda bottle or larger jam or pickle jar would do well), a small low voltage motor, a drive rod (metal or strong plastic) and some copper-clad board (as used for making printed circuit boards).

A new biotechnology company is seeking a new impeller design for a bioreactor. They want it to cause a stir among their competitors by outperforming existing designs! You have been asked to make and test some prototypes to meet demanding standards. You will be expected to make a presentation to the company board of your designs.

An idea to stir your imagination

Try making a rig like the one shown in (A) below and then modify the design to make improvements to it. The impeller can be made by soldering small pieces of copper-clad board on a disc of the same material This is mounted on a rod running down from a small motor. The base of the vessel will need something to hold the rod in place while still allowing it to turn freely. Run an air line from a small aquarium pump into the vessel so the bubbles rise up under the impeller.

The design of the impeller or stirring system would be expected to meet certain criteria, such as:

- air bubble should be as small as possible to make the passage of oxygen into the culture as effective as possible.

- rapid mixing of additives, such as alkali and acid.

- full mixing of solid particles e.g. clumps of cells (can be simulated by fine sand).

- no large central vortex so that air cannot leave the bioreactor without passing through the liquid.

- minimum power input (to reduce costs).

- no dead spaces, to reduce conditions that could become anaerobic.

- minimum shear on cells from the fast movement of the impeller.

- impeller diameter should be within 1/3 to 1/2 of the vessel diameter.

- cells should not clump together.

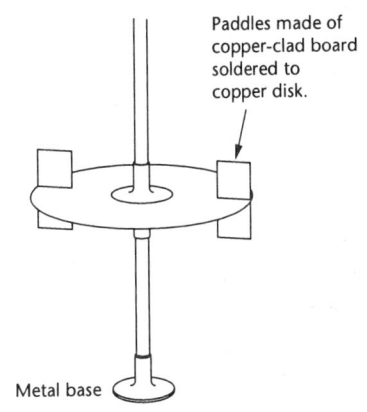

Paddles made of copper-clad board soldered to copper disk.

Metal base

(A) Impeller test rig

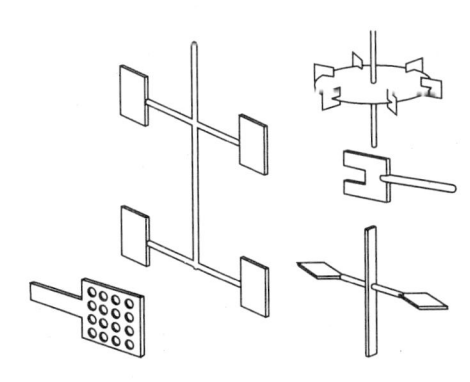

(B) Some Impeller Designs

DESIGN ACTIVITIES—BIOREACTORS AND CELL IMMOBILIZATION

Design Brief: Hold That Cell.

You have been asked by a local alternative fuels company to design and construct a bioreactor model for continuous production of ethanol as a gasoline substitute. You must design your prototype system in such a way that the yeast cells used do not get lost or mixed up with the sugar solution they are converting to ethanol. Luckily, you know of an easy way to immobilize cells in small gelatin beads, which can be used to keep them separate from the sugar solution. The tough part is determining the best way to feed the sugar solution into the vessel so you can have a continuous production of ethanol.

Here are some tips for constructing such a system. Tall, narrow, plastic soda bottles or bottled water containers make excellent bioreactor vessels. (See page 329 in this chapter.) Held (or mounted) upright with the spout pointing down, they can be used as a large column where the bioreaction process can take place. Sensors can be made to monitor the reaction temperature and any other necessary conditions. A way to add sugar solution at the top and then check for ethanol at the bottom will also be needed.

BIOPROCESSING

Bioprocessing methods, used in industry, involve two major procedures: fermentation and bioconversion. These two procedures require supporting technologies, such as fermentors, bioreactors, sensors, and electronic control mechanisms. Fermentation has been traditionally used in the food industry for making beer and wine and recently has been used to produce genetically improved insulin for use in treating diabetes.

Control mechanisms are extremely important for making sure the microorganisms grow well, produce the right product in the greatest amount, and detect contamination. These controls are generally electronic sensors built into the fermentor, with computers keeping track of the information coming from the sensors.

The tools of modern biotechnology are also focused on problems caused by viruses. Viruses are quite different from bacteria and yeast. Viruses incorporate themselves into the DNA of the host organism and use the host's processes for their own reproduction. A virus can remain dormant in the host for some time and only show its presence after years of living in the host genes. Mutations can occur as the virus adapts to its host and learns to resist attacks by the host immune system or medication. Because it uses the host's own genetic material for its mutations, any medicine is likely to kill host cells as it kills the virus. Development of better tools and processes can lead to more effective treatment of viral diseases, such as AIDS and the common cold, and viruses that attack plants.

Bioconversion uses enzymes or cells (biocatalysts) to speed up biological reactions, without becoming a part of the reaction itself. Enzymes have been used to improve fuels, to diagnose conditions and illnesses, to detect the presence of disease-causing organisms in foods and other products, and in cleaning techniques.

Immobilization techniques to recapture the enzymes so that they can be reused include chemical bonding, adsorption, and entrapment. In each of these methods, the goal is to fix the cell so that it does its work, but remains insoluble. Immobilization techniques are also becoming very important for the development of biosensors.

Technological efforts to decrease death have been more readily used than efforts to decrease birth. Therefore, the world population continues to grow and the demand for resources increases. Farming methods, whether for food, fiber, or forest products, need to be made more efficient if the demand is to be met.

DESIGN ACTIVITIES—CATERING TO OUR SWEET TOOTH

Most of us have developed a sweet tooth and crave products that use some form of sugar. Considerable work is being done related to the development of natural and artificial sweetening agents, including those that are ignored or that can not be assimilated by the body.

- Make high-fructose sugar (HFS). Contrast the amount of sweetener required when HFS is used vs. other sweeteners.

- Identify how the use of this sugar changes the nutritional content of the product. Interview a nutritionist about how the taste for sweetness is learned. Determine recommendations on using artificial sweeteners for people at different ages, energy requirements, and potential diseases.

- Prepare a collage of labels from foods that are sweetened.

- Find out how much money is spent on sweetened drinks, candy, and snacks each year in the U.S. and in other countries of the world.

- Identify the costs/benefits of the use of different sweeteners. Be sure to include nutritional as well as economic criteria.

- Identify the impact of snacks and drinks on the nutritional value of the diet.

- Identify some of the developments regarding sweetening agents that are not assimilated by the human body, such as the left-handed sugar molecule. What advantages would these sweeteners provide to individuals as well as to food production companies?

DESIGN ACTIVITIES—HORMONES AND PRODUCTION

Periodically, there has been considerable attention given to the use of hormones to cause bodily changes in animals and humans. All too often, many of us are ill prepared to understand what is actually taking place with the use of hormones, as in the examples below:

- A current controversy is over the use of Bovine Stimulator Hormone to increase milk production in dairy cows. Identify how the hormone works. Interview a dairy farmer, a food broker, and a representative from a consumer group to find out the differences in opinion about what is an acceptable risk.

- It is possible to increase the body's production of muscle through the use of growth hormones. Identify some of the concerns that have been expressed if the hormones are used in production of animals for food.

- Athletes who compete must undergo tests for evidence of the use of steroids for bodybuilding. Why? Research the effects of such use on the human body.

INTEGRATED S/M/T ACTIVITIES—UNDERSTANDING AND FIGHTING VIRUSES

AIDS, cancer, and the common cold have eluded the pharmaceutical industry in coming up with a cure or effective treatment. A better understanding of these diseases is required when difficult decisions are made regarding support for the development of adequate means of treatment, protection, and prevention.

- In groups, select one of these or another disease that currently poses a major challenge to medicine and health management.

- Trace the history of what has been discovered and treatments that have been tried.

- Write to or interview someone who is engaged in research and development. Identify barriers they face and successes they have encountered.

- Prepare a display for your school bulletin board that explains your findings. Describe the scope of the current problem, along with the most recent recommendations on how to protect oneself from exposure to the disease. Include recommendations on how to keep the immune system healthy in order to avoid or delay the progress of the disease if exposed.

DESIGN ACTIVITIES—BIOCONVERSION AND CELL IMMOBILIZATION

Refer to your text to review the concepts of bioconversion, enzymes, and biocatalysts. Review also the different means of immobilization including chemical bonding, adsorption, and entrapment. In many agricultural areas a great deal of chemical fertilizer is used to enhance and promote plant growth. This fertilizer is easily carried along with soil runoff caused by frequent rains. The result is a high concentration of phosphates accumulating in the local rivers and streams. Phosphate is utilized by many different algae commonly found in these waters, which quickly flourish and overgrow. The overgrowth depletes the water of oxygen, eventually killing many marine inhabitants of the streams.

Micro-algae (those other than large seaweeds) can be immobilized and used for a number of purposes, one of which is the removal of phosphates and nitrates from farm waste water.

Design Brief: Waste Eaters

Design a system to remove unwanted phosphates from stream water that involves the use of immobilized micro-algae. The system must be passive in operation, supply sufficient solar radiation for photosynthesis and require low maintenance. Include thought on possible monitoring methods that would indicate when replacement algae is required.

DESIGN ACTIVITIES—DESIGNING YOUR OWN ALGAE BIOREACTOR

In this activity, you will learn about how micro-algae can be grown to produce many things, including human food, fish food, food colorings, gums, and a range of chemicals such as glycerol, amino acids, fats, steroids, and vitamins. You will have an opportunity to design your own bioreactor to grow algae and to test how well it works. You could even use algae to refresh stale air from enclosed spaces such as office blocks or spacecraft.

Algae include the large multicellular seaweeds, which have been a source of food for years in countries like Japan and have been used as a source of chemical gums such as agar and alginates. Alginates have a variety of uses, from producing high-quality varnishes for musical instruments, to stiffening the fabric in roller blinds, to immobilizing cells and enzymes in biotechnology.

Here we are dealing with much smaller types, called the micro-algae. Micro-algae have only recently attracted attention as having economic importance. They have many different forms, some of which are very attractive. *Spirulina,* as the name suggests, is a spiral shape and can be bought in health food shops as a protein supplement. It is grown in large salt lakes in Africa, but more recently farmers have been experimenting with other techniques using plastic tubing. Other algae, including *Dunaliella,* have a red coloration, or pigment, in them. They are grown so that this pigment can be extracted and used as beta-carotene food coloring. *Dunaliella salina* grows in seawater and enjoys the title of the most salt-tolerant organism known. The simple *Chlorella,* a green alga, is grown in shallow lakes to produce a nutritious fish food.

Porphyridium is another marine alga which produces large amounts of a slimy gum, similar to the xanthan gum used as a thickener in foods like mayonnaise. Currently, the gum is used to help extract oil from oil-bearing rocks. It is piped with water down to the rock layers containing the oil. The gum helps to release the oil from the rock particles and so improves the extraction rate.

Blue-green algae can also be used, such as *Nostoc* or *Anabaena.* These produce significant amounts of nitrates which can be used as an organic alternative to fertilizers. Imagine a living product which claimed to provide all the fertilizer requirements for your lawn or vegetable plot for a whole growing season, for a fraction of the cost of chemical alternatives!

- Why do you think growing a pure culture of algae in saltwater might have advantages over freshwater types?

- Why do you think there is a lot of interest in the idea of putting the nitrogen-fixing gene from blue-green algae into crop plants?

A vessel or bioreactor for growing algae has a number of differences from those used to grow bacteria. You cannot have the vessel stirred with an impeller, as this would damage the more delicate cells. Also, the cells need light for their photosynthesis. We are therefore designing a photo-bioreactor stirred with air to give a supply of carbon dioxide to the algae. This means that the water inside must never be far away from the light source or the algae will die.

DESIGN ACTIVITIES—DESIGNING YOUR OWN ALGAE BIOREACTOR CONTINUED

Two basic designs suggest themselves here. One is to have two parallel plates of plastic (Plexiglas™ or Perspex™) with perhaps only about a 4 cm gap between to allow the light through. The shape of the vessel might be determined by studying the flow patterns of water if you bubble air in from the base. These two designs are rather poorly done. Can you improve the designs and avoid dead spaces where the algae can settle out?

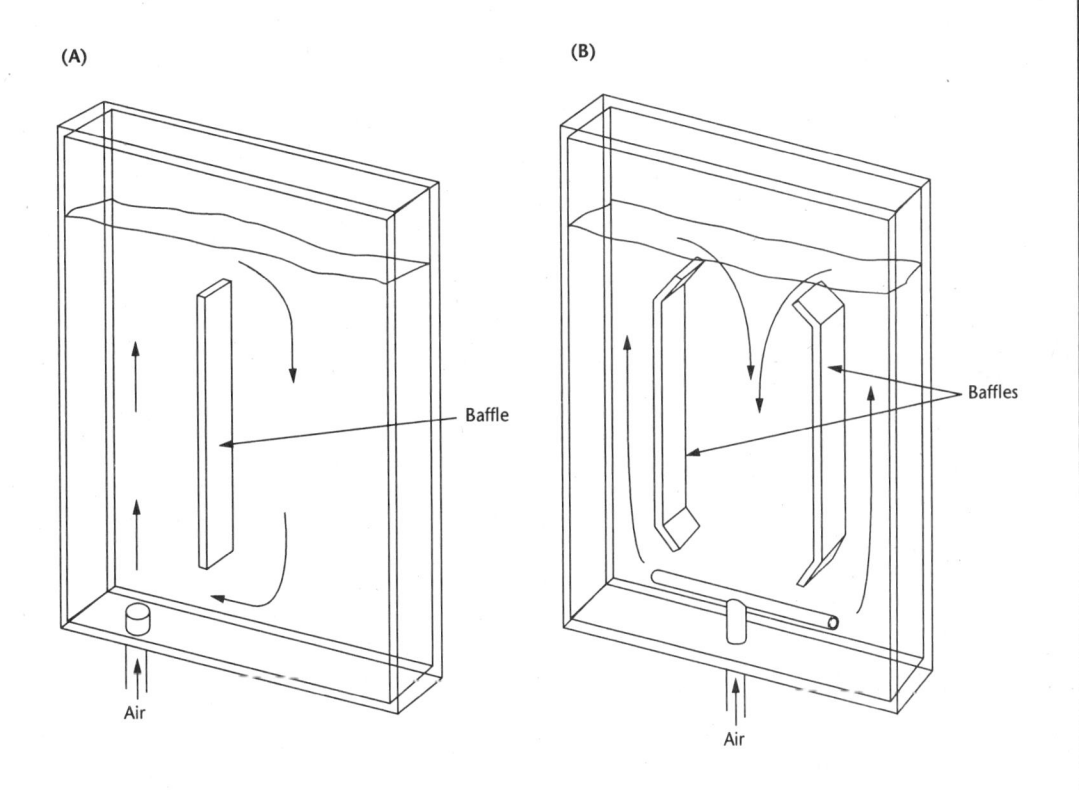

(A)

(B)

Baffle

Baffles

Air

Air

Your experiments on this idea should lead you to suggest a design for the bioreactor which you can then make.

DESIGN ACTIVITIES—DESIGNING YOUR OWN ALGAE BIOREACTOR CONTINUED

A second idea is to use plastic cylinders and tubing to make a photo-bioreactor. The four examples provide here are intended as ideas of what could be developed. They are only representative of what could be done.

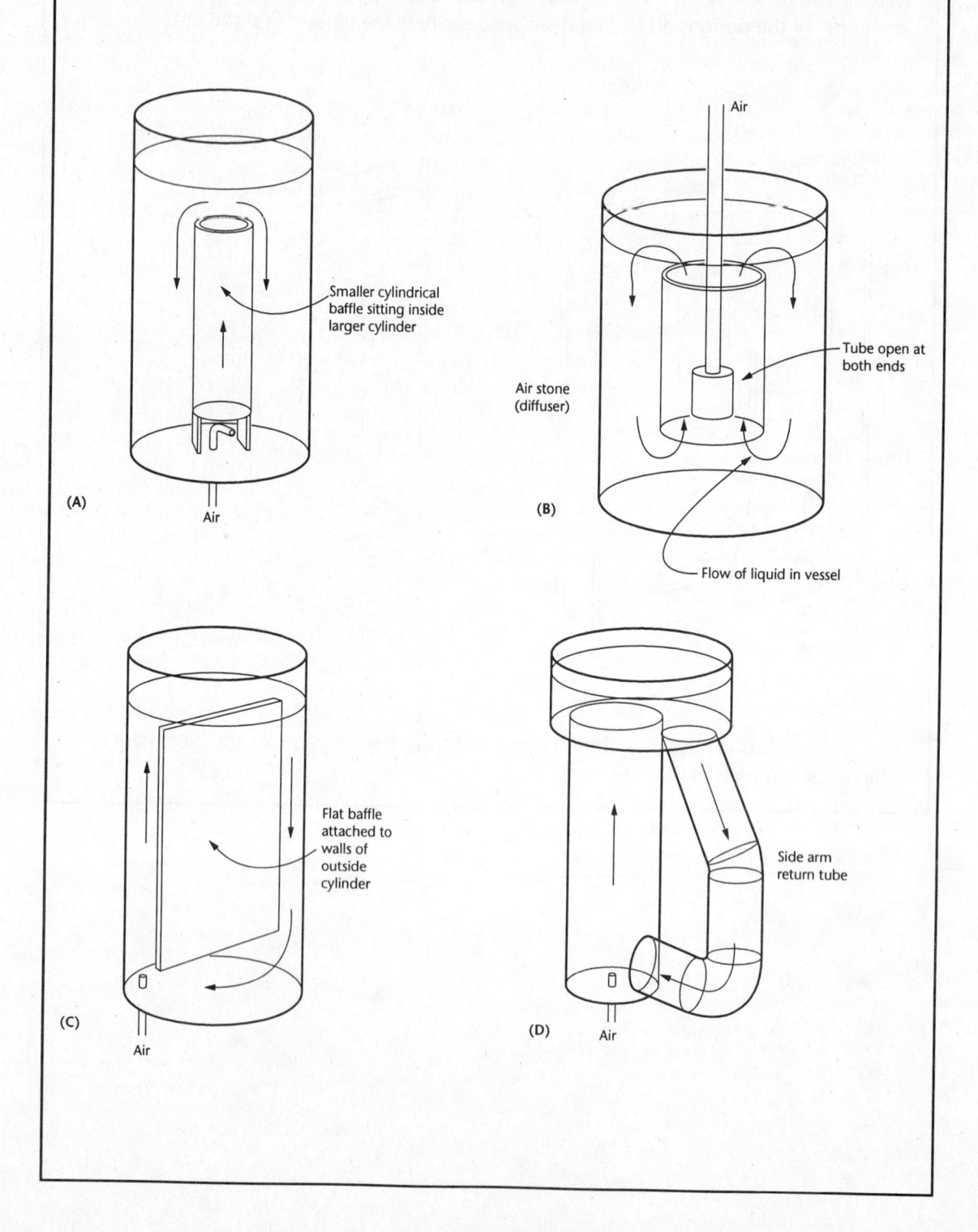

(A) Smaller cylindrical baffle sitting inside larger cylinder. Air.

(B) Air. Air stone (diffuser). Tube open at both ends. Flow of liquid in vessel.

(C) Flat baffle attached to walls of outside cylinder. Air.

(D) Side arm return tube. Air.

DESIGN ACTIVITIES—DESIGNING YOUR OWN ALGAE BIOREACTOR CONTINUED

The use of plastic tubing has been applied by some innovative farmers who are looking for new ways of using their greenhouse space. The idea is simple. Air is bubbled in to the base of a small tower. This causes the liquid, containing the algae, to circulate around a series of tubes which are arranged to face the sunlight.

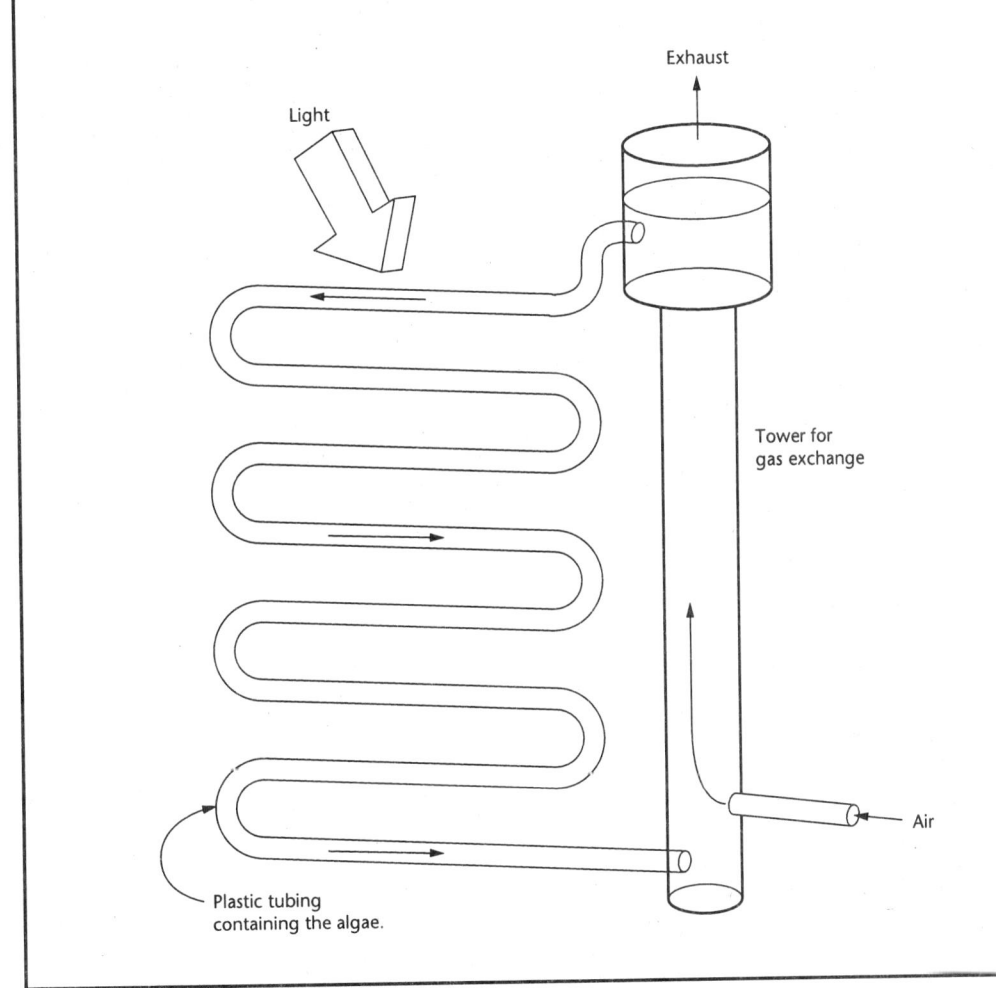

INTEGRATED S/M/T ACTIVITIES

Several developmental efforts are currently focused on identifying the genes that will help to improve plant crop production. The next step is finding a way to splice these genes into the plant's own DNA. This use of biotechnology gives farmers new varieties of plants and animals. Transferring traits between plants and animals normally took years using traditional cross-breeding methods. But so far, only a small number of genes have been successfully transferred into a limited variety of plants. Yet, there is great expectation for the application of biotechnology in plant agriculture. Listed below are some of the topics related to plant agriculture that biotechnologists are currently studying. Consider one of these as a research and development topic that you might pursue.

Research and Development Topics in Plant Agriculture

- Growth, even in extreme heat or cold, without damage
- Growth, where there is too much or too little water, salt, and acid
- Crops for animal food that have high nutritional value and are easy to digest
- Immunity and resistance to certain diseases, pests, and weeds
- Extended growing seasons, so that harvest can occur over a longer period
- Controlled ripening, so the produce can be stored longer
- Stronger walls on fragile, watery fruits and vegetables, thus allowing shipping with less damage
- Cheaper methods for producing flavorings and ingredients that are currently very expensive
- Changes in the type of fats and oils produced
- Increased yield of the produce
- Improved amount and quality of nutrients
- Production of antibiotics which kill pathogenic fungi

BIOTECHNOLOGY IN AGRICULTURE

Biotechnology has been used to help farmers reduce the risk of crop failure, to create new and improved varieties of plants and animals, and to decrease the use of herbicides, pesticides, and fertilizers. This, in turn, means less damage to our environment.

For plants, identical copies can be made through tissue culturing, a technique that allows the biotechnologist to grow an entire plant by using as few as one cell from the original plant. Each of the plants grown in this way came from the one cell of the original plant and are identical to the original plant. The purposes of cloning and culturing plant cells are to increase the crop yield, improve the beneficial traits, and reduce the labor and production costs.

Microorganisms and functional foods have been used to provide many valuable nutrients. Protein produced by bacteria, known as single-cell proteins (SCPs), was first used on a large scale as a food for human consumption in Germany during World War I, and holds the potential to help reduce world hunger. SCP is a valuable food because it has a very high protein content and contains vitamins and other essential chemicals the body needs. Another advantage in using SCPs as food is that they can be grown quickly and are cheap to make. Tiny plant molds contain high levels of mycoprotein and can be produced by having the microorganism grow on cheap waste materials such as wastepaper, straw, or molasses.

Many biotechnology processes are aimed at producing a specific product. But some biotechnological processes are designed to destroy waste and pollution. Most sewage purification processes depend on the work of tiny microbes to break down domestic and agricultural waste products. Biotechnology, as part of the production process itself, can increase the speed at which plastics biodegrade. The use of biotechnology to reduce the effects of oil spills and other similar pollution emergencies is quite valuable.

DESIGN ACTIVITIES—AGRICULTURE/PLANTS AND ANIMALS WITH HYDROPONICS

On many farms, feed for animals can become scarce during the winter months. Farmers would like to have a steady supply of year-round feed for their animals. Hydroponics is a method of plant production that might be used throughout the year to produce animal feeds. Hydroponics is a method of growing plants in nutrient-rich water instead of soil. By using hydroponics techniques, it would be possible to grow oats, barley, or similar grains without ever planting the seeds in soil. This would give a thick mass of plant animal feed that is high in protein and that could be fed to livestock roots, shoots, and all!

Design Brief: Down on the Farm

You have been asked to design and construct a hydroponics system which will produce enough feed for one adult cow. The system should consist of four (4) trays that can produce the amount of feed needed in a single batch. Your system must be able to do the following things:

(a) spray the seeds with a nutrient solution

(b) rotate the trays

(c) provide enough light for growth

(d) maintain the best temperature for growth

(e) maintain proper humidity for growth

Here are some tips for constructing such a system. Seeds might be grown on round trays stacked one above the other. Water, with nutrients, could be sprayed on, and a method could be designed where the excess water is allowed to drip down to the trays below. A sump pump could recirculate the solution back to the top sprayer to be used again. Sensors can be made to monitor the correct growing conditions. Rotating trays might be a useful design feature.

DESIGN ACTIVITIES—AGRICULTURE/TISSUE CULTURE: FOOD SOURCE

All organisms begin life as a single cell. That single cell has the ability to replicate itself into many cells, eventually producing all the direct body cells that make up the adult organism. For most organisms, the ability to generate cells that grow into body parts such as arms and legs lasts only a short time at the beginning of their development stage. However, there are a few organisms that retain this ability even after reaching the full adult stage. Tadpoles, for example, can reproduce their tails, and salamanders can reproduce limbs if they are damaged or lost. Plants also have the potential for regeneration of plant parts. In fact, most plants can be entirely regrown from a single cell taken from the original parent plant. The genetic potential for each cell to divide and grow into a new plant is called totipotency. The technique called tissue culturing takes advantage of this potential, allowing for fast propagation of many plants at once.

Perhaps at some time you have notice on a damaged tree the bumpy growth that formed around a wound. This grown area is called a callus and is made up entirely of actively growing plant cells, all of which have the DNA information to create a whole new plant exactly the same as the parent plant. Biotechnologists have learned to take advantage of this process and can grow entirely new plants from the callus tissue using a special tissue culturing technique. Individual callus cells are first grown on agar having all the nutrients needed for the dividing cells. As the callus cells divide and grow, different plant growth substances are added to the agar, causing stems and roots to form. In this way, a new plant is produced that is an exact replica—a clone—of the parent plant.

Tissue culturing is especially useful in the plant industry for a number of reasons. This process allows for the rapid multiplication of plants in very short time periods and requires low maintenance in a laboratory setting. Tissue culturing can also be accomplished in a very small space, and in a controlled environment that allows for screening of any new and unwanted genetic variations of the clones. The beauty of plant tissue culturing is that it begins by dealing with only one plant. In this way, no matter how many clones are generated from the original plant, all the plants will have the same genetic traits (color, size, texture, etc.). This can be both good and bad.

One problem with generating clones having all the same genetic traits is that if the original plant was susceptible to a certain disease, then all the clones will be too. Another result is that the cloned plants are often not as strong as plants generated through the natural process of cross-breeding between different parent plants. Yet, tissue culturing is frequently the best choice when trying to cultivate plants that are very hard to grow naturally, such as orchids, azaleas, and rhododendron. It is also the best choice for growing food crops in isolated places such as remote research stations, spacecraft, space colonies, or permanent underwater living quarters.

DESIGN ACTIVITIES—AGRICULTURE/TISSUE CULTURE: FOOD SOURCE CONTINUED

Design Brief: From a Callus to the Table

You are the chief Biotechnology Officer for the underwater living station known as Ocean Venture. The government is interested in conducting research on how underwater communities function in isolation for long periods of time. The Ocean Venture mission is to stay in the underwater living station for an entire year, with food cultivated from the seafloor and within the station itself. An area of 3 feet by 5 feet has been provided for growing vegetables during the yearlong stay, and must produce enough food to continually supplement meals for the five-member crew that will live in Ocean Venture.

You need to design a plant manufacturing system using plant tissue culturing as the means for producing enough vegetables to support the crew for their year's stay underwater. The system must operate in the limited space provided, have a light source for the plants, be automated enough to control temperature, nutrients, and light exposure time, and allow for the increase in plant size as they grow. In addition, your system must allow for plant manipulation and transplant once plants are able to sustain themselves outside the tissue culture environment.

DESIGN ACTIVITIES—USING MICROSCOPIC PLANTS OR ANIMALS

Most of the biotechnology processes produce a specific product, but some processes work in the opposite way. To control the pollution in the environment, biotechnology processes are designed to destroy the specific raw materials of pollution. For example, special microbes are being developed that will eat unwanted waste, sometimes producing something useful during the process. This is being done today with microbes that can produce methane gas, while breaking down household sewage.

The use of biotechnology to reduce the effects of oil spills and other similar pollution emergencies is quite valuable. In some cases, nutrients are added to the oil-contaminated water or soil to enhance the ability of naturally occurring bacteria to degrade the oil. Another method makes use of biological materials that will soak up, or adsorb, a wide range of unwanted pollutants. These types of materials are known as **biosorbants.**

- Refer to your text to read about chitosan, a material made from the shells of crustaceans such as shrimp or prawns.

- Investigate how the substance chitin, that comes from the hard outer shells of these animals, attracts and absorbs oil and similar substances.

- If possible, secure a sample of chitosan and conduct experiments to determine how much oil a given amount of chitosan can absorb.

- Determine the cost of the material and project what it would cost if it was used to clean up the results of small, medium, and large oil spills.

- What parts of the world are well suited to the acquisition and preparation of chitosan? What role might the production of chitosan play in improving the economy of some parts of the world, especially in underdeveloped countries?

Biotechnologists are hopeful that the ideas being developed today on waste management will go much farther in time. It is important that efforts continue toward identifying those microorganisms that can naturally break down pollutants and industrial wastes. In the future, new microorganisms can be genetically designed to remove various pollutants. The more hazardous pollutants, such as pesticides and herbicides, remain in the environment for long periods of time and are a challenge to modern biotechnology.

BIOETHICS

In the past ten years alone, biotechnology has had an enormous impact in the areas of agriculture, medicine, and environmental control. Serious questions concerning its regulation and control arise, however. Bioethics is concerned with understanding all the legal, social, cultural, ethical, and economic implications of conducting biotechnology research.

Engineered microorganisms that produce new antibiotics or proteins have been patented for years. Recently, the U.S. Patent Office approved the patenting of modified, or changed, higher, more complex life forms created by scientists in the laboratory. The issue of ownership is only a part of the greater issue of creating new life forms and altering the process by which individual traits are determined.

Other areas of biotechnology need monitoring and control to ensure the safe and appropriate use of this new technology. Gene therapy, DNA fingerprinting for forensic purposes, vaccines from recombinant DNA, and the Human Genome project all require regulation. Methods of regulation are being prepared by a number of government agencies. The Department of Agriculture, Environmental Protection Agency, National Institutes of Health, and the Food and Drug Administration are some of the agencies in the United States that are responsible for monitoring new products. Many nations have comparable agencies and there are some world-wide watchdog groups.

ENRICHMENT DESIGN BRIEFS AND ACTIVITIES

Prepare a display showing products that have been developed for use in growing plants and animals. Display in the following categories:

1. Resistance to damage, even in conditions of extreme heat or cold
2. Growth in conditions where there are high (or low) levels of acid, salt, and water
3. Resistance to certain diseases, pests, or weeds
4. Controlled ripening
5. Better yield
6. Increased tolerance for rough handling by harvesting and processing machines
7. Cheaper methods of production
8. Improved nutritional value

CHAPTER 12
Communication Systems

This chapter places primary focus on communication systems in a technological context. Communication involves a sender and receiver who are willing and able to share information. The participants may be humans communicating with other humans or with machines, or machines communicating with other machines. Communication can take place when the sender and receiver share the same language system and have some common interest and common base of understanding. This requires that sender and receiver use a common code of signals and symbols, agreed upon in advance. The need to communicate arises when some unguessable information must be shared with others. The act of communicating attempts to make the unguessable a matter of common understanding between the two participants.

SENDERS AND RECEIVERS

Early machines used very simple ways, such as cams, gears, and linkages, to send signals to other machines. Later, the use of holes punched in paper cards or paper tape set the stage for even more sophisticated communication through electronic means. Codes such as the international ASCII code were developed. With the computer, all commands had to be programmed by using a machine language. Now that computers are more sophisticated, they are able to translate input programming that comes closer to human language to the 0's and 1's of machine language. Some of the early languages include BASIC, FORTRAN, COBOL, and PASCAL. More recent languages include LOGO, FORTH, and "C."

Machines were developed to translate spoken words into the signals that machines can understand. Now machines (synthesizers) are able to receive as well as send spoken words. These machines actually respond to the individual sound waves of the words that, when decoded, trigger specifically programmed events inside the machine.

TRANSMITTING THROUGH MEDIA

Information in the form of a code or message is transmitted by use of a carrier (medium). A communication medium requires that a message be paired with an appropriate vehicle. The effect of the total message and the amount of information that can be sent is different with each medium. Media can be static or dynamic, transmit rapidly or slowly, allow storage and replay, and be easily replicated or sent to many different receivers at the same time. Those that reach very large numbers of receivers are called mass media. Carriers have different capacities for transmitting signals clearly and accurately and for maintaining separate channels for each message.

The role and importance of carriers can be illustrated by comparing visible light waves with radio waves, both on the energy spectrum. Light waves have a higher frequency than radio waves. Radio, television, microwaves, and infrared and visible light are radiated waves that all travel at the same speed. However, they differ in wavelength, the number of times they vibrate per second. Messages are carried on the wavelength from one vibration to another. The more vibrations per second, the more information can be carried.

Claude Shannon considered the unguessable aspect of a message as synonymous with disorder in communication, or entropy. Entropy as disorder means some of the message is not understood and information is lost. One means of improving the transmission of information is to send more signals than are actually needed (called redundancy). Other examples that cause loss of information are ink that fades, tape that loses magnetism, and a worn and tattered carrier.

Signal entropy is the loss of usable information as it is changed from one form to another, because of slight incompatibility or because of outside interference. Symbols may also lose some of their meaning over time or with translation. Materials may have worn away or decayed; we may only have pieces or parts of the object on which the message was recorded; we may be unable to break the code; or we may lack compatible experiences.

All communication systems have some noise that interferes with information transmission. To maintain good transmission of information, a high signal-to-noise ratio must be maintained.

DESIGN ACTIVITIES—SYMBOLS, CODES AND LANGUAGES

Many different types of symbols are used in D&T activities. Some of these were introduced in earlier chapters. Examples of map symbols are shown here. They can be used to help interpret a topographic map. They can also be used to represent actual features of a section or area of land in symbolic form.

Topographic Mapping Symbols

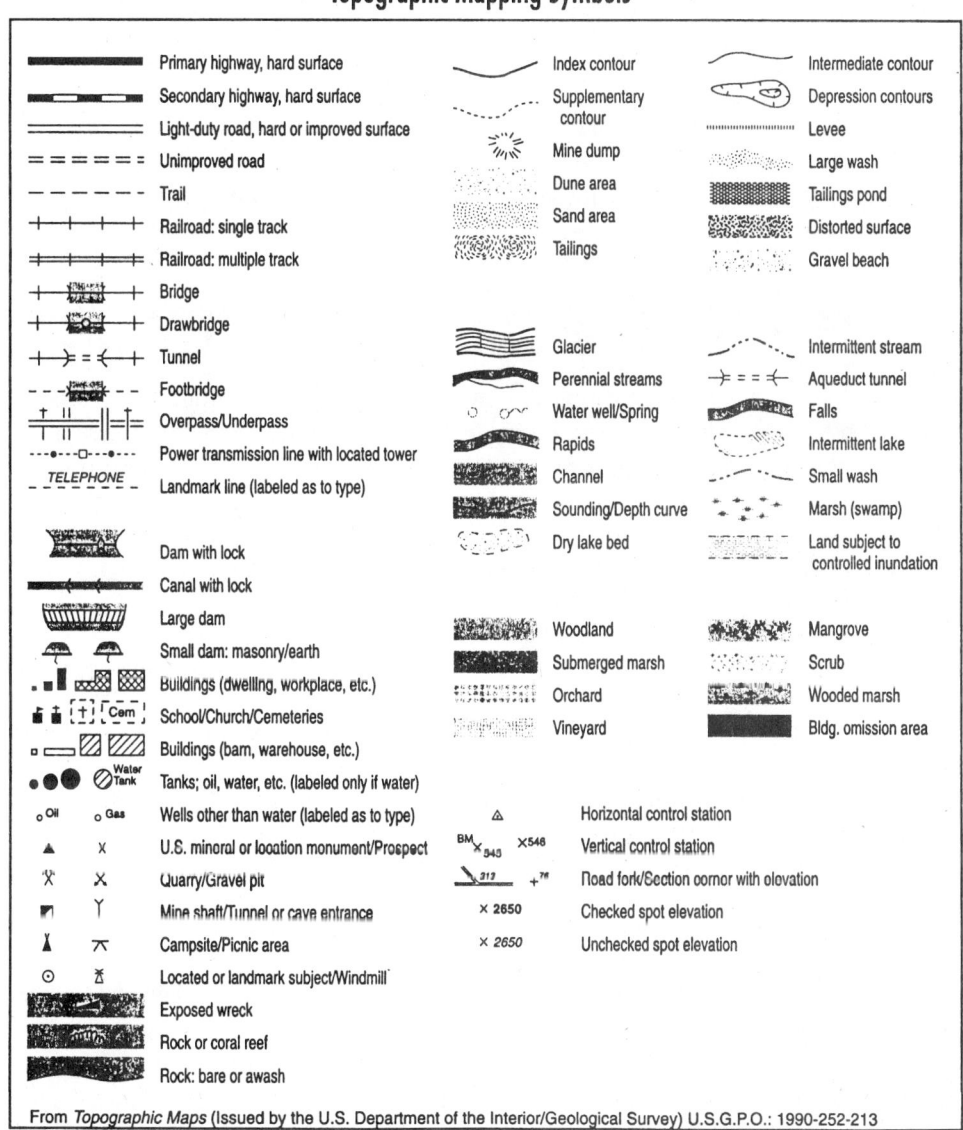

Symbol	Feature
	Primary highway, hard surface
	Secondary highway, hard surface
	Light-duty road, hard or improved surface
	Unimproved road
	Trail
	Railroad: single track
	Railroad: multiple track
	Bridge
	Drawbridge
	Tunnel
	Footbridge
	Overpass/Underpass
	Power transmission line with located tower
	Landmark line (labeled as to type)
	Dam with lock
	Canal with lock
	Large dam
	Small dam: masonry/earth
	Buildings (dwelling, workplace, etc.)
	School/Church/Cemeteries
	Buildings (barn, warehouse, etc.)
	Tanks; oil, water, etc. (labeled only if water)
	Wells other than water (labeled as to type)
	U.S. mineral or location monument/Prospect
	Quarry/Gravel pit
	Mine shaft/Tunnel or cave entrance
	Campsite/Picnic area
	Located or landmark subject/Windmill
	Exposed wreck
	Rock or coral reef
	Rock: bare or awash
	Index contour
	Supplementary contour
	Mine dump
	Dune area
	Sand area
	Tailings
	Glacier
	Perennial streams
	Water well/Spring
	Rapids
	Channel
	Sounding/Depth curve
	Dry lake bed
	Woodland
	Submerged marsh
	Orchard
	Vineyard
	Horizontal control station
	Vertical control station
	Road fork/Section corner with elevation
× 2650	Checked spot elevation
× 2650	Unchecked spot elevation
	Intermediate contour
	Depression contours
	Levee
	Large wash
	Tailings pond
	Distorted surface
	Gravel beach
	Intermittent stream
	Aqueduct tunnel
	Falls
	Intermittent lake
	Small wash
	Marsh (swamp)
	Land subject to controlled inundation
	Mangrove
	Scrub
	Wooded marsh
	Bldg. omission area

From *Topographic Maps* (Issued by the U.S. Department of the Interior/Geological Survey) U.S.G.P.O.: 1990-252-213

Study the symbols and identify which features you can find in your town of region. Use the symbols to sketch a map that represents the town or region where you live. Determine how these symbols and their use is similar to the electronic symbols that have been used to represent electrical circuits throughout your textbook.

INTEGRATED S/M/T ACTIVITIES—CODES AND COMMUNICATION

Successful communication requires a common code and language plus a common area of interest and some degree of common understanding. Without a common area of interest, the sender and receiver have little to talk about or to share. Without some common understanding, there is little likelihood that the messages that are transmitted will have any real meaning. Consider the example provided in your textbook of the dance performed by honey bees to communicate to other bees where they can find flowers (See Figure 12.3). The bee that has discovered the source of nectar communicates through the dance movements and duration the direction and distance to be traveled to reach the flowers.

Conduct an investigation into the means that other animals use for communicating with each other. Determine what research has been done on how such animals as ants, termites, whales, porpoises, or baboons communicate. What use, if any, might be made

DESIGN BRIEF—MACHINE COMMUNICATION

Understanding how machines communicate with each other is sometimes more easily accomplished by looking closely at some early historic developments in communication. In many instances, the sharing of information between machines was for the purpose of control—which will be considered in more detail in the following chapter. In the instances referenced below, you should focus on the specific means by which information was provided, how it was transferred to another machine, and how the information was used by another machine.

The book *Connections*, by James Burke, provides several good starting points for looking at historical instances of machine communication. For example, in Chapter 4, "Faith in Number", Burke shows how the idea of using pins in a revolving cylinder to sound bells was integrated with early machines used to spin and weave cloth. This led to the automated loom, capable of producing intricate patterns by using holes in cards, that in turn led to punched cards being used in the United States census of 1890. All of this set the foundation for the development and growing widespread use of computers today.

Design and develop an exhibit, with working models of the above machines, to show the evolution of the modern computer. Design and develop an exhibit of the evolution of mass production (Chapter 5, "The Wheel of Fortune"), the evolution of plastics (Chapter 7, "The Long Chain"), or another instance of change presented by Burke. In these instances, draw attention to how information was shared between machines—mechanically, pneumatically, electrically, electronically, optically, etc.

INTEGRATED S/M/T ACTIVITIES—MACHINE COMMUNICATION: UNIVERSAL PRODUCT CODE (UPC), OR BAR CODES

Figure 12.4 in your textbook provides an illustration of how a Universal Product Code (UPC), or bar code system, operates at a supermarket checkout counter. Each product has its own bar code which is printed on the package. The barcode can be scanned and the computer will be able to recognize the product and determine its price, remove it from the inventory if the product is sold, and reorder additional quantities when stocks get too low.

The technology facilities represent many opportunities for the use of bar codes. Bar codes can be used to keep track of hardware, materials, and other resources. They can be used in the reference center to monitor the use of books and other materials. What other uses of bar codes could be implemented to organize the technology lab?

Design Brief—Setting Up Bar Code Systems

Check with your teacher to see if a bar code system is available for use in this problem. If so, work with one or two other students to complete the following introductory activity. With suggestions from your teacher, determine which of the above problems is significant and feasible for your class setting. For example, you and your team may choose to set up part of a materials or tool inventory in the model-making area. You might set up a system for all students to have their own bar code. You might choose to establish a tool sign-out system that keeps track of which students have which tools.

Access the bar code software program on the computer you are to use, or secure the software disk from your teacher and install the program on your computer. Set up bar codes for each of the items (tools, materials, people) that you plan to monitor. Print out the bar codes and attach them to tools, tool boards, storage containers, or storage racks. Develop bar code identification cards for your classmates.

Use the bar code scanner provided by your teacher to check the accuracy and dependability of the bar codes you have developed. After the bar codes have been tested, develop a program that will monitor the inventory, use, and resupply of the materials in your technology facilities. If appropriate, develop a program that will monitor which students use which tools and materials. Develop a method of monitoring the cost of the materials that a student has used. Develop a system that will monitor if a student has been checked out on the safety rules of a machine before using it.

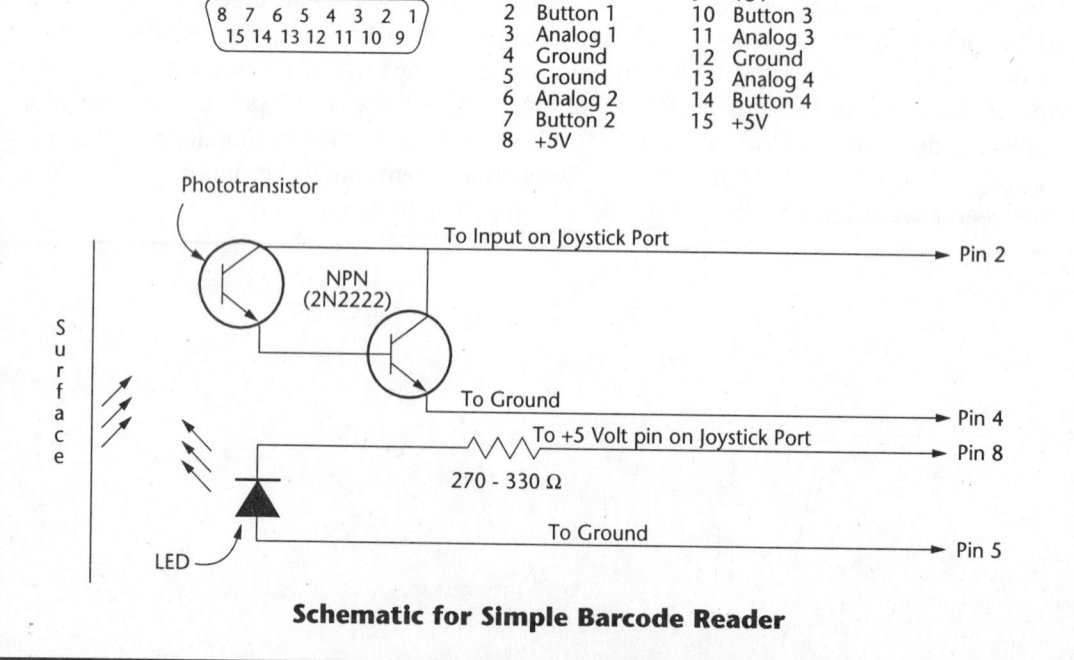

DESIGN ACTIVITIES—READING UPCS, OR BAR CODES

Bar coding is one of the most accurate and efficient means of identifying and categorizing used today. The two most utilized bar code standards are the Universal Product Code (UPC), used to identify products, and POSTNET, which is used by the U.S. Postal Service to identify ZIP codes. There are many other standards. In each one, a number, letter, or character is symbolized by a certain number of bars and spaces. Bar codes vary, depending on their uses. They can be produced to identify almost anything as long as there is someone to program the computer to interpret the symbol and translate it into useful information.

Bar codes consist of bars and spaces. The bars are the darker, nonreflective elements of the code, while the spaces are lighter reflective elements. The code, consisting of various patterns of these elements, may represent only the identification for the item or it may represent only the identification for the item or it may contain other elements necessary to the programming of the reader. Samples of such elements are check digits which are included for error detection, start characters to indicate the beginning of a bar code symbol, and stop characters to indicate the end of a bar code symbol.

Sample UPC Code

Circuitry

Most commercial scanners, such as the ones used in supermarkets, use an invisible infrared laser beam to scan a bar code. The scanner may be either a fixed beam (stationary) or a hand-held unit. A laser beam is just one method of reading a bar code. A device designed to recognize the difference between the bars and spaces can be built without a laser beam. A sample of this can be seen in the following figure.

Joystick Connector

| 8 7 6 5 4 3 2 1 |
| 15 14 13 12 11 10 9 |

Pin	Function	Pin	Function
1	+5V	9	+5V
2	Button 1	10	Button 3
3	Analog 1	11	Analog 3
4	Ground	12	Ground
5	Ground	13	Analog 4
6	Analog 2	14	Button 4
7	Button 2	15	+5V
8	+5V		

Schematic for Simple Barcode Reader

- Phototransistor — NPN (2N2222) — To Input on Joystick Port → Pin 2
- To Ground → Pin 4
- To +5 Volt pin on Joystick Port, 270 - 330 Ω → Pin 8
- LED — To Ground → Pin 5
- Surface

DESIGN ACTIVITIES—READING UPCS, OR BAR CODES CONTINUED

Using the above schematic, a reader can be built which can distinguish between the bars and the spaces. When the reader passes by a dark bar, the light does not reflect back and a high signal (1) is sent to the computer. If a white space is passed, the light will reflect back and send a low signal (0) to the computer. These high and low signals translate into binary code, which is interpreted by the computer program designed to accompany the reader.

Binary Code

Binary code is the language by which machines communicate. It is based on two numbers, 0 and 1. A switch on a port is open (0) when there is no signal and closed (1) when there is a signal. Each individual signal, or switch, is called a bit. A byte of information equals eight bits. The combination of 0's and 1's in a byte of information translates to either an alphanumeric character or some other signal that the computer is programmed to recognize. The ability to translate binary code into decimal code is important when writing a program to accompany the reader. Each of the eight bits has an assigned value.

128 64 32 16 8 4 2 1
●   ●   ●   ●   ● ● ● ●

128	64	32	16	8	4	2	1	Decimal Equivalent
\multicolumn{8}{c}{Binary Code}	
0	0	0	0	0	1	0	1	5
0	0	0	1	1	0	0	1	25
0	0	1	1	0	0	0	0	48
0	0	1	1	1	0	1	1	59
0	1	1	1	0	0	0	0	112
1	0	1	1	0	0	0	0	176
1	1	1	1	0	0	0	0	240
1	1	1	1	1	1	1	1	255

Simplified Bar Code (with five bars)

Binary 0101
Decimal 5

The sum of the assigned values of the high (1) bits equals the decimal equivalent to the binary code. A byte has 256 possible numeric values. Using this information, a bar code with eight bars could be used to identify 256 different items. A simple bar code was created to use with the bar code reader. The code contained five bars. The first bar was used as a standard for the program. The remaining four bars, in varying combinations, were used to identify a total of 16 possible items.

DESIGN ACTIVITIES—MAKING A BAR CODE READER

In the illustrations below, several different means of scanning bar codes are shown. These projects were developed in England by the Staffordshire Design and Technology Team and published by Cambridge University Press in the book *Food for Thought*. If available in your school, you will want to use it as a reference.

Using the information provided in the references and gained through the preceding activities, design and develop either the buggy or a roller-driven system to scan simplified bar codes. For these activities, you will need a reflective opto-sensor and an interface that is compatible with the computer you are going to use.

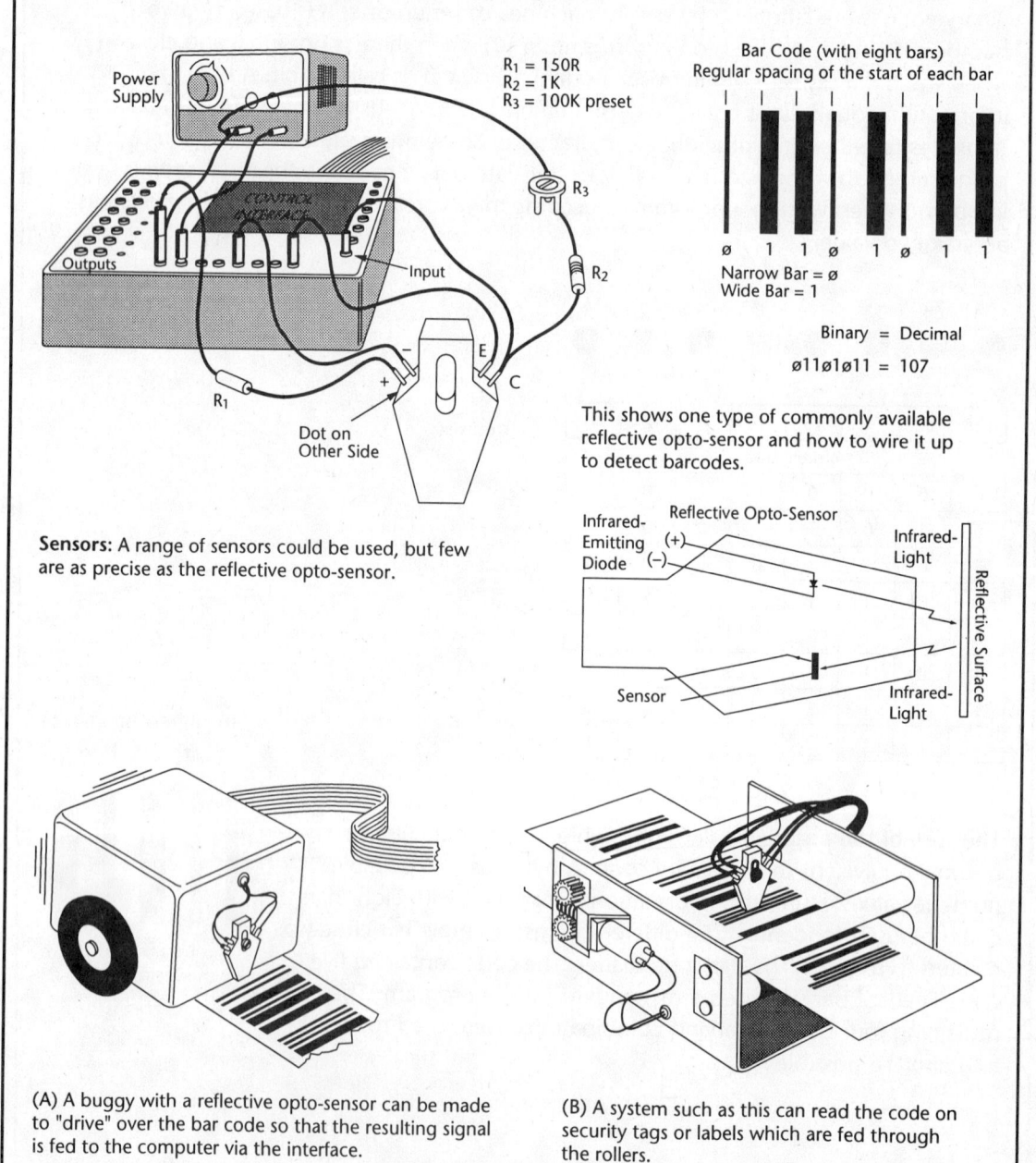

R_1 = 150R
R_2 = 1K
R_3 = 100K preset

Bar Code (with eight bars)
Regular spacing of the start of each bar

ø 1 1 ø 1 ø 1 1

Narrow Bar = ø
Wide Bar = 1

Binary = Decimal
ø11ø1ø11 = 107

This shows one type of commonly available reflective opto-sensor and how to wire it up to detect barcodes.

Sensors: A range of sensors could be used, but few are as precise as the reflective opto-sensor.

(A) A buggy with a reflective opto-sensor can be made to "drive" over the bar code so that the resulting signal is fed to the computer via the interface.

(B) A system such as this can read the code on security tags or labels which are fed through the rollers.

DESIGN ACTIVITIES—MAKING A BAR CODE READER CONTINUED

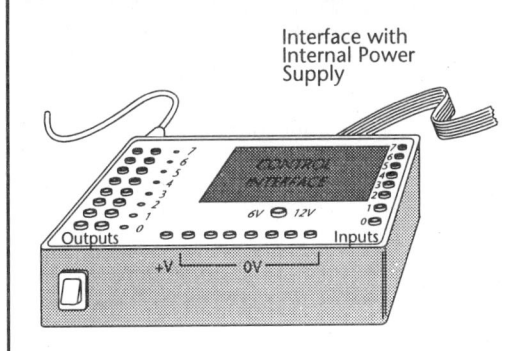

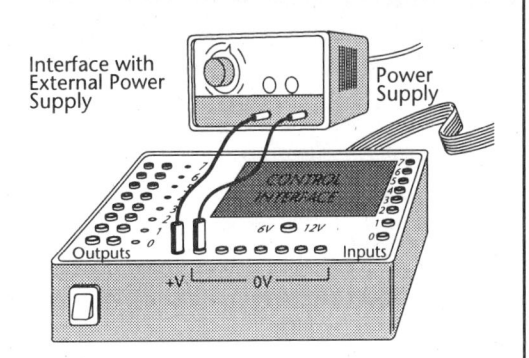

Interface with Internal Power Supply

Interface with External Power Supply

Power Supply

NOTE: The signals from the slotted opto-switch will need to pass through an interface to make them suitable for the computer to read.

Computer Program: Because of the difficulty of programming in different languages, a flow diagram method will be used to describe a software system which could be used to read bar codes with the hardware already discussed.

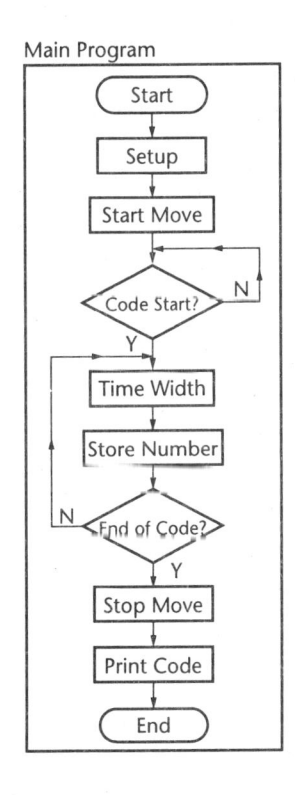

Main Program

Start → Setup → Start Move → Code Start? —N→ (loop back)
Y ↓
Time Width → Store Number → End of Code? —N→ (loop back)
Y ↓
Stop Move → Print Code → End

The flow chart at the left provides an overview of the main program. The different steps represent the major parts of the program that must be included if the program is to operate. Each step in the program must be developed in more detail, as shown in the illustration on the following page.

DESIGN ACTIVITIES—MAKING A BAR CODE READER CONTINUED

NOTE: The signals from the slotted opto-switch will need to pass through an interface to make them suitable for the computer to read.

Computer Program: Because of the difficulty of programming in different languages, a flow diagram method will be used to describe a software system which could be used to read bar codes with the hardware already discussed.

The expanded flow chart, shown at the right, can now be used to develop the computer program that will control the operation of the bar code reading process. The final program must be developed in the language required by the computer and the related hardware that will be used with the bar code reader.

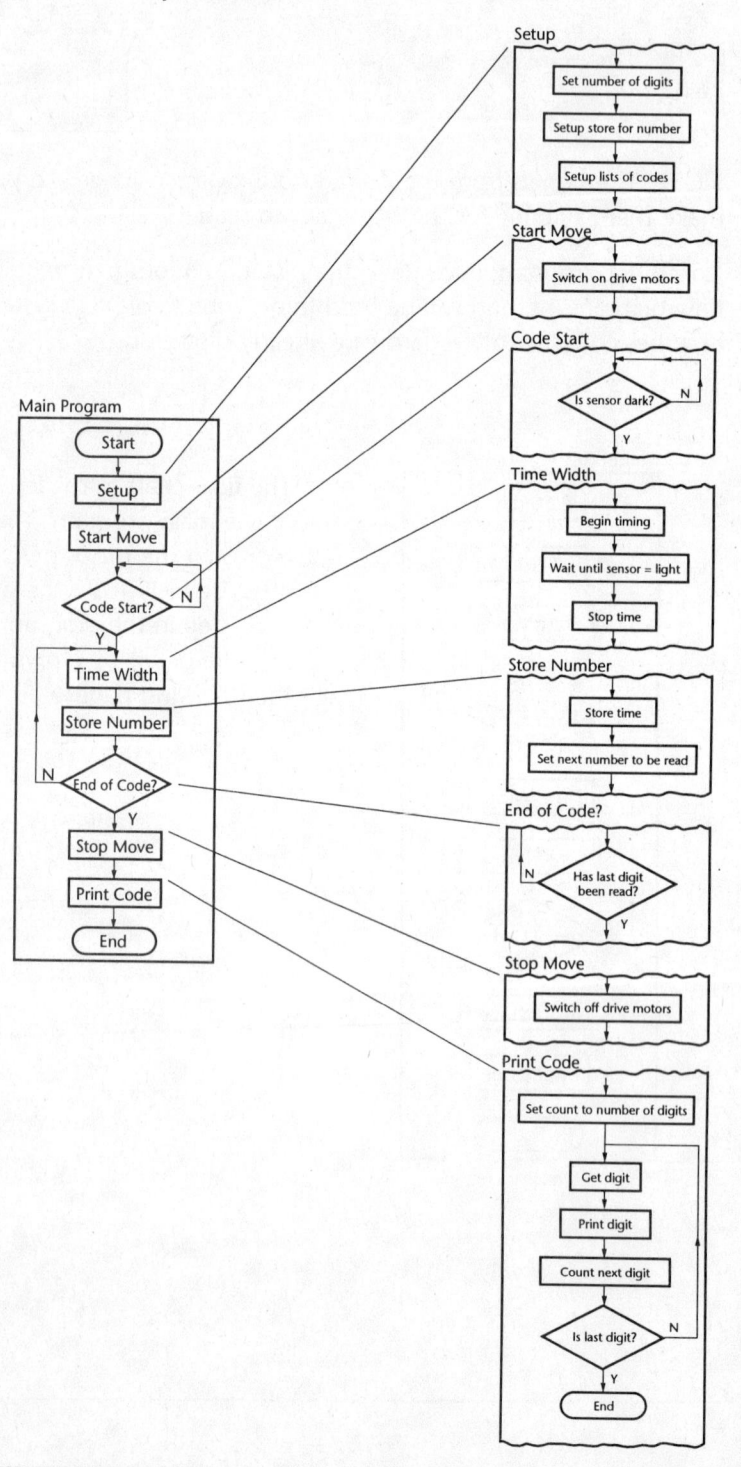

Main Program
- Start
- Setup
- Start Move
- Code Start? (N loops back, Y continues)
- Time Width
- Store Number
- End of Code? (N loops back, Y continues)
- Stop Move
- Print Code
- End

Setup
- Set number of digits
- Setup store for number
- Setup lists of codes

Start Move
- Switch on drive motors

Code Start
- Is sensor dark? (N loops, Y continues)

Time Width
- Begin timing
- Wait until sensor = light
- Stop time

Store Number
- Store time
- Set next number to be read

End of Code?
- Has last digit been read? (N loops back, Y continues)

Stop Move
- Switch off drive motors

Print Code
- Set count to number of digits
- Get digit
- Print digit
- Count next digit
- Is last digit? (N loops back, Y continues)
- End

DESIGN ACTIVITY—RESEARCH AND DEVELOPMENT ON MACHINE COMMUNICATION AND SPEECH SYNTHESIS

Even very complex information machines, such as the synthesizer and the computer, are still only machines. They can respond only to signals.

In your textbook, an example is provided on the development of a speech synthesizing device (see Figure 14.22). Consider this as a starting point for a research and development project on how speech synthesis works and how you might use it to generate a spoken message to announce in common language what is actually encoded in different bar codes.

DESIGN ACTIVITIES—USING SELECTED MEDIA, MESSAGES, AND CARRIERS

Medium	Message Symbols/Signals	Carrier Vehicle
Print	Words	Paper
Television	Electronic signals	Radio waves
Telephone	Electrical signals	Wire, optic cable
Facsimile	Images, words, electronic signals	Wire, optic cable, radio waves
Voice	Auditory symbols	Sound waves
Recordings	Magnetic or optic signals	Tapes, disks
Data processing	Holes or pins to make patterns or magnetic signals	Cards, tapes, drums, or disks
Painting	Figures in symbolic patterns	Canvas, paint
Photographs	Figures in symbolic patterns	Paper, chemicals

Design Brief

As a class, design and develop a display of the media, messages, and carriers presented above. Include a historical treatment of each. Show what changes, if any, there have been in these early forms and how they were used. Contrast these with their current forms and uses. Design the display for students who are at least three years younger than you and who have little experience with technology as a subject.

DESIGN ACTIVITIES—ELECTRONIC COMMUNICATION

There are many new developments in electronic communication that help you communicate with others as you pursue your design projects. You will find these helpful as you investigate possible topics for study, or as you attempt to find answers to specific questions, and the source of materials you may need to fabricate your design. You will need to determine what electronic means of communicating are available to you in the school or through local resources.

- Design and develop a message to be transmitted by standard telephone.
- Design and develop a message to be sent by fax.
- Design and develop a message to be sent by e-mail.
- Design and develop a concept and procedures map to guide you in accessing the Internet.
- Develop a drawing and symbolic representation of an electronic system you developed.
- Design and develop a home page for the technology education program in your school.

INTEGRATED S/M/T ACTIVITIES—INFORMATION HIGHWAYS

A great deal has been written regarding the development of new information highways to improve long-distance communication. The use of information highways is expected to change significantly how we access data and interact with people around the world.

Design Brief

Collect materials on the new means of moving information locally, nationally, and internationally. Determine what is needed to access information through an electronic information network. Design and develop a display that will help your classmates understand how that network operates. Design and develop a set of instructions that communicate to others how they can use that network to get access to information related to problems of interest to them.

DESIGN BRIEF—COMMUNICATING VIA OPTIC CABLE

The use of optic cable has become rather commonplace. Using optic cable, or optic fiber as it is often called, significantly increases the amount of information that can be sent over a carrier in a given length of time. Several manufacturers of equipment and materials for technology education provide activities related to optic fiber and how it is used for communicating messages. These include learning activities from such companies as Science Concepts, SCAN, Modern School Supply, Paxton Patterson, Synergistics, and Unilab.

Check with your teacher to see what learning activities might be available for you and your classmates. Conduct an experiment to determine the effectiveness of transmitting information by fiber cable as compared to transmitting information by metal wire.

FEEDBACK

Feedback is the term used to describe a contact from receiver to sender. Feedback closes the loop of a communication or control process. Information provided by the action of the receiver indicates that the message was received and can be used to modify future messages. Feedback from and to machines is based on a deviation from an existing situation to a new situation. Feedback and two-way sharing of information provide the user with increased ability to interact with the communication system. Interactive systems enable the user to direct, or query, the system to get information of interest.

Morse's invention of the telegraph gave people the capability of sending coded messages over metal wire at the speed of light. The binary code that was developed for the telegraph was crucial in developing systems of information and communication.

Technological activities tend to evolve into systems and then into still larger systems. A communication system may be very simple, such as a doorbell, or highly sophisticated, such as the telephone system that links a large portion of the people of the world. Communication systems may also be established between machines. Automated production requires a highly sophisticated system.

Some communication systems use synchronous satellites in an orbit around the Earth. A growing number of computer networks support information highways when such networks are linked.

All aspects of a system are interdependent. Each element needs all the other elements to work. This interdependency may be evident only when one part of a system breaks down.

The exchange of money is another example of a communication system that is dependent on production and transportation systems. The medium of exchange varies and has included salt, shells and sand dollars, coins, paper money, credit cards, and (currently) electronic "blips."

DESIGN BRIEF—USING FEEDBACK IN COMMUNICATION

Effective communication is determined, to a great extent, by the feedback that you are able to gain from the receiver of the message(s) you have sent. In instances where people are the receivers, you will need to develop appropriate means to secure the feedback of the information you want. For example, if you are making a presentation, you will want to monitor the reactions of your audience. You may pose questions to see if key ideas you want to communicate have actually been understood. If your presentation has been made to viewers without direct contact, you could create a questionnaire to secure data on how well the message got across to your audience.

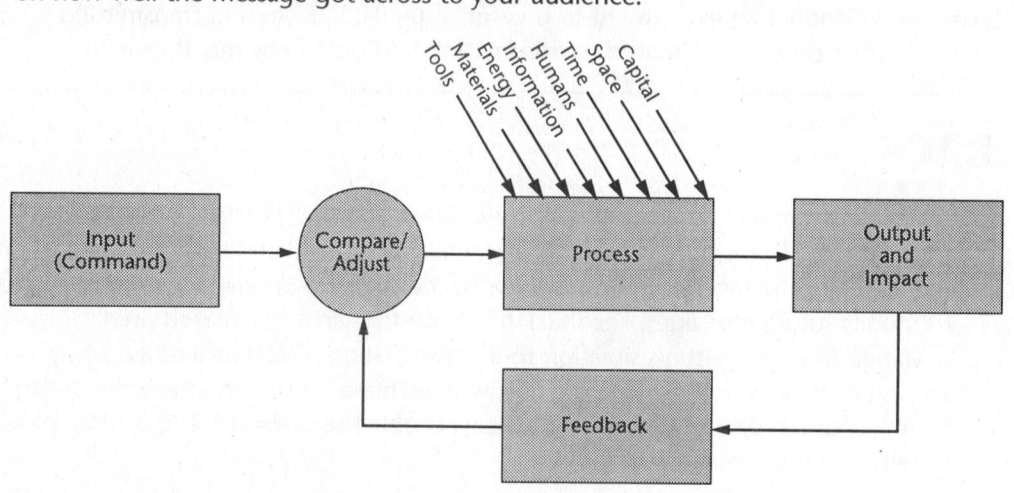

The General Communication Model with the Feedback Element

It is also helpful to consider a marketing effort as a form of communication, usually without the benefit of direct contact with your audience. Marketing surveys are often used to determine the reactions of certain groups to a product to determine if individuals might be interested in purchasing the product. The marketing survey is an important form of feedback for those in design and technology who are interested in changing their products to make them more salable.

Design Brief

Design and develop (1) a questionnaire to use with the audience of one of your presentations, or (2) a marketing survey for one of the products that you or a class member have developed. Determine what questions you want to ask regarding the interest of the individuals and what they might consider a fair price for the product they are being shown. Refer to the communication model above and determine how the feedback you secure will be used to make changes in your presentation of your product. Determine who could help you in developing your questionnaire or survey.

FORMS OF COMMUNICATING

Graphic communication refers to the visual forms of sharing information, usually in some form of printed or visual display of ideas. One form of graphic communication is the portfolio. A portfolio is used to convey and record ideas during the design and implementation of a project. Your message might include text, drawings, photographs, models, sounds, and demonstrations. If your portfolio includes text, you will probably input that information by typing it in a word processing program. Images might include sketches, renderings, illustrations, technical drawings, CAD drawings, charts, graphs, photographs, or animations.

After images are captured through scanning, they can be manipulated in a variety of ways. A variation of animation called morphing, fills in between the two images with a gradual transition from one to the other. Because digital audio and video devices record digitally, the information can easily be stored and manipulated by desktop computers. Conventional analog audio and video recordings can be converted into digital code.

For print media, text and images are combined and prepared for output. Page layout (desktop publishing) software can understand and manipulate the machine coding for both text and image information. Text size, font, style, line spacing, and color can be altered. Images can be cropped, scaled, or rotated. The design decisions you make can enhance and emphasize, or muddle and lessen, your intended communication. Regardless of the venue, the designer (or message sender) must make decisions regarding timing, sequencing, and transitions between elements.

In order to share your portfolio with others, you will publish it. Output from a computer will most usually take the form of print or graphic representations. Print can be inexpensive to reproduce, is easily transported, is commonly understood, and requires no special equipment or technological capability on the part of the receiver. However, print also has limitations. It does not include sound or motion, and generally offers little interaction beyond reading.

The addition of sounds, narrations, animations, movies, and special effects in multimedia presentations requires more sophisticated output options. Output may be on computer system or videotape.

Feedback coupled with two-way exchange of information results in dynamic, interactive communication systems. Interactive systems move users from normally passive to more active roles in communication. Interactive communication systems are now commonly used on personal computers (PCs). Special systems, such as virtual reality, that allow the user to enter a computer-generated world, continue to be developed. Over the past few years, a range of more powerful and less expensive video equipment has been integrated with personal computers to create what has become known as desktop video. The combination of television and other media with computers continues to result in new forms of communication. Providing interactive communication through the use of simulations is becoming rather common and provides power and productivity that is difficult to accomplish through other media.

The communication system that allows us to monitor the world's weather also provides maps of weather systems as they develop and travel. Forecasting weather would be improved significantly with a reliable, large-scale computer model of the world's weather.

Attempts to communicate with people from different cultures through a common graphic language can be seen in road signs. The sophistication in this approach lies in the simplicity of the images. Special sets of symbols that have common meaning to the senders and the receivers are being developed regularly. The use of drawings for communication is very common. Drawings in the form of plans, charts, and graphs can be very helpful in presenting complex data and information.

Visual communication can take three-dimensional forms, such as in models, displays, and exhibits. Packaging is a common form of communicating through three-dimensional objects. Often, the package is designed with careful attention to the ease and satisfaction of the user and the durability and functioning of the product. The package also attempts to persuade the consumer to buy the product. Producers are required by law to identify the ingredients of some products and give clear warning if the product poses potential risks to safety, health, or the environment.

DESIGN ACTIVITIES—TELECOMMUNICATION: TRANSMITTING MESSAGES ON ENERGY WAVES

- Telegraph—an apparatus or system for transmitting signals in code by electric impulses sent by wire or radio.

- Telemetry—the process of measuring and recording television images and readings of instruments at long distances.

- Telephone—a system or instrument used to convert speech to electrical impulses to be sent long distances by wire or other carrier.

- Telescope—a device for viewing distant objects by means of lenses.

- Teleshopping—a network of computer systems that allows shopping for a wide variety of items, from your home.

- Television—the process of transmitting visual images by electric impulses superimposed on radio waves to be projected on a luminescent screen (TV set).

- Teletext—the process by which users can call up pages of text and graphics and receive the information, superimposed on their regular TV screen.

Design and develop a display of one of the above means of telecommunication. Include in the display a working model, related graphic materials, and images that can be used in an exhibit for your school. Work with your teacher to determine the site within the school where the exhibit will be set up. For example, if the exhibit is to be used in a hallway, the display may be as shallow as 18 inches. If the exhibit is to be used in a library, the space possibilities and requirements would be quite different.

Design and develop a survey or other means of securing feedback from the viewers and users of the exhibit. Determine what information you want to secure from the participants and what use you will make of the information that you collect. Use the information to make changes in the displays and exhibit, and conduct another survey to see what changes, if any, are apparent in the responses of the participants.

DESIGN ACTIVITIES—DESIGNING AND DEVELOPING A VIDEO PRODUCTION

You have joined a team to develop a video presentation on your school that can be shared with other schools. As a group, review the script provided by your teacher. Determine if the script will have a beginning, middle, and ending. Are speakers clearly identified? Is the script to be used as a voice over (VO) of an existing video, or is the audio portion to be shot at the same time the video is recorded, sound on tape (SOT)? Once the script is prepared, a director's Video Script (see enclosed form) must be developed. The director's script basically describes what you will see and hear during the entire video. After the director's script has been prepared, you and your team will need to complete the following:

- Record narration

- Record video
  (Use Field Footage Log)

- Select and record background sound track music

- Select editing approach
  (Assemble vs. insert editing)

- Lay black

- Edit the final video

- Make final review of the edited video

- Set up for final presentations

You should acquire from your teacher the video production equipment and software such as Video Director for simple video production, Alchemy as a sound design and analysis tool, and Sound Edit for synchronizing sound and motion and adding sound effects. Check with your teacher to see if more sophisticated digital video systems, such as Spigot Power or Video Vision Studio, are available for advanced video work.

You may want to refer to the article on "The Making of *Who I Am*" a step-by-step approach to producing a video that was published in *TIES Magazine* (Nov/Dec 1991, pgs. 44-49.) Mike Supko describes how the "*Who I Am*" tape about fifth graders was produced by a high school video team.

VIDEO SCRIPT

PRODUCTION/PROJECT _____ **PAGE** ____ **OF** ____
DATE _____

VIDEO	INSTRUCTIONS	AUDIO

FIELD FOOTAGE LOG

PRODUCTION/PROJECT _____

PAGE ____ OF ____
DATE _____

SCENE	TAKE	TIME	SHOT DESCRIPTION	COMMENTS

DESIGN BRIEF—SENDING A MESSAGE VIA TELECOMMUNICATION

You may have seen an interesting example of telecommunicating in the movie *E.T.* To call home, E.T. made a telecommunication device from stuff found around the house.

NOTE: The device in the movie was actually developed by Henry Feinberg, Coordinator of Science Exhibits for American Telegraph and Telephone Company. Mr Feinberg's device, shown below, was published in several magazines, including the inaugural issue of *TIES Magazine* (Fall, 1989, pgs. 13-16).

1. Row of bobby pins to contact saw blade through openings in painted surfaces
2. Rubber band to return knife to resting position
3. Rope to tree branch
4. Safety pins through rope to limit movement
5. Wooden coathanger
6. Small rubber band
7. Fork hinged to knife to form ratchet
8. Butter knife bent up at the end
9. Painted circular saw blade. Holes scratched in paint form read-only memory
10. Golf umbrella handle
11. UHF TV tuner, adapted to be frequency modifier
12. Coffee can resonator
13. Funnel waveguide and matching section
14. Cable of wires from keyboard contacts to bobby pin feelers
15. Speaker mike from handie-talkie to pick up sound from Speak and Spell
16. Golf umbrella lined with aluminum foil to act as parabolic reflector
17. Modified readout
18. Speak and Spell
19. Kid's CB walkie-talkie
20. Antenna replaced by coax

Design and develop a display on telecommunication that includes a model of Mr. Feinberg's device, to help young children understand how the device works and how it is similar to other transmitting devices.

DESIGN ACTIVITIES—DESIGNING COMMUNICATION SYSTEMS

Below is an illustration of Samuel Morse's telegraph as shown in Figure 7.19 in your textbook. Refer to the "History of Science and Technology" activity in Chapter 7 of this book. Form teams to build two working models of Morse's telegraph that will make marks on the paper strips when signals (dots and dashes) are sent and received. The signals should cause the electromagnet on each device to move the pendulum and pencil to record the marks. The suspended weight at the top of the device is to move the paper as the incoming message is recorded.

Set up the two devices to create a communication system. Prepare a coded message (using Morse Code) to be placed in the Transmitter. Transmit the message to the other device.

You can use a dry-cell battery as the energy source for your model of the recorder. The dry cell is the answer to the question asked in your textbook ". . . what is wrong with this drawing?" The dry cell was not invented until many years after Morse had completed his work. The dry-cell battery would have been a great help to Morse, because one of the problems he faced was how to provide dependable electrical power for his device.

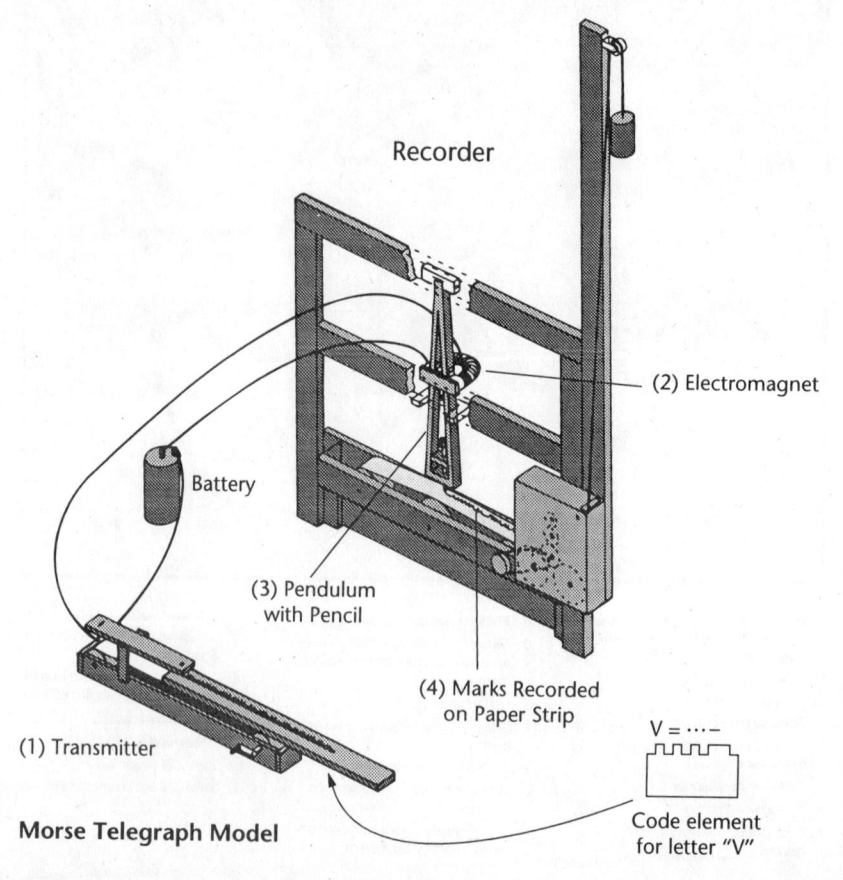

Morse Telegraph Model

- Recorder
- (1) Transmitter
- (2) Electromagnet
- (3) Pendulum with Pencil
- (4) Marks Recorded on Paper Strip
- Battery
- V = ···−
- Code element for letter "V"

NOTE: The transmitter shown here preceded the hand operated "code key" that became standard with later telegraph transmitters. In the original invention Morse used small pieces of metal with a different profile for each letter of the alphabet. For example, the letter "V" in Morse Code is ···—. Its profile is shown above. Morse did not think messages could be sent by hand.

DESIGN ACTIVITIES—DEVELOPING A SCANNING DEVICE

Context: Computers are often used to create, store and manipulate many different kinds of drawings, images and photographs. Images can be directly created using a variety of drawing tools available for computers, or they may be "imported" for further enhancement and modification. The process of importing a picture or drawing on a piece of paper into a computer is called scanning. Scanning is a method in which a picture is digitized; converting the image into digital information that the computer can use.

Design Brief: Develop a means to scan images that have been printed on paper and convert them to a digital format for storage and display on a computer.

Possible Solution: The information that follows provides a general introduction on how a simple scanner operates NOTE: You may find it necessary to pursue a more in-depth investigation on different aspects of the scanner and the process of scanning.

The scanner, shown in simple form in Figure 12.11 in your textbook, and as a drawing below, operates when the image on the drum is moved under the photo sensor. Each rotation of the drum results in one scanned line of information. The computer then captures and processes the information to produce the same image on the computer screen.

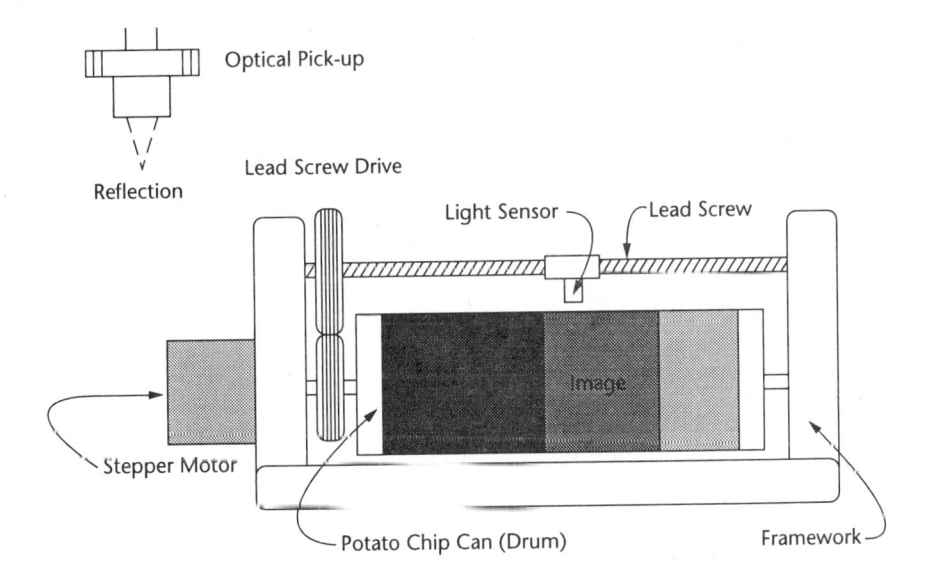

First, let us consider how the drum of the scanner moves and how it is controlled. The drum of the scanner is rotated by a stepper motor. Rather than spinning as a standard motor, a stepper motor rotates in small increments or steps—hence the name, "stepper motor". Each step is controlled by a coil that can be turned on and off to operate like an electromagnet.

DESIGN ACTIVITIES—DEVELOPING A SCANNING DEVICE CONTINUED

The simplified stepper motor shown in diagram form that follows, uses four coils. Each coil when triggered will cause the motor to rotate 90°. For example, when a signal is sent to pin 2 the transistor is turned on and current is sent to the top coil causing the motor to turn 1/4 of a turn. A signal would then be sent to pin 3, then pin 4, and finally pin 5. This set of four signals would cause the motor to rotate once. If you wanted to have the motor rotate ten times, you would need to program the computer to send "ten sets of four signals" to the motor.

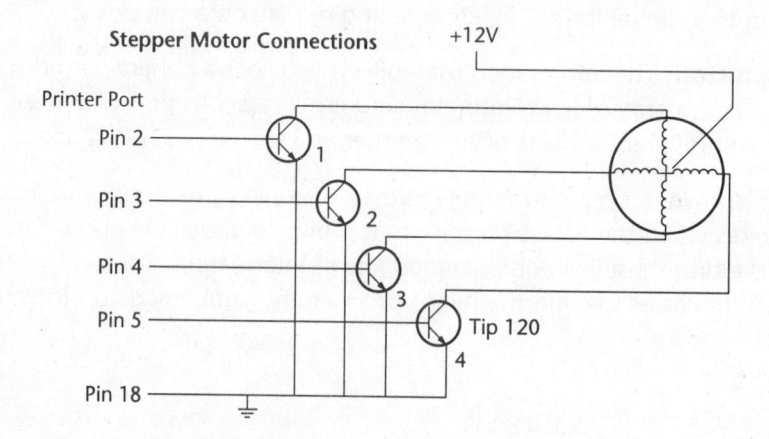

Stepper Motor Connections

For all of this to happen, and the motor to rotate, a software program needs to send a sequence of binary numbers as an output through the printer port to the stepper motor. The diagram below left shows the binary symbols for the decimal numbers of 1, 2, 4, 8. The sequence of these four symbols in the software will cause signals to be sent to the stepper motors to cause them to complete one rotation.

Binary Code	Decimal Equivalent
0000000●	1
000000●0	2
00000●00	4
0000●000	8

Note: You may want to refer again to the information on "binary code" on page 357 in this book. Remember that the combinations and permutations of the eight binary numbers can generate digital numbers from 0 to 255.

DESIGN ACTIVITIES—DEVELOPING A SCANNING DEVICE CONTINUED

In the preceding example, you saw how a simplified stepper motor could be rotated by four signals in sequence. The real stepper motor used in the scanner works in a similar manner. Four signals sent through four transistors acting as electronic switches will cause the four coils to move the motor through four small steps. The real stepper motor that was used had 200 coils and consequently moves in small steps of 1.8°, (360°÷200 = 1.8°). Each signal causes the stepper motor to rotate 1.8° and a sequence of four signals will move the motor 7.3°. A complete revolution of the stepper motor would require 50 of these four-step sequences.

To accomplish this the computer and software will send signals through the printer ports to the transistors. The sequence of signals is shown below. This sequence could be continued as many times as specified by the software program.

Binary Code	(sends)	Signal	(triggers)	Transistor	(energizes)	Coil	(rotates)	Motor
0000000●		Pin #2		#1		#1		1.8°
000000●0		Pin #3		#2		#2		1.8°
00000●00		Pin #4		#4		#4		1.8°
0000●000		Pin #5		#8		#8		1.8°
								7.2°

Now that the scanner is rotating, it is necessary to scan the image on the drum and convert it to digital signals. To do this, a software program is required that can complete another series of tasks. First, it will be necessary to take the information from the optical sensor and convert it to a value that can be used by the computer to display the image on the screen. Second, it is essential that the software put a dot on the screen corresponding to the dot that is read by the sensor. Third, the drum must advance to the next dot to be read. Fourth, the computer must advance a line on the screen each time a scan line is completed on the image.

DESIGN ACTIVITIES—DEVELOPING A SCANNING DEVICE CONTINUED

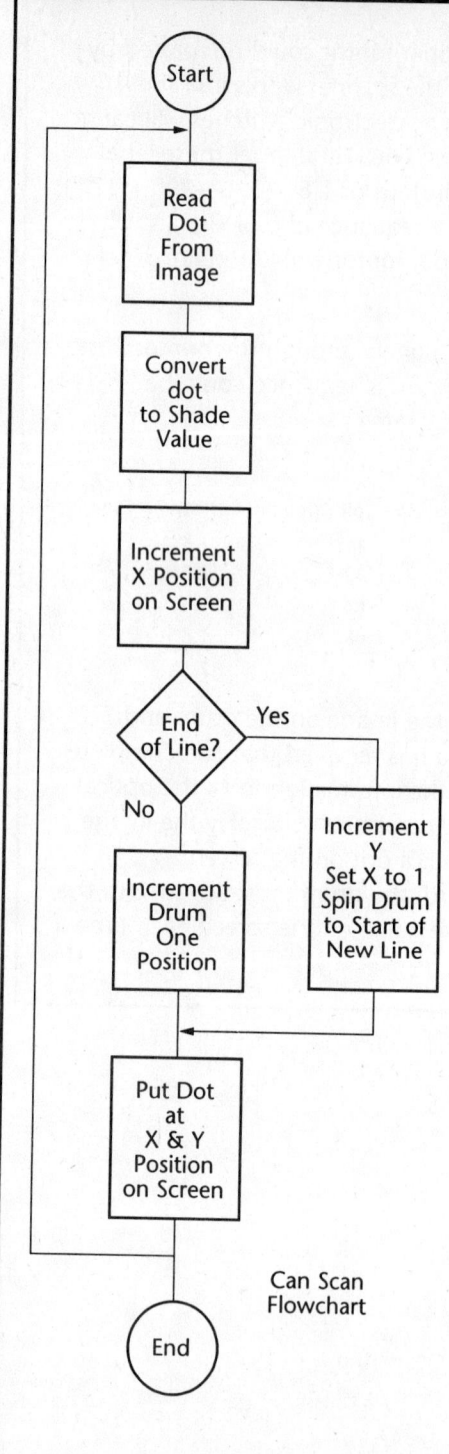

Can Scan Flowchart

[Flowchart: Start → Read Dot From Image → Convert dot to Shade Value → Increment X Position on Screen → End of Line? If No → Increment Drum One Position → Put Dot at X & Y Position on Screen → (loop back to Read Dot From Image); If Yes → Increment Y, Set X to 1, Spin Drum to Start of New Line → Put Dot at X & Y Position on Screen → End]

The flowchart shown at the left indicates the flow of the program and the operations to be accomplished. The flowchart helps to identify what the computer program is to accomplish. Each step included in the flowchart could represent several or many lines of programming.

The sensor for the scanner includes a light source and phototransistor mounted in the same housing. The signal returned by the sensor varies in current, depending upon the amount of light that is reflected—the darker the image, the less light reflected. This signal is then fed into the game port of an IBM-compatible computer. The game port is used to tell the computer the position of a joystick. A joystick is capable of returning a signal that varies in current, depending upon its position. Basically, the joystick has been replaced with the optical sensor.

Once a signal is received, the software determines the location on the drum that it is reading, and determines the equivalent location on the computer screen. The signal from the sensor is converted into a dot of one of 16 levels of gray. The next step is for the computer to rotate the drum another increment and read the next position. The computer keeps constant track of both the drum position and the position of the image on the screen. When the drum reaches the edge of the image, the computer rotates the drum to the next starting position. Thus, row by row an image is developed on the screen.

NOTE: The homemade device can scan an 8" x 8" image. It is designed to sense and generate 200 dots as it travels the 8" circumference of the drum. The total dots sensed and generated on the computer screen as pixels you be 40,000. Commercial scanners can easily produce 1,200 dpi (dots per inch). How many dots and pixels would that be for the 8" x 8" image?

DESIGN ACTIVITY—DESIGNING AND DEVELOPING A PORTFOLIO

You may find that designing and developing a portfolio will be unfamiliar and difficult work. Provided here is a fairly straight-forward example that show how a portfolio can help in documenting ideas, approaches, and possible solutions to a design problem. In your portfolio, you may wish to use a different approach for format, notes and notations, documentation and illustrations. It is very important to include statements of how you assessed your solution(s) and how you went about arriving at that solution or solutions.

The illustration below revisits Figure 2.43 of your text and represents the general organization for design portfolios. The sample pages that follow depart somewhat from that organization but still include the important and key components for a portfolio.

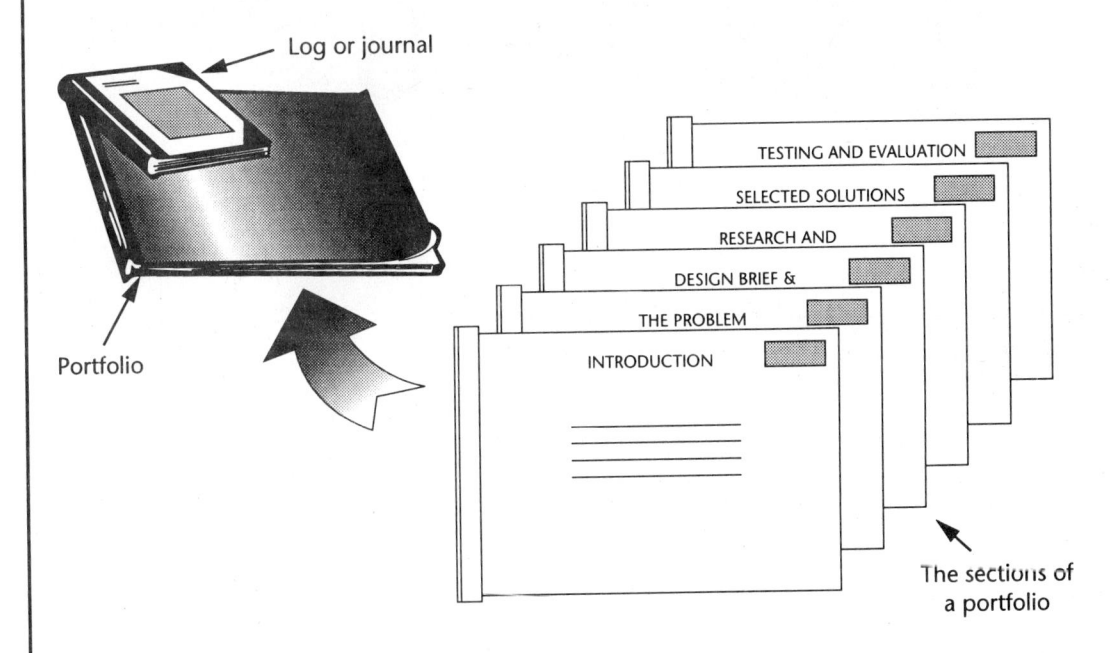

- Log or journal
- Portfolio
- The sections of a portfolio:
  - TESTING AND EVALUATION
  - SELECTED SOLUTIONS
  - RESEARCH AND
  - DESIGN BRIEF &
  - THE PROBLEM
  - INTRODUCTION

NOTE: You will want to check with your teacher on the availability of video materials that can show you how to develop and illustrate a portfolio.

An example portfolio on "Toys" is presented on the following pages. Each sheet of the portfolio was approximately 11" x 17". The portfolio was developed by Andrew Birkin when he was fourteen. Not all of Andrew's work is shown. The final portfolio was about 20 pages long and was organized some what differently than the suggested format shown above. The final document, however, included all the key components of a portfolio.

DESIGN ACTIVITY—DESIGNING AND DEVELOPING A PORTFOLIO CONTINUED

TOYS

Portfolio Cover

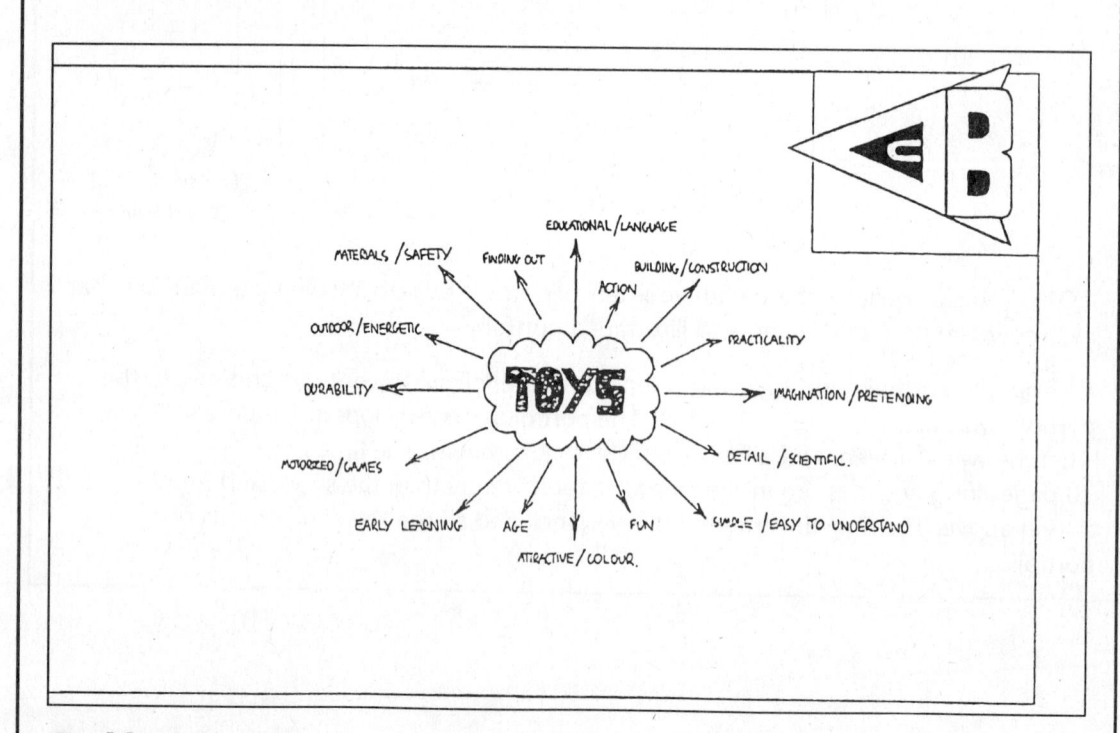

Mind map around "TOYS":
- MATERIALS / SAFETY
- FINDING OUT
- EDUCATIONAL / LANGUAGE
- ACTION
- BUILDING / CONSTRUCTION
- OUTDOOR / ENERGETIC
- PRACTICALITY
- DURABILITY
- IMAGINATION / PRETENDING
- MOTORIZED / GAMES
- DETAIL / SCIENTIFIC
- EARLY LEARNING
- AGE
- FUN
- SIMPLE / EASY TO UNDERSTAND
- ATTRACTIVE / COLOUR

Problem Context

DESIGN ACTIVITY—DESIGNING AND DEVELOPING A PORTFOLIO CONTINUED

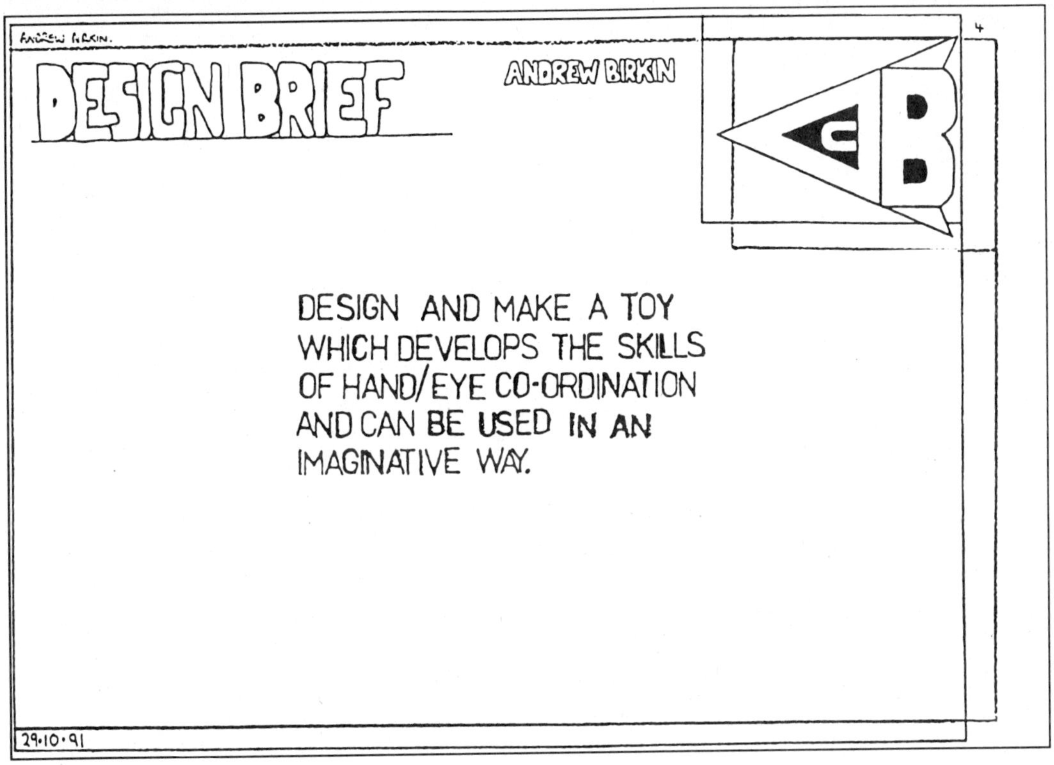

Design Brief

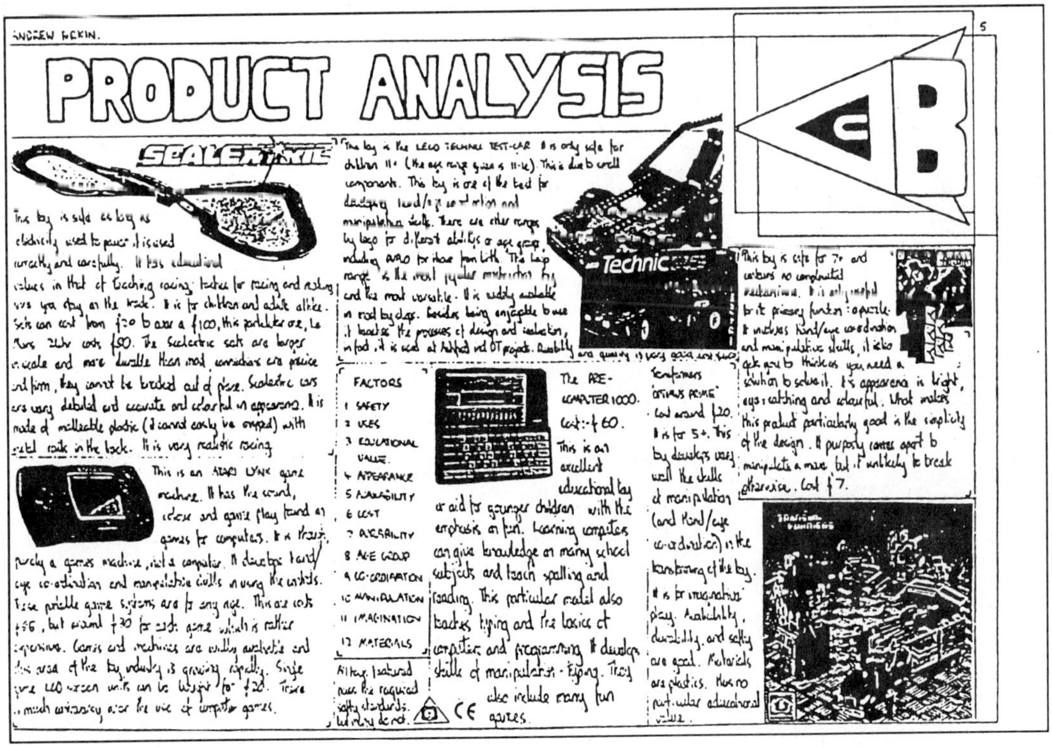

Product Analysis

DESIGN ACTIVITY—DESIGNING AND DEVELOPING A PORTFOLIO CONTINUED

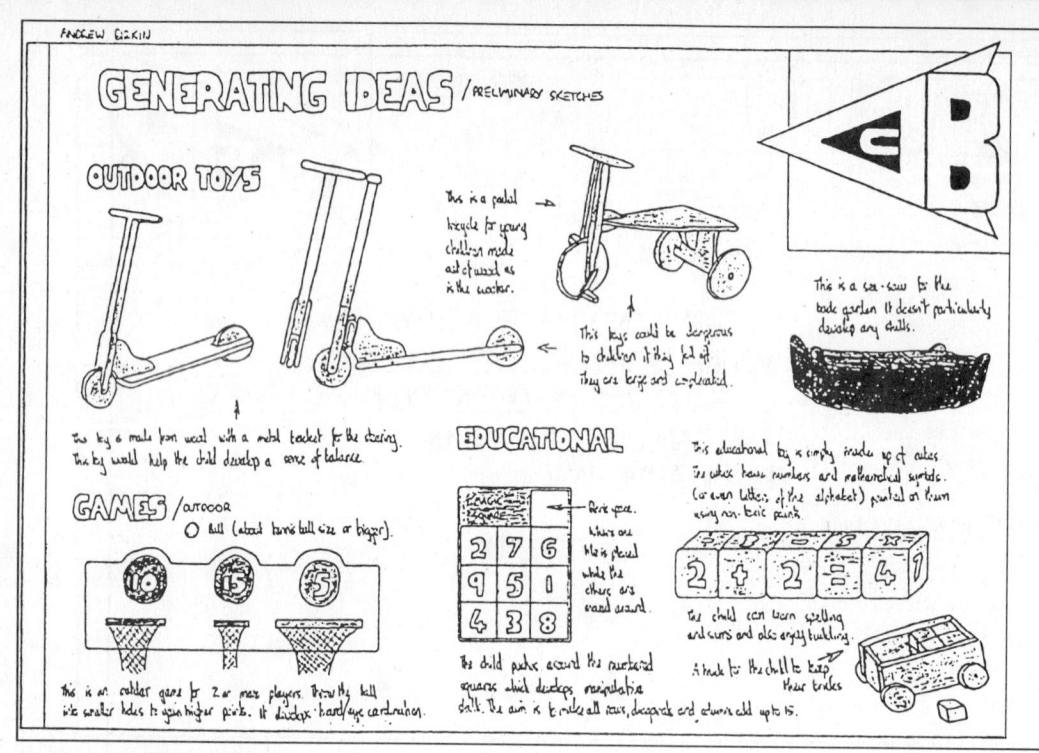

Generating Ideas

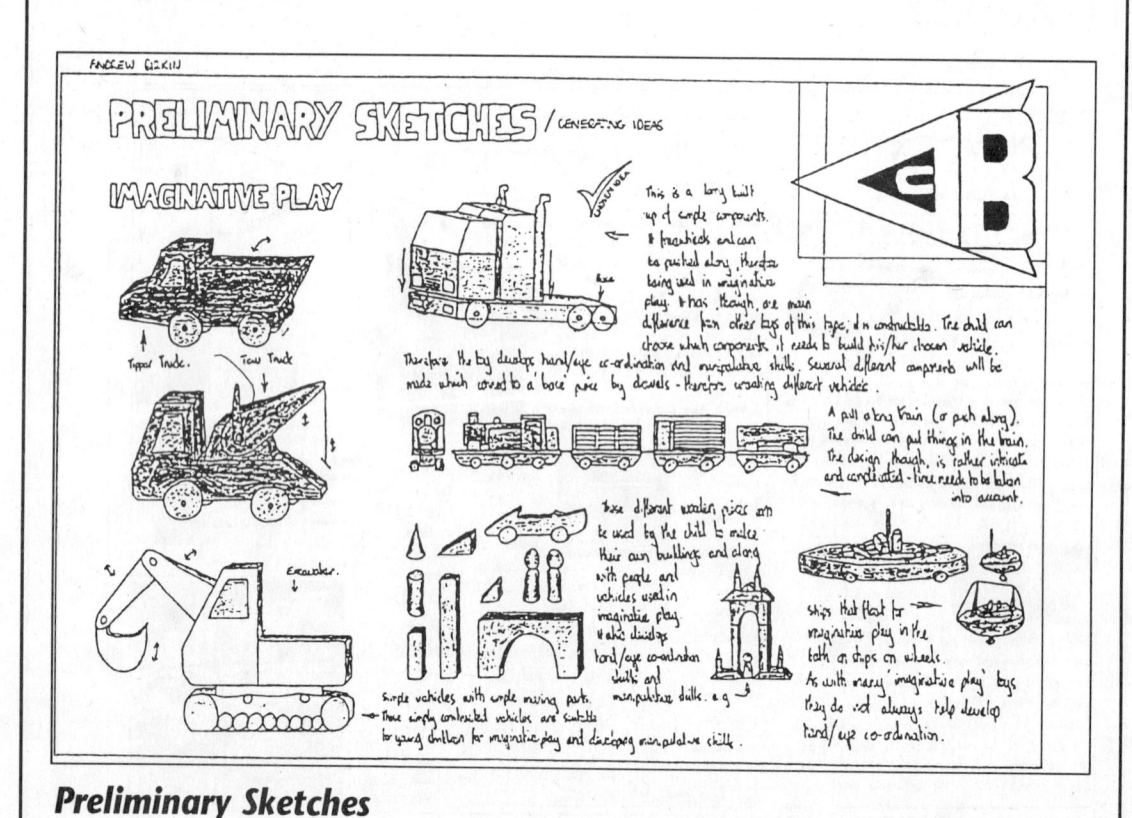

Preliminary Sketches

DESIGN ACTIVITY—DESIGNING AND DEVELOPING A PORTFOLIO CONTINUED

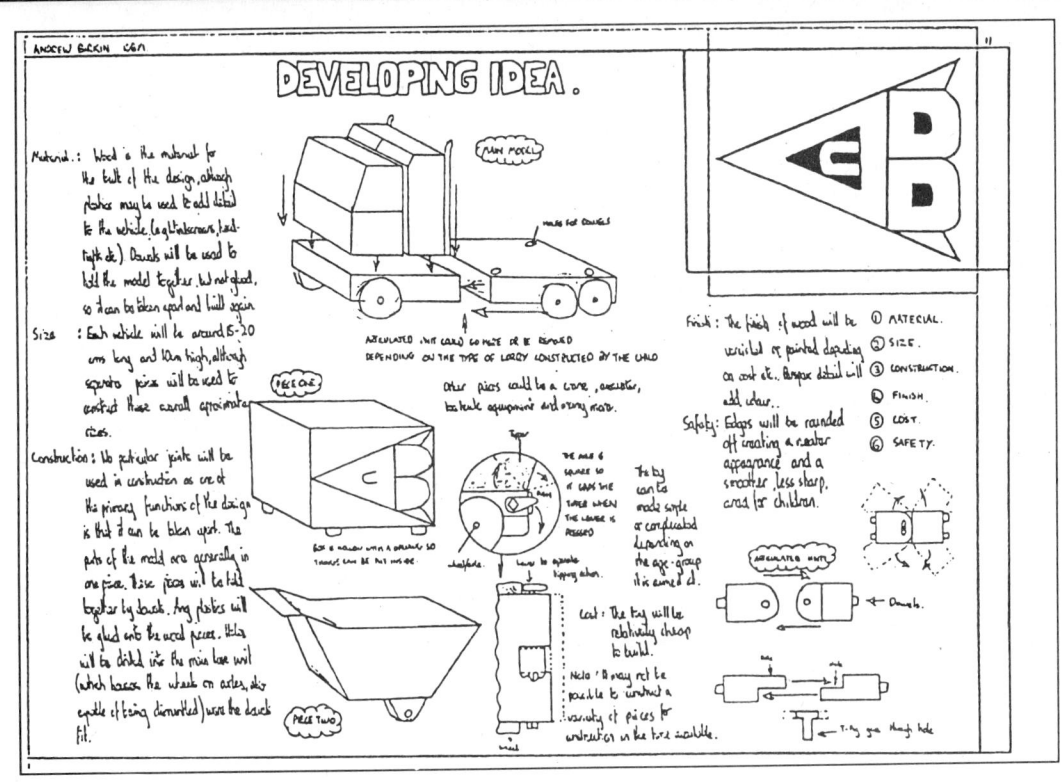

Developing Ideas

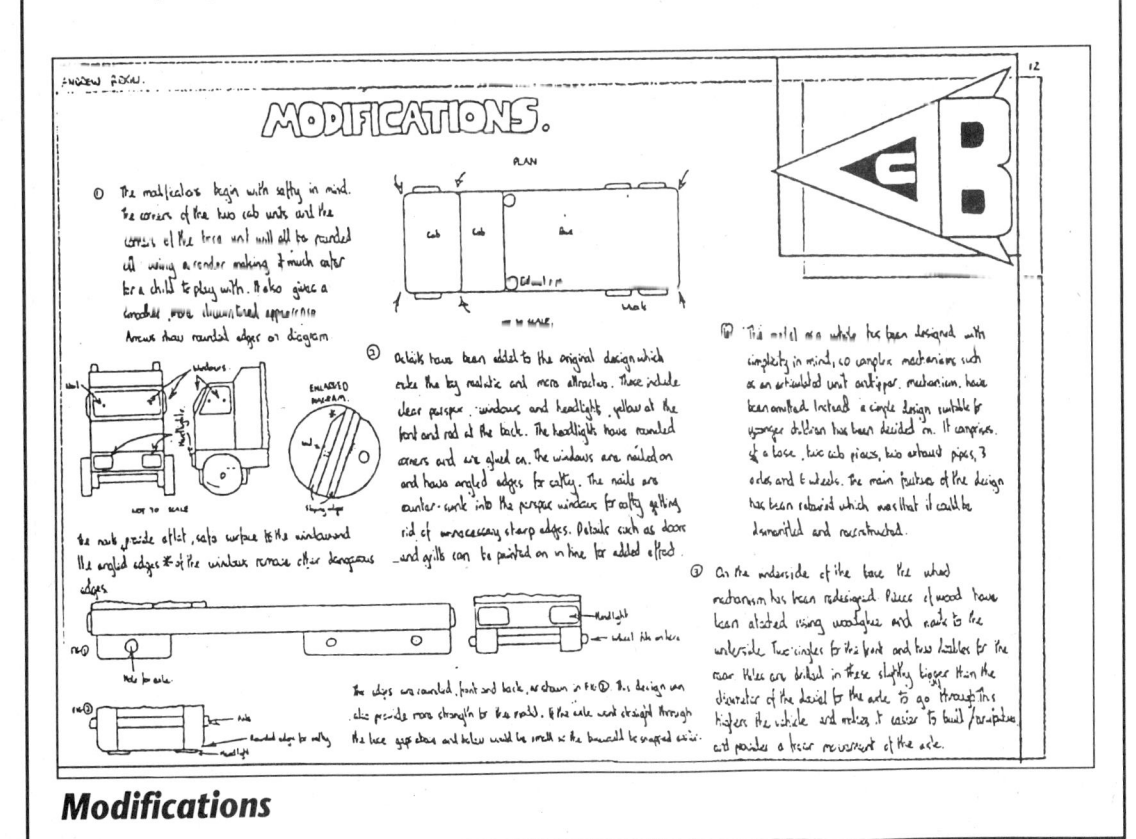

Modifications

DESIGN ACTIVITY—DESIGNING AND DEVELOPING A PORTFOLIO CONTINUED

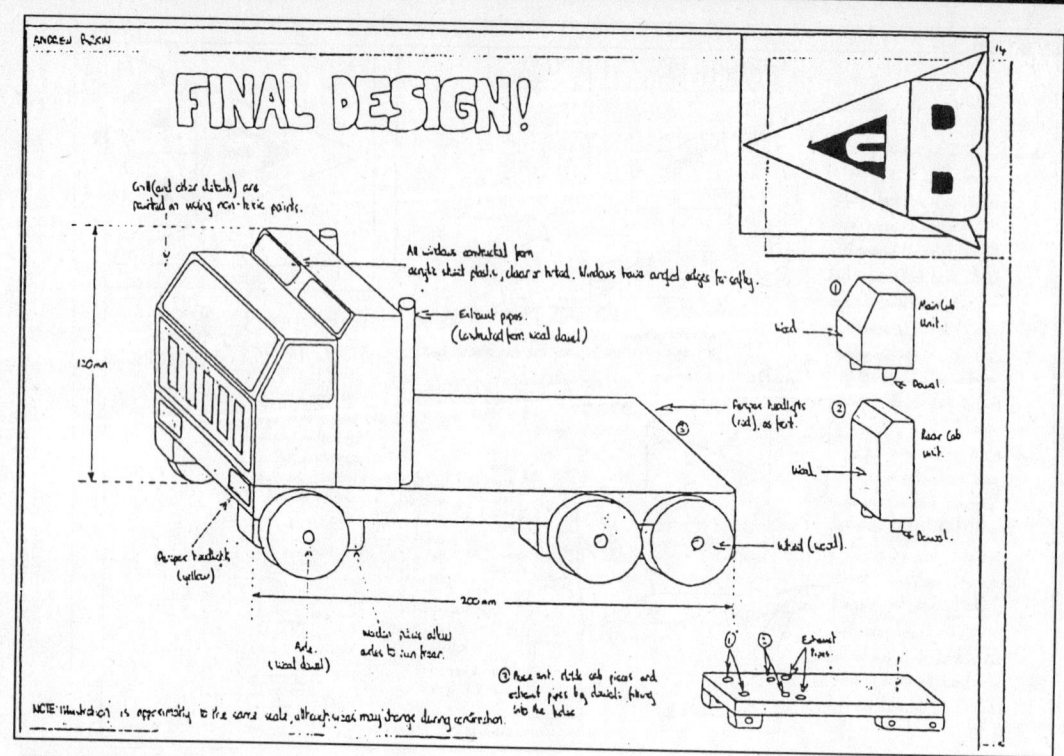

Final Design

Testing and Evaluation

FINAL EVALUATION

I am generally pleased with the results of this project. The model of the toy truck was quite sturdy and it should stand up to rugged use by most children of the age for which it was designed. The smoke stacks behind the truck cab will need to be attached more firmly, perhaps attaching them to the cab will provide the added reinforcement.

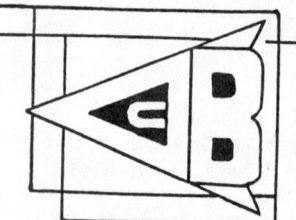

The end product ended up to be far more conventional than I anticipated. I think my solution was shaped too much by my interest skills in woodworking. I tended to use a material I was familiar with, rather than looking at a wider range of materials.

I am particularly pleased with what I learned in this design problem and think I am now ready to pursue problems using a wider range of approaches and that consider more inventive products that could yield more innovative results.

DESIGN BRIEF—DEVELOPING A PORTFOLIO VIA DESKTOP PUBLISHING

After you are familiar with designing and developing a portfolio, you may want to turn to electronic publishing techniques. You can use a personal computer and desktop publishing software to facilitate your portfolio work. In most instances, you will find it most productive and effective to merge electronic and hand-drawn images in your finished document. Some of the most common programs for desktop publishing include Adobe® PageMaker®, and Quark XPress. More and more schools are including one of these publishing tools in their design and technology programs.

DESIGN ACTIVITIES—DESIGNING AND DEVELOPING A PRESENTATION

You may also find it very helpful to use some software programs in the design and development of your presentations on your design problems. Some of the commonly used programs that are increasingly available in schools include Powerpoint, Posterworks, Ray Dream Studio, Draw Slate II, and Adobe Persuasion. Any of these will help you create more attention-holding visuals and professional presentations.

DESIGN BRIEF—USING CHARTS AND GRAPHS FOR COMMUNICATION

In your design and technology work, you will need to present facts, figures, and the interrelationship of information that can only be achieved effectively by using charts, graphs, and diagrams. You can use many different charts to present your information. Several examples are shown below. Refer to the materials provided by your teacher, such as *How to Draw Charts and Graphs*, by Bruce Robertson. Select an appropriate approach to present information you have collected on (a) the response to a market survey, (b) the results of testing a product, or (c) the operation of a product or system. Design and develop a chart that conveys the information in as simple and straightforward a manner as possible.

Charts of Relationship

Line charts are usually single lines with intervals plotted along the lines at irregular points. They include *thermometer charts*, *linear charts*, and *time lines*.

Flowcharts are either intervals plotted on one or more lines or a series of parallel lines of varying length. They include *chronologies*, *progress*, *schedule*, *process*, and *procedure charts*, and *time lines*.

Tree charts are lines beginning in a single source and branching into a group of arms. They include *fan charts*, *family tree charts*, *pedigree charts*, and *genealogy charts*.

Organizational charts have links between points, indicating the relationships of the items in the chart.

Matrix charts are usually rectangular grids into which data is placed against their vertical and horizontal values. They include *classification charts*, *tabulation charts*, *distance charts*, *table charts*, and *placement charts*.

Scatter charts are a form of matrix chart. They include *placement charts*, *triangular charts*, *trilinear charts*, *correlation charts*, *position charts*, *bivariate charts*, *shotgun charts*, and *scatter plot charts*.

Charts of Length, Area, and Volume

Charts of length
The terms bar and column are interchangeable. Column usually refers to a vertical arrangement, but bar can mean either. *Histograms* are column charts, usually without vertical divisions, and resemble stepped graphs. They include *ranked charts*, *rating column charts*, and *frequency distribution bars*.

Ranged bars as shown in the following examples, are charts in which the positions of the bars are the result of a particular axis or direction.

Population pyramids, *bilateral*, and *two-way histograms* are paired bars ranged from a center line.

Deviation bars and *two-directional bars* are bars set against a single-value line (often zero).

Radial bars, *polar coordinated bars*, and *star charts* are all bars that begin at a common center and radiate outward.

Range bars, *slide bars*, and *floating bars* are bars set against a background scale and located according to the range of their extremes.

Divided bars, *composite bars*, *segmented bars*, *banded bars*, *multiple bars*, *component bars*, *area bars*, *subdivided bars*, *relative part bars*, and *strata surface bars* are all bars containing subdivisions within the bar.

Charts of area
Pie charts are circular area charts containing segments representing parts of the whole. They include *sector charts*, *cake charts*, *circle charts*, and *divided circle charts*. *Block charts* and *unit charts* are charts that use regular areas to express values.

Charts of volume
These are expressed as cubes, spheres, or columns.

DESIGN BRIEF—USING CHARTS AND GRAPHS FOR COMMUNICATION CONTINUED

Graphs

Graphs are usually rectangular grids with the vertical axis representing values and the horizontal axis representing time. They include *rectilinear, coordinate, arithmetic line, frequency, fever,* and *alignment charts*, as well as *time series plot graphs* and *nomographs*.

Graphs plotted on logarithmic scales include *semi-log charts*, where one axis is a logarithmic scale, and *log-log*, if both are. *Ratio charts* and *rate-of-change charts* have similar scales.

Graphs on a circular grid include *radial, circular, polar,* and *polar coordinate charts*.

Graphs with shaded areas between the curve and a single value line (usually zero) include *deviation area graphs* and *silhouette charts*.

Graphs with two curves in which the areas between each curve are shaded include *net difference surface graphs* and *high-low charts*.

Charts in which the areas between the curves are shaded include *area, surface, multiple strata, subdivided, accumulated area, divided area, banded,* and *combined surface graphs*, as well as *stratum charts*. Values may be measured from the baseline up the vertical axis or between each curve independently.

Graphs with adjusted individual valuations include *progressive average, moving average,* and *moving total curves*.

Graphs with both axes scales of 100, so the valuations are percentages of the totals, are known as *Lorenz charts*.

Graphs in which the curve moves forward both vertically and horizontally between points include *stepped graphs* and *stair charts*.

Maps

Isoline maps
These consist of lines joining up all points of similar value. The area between one isoline and the next contains the range of values. Isoline maps are the most common way of depicting change on a map surface, and they include *isopleth, contour,* and *line relief maps*.

Area-shaded maps
These contain various tones representing different values within each area. They include *choropleth* and *crosshatched maps*.

Distribution maps
These show the distribution at particular points. They include *dot maps* and *plot maps*.

Flow maps
These contain particular or general lines of flow.

Grid maps
These are maps that have superimposed grids into which data is placed.

DESIGN ACTIVITIES—DESIGNING PRODUCT PACKAGING

In preparation for creating a package for one of your products, collect a number of packages of different sizes and shapes for study. Select several packages of appropriate size but different shapes from your collection. Carefully take the packages apart so they can be laid out flat. As indicated in Figure 3.13 in your textbook, the shape of the box laid out flat is called the pattern or development, similar to the electric car model in Figure 3.14.

Study these packages to determine how they were fabricated. Refer to these shapes to see how your package could be made and where the fold lines and flaps would be positioned. Refer to pages 382–383 in your textbook to review the section on packaging and the Guidelines for Effective Marketing Packages. Apply these guidelines by using the work sheet provided below, to ensure that your package conveys a visual message that is appropriate to your product.

Design a package for a toy product developed for young children or for a food product developed for teenagers. Determine the size and shape of packages needed. Develop a 2-D pattern for one of the packages. Conduct tests to see if the pattern provides you with a package of appropriate size and shape. Plan the graphic message you want to use on the package to draw attention to the product. Determine what information about the product must be included, by law, on the package. Determine how you will incorporate that information on the package. Develop and render the final package design on card stock. Cut out and shape the package in its final 3-D size and form.

Work Sheet for Effective Marketing Packages

- **Package Simplicity**   Poor 1 2 3 4 5 Good
    - Package design is simple.
    - Amount of information on the package is limited.
    - Drawings and graphics are simple.

- **Attention and Attraction**   Poor 1 2 3 4 5 Good
    - Package catches buyer's attention.
    - Package communicates as quickly as possible.
    - Package helps consumer understand package contents.

- **Package and Product Compatibility**   Poor 1 2 3 4 5 Good
    - Package is compatible with the product.
    - Package reflects the image of the product.

- **Package Appeal**   Poor 1 2 3 4 5 Good
    - Package has an aesthetic appeal to the consumer.
    - Package is more eye-catching than competing packages.

DESIGN BRIEF—ANALYSIS OF INFORMATION ON PACKAGES

In this design brief, you will have the opportunity to look at several different types of products, their ingredients, and product claims. You can then use this as background when you add pertinent information to the packages you design.

Collect a number of packages of different sizes and shapes. Determine a product or material from your design and technology project for which a package is needed. Select several packages of appropriate size but different shapes from your collection. Carefully disassemble the packages so that they lay flat. Study these packages to determine how they were fabricated. Refer to these shapes to see how your package could be made and where the fold lines and flaps would be positioned. Again, refer to the Guidelines for Effective Marketing Packages on page 383 of your textbook. Use these guidelines and the information from your analysis of packages to design a package that conveys a visual message that is appropriate to your product. Remember, the most effective packages are usually rather simple and straightforward.

You will also want to transfer the shape of your package to a blank sheet of paper to serve as a format on which you can develop the message for your package. What information about your product must be included on the package? What information can be added as a courtesy or help to the potential buyers of your product? What information is relatively unimportant to the buyers/users of your product?

Attach a sketch, photograph, or digital image of your package design in the space provided here.

DESIGN BRIEF—COMMUNICATING THROUGH EXHIBITS AND DISPLAYS

Design and develop an exhibit that will help younger students understand more about design and technology. The students will be attending your school next year and will be involved in design and technology activities. What information will you need about the students? What information will you plan to share with them?

Use the software program on 3-D design provided by your teacher to develop a computer model of your exhibit. Use the program to allow you to simulate what the exhibit would look like to the viewer before actually building the exhibit. Determine what changes you plan to make before you build the model of your exhibit. Print out some of these views to use in your project portfolio.

Build a 3-D model of the exhibit. Compare the physical model to the simulation to determine how closely they match. If apppropriate, your teacher may have you and your group develop a full-size version of the exhibit.

INTEGRATED S/M/T ACTIVITIES

- Determine what math is related to the design and development of packages that are developed from flat sheets of materials into boxes.
- What are some standard sizes of cans and boxes that are used for food?
- How would you change the size of a No. 10 can to optimize the quantity of contents that could be stored in the can?
- What would be the optimal box size to store 20 oz. of granola using the least amount of cardboard?
- Are cereal boxes made to optimize their volume while minimizing the materials used in them? Why are boxes for cereal made the sizes they are.
- What advantages are there for forming containers of plastic that are square instead of round?
- Why are tin cans made round rather than square?
- What are the daily nutritional requirements for a teenager?
- What does the required labeling of food include? Why?
- What is required in the labeling of a product for young children? Is the labeling adequate? Why? What would you change?

CHAPTER 13
Control Technology Systems

Control is an important part of our lives, and you engage in control activities many times every day. Control technology represents the technical means by which we direct and regulate different systems.

CONTROL SYSTEMS

Systems Approach to Control Systems

The **systems approach** involves looking at the major parts, or building blocks, of **input, process,** and **output** that make up any system. The systems approach, can be shown in general form as a block diagram or in specific form as a transistor-controlled circuit.

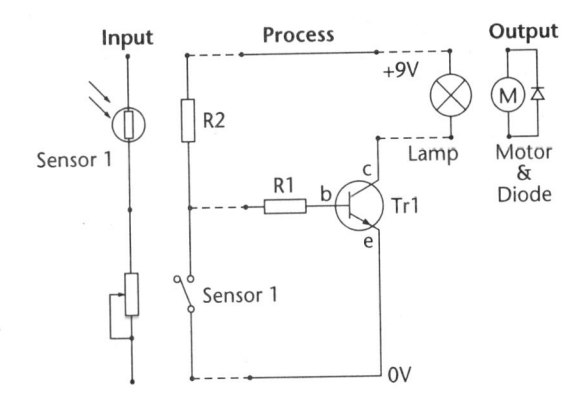

A Basic Control Circuit

NOTE: The resistor R1 (normally about 1–5 K) limits the base current and prevents overheating. Negligible current flows through the lamp when the transistor is switched off. However, when the transistor is fully on, the potential difference between the collector and emitter is almost zero (approximately 0.2 volts) so that the lower terminal of the lamp is effectively connected to the ground. A large collector current then flows; the voltage across the lamp is almost the whole supply voltage. This circuit is designed to act as a switch. It ensures that the transistor only operates in two states—fully on or fully off.

INTEGRATED S/M/T ACTIVITIES—AN EARLY EXAMPLE OF CONTROL TECHNOLOGY

Machines that operate automatically have been around long before James Watt developed his improved version of the steam engine. One improvement that Watt made on the steam engine was to add an automatic control device to regulate the speed of the engine, as shown in the illustrations below.

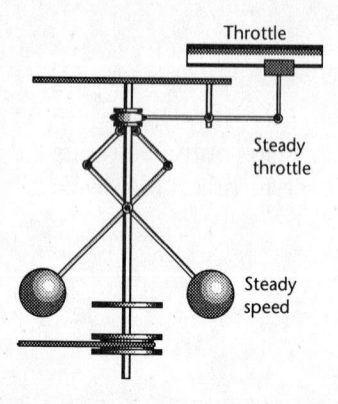

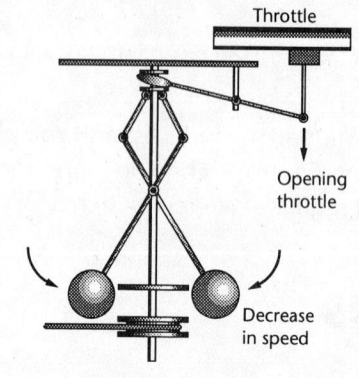

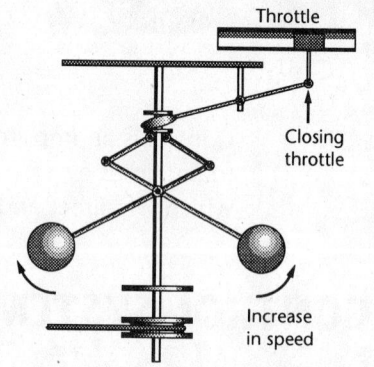

(A) The flyball governor maintaining the desired speed.

(B) Opening the throttle because the engine is slowing down.

(C) Closing the throttle to slow the engine from running too fast.

Using your earlier work with mechanisms, design and develop a working model of a flyball governor. Indicate how the mechanism could be used to control the speed of a gasoline engine used on a lawn mower.

DESIGN BRIEFS—SYSTEM INPUT DEVICES

System inputs can take many different forms. For control systems, all inputs are energy that is converted into information. All input devices provide a means of sensing a condition you want to monitor. For example, you may want to monitor conditions related to the temperature, humidity, or light level of an environment, or monitor the movement of something—an object, wind, or water. You will make a number of key decisions in the design of a control system. One of these key decisions is the choice of the system inputs in the form of the sensor or sensors that can monitor the condition you wish to control.

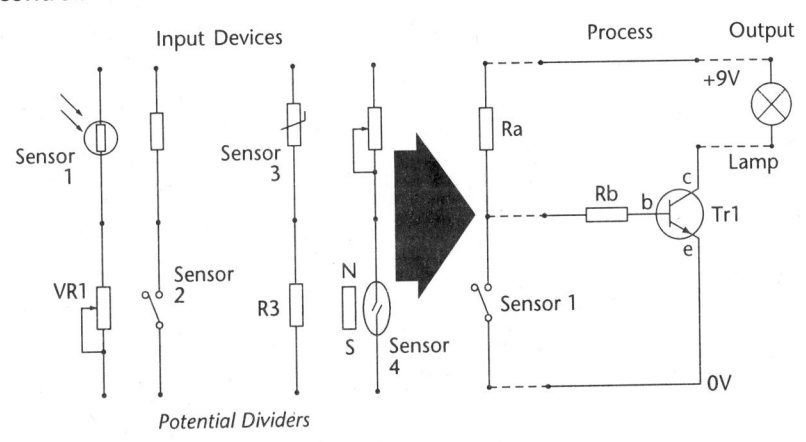

The input signal to the base of a transistor is often supplied from the center tap of a potential divider consisting of a sensor/resistor combination connected in series across the power supply. A change in sensor resistance causes a change of voltage at the center point of the potential divider. When the voltage is high enough (approximately 0.7 volts), the current flowing in the base is sufficient to turn on the transistor.

Design Activity

Collect a range of the sensors and input devices that have been introduced. Identify other devices that could be used to provide input for your control systems. Design a sensor/resistor combination for each of the devices that provides an input for a control system. Determine the combination needed to operate when the device is "on" (sensing the presence of something) and when it is "off" (sensing that something is not present.)

DESIGN ACTIVITIES—SYSTEM PROCESS DEVICES

Process devices take the input signals and convert them to output signals that can **control** a system. Such control can take the form of **switching** on a light, **adjusting** the volume of an amplifier on a stereo, or **changing** a signal to be sent to another control device.

In much of your design and technology work, you will use electronic circuits for your process devices. There are a variety of electronic process devices. We will consider several—the transistor, the silicon-controlled rectifier, and ICs (the 555 timer and the 741 operational amplifier).

Transistors. Transistors are components with three terminals, usually called the base, emitter, and collector.

Transistors are manufactured in different ways, but the most common transistors come in a small metal can with a protruding tab on the rim.

Transistors operate when a small current flows between the base and emitter and the transistor switches on; this allows a much larger current to flow between the collector and emitter. When this collector current reaches its maximum, the transistor has reached its peak amplification and is described as saturated. The ratio of collector to base current is known as the current **gain** of the transistor, or its **amplification**.

With the components and materials provided by your teacher, set up the circuit shown at the right. Connect the collector and emitter legs of a 2N222 transistor as shown. What happens?

Complete the circuit as shown in the illustration at the right. Can the circuit operate?

NOTE: To turn the transistor on, a small current has to flow between base and emitter. This can be supplied by adding a small resistor that is connected between the base of the transistor and the positive side of the battery. The very small current that flows into the base causes a much larger current to flow between collector and emitter, so the lamp is turned on.

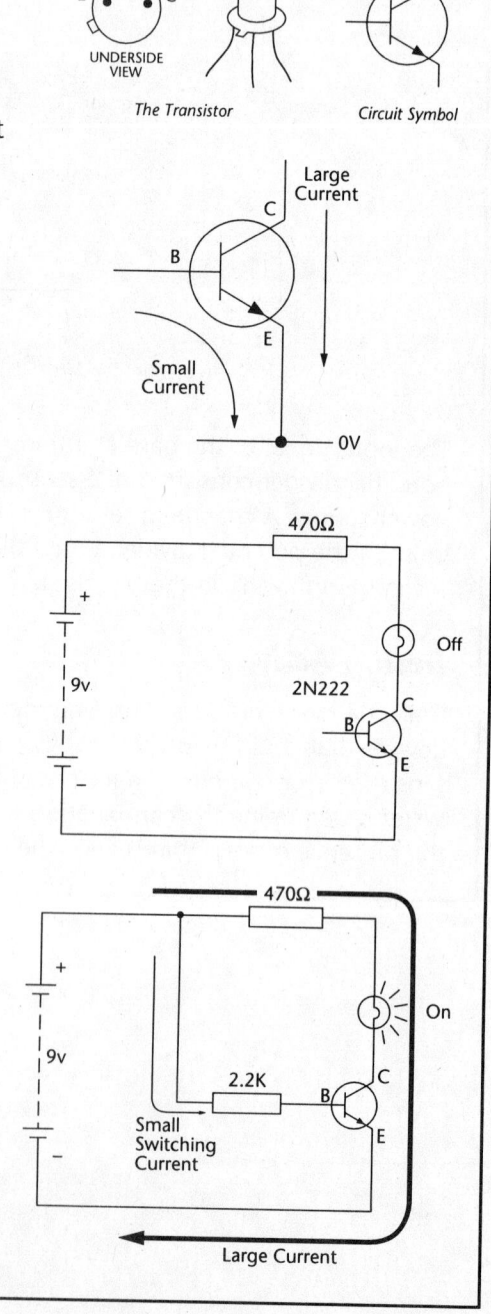

DESIGN ACTIVITIES—
THE SILICON-CONTROLLED RECTIFIER (SCR)

The Silicon-Controlled Rectifier (SCR)

The SCR operates somewhat like a transistor, although with one big difference. Once the SCR is turned on, it stays on.

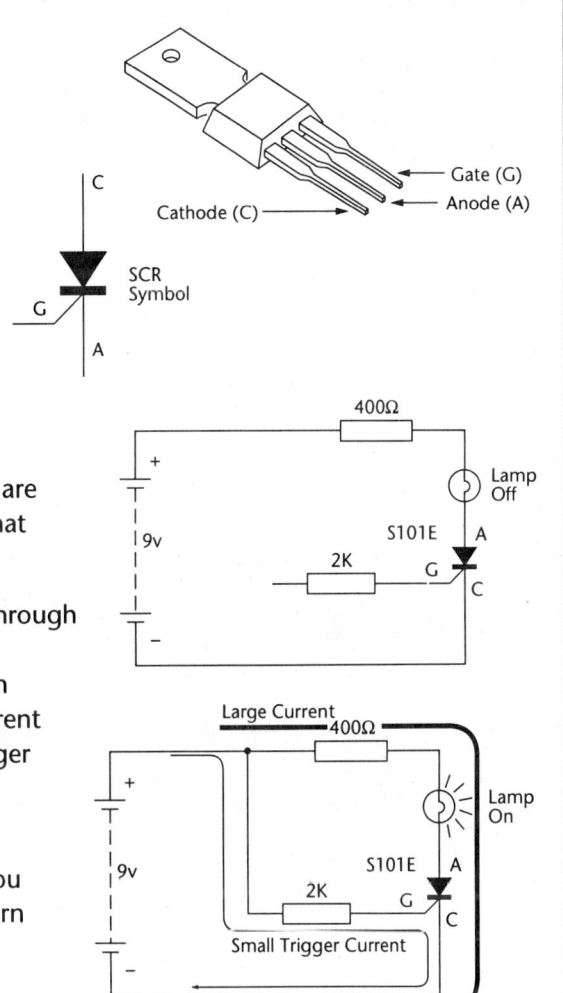

Like a transistor, the SCR has three legs, with similar functions but different names. The names came from terms that were used during the early development of electronic tubes. The legs are named **gate** rather than base, **anode** rather than collector, and **cathode** rather than emitter.

Connect the anode and cathode of the SCR are connected into a lamp circuit, as shown. What happens? Does the current flow?

NOTE: A small current flowing to the gate through a resistor will cause the SCR to turn on, (or trigger) causing a larger current to flow from the anode to the cathode (conventional current flow). Unlike the transistor, however, the larger current will keep flowing even if the gate current is stopped.

Set up the circuit shown at the right. Can you make it operate? Can you make the lamp turn off?

DESIGN ACTIVITIES—
THE SILICON-CONTROLLED RECTIFIER (SCR) CONTINUED

NOTE: Transistors return to a normal state of being turned off. The SCR must be turned off. This is accomplished by turning off all current, even for a very short period of time. This can be done by using a switch that turns off the current from the battery. When the switch powers up the circuit, the SCR can be turned on again only if current is sent to the gate leg again.

Use the concept of "bypassing" to design another way to turn the SCR off. How does the circuit operate? Does the SCR turn off if bypassed for even a very brief time?

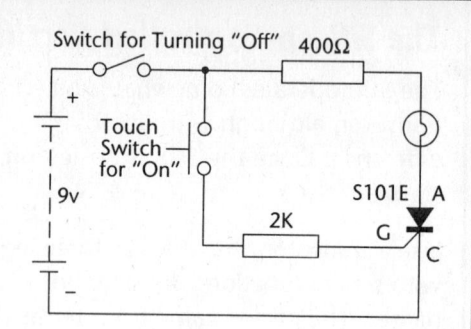

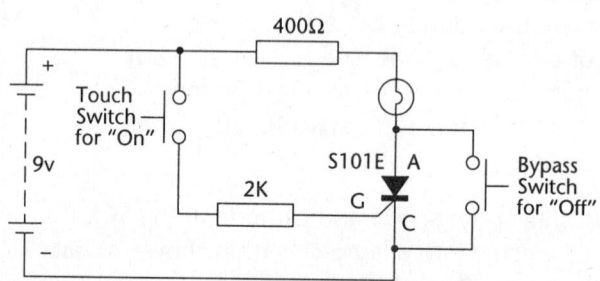

NOTE: SCRs can carry several times more current than transistors. The SCR gate will need to be protected with a resistor.

BE CAREFUL: If the SCR is carrying a large current, it will get hot, and you may get burned. You may also need to connect the SCR to a heat sink to help dissipate the unwanted heat and protect the SCR from damage.

DESIGN ACTIVITIES—TIMING CIRCUITS

Timing Circuits

In work with control systems, you will have occasional need for timing circuits. Electronic timing circuits use capacitors to introduce "delay" for timing functions.

Set up the circuit shown in the diagram at the right. A capacitor has been connected between the base leg of the transistor and the positive side of the battery (or power supply).

Determine what happens when the input switch is closed. Does the lamp light? Does it light immediately or is there a delay? What happens when the input switch S_1 is opened? Does the lamp change immediately or is it delayed?

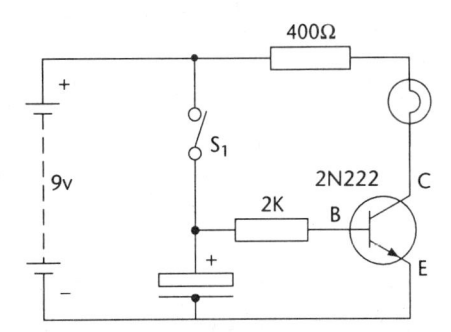

> **NOTE:** You can use this approach to design a circuit that will remain on for a period of time after you have turned the device off. You may find it interesting that a capacitor operates quite like an electric counterpart to a pneumatic accumulator. You can use a pneumatic accumulator coupled with a flow regulator or restrictor (pneumatic resistors) to provide a time delay in a pneumatic circuit.

Use the circuit you developed above (or one from your teacher) to see what happens when different size capacitors are used. Try capacitors with values of 0.01 µF to (10nF), 1.0 µF, and 100µF.

> **NOTE:** These capacitors are progressively 100 times larger than the one before. The larger capacitors will be electrolytic and you must pay attention to their polarity when connecting in a circuit.

What happens when a larger capacitor is used? Does the lamp stay on for a longer or shorter period? You can also experiment with different size resistors to see what happens. With a 1000 µF capacitor, try the following resistors with values of 2 K, 5 K, and 10 K.

DESIGN ACTIVITIES—TIMING CIRCUITS CONTINUED

Timing circuits can also be designed to link capacitors and relay coils. With the components provided by your teacher, set up a circuit patterned after the one shown to the right. What happens to the relay when the switch S_1 is opened? Notice that the capacitor is connected in parallel with the relay. Can you explain why? **Hint:** The current from the capacitor affects the relay in a manner similar to the way the capacitor in the transistor circuit above affected the transistor.

Set up the circuit shown in the following illustration with a capacitor and a relay in series. This arrangement works somewhat differently and causes the light (or other output device) to remain on for a period of time and then to shut off automatically.

Can you explain why? Refer to the circuit shown at the right and consider the following:

When switch S_1 is closed, the capacitor is charged because current will flow through the relay coil. At first, the charging current is high, but the current gradually decreases until the capacitor is charged. At that point, the current flow reaches zero. When you closed S_1, the relay was energized and the lamp came on. The flow of current in that part of the circuit gradually decreased to the point that the relay de-energized and turned off the lamp. The circuit can be reset by opening S_1 and then pressing push switch PS_1 to discharge the capacitor. When S_1 is closed again, the circuit will repeat the above operation.

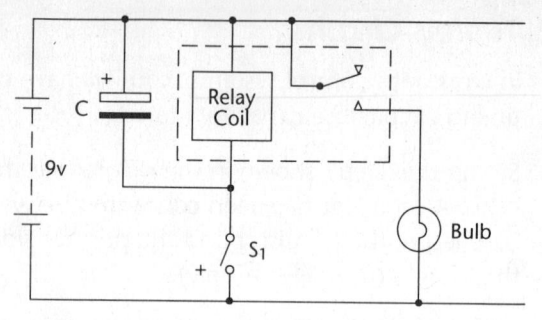

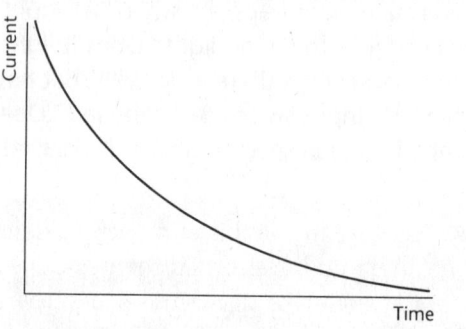

Graph showing relationship of current and time for the discharging of a capacitor

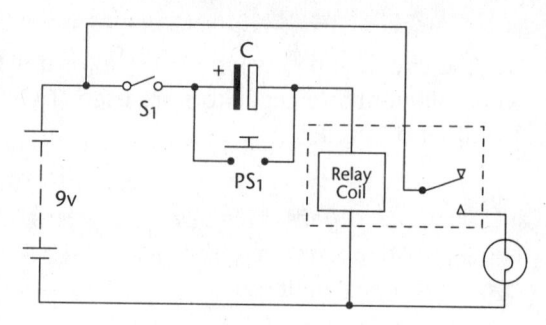

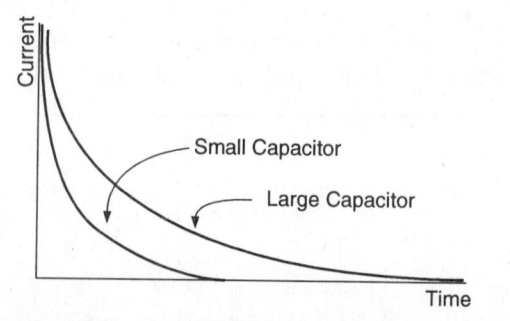

NOTE: The length of time the lamp is on is determined by the size of the capacitor in the circuit, as shown in the graph.

DESIGN ACTIVITIES—TRANSISTOR-CONTROLLED RELAY

Set up the circuit shown below. In such circuits, it is handy to combine transistors and relays. The transistor can be used to control the relay that, in turn, can control devices that use more power than a transistor can handle. The combination of the two also provides another timing capability—creating a delay before the relay operates and the bulb or other output device is switched on. A three-part explanation of this circuit follows:

1. When you close switch S_1, capacitor C and resistor R form an active circuit. Capacitor C begins to take a charge, and the voltage across it increases. With an increase of voltage across C, the voltage across R decreases.

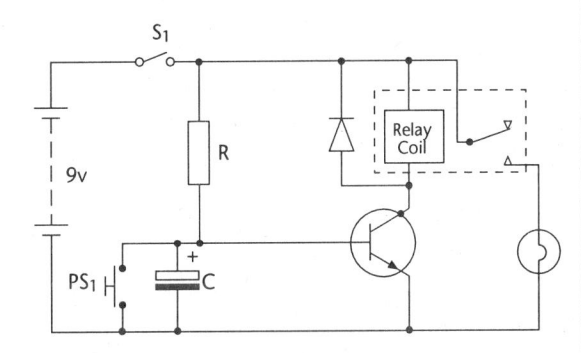

NOTE: C and R will divide the voltage available from the supply (in this case, 9 volts). The total voltage across C and R will always be equal to the supply voltage. If the resistor is large, then the amount of voltage for the capacitor is reduced. Similarly, if the capacitor is large, the voltage for the resistor is reduced.

2. A transistor operates when a current is supplied to its base. The transistor does not turn on, however, until the voltage across the base reaches about 0.6 volts. When S_1 is closed, the capacitor begins to charge and the voltage increases. When the voltage reaches 0.6 volts the transistor starts to turn on, and as the voltage goes slightly higher, the transistor comes on completely and operates the relay.

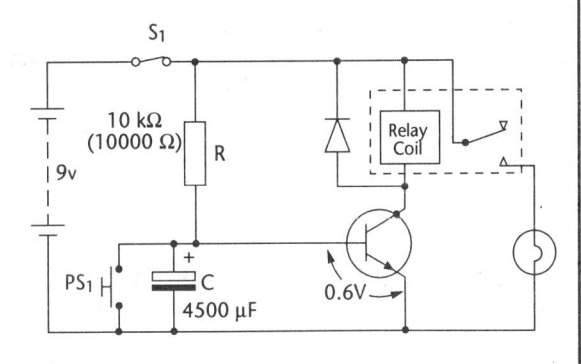

3. You can reset the circuit by opening S_1 and then pressing PS_1 to discharge the capacitor. When you close S_1 again, the circuit will repeat the operation described above.

DESIGN ACTIVITIES—DETERMINING R.C. TIME CONSTANTS

You will find it helpful to know how to determine the time it takes for a capacitor and resistance arrangement to charge. This is called the R.C. time constant and represents the time it takes a capacitor to reach about two-thirds of the supply voltage. To calculate the time constant for a given R.C. circuit, use the following equation:

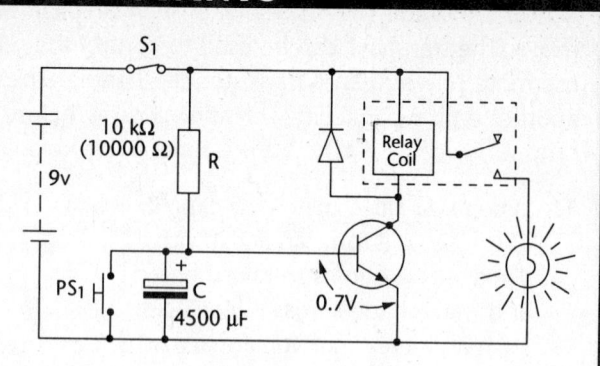

t = C x R

(When C is expressed in farads and R is expressed in ohms.)

Refer to the diagram at the right that shows the resistor and capacitor from the circuit shown above.

> NOTE: As you begin to determine the time constant, remember that 4500 μF must be divided by 1,000,000 to change μF to F, and 10 K Ω must be multiplied by 1,000 to change K Ω to ohms.

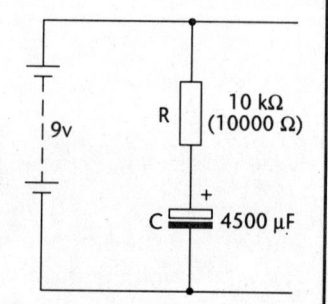

What will be the R.C. time constant for these components?

DESIGN BRIEFS

- Design and develop a circuit that uses a transistor or an SCR to turn on a light in the garage or hallway that will stay lit until it is turned off by a switch inside the house or apartment.

- Design a circuit that uses a relay and capacitor to accomplish the above function.

- Design and develop a circuit that will sound an alarm 30 seconds after someone opens the door to your bedroom. Design a circuit that will sound an alarm after a delay of a minute.

INTEGRATED CIRCUITS

Up to this point, all the circuits discussed have been constructed from discrete (separate) components such as resistors, capacitors, and transistors. Integrated circuits (ICs) are different in that they are complete circuits in small containers. ICs are made of very small chips of silicon formed to create hundreds of components—resistors, capacitors, and transistors. There are hundreds of different ICs. Two ICs, the 555 timer and 741 operational amplifier, or op amp, have proven to be very useful in design and technology projects and will be considered here.

The 555 Timer—Integrated Circuit

The circuits presented earlier, although useful in your design work, have a key disadvantage. They must be reset manually after each sequence, usually by pressing a switch to discharge the capacitor. Additionally, the time delays that can be created will be relatively short. These disadvantages can be overcome by using the 555 timer integrated circuit (IC).

DESIGN ACTIVITIES—
USING THE 555 TIMER (MONOSTABLE OPERATION)

The circuit shown at the right will switch the lamp (or other output device) on for a specific time and then turn it off. You can determine the length of time the unit is to remain on (RC factor) and choose the resistor and capacitor accordingly. The internal circuit of the 555 timer allows you to send a signal to start the process and to send another signal from the RC part of the circuit to turn the device off.

You press PS_1 momentarily to start the timing process. When PS_1 is pressed, pin 3 on the 555 timer goes from 0 volts (its normal state) to +9 volts, instantaneously. This in turn activates the relay which switches on the lamp. The relay will remain activated (and the lamp will remain on) for a given period of time, depending on the size of the timing components, R and C. The capacitor will then discharge to a point where the current flow will not hold the relay. The relay then turns off and pin 3 will return to 0 volts.

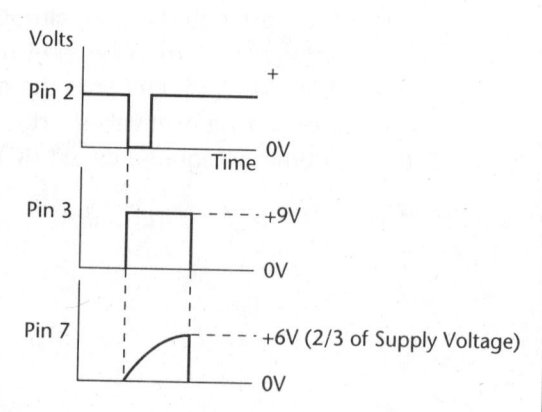

The graph shows the above process and indicates the voltages for pins 2, 3, and 7 during that time period. The internal design of the IC allows the capacitor to be automatically discharged when the relay switches off, thus making the circuit ready for the next timing process.

Design Brief

Design and develop a 555 timer that will operate an output device on a 5 second interval. What changes would be necessary to provide a 15 second interval?

> **NOTE:** Monostable means that the output of the IC (the voltage at pin 3) has one stable state (0 volts). The voltage can be changed (as in this example to 9 volts, but output will go back to 0 volts (its stable state) after a predetermined period of time.

DESIGN ACTIVITIES—
USING THE 555 TIMER (ASTABLE OPERATION)

The 555 timer can also be used as an oscillator to achieve astable operation. Astable means that the system oscillates back and forth and has no stable state. The oscillation caused by the RC factor of the resistors and capacitor creates an output of the 555 timer circuit that changes continuously between 0 volts and +9 volts. In Circuit A below, the output of the device continues to go low (0 volts) and high (+9 volts), and the lamp continues to flash off and on.

To calculate the frequency of an astable timer, you will complete the procedure shown here:

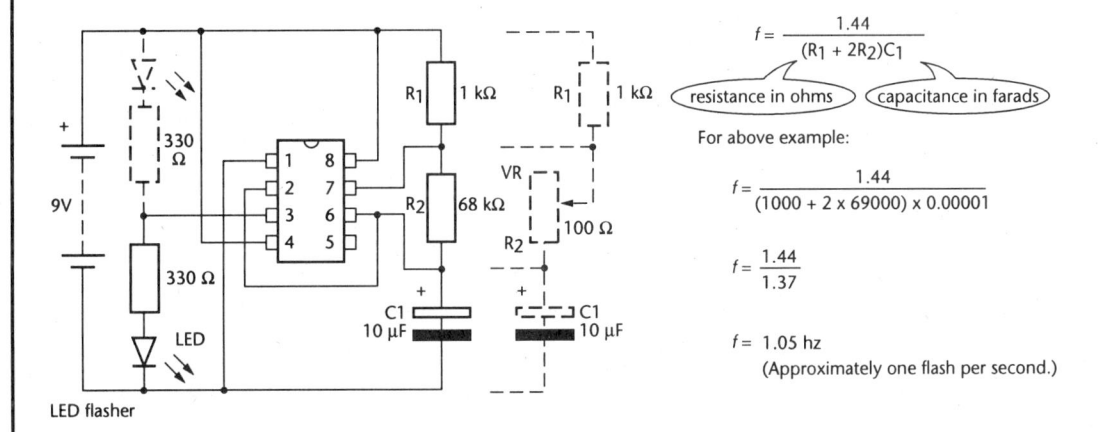

$$f = \frac{1.44}{(R_1 + 2R_2)C_1}$$

(resistance in ohms) (capacitance in farads)

For above example:

$$f = \frac{1.44}{(1000 + 2 \times 69000) \times 0.00001}$$

$$f = \frac{1.44}{1.37}$$

$$f = 1.05 \text{ hz}$$

(Approximately one flash per second.)

LED flasher

Design Brief

Design and build a circuit so that it will operate across a range of frequencies. You can change the frequency of the astable (oscillator) by using a variable resistor to replace R_2, as shown in the circuit above and the phantom drawing at the right.

The above circuit also shows how the circuit can be adapted if you want to use it as a low-power flasher. This can be accomplished by replacing the standard lamps with LEDs. The LEDs will use less power as they flash on and off, first one and then the other. You can use one LED and its resistor, or install a second LED with its resistor, as shown in the dotted line (phantom) drawing near the battery.

Design and develop an astable timer circuit using a 555 chip that will cause one LED to flash on 5 second intervals.

Design and develop an astable timer that will flash two LEDs, first one and then the other, on an interval of 12 seconds. Can you design a circuit that will cause the top LED to flash on for 12 seconds and the bottom one to flash on for approximately 24 seconds?

The 741 Operational Amplifier

As indicated earlier, the 741 operational amplifier, or op amp, has proven to be very useful in design and technology projects. It is particularly useful because it can serve as an amplifier, and it can do mathematical operations, such as subtraction and addition.

As with all ICs, the op amp chip contains very small and complex circuits. The circuits are so small you can't see them, nor could you repair them if they ceased to work. For your design and technology work, you will only need to understand what the op amp can do. You need not be too concerned about its internal parts and how they work. (If you are interested, there are numerous technical books on electronics to which you can turn.)

On page 392, you were introduced to the concept of amplification of a transistor. Amplification (gain) from using a transistor deals essentially with current gain. With an op amp, the amplification is related more to voltage gain.

An amplifier is usually represented by a triangular symbol, as shown here. The standard amplifier has one input and one output. The input receives the input signal and the output provides the amplified output signal.

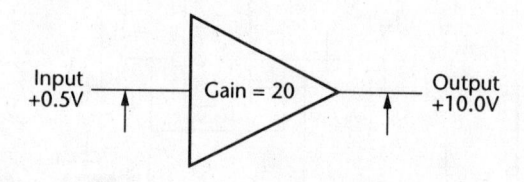

For example, an amplifier might have a gain of 20. If the voltage at the input is 0.5 volts, the output would be +10 volts (0.5 x 20 = 10).

An op amp is different from a standard amplifier because it has two inputs rather than one. The inputs of op amp are called inverting and non-inverting inputs. Op amps are designed to amplify the difference between the voltages of the two inputs.

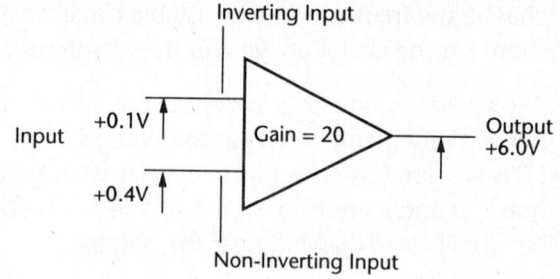

In the example at the right, the non-inverting input of an op amp is supplied with +0.4 volts. The inverting input is supplied with +0.1 volts. The op amp will amplify the difference of 0.3 volts to provide an output of +6.0 volts (0.3 volts x 20 gain = 6.0 volts).

Consider, however, what happens if the input voltages are reversed—the output is also reversed and the +6.0 volts becomes -6.0 volts. As shown in the diagram above, the non-inverting input of an op amp is supplied with +0.4 volts and the inverting input is supplied with +0.1 volts. The op amp will amplify the voltage difference (which is now -0.3 volts) with a gain of 20 to provide an output of -6.0 volts. By the design of the op amp, when the larger voltage is fed to the inverting input, the device **inverts** the output and makes it go negative.

DESIGN ACTIVITIES — DEVELOPING A PRACTICAL OP AMP CIRCUIT

As you have seen in earlier activities, design and technology projects make considerable use of switching devices for purposes of control. The circuit shown below provides a rather sensitive light-activated device that will control a relay switch. The relay switch could be used to control a variety of other devices when attached to the terminals of the relay. We will give this more attention later in the activity. First, turn your attention to the op amp circuit.

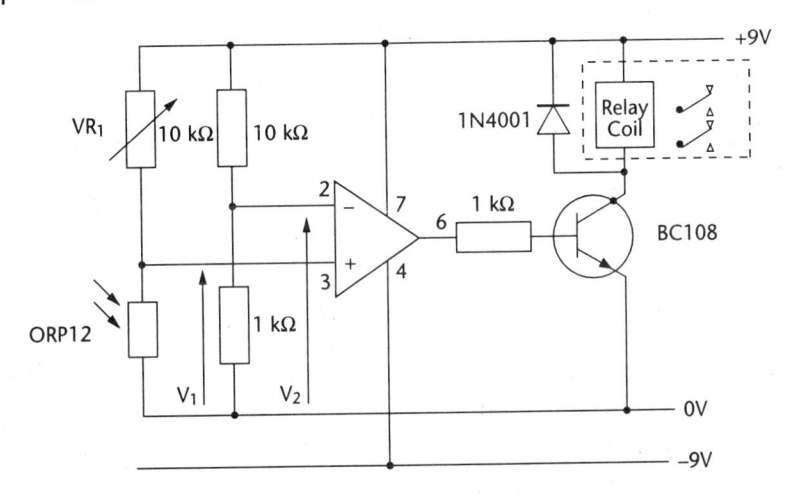

Study the drawing of the op amp circuit above, and consider the following:

- If you place the LDR (ORP 12) in the light, its resistance becomes low and the voltage across it also becomes low.
- Whenever voltage V_1 is lower that V_2, the output of the op amp will be negative.
- Because the voltage to the base is negative, the transistor remains off and the relay will not be activated.
- If you place the LDR in the shade, its resistance rises and the voltage across it also rises.
- As V_1 rises above V_2, the output of the op amp goes positive and sends positive voltage to the base of the transistor.
- The transistor now turns on and the relay is activated.

NOTE: If you replace R_1 with a variable resistor (VR_1), you will be able to adjust the circuit so that it operates at a desired light level.

This circuit can also be used with other sensors and input devices. Refer to Figure 7.5 in your text and your work from the Information chapter of the Student *Portfolio and Activities Resource*. Obtain the following devices from your teacher: moisture sensor, reed switch, thermistor, and microphone. Set up the test voltage divider circuit shown at the right and substitute the different sensors for S_1.

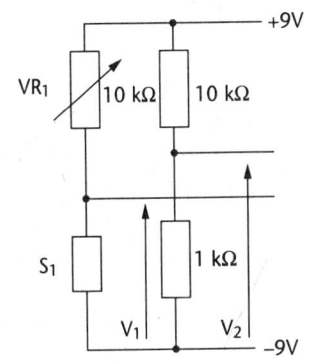

DESIGN ACTIVITIES — DEVELOPING A PRACTICAL OP AMP CIRCUIT CONTINUED

Replace the LDR with the moisture sensor. With a digital voltmeter, determine the readings of V_1 and V_2 when the moisture sensor is active (wet) and inactive (dry). Complete this test and record your findings for each of the devices in the space provided below.

INPUT DEVICES

State/Name	Inactive	V1	V2	Active	V1	V2
Moisture sensor	moisture absent (dry)	___	___	moisture present (wet)	___	___
Reed switch	magnet absent	___	___	magnet present	___	___
Thermistor	low heat	___	___	high heat	___	___
Microphone	sound absent (quiet)	___	___	sound present (noisy)	___	___

Review your results and answer the following:

- Which devices provide a marked change in resistance between their active and inactive states? _____
- Which devices provide a smaller change in resistance between their active and inactive states? _____

Determine if adjusting the variable resistor (VR_1) will cause V_1 to rise above V_2 for the thermistor and the microphone. Is the setting of VR_1 at a high or low setting? _____

Use the op amp circuit you have developed (or one provided by your teacher) and use the sensors you tested as input components to the circuit to replace S_1. Modify the resistance in the voltage divider circuit, as needed, so that your sensor will cause the IC and transistor to activate the control relay.

NOTE: If you plan to apply the 741 op amp in other circuits in your design and technology work, you may want to try out other experiments that illustrate the versatility of the 741. You can check with your teacher for additional information and activities.

SYSTEM OUTPUTS

The second focus of our attention now turns to the third part of a control system—its outputs. There can be many possible outputs of a control system, but all of the outputs change energy from one form to another. For example, you may design a control system to create an output of light, sound, heat, or movement. If the output is to be sound from a small buzzer, or light from a small lamp, you can design control systems that have small energy requirements for their operation. If you need to light a larger bulb or turn on a heating device, the power requirements are much greater and the control devices must be heavier duty. For these and similar applications, you can use an intermediate control device. As shown in the earlier Process Output section, the output signal of a light-duty control system can provide an input signal to a second heavy-duty control system. For example, the output signal from the first system can be transmitted to a transistor switch to control a fan. Similarly, you might use the same system to activate a heavy-duty relay to control a heater.

DESIGN BRIEFS—OUTPUT DEVICES

The concept introduced above illustrates the third of the key decisions you will make in designing control systems—determines what the "system output" will be. To complete the design of your control circuits, you will need to identify the power requirements of the output devices you plan to use.

Using the form provided below, identify and describe the device(s) provided by your teacher. Try to select devices that you plan to use for one of your designs. For each device, identify the power requirements for operating the device. Finally, identify and describe the function the device actually performs.

Device—Description	Power Requirements	Functional Output
buzzer, piezo-electric	12 volts, 1 amp	vibrating sound of approximately 5 decibels (dBs), and generally audible at about 10 feet
pneumatic cylinder, double action, 1 inch in diameter, 8 inches long	10-20 psi	linear movement
LED (light-emitting diode), green, small, flashing	7-9 volts, .1 amps	intermittent flashing green light, fractional lumen

DESIGN BRIEFS—OUTPUT DEVICES CONTINUED

DESCRIPTION AND REQUIREMENTS FOR SYSTEM OUTPUT DEVICES

Device—Description	Power Requirements	Functional Output

(Develop more sheets as needed.)

Design and Development of Control Systems

In this section, you will have the opportunity to apply what you have learned from the section on Resources and the preceding chapters on Systems as you design different control systems. Your design and development work in control technology will involve you with two basic types of systems: open loop and closed loop systems.

In the design of control systems, it is important to focus on the end result you are trying to accomplish. You should be most concerned with the outputs of the control system and how they will be used to control another system. In most instances, it will be very helpful if you make this decision early on. This will allow you to determine what the specific output device for your system will be.

In a similar manner, you will need to choose the input device. If you will be using a sensor, you will need to choose it almost at the same time you are deciding on an output device. Knowing what specific sensor and output devices you will use will allow you to determine the input and output requirements of your control system. All of this sets the stage for you to design the process part of your control system.

DESIGN ACTIVITIES—DESIGNING CIRCUITS

Designing Circuits

In the chapter on Information, two approaches to developing electronic circuits were introduced. The two standard circuits, shown below and included in Figure 7.10A and B, were utilized to serve as processors. The circuits use a change in resistance to operate—one requires a sensor that causes an increase in resistance, and the other requires a sensor that causes a decrease.

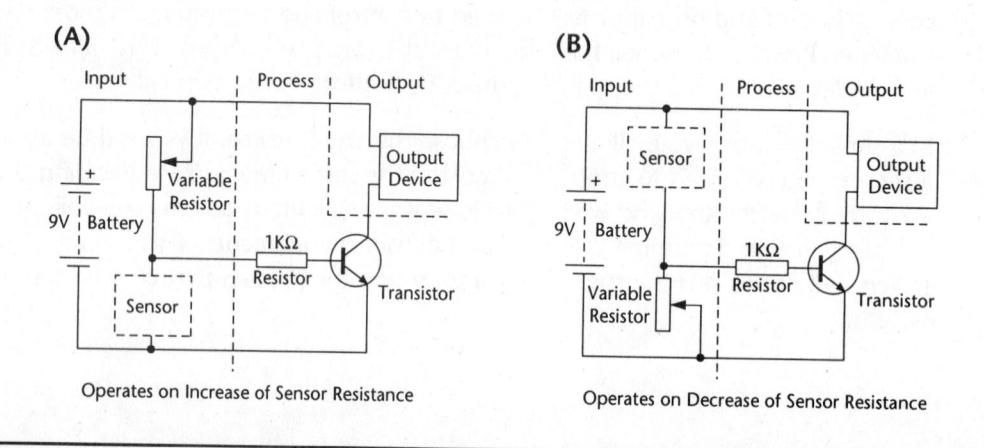

(A) Operates on Increase of Sensor Resistance

(B) Operates on Decrease of Sensor Resistance

DESIGN BRIEFS

- For the two circuits above, identify which of the different sensors available to you will operate with an increase in resistance, and which will operate with a decrease in resistance.

- Identify the different output devices that are available to you. Which of the devices will operate on the circuit that uses an increase in resistance, and which will work on the circuit that uses a decrease in resistance?

DESIGN ACTIVITIES

Throughout the book, you have seen and used the concepts of input, process, and output. These are revisited below as the three basic parts required in all control circuits. In the problem that follows, you can apply the concept of change in resistance and what you have learned about input, process, and output as you design a control circuit.

Problem: You have a summer job at the beach coordinating the distribution of leaflets to swimmers and sunbathers urging them to try a new product called SunBlocR. The job requires you to be at work very early but only on days when the sun shines. On days when the weather is overcast, you can sleep in. However, if it is raining in your area, you must get up at dawn to bring in the flyers for the day so they don't get wet, and then call the other members of the work team and notify them not to come to work.

Design Brief: Design an alarm that will wake you if the sun is shining in the morning, or if it is raining after daybreak.

Proposed Solution: The problem will require the use of logic devices. The alarm must sound IF the <u>sun is bright</u> OR if <u>it is raining</u> AND <u>it is light outside</u> (after daybreak). You can use a detailed block diagram to work out how the circuit will work and which components you need.

Choosing Components: You can use discrete components as shown above, or you can refer to the modular components in your textbook (see Figure 13.4B) to identify what is needed for this job. Choose the other modular units required for this problem.

INPUT	PROCESS	OUTPUT
Must sense when the sun is shining or if it is raining after it gets light in the morning.	Must switch on the output when the input senses bright light but no moisture. It must also switch on if it senses rain and it is not dark.	Must sound buzzer and turn on the light when the process unit switches on.

DESIGN ACTIVITIES CONTINUED

Circuit Design Notes

NOTE: You face the problem of two different circumstances that are to wake you in the morning. You will need a circuit that can sense if it is raining and it is getting light (it is no longer dark) outside. You also need a circuit that can sense if the sun is bright (it is not overcast). These two circumstances will require two different inputs and a logic circuit that can use these inputs to sound the buzzer. You should sketch out your circuit design using symbols for electronic sensors, logic gates, and the device you plan to use for your alarm.

You also face the problem of needing a circuit that will sound your alarm if it begins to rain anytime after dawn, when the flyers for the day are delivered. You will need a circuit that will be rather sensitive to any rainfall so that you can get dressed and bring the flyers in before they are damaged by the rain. The circuit below can provide the sensitivity you need.

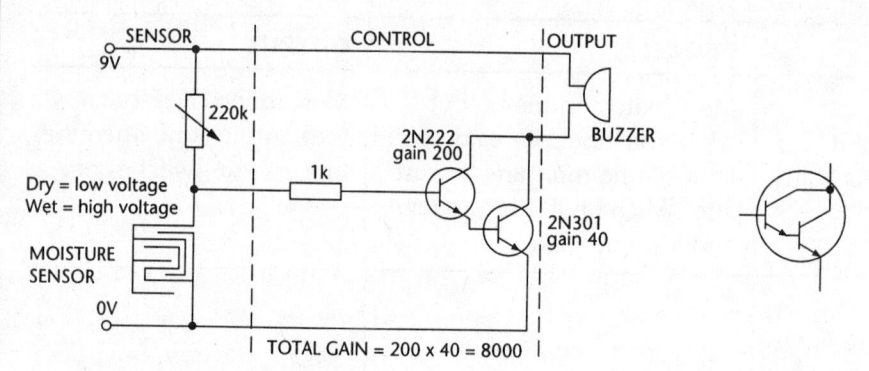

```
     SENSOR    |    CONTROL    | OUTPUT
  o─9V─────────┬───────────────┬──────────
               │               │
              220k            BUZZER
               │               │
               │      1k      2N222
  Dry = low    ├────/\/\──────│ gain 200
  voltage     │               │
  Wet = high  │              2N301
  voltage     │              gain 40
  MOISTURE    │
  SENSOR      │
  ───0V───────┴───────────────┴──────────
     | TOTAL GAIN = 200 × 40 = 8000 |
```

The circuit uses two transistors that work together in a special way. The circuit is so well known that it has its own name (Darlington pair). As presented earlier, you know that transistors can be used to amplify signals from sensors and they can be used as switches. The Darlington pair performs both of these functions together. (The symbol at the right represents a Darlington pair that are manufactured as one device.)

To amplify a signal, the Darlington pair arrangement uses a sensitive high-gain transistor (a BC 108). (In your application, the signal comes from a moisture sensor.) The signal is used to switch on a less sensitive low-gain transistor (a BFY 51) to sound the alarm. The circuit works by using one transistor to control the other. The circuit also works because it takes advantage of the different characteristics of the two transistors, in this case achieving a total gain of 8,000 This means the output is 8,000 times greater than the input of the circuit.

DESIGN ACTIVITIES CONTINUED

The 2N222 is good at sensing weak signals but is not very good at providing enough current to turn on devices such as an alarm. The 2N301 does not respond well to tiny signals but is good amplifying a signal to provide current that can switch on alarms and other high current devices. Your circuit will work well if you:

- Use the signal (which is a small change in resistance in the sensor) to switch the 2N222 on or off, and

- Use the 2N222 to switch the 2N301 on or off.

You plan your circuits, you will want to show the process in a general block diagram similar to the one shown in your text in Figure 13.4A.

Circuit Diagram: Using the information provided above, make a sketch of your proposed circuit. Select the components you need for the circuit and show how the components will fit together. You may want to refer to the simple circuit in Figure 13.4C as a starting point.

Describe how your circuit will work. Identify what logic gate or gates you have decided to use, describe the function they will serve, and provide a truth table that will show how the alarm will sound when the correct conditions are met.

Modeling

You will find it important and helpful to "model" the circuit you have designed. Doing this early in the building process provides a quick way to test whether the circuit operates correctly. The illustrations in Figure 13.4D in your text show two forms of modeling. You may use a home-built approach or a commercial prototyping-board approach.

DESIGN ACTIVITY

Design and develop a model of your circuit. Check with your teacher to see what materials are available in the design and technology facilities. You may want to use a home-built device for one of your first models. If the resources are available, you may want to develop a later model using the prototyping-board approach. You may find it helpful to refer again to the illustrations in Figure 13.4D in your textbook.

NOTE: You will find that both modeling approaches allow you to create a working circuit without soldering components together. In addition to speeding up the developing and testing of your devices, you will be less likely to damage any electronic components that are heat-sensitive, such as transistors.

DESIGN ACTIVITY—DEVELOPING CIRCUITS

After you have built and tested a model of your circuit, you are ready to build the circuit in a more permanent form. The most-used permanent circuit is called a printed circuit and involves making a printed circuit board (PCB).

In planning your PCB, you will need to lay out and draw the circuit to the proper size to fit the board that you have. Use the sketches and notes (your thinking on paper) to help avoid making mistakes in your fabrication work. You will want to refer to the guidelines and procedures provided on pages 391 and 392 and in Figures 13.5 and 13.6 of your text. You will need to receive direct instructions on making a PCB from your teacher.

CAUTION: Some of the materials used in developing and etching a PCB are toxic. You must exercise caution and follow the safety rules regarding the use of the tools, materials, and processes.

NOTE: Be sure to use a pair of pliers as a heat sink to protect transistors and other heat-sensitive electronic components. Holding the component with pliers will draw excess heat away from the component, reducing the likelihood that the component will be damaged.

Applying Control Technology Systems

There are three types of control systems, open-loop systems, closed-loop systems, and self-regulating systems. Open-loop systems are the simplest. Figure 13.7 in your textbook shows a toaster as an example of an open-loop system. After you set the control (a bimetallic device that operates from the heat of the toaster), the process runs its course. This makes it an open-loop system.

Closed-loop systems provide a means of checking to see if a desired action has been carried out correctly. Feedback provides the means of checking the action of a system. Figure 13.8 in your textbook shows a sound system as an example of a closed loop-system that allows the operator to determine if the sound is of appropriate loudness and quality.

Self-regulating, or cybernetic, systems are very important in technology because they provide the capability of machine-controlled processes that can relieve humans from repetitive and boring work. In your textbook, the steam engine, the windmill, and the refrigerator, as well as the toy gyroscope (introduced to show the **gyroscopic action** that is used in the cybernetic control of airplanes) are examples of a wide range of self-regulating systems we use regularly.

DESIGN ACTIVITIES — AN EARLY SELF-REGULATING SYSTEM

As indicated in your textbook, inventor Lawrence Sperry entered an international competition that was held during the early development of the airplane. Sperry's invention used a gyroscope that was attached to the airplane's controls to make the airplane self-correcting.

Design and develop a system that uses a gyroscope to keep a model airplane flying level. Conduct an investigation of how gyroscopes work. Build a working model of your system that demonstrates how the system would control the test model shown below.

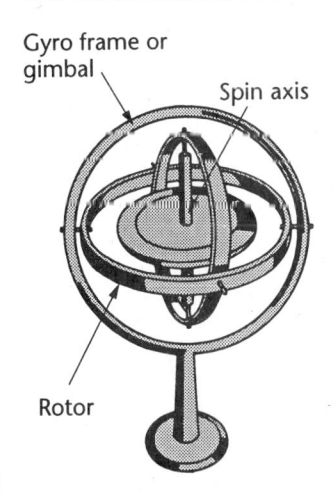

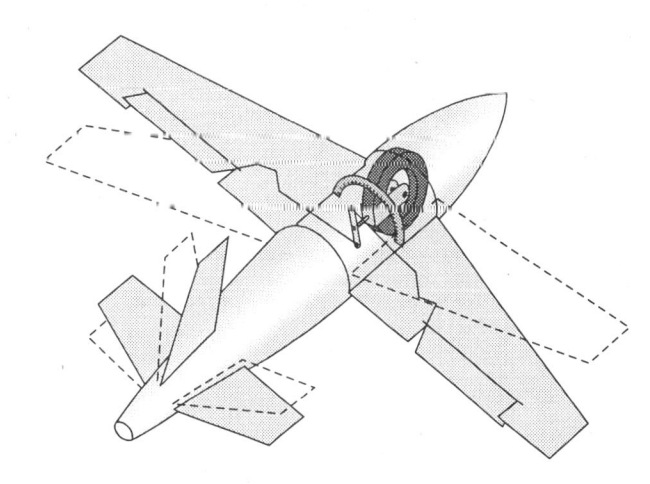

(A) Toy Gyroscope

(B) Controls of an Airplane

Cybernetics is defined as "the automatic control of a machine toward a desired goal." Describe how Sperry's gyroscope resulted in a cybernetic, or self-regulating, system that could keep an airplane flying straight and level without human control.

Feedback in Control Systems

An automatic machine will "know" when it has reached the desired goal because of feedback. The feedback provides the capability of making adjustments until the machine reaches a **steady state** of operation. The steady state of an airplane is established by the level position of the airplane when the gyroscope is first turned on. The gyroscope does not want to change its position, so each movement of the airplane is counteracted by the gyroscope so it can maintian its original level position. The above is accomplished if the system has the capability of setting an adjustment and then comparing the output of the system to see if it matches that setting.

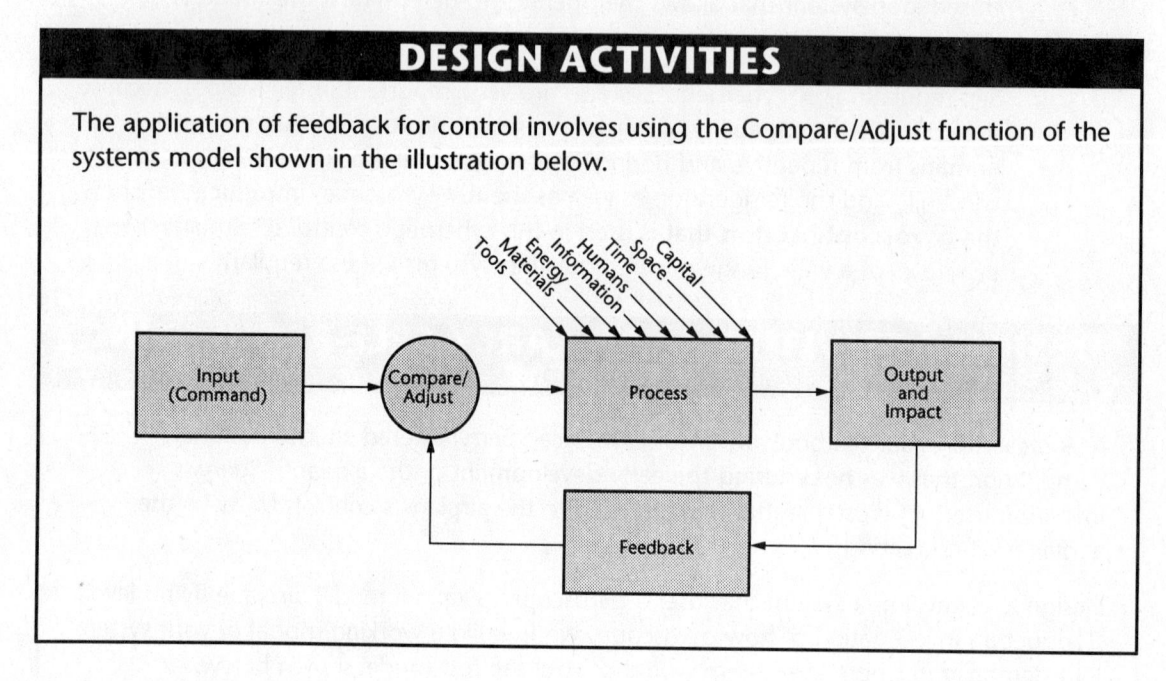

DESIGN ACTIVITIES

The application of feedback for control involves using the Compare/Adjust function of the systems model shown in the illustration below.

DESIGN ACTIVITIES CONTINUED

As an example, a thermostat could be used to compare and adjust the temperature in the greenhouse. Similarly, a thermostat might also be used to control the ventilation in the greenhouse when the temperature gets above a desired level.

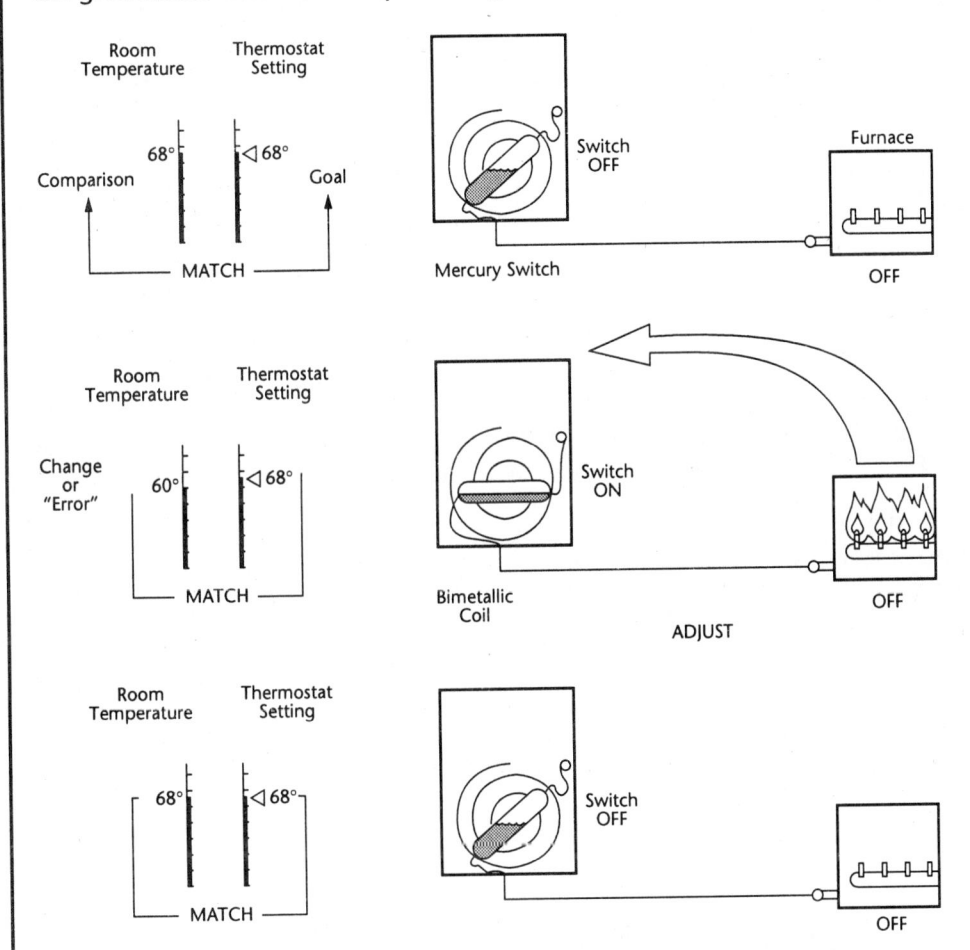

Heating System Showing Compare/Adjust Function.

Design and develop one of these or some other appropriate controls for use in a small greenhouse. Be sure to determine the setting that is most appropriate and the means you will use to compare the output of your system to that setting.

Design and develop a hydroponics system for the greenhouse that involves the monitoring and controlling of such conditions as nutrient levels, pH factors, temperature, humidity, light levels, and time of day.

DESIGN ACTIVITIES

As another application of feedback for control that uses the Compare/Adjust function, consider the following problem.

Members of your family have become interested in gardening and want to use a small greenhouse to give plants an early start while the weather is still too cool for planting outside. There are a number of interesting control problems related to even a small greenhouse. Three possibilities include providing water to the plants, providing adequate lighting, and controlling the temperature of the greenhouse. Each of these control functions will require the capability of comparing/adjusting the system, as in the example of providing water to plants to keep them from becoming too dry.

Working in teams, design and develop means of controlling these three systems.

NOTE: Keep your solutions to these problems so you can use them in the logic-based smart greenhouse system introduced on page 419.

INTEGRATED S/M/T ACTIVITIES

Consider the following as possible concerns about the greenhouse and the plants that will be placed in it. What other ideas or concerns do you think are important for improving the greenhouse?

What is a suitable range of temperatures for the plants in the greenhouse?

What nutrients do the plants require?

What influence does the chemistry of the soil have on the plants?

How do plants grow in a hydroponics greenhouse without soil?

How can you determine what size the greenhouse should be?

How often should the air be exchanged?

What effect does the temperature of the soil have on plant growth?

What effect does artificial light vs. natural light have on the plants?

Conduct the necessary research and investigation to design, develop and implement scientific experiments to answer the above questions. You may want to talk with your biology teacher to discuss how these questions might be restated to make it easier to conduct your scientific inquiries.

Developing Smart Machines

The work on "smart" machines has resulted in machines that can perform jobs requiring some decision-making. The following activities introduce the basic means that can be used to develop machines that think.

Automatic control is not possible unless the machine is able to determine when the changes it makes are enough to reach the goal. Machines cannot "think" as people do. Cybernetic machines do operate on the principle of **machine logic.**

Production and Controls

As people began to want more and more technological products, key mass production techniques such as interchangeable parts emerged. Mass production required high quality which, in turn, required information (feedback) on how accurately the items and parts were being made. As more and more complicated products were made, the manufacturing and quality control processes became more intricate. The most common answer to these problems was the continued division of labor and specialization on the assembly line. In this system, one person was employed to do one step of the process and to attend to feedback from only a few individuals at quality control stations on the line. This approach was often boring to the worker and expensive to the employer.

DESIGN ACTIVITY

There are many instances in industry where automation and control are used in production. This could include filling food containers, stacking or sorting packages for storage, moving parts on a production line, and the control of the nutrients, light, and heat for hydroponics. The example described in your text and illustrated below shows the process of automatically filling containers, such as cereal boxes.

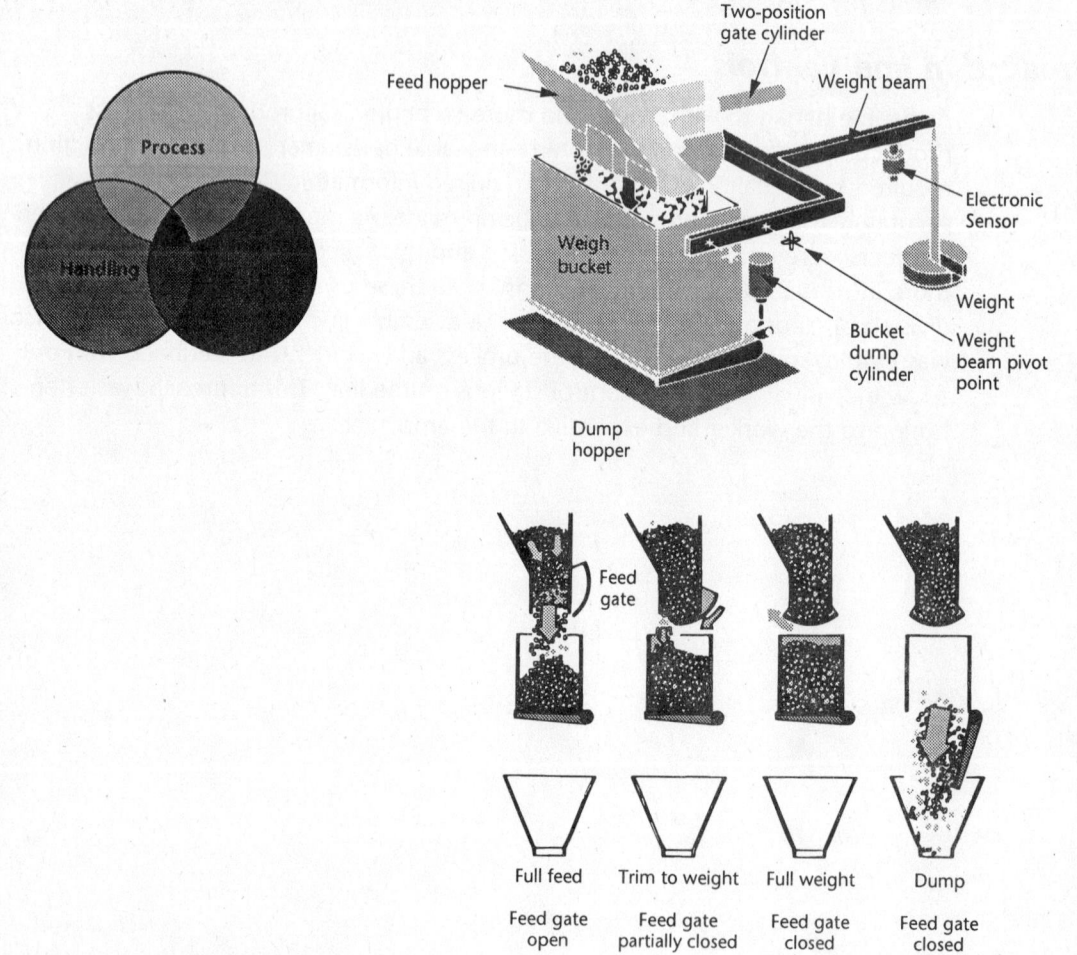

Full feed — Feed gate open
Trim to weight — Feed gate partially closed
Full weight — Feed gate closed
Dump — Feed gate closed

Cereal Box Filling System

Design and develop a means of completing a similar process using a device of your own design or one that improves on the system representing the cereal box filling operation on a production line shown above. Be sure to clarify the problems related to the automatic operation as you design your control system.

DESIGN ACTIVITIES

There has been a lot of talk about smart machines and systems and the role they can play to take over responsibility for specific tasks. Some of these machines have become very sophisticated, and many have been used for some time and operate on simpler yet similar bases. Consider the following as example problems that could be approached by using logic control devices:

- Provide a safety guard for an automatic stamping machine that will ensure the operator will have both hands out of the way when the machine goes through its stamping process.

- Provide an automatic door opener that can be operated by individuals approaching the door from either side.

- Provide a means for helping an attendant in a parking lot monitor exits that are out of sight and determine if any gate has been left open or if the wooden arm has been broken.

- Provide a means to ensure that both sets of doors on an elevator are closed before the elevator car is moved to a different floor.

- Provide a means of turning off the doorbell on your home so that you will not be bothered at night.

- Design and develop appropriate logic systems that can integrate the three control systems of the greenhouse problem introduced on page 416.

- Identify several circumstances where logic systems might be used in your home, at school, or in the community.

Computers and Control Technology

Over the past few years computer control devices and programs have become more and more available. The first computers were analog in nature and were developed to measure processes. The speedometer in an automobile is an analog device that allows for the measuring of speed. Other examples of analog devices are the gas gauge in cars, a clock with hands, and a pressure gauge in a boiler. **Analog devices** do continuous sensing and measuring of something that is happening.

The early analog computers were quite large and were limited in their applications. Many of the tasks for which analog computers were used have now been taken over by digital computers. This is possible since the speed of the digital computer allows individual measurements to be made thousands of times per second. These discrete measurements merge into virtually a continuous process that can be used for the monitoring and controlling of systems.

Designing Computer Control Systems

Over the past decade or so, there have been a number of interesting developments that now provide you with the capability of using computers to control the machines, systems, and environments you create in your design and technology work. Several companies now provide control systems with the related software and hardware. You can check with your teacher to see which of the systems are available for you to use.

The examples provided on the following pages builds upon concepts introduced earlier in Chapter 10 on the design of a remote-control vehicle for handling and storing toxic materials. (See page 309.) This earlier example used a buggy that can be controlled through the use of the Logicator™ system and the Smart Box™ developed by the Economatics company. These are described in more detail and applied in the two applications that follow.

Logicator is a graphics programming system that uses a design process approach for the development of control programs. The first of the applications related to the design and development of a "stairlift" project for moving elderly or injured people from one floor to another.

The Situation

"I have an elderly aunt living on her own in a large house. She has recently broken her hip and is unable to climb the stairs. A stairlift will enable a disabled people like her to use the stairs and so have access again to their second floor."

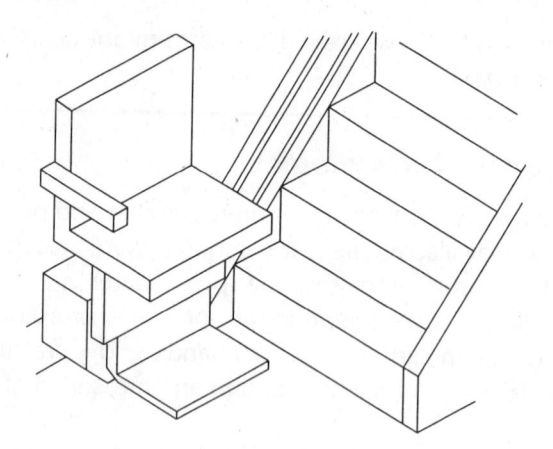

Developing the System

In programming it is helpful to use "Macros" so that you can break up a task into little bits, think about what each bit should do and then join them together like a jigsaw. In the example below-left, the stairlift system uses two Macros one for UPSTAIRS, one for DOWNSTAIRS. The subroutines for the Macros are shown in the bottom illustrations. Using Macros makes it easier for you to change your program. You can access a Macro and make any necessary changes without changing any other part of the general program.

The "key" decision cells that precede the Macros allows you to test the system by pressing one of the keys on the keyboard. When you develop a working model of the system, you will this function will be taken over by a "go" button on the chair arm.

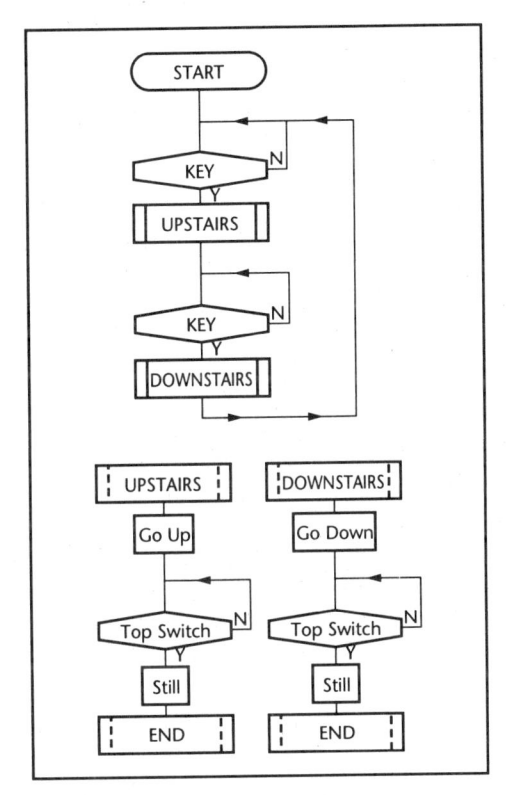

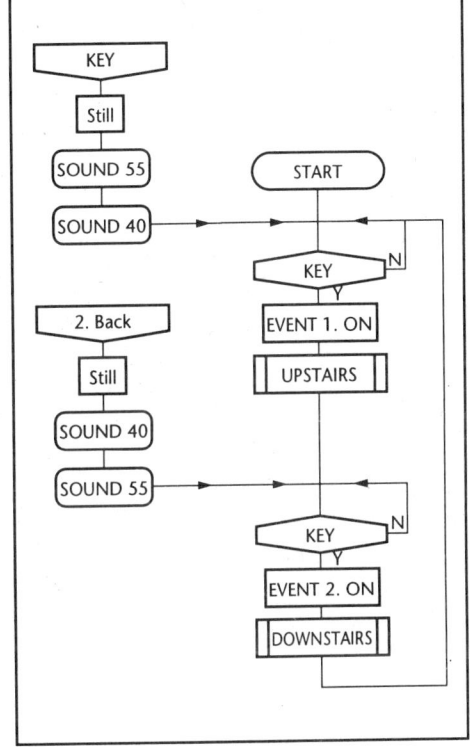

Using Sensors

In an initial approach, a student used timers so that the system would stop automatically when it reached the top of the stairs. However, because of the different loads (due to the different weight of the people who might use the system) the speed of the chair varied, and the chair stopped in a slightly different position.

The second program, shown above and to the right, represents an improved design that uses sensors to provide a safety system. With switches mounted in "bumpers" on each side of the chair, the systems can sense obstacles on the stairs and will stop automatically. The dhair will remain at rest until the "go" button is pressed again.

Design Brief

Design and develop a version of a chairlift that can be operated (start and stop) by the sound of a persons voice. Consider a control system that can use a "high" pitch of a person's voice to start the movement of the chair up the stairs, and a 'low" pitch to start the movement down the stairs.

The activities in Chapter 10, mentioned above, introduced you to the problem of designing a vehicle (patterned after Figure 9.12 in your text) that could move loads of toxic materials in a vast underground storage system. The system is intended to operate by remote control so that human operators will not be exposed to the toxic materials.

The activities that follow use an additional control-related system called "Logicator" and a compatible interface called the "Smart Box". (All of these products were developed by Economatics Ltd. and are available through Modern School Supply.™

Design Brief

Use the Economatic's Buggy, or one of your own design, and connect it through the Smart Box to a computer that can operate the Logicator program. Working individually or in pairs, design and develop a program that will control the vehicle so that it will move and store barrels of toxic materials in a set of pathways that represent an underground storage system. If time permits, you and your team can create a model of the storage system that is covered, representing that the system is underground. This will allow you to see if the system will run automatically without human intervention. It could also provide the opportunity for you to experiment with using a small video camera mounted on the Buggy as a means of monitoring what is taking place inside the model storage system. You will want to complete the activities provided in Appendix I.

DESIGN ACTIVITIES—DEVELOPING A WORKING BAR CODE READER AND PROGRAM

Different types of circuitry have been covered in previous sections of the text. It is important to be able to use and manipulate the information and signals produced by these circuits. The circuit schematic viewed previously on page 358 allows a computer to receive a signal through the game port. This signal can be translated into a usable form that has practical applications.

The program for the bar code reader can be written in any language that gives the user access to the signals being sent through the ports. The following are flowcharts for a program used with the previously mentioned circuit and written in Microsoft® Visual Basic™ version 2.0.

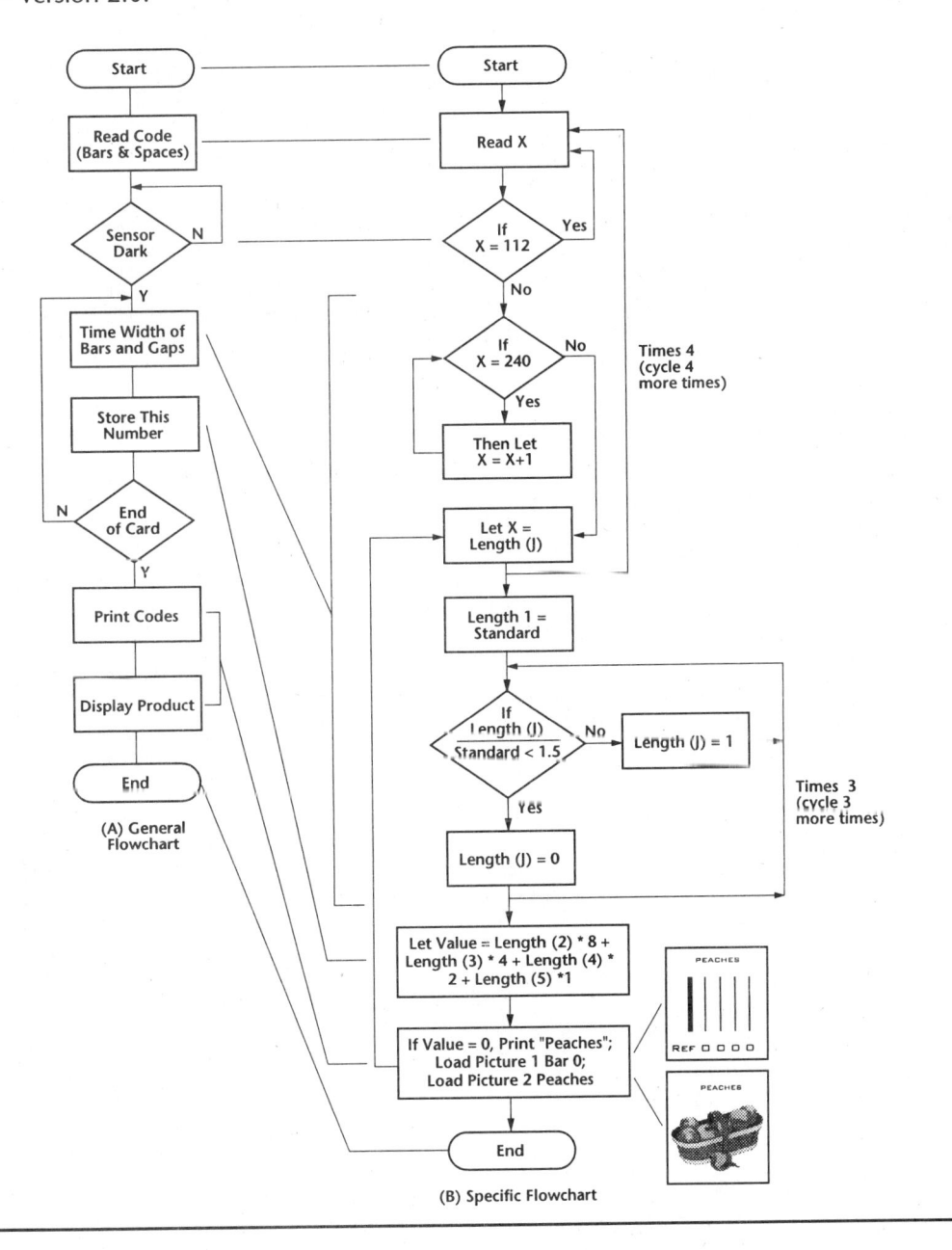

(A) General Flowchart

- Start
- Read Code (Bars & Spaces)
- Sensor Dark? N → back to Read Code; Y ↓
- Time Width of Bars and Gaps
- Store This Number
- End of Card? N → back; Y ↓
- Print Codes
- Display Product
- End

(B) Specific Flowchart

- Start
- Read X
- If X = 112, Yes → continue; No ↓
- If X = 240, No → loop back; Yes ↓
- Then Let X = X+1
- Let X = Length (J)
- Length 1 = Standard
- If Length (J)/Standard < 1.5, No → Length (J) = 1; Yes ↓
- Length (J) = 0
- (Times 3, cycle 3 more times)
- Let Value = Length (2) * 8 + Length (3) * 4 + Length (4) * 2 + Length (5) *1
- If Value = 0, Print "Peaches"; Load Picture 1 Bar 0; Load Picture 2 Peaches
- End

Times 4 (cycle 4 more times)

DESIGN ACTIVITIES—DEVELOPING A WORKING BAR CODE READER AND PROGRAM CONTINUED

The following is a sample program which can be used as a guideline.

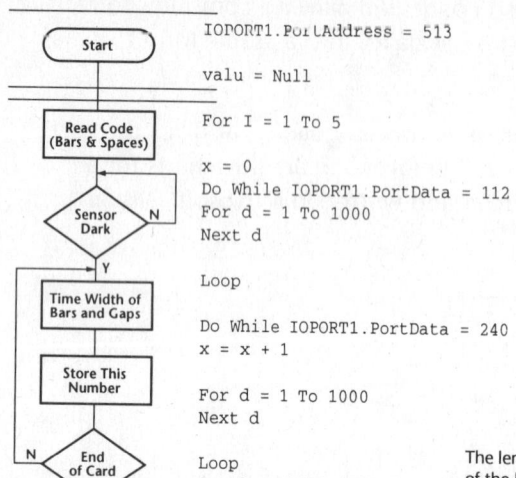

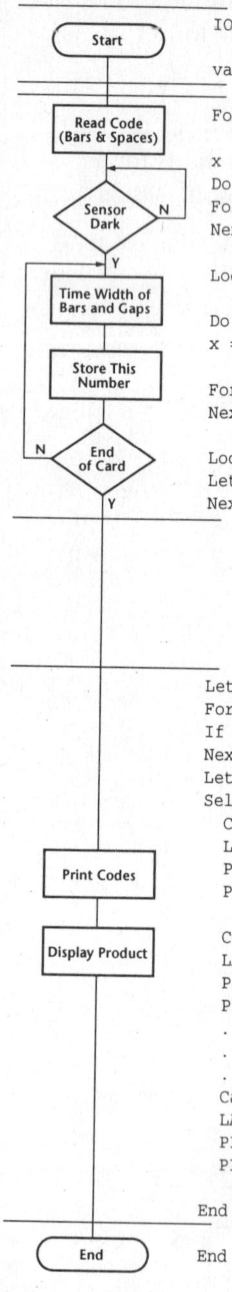

Flowchart:
- Start
- Read Code (Bars & Spaces)
- Sensor Dark? (N loops back, Y continues)
- Time Width of Bars and Gaps
- Store This Number
- End of Card? (N loops back, Y continues)
- Print Codes
- Display Product
- End

```
IOPORT1.PortAddress = 513

valu = Null

For I = 1 To 5

x = 0
Do While IOPORT1.PortData = 112
For d = 1 To 1000
Next d
Loop

Do While IOPORT1.PortData = 240
x = x + 1
For d = 1 To 1000
Next d
Loop
Let length(I) = x
Next I


Let STANDARD = length(1)
For J = 2 To 5
If length(I)/STANDARD < 1.5 Then length(I) = 0 Else length(I) = 1
Next J
Let valu = (length(2) * 8) + (length(3) * 4) + (length(4) * 2) + (length(5) * 1)
Select Case valu
  Case 0
    LABEL1.Caption = "PEACHES: GEORGIA - $0.69/LB."
    PICTURE1.Picture = LoadPicture("c:\vb\graph\BAR0.bmp")
    PICTURE2.Picture = LoadPicture("c:\vb\graph\PEACHES.BMP")
  Case 1
    LABEL1.Caption = "CARROTS: FLORIDA - $0.39/BUNCH"
    PICTURE1.Picture = LoadPicture("c:\vb\graph\BAR1.bmp")
    PICTURE2.Picture = LoadPicture("c:\vb\graph\CARROTS.BMP")
    .
    .
    .
  Case 15
    LABEL1.Caption = "ONION:BERMUDA - $0.39/LB."
    PICTURE1.Picture = LoadPicture("c:\vb\graph\BAR15.bmp")
    PICTURE2.Picture = LoadPicture("c:\vb\graph\ONION.BMP")
End Select
End Sub
```

The port address is the location of the switch on the game port which sends a high or low signal to the computer. The address "513" is in decimal notation. This address is also known as "201H" in hexadecimal notation.

The port data will equal either 112 or 140, depending on whether the reader is passing a space or a bar. For this program and circuit, a space will give a reading of 112 and a bar will give a reading of 240.

When the computer gets a reading of 240, it will begin to count until it gets a reading of 112 again. This final count becomes the length of the first bar. This step is repeated until all five bars have been measured and five lengths have been assigned.

The length of the first bar is used as a standard to compare to the rest of the bars. The first bar was always a narrow bar. The Wide bars were all at least twice as wide as the narrow bars (wide-to-narrow ratio). The wide bars were assigned a value of 1 and the narrow bars were assigned a value of 0 after being compared to the standard. (The length of a narrow bar divided by the standard should equal approximately 1. The value may not be exact, depending on the speed of the reader as it passed across the bar code. A wide bar divided by the standard should be < 1.5).

A decimal value is calculated for each bar code. Using "select case," predetermined labels and graphics can be assigned to the value. The labels and values will appear on the operator's screen when the bar code is read. These graphics can be created in any drawing program that allows you to save in a BMP format.

DESIGN ACTIVITIES—DEVELOPING A WORKING BAR CODE READER AND PROGRAM CONTINUED

The operator's screen could possibly look similar to the one below. The read button would execute the program listed on the previous page. When the item is recognized by the computer, the bar code, a descriptive label, and a picture of the item would appear on the screen. Separate programs could be written to add or delete inventory for the identified item. A program could also be written to list the inventory information.

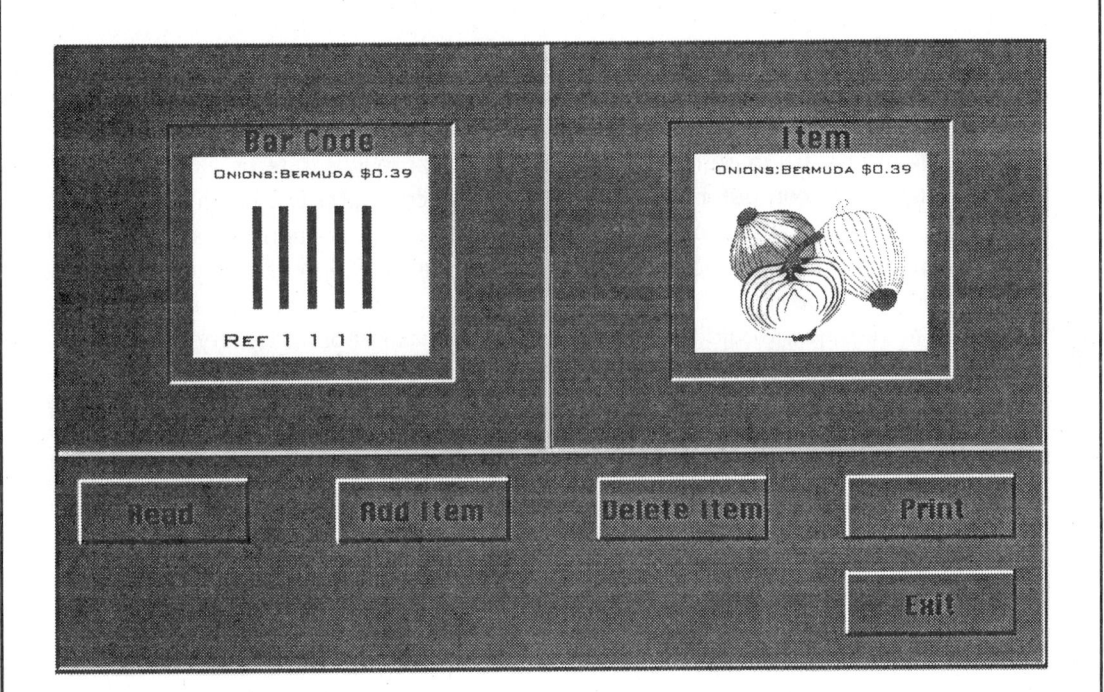

INTEGRATED SYSTEMS

Automatic and self-regulated operation of systems can be achieved when all three concepts of process, handling, and control operate as an integrated system. The control parts of the system include the sensing devices that provide information. These are used to control and to change the processes. Other sensing devices provide information to direct the handling of the materials, products, or people. The materials may be moved, stored, or converted through the intended materials conversion processes. Thus, process, handling, and control can be united into one functioning integrated system.

Consider, for example, the operation of a large airport. Without computer-controlled, integrated systems, the current operations of the terminal, flight scheduling, ground control, and airplane operation would be impossible. The work of humans in designing and controlling large integrated systems is made easier by the computer in two ways. First, the computer is used to construct a simulation of the system during the design and improvement phases. Second, the computer is used to record the data during the operation of the system. Through simulation, the system can be modeled and experimented upon safely and economically. It would be unwise and sometimes impossible to try out a new approach without first conducting a simulated trial run. How would you like to be the first customer through a brand new, untested terminal, or the first passenger on a new airplane that had never been tested?

DESIGN ACTIVITIES—DEVELOPING INTEGRATED SYSTEMS

Design and develop working models of subsystems of such an airport that:

- uses a bar code approach to monitoring and controlling the flow, storage, and dispatching of passenger luggage.

- plans and tracks the flight plans and operations of airplanes as they depart the airport and fly to another airport.

- monitors inventory and orders food and other resources for the airport cafeterias.

- controls the movement of people via a mag-lev vehicle to and from the parking areas.

- monitors and controls the supply of water and nutrients to all the plants used for decoration within the terminals.

- posts the arrival and departure information (city, arrival time, departure time, airline carrier, gate number, and status of the flight).

NOTE: Systems cannot operate in a self-correcting manner unless (1) controls can be adjusted to set the desired outcome of the system, (2) feedback signals can be interpreted and compared to the adjusted setting, and (3) the parts of the system work together in responding to the settings, feedback, and comparisons.

REVIEW AND ASSESSMENT ACTIVITIES

- Identify the different components of a control system and the role that each of them plays in its operation.

- Explain what is meant by the statement, "the output of one system can serve as the input for another."

- Identify the different sensors and other devices that can be used for the input aspect of a control system. Describe how they function.

- Identify the different devices that can be used for the output aspect of a control system. Describe how they function.

- Explain how the process circuit of a control system can be controlled by a change of resistance in the input device.

- Describe the differences of open-loop, closed-loop, and self-regulating systems.

- Describe the role that the adjust/compare aspect of a control system plays and how it relates to the feedback aspect of the system.

- Describe how AND, OR, and NOT logic circuits operate and provide some examples of how they can by applied

- Explain the significance of integrating process, handling, and control in an automated manufacturing operation.

- Describe the role that flowcharting can play in planning for computer programming.

- Identify and describe some of the large systems that require the use of computers in order to operate.

UNIT Four

The Impact of Technology

CHAPTER 14
Investigating, Developing, and Improving

As the design process has been applied, over time, to a number of different issues, technology grew and it continues to develop. Products, systems, and environments are improved through investigation when humans are dissatisfied or when they want to explore beyond what is currently known. New tools, materials, and processes are developed to support this investigation.

INVESTIGATING THROUGH EXPLORING

Early in human history, people developed instruments for determining direction by observing the sun, stars, and seasonal variations. The sundial and ship's bearing dial were used to determine the time of day and a ship's orientation to the north. The invention of the hinged rudder allowed a ship's direction to be better controlled in the changing currents of the open sea. The magnetic compass provided a direction indicator for sailing because the compass aligned itself with the Earth's magnetic field. However, the compass points to magnetic north and the ship's bearing dial points to "true" north. This problem confused early explorers, but not enough to slow down exploration by sea.

Merely knowing their bearing, or direction, was useful, but sailors also needed to determine location. Devices invented for this purpose included the cross staff, the astrolabe, the quadrant, and the sextant. All four devices measure the angle, or height, of the sun above the horizon. Because the sundial was not an accurate timekeeper, the development of the clock was a major boost to travel. By combining accurate information about time, with a reading from an astrolabe or sextant, the ship's position could be accurately located on a map. Centuries later, mapmakers designated that Greenwich, England, as the "starting point" for the measurement of time and location.

Information from early navigation was used to turn simple, hand-drawn maps into accurate maps and charts. Two of the first maps were the Polynesian stick chart and the Portuguese rotarios. In order to represent the features of a round world on a flat surface, such as paper, Mercator developed the Mercator projection technique.

Until the development of the rocket, exploration of space was limited to information gathered from land-based telescopes and radio equipment. The earliest telescopes, such as the kind that Galileo used, were of the refractor type. Approximately 50 years later, Sir Isaac Newton invented the reflector telescope. It was not until 1931 that the first radio telescope was built by Jansky.

Eventually, people became curious about the seas themselves and what might lie below their surface. Undersea exploration was held back for years, due largely to the lack of suitable technology to support human life in that environment. Once stronger metals were developed, deep-sea exploration vehicles became possible.

Maps of the ocean floor and currents have been drawn and seismographs have been used to chart the Earth's structure. Right now, however, we have a more accurate understanding of the makeup of the solar system than we do of the Earth itself.

Early microscopes, developed to investigate micro (small) space, were optical. In recent years, powerful electron-type microscopes have enabled us to explore the structure of molecules themselves. Recent developments in the use of lasers indicate that it may soon be possible to see even more clearly into the micro space of our world. Ultrasonic beams, X-ray scanners, and infrared photography can now be used instead of surgery to determine the causes of health problems.

Historians search for evidence in the technological remains of past activities, called artifacts. Historians and archaeologists rely on special instruments to study the artifacts left by previous generations. One such instrument measures the amount of radioactive carbon that remains in the object, to determine where the radioactive carbon atoms are in their decay sequence. This information provides a fairly accurate index of the length of time that the material has been decaying. The archaeologist uses many other technological tools, such as the airplane, camera, electronic mine detector, X-ray spectrum analyzer, and radioactive sampler.

INTEGRATED S/M/T ACTIVITIES—INVESTIGATING THROUGH EXPLORING

Over the ages, there have been many developments in technology that have supported investigation and exploration. By providing the tools, devices, and machines needed to travel to new places, or to transport these objects to environments too hostile for humans, technology has provided not only artificial eyes, ears, and other sense organs for science, but also the means for mobility.

Select one of the devices or topics that follow and conduct your own research and investigation into how the device was created, how it developed, and how it was used in ways not considered when it was first developed. Consider such tools, materials, and machines as the following:

- the bearing dial of a ship
- the magnetic compass
- the clock
- early maps and charts
- the reflector telescope
- the optical microscope
- the scanning electron microscope
- the diving bell
- the ultrasonic scanner
- infrared photography
- the X-ray spectrum analyzer
- others _____

- the hinged rudder
- the sextant
- the rotarios
- the refractor telescope
- the radio telescope
- the transmission electron microscope
- the field ion microscope
- the bathysphere
- the X-ray scanner
- radioactive carbon dating
- the radioactive sampler
- others _____

DESIGN ACTIVITIES—TECHNOLOGICAL DEVELOPMENTS

- Select a tool or device that has played a key role in an important technological development. Some examples might include (a) the early rockets and what they contributed to space travel and to modern warfare, (b) the printing press and what it has contributed to publishing and propaganda, and (c) the transistor and what it has contributed to computers and smart weapons. Trace the history of the development of the device that you selected. Write an illustrated paper on the changes in the device over time. Include, as well, the contributions it made to the knowledge, capabilities, and expectations that people had, as a result of the development of the tool.

- A student from China is enrolling in your school next week. In groups of three to four, create maps of your neighborhood or town for this new student, to show aspects that will help him/her explore the unfamiliar territory.

- Consider the following problems and design a means to support exploration in such hostile environments as:

    volcanoes   ocean floors   the moon
    Mars   the Arctic/Antarctic the deserts

INVESTIGATING THROUGH FORECASTING

Humans have always tried to see into the future, whether by predictions or the more recent ways to explore, called forecasting. Forecasting uses current and past information, and often employs trend analysis. The computer is an important tool in a variety of trend analysis activities. Modern futurists project the future by describing possibilities and "alternative futures," hoping that people will use this information to choose wise courses of action in the present time. Short-ranged studies of the future tend to be more reliable than mid-range or long-range projections, because of the greater potential for the unknown and unexpected.

One method of studying the future is based on analyzing information about past developments and trends of the area of interest. A second method involves the use of analogies. Using the data on what has happened with a given object, process, or event, you can project what may happen to an analogous or similar, thing. A third future study method relies on conducting surveys, or polls, such as the Delphi survey. This process polls experts on a given topic and recirculates the opinions of the group until a consensus is reached.

Future histories are another means of studying the future, by pretending to be alive at a time far in the future. A future history is written to describe the events that must happen to lead up to that imaginary time in the future. Scenarios are similar in that they begin with imaginative "pictures" of what could happen in the future. Usually, several scenarios are developed for a single problem. Scenarios ordinarily identify a set of events and how they lead to other events.

Modeling, as a method for future studies, involves trying to translate ideas into more concrete and visible forms. When enough information has been gathered and when the data can be reduced to a mathematical form, the computer becomes a valuable tool for creating models. The models can be varied to show different alternatives. Projecting into the future by modeling is possible only if the model can be used to (a) describe its component parts, (b) illustrate how those parts fit together, and finally (c) provide some of the instructions or rules for creating something from the model and its component parts.

Forecasting of the future is a useful technique for design and technology. Forecasting depends on technological tools, but differs somewhat from other exploring activities. Choose a topic of interest and implement a future-oriented exploration through the following sequence of actions used in all forecasting:

(1) collect information

(2) analyze data

(3) identify probabilities

(4) forecast the possibilities

DESIGN ACTIVITIES—TRENDS

Trends are a means of looking at the past and present in order to identify possible patterns that might project into the future.

Select an area of interest for which you wish to identify a possible trend(s). Perhaps you are interested in how the bicycle has changed and how it may continue to change in the future. (1) Study events and developments from the past related to the bicycle. Identify any significant changes (the changes in materials used), increases in the number of bikes, or the adding of new innovations (tires, brakes, gearing). (2) Attempt to identify if there was a pattern of growth or change for one or more of the above. If so, plot out that pattern of change up to the present in a chart or graph. (3) Identify if that pattern sets a trend, or direction, that may extend into the future. (4) If there is a trend, project where it might lead in the future.

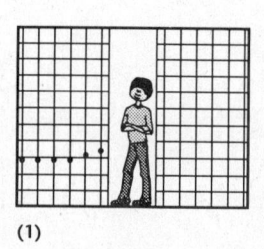

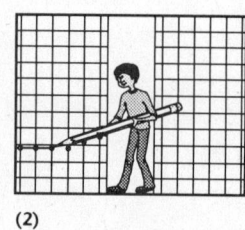

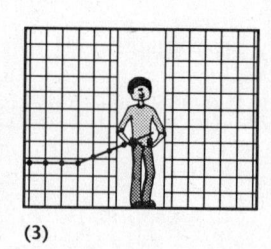

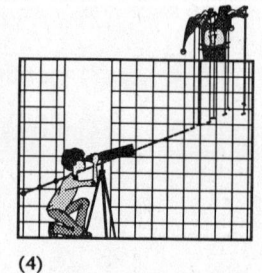

(1) (2) (3) (4)

- You are considering a career using computers. Conduct research on trends in the use of computers to use in developing a report to use in your career planning.

- Conduct research on the development of an appliance or machine you use at home or in school. Project developments that are possible and probable in the future.

- Consider the following products, materials, and machines and design a means to forecast future trends and innovations related to:

airplanes	trains	automobiles
bicycles	skates	computers
television	multimedia	clothes
electronics	the Internet	food

DESIGN ACTIVITIES—ANALOGIES

Analogies use events or trends that have similarities between them as a means of looking at one pattern of events in order to identify possible patterns in related events.

After you have identified a trend, you may be able to use it as an analogy to look at something else of interest. Trends in materials and processes for new products, especially those in space, can be used as analogies for looking at commercial products. For example, you might look at developments in television. (1) First you study the important developments in video equipment, (2) you identify the directions and patterns of change. (3) Next, chart the trends to use as an analogy, such as the definition and clarity of high-cost video for recording events in space lab experiments. The trends of the past developments can serve as an indicator of a trend for later events (the definition and clarity of video equipment for the home). (4) Finally, the second trend of events should show a similar pattern of change. If the analogy works, the earlier trend will provide a pattern for projecting the events yet to come.

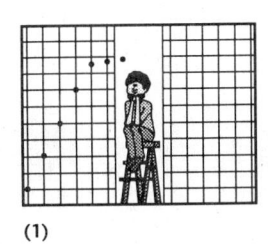

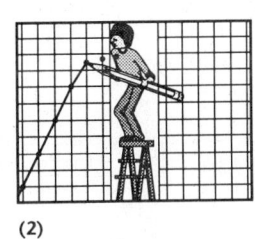

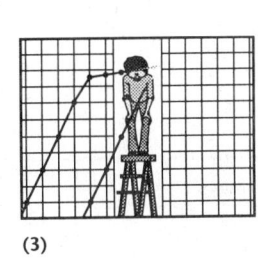

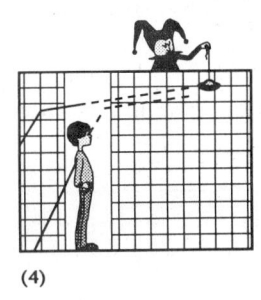

(1) (2) (3) (4)

- Based on trends for purchasing computer-related materials (games, software, hardware) nationally, project the amount of time and the type of activities individuals will pursue using their computers. Determine what products have the most potential for sales, based on the projected activities.

- Look into the development of such products as records, tapes, and other devices for recording music. Project developments in compact disc production and consumption for the next ten years.

- Consider the trends of the following products, materials, and machines and determine how they might serve as an analogy for trends of the other innovations:

computers in business	computers in the home
communications in the space effort	communication for the general public
airplanes for the military	airplanes for commercial use
new materials from research and development	new materials in products and structures
microminiaturization in electronics	new products and innovations
developments in solar research	changes in home design and construction

DESIGN ACTIVITIES—SURVEYS

Surveys use polls and questionnaires to obtain the opinions of experts in an area to be studied, to identify possible future developments.

The Delphi study starts by conducting a survey with experts in the field. (1) If you want to know what changes might take place in the field of transportation, you could survey, or interview, people who have knowledge about technological, economic, and political aspects of transportation. (2) You could collect information on the impact that the political and economic systems have upon the technological aspects of transportation. You might attempt to determine what impact new developments might have on individuals, society, and the environment. (3) After gathering information from your survey, you would share the statements made by the large group with all the participants. Based on how others responded, the participants may change their ideas and provide a new set of data. (4) The revised ideas of the total group are then shared with everyone else. This, in turn, may cause some participants to reconsider what they said and give you new responses. (5) This cycle can be repeated until there is no significant change in the positions taken on the ideas. The large part of your sample will now share some agreement as to what the transportation systems of the future might look like and what their impacts might be. A smaller group may still disagree.

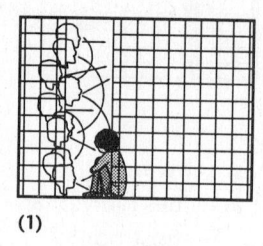

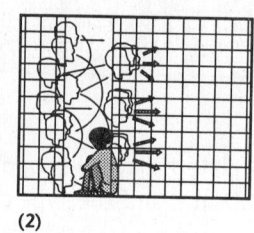

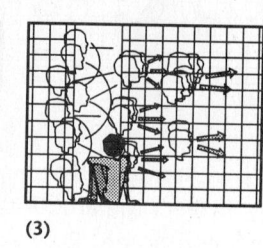

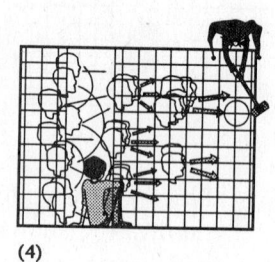

(1) (2) (3) (4)

- You and a group of your classmates would like some alternative to eating lunch in the cafeteria at school. You have talked with the local vendor, who sells snacks and other foods from his truck parked near the school. He said he would offer a wider selection if he knew what students and teachers would buy. Your class has agreed to determine what students and teachers would be most likely to buy for lunch from the vendor.

- Conduct a library search for guidelines, and design and conduct a Delphi study. Gather the information for creating the most nutritious and appealing lunch that could be safely and economically sold by a vendor. The survey should include students and teachers, as well as experts on food processing and safety, business, and nutrition. Design your survey to tap the expertise of each participant.

- Choose one of the most promising designs that has been developed by students in your class, as you have carried out the design activities from previous chapters. Conduct a marketing survey to determine the likelihood that the product would be salable if you decided to mass-produce it. Identify which groups of buyers would be most likely to want it. Also, in your survey, gather opinions on whether modifications in color, shape, and size would make your design more attractive to a buyer.

DESIGN ACTIVITIES—FUTURE HISTORIES

Future histories allow a backward look from a point in time in the future to the intervening events that extend from the present and lead up to that future time. In writing a future history, you travel by imagination to a future time and place, and then look back to the present.

Consider, for example, (1) what might our means of communicating look like in the year 2020? With the changes that are now taking place, you project that there will be widespread use of personal communicators similar to those seen on Star Trek. (2) With this image in mind, you will need to project yourself to that point in time, and from that vantage point, write a history of the events that will lead up to that future time. You will need to study what new developments are taking place related to the technical aspects of communication, such as electronics and fiber optics. You will need to consider the research on the biological nature of communication and the possibilities of a biocomputer. From your investigations, you begin to describe what will be found in 2020 and the events that must take place in order for the evolution of these new means of communication to evolve. (3) In your future history, you should link the events together like links of a chain. When you finally work your way back to the present, you can check out whether the chain of events is logical. (4) As you study the future, it will help to write several future histories that might lead to the final future event. This will make it easier to present several different future history perspectives that, in turn, will help foster discussion and debate. From this process should emerge a considered and plausible treatment of the topic of study.

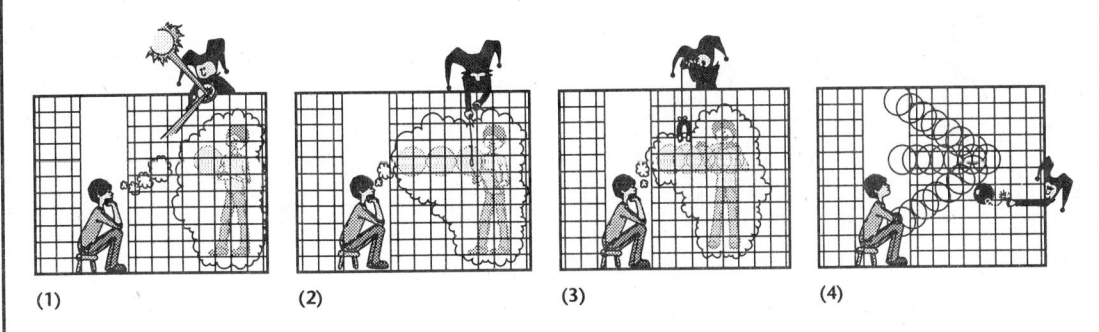

(1) (2) (3) (4)

- Conduct necessary research on how a "humachine" system might be developed for work or travel. Plot out the history that would be needed in order for this system to evolve.

- Write a description of your life in 30 years, as you live in your home under the ocean. Be sure that you describe your everyday behaviors and the goods and services you use. Your description should be a projection of scientifically feasible events. Plot out the history of the 30 years of your life to describe how you got to this point.

- Consider other periods of time and what would lead up to new technological developments. What would your home of the future look like when you are Aunt Sarah's age? How might you travel in the year 2025, if a supersonic "space plane" is used that could reach Australia in less than two hours?

Unit 4   The Impact of Technology

DESIGN ACTIVITIES—FUTURE SCENARIOS

Future scenarios allow a more complete treatment, or picture of a future time. Such scenarios can be used to identify and describe sets of related events. Future scenarios are broader based and more complete than the more specific future histories.

(1) A future scenario often starts like a future history by imagining a point sometime in the future. Such a scenario would also be built upon several related future histories. In all cases, you try to envision a set of related events at a given time in the future. (2) You continue to build your future scenario by identifying more and more possible events connected with a topic of interest. For example, you might want to develop one or more scenarios that attempt to portray what your hometown might look like in 50 years. One scenario could consider the possible change if a regional development plan provided guidance and direction. A second could consider what might happen if things just evolved over time. A third scenario might consider the changes created by the introduction of a major industry into the community. Other scenarios could be developed that consider developments of interest or concern.

As you develop your future scenario, project events for the same general time in the future. (3) After drawing together the many related events, try to describe how they are connected. You join them like links in a chain. Your description should provide some insight about what the community might become and what it will be like for the people who live there. (4) As more and more connections are made between the various events, your description of the time slice will become more complete. Each of these descriptions provides you with a future scenario.

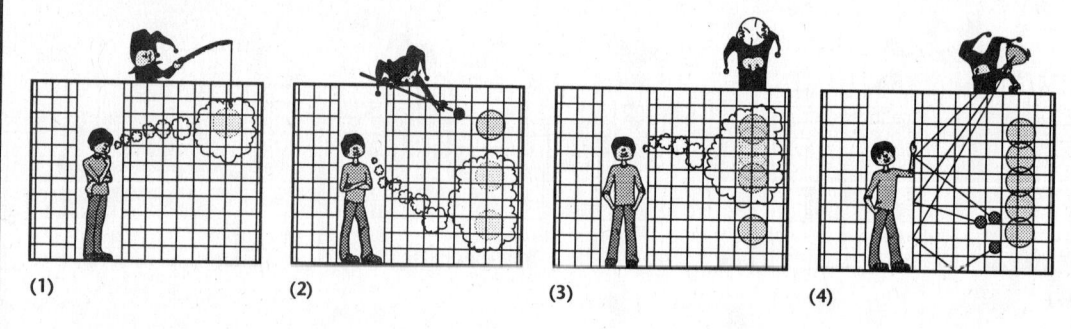

(1)   (2)   (3)   (4)

- Conduct the necessary research on how human/machine systems in the scenario described on page 432 in your textbook might be used for recreation or communication. Write out the series of events that would be needed for this scenario to occur.

- Using some of the concepts you have learned about biotechnological developments in agriculture, write a scenario that describes how food is grown and distributed in order to combat hunger and malnutrition in the world.

- Consider what a future scenario would look like if you actually were living in 1950 and were trying to understand what developments might take place in the year 2000. Ask your grandparents, or others who were teenagers at that time, what they remember and what they thought might take place in the future. How might they have used future scenarios to better understand some of the developments of the past 50 years? What problems are there in making projections in one period of time for a future time?

DESIGN ACTIVITIES—MODELING

Modeling as part of future studies provides the means of simulating some selected aspects of the real world and manipulating that simulation to see what events and results emerge. Before you can model some aspect of the future, we must identify what parts there are and how these parts interrelate. A model is considered adequate because it (a) describes its component parts, (b) illustrates how those parts fit together, and finally (c) provides some of the instructions or rules for creating something from the model and its component parts.

This approach to modeling is similar but more sophisticated to the modeling you have done in earlier chapters. With modeling, you try to translate ideas into more concrete and visible forms. When enough information has been gathered over a period of time and when the data can be reduced to a mathematical form, the computer becomes a valuable tool for creating models. The models can be varied to show different alternatives.

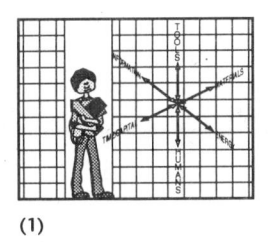

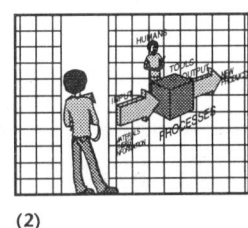

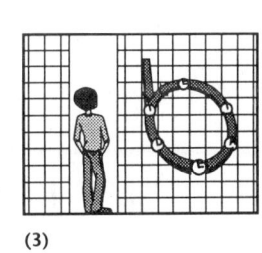

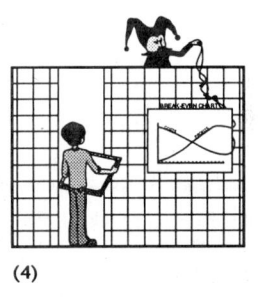

(1)   (2)   (3)   (4)

- Conduct the necessary research that will help you develop a model for evacuating the school building in the event of a fire or accident. Your model should help show how changes to one part of the system or operation can create changes in other parts of the system. For example, what would happen if the fire started in one location vs. another? At one time of day vs. another?

- Secure a copy of SimCity™ from your teacher. Use this simulation to help you gain experience in how a simulation operates. Study about simulations as serious games to help you understand how models are used in developing simulations. Design and develop a simulation that would help sixth grade students understand how one of the industrial processes illustrated in your textbook actually operates.

- Conduct research into other models and simulations that are available for you to use in your study of future developments of technology.

EXPANDING KNOWLEDGE FOR IMPROVING FUTURE INVESTIGATIONS

Technology has developed over time, and the products, environments, and systems developed at any time reflect the knowledge and attitudes available at the time in which they were designed. For centuries, the expansion of knowledge came through the trial and error approach. Gradually, accepted procedures for gathering and reporting new information and testing old ideas were developed. This method was called the scientific approach and is the expected process for scientists today as they do pure research. The primary aim of the investigator who does basic, or pure, research is more complete knowledge or understanding. No concern is given to how the knowledge will be used.

Most of the work that is done in technology can be called applied research, and its aim is to use knowledge. Applied research is also used to test and evaluate the prototype solutions to a design process. Here, too, formal methods can increase the likelihood that the product is given a fair test and will perform as intended most of the time. The procedures for both pure and applied research require attention to detail, attempts to guard against the investigator's biases, and clear communication of results so that others could replicate the work.

DEVELOPING—PUTTING KNOWLEDGE TO WORK

Development is the planned use of knowledge from research and experience, for the purpose of achieving a desired goal. The three parts of development are discovery, invention, and innovation. A discovery is new insight into the uses of something that already exists. An invention is something that a person makes that did not exist before. An innovation occurs when a person takes several things that already exist and brings them together to produce a new device or process. Development is a system that recycles almost continuously in search of improvements.

Some of the outcomes of development are consumables and others are more permanent and have an impact on further developmental work. The three general categories of outcomes are new or revised products, processes, and systems. For a few highly creative geniuses, the processes of discovery, invention, and innovation seem to come easily. For most people, however, breakthroughs come only after a lot of hard work and frustration. For both, having a body of knowledge and keen skills of observation are necessary.

IMPROVING—MAKING THINGS BETTER

A developer seldom finds the best answer to a proposed problem and then uses the solution without changes. Ordinarily, there are continual attempts to improve solutions through optimization. This is the process of seeking the most favorable condition or solution to a problem, or a goal, and usually involves trade-offs between two or more conflicting criteria. Decision-making within technology is often similar to optimization. Many times there are competing goals and criteria, and one type of risk must be weighed against another. A choice between two behaviors, both of which are based on probability, requires that you decide what is an acceptable risk.

Iterating is the process of developing and improving an idea, process, product, or system by sending it through a development stage more than once. The procedure is similar to the recycling and feedback used in the Delphi survey. Recycling an idea for its improvement through iteration techniques is part of the ongoing design and problem-solving process. The failure of a product to perform in an idealized way provides valuable information about changes that could be made in the process and/or the product. The designer uses the mismatch or error as information to be sent back into the design process for the improvement of the product. This process continues until the risk level for error is at an acceptable level.

DESIGN ACTIVITIES—RESEARCH AND DEVELOPMENT EFFORTS

It should be apparent to you by now that there are an unlimited number of problems that remain to be pursued. Many old problems have not been solved. New developments that provide an answer to a problem will always create additional new problems to be solved. Many of these problems we encounter on a daily basis. For example, in your technology education facility there are many problems that interfere with the optimum operation of this design and technology course, as well as problems that interfere with you and your classmates working effectively and efficiently in the facilities. One instance, introduced earlier, considered the problem of determining what hardware you might need to solve a specific problem, if that hardware was available and, if so, where it was stored in the facilities. A research and development project that focused on the design and development of a parts storage, tracking, retrieval, and replenishing system has much to offer, both in learning new concepts and skills for a student and in improving the way that your facilities operate.

As a class, design and conduct a survey of all students taking technology education courses in your school to determine the problems they have encountered in their design and technology work. Analyze the data to determine which of the problems might be solved through student-initiated projects. Plot out the problems in terms of short-, medium-, and long-term efforts. Identify which problems could/should be undertaken during the initial phase of facility/course improvement. Develop a set of criteria that can be applied to the problems. You will want to include cost, time required, number of students affected, amount of time saved for students, and number of possible consequences resulting from implementing the proposed solution.

Apply the criteria to rank the problems in terms of those most feasible to pursue on an immediate basis. Working with your teacher, identify the problems that fit best within an overall long-term plan of improvement. Form small research and development project teams to tackle one of the problems that holds promise for program and facility improvement.

Conduct your research and development effort and create a model of the proposed solution(s). When a selection of the proposed solutions is available, develop a scenario of how your facility will operate if the solutions were implemented. After the scenarios have been critiqued, your teacher may decide to have you develop a future history that will explore how the proposed changes might be implemented in your school and what the possible results and consequences might be if the changes were actually instituted.

You will want to save the work you have done on the modeled solutions, future scenarios, and future histories so that they can be used in the decision-related activities that will be considered in the following chapter.

DESIGN ACTIVITIES—ASSESSMENT OF QUALITY OF PRODUCT DESIGN

As you engage in assessing the quality of your designs or the design work of others, consider the following questions. The answers you are able to make should provide you with an overall impression of how well your design works and how much modification it might need.

1. Does it cost as little as possible (considering resources for production, maintenance, and replacement)?
2. Is the design as simple as possible, while still providing the required and wanted features?
3. How reliable and dependable is the product and how long will it last?
4. Is the product appropriately rugged and durable?
5. Does the product function as it is intended?
6. Is the product safe while in operation, as well as when stored?
7. Is it attractive and pleasing to use?
8. Is the design appropriate for the ergonomics and developmental level of the intended user?
9. Can the product easily be taken apart to replace parts that break down, rather than having to replace the entire product?
10. Does the design allow for recycling of materials once the product is no longer wanted?
11. If failure of the product has costly consequences, does the design include ways to guard against breakdown or methods to protect the user, should failure occur?

ENRICHMENT DESIGN AND TECHNOLOGY ACTIVITIES

Design Activities

- Choose a consumable material, tool, or system in which you are interested. Trace the development process as improvements were made over the last 50 years.

- Select a product that you use daily. Assess the design, using the criteria given in this chapter. Weigh the value of the criteria that the product meets readily against those criteria it misses. Compare these findings against a similar product of another brand. Decide which is the best design, overall.

INTEGRATED S/M/T ACTIVITIES

- Design and conduct a research study to gain information on a topic of interest to you. Include all the steps of the scientific research method.

- Conduct applied research procedures to test gathered data for improving the design of the product analyzed above.

- Identify interest groups that regularly communicate their findings on a topic of interest to you. Use data banks and available information networks.

- Choose the best antitheft device and best automobile to use in your geographical area. Use all available data on theft of autos, effectiveness of various devices, insurance costs, etc. Decide on an acceptable level of risk. Identify the criteria, other than safety from theft, that you want the car to meet. Choose the best car and device, given all information and criteria. Write out the process, showing the weight you gave to each criterion. Illustrate your decision-making process.

REVIEW AND ASSESSMENT ACTIVITIES

- Name some inventions and innovations that increased people's abilities to tell the direction in which they were traveling and to determine their location on Earth. Describe how each device works.

- What are the barriers to human travel in space? under the sea?

- Describe at least one method used to determine the age of artifacts from an ancient time.

- Compare and contrast three different methods for investigating the future.

- Distinguish between discoveries, inventions, and innovations. Give examples of each.

- What is the difference between pure and applied research? Identify how each contributes to technological development.

- Describe an instance in which you attempted to optimize the match between two or more variables. Discuss your decision-making process.

- Cite at least five criteria for good design.

CHAPTER 15
Consequences and Decisions

Technology has changed our world and will do so in the future. With each generation of humans, the rate of change is quickening. Technology has had many different effects on people, some of which have been desirable and intended, and others which have not. Some of the effects are immediate, while others are delayed. If technology is to be used to achieve our desired purposes, we must become better at predicting consequences before we act. To make intelligent decisions, however, we must have knowledge.

LOOKING TOWARD THE FUTURE

Making decisions from the projections for the future is a complex process. One approach to using projections is decision networking. This is the identification of events that must happen if a goal is to be reached. When all the necessary events are placed on a chart, the result is called a decision tree. Like a tree on its side, each branch (event) leads to other branches (events). When the total chart or picture of events is plotted, it becomes more clear what people will need to do to reach the goal.

Decisions are made about acceptable risks regarding the intended/unintended, and desired/undesired outcomes. A study of the immediate/delayed impacts of potential technological developments on individuals, society, and the environment is conducted. The Office of Technology Assessment (OTA) was established to investigate the possible effects of new technological developments. Concern about regulations and assessment of technological consequences is needed as nations throughout the world trade with each other. Special interest groups and consumer unions also help watch over new technologies that might be dangerous.

The consequences of technology can be divided into three general categories: personal consequences, social consequences, and ecological consequences.

Success in making and using tools changed our ancestors in specific and important ways. Early humans who could use tools were more likely to survive in difficult environments, and live long enough to reproduce and nurture their children. With the development of a reliable food supply and adequate stores to protect against emergencies, human efforts could be turned to tasks other than survival and they could build a shared culture.

Tools extend our use of physical capabilities, including strength. Consequences including our bodies getting "soft," improved availability of a variety of food, increased exposure to new types of additives and potential toxins, earlier maturity, longer life expectancy, threat of large-scale war, increased size of population, and complex new social and ethical decisions.

Technology changes people emotionally, as well as physically. Tools for measuring time have changed our ideas about what is important. With modern biotechnology, agriculture is being changed by attempts to hurry up or slow down growth and maturation according to human wants and needs. One of the goals of many design and problem-solving efforts is that of efficiency. Processes that once took years, days, or hours to accomplish now take minutes. People must decide how to use the time that is left over from labor. When people have many of their basic needs satisfied by the results of technological systems, they have time and energy to turn to issues of belonging, achievement, esteem, and higher-order motives.

Increased availability of information from a wide variety of sources has a profound effect on people's lives. People can be less dependent as they interpret information for themselves, rather than rely on a few leaders for an interpretation. Just as there once were divisions between people based on who could and could not read and write, now there are divisions based on access to information sources. Those who have access to information have more power to decide for themselves and others.

The knowledge explosion can be exciting, as well as overwhelming! People might be experts in one area, but at the same time ignorant in other areas. The development of information tools has led to more highly developed intellect. Having access to information does not mean that people always take advantage of what is available.

Beginning with the very first invention, technology has caused social changes. Invention of the wheeled plow led to the development of a communal life-style. Working together allows people to specialize, and protects them from fluctuations in factors that influence production and markets. People were required to give up some of their individual freedoms to benefit from group cooperation.

Invented more than a thousand years ago, the stirrup changed the course of history. The stirrup allowed the rider to stay on the horse more easily. The stirrups gave soldiers the power to overwhelm other, less equipped soldiers. Thus, Charlemagne built an empire that lasted for a century. The mounted troops were given portions of the land, complete with knights, serfs, and castles.

Environmentalists and ecologists are beginning to make us aware of what humans have been doing to our natural resources for centuries. For generations, people have been using raw materials, processing them and pouring wastes in the rivers, oceans, air and soil, and threatening nature's delicate balance. Because it takes such a long time for ecological consequences to be discovered, it is difficult to know today how serious the situation will be in the future.

Some scientists point out that humans have always had an effect upon the environment. Wherever humans have migrated, the balance of nature has been changed. Concern about what happens when a species dies out has become even more intense as we have developed the tools to study DNA. Genetic diversity is seen as a safeguard as we face issues that have not occurred in the past. There are difficulties in predicting and determining the possible consequences of technology. Effects may not become apparent until long after a harmful chain of events has started, and we may not be able to stop the sequence, once begun.

Many of the by-products of technological activities are materials that do not occur naturally in the environment. Toxic chemicals that do not naturally break down into safe products have potentially high economic and ecological costs. Each of these issues is complex and will need attention to both prevention of further damage and efforts to repair what has been done.

We can learn to use technology assessment to try to foresee the immediate and delayed effects of a proposed technological event. Delayed, or second-order effects, often occur in a sequence. Technology assessment is used to study, and hopefully, project strings of possible effects.

DESIGN ACTIVITIES—DECISIONS

Making decisions that consider future projections is often a difficult and complex process. Decision networking, one approach that was introduced in the textbook, uses future projections as a way to improve making choices. Decision networking involves the identification of events that must happen if a goal is to be reached. An example was provided that considered what must happen if people in the United States are to decrease their use of nonrenewable energy resources. If this goal is to be achieved, a number of prior events must take place, such as a reduction in the consumption of gasoline. This can be achieved if more economical gasoline cars are used, if electric cars are used, or if alternative means of transportation are developed. In a similar manner, all the possible events that could help reach the stated goal must be identified, and then the essential, or necessary, events are selected.

When all the necessary events are placed on a chart, the result is called a decision tree. Like a tree on its side, each branch (event) leads to other branches (events). Plotting out the decision networks makes it far easier to discuss the projected network of events and identify what might support or disrupt the events. In this manner, it becomes easier to understand what the involved people will need to do to reach the desired goal.

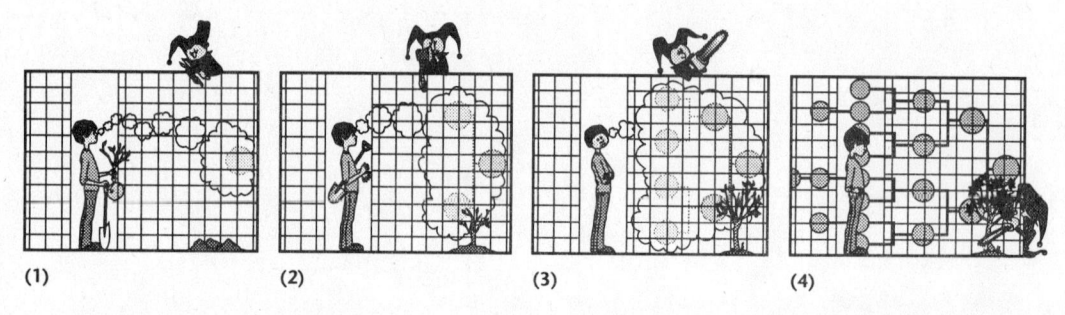

(1) (2) (3) (4)

- Use the decision networking approach to learn what is required to cut in half the amount of energy used in your home. List each energy-saving idea and its related costs, along with the steps needed to implement each idea. Decide which steps must be completed first, second, third, etc. Lay out the decisions in graphic form for the network.

- Work with a number of your classmates to determine how to reduce the energy costs for your school. Develop your decision tree as a part of a presentation that could be made to the school administration and the Board of Education.

- Consider the following problems and opportunities for using decision networks to facilitate the making of choices for complex problems:

    – Plan for improving local recycling system
    – Community system to support bicycling
    – System to monitor violence on television
    – Plan to reduce community use of cars
    – Plan to improve nutrition of students
    – Plan to increase student access to Internet
    – System to improve sharing of design and technology activities
    – Plan to improve technological decision-making

DESIGN ACTIVITIES—TECHNOLOGY ASSESSMENT

We are informed by the media that new products of technology are being developed each day. Too often, new products and processes are being discovered faster than we can learn how to deal with the possible consequences of their adoption and use. For example, nuclear power plants are being developed even though we are not yet sure of their long-term effects on human health. Similarly, genetically engineered products are being developed with little understanding of the results of those efforts. Either of these examples could be very good for humans and society, or very bad. The complexity of making decisions about technology makes it very important that the possible effects of new technologies be evaluated before they are put to use. Technology assessment is the process of systematically evaluating new technologies. It includes the study of the immediate and delayed effects which result when an aspect of technology is introduced or changed. Technology assessment helps in considering the acceptable risks regarding the intended/unintended and desired/undesired outcomes of decisions and choices. A study of the immediate/delayed impact of potential technological development on individuals, society, and the environment are also considered a part of technology assessment.

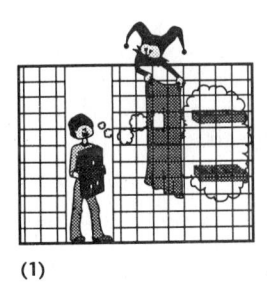

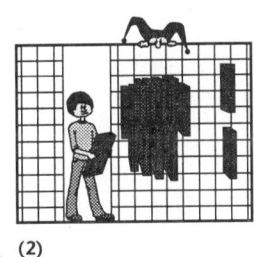

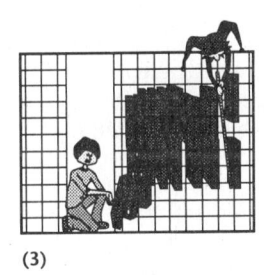

(1) (2) (3) (4)

- Conduct a study of the impact of the telephone. Write a report on these impacts as though the study was conducted very soon after the telephone became popular.

- Identify other problems of interest to people in your community regarding possible future developments. As a Technology Assessment team, conduct the necessary research to determine what changes one of the future developments might make in the setting or environment of the community.

- Consider the impacts of the choices made in the preceding decision-making activities. Consider the intended/unintended and the desired/undesired outcomes of your decisions. Also, consider the immediate/delayed impacts of the following systems and plans:

  - Plan for improving local recycling system
  - Community system to support bicycling
  - System to monitor violence on television
  - Plan to reduce community use of cars
  - Plan to improve nutrition of students
  - Plan to increase student access to Internet
  - System to improve sharing of design and technology activities
  - Plan to improve technological decision-making

DESIGN ACTIVITIES—THE EFFECTS OF TECHNOLOGY

If you are to make good decisions related to technology, it is important that you understand the possible consequences of actions or technologies in order to anticipate their possible effects. Unintended, unknown, and delayed consequences may prove even more important in the long run than the direct and intended effects. The projection of such effects will be essential to support the making of complex and difficult decisions about technological developments and their impact on people, society, and the environment. The multiple-order consequences chart, shown below, identifies the complexity of long-term effects of three technological developments that have been widely adopted in current society.

	Automobile	Improved Refrigeration	Television
First-Order Consequences	People have a means of traveling rapidly, easily, cheaply and privately door to door.	Food can be kept for longer periods in the home.	People have a new source of entertainment in their homes.
Second-Order Consequences	People patronize stores at greater distances from their homes. These are generally bigger stores that have large clienteles.	People stay home more because they don't need to go out.	People stay home more, rather than go out to local clubs and places where they would meet others.
Third-Order Consequences	Residents of a community do not meet as often and therefore, do not know each other as well.	Same as at left. (Also, more free time becomes available.)	Same as at left. (Also, people become less dependent on other people for entertainment.)
Fourth-Order Consequences	Strangers to each other, community members find it difficult to unite to deal with common problems. Individuals find themselves increasingly isolated and alienated from their neighbors.	Same as at left. (Also, additional free time increases demand for recreation and entertainment.)	Same as at left.
Fifth-Order Consequences	Isolated from their neighbors, members of a family depend more on each other for satisfaction of most of their psychological needs.	Same as at left.	Same as at left.
Sixth-Order Consequences	When spouses are unable to meet heavy psychological demands that each makes on the other, frustration occurs. This may lead to divorce.	Same as at left.	Same as at left.

DESIGN ACTIVITIES—THE EFFECTS OF TECHNOLOGY

Assess the effect that three technological products—the bike, computer games, and pre-packaged dinners—have had on people.

- What current impact do these products have on you?

- What long-term impact and consequences (physical, emotional, and social effects) could these have on you?

Determine other technological products that have had a significant effect on people and conduct a study of their impact on people, society, and/or the environment.

Determine several technological products that currently are having a significant effect on people. Project an assessment of the different levels of consequences that might emerge from the broad adoption of those technologies.

Determine an emerging or proposed technological product or process that could have a significant effect on individuals and society in the near future. Implement a future-oriented study of the potential impact of this product on people, society, and/or the environment. Use the multiple-order consequences chart to present some of the delayed and unintended results that could emerge from adopting the product or process.

INTEGRATED S/M/T ACTIVITIES

Make a collage of the ingredients of some of the products you use. Include cosmetics, food, household cleaners, etc. From the list of ingredients, stage a contest to see whether people in your school can tell what the products are. Find out what some of the ingredients are and what their functions are in the products. Categorize the ingredients according to the following functions:

| color | thickness | smell | flavor | preservative |
| nutritional | value | texture | extender | |

How could you determine the effects these products and ingredients have on people?

DESIGN BRIEF—ECOLOGICAL IMPACTS

The World Watch is an organization that regularly assesses what is happening in most of the world's ecological systems. Choose a system that has been studied by this group and gather information on the most recent indicators of the health of that system. Develop a plan for action, that can be accomplished by students in your school, that will affect that system. Develop a list of ways people can make changes locally, yet have global consequences. Create a video or program for adults in your community to report your results and indicate what they can do to make a change.

INTEGRATED S/M/T ACTIVITIES—THE MATHEMATICS OF POPULATION AND CONSUMPTION

Read and analyze the following problem of population and consumption introduced on page 457 of your textbook. Form in small groups to discuss the issue and related problems.

THE ISSUE:

1. World population has doubled since 1950. In terms of new people, the planet gains the equivalent of a New York City every month.

2. The rate of net increase of population is also increasing. In 1993, the increase was 87 million people; in 1950, it was 37 million.

3. Ninety-five percent of the world's babies are born into the poorest countries of the world. However, the population in the United States is expected to double in the next 60 years.

4. Because of our population size, energy and other resource use, and creation of waste and pollutants, THE UNITED STATES HAS BEEN CALLED THE MOST OVERPOPULATED NATION IN THE WORLD.

5. In terms of yearly energy use, the consumption of 3 million United States citizens is equal to that of 90 million Indian citizens.

6. Considering the expected consumption of natural resources of a newborn over its expected lifetime, a baby born in the United States costs the planet as much as 30-40 babies born in developing countries.

CHANGES NEEDED IN ORDER TO FOSTER SUSTAINABLE DEVELOPMENT:

1. Reduce the demand for energy use.

2. Equalize the birth rate and the death rate.

3. Diminish resource use and the creation of wastes by reducing the demand for consumer products, reusing resources, and recycling materials.

4. Recognize that happiness and well being do not come from the accumulation of possessions.

5. Recognize that "more" does not mean "better" and that the fact something can be done does not mean it should be done.

After the analysis and discussion of the issue and problems, identify some of the means by which these problems might be addressed. Determine what this problem could mean for the providing of food worldwide. What does this problem mean for the issue of birth control? What other issues will be introduced and influenced by this issue and its problems?

Source of data: *The Zero Population Growth Reporter*, Vol. 26, No. 1, February, 1994

INTEGRATED S/M/T ACTIVITIES

Form discussion and work groups to consider some of the ecological consequences that change the balance between the living and the non-living things in the biosphere. Select any of a range of problems that have important consequences for the environment. Several possible topics are listed below:

- Excess burning of fossil fuels
- Dumping of waste materials and garbage into rivers, lakes, and soil
- Nuclear testing and its resulting atomic fallout
- Use of pesticides and weed killers
- Oil leaks from shipwrecks or offshore drilling
- Storage of nuclear waste
- Deforestation of the world's woodlands
- Acid rain
- Greenhouse effect

Determine what some of the positive effects have been on humans and animals that have been omitted from the above list.

DECISIONS—MAKING TOUGH CHOICES

Decision-making skills are soft technologies that can be used to determine if the technology of the future will result in the consequences we desire. A decision is a choice among alternatives in the face of uncertainty. Your decision is an educated guess about meeting current and future needs. There is always an element of uncertainty in making decisions. Most decisions in our technological world are selected from dozens of possible choices. Making decisions leads to accepting responsibility. When people make a decision, they must accept the consequences.

One type of decision is a choice among several alternatives, all of which seem to have desirable consequences. Usually, the more you know about the options, the easier it is to make a choice. A second type of decision is that made when one alternative is what you clearly want, and the other is something you wish to avoid. This kind of decision is easiest to make, but only if your goals are clear.

Some criteria are more important than others. Not all alternatives are equal in weight. People make judgments about just how much of a risk they are willing to take, as they weigh the probabilities of an outcome.

A third type of decision is the kind that people must make when all the choices seem to lead to undesired consequences. This is the most difficult decision because it requires you to decide which alternative has the least negative consequences. Making choices from several undesired alternatives places added importance on techniques such as risk assessment as a means of helping to make the best decision possible.

When we make any decision, we make our best fit—we try to optimize the probability of achieving the outcomes we want. Yet there are no guarantees that even the best choice will work out as you hope. Different people see different effects and place different values on them. Often, they want other people to take the negative consequences, not them.

In the face of uncertainty and change, we must make decisions based on the best information we can get. We will make some mistakes, but we can learn from past errors and avoid repeating them.

The four general bases for decision-making are authority, feelings, logic, and experience. In the first approach, people make choices based on the advice of others. As technology becomes more complex, we often must rely on specialists in a given field. It is imperative that we check out the reliability of the expert and assess any biases that may influence the interpretation of the information.

A second approach involves making a choice based on feelings, on what "feels right." This is a kind of personal sense of what is best. There may be no reliable facts available and no authority to consult. Strong emotions are signals that expectations and rules, developed in the past, are being used to perceive the current situation. If you do feel strongly about something, it is useful to tune into what you are thinking at the time. You can consider probabilities and you can handle more information at once. You can consider other people's feelings as well as your own.

As a third way to decide, you can rationally consider the consequences of the decision. Using this method, people logically weigh the probable effects of a choice and judge the worth of each effect. The process usually involves if-then statements.

A fourth method for making decisions is to use personal experience. The actions and past consequences are used as a guide for new decisions. Only when we sense a problem do we look around for new ways of responding. This is the source of most technological efforts.

Each of these methods of choosing may be used to make decisions about technology, whether on a personal, national, or global scale.

Each method of decision-making has certain advantages and disadvantages. Decision-making requires a consideration of goals, resources, actions, and results. As you know from your design work, each involves thinking through the problem and making a plan. Goal-setting requires that you have an indication of what you wish to achieve, and what short-term and long-term outcomes you want to achieve, and what undesirable consequences you wish to avoid. Decisions also require that necessary actions be considered, as well as the resources that will be needed. Also needed is an analysis of what might happen.

It is often helpful to consider a sequence of effects of your actions. These are called first-order effects, second-order effects and so on. It is useful to recognize that every other person could make the same decision you do. What are the potential effects if they are multiplied by everyone acting as you want to act?

A decision chart may help you focus on the necessary information, but it will not make a decision for you. Often decisions are reached by a continuous cycling of the process. After going through the process several times, the best choice may become evident.

Decisions involve personal, social, and ecological factors. Each factor may bring certain limitations to the decision-making process. Sometimes our choices are limited by factors we cannot change, by external constraints. Internal controls are those things which you are able to change, at least in theory. The internal control often is your own willingness to make an extra effort.

Humans decide which factors to consider. The ultimate decisions are human ones. Making the "right" decisions includes many things—what is ethical and moral as well as what is technically correct (true). Decisions that people make do not always fit what they say they value. Actions do not always correspond to words.

Centuries ago, the world population was small. Decisions could be made in terms of the immediate effects upon the local group. Today, however, we are becoming more aware of how far-reaching our decisions actually are. Decisions made in one part of the world may have profound effects on other parts of the world.

We are beginning to see that many of the earth's resources are limited (finite). We realize that decisions must be faced about sharing these resources with billions of other people for now and for future generations.

Ultimately, the "right" or "best" decision is the result of human judgment. The process is becoming more difficult all the time as we become aware of the interconnectedness of our decisions. The decisions we make about technology may have serious consequences for the rest of the world and for future generations.

DESIGN ACTIVITIES—MAKING DECISIONS

As introduced in the textbook, one way to make decisions is to chart the possible goals, actions, resources, and their results. This approach is similar to the design approach discussed throughout the book. Decision components can be listed in order to show the interrelations among the action and consequences. This may cause you to rethink your original goals.

Using a decision chart may help you focus on the necessary information, goals, and other important concerns, but it will not make a decision for you. Decisions are seldom made in a straight line sequence of goals, actions, resources, and results. Most often, as indicated many times earlier, decisions are the result of iterating and recycling through the problem-solving process many times before the best choice, or at least the best choice under existing conditions, becomes evident. The following chart compares alternatives for choosing the most appropriate approaches to gardening and shows the complexity of what seems to be a relatively simple problem.

Goals	Actions	Resources	Results
Produce fresh vegetables, get exercise	Gardening, planting (mulching or hoeing)	Seed, tools, fertilizer, time, growing season	Fresh vegetables, sore muscles
Produce fresh vegetables, save money and time	Pest control (spraying or bug eaters)	Tools (sprayers), chemicals (pesticides)	Larger yields, reduced costs, killing bees and birds
Produce fresh vegetables, get suntan	Cultivation (no till or weeding)	Tools (hand, power), chemicals (nitrogen, herbicides)	Increased yield, good suntan, health risk from chemicals and sun
Produce fresh vegetables, stay out of sun	Gardening (greenhouse or hydroponics)	Greenhouse, equipment, chemicals	Vegetables year-round, increased costs, work, knowledge, health risks from chemicals but not from sun

Use the example provided above and plot out the goals, actions, resources, and results for one or more of the problems that were introduced earlier in this chapter.

LOCAL PROBLEMS

Plan for improving local recycling system

Plan to improve nutrition of students

Community system to support bicycling

Plan to increase student access to Internet

System to monitor violence on television

System to improve sharing of design and technology activities

Plan to reduce community use of cars

Plan to improve technological decision-making

GLOBAL PROBLEMS

Excess burning of fossil fuels

Dumping of waste materials and garbage into rivers, lakes, and soil

Nuclear testing and its resulting atomic fallout

Use of pesticides and weed killers

Oil leaks from shipwrecks or offshore drilling

Storage of nuclear waste

Deforestation of the world's woodlands

Greenhouse effect and acid rain

DESIGN ACTIVITIES—QUANTITATIVE APPROACHES TO DECISION-MAKING

Some decisions can be made by using approaches that rely on more quantitative descriptions and data. One such approach uses the four elements of models, criteria, constraints, and optimization. All of these concepts have been introduced in the textbook. They are brought together here as alternative means to decision making that can be used when appropriate.

Consider the following as you engage in using quantitative approaches to making decisions.

In this context, the term model refers to theoretical models, introduced in Chapter 3 (see page 58 in your textbook). The model is a mathematical, or quantitative, description of the problem to be solved. Consider the following examples. It would be possible to quantify the work that can be accomplished by the crane introduced on page 297 in this text), or the speed of operation of the elevator introduced in Chapter 6 on energy (see page 160 in this text), or the output of ginger ale from the bioreactor introduced in Chapter 11 on biotechnology (see page 329 in this text). These examples represent many instances where the operation and output of the system can be described mathematically (quantified) to provide a model of the system.

The criteria for the problem represent the goals and objectives to be achieved through the decision-making process. For example, in the elevator problem, the speed of the elevator, its doors, and the time provided for loading will have to be balanced with safety concerns.

The constraints of the problem are additional factors to be considered in identifying and implementing a solution. The time required for a full load of passengers to enter or exit the elevator is one factor. A second factor is the speed at which the passengers can travel comfortably. The constraints help to identify the boundaries within which we can expect to find a workable and acceptable solution to the problem at hand.

The optimization of the problem solution can now be pursued. We describe the problems in the form of a model which can help us determine what we really want to achieve (the criteria). We can then set the boundaries of what is permissible (the constraints) to search for the best (optimum) solution.

QUANTITATIVE DECISION-MAKING CHART

MODEL	CONSTRAINTS

CRITERIA	OPTIMIZATION

COMPREHENSIVE DECISION-MAKING CHART

GOALS	ACTIONS	RESOURCES	RESULTS

LIMITATIONS ON DECISIONS | BASIS FOR DECISION-MAKING

Controls

Constraints

Authority

Feelings

Consequences

Experience

IMPACTS AND CONSEQUENCES

Immediate	Desired	Intended
Delayed	Undesired	Unintended

REVIEW AND ASSESSMENT ACTIVITIES

- Describe a decision tree. Indicate how you would construct one.

- What is the purpose of technology assessment? How is it done?

- Give an example of an acceptable risk.

- Cite three examples of personal consequences that have occurred because of a technological product or event. Do the same for social and ecological consequences.

- Describe some of the impacts of the development of print on the lives of humans centuries later. Describe your life if there were no television, books or magazines, radio, or automobiles.

- List some of the activities you do alone and with a group. How do you think this list differs from what your ancestors, 200 years ago, might have done?

- Identify some of the concerns that people have about future consequences for current decisions and behaviors related to technology.

- Make a list of the constraints and controls that place limits on the decisions that are possible for you to make.

- Describe the types of alternatives that are involved in choices people make.

- What are the major sources that people consult when they decide?

- Give some examples of situations in which ethical and moral values must be considered in making a decision.

APPENDIX A: Isometric Grid

APPENDIX B: Suggested Model-Making Materials

Material	Advantages	Disadvantages
Paper and Cardboard	Available in many colors and thicknesses, and many different surface finishes; Easily cut and shaped.	Lacks strength. Can be affected by humidity. Restricted to sheet form.
Wood; basswood	Relative inexpensive and easily worked with hand tools and selected machines. Good for structural work. Bonds well.	Difficult to create very fine details. Does not provide good surface and will require many coats of paint.
Acrylic	Easily worked with hand tools. Can be machined by turning and milling. Very fine details can be produced. Can be heat-formed. Bonds well.	Somewhat expensive, especially if used in thicker sections. Does not vacuum-form well. Can fracture during machining processes.
Polystyrene	Easily worked with hand tools. Can be cut by scoring and cracking. Can be vacuum-formed easily. Bonds extremely well. Can be fabricated easily.	Very sensitive to heat: machining can be a problem. Cellulose paint must be left for a long period after spraying.
Aluminum	Easily machined by turning or milling. Very fine details can be produced. Great strength in thin-walled shells. Adhesive bonding possible.	Normally requires the use of machine tools. Considerable material might have to be removed to achieve realistic weight. Fabrication can be difficult.
ABS	ABS has many advantages including all listed for the above materials.	Usually is relatively expensive for model making.
Plaster of Paris	Can be poured into a mold to replicate a shape or form. Easily shaped by forming tools.	Materials can become brittle. Can require several coats of finish.

NOTE: Polystyrene is very easy to use and one of the least expensive of the above materials. It is widely used in model-making.

APPENDIX C: Properties of Materials

The properties of materials are described by different terms. It is important that they have exact meanings. These terms are often used interchangeably in general conversation. For our purposes in D&T, we should comprehend what each team means and then use the terms accurately.

The most commonly used terms are defined below.

- **Hardness** is the resistance of the material to being cut or dented.

- **Toughness** indicates the amount of energy the materials can absorb without breaking. Toughness measures the ability of a material to withstand shocks. It is the opposite to brittleness.

- **Tensile strength** represents the maximum force the material can stand in tension (pulling apart), compression (crushing), torque (twisting) and shear (sideways pressure), without breaking.

- **Malleability** is the amount of shaping that can be done to a material by hammering, rolling or pressing without it breaking.

- **Ductility** represents the capability of a material to be stretched and elongated without breaking.

- **Elasticity** is the length to which the material can be stretched and then return to its original length when released. The elastic limit is the point beyond which it remains stretched.

- **Heat and electrical conductivity** provides a measure of how well the material will conduct heat or electricity.

APPENDIX D: Common Adhesives

PVA Polyvinyl acetate

This is the most popular wood glue. It is sold ready to use, is easy to apply, non-staining and strong, providing that the joints fit well. Any excess should be wiped off after cramping with a damp cloth. It is not waterproof.

Synthetic resin

This is a stronger wood glue than PVA and also waterproof. It is chemically activated plastic resin that must be mixed with water and a hardener. Cascamite has the resin and hardener ready mixed in the form of a white powder. Aerolite 306 has a liquid hardener supplied in a separate bottle. Synthetic resins will fill small gaps in joints.

Epoxy resin

This is a very versatile, but expensive adhesive that will bond almost any clean, dry materials. Equal amounts of resin and hardener are mixed to start the chemical hardening process. Hardening begins immediately, but full strength is achieved after two or three days depending on the temperature.

Contact adhesive

This is used for gluing sheet material, such as melamine to work surfaces. Both surfaces are coated with a thin layer which is left for approximately 15 minutes to become touch-dry. Adhesion takes place as soon as contact is made between the surfaces, there is no provision for re-positioning. Contact adhesive must only be used in a well-ventilated area.

Latex adhesive

This is a cheap adhesive suited to fabrics, paper, card and upholstery. It is non-toxic and has no fumes and is therefore ideal for younger children.

Acrylic cement

This is an adhesive purpose made for acrylic and available in two forms. One is a solvent adhesive that is supplied ready for use. The other is a two part polymerising adhesive that requires mixing before use.

Polystyrene cement

This is an adhesive that is especially made for rigid polystyrene and is usually supplied with polystyrene model kits. The glue should be used sparingly to ensure that the solvent in the glue does not dissolve or distort the plastic parts.

Rubber solution

Supplied as part of a bicycle puncture repair outfits. This adhesive is available through hardware supply stores.

CNA Cyanoacrylate Glue (Superglue)

These glues require only 10 to 15 seconds to produce a satisfactory bond. The glue should be used sparingly since excess glue tends to produce a weak joint. Avoid getting the glue on your fingers as it can bond them together or to other objects.

Gluing hints

1. Do not apply any form of finish to the gluing surfaces.

2. Ensure that the gluing surfaces are free from dirt, dust, oil and moisture.

3. Assemble all joints dry before reassembling with adhesive. Have all the clamps and assistance that you will need to hand before you begin to apply glue.

4. Check the above chart for the correct adhesive for the job. Read the adhesive manufacturer's instructions and warnings.

SAFETY - Many modern adhesives are solvent based, they give off fumes that are both addictive and very harmful. Be sure that you have plenty of ventilation. Avoid excessive skin contact. Always take note of the manufacturer's warnings.

Appendix E: Adhesives Application Chart

Adhesives Application Chart

MATERIAL	Leather	Rubber	Fabric	Polystyrene	Melamine	Expanded Polystyrene	Acrylic	Metal	Wood	Paper
Paper	Contact Cement / Epoxy Resin	Contact Cement / Latex Adhesive	PVA / Contact Cement	Contact Cement	Contact Cement	PVA	Epoxy Resin	Epoxy Resin	PVA or Synthetic Resin	PVA
Wood	Contact Cement / Epoxy Resin	Contact Cement / Latex Adhesive	PVA / Contact Cement	Contact Cement	Contact Cement	PVA	Epoxy Resin	Epoxy Resin	PVA or Synthetic Resin	
Metal	Contact Cement / Epoxy Resin	Contact Cement / Latex Adhesive	Contact Cement	Contact Cement	Contact Cement	PVA	Epoxy Resin	Epoxy Resin		
Acrylic	Contact Cement / Epoxy Resin	Contact Cement / Latex Adhesive	Contact Cement	Contact Cement	Contact Cement	PVA	Acrylic Cement			
Expanded Polystyrene	Contact Cement / Epoxy Resin	Contact Cement / Latex Adhesive	Contact Cement	Contact Cement	Contact Cement	PVA				
Melamine	Contact Cement / Epoxy Resin	Contact Cement / Latex Adhesive	Contact Cement	Contact Cement	Contact Cement					
Polystyrene	Contact Cement / Epoxy Resin	Contact Cement / Latex Adhesive	Contact Cement	Polystyrene Cement						
Fabric	Contact Cement / Epoxy Resin	Contact Cement / Latex Adhesive	Contact Cement							
Rubber	Contact Cement / Epoxy Resin	Rubber Solution								
Leather	Contact Cement / Epoxy Resin									

APPENDIX F

Common Plastics and Polymers

THEIR PROPERTIES, USES, AND COMMON FORMS

Common Name and Abbreviation	Chemical Name	Properties	Uses	Common Forms
Low density polyethylene (LDEP)	Low density polyethylene	Tough, flexible, soft Good chemical resistance Good electrical insulator Fades in light unless treated service temperature 60°C wide range of colors	Flexible squeeze bottles, toys, antenna lead insulation, plastic bags and sheets	Powder, granules, film, sheets
High density polyethylene (HDPE)	High density polyethylene	Stiff and hard, can be sterilized Good chemical resistance High impact and shock resistant service temperature 80°C wide range of colors	Bowls, buckets and other housewares, milkcrates, barrels, tanks, pipes, some machine parts	Powder, granules, film, sheets
Polyvinyl chloride (PVC)	Polychloroethane	Soft, flexible Good electrical insulator wide range of colors	Synthetic leather, sealing compounds, dip coating, pipes, electrical wiring insulation, wall covering (vinyl wallpaper), flooring (vinyl tile)	Powder, pastes, liquids, sheets
Rigid polyvinyl chloride (PVDC)	Rigid Polychloroethane	Stiff, hard, tough, lightweight Good for fabrication work Good acid and alkali resistance wide range of colors	Bottles, containers, pipes, rain gutters, audio records, shoe soles, roofing material	Powder, paste, liquids, sheets
Polystyrene	Polyenylethene	Stiff, hard, can't be made impact resistant wide range of colors	Disposable cups, plates, food containers, model kits, kitchenware, toys	Powder, granules, sheets
Expanded Polystyrene	Expanded Polyenylethene	Lightweight, very buoyant Good sound and heat insulator Absorbs shocks, crumbles easily Burns with poisonous gas	Heat and sound insulation, packaging materials, floatation material for small boats and canoes	Sheets, slabs, beads
Acrylic or Polymethyl methacrylate (PMMA)	Polymethyl methacrylate	Stiff, hard, crystal clear, Durable outdoors, easily machines, cemented and polished, Good electrical insulator, impact resistant, can be bent and formed easily at about 160°C, scratches easily	Watch and clock covers (lenses), simple optical lenses, aircraft canopies, record player covers, window materials, skylights, furniture	Rods, tubes, sheets
Nylon	Polyamide	Hard, tough, wear resistant, self lubricating High melting point Resistant to oils, fuels and chemicals	Gears, bearings, clothing, packaging, power tool casings, combs, general communication equipment	Powder, granules, chips, rods, tubes, sheets, extruded sections
Polyester resin	Polyester resin	Stiff, hard, brittle when used alone strong and resilient when laminated with glass or carbon fibers	Boats, canoes, car bodies, furniture, encapsulating and embedding	Liquid and pastes
Epoxy resin (EP)	Epoxy resin	Good insulator Good adhesive	Two compound glues for metals Glue for wood	Powders and pastes

APPENDIX G: Units of Measure

For metric or SI (Systeme International) units, you can place prefix letters in front of them to indicate fractions or multiples of ten. For example, km stands for kilometer (1000 meters) and mm stands for millimeters (thousands of a meter).

Prefix	Symbol	Value (powers of ten)	Value (decimal fractions)
pico	p	10^{-12}	0.000 000 000 001
nano	n	10^{-9}	0.000 000 001
micro	m	10^{-6}	0.000 001
milli	m	10^{-3}	0.001
Base Units*			
kilo	k	10^{3}	1 000
Mega	M	10^{6}	1 000 000
Giga	G	10^{9}	1 000 000 000
Terra	T	10^{12}	1 000 000 000 000

*Examples of base units are: meters, ohms, farads, watts

APPENDIX H: Trigonometric Functions

Angle	Sin	Cos	Tan	Angle	Sin	Cos	Tan
0	.000	1.000	.000				
1	.017	.999	.017	46	.719	.695	1.04
2	.035	.999	.035	47	.731	.682	1.07
3	.052	.999	.052	48	.743	.669	1.11
4	.070	.998	.070	49	.755	.656	1.15
5	.087	.996	.087	50	.766	.643	1.19
6	.105	.995	.105	51	.777	.629	1.23
7	.122	.993	.123	52	.788	.616	1.28
8	.139	.990	.141	53	.799	.602	1.33
9	.156	.988	.158	54	.809	.588	1.38
10	.174	.985	.176	55	.819	.574	1.43
11	.191	.982	.194	56	.829	.559	1.48
12	.208	.978	.213	57	.839	.545	1.54
13	.225	.974	.231	58	.848	.530	1.60
14	.242	.970	.249	59	.857	.515	1.66
15	.259	.966	.268	60	.866	.500	1.73
16	.276	.961	.287	61	.875	.485	1.80
17	.292	.956	.306	62	.883	.469	1.88
18	.309	.951	.325	63	.891	.454	1.96
19	.326	.946	.344	64	.898	.438	2.05
20	.342	.940	.364	65	.906	.423	2.14
21	.358	.934	.384	66	.914	.407	2.25
22	.375	.927	.404	67	.921	.391	2.36
23	.391	.921	.424	68	.927	.375	2.48
24	.407	.914	.445	69	.934	.358	2.61
25	.423	.906	.466	70	.940	.342	2.75
26	.438	.898	.488	71	.946	.326	2.90
27	.454	.891	.510	72	.951	.309	3.08
28	.469	.883	.532	73	.956	.292	3.27
29	.485	.875	.554	74	.961	.276	3.49
30	.500	.866	.577	75	.966	.259	3.73
31	.515	.857	.601	76	.970	.242	4.01
32	.530	.848	.625	77	.974	.225	4.33
33	.545	.839	.649	78	.978	.200	4.70
34	.559	.829	.675	79	.982	.191	5.14
35	.574	.819	.700	80	.985	.174	5.67
36	.588	.809	.727	81	.988	.156	6.31
37	.602	.799	.754	82	.990	.139	7.12
38	.616	.788	.781	83	.993	.122	8.14
39	.629	.777	.810	84	.995	.105	9.51
40	.643	.766	.839	85	.996	.087	11.43
41	.656	.755	.869	86	.998	.070	14.30
42	.669	.743	.900	87	.999	.052	19.08
43	.682	.731	.933	88	.999	.035	28.64
44	.695	.719	.966	89	.999	.017	57.28
45	.707	.707	1.000	90	1.000	.000	Infinity

$$\sin \angle = \frac{\text{opposite side}}{\text{hypotenuse}} \qquad \cos \angle = \frac{\text{adjacent side}}{\text{hypotenuse}} \qquad \tan \angle = \frac{\text{opposite side}}{\text{adjacent side}}$$

For angle greater than 90°, $\sin \angle = \sin(180° - \angle)$, $\cos \angle = -\cos(180° - \angle)$, $\tan \angle = \tan(180° - \angle)$.

APPENDIX I

Designing a Computer-Controlled System

The following materials are drawn from *The Kickstarts Book*® activities dealing with the remote control of a mobile Buggy. The materials are provided through the courtesy of Economatics (Education) Ltd. of Sheffield, England.

The *Kickstarts Book,* the Logicator software and the Smartbox hardware are available through:

Modern School Supply
P.O. Box 958
Hartford, CN
(800) 243-2329

INTRODUCTION BUGGY: 1

Driverless vehicles are used for all kinds or purposes.

a) An autocarrier, designed to transport materials and components around a factory. It is controlled by an onboard computer.

b) An intelligent vehicle designed to gather mineral samples from the surface of Mars.

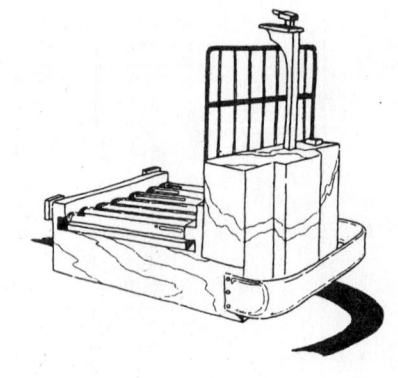

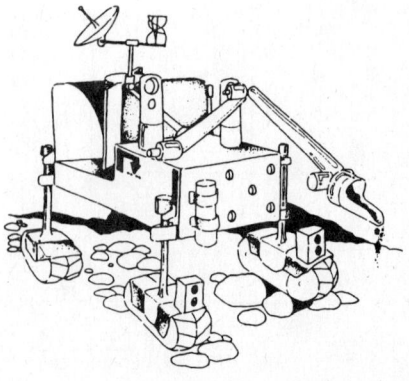

c) A remote controlled vehicle that grabs suspicious looking objects and takes them away for disposal. It is operated by a bomb disposal expert who stays safely out of harm's way.

You can program the Buggy model to move in any direction. With its forklift attached, it can fetch and carry objects for you. If you attach its bumpers, you can program it to detect obstacles and move round them.

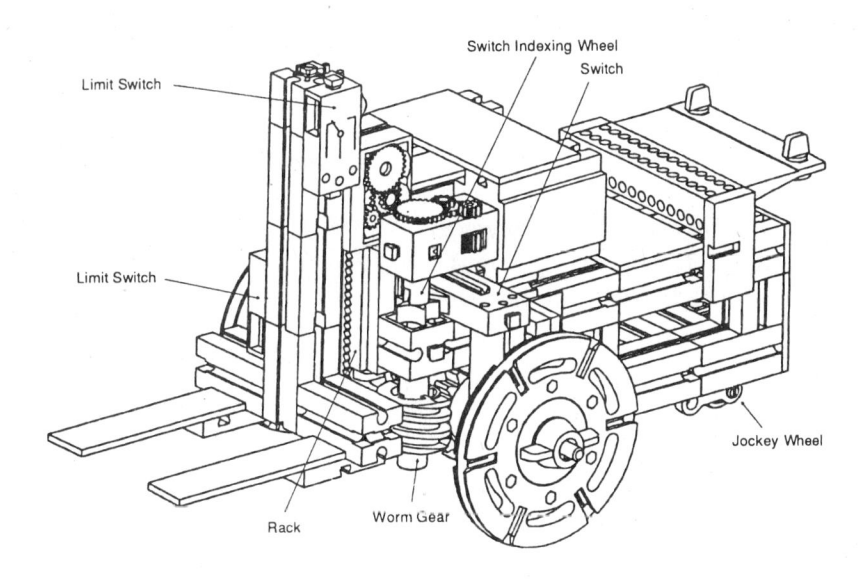

How the Model Works

Each one of the two large wheels on the Buggy is driven by a separate motor. This allows you to steer it in different directions. A small jockey wheel on the back, swivels freely as the Buggy turns.

The rotary movement of the motor is transferred to the wheel by a worm gear mechanism, which also reduces the speed of the movement.

Each motor has a switch indexing wheel and switch connected to it. As the motor turns, the switch sends pulses to the computer. These can be counted and used in procedures for accurate control of the Buggy.

The third motor on the Buggy operates the fork lift by a rack and pinion mechanism. Two limit switches are attached to the fork lift. You can use these to control how far it moves in either direction.

Objects that you want the Buggy to carry can be placed on the pallet.

CHECK THE MODEL NOW TO MAKE SURE THAT EVERYTHING IS IN THE RIGHT PLACE.

BUGGY: 2—LOGICATOR

2.1: Connect the motors and switches on the Buggy to your interface box.

2.2: Driving Forward And Backward

To drive the Buggy forward, you need to switch on both motors to turn the wheels forwards. (See Fig. 1.)

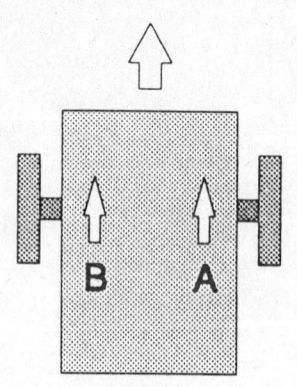

Fig. 1

Open a function cell somewhere away from the start cell. (See Fig. 2.)

Label it "forward" and set the output bit pattern to drive both motors forwards. Use the Test button to help you find the pattern you need. When you have set it, click on OK.

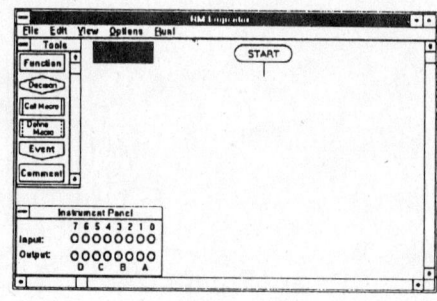

Fig. 2

Now open another cell labeled "backward" and set the output bit pattern to drive both motors backwards.

You now have two test cells that you can use for direct control of the Buggy. (See Fig. 4.)

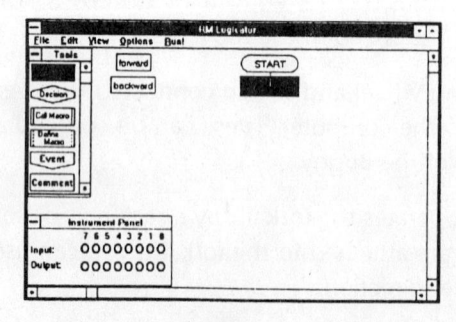

Fig. 3

Fig. 4

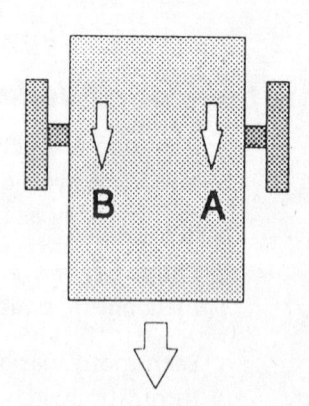

Test the Buggy by opening one of the cells and clicking on the Test button to make the Buggy move.

Try it both forward and backward to check that it runs smoothly.

2.3: Turning Right And Left

To make the Buggy turn right, you need to drive the right motor backwards and the left motor forwards. (See Fig. 5.)

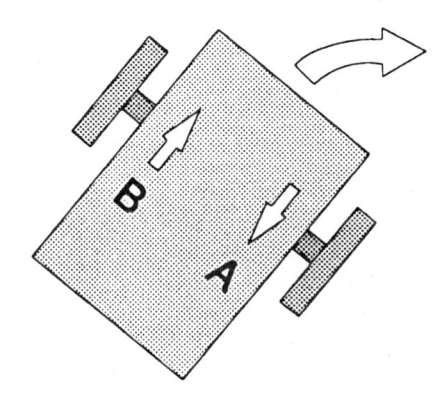

Fig. 5 - Turning Right 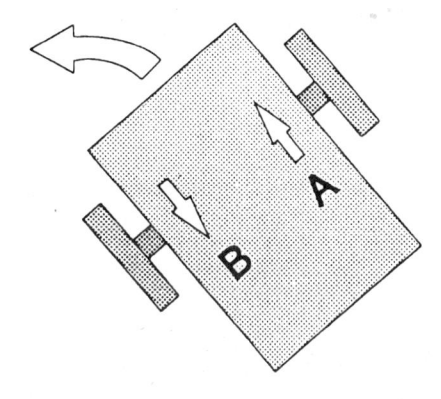   **Fig. 6 - Turning Left**

To make the Buggy turn left, you need to drive the left motor backwards and the right motor forwards. (See Fig. 6.)

Make two new test cells, labeled "left" and "right". Use the Test button to help you to set the correct output bit pattern for each cell.

Practice driving the Buggy by direct control. Open one of the cells and use the Test button to drive the Buggy in that direction.

Try driving it like this in all four directions.

SAVE THIS FLOWSHEET.

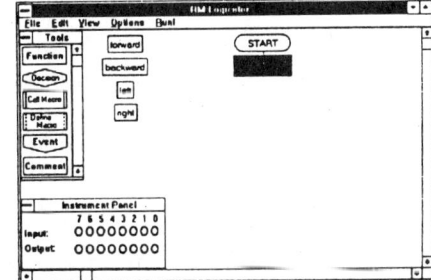

Fig. 7 - Flowsheet with four test cells

BUGGY: 3—LOGICATOR

3.1: Using A Counter

You can control how far the Buggy moves in any direction, by using the Count command to count the pulses from one of the counters which are connected to the motors that drive the Buggy.

Each counter is made up of a switch indexing wheel and a switch. (See Fig. 8.)

Check that both of these counters are working correctly. Open your "forward" test cell and click on the test button. Watch the indicator lights on your interface box. The lights on the two lines connected to the counters should be flashing. If they are not flashing, check that the switch and wheel are positioned correctly as shown in Fig. 8.

Fig. 8

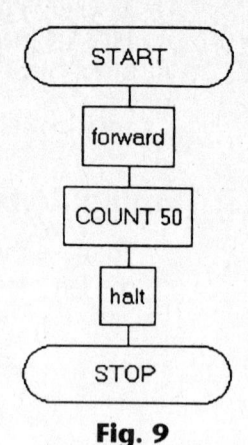

Fig. 9

Now write the routine shown in Fig. 9.

To save time, you can copy your "forward" test cell into the routine.

Set the count 50 cell to count 50 pulses on the input line connected to one of the counters.

Run the routine and measure how far the Buggy moves.

Delete the "forward" cell in the routine and copy in your "right" test cell in its place (See Fig. 10.)

Run this routine and check how far the Buggy turns. Alter the number in the Count cell so that the Buggy turns through 90 degrees.

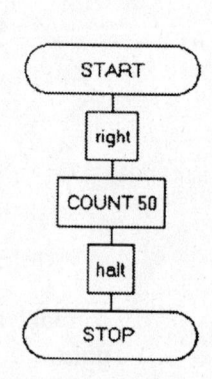

Fig. 10

> **HELP!**
> To COPY a cell, highlight it. Then hold down CTRL and click and drag it to where you want to place a copy.
>
> The copy has exactly the same label and bit pattern as the original.

3.2: Full Control Of The Buggy

Write the routine shown in Fig. 11. Copy cells to save yourself time.

The Count cell in each macro contains a variable, N for straight movement and T for turning. This means that you can use the macros in any routine for moving the Buggy.

All you need to do is give values to the variables. You would normally do this at the start of the routine, but you can also set new values at any point in the routine.

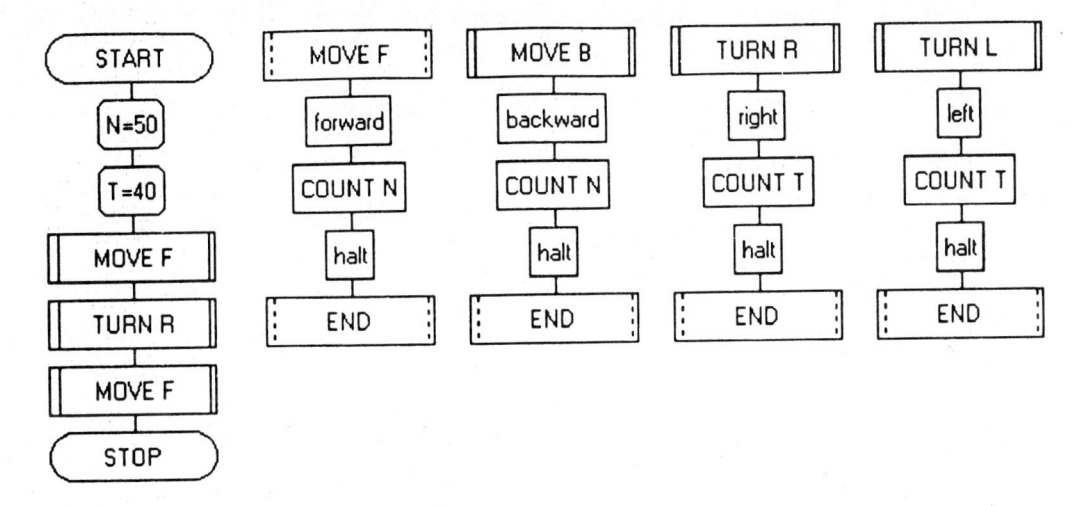

Fig. 11

3.3: Giving The Buggy A Route

a) Run the routine. Then extend it to make the Buggy move through a complete square.

b) Change the values of the variables to make the Buggy move through a different shape. Draw the shape on paper first, to work out the moves that you need.

SAVE THIS FLOWSHEET.

BUGGY: 4—LOGICATOR

4.1: Load the flowsheet you have written to control the Buggy. Save it as version 02. This way, you can develop the system and also have access to the macros that you have already written.

4.2: Using The Fork Lift

Check that the motor which operates the fork lift, and the two limit switches are connected to your interface box.

Notice that the upper switch on the forklift limits its downward movement.

Then write the two routines shown in Fig. 12.

Run each routine in Graphic Run with zero delay, as quick response to the limit switches is important.

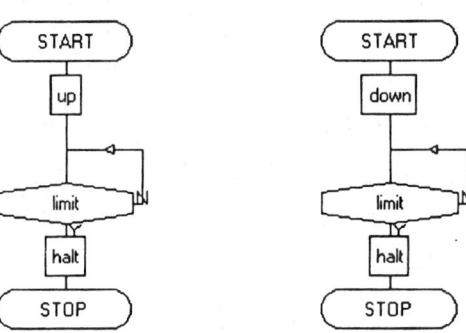

Fig. 12

Check that the forklift works properly. Adjust the position of the limit switches if necessary.

Now convert the two routines into two macros as shown in Fig. 13.

Notice that the limit switch is tested at the start of the macro, so that the forklift doesn't move if it is already in the required position. This is an important safety feature.

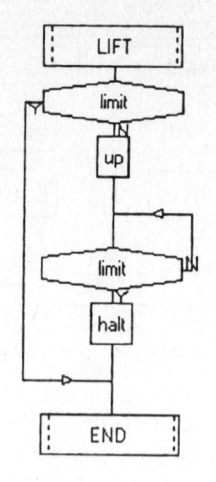

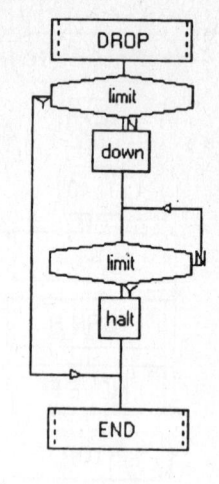

Fig. 13

You can now write a routine to combine the forklift with Buggy movement.

Write the routine shown in Fig. 14.

Place the pallet about 50mm in front of the Buggy. Run the flowsheet. The Buggy should move forward, pick up the pallet, move back and drop it.

Make any adjustments necessary and then run it again.

4.3 Delivering The Mail

Use what you have learned about controlling the Buggy, to design a system for the situation shown in Fig. 15.

Fig. 14

Mark out the corridor and offices on a table or on the floor. Choose suitable distances for yourself. Make the corridor wide enough for the Buggy to turn around. When you have tested your system and made sure that it works, prepare a report on it for the office manager. Include a copy of the flow sheet.

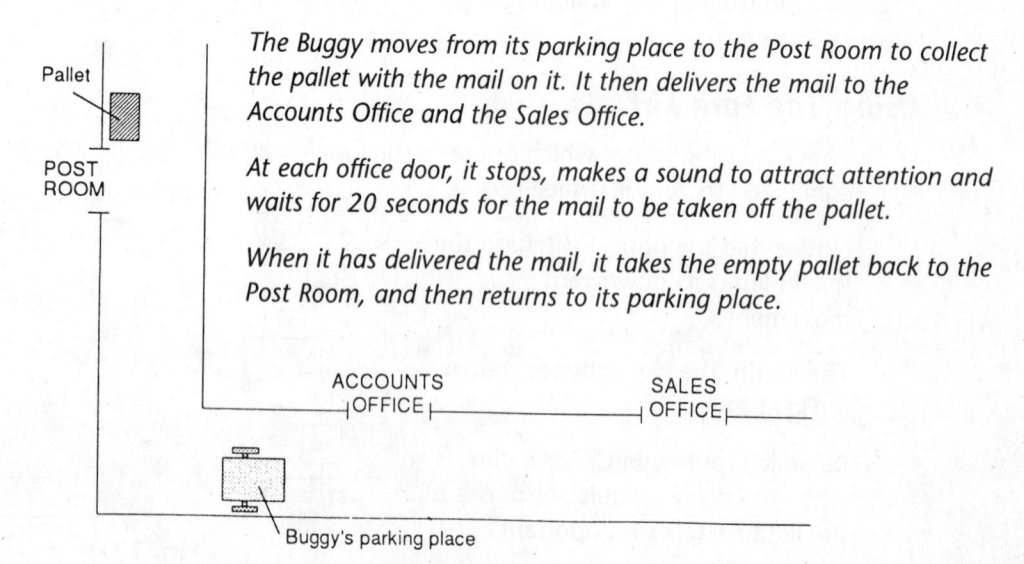

The Buggy moves from its parking place to the Post Room to collect the pallet with the mail on it. It then delivers the mail to the Accounts Office and the Sales Office.

At each office door, it stops, makes a sound to attract attention and waits for 20 seconds for the mail to be taken off the pallet.

When it has delivered the mail, it takes the empty pallet back to the Post Room, and then returns to its parking place.

Fig. 15

BUGGY: 5—LOGICATOR

5.1: Load the flowsheet that you wrote to control the movement of the Buggy. Save it as version 03. You can now make use of your existing macros in a new procedure.

5.2: Using The Bumpers

Remove the forklift from the front of the Buggy, and reassemble it into the bumpers as shown on the construction leaflet for the Buggy.

Connect the two switches on the bumpers to your interface box.

Push each of the yellow plates and check that the appropriate light on your interface box lights up.

Make sure that the yellow plates spring back off the switches when you release them. Write the routine shown in Fig. 16.

Put a reasonably heavy obstacle, such as a book, in front of the Buggy and run the flowsheet in Fast Run.

The Buggy should stop when it detects the obstacle.

Move the obstacle and then run the flow sheet again to check that the Buggy stops if either or both of the bumpers are pressed.

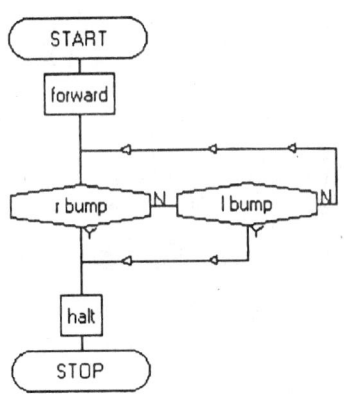

Fig. 16

You can now make the Buggy stop if it detects an obstacle in its path. If you use the macro shown in Fig. 17 you can make the Buggy detect an obstacle and then move round the side of it.

Example numbers. Work out the best ones for yourself

Put the obstacle in front of the Buggy and run the flow sheet in Fast Run.

SAVE YOUR FLOWSHEET.

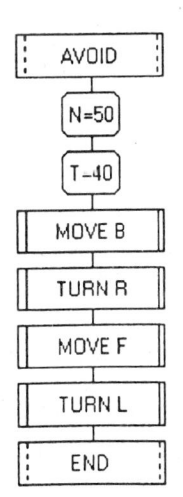

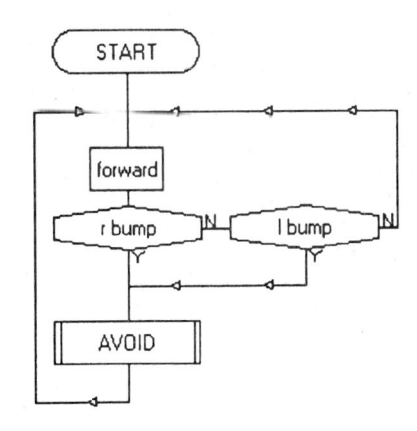

Fig. 17

5.3: Making Use Of The Buggy's Two Bumpers

Build an obstacle route as shown in Fig. 18.

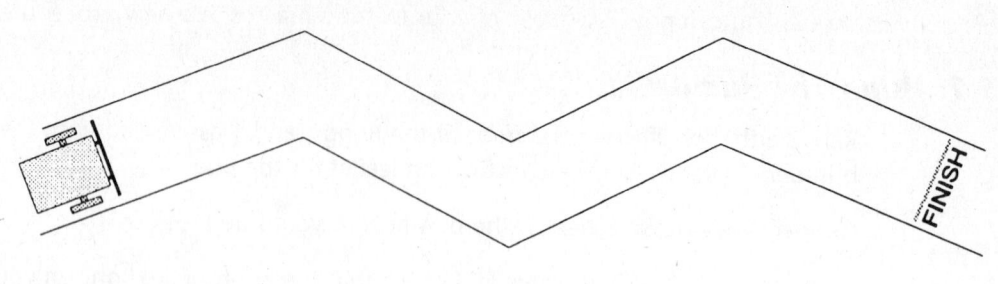

Fig. 18

Design a flow sheet to allow the Buggy to move from start to finish. Make use of the fact that the Buggy has two separate bumpers.

BUGGY: 6—LOGICATOR

6.1: Into The Labyrinth

You can program a Buggy with bumpers to negotiate a maze. This makes an interesting exercise in control and also introduces you to some basic principles of robotics.

You will need a single bumper now, so connect both bumper switches together into your interface box.

6.2: Buggy Geometry

As it negotiates the maze, the Buggy will need to retreat from a wall and turn in a confined space, so you need to know some basic dimensions before you can start to program it.

Measure the distances shown in Fig. 19.

a) Center of Buggy to the front of the bumpers when they are pressed.

b) Center of Buggy to the front corner when the bumpers are not pressed.

c) Center of Buggy to back corner.

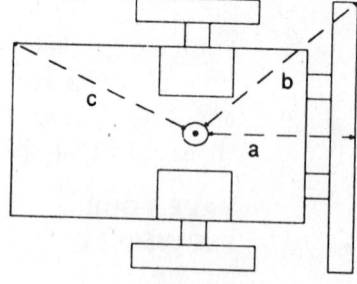

Fig. 19

Use these dimensions to work out:

d) Buggy's safe turning distance. This is: either distance b or c (whichever is the greater) plus a small safety margin of approximately 10mm.

e) Buggy's retreating distance. This is the smallest distance that the Buggy needs to back off from a wall to allow it room to turn. It is: distance d minus distance a.

Keep a record of all five distances.

You will be using the Count command to give the Buggy instructions, so you need to convert the retreating distance to a number of pulses from the counter.

Work out for yourself an accurate way to do this conversion.

You could place the Buggy a measured distance from an obstacle and write a routine to count the switch pulses until it hits the obstacle.

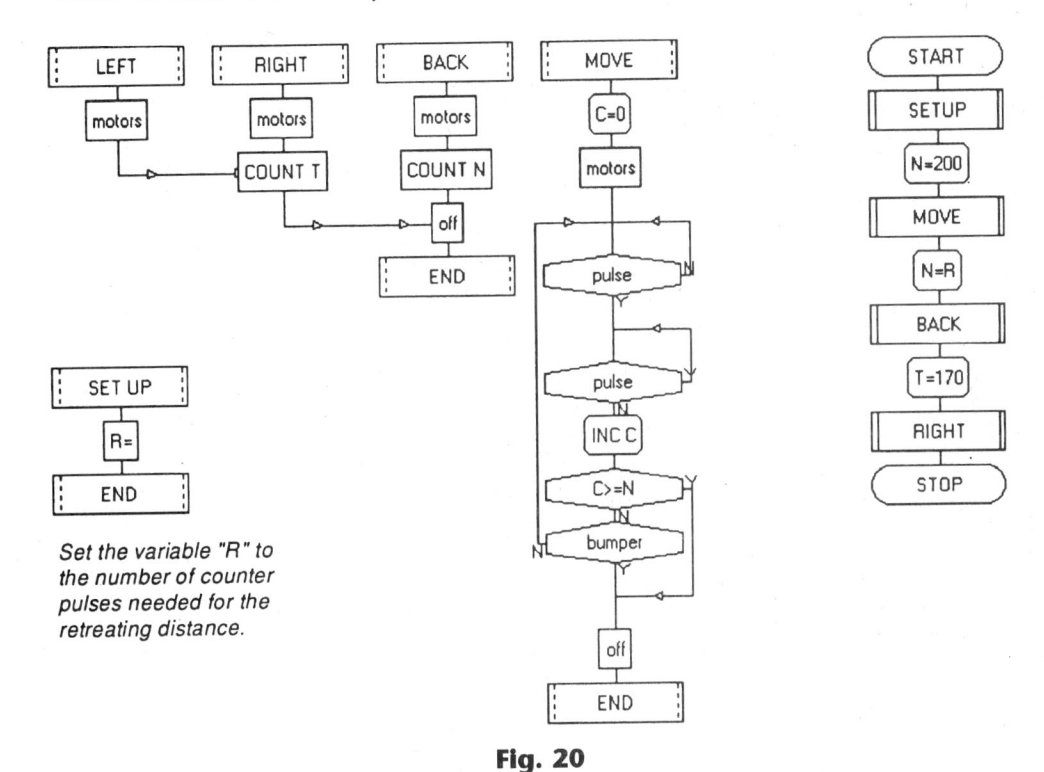

Set the variable "R" to the number of counter pulses needed for the retreating distance.

Fig. 20

Now write the flowsheet shown in Fig. 20.

You can use this flow sheet to check that you have given the Buggy an accurate retreating distance. Put an obstacle in front of the Buggy and run the flowsheet in Fast Run.

When the Buggy hits the obstacle, it should back off and turn through 360° without touching the obstacle. If necessary, change the value of the variable R.

SAVE THIS FLOWSHEET.

BUGGY: 7—LOGICATOR

7.1: Negotiating A Corner

You can now build the beginning of a maze for the Buggy. The width of the maze corridor is important. It must allow the Buggy room to maneuver. Calculate the maze corridor width by: 2 x distance d (the safe turning distance) plus a small safety margin.

Make a corner as shown in Fig. 21. Then write the MOVE TO WALL macro and edit your main routine as shown in Fig. 22.

Place the Buggy as shown in Fig. 21. Run the flowsheet. When it hits the wall, the Buggy should turn 90° right to check if it can move that way. If it then hits another wall, it should turn 180 left and check again.

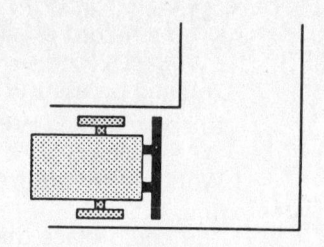

Fig. 21 - Left-hand corner

Now make a right-hand corner as shown in Fig. 23.

Will the Buggy negotiate this corner using the same flow sheet? Try it.

7.2: Negotiating A Series Of Corners

You can now develop the system to allow the Buggy to tackle a maze made up of a series of corners (See Fig. 24.)

This means that the procedure for negotiating a corner has to be restarted from the beginning after each corner has been successfully passed.

Edit your main routine and MOVETOWALL macro as shown in Fig. 25.

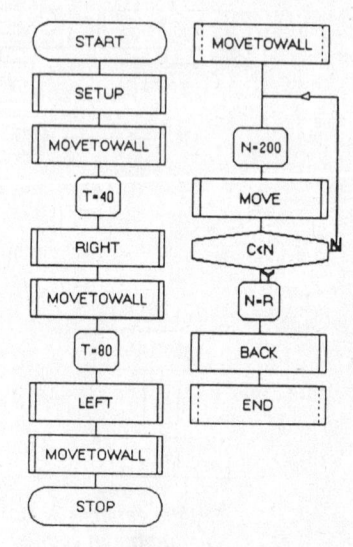

Fig. 22 - Left-hand corner

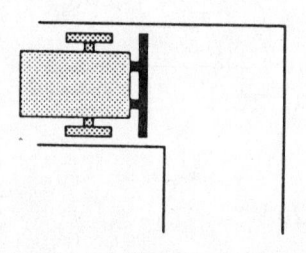

Fig. 23 - Right-hand corner

The variable D is the minimum distance that the Buggy has to travel before it can be sure that it hasn't hit a wall and that a corner has been successfully passed.

Calculate this distance by: maze corridor width minus distance a (the distance from the centre to front of the Buggy).

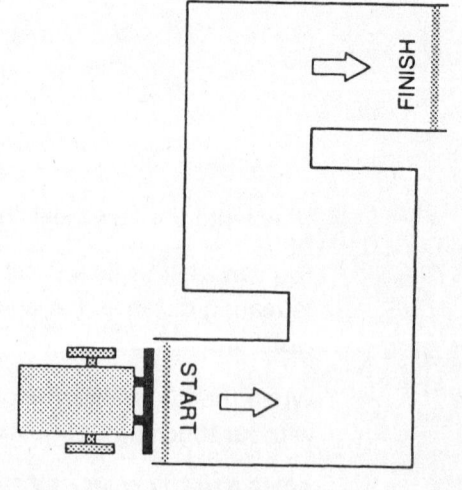

Fig. 24

Convert the distance into a number of counter pulses and set the variable D to this number in the SETUP macro.

Build a maze as shown in Fig. 24. Run the flowsheet and check that the Buggy can move from start to finish.

When you have proved that the Buggy can negotiate a series of corners, close off the "finish" end of the maze. Then delete the stop cell from the main routine and draw a repeat loop back to the beginning.

Run the flowsheet and see how the Buggy behaves when it reaches the finish this time.

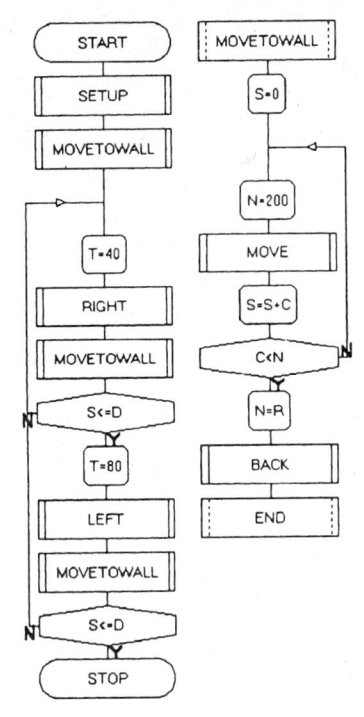

Fig. 25

Appendix J: Selected Reference Books and Resource Materials

A Kick in the Seat of the Pants
von Oech, Roger
Perennial Library (1986)

A Whack on the Side of the Head
von Oech, Roger
Warner Books (1983)

Advanced Design and Technology
Norman, E. et. al.
Longman (1990)

Aerodynamics of Model Aircraft Flight
Simons, M.
Argus Books Limited (1988)

Airplanes of The Future
Berliner, D.
Lerner Publications Co. (1987)

All About FORTH: An Annotated Glossary
Haydon, G.
Mountain View Press (1984)

An SPC Primer
Pyzdek, Thomas
ASQC (1984)

Application of Biotechnology
Fowle, J.
Westview Press, Inc. (1987)

Applied Hydraulics for Technology
Kanen, J.
Hott, Rinehart, & Winston (1986)

Applied Photography
Dennis, E.
Delmar Publishers Inc. (1985)

Applying Autocad
Wohlers, T.
Glencoe (1992)

Appropriate Technology Sourcebook
Saxenian, M. & Darrow, K.
A Volunteers in Asia Pub. (1986)

Architectural Graphic Standards
Ramsey & Sleeper
John Wiley & Sons (1989)

Architecture
Spence, W.
Glencoe (1992)

Asimov's Bibliographical Encyclopedia of Science & Technology
Asimov, Isaac
Doubleday & Co., Inc. (1982)

Asimov's New Guide to Science
Asimov, I.
Viking Press (1985)

AutoCAD: A Tutorial
Avizius, A.R.
McGraw-Hill, Inc. (1991)

Beyond Mechanization
Hirschorn, L.
MIT Press (1984)

Bioethics
Goldstein, D.
Gale Research Co. (1982)

Biomechanics
Dreighbaum, E. and Barthels, K.
Burgess (1981)

Biotechnology: Strategies for Life
Antebi, E.
The MIT Press (1985)

Book for Women Who Invent or Want To
Wallace, E.
The Women Inventors Project (1987)

Build a Remote Controlled Robot
Shircliff, D.
TAB Books, Inc. (1986)

Build Your Own Working Robot
Heiserman, D.
TAB Books, Inc. (1987)

Building: From Caves to Skyscrapers
Salvadori, M.
Athenium (1979)

Building Structures
Ambrose, J.
John Wiley & Sons (1988)

Building the Medieval Cathedrals
Watson, P.
Cambridge University Press (1976)

Card Engineering
Honeybone, Ian
Nippan Publication Books (1990)

Castle
McCauley, D.
Houghton Mifflin Co. (1977)

Cathedral
McCaulay, D.
Houghton Mifflin Co. (1973)

Circuits, Signals, & Systems
Siebert, W.
McGraw-Hill (1986)

City
McCaulay, D.
Houghton Mifflin Co. (1974)

Clothing: Fashion, Fabrics, Construction
Weber
Glencoe/ McGraw Hill (1992)

CMOS Cookbook, 2nd ed.
Lancaster, D.
SAMS (1990)

Computer Interfacing With Pascal
Eckel, B.
David Thompson (1988)

Computer Numerical Control
Seames, W.
Delmar Publishers, Inc. (1986)

Connections
Burke, J.
MacMillan Publishers (1978)

Control Technology: Teachers Handbook
Fox, G.J.
Hodder and Stoughton (1986)

Craft, Design and Technology Foundation
Finney, M.
Collins Educational (1986)

Creativity Design and Technology
Horton and Lawson
Davis Publications, Inc. (1989)

Day the Universe Changed, The
Burke, J.
British Broadcasting Corp. (1985)

Design and Problem Solving
Hutchinson, P. and Sellwood, P.
Thomson Learning Tools (1996)

Design and Problem Solving in Technology
Hutchinson, J. and Karsnitz, J.
Delmar Publishers (1994)

Design and Technology
Caborn, C. et. al.
Nelson (1989)

Design and Technology: Children's Engineering
Dunn and Larson
The Falmer Press (1990)

Design For The Real World: Human Ecology & Social Change
Papanek, Victor
Academy Chicago Publishers (1985)

Designing for Humans: The Human Factor in Engineering
Burgess, John H.
Petrocelli Books (1986)

Desktop Publishing & Typesetting
Kleper, M.
Windcrest Books (1991)

Desktop Video Production
Brown, M.
Windcrest Books (1991)

Diagrams and Charts
Bounford, Trevor
Outline Press (1991)

Digital Electronic Circuits
Glasford, G.
Prentice Hall (1988)

Discovering Food
Kowtaluk, Helen
Glencoe/McGraw Hill (1992)

Electricity & Electronics
Faber, R.
John Wiley & Sons (1982)

Electronic Devices and Circuits
Berube
Merrill (1993)

Energy For a Sustainable World
Goldemberg, J.
World Resources Institute (1986)

Energy for Development
Goldemberg, J.
World Resources Institute (1987)

Energy Fudamentals
Lord, J.
Enterprise for Education. Inc, (1986)

Energy Technology
Bohn, R.
Glencoe (1992)

Engineering—An Introduction to a Creative Profession
Beakley, G.C. & Leach, H.W.
MacMillan Publishing Co.(1982)

Envisioning Information
Tufte, E.
Graphics Press (1990)

Envisioning Information
Tufte, Edward
Graphics Press (1990)

Ergonomics for Beginners
Dul, J. and Weerdmeester, B.
Taylor and Francis (1991)

Eureka! An Illustrated History of Invention From the Wheel to the Computer
de Bono, Edward
Holt, Rinehart, & Winston (1974)

Extraordinary Origins of Everyday Things
Panati, Charles
Harper & Row (1987)

Fasten It!
Self, C.
TABBooks (1984)

Fiberoptics and Laser Handbook, The
Safford, E.
TAB Books, Inc. (1984)

Film and Video Budgets
Wiese, M.
Michael Wiese Film Productions (1988)

Films and Special Effects
Mottram, P. & Meredith, S.
Usborne Pub. (1984)

Finding Facts Fast: How to Find Out What you Want & Need to Know
Todd, Alden
Ten Speed Press (1979)

Focus on Designing
Hubel, V. and Lussow, D.
McGraw Hill Ryerson (1984)

Food Science & You
Mehas, Rodgers
Glencoe/McGraw Hill (1994)

Forecasting the Future: Exploring Evidencefor Global Climate Change
National Science Teachers Association (1995)

From Leaves to Lasers, Cars to Computers
MacCaulay
Houghton Mifflin Co. (1988)

From Mangle to Microwave
Hardyment, C.
Polity Press (1988)

Full House
Brown, Lester & Kane, Hal
W.W. Norton & Co. (1995)

Future Days: A Nineteenth-Century Vision of the Year 2000
Asimov, Isaac
Henry Holt & Co. (1986)

Gadgeteer's Goldmine: 55 Space Age Project.
McComb, G.
TAB Books (1990)

Glue It!
Giles, C. & Giles, B.
TAB Books (1984)

Graphic Communication Technology
Karsnitz, J.
Davis Publications Inc. (1992)

Graphic Design
Potter
Usborne Publishing (1987)

Habitats Tomorrow
Cornish, E.
World Future Society (1984)

Handbook of Invention and Discovery
Reid, S.
Usborne (1986)

Handbook of Photography
Lovell / Zwahlen
Brenton Publishers (1984)

Handbook of Radio Publicity & Promotion
MacDonald, J. and Holsopple, C.
TAB Books (1984)

High Performance Interactive Graphics
Adams, L.
TAB Books, Inc. (1988)

Homes Today & Tomorrow
Sherwood, Ruth
Glencoe/ McGraw Hill (1996)

Homes with Character
Craig, Hazel Thompson
Glencoe/ McGraw Hill (1995)

How Bridges Are Made
Kingston, J.
Facts on File Pub. (1985)

How to Create Effective TV Commercials
Baldwin, H.
NTC Business Books (1988)

How to Design Trademarks & Logos
Rowe, M.
North Light Books (1988)

How to Draw Charts and Diagrams
Robertson, B.
North Light Books (1988)

How to Invent: A Text for Teachers and Students
Shlesinger, B. Edward, Jr.
IFI/ Plenum Data Corporation (1985)

How to Make Printed Circuit Boards
Graf, C.
TAB Books, Inc. (1988)

Human Factors in Design
Burgess, J.
Tab Books (1989)

IC Op-Amp Cookbook 3rd ed.
Jung, W.
Howard W. Sams & Company (1990)

IC Timer Cookbook 2nd ed.
Jung, W.
Howard W. Sams & Company (1990)

Information Age
Kelly, K.
Harmony Books (1988)

Interfacing
Derenzo, S.
Prentice Hall (1990)

Interfacing the Apple
Faughn, J.
Kern International, Inc. (1986)

Interfacing to the IBM Computer
Eggebrecht, L.
Howard W. Sams & Co. (1983)

Introducing Design and Communication
Hutchinson & Tufnell (1986)

Introduction to Electronics Design
Mitchell, F.H. Jr. & Sr.
Prentice Hall (1988)

Introduction to Engineering Technology
Pond, R.
Merrill Publishing Company (1990)

Inventing, Inventions, & Inventors
Flack, Jerry D.
Teacher Ideas Press (1989)

Invention and Discovery
Reid, Struan
Usborne Publishing Ltd. (1986)

Inventioneering
Stanish, Bob & Singletary, Carol
Good Apple, Inc. (1986)

Lasers: The Light Fantastic
Horn, D.
TAB Books, Inc. (1987)

Learning About Energy
Rose, D.
Plenum Press (1986)

Learning CAD with AutoCAD
Spaulding, W.
TAB Books, Inc. (1988)

Life In a Medieval Village
Morgan, G.
Cambridge University Press (1975)

Making the Future Work
Budget-Meakin, Catherine (ed.)
Longman (1992)

Manufacturing System Design
Wright, T.
Society of Manufacturing Engineers (1990)

Manufacturing Technology
Komacek, S.
Delmar Publishers Inc. (1992)

Manufacturing Technology
Daiber, R.
Glencoe/ McGraw-Hill (1991)

Mechanical Drawing 11th ed.
Helsel, Urbanick
McGraw Hill (1992)

Medieval Castles
Cairns, C.
Cambridge University Press (1987)

Megatrends
Naisbitt, J.
Warner Books (1984)

Micro Interfacing Circuits
Penfold
Bernard Babani, Ltd. (1984)

Microcomputer Electronics
Metzger, D.
Prentice Hall (1989)

Microphones
Clifford, M.
TAB Books, Inc. (1986)

Mothers of Invention: From the Bra to the Bomb
Vare, Ethlie Ann & Ptacek, Greg
William Morrow & Co., Inc. (1988)

Nuclear Energy
Murray, R.
Pergamon Press (1988)

On the Wings of A Dream
NASA
NASA (1991)

Optoelectronics: Fiber Optics and Lasers
Tischler, M.
Glenco (1992)

Out of The Crisis
Deming, W. Edwards
ASQC (1986)

Paper Engineering for Pop-Up Books
Hiner, M.
Tarquin Publications (1985)

Passive Solar Energy in Buildings
Sullivan, P.
Elsevier Applied Science Publishers (1988)

Patenting & Marketing Your Invention
Rivkan, Bernard
Van Nostrand Reinhold Co., Inc. (1986)

Physics for Kids—49 Easy Experiments
Wood, R.
TAB Books (1990)

Playground Design
Eriksen, A.
Van Nostrand Reinhold Books (1985)

Practical Robotics: Systems Interfacing
Worthington, J.
Prentice-Hall (1986)

Practical Techniques for the Graphic Artist
Mulherin, J.
North Light Books (1987)

Principles & Practices of TQM
Cartin, Thomas J.
ASQC (1993)

Product Design and Engineering
Wright, T.
Society of Manufacturing Engineers (1990)

Production Systems Technology
Harms, H.
Glencoe (1992)

Production Technology
Komacek, S.
Davis Publications Inc. (1992)

Robot Builder's Bonanza
McComb, G.
TAB Books, Inc. (1987)

Shooting Video
Rosen, F.
Focal Press (1984)

Slides: Planning and Producing Slide Productions
Bishop, A.
Eastman Kodak Company (1986)

SPC Simplified: Practical Steps to Quality
Amsden, Butler & Amsden
ASQC (1991)

Starting Design and Technology Series
Cave, J. (ed.)
Cassell (1990)

Statics and Mechanics of Materials
Hibbeler, R.C.
Macmillan Publishing Co. (1993)

Steven Caney's Invitation Book
Caney, Steven
Workman Publishing Co., Inc. (1985)

Studio Tips and Tricks
Stear, G. and Martin, J.
Outline Press (1989)

Technology in America- 2nd Ed.
Pursell, C.
MIT Press (1990)

Technology in School
Cave, J., Routledge, & Kegan, P.
Boston (1986)

Technology of Industrial Materials
Kazanas, H. et.al.
Bennett (1974)

The Art of CreativeThinking
Nierenberg, G.
Simon & Schuster, Inc. (1982)

The Art of Desktop Publishing
Thomas, W.
Bantam Books (1987)

The History of Invention
Williams, Trevor I.
Facts on File Publications (1987)

The Inventa Book of Mechanisms
Catlin, D.
Valiant Technology Ltd. (1994)

The Invention of Ordinary Things
Wulffson, Don. L.
Lothrop, Lee, & Shepard Books (1981)

The Inventor's Handbook: How to Develop, Protect, & Market Your Invention
Park, Robert
Betterway Publications, Inc. (1986)

The Memory Jogger Plus+
Brassard, Michael
ASQC (1989)

The Tech & Tools Book: A Guide to Technologies Women Are Using Worldwide
Sanhu, et.al
IWTC/IT Publications (1986)

The Timetable of Technology
Ayensu, Edward (ed.)
Hearst Books (1982)

The Way Things Work
Macauly, David
Houghton Mifflin Co. (1988)

The Way Things Work: An Illustrated Encyclopedia of Technology
Simon & Schuster (1967)

The World Almanac Book Of Inventions
Giscard d-Estaing, Valerie-Anne
World Alamanac Publications (1985)

TQM: A Step-by-Step Guide to Implementation
Weaver, Charles N.
ASQC (1991)

Transportation Energy & Power Technology
Schwaller, A.
Delmar Publishers Inc. (1989)

Understanding Electricity and Electronics
Buban, Schmitt, & Carter
Glencoe (1992)

Understanding Electronic Photography
Larish, J.
TAB Books (1990)

Understanding Electronics
Warring, R.
TAB Books, Inc. (1989)

Ventura Publisher: A Creative Approach
McClure, E.
Windcrest (1992)

Weather Forecasting
Ramsey, D.
TAB Books (1990)

Why Buildings Stand Up
Salvadori, M.
McGraw-Hill Book Company (1980)

Why Your House May Endanger Your Health
Zamm, A.
Simon and Schuster (1980)

Appendix K: Selected Publishers and Vendors of Technology Education Resource Materials

A & C Black Ltd.
35 Bedford Row
London, U.K. WC1R 4JH

Academy Chicago Publishers
425 N. Michigan Ave
Chicago, IL

Addison-Wesley Publishing Co.
Rte 128
Redding, MA 01867

ASQC (American Society for Quality Control)
611 E. Wisconsin Ave,
P.O. Box 3005
Milwaukee, WI 53201-3005

Bantam Books
51 Madison Ave.
New York, NY 10010

Barnes and Noble Books
10 East 53rd Street
New York, NY 10022

Beekman House
One Park Avenue
New York, NY 10016

Benchmark Books
67 Fairhaven Ave.
West Mersea, Colchester U.K.
CO5 8BT

Bergwall Productions, Inc.
P.O. Box 2400;
540 Baltimore Pike
Chadds Ford, PA 19317

BSCS (Biological Sciences Curriculum Study)
Pikes Peak Research Park
5415 Mark Dabling Blvd.
Colorado Springs, CO 80918

Burgess Publishing
7108 Ohms Lane
Minneapolis, MN 55435

Cambridge University Press
40 West 20th Street
New York, NY 10001

Cassell Publishers Ltd
Artillery House, Artillery Row
London, UK SW1 P1RT

Charlesbridge Publishing
85 Main Street
Watertown, MA 02172

Collins Educational
77-85 Fulham Palace Rd.
Hammersmith, U.K. W6 8JB

Columbia University Press
2960 Broadway
New York, NY 10027

Creative Educational Society
123 S. Broad St., PO Box 227
Mankato, MN 56001

Creative Learning Systems
16510 Via Esprillo
San Diego, CA 92127

D. C. Heath and Company
125 Spring St.
Lexington, MA 02173

D&T Initiative
The College of New Jersey
Trenton, NJ 08650-4700

Davis Publications, Inc.
50 Portland St.
Worcester, MA 01608

Delmar Publishers
3 Columbia Circle, Box 15015
Albany, NY 12212-5015

Dover
180 Varick St.
New York, NY 10014

E. J. Arnold and Son
29 W. 35th St.
New York, NY 10001

Edmund Scientific Company
101 E. Gloucester Pike
Barrington, NJ 08007-1380

Educational Learning Systems
9899 Hilbert St.,
Suite C,
San Diego, CA 92131

Educational Service Inc.
P.O. Box 219
Stevensville, MI 49127

Eyre Methuen Ltd.
11 New Fetter Lane
London, U.K. EC4P 4EE

Facts on File Publications
490 Park Avenue South
New York, NY 10016

Fitzhenry and Whiteside Limited
10 East 53rd Street
New York, NY 10022

Folens Publishers
Albert House,
Albert Business Centre
Boscombe Road, Dunstable, U.K.
LU5 4RL

G. P. Putnam's Sons
200 Madison Ave.
New York, NY 10016

Gibbs M. Smith, Inc.
PO Box 667
Layton, UT 84041

Glencoe/McGraw-Hill
P.O. Box 543
Blacklick, OH 43004-9902

Golden Press
Rockerfeller Center
New York, NY 10020

Graphics Press
P.O. Box 430
Cheshire, CN 06410

Harcourt, Brace and World, Inc.
1250 Sixth Ave
San Diego, CA 92101

Harper & Row Publishers
10 East 53rd Street
New York, NY 10022

Heinemann Educational
22 Bedford Square
London, U.K. WC1B 3HH

Her Majesty's Stationery Office
49 High Holborn
London, U.K. WC1V 6HB

Hobsons Scientific
521 Fifth Ave, 17th Floor
New York, NY 10175

Hodder and Stoughton
Mill Road
Dunton Green, Seven Oaks,
Kent, U.K.

Holmes McDougall
137-141 Leith Walk
Edinburgh, U.K. EH6 8NS

Holt, Rinehart and Winston
1627 Woodland Ave
Austin, TX 78741-9989

Houghton Mifflin Company
2 Park Street
Boston, MA 02107

Hulton Educational Press
Raans Road
Amersham, Bucks, Bucks

Hutchinson Press
62-65 Chandos Place
London, U.K. WC2N 4NW

International Marine Publishing co.
Div. of McGraw Hill,
PO Box 220,
Camden ME 04843

IWTC/IT Publications
777 United Nations Plaza
New York, NY 10017

J. B. Lippincott Company
227 E. Washington St.
Philadelphia, PA 19106-3780

J. Weston Walch
P.O. Box 658
Portland, ME 04104

John Deere Publishing
John Deere Road
Moline, IL 61265

John Murray Press
50 Albemarle St
London, W2X 4BD U.K.

John Wiley and Sons Inc
605 Third Avenue
New York, NY 10158-0012

Klutz Press
2121 Stanton Court
Palo Alto, CA 94306

Little Brown and Company
200 West St.
Waltham, MA 02254

Longman
Burnt Mill, Harlow
Essex, U.K. CM20 2JE

Lothrop, Lee and Shepard Books
105 Madison Avenue
New York, NY 10016

Macdonald Educational
49-50 Poland Street
London, U.K. W1

McGraw Hill Book Company
Princeton Road
Hightstown, NJ 08520

McGraw Hill-Ryerson Ltd.
New York, NY

Meridian Education Corp.
236 East Front Street
Bloomington, IL 61701

Monday Morning Books
Box 1680
Palo Alto, CA 94302

National Council of Teachers of Math
1906 Association Drive
Reston, VA 22901-1593

National Geographic Society
1145 17th St. NW
Washington, DC 20036

National Science Teachers Association
1840 Wilson Blvd
Arlington, VA 22201-3000

Nelson
1120 Birchmont Road
Scarborough, Ontario, Canada
M1K 5G4

Nelson
Walton on Thames
Surrey, UK

Nippon Publications
1123 Dominguez Street
Carson, CA 90746

North Light Books
1507 Dana Ave
Cincinatti, OH 45207

Outline Press Ltd.
115J Cleveland Street
London, UK W1P 5PN

Oxford University Press
200 Madison Ave
New York, NY 10016

Pendragon House
2595 East Bayshore Road
Palo Alto, CA 94303

Preservation Press
1785 Massachusetts Ave, NW
Washington, DC 20036

R. R. Bowker
245 West 17th Street
New York, NY 10011

Random House Inc.
201 E. 50th St., 22nd Flr.
New York, NY 10022

Scientific American Inc.
415 Madison Ave
New York, NY 10017

Simon and Schuster
1230 Avenue of the Americas
New York, NY 10020

Small World Technologies
P.O. Box 607
Hillsboro, OR 97123

Tab Books Inc.
P.O. Box 40, Blue Ridge
Summit, PA 17294-0850

Taylor and Francis
1900 Frost Rd, Suite 101
Bristol, PA 19007

Teacher Ideas Press
P.O. Box 6633
Englewood, CO 80155

Ten Speed Press
P.O. Box 7123
Berkeley, CA 94707

The Falmer Press
1900 Frost Rd, Suite 101
Bristol, PA 19007

The Science Source
P.O. Box 727
Waldoboro, ME 04572

Thomas Alva Edison Foundation
18280 W. Ten Mile Road, Suite 143
Southfield, MI 48075

Thomson Learning TOOLS
5101 Madison Road
Cincinatti, OH 45227

Treasure Press
59 Grosvenor Street
London, U.K. W1

TTS (Technology Teaching Systems)
Unit 4, Holmwood Park
Holmwood, UK 542 SUY

Usborne Publishing Ltd
20 Garrick Street
London, UK WC2E 9BJ

Valiant Technology Publications
Dimensions in Learning Inc.
435 Thomas Ave
Forest Park, IL 60130

W. Foulsham & Co. Ltd.
Yeovil Road
Slough, Berkshire, U.K. SL1 4JH

Walker and Co.
720 Fifth Avenue
New York, NY 10019

Western Publishing Company
5945 Erie St.
Racine, WA 53404

Young Discovery Library
1911 Shady Lane
Oreland, PA 19075